ENTERTAINMENT-EDUCATION
AND
SOCIAL CHANGE

ENTERTAINMENT-EDUCATION
AND
SOCIAL CHANGE

History, Research, and Practice

Edited by

Arvind Singhal
Ohio University

Michael J. Cody
University of Southern California

Everett M. Rogers
University of New Mexico

Miguel Sabido
Nuevo Sol Productions

Routledge
Taylor & Francis Group
New York   London

Senior Acquisitions Editor: Linda Bathgate
Editorial Assistant: Karin Wittig Bates
Cover Design: Sean Sciarrone
Textbook Production Manager: Paul Smolenski
Full-Service Compositor: TechBooks

This book was typeset in 10/12 pt. ITC Garamond, Italic, Bold, Bold Italic.
The heads were typeset in ITC Garamond, Bold and Italics.

First published by
Lawrence Erlbaum Associates,
10 Industrial Avenue
Mahwah, NJ 07430
Reprinted 2010 by Routledge

Routledge
Taylor & Francis Group
270 Madison Avenue
New York, NY 10016

Routledge
Taylor & Francis Group
2 Park Square
Milton Park, Abingdon
Oxon OX14 4RN

Library of Congress Cataloging-in-Publication Data

Entertainment-education and social change : history, research, and practice/edited
    by Arvind Singhal. . . [et al.].
        p.   cm.
    Includes bibliographical references and index.
    ISBN 0-8058-4552-6 (casebound)—ISBN 0-8058-4553-4 (pbk.)
        1. Soap operas—Social aspects—Developing countries.   2. Television in
    education—Developing countries.   3. Radio in education—Developing countries.
    I. Singhal, Arvind, 1962–

PN1992.8.S4E58   2004
791.45′6—dc22   2003017993

Contents

Preface   xv
List of Tables, Figures, and Photos   xix

I   HISTORY AND THEORY

1 The Status of Entertainment-Education Worldwide   3
       Arvind Singhal and Everett M. Rogers

       What is E-E and What Can It Do?   5
       Growing Institutional Interest in E-E Practice and Research   6
       The Rise of Multiple Forms of E-E   8
       Increasing Theoretical Vigor and Sophistication   12
       Understanding Resistances to E-E   13
       From Individual to Multilevel Explanations of Behavior Change   14
       Methodological Pluralism   15
       Conclusions   17
       References   18

2 A History of Entertainment-Education, 1958–2000   21
       David O. Poindexter

       Editors' Introduction   21
       Getting to Know U.S. National Television   22
       The Population Communication Center   23
       International Population Communication: 1973–1981   26
           Dialogo in Costa Rica   26
           Mexico and Miguel Sabido   26
           Continuing Sabido's Work   28
       Taking the Sabido Methodology to the World   28
           India: First Transfer of the Sabido Methodology   29
           Kenya: A Second Transfer From Mexico   30
           Opening in Brazil   31
       Founding Population Communications International   31

India   32
The Philippines   32
China   32
Tanzania: The First Full-Fledged Model   32
St. Lucia   34
India and Pakistan   34
Later Projects   35
Lessons Learned   35
References   36

3   Entertainment-Education as a Public Health Intervention   39
    Phyllis Tilson Piotrow and Esta de Fossard

    Uses of Entertainment-Education   41
    Challenges of Entertainment-Education   43
    The Importance of Social Norms   46
    Addressing Poverty   48
    Linking Health With Social Issues   50
    Advantages of Serial Dramas   51
       How to Link Health with Social Issues   52
    Conclusions and Lessons Learned   55
    References   56

4   The Origins of Entertainment-Education   61
    Miguel Sabido

    Editors' Introduction   61
    Beginnings   62
    MacLean's Theory of the Triune Brain   64
    Nodes   65
       Reptilian Nodes   65
       Limbic Nodes   66
       Intellectual Nodes   66
    Flow   67
    What is Tone?   67
    Integration With Other Theories   68
       Bandura's Social Learning Theory   68
       Bentley's Dramatic Theory   68
       Jung's Theory of Archetypes   69
    Applying Entertainment-Education Theory to Television
       Soap Operas   69
       The Role of Communication Research   71
    Lessons Learned   71

Conclusions   73
References   74

5 Social Cognitive Theory for Personal and Social Change by
   Enabling Media   75
   Albert Bandura

   Editors' Introduction   75
   Dual Path of Influence   76
   Social Cognitive Theoretical Model   77
      Social Modeling   78
      Perceived Self-Efficacy   78
      Collective Efficacy   80
      Goals and Aspirations   81
      Outcome Expectations   81
      Perceived Facilitators and Impediments   82
   Translational and Implementational Model   82
      Differential Modeling   82
      Vicarious Motivators   84
      Attentional Involvement   84
      Symbolic Coding Aids   84
      Environmental Support   84
   Social Diffusion Model   85
      Cultural and Value Analyses   87
   Global Applications of the Sociocognitive Model   87
      Promoting National Literacy   88
      Environmental Sustainability by Stemming Population
         Growth   90
      Generalization Through Functional Adaptations   91
      Control on Other Independent Variables   93
   Sustainability by Modification of Consummatory Lifestyles   94
   References   95

6 Celebrity Identification in Entertainment-Education   97
   William J. Brown and Benson P. Fraser

   The Role of Celebrities in Today's Society   98
      Celebrity Endorsements   99
      Celebrity Causes   100
   Identification as a Social Change Process   101
   Theoretical Framework for Celebrity Identification   104
      Dimensions of Celebrity Identification   105
      Antecedents and Consequences of Identification   106

Featuring Celebrities in Entertainment-Education 108
Implications and Conclusions 110
References 111

7 The Theory Behind Entertainment-Education 117
Suruchi Sood, Tiffany Menard, and Kim Witte

The Present Research 118
Theoretical Characteristics of Entertainment-Education
Programs 119
Entertainment-Education Theories 123
Steps/Stages Models 123
Social Psychological Theories 124
Psychological Models 126
Drama Theories 128
Audience-Centered Theories 129
Contextual Theories 130
Hybrid Models 131
Methodological Characteristics of Entertainment-Education
Programs 133
Formative Research 133
Measuring Exposure 133
Characters 143
Future Directions for Entertainment-Education
Theoretical Research 143
References 145

II RESEARCH AND IMPLEMENTATION

8 No Short Cuts in Entertainment-Education: Designing
Soul City Step-by-Step 153
Shereen Usdin, Arvind Singhal, Thuli Shongwe,
Sue Goldstein, and Agnes Shabalala

Editors' Introduction 153
The Formative Research Process for *Soul City IV* 156
Translating Formative Research Findings 157
Scriptwriting 158
The Domestic Violence Storyline 160
Decisions About the Characters 164
Decisions About Situations 167
Advocacy and Social Mobilization 169

Impacts of *Soul City IV*   170
Conclusions   173
References   175

9 Organizing a Comprehensive National Plan
for Entertainment-Education in Ethiopia   177
William N. Ryerson and Negussie Teffera

Editors' Introduction   177
The Whole Society Strategy   178
Ethiopia   179
Getting Started   180
Implementing the Entertainment-Education Strategy   181
Planning Workshops   182
Formative Research   183
Training Workshops   184
Production of the Entertainment-Education Radio Dramas   185
Objectives   185
 Stage Dramas   185
 Video Production   186
 Poems and Short Stories   186
 Capacity Building Through Training   186
 Launching the Serial Dramas   187
 Working With Save the Children USA   187
 Working With UNDP   187
 Working With IPAS Ethiopia   188
 Working With the World Bank   188
Monitoring and Evaluation   188
 Isolating the Effects From Other Activities   188
 Data on Client Numbers   189
Lessons Learned   189
References   189

10 Evolution of an E-E Research Agenda   191
*Bradley S. Greenberg, Charles T. Salmon, Dhaval Patel, Vicki
Beck, and Galen Cole*

The Parameters of E-E   192
Toward a Research Agenda   195
A Continuing Research Agenda for E-E   198
The 2000 CDC Conference on Entertainment-Education   201
Conclusions   203
References   204

11 Working With Daytime and Prime-Time Television Shows in
   the United States to Promote Health   207
   Vicki Beck

   Informing and Motivating Viewers About Health   208
      Tony's HIV   209
      Breast Cancer on *The Young and the Restless*   210
      Health Effects of Primetime Television   212
   An Entertainment-Education Program
      for Public Health   212
   The CDC Entertainment-Education Program   214
   The Healthstyles Survey   215
   Entertainment Industry Resources   216
   Collaborations and Their Results   218
   Recognition of Exemplary Health Storylines   219
   Conclusions   221
   References   222

12 Entertainment-Education Television Drama
   in the Netherlands   225
   Martine Bouman

   Rise of the E-E Strategy in the Netherlands   227
   Beyond Entertainment   230
   E-E Partnership Arrangements   230
   Steering Power   232
   Is It Entertainment-Education?   233
   Theoretical Design   234
   The Creative Design Process   236
   Implementation   238
   Lessons Learned   240
   References   241

13 Entertainment-Education Programs of the BBC and BBC World
   Service Trust   243
   Michael J. Cody, Sangeeta Fernandes, and Holley Wilkin

   The British Broadcasting Corporation   244
   The Threat of Commercial Television   245
   The BBC Soap Operas and Other Programs   246
      The EastEnders   247
      Using Web sites   250
      Using Multiple Media   251

The BBC World Service Trust   253
    Combating Leprosy   254
    Other E-E Interventions   256
Conclusions   258
Author's Note   259
References   259

14 Social Merchandizing in Brazilian Telcnovelas   261
    Antonio C. La Pastina, Dhaval S. Patel, and Marcio Schiavo

Social Merchandizing   262
The Brazilian Telenovela   263
Television Globo Network   264
The Current State of Social Merchandizing   266
Social Merchandizing Prosocial Themes   267
Malhação   269
Laços de Família   270
TV Globo's Broadcasting Time Slot Structure   271
Lessons Learned   273
    Production Process   273
    Multiple Approach   274
    Organic Nature   274
    Intentionality   275
    Evaluation   276
    Recommendations   276
References   277

15 Delivering Entertainment-Education Health Messages Through
   the Internet to Hard-to-Reach U.S. Audiences in the Southwest   281
   Everett M. Rogers

Potential of the Internet for E-E   283
Effects of the Entertainment–Education Strategy   284
Diffusion of the Internet and the Digital Divide   286
Appropriate Web Content for New Internet Users   287
Health Information Needs of Internet Users   288
Breast Cancer and Mammography Screening   289
Reaching Hispanic People in the Southwest With Internet
    Health Messages   290
Investigating Internet-Delivered E-E for Breast Cancer
    Screening   292
Conclusions   293
References   294

III ENTERTAINMENT-EDUCATION INTERVENTIONS AND THEIR OUTCOMES

16 Entertainment-Education in the Middle East: Lessons From the
Egyptian Oral Rehydration Therapy Campaign   301
Rasha A. Abdulla

An Overview of Entertainment–Education in Egypt   302
   E-E Television in Egypt   303
   E-E Television Spots   304
The Egyptian ORT Campaign   305
   What Is ORT?   306
   The ORT Campaign E-E Strategy   306
The ORT Campaign and Communication Theory   315
   Social Marketing   315
   Diffusion of Innovations   315
   Social Learning Theory   317
Lessons Learned   317
References   319

17 The Turkish Family Health and Planning Foundation's
Entertainment-Education Campaign   321
Yaşar Yaşer

Campaign Objectives   322
Campaign Strategy   323
Media Reach and Media Mix   324
Campaign Effects   325
Social Marketing   328
Conclusions   329
Reference   329

18 Cartoons and Comic Books for Changing Social Norms:
Meena, the South Asian Girl   331
*Neill McKee, Mira Aghi, Rachel Carnegie,
and Nuzhat Shahzadi*

The Birth of *Meena*   332
Background and Rationale   334
Cartoons and Comic Books for Social Change   336
Creative Development and Formative
   Research Process   337
Using *Meena* to Foster Social Change   340
Evaluation of *Meena*   345

Lessons Learned 347
References 348

19 Air Cover and Ground Mobilization: Integrating
Entertainment-Education Broadcasts With Community
Listening and Service Delivery in India 351
*Arvind Singhal, Devendra Sharma, Michael J. Papa,
and Kim Witte*

Historical Background: From *Tinka* to *Taru* 355
The *Taru* Project 357
  Orchestrating Audiences Through Folk Performances 358
Researching *Taru* 362
  Taru's Listenership 362
  Community Case-Study and Field Observations 363
Impact of *Taru* 365
  Parasocial Interaction With *Taru* 366
  Social Learning Through Peer Conversations 369
  Collective Efficacy Stimulated by *Taru* 370
  Nonlinearity of Social Change: Power, Resistance, and
    Paradoxical Behaviors 372
Conclusions 373
References 374

20 Entertainment-Education Through Participatory Theater:
Freirean Strategies for Empowering the Oppressed 377
Arvind Singhal

Participatory Communication 379
Paulo Freire's Dialogic Pedagogy 381
Freire in Practice: Augusto Boal's Theater of the Oppressed 383
Participatory Theatrical Techniques 385
  #1. Image Theater 385
  #2. Forum Theater 386
  #3. Invisible Theater 388
  #4. Legislative Theater 389
Participatory Theater: Serving the Oppressed 390
  Drama AIDS Education in South Africa 390
  Theater for Empowerment in India 393
  A Pedagogy of Prevention in Brazil 395
  Participatory Mass Media E-E in Brazil 396
Conclusions 396
References 397

21 Soap Operas and Sense-Making: Mediations and Audience
   Ethnography   399
   Thomas Tufte

   E-E and Communication for Social Change   400
   Participation and Community Involvement   403
   E-E and HIV/AIDS   404
   Bridging Paradigms?   404
   From Media to Mediations   405
   Anglo-Saxon Tradition of Cultural Studies   407
   Telenovelas: Touching Everyday Experience   408
      Research Findings   410
   Conclusions   413
   References   413

22 Entertainment-Education and Participation: Applying
   Habermas to a Population Program in Nepal   417
   J. Douglas Storey and Thomas L. Jacobson

   Communicative Action and Participation   419
   Habermas' Theory and Participatory Communication   422
   Nepal's Population Program   424
   Communicative Action and Nepal's Population Program   425
      Interpersonal Communication/Counseling   425
      Mass Media   427
      Networks for Behavior Change   429
   Research on Program Impacts   430
   Conclusions   431
   References   432

Epilogue   435
About The Authors   439
Author Index   446
Subject Index   454

Preface

This book evolved out of several previous efforts to tell the story of entertainment-education (E-E). Arvind Singhal and Everett M. Rogers collaborated in a 1999 book, *Entertainment-Education: A Communication Strategy for Social Change*. Singhal and Rogers' volume focused on the history and theory of entertainment-education, and on the research-based findings about this strategy and its effects.

Our interest in entertainment-education, however, dates back to over 17 years ago, when editors of this volume—Singhal, Rogers, and Cody—and our colleague, Bill Brown, spent hours at the University of Southern California (USC) watching episodes of *Hum Log* (the first entertainment-education soap opera in India), discussing parasocial interaction, pro-social uses of the media, and much more. These discussions eventually led to interviews conducted with Miguel Sabido; the initiation of research projects in India, Tanzania, and China; and collaboration with family planning and health communication experts around the world, including David Poindexter, Phyllis Piotrow, David Andrews, Bill Ryerson, Martine Bouman, and Garth Japhet and his fellow visionaries at Soul City. The first of three international conferences on entertainment-education was held in 1989 at USC. A number of "Soap Summits" have taken place in New York and Los Angeles, and today a growing network of researchers, writers, and entertainment professionals use E-E to further a range of interests.

In 2001, Miguel Sabido, the key figure in formulating the theoretical basis for entertainment-education, served as a visiting professor at USC, where he taught a course on entertainment-education. With his USC colleague, Michael J. Cody, plans were laid for this volume.

Then, in May 2002, Singhal and Rogers collaborated in guest-editing a special issue (Volume 12/2) of the journal *Communication Theory* devoted to entertainment-education. With the help of Michael J. Cody, the editor of this journal, the 2002 special issue contained articles representing promising new approaches to entertainment-education. Many of these articles had previously been presented at the third International Entertainment-Education

Conference, held in 2000 in Arnhem, the Netherlands, and led by Martine Bouman.

The co-editors of this volume felt that despite these previous publications and other attempts to pull together a synthesis of what was known about entertainment-education, a more comprehensive effort was needed. *Entertainment-Education and Social Change: History, Research, and Practice* represents a resource book that introduces its readers to E-E literature written from varied perspectives. Chapter authors include E-E theoreticians, practitioners, and researchers, and display a wide range of nationalities and theoretical orientations. This diversity of thought is typical of entertainment-education today, a movement that has moved far beyond its beginnings. Only a few years ago, the main research question being asked by E-E scholars was, "Does it have an effect?" Once that issue was settled beyond dispute, further study of entertainment-education explored *why* and *how* E-E has its effects on audience individuals. E-E researchers, while pursuing these later questions, were led to consider new theories and to utilize different methodologies. Here we report results from these contemporary studies of entertainment-education.

We thank the following people for their vital contributions to this book: Linda Bathgate, our editor at Lawrence Erlbaum Associates, who had faith in this project from the first; Sergio Alcaron, who translated Miguel Sabido's chapter; the chapter authors, whose work is displayed here; two doctoral students at USC, Holley Wilken and Sangeeta Fernandes, who edited all of the chapters in this volume; Wanda Sheridan, Administrative Coordinator of the School of Communication Studies, Ohio University, who helped in finalizing the book; Peter Gill and Lori McDougall of the BBC World Service Trust in India, who provided the photographs and data that accompany Chapter 1; and Mkhonzeni Gumede of DramAidE, South Africa, who provided the photograph of participatory theater in a school in KwaZulu–Natal Province.

We also thank Phyllis Tilson Piotrow and Patrick L. Coleman at Johns Hopkins University, Vibert Cambridge at Ohio University, and Martine Bouman at the Netherlands Entertainment-Education Foundation, for advancing a global E-E agenda and sponsoring International E-E conferences; and David Andrews, Kate Randolph, and Irwin "Sonny" Fox at Population Communications International, for leadership in implementing E-E interventions worldwide and for pioneering the "Soap Summits" in New York and Los Angeles.

We express our gratitude to the supportive faculty at USC who advocate the use of E-E in the United States, and its evaluation: Marty Kaplan, Director of the Norman Lear Center; Vicki Beck, Director of the Hollywood, Health and Society Office; Doe Mayer, Professor in the USC School of Cinema and

Television; Patricia Riley, Director of the School of Communication; and Geoff Cowan, Dean of the Annenberg School for Communication. Finally, we thank Everett Rogers-King, who compiled the Author and Subject Indexes for this book.

—Arvind Singhal, Athens, Ohio
—Michael Cody, Hermosa Beach, California
—Ev Rogers, Albuquerque, New Mexico
—Miguel Sabido, Acapulco, Mexico

List of Tables, Figures, and Photos

TABLES

Table 3.1. Entertainment-Education Programs Supported by the Johns Hopkins University's Center for Communication Programs, 1986 to 2002, by Type and Region   41

Table 7.1. Theoretical Characteristics of Selected Entertainment-Education Programs   120

Table 7.2. Methodological Characteristics of Selected Entertainment-Education Programs   134

Table 14.1. Social Merchandising in *Malhação* in 2000   270

Table 14.2. Social Merchandising in *Laços de Família* in 2000   271

Table 14.3. Telenovelas on Globo Network   272

Table 15.1. Effects of Selected E-E Health Interventions on Behavior Change   284

Table 19.1. The Main Characters of *Taru*   361

Table 19.2. Longitudinal Assessment Through Four Rapid Random Surveys in Begusarai District of Bihar State to Gauge (1) Listenership to *Taru*, (2) Listeners' Perceptions of Similarity of *Taru*'s Characters to Them, and (3) Listeners' Intentions to Change Their Behaviors as a Result of Listening to *Taru*   363

Table 20.1. Participatory Versus Nonparticipatory Communication Strategies   380

FIGURES

Figure 5.1. Paths of influences through which communication affect psychosocial changes both directly and via a socially mediated pathway by linking viewers to social networks and community settings.   77

Figure 6.1. Two-dimensional celebrity profile.   106

Figure 6.2. Antecedents to, and consequences of, celebrity identification.   107

Figure 8.1.   Those exposed to the *Soul City* series were more likely
to bang pots to protest domestic violence.   173
Figure 12.1.   Stages of collaboration in entertainment-education.   230
Figure 12.2.   Five stages of creativity.   237
Figure 12.3.   Symmetry and asymmetry of power in
entertainment-education.   239
Figure 16.1.   The logo of the Egyptian ORT campaign was chosen
based on input from the target audience.   309
Figure 16.2.   Percentage of ORT awareness and use in Egypt,
1983–2000.   311
Figure 16.3.   Infant and under five mortality rates in Egypt,
1970–2000.   314
Figure 16.4.   Infant and under five mortality rates as a result of
diarrheal-related diseases in Egypt, 1970–2000.   314

PHOTOS

Photo 1.1.   Detective Vijay played by actor Adil Khandkar.   04
Photo 1.2.   The two *Haath Se Haath Milaa* buses, each equipped
with bunk beds, cooking facilities, television cameras, and a
presenter.   10
Photo 1.3.   Daman (left) and Sugandha (right), the two presenters
that accompany the male and female *Haath Se Haath Milaa*
buses, respectively.   11
Photo 2.1.   Miguel Sabido (left) and David Poindexter (right) in
Mexico City in September 2002, celebrating the 25th anniversary
of their first meeting.   27
Photo 3.1.   The Bangladesh serial drama, *Shabuj Chhaya*, attracted
more than 600,000 letters.   40
Photo 3.2.   Community performances and street theater are
important E-E components of Ghana's "Stop AIDS, Love Life"
campaign.   43
Photo 3.3.   In Egypt's television drama series *And the Nile Flows
On*, a young religious leader helps other men understand the
need for child spacing.   46
Photo 3.4.   Young actors in Peru's *Time for Love* series depict the
consequences of careless love versus concern for partners.   48
Photo 4.1.   Miguel Sabido being interviewed by a reporter about
his tonal theory in Mexico City in September 2002.   62
Photo 5.1.   Miguel Sabido and Albert Bandura discuss social
cognitive theory and its applications in entertainment-education
programs at the University of Southern California in 2001.   83

Photo 6.1. Robert Lopez, more commonly known as "El Vez," interacts with his fans at an Elvis concert. 102

Photo 8.1. Neighbors collectively bang pots and pans to protest Thabang's abuse of Matlakala. 154

Photo 8.2. An altercation between Thabang and Matlakala which escalates into physical abuse of Matlakala. 161

Photo 8.3. Upon hearing the battered woman's story, Matlakala realizes what lies in store for her in the future. 165

Photo 8.4. Intergenerational socialization of domestic violence as Thabang tells his son Bheki that a man must always be the "captain of his ship." 168

Photo 9.1. Focus group research for the E-E radio serial, *Dhimbiba*, being conducted in Ethiopia by Birhan Research for the Population Media Center. 184

Photo 9.2. Abdulnasser Hajihassen, producer of the Oromiffa language E-E radio soap opera, recording an episode of *Dhimbiba* in a studio in Addis Ababa. 186

Photo 11.1. The doctor tells Tony his HIV test showed that he is HIV-positive. 209

Photo 11.2. Tony discusses his HIV status with his fiancé Kristin in the AIDS storyline on *The Bold & the Beautiful*. 210

Photo 11.3. Tony and Kristin marry and visit an orphanage in Africa where they adopt a young child, Zende, whose mother died of AIDS. 211

Photo 12.1. Maarten, played by Hugo Haenen, and Laura, played by Linda de Wolf, two central characters in the Dutch television series *Villa Borghese*. 226

Photo 12.2. The cast of *Costa!* (Left: Katja Schuurman; middle: Georgina Verbaan; right: Froukje de Both) 227

Photo 15.1. A community outreach trainer from the La Plaza Telecommunity demonstrates computer and Internet use to an elderly Hispanic woman in Taos County, NM on his laptop computer, by showing her *Meet the Montoyas*, a *fotonovela* on diabetes. 282

Photo 17.1. Ömer and his large family in the Turkish Family Planning film *Berdel*. 326

Photo 18.1. Meena notices she gets less food than her brother, Raju, and begins to ask why. 332

Photo 18.2. Meena convinces the community about the importance of girls' education by using her counting skills to catch a chicken thief. 336

Photo 18.3. Of the multiple images of South Asian girls that were pretested, audiences preferred the drawing on the right, which inspired the final image of Meena. 338

Photo 19.1.   Shailendra, the rural medical practitioner in Village
    Kamtaul, standing next to a *Taru* poster.   **354**
Photo 19.2.   A 15 feet by 8 feet wall-painting on the Patna-
    Muzzafarpur Highway, promoting the broadcasts of *Taru*, and the
    rural medical practitioner network of Janani.   **355**
Photo 19.3.   Some 800 people from eight neighboring villages
    gathered near Abirpur Village to watch a folk performance about
    Taru, prior to the broadcast of the radio soap opera.   **359**
Photo 19.4.   (Left to right) Usha Kumari, Sunita Kumari, and
    Kumari Neha, members of the Abirpur young women's listening
    club, who regularly listen to *Taru* on the transistor radio that they
    won in the quiz competition following the *Taru* folk performance
    in their village.   **360**
Photo 19.5.   Sunita (standing right), the wife of RHP Shailendra
    Singh, who was inspired by Neha (a friend of Taru) in the radio
    serial, to begin an adult literacy class for lower-caste women in
    Kamtaul Village.   **367**
Photo 20.1.   Brazilian educator Paulo Freire, who developed
    pedagogical techniques to empower the oppressed.   **382**
Photo 20.2.   Augusto Boal, founder of the Theater of the
    Oppressed (TO), which applies Freire's principles to empower
    the poor, the weak, and the vulnerable.   **384**
Photo 20.3.   Secondary school students in KwaZulu-Natal
    Province, South Africa, perform an HIV/AIDS play for other
    students, parents, teachers, and community leaders as part of
    DramAidE project's open day celebrations.   **392**
Photo 22.1.   A female health worker counseling a mother and her
    child after a medical examination at the Bhaktapur Health Post in
    Nepal.   **426**
Photo 22.2.   A listeners' group gathered in Mainapokhar, Nepal, to
    listen to the radio serial, *Cut Your Coat According to Your Cloth*.   **428**
Photo 22.3.   A street theater performance on family planning in
    Mainapokhar, Nepal, conducted on National Condom Day 2001.   **429**

I

History and Theory

1

The Status of Entertainment-Education Worldwide[1]

Arvind Singhal

Ohio University

Everett M. Rogers

University of New Mexico

Detective Vijay is commissioned by an urban Indian family to check out the background of a young rural woman, whom they wish their son to marry. When Vijay arrives in her village, he discovers the young woman is missing and her family is trying to cover up her disappearance. When her body is found in the village well, Vijay investigates the death. Through a maze of intrigue and suspense, Vijay discovers that the young woman was a childhood friend of a village outcast who was ostracized by the community because he was HIV-positive (Photo 1.1). She was killed because of her association with an HIV-positive person.

The above plot is part of a 120-episode entertainment-education detective series titled *Jasoos Vijay* (Detective Vijay), broadcast in India[2] to raise

---

[1]This chapter draws upon Singhal and Rogers (1999; 2002).

[2]*Jasoos Vijay* is part of an intensive HIV/AIDS media initiative involving the Indian government's National AIDS Control Organization (NACO), Prasar Bharati (the Indian national broadcaster), and the BBC World Service Trust (BBC WST). This HIV/AIDS initiative, funded by the British government's Department of International Development (DFID), focused on five low HIV-prevalence Indian states: Rajasthan, Haryana, Delhi, Uttar Pradesh, and Uttaranchal. The India HIV/AIDS initiative, the largest media health initiative ever funded by DFID, includes a strong entertainment-education component: (1) the detective television

PHOTO 1.1. Detective Vijay played by actor Adil Khandkar. (*Source*: BBC World Service Trust. Used with permission.)

awareness about HIV/AIDS, to shift social norms about the disease, and to reduce stigma (Singhal & Rogers, 2003). Watched regularly by 125 million viewers, *Jasoos Vijay* is among the Top Ten rated television programs in India, and a major revenue earner for Doordarshan, the Indian national television network. Broadcast for 10 months from June 2002 to April 2003,[3] each month, Vijay solves one case. So *Jasoos Vijay* is really a collection of 10 detective case stories.[4] In this interactive, fast-paced drama series, each episode ends with a cliffhanger and an epilogue delivered by Om Puri, a famous Indian film celebrity. Puri summarizes plot developments, focuses viewers' attention on the key HIV/AIDS dilemmas, and urges viewers to send a written response to the central question posed. Puri receives 1,000 letters and e-mails each week.

---

series, (2) a reality-based television program that follows the lives of 80 youthful audience members who journey on buses across the four states, (3) radio talk shows, and (4) public service announcements on HIV prevention.

[3] In the five low HIV-prevalence Indian states—Rajasthan, Haryana, Delhi, Uttar Pradesh, and Uttaranchal—*Jasoos Vijay* is broadcast thrice a week in 10-minute segments. The weekly omnibus of 30 minutes length is broadcast on Doordarshan's national network each Sunday night.

[4] This description of *Jasoos Vijay* draws upon author Singhal's conversations with Peter Gill, Lori McDougall, Sangeeta Sharma Mehta, and Jyoti Mehra of the BBC World Service Trust in New Delhi in 2001 and 2002. Author Singhal participated in the message design workshop for this HIV/AIDS media initiative in New Delhi in January, 2002.

Jasoos Vijay represents an innovative entertainment-education vehicle. It is comprised of engaging narratives centering on a key protagonist, with multiple cliffhangers and denouements. Various theory-based strategies are employed to enhance the entertainment-education narrative: the use of a celebrity epilogue-giver; the posing of multiple dilemmas (such as "How did she die?") to stimulate audience reflection and elaboration; an emphasis on mystery to build suspense and audience involvement; and the raising of key social dilemmas surrounding HIV/AIDS, designed to deconstruct prevailing social values, beliefs, and norms about HIV/AIDS. A study of *Jasoos Vijay* in five North Indian states—Rajasthan, Haryana, Delhi, Uttar Pradesh, and Uttaranchal—estimated a viewing audience of 36 million in these five states. Of these, an estimated 5.6 million (16%) reported a positive change in their sexual behavior four months after the broadcasts of *Jasoos Vijay* began. The cost per behavioral change was 5 cents (U.S.) (personal communication, Lori McDougall, December 9, 2002).

Jasoos Vijay shows that the entertainment-education strategy continues to evolve and reinvent itself around the globe. This chapter overviews the current status of entertainment-education interventions as they are implemented around the world. We show that this strategy is currently widespread and growing.

WHAT IS E-E AND WHAT CAN IT DO?

Entertainment-education (E-E) is the process of purposely designing and implementing a media message to both entertain and educate, in order to increase audience members' knowledge about an educational issue, create favorable attitudes, shift social norms, and change overt behavior (Singhal & Rogers, 1999; Singhal & Rogers, 2002). Entertainment-education is not a theory of communication. Rather, it is a communication strategy to bring about behavioral and social change. Several communication theories, however, provide a basis for the E-E strategy.

The general purpose of entertainment-education interventions is to contribute to the process of directed social change, which can occur at the level of an individual, community, or society. The entertainment-education strategy contributes to social change in two ways. First, it can influence members' awareness, attitudes, and behavior toward a socially desirable end. Here the anticipated effects are located in the individual audience members. An illustration is provided by a radio soap opera, *Twende na Wakati* (Let's Go with the Times), in Tanzania that convinced several hundred thousand sexually-active adults to adopt HIV prevention behaviors (such as using condoms and reducing their number of sexual partners) (Rogers et al., 1999). Second, it can influence the audience's external environment to help create the necessary conditions for social change at the system level. Here the major effects are located in the interpersonal and social–political sphere of the audience's external environment. The entertainment-education media can serve as a social mobilizer, an advocate, or an agenda-setter, influencing public and policy initiatives in a socially-desirable direction (Wallack, 1990). Soul City's domestic violence series mobilized community action, women's marches, and speeded passage of domestic violence legislation in South Africa through media, public, and policy advocacy (see the chapter by Shereen Usdin and others in this volume).

E-E projects benefit from formative, process, and summative research, which amounts to approximately 10% of the total budget of these projects. Formative evaluation research is conducted with the intended audience in order to design the entertainment-education intervention. *Formative research* is conducted while an activity, process, or system is being developed or is ongoing, in order to improve its effectiveness (Singhal & Rogers, 2001). Research-based information about the characteristics, needs, and preferences of a target audience sharpens the design of entertainment-education (see the chapter by Shereen Usdin and others in this volume).

Entertainment-education interventions are further strengthened through such process evaluation activities as the analysis of audience letters, monitoring of clinic data (to track family planning adoption, for example), and content analysis of the entertainment-education messages (to determine if the scripts are consistent with desired educational goals). Feedback can thus be provided in a timely manner to entertainment-education media producers for appropriate mid-course corrections.

Summative evaluation research measures the effects of the entertainment-education campaign on audience behavior. For example, an entertainment-education radio soap opera, *Tinka Tinka Sukh* (Happiness Lies in Small Pleasures), in Hindi-speaking North India was evaluated by a field experiment (using pre-post, treatment-control audience surveys), content analysis of the episodes and of listeners' letters, and a case study of one village in which the program had strong effects (Papa et al., 2000).

GROWING INSTITUTIONAL INTEREST IN E-E PRACTICE AND RESEARCH

The authors of this chapter, Arvind Singhal and Everett M. Rogers, became involved in investigating the impacts of E-E soap operas in developing nations relatively early (beginning in 1984–85), and have since followed the evolution of this genre closely, providing overviews and syntheses of research on E-E

(Singhal & Rogers, 1999, 2002). Since our involvement in E-E began in the mid-1980s, over 200 E-E interventions, mainly for health-related educational issues and mostly broadcast as radio or television soap operas, have been implemented, mainly in the developing countries of Latin America, Africa, and Asia.

In the initial era of E-E, two main organizations drove the international diffusion of E-E projects: Population Communications International (PCI), a non-governmental organization headquartered in New York City, and Johns Hopkins University's Center for Communication Programs (JHU/CCP). PCI helped launch television soap operas such as *Hum Log* (We People) in India, and radio soap operas like *Ushikwapo Shikimana* (When Given Advice, Take It) in Kenya, *Twende na Wakati* (Let's Go With the Times) in Tanzania, and *Taru* in India (see David Poindexter's chapter in this volume; and Arvind Singhal and others' chapter in this volume). Johns Hopkins University's Center for Communication Programs (JHU/CCP) launched several dozen entertainment-education projects in numerous countries of Asia, Africa, and Latin America (see the Phyllis T. Piotrow and Esta de Fossard chapter in this volume).

Today, numerous other organizations are involved in utilizing and diffusing the E-E strategy. The Centers for Disease Control and Prevention (CDC) in Atlanta, as part of its Global AIDS Program, utilizes entertainment-education soap operas in its MARCH (Modeling and Reinforcement to Combat HIV) Project in four African countries: Botswana, Ethiopia, Ghana, and Zimbabwe (Galavotti, Pappas-DeLuca, & Lansky, 2001). The BBC World Service Trust, in cooperation with the Indian government's National AIDS Control Organization (NACO) and Prasar Bharati (the Indian broadcasting agency), launched a major E-E initiative in India in 2002, which included the *Jasoos Vijay* series (discussed at the top of this chapter). The Population Media Center, an NGO headquartered in Burlington, Vermont, has E-E initiatives underway in Ethiopia, Philippines, Sudan, and Swaziland (see the William Ryerson and Negussie Teffera chapter in this volume).

The entertainment-education strategy has been widely invented and recreated by media professionals in various countries. Notable is the work of the Soul City Institute for Health and Development Communication in South Africa, Media for Development Trust in Zimbabwe, Africa Radio Drama Association in Nigeria, Puentos de Encuentro in Nicaragua, Minga Peru in Peru, and the Netherlands Entertainment-Education Foundation in the Netherlands. Soul City materials, through local in-country partnerships, are being produced and distributed in neighboring Botswana, Zimbabwe, Lesotho, Swaziland, Namibia, and Zambia.

Several communication departments are now particularly oriented to studying or teaching about the E-E strategy. The Annenberg School for Communication at the University of Southern California, since 1999, has taken the study of entertainment as its main theme by establishing the Norman Lear

Center.[5] Also, the College of Communication at Ohio University; the Department of Communication and Journalism at the University of New Mexico; Johns Hopkins University's Bloomberg School of Public Health; the College of Communication and the Arts, Regent University; the Department of Film and Media Studies at the University of Copenhagen; the Centre for Cultural and Media Studies, University of Natal, Durban, South Africa; and various other institutions around the world are increasingly engaged in teaching and research on entertainment-education. Today a map of the world would show E-E almost everywhere.

THE RISE OF MULTIPLE FORMS OF E-E

The E-E strategy began in developing countries, mainly in the form of radio and television soap operas dealing with health-related topics, where donor support was often provided, and where societies were not media saturated. Today there exist multiple types of E-E, and the E-E strategy has been applied very widely.

Some E-E interventions are national campaigns, while others are designed for a very specific, local audience. Yet others go beyond a national scope to include a much broader "cultural" space. For example, the Soul City E-E intervention reaches 80% of its target audience in South Africa (Soul City, 2001). In contrast, E-E street theater interventions in India and in Bolivia reached only a few hundred people per performance (Valente & Bharath, 1999; Valente, Poppe, Alva, de Briceno, & Cases, 1995), although over a period of several years one South Indian street theater group, Nalamdana, reached over one million people (Singhal & Rogers, 2003). Other E-E campaigns, such as the UNICEF-sponsored *Meena* Project, were targeted to a "cultural" space comprising several South Asian countries (see the Neil McKee and others' chapter in this volume). Similarly, *Heart and Soul*, an E-E radio and television soap opera produced in Kenya in 2002 through a collaborative arrangement among 25 UN agencies, reached an audience of over 50 million people in 23 African countries.

E-E programs vary widely in terms of the extent to which they use (1) formative research, and (2) human communication theories in their message design. For instance, E-E interventions like *Soul City* in South Africa spend 18 months to develop one annual campaign cycle[6] by conducting extensive formative research (see the chapter by Shereen Usdin and others

---

[5]In fact, the entire University of Southern California adopted entertainment as its core specialty. Thus, the USC Law School offers a specialization in entertainment law, the USC Engineering School focuses on the technology of entertainment production, and so forth.

[6]One *Soul City* campaign cycle includes a 13-episode prime-time television series, a 60-episode radio series in nine different languages, and one million copies each of three glossy

in this volume). Detailed message design and planning processes are carried out, including thorough pretesting of messages and materials. Also, E-E soap operas, especially those patterned after Miguel Sabido's methodology (for example, *Hum Log* in 1984–1985 in India), purposely incorporated principles of Bandura's social learning theory in the design of positive, negative, and transitional role models (Nariman, 1993; Singhal & Rogers, 1999). On the other hand, some E-E interventions incorporate little formative research or theoretical inputs, and rely heavily on the intuition and creativity of the production staff.

E-E interventions also vary widely in terms of their intensity and their ability to deliver dose effects (in which greater audience exposure to the intervention leads to stronger effects). E-E messages may be incorporated as a few lines of dialogue in an existing media program (as in the case of the designated driver concept, promoted in the Harvard Alcohol Project, which was incorporated in the episodes of 75 television programs in the late 1980s). The E-E strategy may be used in one episode of a popular prime-time series, such as the discussion of Walter's vasectomy in the CBS sitcom *Maude*, or in a long-running E-E series such as the BBC's *The Archers*, which broadcast over 8,000 episodes since its launch in 1951. The effects of these E-E interventions vary considerably depending on whether audiences experience a one-time, live street theater performance versus an ongoing, long-running television E-E soap opera.

E-E interventions operate in very different contexts. The situated context of an E-E intervention undoubtedly impacts <u>what</u> effects they have and <u>how</u> and <u>why</u>. For instance, E-E faces special challenges and resistances in media-saturated societies such as the United States (Sherry, 2002).

Currently, a wider range of E-E forms are being implemented and evaluated both overseas and in the United States (see Bradley Greenberg and others'; Suruchi Sood and others'; Antonio Pastina and others'; Yasar Yaser's; and Doug Storey & Tom Jacobson's chapters in this volume). The CDC Sentinel Health Awards for Daytime Drama, bestowed at the annual Soap Summits hosted by Population Communications International in Los Angeles and New York, reward the effective application of the E-E strategy in Hollywood soap operas. For example, in 2002 the Sentinel Award went to *The Bold & the Beautiful* episodes about Tony, a young American who is diagnosed with HIV/AIDS (see the Vicki Beck and others' chapter in the present volume). Celebrities can play an important role in E-E by providing positive role models for healthy behavior (see the William Brown and Benson Fraser chapter in this volume). Oral rehydration therapy (ORT) television spots in Egypt effectively illustrate the E-E strategy and the use of celebrity performers (see the Rasha Abdullah chapter in this volume).

---

comic booklets (total 3 million), each distributed through 10 partner newspapers, NGOs, and government departments.

Incorporating Reality Television in E-E[7]

Reality television series such as *Survivor, Temptation Island*, and *Big Brother* obtain very high audience ratings worldwide, but valorize lewdness, sexual irresponsibility, greed, and other antisocial messages. Can entertainment-education practitioners leverage the popularity of the reality television format for disseminating educational messages?

Complementing the *Jasoos Vijay* entertainment-education detective series in India (discussed at the top of the present chapter) and designed to promote HIV/AIDS prevention, care, and support, is a youth reality television show, *Haath Se Haath Milaa* (Hand in Hand Together), set aboard two buses (one for boys, one for girls) that journey over five targeted low HIV-prevalence Indian states—Rajasthan, Haryana, Delhi, Uttar Pradesh, and Uttaranchal. Each bus, at any given time, carries two *humsafars* (cotravelers), with each pair of *humsafars* spending no more than two weeks on the bus (Photo 1.2). The buses, equipped with bunk beds, cooking facilities, television cameras, and a presenter, visit cities, villages, university campuses, ancient forts, farms, and temples, signifying the youth journey of a lifetime. During this journey, the *humsafars* learn the skills to live life to the fullest, to protect themselves from HIV/AIDS, and to have more compassion for those living with AIDS. Each week,

PHOTO 1.2. The two *Haath Se Haath Milaa* buses, each equipped with bunk beds, cooking facilities, television cameras, and a presenter. (*Source:* BBC World Service Trust. Used with permission.)

---

[7]This case draws upon Singhal and Rogers (2003, p. 329).

PHOTO 1.3.   Daman (left) and Sugandha (right), the two presenters that accompany the male and female *Haath Se Haath Milaa* buses, respectively.
(*Source*: BBC World Service Trust. Used with permission.)

the presenters provide the *humsafars* with a creative, entertaining challenge:
for instance, who is least embarrassed to buy a condom; a role-playing game
wherein each repulses the advances of the opposite sex; and so forth.

The boys' and the girls' buses take different routes but come together at various locations for interaction between the two groups. While on separate-sex
buses, boys were asked questions about girls, and girls about boys. Each
week, the reality-based sequences were filmed, edited, and broadcast in forty
30-minute episodes during the 10-month period in 2002 to 2003 overlapping
with *Jasoos Vijay's* broadcasts. The bus-based reality television presentation
is complemented with a *Haath Se Haath Milaa* media fair, including performances by local musicians, village poets, and Bombay film-based celebrities.
Celebrity endorsements for HIV/AIDS prevention are also included in each
week's episode, and competitions are held for audience members on the issues
of AIDS, health, and lifeskills (Photo 1.3). Finally, after 40 weeks, the buses,
carrying all 80 *humsafars* (40 boys and 40 girls) arrived in Delhi to meet with
the Prime Minister of India.

Haath Se Haath Milaa is an exemplar of how popular entertainment formats
can be suitably adapted for educational purposes. This program had 8 million
viewers in the five North Indian states in which it was broadcast. An estimated
1.1 million (12%) reported a positive change in sexual behavior four months
after the broadcasts began. The cost per behavior change was 13 cents (U.S.)
(personal correspondence, Lori McDougall, December 9, 2002).

INCREASING THEORETICAL VIGOR AND
SOPHISTICATION

Barring some exceptions, the dominant theoretical basis for most E-E research in the past was Bandura's social learning theory (also called social cognitive theory). Today, connections are formed by entertainment-education with additional theories, involving a wider range of communication scholars.

How did social learning theory initially dominate E-E theorizing and practice? The modern history of E-E is revealing in this respect. When the first recognizable entertainment-education (E-E) interventions were launched on radio with the Australian Broadcasting Corporation's *The Lawsons* (in 1944),[8] the BBC radio series *The Archers* (in 1951), and then the Peruvian *telenovela* (television soap opera) *Simplemente Mariá* (in 1969), communication scholars were not involved in the design or in the evaluation of effects (Singhal, Obregón, & Rogers, 1994). The communication discipline was not yet involved. Theorizing about E-E was yet to begin.

After the broadcast of *Simplemente Mariá* in Mexico in 1970, Miguel Sabido, a creative writer–producer–director at Televisa, the private Mexican television network, carefully deconstructed this Peruvian *telenovela* in order to understand its theoretical basis, so that he could then produce a series of seven E-E television programs for Televisa (the Mexican television network), which were each evaluated as to their impacts (Nariman, 1993; Singhal & Rogers, 1999). In designing his E-E *telenovelas*, Sabido drew especially on Albert Bandura's (1977; 1997) social learning theory (which later evolved into social cognitive theory). This theoretical approach has since tended to dominate most theoretical writing and research about entertainment-education, and Sabido's methodology for the design of E-E programs, especially soap operas, influenced most later work on entertainment-education by communication professionals around the world. A natural fit exists between Bandura's theory and entertainment-education interventions, which often seek to influence audience behavior change by providing positive and negative role models to the audience.

Theoretical understanding of entertainment-education interventions has been considerably broadened by inviting consideration of social cognitive

---

[8] *The Lawsons* was an entertainment-education radio serial broadcast by the Australian Broadcasting Corporation (ABC) in its *Country Hour* program, beginning in 1944. Pre-dating the well-known BBC radio series, *The Archers*, by seven years. *The Lawsons* was designed to promote the diffusion of agricultural innovations among Australian farm families. In 1949, *The Lawsons* evolved into *Blue Hills*, another E-E serial that was also broadcast daily in ABC's *Country Hour* for 6,000 episodes over 27 years. Both *The Lawsons* and *Blue Hills* were written by Gwen Meredith, based on extensive research on agricultural and other development topics (personal correspondence, Esta de Fossard, May 15, 2002), and played a role in inspiring the highly acclaimed BBC radio series *The Archers* which began broadcasting in 1951.

theory (see the Sood et al. chapter in this volume) as well as other communication theories that have, or may, contribute to improved understanding or to the design of future E-E programs: social learning/social cognitive theory (see Albert Bandura's chapter in this volume); the elaboration likelihood model (Slater & Rouner, 2002); audience involvement (Sood, 2002); dramatic theories (Kincaid, 2002); social constructivism (Sypher et al., 2002); uses and gratifications, agenda-setting, knowledge-gap, cultivation analysis, and diffusion of innovations (Sherry, 2002); and Habermas' theory of communicative action (see the Storey and Jacobson chapter in this volume).

Past investigations of E-E largely provided cognitive and rational explanations of effects, utilizing the hierarchy-of-effects, stages-of-change, and other models. E-E investigations today are focusing more on the rhetorical, play, and affective aspects of E-E, which emphasize the entertainment, rather than the education, aspects of E-E (Stephenson, 1988; Singhal & Rogers, 2002).

E-E almost necessarily involves the use of narratives, suggesting the possibility of utilizing Walter Fisher's (1987) "narrative" theory to investigate the rhetorical nature of E-E discourses. Most E-E programs deal with the affective and emotional aspects of human communication (Papa et al., 2000; Rogers et al., 1999). Theoretical investigations of E-E are currently taking the role of emotions more seriously (Singhal & Rogers, 2002). Emotions are an important form of human experience, which can trigger, for instance, changes in preventive health behaviors. This potential is often underestimated, understated, and overlooked (Zillman & Vorderer, 2000). For instance, witnessing the death from AIDS of a favorite soap opera character, and seeing the grief of his parents, infected widow, and child, may serve as a more powerful trigger for adopting a prevention behavior than rationally-structured media messages promoting condom use and other safer sex behaviors (Airhihenbuwa, 1999; Singhal, 2001).

UNDERSTANDING RESISTANCES TO E-E

E-E scholars and practitioners are now more mindful about potential resistances to entertainment-education by message producers in the message environment, and in message reception by audiences.

On the message production side, strong resistance exists to initiating E-E interventions. Most commercial broadcasters fear charting what they perceive to be unknown territories. Time-tested media formulae generate audience ratings and profits. Commercial broadcasters fear that advertisers and audiences will be turned off if a radio or television program is perceived as playing an educational role. They are apprehensive about possible controversy, and thus losing their audience. Such resistances operate particularly in more media-saturated commercial broadcasting environments, such as the United States, where the total audience is relatively fragmented (see the Greenberg et al. chapter in this volume).

E-E scholars and practitioners are mindful of resistances on the message production side, and increasingly pay attention to how E-E projects are formulated, funded, researched, produced, distributed, and broadcast (Bouman, 2002). Martine Bouman's chapter in this volume pays attention to possible means of bridging the divide between "peacocks" (television professionals) versus "turtles" (health communication experts).

Most E-E scholars acknowledge that entertainment-education is only one of many competing, and conflicting, discourses that exist in a given message environment. In highly-saturated media societies like the United States, and to a lesser degree in many developing countries, entertainment-education messages face competition from, and are resisted by, other media programs (Sherry, 2002). These are often of the "entertainment-degradation" or "entertainment-perversion" type. Examples in the United States include television programs such as the *Jerry Springer Show*, and reality television shows like *Survivor*.

Resistance also operates at the message-reception end of the process as audience members selectively expose themselves to E-E messages, selectively perceive them, selectively recall them, and selectively use them for their own purposes. One example of such audience-centered resistance is the *Archie Bunker effect*, defined as the degree to which certain audience individuals identify with negative role models in E-E interventions (Singhal & Rogers, 1999). In investigating Norman Lear's popular situation comedy *All in the Family*, Vidmar and Rokeach (1974) noted that Archie Bunker, a bigoted character, reinforced, rather than reduced, racial and ethnic prejudice for certain already prejudiced viewers. Highly-prejudiced persons, as compared to lowly-prejudiced individuals, were more likely to watch the television program, and to perceive Archie as a "lovable, down-to-earth, honest, and predictable" person. They were more likely to condone his use of racial slurs than were low-prejudiced viewers (Vidmar & Rokeach, 1974). An Archie Bunker-type effect has been observed in many entertainment-education programs, although it usually is characteristic of only a very small percent of the audience. For instance, some women viewers of the Indian television soap opera, *Hum Log*, identified Bhagwanti, a negative role model for gender equality, as the character most worthy of emulation.

FROM INDIVIDUAL TO MULTILEVEL EXPLANATIONS OF BEHAVIOR CHANGE

Theoretical investigations of entertainment-education go beyond the exclusive use of individual-level theories and models of preventive health behaviors such as stages-of-change, the hierarchy-of-effects model, and social cognitive theory to more multilevel, cultural, and contextual theoretical explanations (McKinlay & Marceau, 1999). Metaphorically speaking, entertainment-education scholars are increasingly moving beyond investigating the bobbing of individual corks on surface waters, so as to focus on understanding the strong undercurrents that determine where cork clusters are deposited along a shoreline (McMichael, 1995).

Some recent E-E investigations have gone beyond studying individual-level behavioral changes to investigate E-E-instigated changes at the system or community level (for example, Papa et al., 2000). In an ongoing community-level investigation in the Indian State of Bihar, a popular E-E radio soap opera *Taru*, accompanied by such ground-based activities as folk performances, group listening, and the availability of local health services, brings about changes in group, community, and organizational norms (see the Arvind Singhal and others' chapter in this volume). This year-long E-E radio soap opera is leading to enhanced levels of *collective efficacy*, defined as the degree to which people in a system believe they can organize and execute courses of action required to achieve collective goals (Bandura, 1997). Deeply-ingrained cultural norms can be altered only by concerted action of the collectivity. Seldom can a system's norms be altered only by individual efforts.

E-E interventions can model either (or both) individual *self-efficacy* (defined as an individual's perception of his or her capability to deal effectively with a situation, and one's sense of perceived control over a situation) or collective efficacy. In the popular E-E television series *Soul City* in South Africa, a new collective behavior was modeled to portray how neighbors might intervene in a domestic violence situation (see the Shereen Usdin and others' chapter in this volume).

In essence, theoretical investigations of E-E now focus not only on *what* effects E-E programs have, but also try to better understand *how* and *why* entertainment-education has such effects. There is an increased focus on how audience members negotiate the message content, especially as the message reception environment hinders or enables the impact of the E-E message (see the Thomas Tufte chapter in this volume). There is growing evidence that interpersonal communication of E-E message content, once it is received by audience individuals from a mass media channel, can greatly magnify E-E effects on behavior change (Rogers et al., 1999).

METHODOLOGICAL PLURALISM

Most past research on entertainment-education effects relied mainly on audience surveys, sometimes coupled with content analyses of E-E messages, and with analyses of audience letters. Singhal and Rogers (1999) and Sypher and others (2002) pointed to the advantages of employing methodological pluralism in complementing survey techniques with more qualitative methods, including the use of focus group interviews, participant observation, in-depth interviews, letters from audience members, and semiotic analyses.

Audience letters and e-mails represent a rather "pure" form of audience feedback, and E-E scholars should consider tapping the research potential of these messages more fully. Such letters are usually unsolicited, unprompted (and hence free of possible researchers' biases), and in the writer's own language, and thus provide rich insights about how an E-E intervention affects the audience (Law & Singhal, 1999; Sood & Rogers, 2000). Such data also cost very little to gather. Over 400,000 letters from viewers were received by Doordarshan, the government television network in India, in response to an E-E soap opera, *Hum Log*, providing rich insights about the program's popularity and its effects on highly involved audiences (Singhal & Rogers, 1999).

In the Amazon rainforest of Peru, the entertainment-education program *Bienvenida Salud!* attracted hundreds of letters each month (Sypher et al., 2002; Elias, 2002). Many letters are written on tree bark (one letter was about a meter long) with vegetable, stone, and natural colors used as ink. Minga Peru, the nongovernmental organization that produces the radio program, made arrangements with boat companies to ferry listeners' letters from the interior of the Amazon jungle to Iquitos, the headquarters of Minga Peru. Letter-writers do not pay for this postal service; Minga Peru pays a small fee for each letter that is delivered. When one of the present authors (Singhal) asked Eliana Elias, Executive Director of Minga Peru, about this emphasis on audience letters, she replied: "Asking for letters is not only a strategy to measure audience effects, it is also a way to prepare the scripts of the programs and a way to change the passive consumers of the program into active producers" (personal conversation, October 16, 2002). Indeed, the educational theme of each episode of *Bienvenida Salud!*, produced in-house in the organization's well-equipped studio in Iquitos, is carefully distilled from previous audience letters.

Telephone hotlines also represent a useful means for obtaining feedback from audiences in E-E interventions. A popular song, "I Still Believe," performed by Lea Salonga in the Philippines, was used to encourage telephone calls from adolescents to "Dial-a-Friend," where they could receive personal information and advice about contraception and other sexually-related topics. Trained professional counselors maintained four hotlines, which averaged over 1,000 calls per week (Rimon, 1989). Telephone helplines for abused women also supplemented the *Soul City* prime-time television series on domestic violence in South Africa. Some 180,000 calls were answered in five months (when the *Soul City* series on domestic violence was broadcast in late

1999). Monitoring of the call data suggested that in places like Johannesburg, only 5 percent of the calls could be answered during peak times; the remaining 95% encountered a busy signal (Soul City, 2000).

E-E researchers increasingly realize the importance of measuring the degree to which E-E interventions spur interpersonal communication between audience and non-audience members (a measure of the indirect effects of an E-E intervention in a version of the two-step flow process). To more adequately gauge these indirect effects of E-E interventions, we recommend that during the production of E-E messages, markers should be incorporated in the E-E intervention. Markers are distinctive elements of a message that are uniquely identifiable (Singhal & Rogers, 2002). The simplest way of introducing a marker in an E-E intervention is to rename an existing product. For instance, in the popular St. Lucian family planning radio soap opera *Apwe Plezi* (After the Pleasure), a new condom brand called "Catapult" was introduced. This new name was identified by 28% of the radio program's listeners, validating their claim of direct exposure to the radio program, and by 13% of the nonlisteners, suggesting that the message diffused via interpersonal channels (thus providing a test of diffusion of innovations theory) (Vaughan, Regis, & St. Catherine, 2000).

Alternatively, a marker or tracer might consist of creatively naming characters in an E-E program, like the skirt-chasing character Scattershot in *Nasebery Street*, a radio soap opera about sexually responsible fatherhood in Jamaica (Singhal & Rogers, 1999). Scattershot became a common term in Jamaican discourse, as in "Oh, you Scattershot you," providing an opportunity for researchers to trace the direct and indirect effects among audience individuals of listening to the radio program.

The most powerful markers model new culturally-appropriate realities to break oppressive power structures in society, exemplified by the collective pot banging by neighbors in the South African entertainment-education series, *Soul City*, so as to stop wife/partner abuse. Markers, which model new realities, not only enhance the message content of an E-E intervention, but also provide additional validation for whether or not audience members were directly or indirectly exposed to the E-E intervention.

CONCLUSIONS

E-E today is a worldwide phenomenon, with almost every nation having, or having had, an E-E project. Diverse opinions now characterize the E-E field, including the voices of enthusiasts, dissenters, and skeptics. More organizations are engaged in E-E practice, and teaching and scholarship on E-E now occurs in university-based schools of communication, public health, and international development. Evaluations of these E-E interventions have become increasingly sophisticated, employing multiple theoretical perspectives and research methods. In the past decade or so, the E-E strategy emerged as an important issue in the fields of communication, health, and development practice and research.

In the future, E-E will more closely integrate "modern" and "traditional" entertainment outlets, and "big" and "little" media technologies. The Internet opened new possibilities with respect to conveying E-E interventions (see the Everett Rogers chapter in this volume). Such Web-based delivery of an E-E intervention allows for tailoring, defined as the individualization of a communication message to audience members (Singhal & Rogers, 2003).

The field of entertainment-education will go beyond its mass-mediated (television, radio, film, video, and print) formats to include crafts, art, textiles, murals, toys, and other creative expressions. For instance, in South Africa, "positive pottery" (made by HIV-positive people) includes colorful AIDS ribbons etched with traditional African motifs.

In the future, E-E interventions are likely to see more integration with participatory communication approaches (see the Arvind Singhal chapter in this volume). The work of Brazilian theater director Augusto Boal, who founded the Theatre of the Oppressed (TO) movement, is particularly relevant here. TO's techniques, based on Paulo Freire's principles of dialogue, interaction, problem-posing, reflection, and conscientization, are designed to activate spectators ("spect-actors") to take control of situations, rather than to passively allow actions to happen to them (Boal, 1979).

In the future, we believe entertainment-education will also go beyond the boundaries of its mainstay messages—reproductive health, family planning, and HIV prevention—to include other pressing social issues such as peace, conflict mediation, terrorism, race relations, and reconstruction. The role of E-E will likely be further realized in understanding the struggles for liberation and empowerment, especially the use of songs and other expressions as means of protest, resistance, dialogue, debate, and coping.

In essence, the future of E-E practice and research is one of exciting possibilities, challenges, and debates, as evidenced by the chapters that follow.

REFERENCES

Airhihenbuwa, C. O. (1999). Of culture and multiverse: Renouncing "the universal truth" in health. *Journal of Health Education, 30*(5), 267–273.

Bandura, A. (1977). *Social learning theory*. Englewood Cliffs, NJ: Prentice-Hall.

Bandura, A. (1997). *Self-efficacy: The exercise of control*. New York: Freeman.

Boal, A. (1979). *The theatre of the oppressed*. New York: Urizen Books.

Bouman, M. (2002). Turtles and peacocks: Collaboration in entertainment-education television. *Communication Theory, 12*(2), 225–244.

de Fossard, E. (2002, May 15). Personal email correspondence.

Elias, E. (2002, October 16). Personal conversation in Iquitos, Peru.

Elias, E. (2002, October). *Comunicar para icarar: El modelo Minga de communicación para la salud desde la cultura.* Paper presented to the International Conference on Reproductive Health in the Amazonian Region, Iquitos, Peru.

Fisher, W. (1987). *Human communication as narration.* Columbia, SC: University of South Carolina Press.

Galavotti, Christine, Pappas-Deluca Katina A., & Lansky Amy (2001). Modeling and reinforcement to combat HIV: The MARCH approach to behavior change. *American Journal of Public Health, 91*(10), 1602-1607.

Kincaid, D. L. (2002). Drama, emotion, and cultural convergence. *Communication Theory, 12*(2), 136-152.

Law, S., & Singhal, A. (1999). Efficacy in letter-writing to an entertainment-education radio serial. *Gazette, 61*(5), 355-372.

McDougall, L. (2002, December 9). Personal e-mail correspondence.

McKinlay, J. B., & Marceau, L. D. (1999). A tale of 3 tails. *American Journal of Public Health, 89,* 295-298.

McMichael, A. J. (1995). The health of persons, populations, and planets: Epidemiology comes full circle. *Epidemiology, 6,* 636-663.

Nariman, H. (1993). *Soap operas for social change.* Westport, CT: Praeger.

Papa, M. J., Singhal, A., Law, S., Pant, S., Sood, S., Rogers, E. M., & Shefner, C. L. (2000). Entertainment-education and social change: An analysis of parasocial interaction, social learning, collective efficacy, and paradoxical communication. *Journal of Communication, 50*(4), 31-55.

Rimon, J. G., II (1989, December). Leveraging messages and corporations: The Philippine experience. *Integration, 22,* 37-44.

Rogers, E. M., Vaughan, P. W., Swalehe, R. M. A., Rao, N., Svenkerud, P., & Sood, S. (1999). Effects of an entertainment-education radio soap opera on family planning in Tanzania. *Studies in Family Planning, 30*(3), 193-211.

Singhal, A. (2001). *HIV/AIDS and communication for behavior and social change: Program experiences, examples, and the way forward.* Geneva, Switzerland: UNAIDS.

Singhal, A., Obregon, R., & Rogers, E. M. (1994). Reconstructing the story of *Simplemente María,* the most popular *telenovela* in Latin America of all time. *Gazette, 54,* 1-15.

Singhal, A., & Rogers E. M. (1999). *Entertainment-education: A communication strategy for social change.* Mahwah, NJ: Lawrence Erlbaum Associates.

Singhal, A., & Rogers, E. M. (2001). The entertainment-education strategy in campaigns. In R. E. Rice and C. Atkins (Eds), *Public Communication Campaigns* (pp. 343-356). Third Edition. Thousand Oaks, CA: Sage.

Singhal, A., & Rogers, E. M. (2002). A theoretical agenda for entertainment-education. *Communication Theory, 12*(2), 117-135.

Singhal, A., & Rogers, E. M. (2003). *Combating AIDS: Communication strategies in action.* Thousand Oaks, CA: Sage.

Sherry, J. L. (2002). Media saturation and entertainment-education. *Communication Theory, 12*(2), 206-224.

Slater, M., & Rouner, D. (2002). Entertainment-education and elaboration likelihood: Understanding the processing of narrative persuasion. *Communication Theory, 12*(2), 173-191.

Sood, S. (2002). Audience involvement and entertainment-education. *Communication Theory, 12*(2), 153-172.

Sood, S., & Rogers, E. M. (2000). Dimensions of intense parasocial interaction by letter-writers to a popular entertainment-education soap opera in India. *Journal of Broadcasting and Electronic Media, 44,* 386-414.

Soul City (2000, September). *The evaluation of Soul City 4: Methodology and top-line results*. Paper presented at the Third International Entertainment-Education Conference for Social Change, Arnhem, The Netherlands.

Soul City (2001). *Series 4: Impact Evaluation—AIDS*. Parkstown, South Africa: Soul City Institute for Health and Development Communication.

Stephenson, W. (1988). *The play theory of mass communication*. New Brunswick, NJ: Transaction Books.

Sypher, B. D., McKinley, M., Ventsam, S., & Valdea Vellano, E. E. (2002). Fostering reproductive health through entertainment-education in the Peruvian Amazon: The social construction of *Bienvenida Salud! Communication Theory, 12*(2), 192–205.

Valente, T. W., & Bharath, U. (1999). An evaluation of the use of drama to communicate HIV/AIDS information. *AIDS Education and Prevention, 11*, 203–211.

Valente, T. W., Poppe, P. R., Alva, M.E., de Briceno, R.V., & Cases, D. (1995). Street theater as a tool to reduce family planning misinformation. *International Quarterly of Community Health Education, 15*(3), 279–289.

Vaughan, P., Regis, A., & St. Catherine, E. (2000). Effects of an entertainment-education radio soap opera on family planning and HIV prevention in St. Lucia. *International Family Planning Perspectives, 26*(4), 148–157.

Vidmar, N., & Rokeach, M. (1974). Archie Bunker's bigotry: A study in selective perception and exposure. *Journal of Communication, 24*(1), 36–47.

Wallack, L. (1990). Two approaches to health promotion in the mass media. *World Health Forum, 11*, 143–155.

Zillman, D., & Vorderer, P. (Eds.) (2000). *Media entertainment: The psychology of its appeal*. Mahwah, NJ: Lawrence Erlbaum Associates.

2

A History of Entertainment-Education, 1958–2000

David O. Poindexter
Population Media Center

EDITORS' INTRODUCTION

Here one of the pioneers of entertainment-education (E-E), David Poindexter, the former President of Population Communications International, provides a look inside the kitchen of the international diffusion of this important strategy. The key role of Miguel Sabido in developing a methodology for E-E broadcasts, and of PCI in initiating Hum Log *in India, the first E-E project outside of Mexico, are explained.*

My drift into the worldwide entertainment-education (E-E) movement began in 1958 when I was asked to go for training in an early E-E experiment being mounted by the U.S. Methodist Church. Called *Talk Back*, it consisted of thirteen 13-minute dramas. Each posed a problem that people encounter as they live their lives, but offered no solutions. *Talk Back* was to be syndicated to the U.S. television media for public service play. A panel of professionals would follow each episode in order to help the audience members develop better ways of coping with a given crisis when it arose in their lives. It was expected that church and NGO groups would carry on discussions of the problem posed. *Talk Back* represented one of the more effective attempts of the church to utilize the then new medium of television.

In each television market, a three-person group would place, publicize, and assist in utilization of the television series. In my market, Portland, Oregon, the other two persons involved shortly moved out of the state and I was then asked to take over the project. The program was telecast in 1959 and I was on my way to being "hooked" on the E-E strategy.

The NBC affiliate in Portland belonged to a group of radio and television stations in the four largest Pacific Northwest cities. The owner of the company was a particularly enlightened person, Mrs. A. Scott Bullitt. She and her Public Service Director, Gloria Chandler, opened many doors for E-E broadcasting including *Talk Back*, and Mrs. Bullitt traveled frequently from Seattle to serve on the media committee that I chaired for the Greater Portland Council of Churches. The next six years provided me with an invaluable introduction to the language and processes of television and radio broadcasting. In 1965, I was invited to join the staff of the National Council of Churches' (NCC) Broadcasting and Film Commission (BFC) in New York City.

GETTING TO KNOW U.S. NATIONAL TELEVISION

While in New York, I was immersed in work with television both in New York and Hollywood, where the BFC also had offices. I worked as the NCC's official liaison with CBS News. In those years, CBS mounted some highly creative religious programs on Sunday morning, led by a CBS News Vice President, Miss Pamela Ilott. She was a unique mix of creativity, innovation, and management.

Two events stand out from those years. The first was a 30-minute drama written for a summer series on religion and the arts. The playwright was Jean-Claude Van Italie, whose *America Hurrah* in 1966 was cited as the outstanding drama of the year, on or off Broadway. Titled *Hobbies, or Things are Fine with the Forbushers*, the teleplay was an incisive examination of the U.S. psyche, American culture, and the country's actions in Vietnam. It was the first program on any U.S. television network to analyze our country's Vietnam involvement. Top management at CBS News resisted *Hobbies*. They asked: "Can't you deal with other public issues as well?" Jean-Claude said, "No, either you take my drama as is or not at all." I hauled up the church's "big guns" and the program aired.

In 1967, a five-week series titled, *Choice: The Imperative of Tomorrow*, was broadcast. It dealt with the knowledge explosion, the information explosion, the population explosion, and the aspiration explosion, coupled with the pervasive social problems of global poverty, environmental degradation, the gender gap, and more. Some 45 nongovernmental organizations in North America, ranging from AARP to Zonta, including the churches, were involved. In 45 metropolitan areas in both the U.S. and Canada (the program was carried simultaneously on CBC-Canada), local committees were formed. The broadcasts were on Sunday. In each market, hundreds or even thousands of viewing and discussion groups telephoned their conclusions to a local committee. By the following Sunday, some of the most important returns were incorporated in the telecast. The notion of coupling a radio or television broadcast with local discussion groups was shown to have considerable impact.

THE POPULATION COMMUNICATION CENTER

In 1969, a good friend of mine, Rodney Shaw, became convinced that the population bomb posed a big, if not bigger, threat than nuclear warfare. Shaw founded the Department of Population Problems in the Methodist Church. Rodney believed that because of the population explosion, the world was headed toward disaster unless hundreds of millions of people in their childbearing years made sensible, reality-relevant family size choices. Massive ongoing radio and television campaigns were needed to educate and motivate couples and individuals worldwide.

"You," he said to me, "know something about media. What would you do?" I wrote him a proposal outlining my ideas. Rodney said, "This makes good sense to me. If I find the money, will you work to implement it?" "Yes," I said.

I started the population project on July 1, 1970. My initial primary goal was to get the issue into prime-time television entertainment programming. Instinctively, I knew that drama and comedy were vehicles to get population messages to American viewers more effectively than news stories and documentaries.

Five strata must be addressed in order to implement a change in U.S. network television: (1) the corporations that own the networks; (2) top management of each network; (3) production houses that produce television programs for the three commercial networks; (4) the producers themselves; and (5) perhaps most important, although least powerful, the scriptwriters.

My title was Director of the Population Communication Center, which was supported both by the church's Department of Population Problems and by the Population Institute, the fledgling organization that Rodney Shaw had started. The Institute was essential because if I wished to establish a working relationship with national television networks, I could not do so wearing the hat of one religious group. I targeted the chief operating officers of the companies that owned the networks.

In March 1971 I assembled members of a blue ribbon committee and senior officers of the three companies at a luncheon in the Waldorf Towers in

New York. This was during the second year of the three-year U.S. National Commission on Population Growth and the American Future. Republican Senate member on the Commission, Bob Packwood, and the Chair, John D. Rockefeller, III addressed the luncheon. Other blue ribbon committee members included the then U.S. Ambassador to the U.N., George H. W. Bush, a staunch advocate of population programs, and Emerson Foote, a distinguished elder statesman of U.S. advertising. Also present were Dr. Frank Stanton, Chief Operating Officer of CBS, Jim Haggerty, Corporate Vice President of ABC, and Robert Kasmire, Corporate Vice President of NBC.

Senator Packwood laid out the nature, dimensions, and implications of domestic and international population growth. After 10 minutes, Dr. Stanton said, "Senator, you don't need to convince me, or I'm sure, my colleagues, of the seriousness of this problem. But you are talking to the wrong people. You ought to be out on the Coast talking to the creative people." I read from a letter from Harry Ackerman, who had served as programming vice president of CBS-TV during its golden age: "There is very little that any writer or producer on the coast can accomplish on your subject until you can achieve a climate of support and approval at the networks." Dr. Stanton said: "Okay, that's fair. I can't speak for my colleagues at the other two networks, but so far as we at CBS are concerned, as of this moment, you have top management's support and approval." Then he leaned far across the table, aimed his index finger at my face, and said, "so long as it is a quality program." "Dr. Stanton," I replied, "unless it is a quality program, I don't want it on the air!" He responded: "We understand each other."

Both Kasmire and Haggerty said that we had the backing of their networks. Senator Packwood followed up: "Will you put it in writing?" They gulped and said, "Yes."

My next stop was to visit the West Coast creative people to whom Dr. Stanton had referred. When I arrived in Los Angeles with the written guarantees of support and approval for quality prime-time network programs dealing with the population issue, the creative community was astounded. The question was how to proceed. A particularly experienced advisory committee, including Robert F. Lewine, President and CEO of the Television Academy; Harry Ackerman, prominent producer and industry leader for decades; Gerald Leider, President, Warner Brothers Television; Roy Huggins, who headed a company that was part of the MCA Universal Group; and Thomas Sarnoff of the famous family who ran NBC on the West Coast, recommended an all-day meeting to brief the Los Angeles production community and propose a script awards and an annual awards banquet. Speakers at the annual banquets included Dr. Paul Ehrlich, author of *The Population Bomb*, Ambassador Andrew Young, and Professor Margaret Mead. Emcees included Jackie Cooper, Jack Lemmon, and Carl Reiner.

A major daylong event in November 1971 was held in the Grand Ballroom of the Century Plaza Hotel. Some 500 people who managed the U.S. television and film industry participated. Presenters included MIT Professor Dennis Meadows, who presented his "The Limits to Growth" study; General William H. Draper, Jr.; the Right Honorable Lord Caradon; Walter Hickel, who had just been released by President Nixon as his Secretary of the Interior; and Hugh Downs, who we introduced as "Yesterday's host of *Today*." The script contest awarded $5,000 to the writer of the best half-hour television program telecast over a network that dealt with the population issue, $10,000 to the writer of the best program of an hour or longer, and $5,000 to the writer of the best episode or series of episodes in a soap opera. These prize amounts in the early 1970s were serious money, representing more than a writer might earn for writing a script for a production company.

The event was a springboard for a follow-up event held in March, 1972 in the Grand Ballroom of New York's Plaza Hotel. The Committee for this event included the presidents of the three commercial television networks plus PBS's predecessor, NET. John D. Rockefeller III, presented the pending recommendations of the U.S. National Commission on Population Growth and the American Future. Dr. Frank Stanton gave a luncheon address on television's responsibilities for a major national issue. The Script Awards Contest was announced for the next year.

Having secured the backing of television's owners, plus the West and East Coast television establishment, it was now time to connect with the actual groups who were producing television shows.

A series of luncheons were held for five days running at the Beverly Hills Hotel in Los Angeles. Invitees were the top executives of the major production studios, plus senior television creative people. The presenter for the first four days was Philander Claxton, senior population officer of the U.S. government, and Congressman Moe Udall presented on the fifth day.

That day, the top-rated CBS dramady, *Maude*, began a storyline about an unexpected and undesirable pregnancy. The result was "Maude's Dilemma," Parts 1 and 2. During the fall of 1972, *Mash, Maude, Mary Tyler Moore*, and *All In The Family* carried the population issue. The two-part story on *Maude* had the most impact because of the uproar surrounding it. The two episodes discussed the whys and why-nots of pregnancy, various forms of contraception, and at the end of the second week arrived at Maude's decision to have an abortion.

Between the original telecast in November, 1972 and a rerun the following August, the program was seen by 140 million viewers, 80 million of whom saw it in both November and August. In following years, we carried on intensive activities with U.S. television programmers. Population-related attention was included in prime-time television programming.

When we began the effort in Hollywood, it was by no means clear that the baby boom was over, as was stated by the U.S. National Commission on Population Growth and the American Future. Within a few years, U.S. culture changed. Numerous factors were undoubtedly involved, including our messages that were carried in the heart of U.S. television programs, articulated by such American favorites as Mary Tyler Moore as Mary Richards, Rob Reiner as Meathead, and Bea Arthur as Maude.

INTERNATIONAL POPULATION COMMUNICATION: 1973–1981

From its inception, it was clear that the Communication Center had to move beyond the United States into the high-population growth rate countries. In the United States, the appropriate medium was network television, and the format was primarily comedy and drama. The modus operandi was to build constructive relationships with the professionals who were writing, producing, and telecasting these television programs.

Dialogo in Costa Rica

A model radio program entitled *Dialogo* in Costa Rica was led by Jose Carlo, who served on our staff in the mid-1970s. *Dialogo* (Dialogue) was a radio talk show that tackled hitherto taboo topics like sex, contraception, and family planning. During this period, I took Jose Carlo to Stanford University's Institute for Communication Research to meet Professor Everett M. Rogers. Two of his colleagues, Dr. Peter Spain, and a Chilean MA student, Felipe Risopatron, conducted an audience survey in Costa Rica investigating the effects of the radio program. *Dialogo*'s impact on its audience was substantial, especially upon the most poor, most rural, and least-educated people (Risopatron & Spain, 1980). The *Dialogo* strategy required the creation and funding of a sizable infrastructure, which was beyond our Center's resources.

Mexico and Miguel Sabido

I continued to look for my "how-to" answer until 1977, when in September, I looked next door, in Mexico. There, I found a most incredible human being/social scientist/broadcast professional, Miguel Sabido (Photo 2.1).

I started at the top of Mexico's gigantic television conglomerate, Televisa. The network's President Emilio Azcarraga Milmo issued the invitation. However, Azcarraga was on a summer holiday on his yacht in the Mediterranean when we arrived in Mexico City. His assistant, Gaspar Rionda, sent us directly to meet a person who would infuse content into my mission and change the course of my life. Miguel Sabido proceeded to give us a three-hour lecture, professionally translated, outlining his social content communication methodology with references to Albert Bandura's social learning theory and Eric Bentley's dramatic theory. At that point in the development of Sabido's

PHOTO 2.1.   Miguel Sabido (left) and David Poindexter (right) in Mexico City
in September 2002, celebrating the 25th anniversary of their first meeting.
(*Source*: Population Media Center. Used with permission.)

methodology, Paul MacLean's psychoneurological theory and Carl Jung's
archetypes theory had yet to find a place in his approach.

Our meeting with Sabido occurred just one week after the premier of
Acompáñame, the world's first family planning television serial drama. Here
was a theoretical framework, a methodology for television production, and
an on-air production that represented this unique approach. To say that our
attentions were riveted is an understatement. I said: "Here, for the first time, is
something that makes total sense to me and it has the earmarks of being a valid
way to proceed within the realities of a high population growth developing
country."

On the September day that I encountered Miguel Sabido, the population
growth rate of Mexico was 3.1% per annum, which meant the nation's population would double in a little more than two decades.

Miguel Sabido said to me: "Because of our serial drama, the population
growth rate of Mexico will come down 0.4% in the next year." Miguel was
suggesting that Mexico would experience such an unprecedented decline
in the population growth rate because of a one-half hour a day television
program, five days a week, in addition to the effects of the national program
of family planning.

In May 1978, I returned to Mexico. *Acompáñame* had completed its
9-month run. Enrollments in family planning clinics in Mexico had been raised

by 33% from the previous year, about half a million women. Sales of over-the-counter contraceptives (like condoms and oral pills) had increased 23%, compared to a 7% rise the preceding year. Mexico's population growth rate declined from an estimated 3.1% to 2.7% in one year. Some of this decline was undoubtedly due to the contemporaneous changes that occurred while *Acompáñame* was being broadcast, such as the national family planning program in Mexico, then in its fourth year. Later evaluations of E-E programs in other nations, like Tanzania, would use more sophisticated research designs to remove the effect of these contemporaneous changes.

Continuing Sabido's Work

I had letters sent to Televisa President Emilio Azcarraga, encouraging him to broadcast another E-E soap opera. Several U.S. senators, the Director–General of the BBC, and the Secretary–General of the Commonwealth Broadcasting Association dispatched letters. The Right Honourable Lord Caradon, Chair of the International Advisory Council of the Population Center, sent the letter that did the trick. I then received a telephone call from Miguel Sabido. "David", he said, "last evening Mr. Azcarraga invited us to his office. He questioned us about *Acompáñame* and the research results (on its effects). He was terribly pleased to receive the letter from Lord Caradon. He authorized us to begin preparation for the next E-E *telenovela* and the first social content *radionovela*. Sabido created telenovelas entitled *Vamos Juntos* (We Go Together); *Caminemos* (Let's Walk), which dealt with adolescent sexuality; *Nosotras las Mujeres* (We the Women); and *Por Amor* (For Love).

During this period of working closely with Miguel Sabido, in which Miguel was strengthening and expanding his entertainment-education methodology, I was reporting regularly to the Advisory Committee of the Population Center. I encountered vast skepticism. Richard K. Manoff, a member said, "Poindexter, forget it. What you say the Mexicans are doing, we couldn't do in our own country." Sabido produced a video containing a storyline extracted from *Acompáñame* plus two separate episodes of the show with English subtitles. I played this video for my Advisory Committee. They were enthusiastic. Arthur Reef, Chair of the U.S. Committee for the International Institute of Communication (IIC) declared that there must be a Televisa presentation at the next IIC annual meeting.

TAKING THE SABIDO METHODOLOGY TO THE WORLD

At the forthcoming IIC Conference in Strassbourg, France, I met Inder K. Gujral, a senior government official, later to serve as India's Prime Minister. He extended an invitation to bring Sabido and his E-E approach to India.

In December 1981 in the home of Inder Gujral in New Delhi, I made a presentation to the senior officials from the Ministry of Information and Broadcasting, the Ministry of Health and Family Welfare, as well as private sector leaders. The Sabido video helped me make a powerful case for the adoption by India of this E-E methodology. But at the end of the evening, all I got were limp handshakes and perfunctory goodbyes.

Six weeks later, my U.N. colleague Jyoti Singh asked me what I had accomplished in India. I told him my impressions. He replied, "You stupid American. Those were Indian civil servants. Just because they didn't give you their opinions doesn't meant they don't have them. Get back to India." When I did, I found out that the Indian civil servants had been really excited.

I was quick to learn that the Sabido methodology cannot be grafted onto a large diverse group. Rather, it is designed to be utilized by a production/research group that is going to mount an E-E drama in a specific place dealing with a specific social problem. In May 1983, a Mexican team led by Miguel Sabido spent the better part of a month in India meeting with a large group that was assembled not to develop an E-E project, but only to listen to a savant from the West. At the end of the visit, had nothing further occurred, the project would have been dead. However, we were saved for three reasons: (1) Prime Minister Indira Gandhi had determined that, for political reasons, she needed to expand national television; (2) a hardware technology for covering India with download/re-transmitting ground stations allowed India over 10 months to move from 14% television coverage of their land area to more than 70%, and (3) the Sabido team met with Prime Minister Gandhi, and they sold her on the importance of Sabido's methodology for India (for a photograph of this historic meeting, see Singhal & Rogers, 1999).

The Secretary of the Ministry of Information and Broadcasting, S. S. Gill, was favorably oriented to the Sabido methodology. By late 1983, an Indian (and Kenyan) team was in Mexico City for a training session with Miguel Sabido. Gill began his own orientation at Televisa in January 1984.

India: First Transfer of the Sabido Methodology

Events in India moved rapidly following Gill's return. He decided that regulations would be "bent" so that he could mount a commercially sponsored program in prime-time. He assembled an untraditional team headed by a female advertising entrepreneur to secure sponsors, his own hand-picked writer, a producer from the Bombay film industry, and a staff member from Doordarshan, India's national television system.

Mrs. Gandhi wanted national television. First, Gill put the hardware of television transmission into place. Then a program of compelling entertainment value was essential if he were to deliver a mass audience of new television owners. In July 1984, *Hum Log* (We People) went on the air in India. It delivered the national audience Mrs. Gandhi desired. Ratings of *Hum Log* were unprecedented. At certain climactic points in the plot, 90% of the potential audience was watching. *Hum Log* broadcasts continued for 18 months.

Singhal and Rogers (1989) found that 70% of the viewers indicated they had learned from *Hum Log* that women should have equal opportunities, 68% had learned that women should have the freedom to make their personal decisions in life, and 71% had learned that family size should be limited. Over 400,000 viewers were stimulated to write letters to the Indian television network or to various characters in the soap opera. Ninety percent of these letters dealt with plot suggestions, asked for help or advice, or reported actions that had been stimulated by viewing *Hum Log*.

Hum Log demonstrated that Indian television could attract large audiences and sell products, such as Maggi Two-Minute Noodles, an entirely new food product in India that was only advertised on the *Hum Log* broadcasts. Until now, the world's largest pool of professional visual production talent had been almost totally walled off from Indian national television. Virtually overnight, a thousand new organizations sprang up. A marketer with a product to sell, a filmmaker with a television program, and an advertising agency/packager: They headed for Doordarshan television headquarters at Mandi House in New Delhi. So *Hum Log*, the first E-E soap opera in India, changed not only the behavior of the national population, but also the nature of Indian television (Singhal & Rogers, 1999).

Kenya: A Second Transfer From Mexico

After their return from a training session with Miguel Sabido in Mexico City, I did not hear from the Kenyan team until the following September (1984). When they returned from Mexico City, Kenya's Catholic bishops were generating opposition to family planning and everyone was intimidated. But in August 1984, Kenyan President Daniel Arap Moi called a national conference on population. Now the course was clear to produce E-E television and radio serial dramas.

At Broadcast House, the headquarters for the government broadcasting network in Nairobi, all studios were fully booked. The only option was an all-night train ride to Mombasa where there was a television studio. The studio could not film in color and had no editing facilities. Editing the soap opera series entailed the overnight trip to Nairobi, plus standing in line to get into the editing room at Broadcast House.

A radio studio was available in a stadium built for the All-African Games. The problem was that it was several miles away from downtown Nairobi. Transport was required and it had to be scrounged. Despite these obstacles, the television serial *Tushauriane* (Come with Me) went on the air in mid-May,

1987. The radio serial *Ushikwapo Shikamana* (When Assisted, Assist Yourself) premiered in late 1987.

Tushauriane was the highest rated television program in the history of Kenyan television. It premiered under the aegis of Mwai Kibaki, Kenya's Vice President. He was replaced, at which point the E-E program ended. Nevertheless, 60 episodes had been recorded and broadcast. Later, on two occasions, these 60 episodes were rebroadcast, each time to huge audiences. *Ushikwapo Shikamana* managed to persevere, ultimately broadcasting more than 200 episodes on radio. Its director, Tom Kazungu, became a missionary for Sabido's approach, providing technical assistance to later E-E projects in Tanzania, St. Lucia, and in other nations.

By the time the two soap opera series ended, contraceptive use in Kenya had increased 58%, and desired family size had fallen from 6.3 to 4.4 children. Many other factors also were important in this behavior change, but the broadcasts played an important role.

The original *Tushauriane* producer, Greg Adambo, now out of government service and working in the private sector with commercial sponsorship, is preparing another television drama. Many of the original actors will again play their roles. *Ushikwapo Shikamana*, with funding from the Ford Foundation and under the aegis of Population Communications International, is currently back on the air in Kenya and attracting a large listening audience. Perseverance pays off.

Opening in Brazil

An invitation to the Population Center in August 1984 resulted in an exploratory visit to Brazil. The result was a formal agreement with TV Globo, the huge commercial network, that beginning in 1987, targeted population, family planning, and family size content that would appear in TV Globo's hour-long prime-time telenovelas that are broadcast for three hours on five nights a week. Since 1987, Brazil's fertility rate fell from approximately 3.5 children per woman to slightly more than 2 children. TV Globo's programs played an important role in this fertility rate decrease.

FOUNDING POPULATION COMMUNICATIONS INTERNATIONAL

My institutional base from 1970 until 1984 was the Communication Center of the Population Institute (PI). In 1984, the Communication Center was restructured into Population Communications International (PCI), and I became president and chief executive.

India

PCI initiated a second E-E television series in India. Titled *Humraahi* (Come Along with Me), this television program was a collaborative effort of Roger Pereira and his communication company; Harish Khanna, President of the Population Foundation of India and previously the Director-General of Indian Television; J. R. D. Tata, Chairman of India's largest industrial conglomerate; and PCI. It focused on improving the status of women in India, a social change that has consequence for population size.

This serial was the top-rated program on Indian television with an estimated audience of 230 million viewers. The most popular episode featured the death of a teenage mother in childbirth, who was forced to get married by her patriarchal father and forced into an early pregnancy by her patriarchal husband.

The Philippines

In the Philippines, Cecile Guidote Alvarez produced a television serial, *Sali Sing Buhay* (Interweaving Lives), as well as a radio serial and printed insert in the nation's most widely circulated comics publication.

China

An invitation from the Deputy Minister of Family Planning to PCI initiated negotiations in China in 1989. Communicating the Sabido methodology was complicated at first. Then Chinese television broadcast its first serial drama, *Ke Wang* (Aspirations), a 52-week series about the Cultural Revolution (Wang & Singhal, 1992). It was riveting and the audiences were unprecedented. The authorities in Beijing set up China Population Information Service as our counterpart agency. Funding became available from a private U.S. family foundation, the Ford Foundation, the UN Population Fund, and others.

The television series that resulted was titled *Zhonguo Baixing* (Ordinary Chinese People). It dealt with the status of girl children and women. Professor Arvind Singhal of Ohio University collaborated with the Center for Integrated Agriculture Development (CIAD) in Beijing to conduct an investigation on the audience effects of *Zhonguo Baixing*. This research indicated that the television series was highly popular and raised consciousness among its viewers about the importance of (1) raising gender equality, (2) abrogating harmful social and cultural practices, and (3) boosting self and collective efficacy (Singhal, Ren, & Zhang, 1999).

Tanzania: The First Full-Fledged Model

In 1990 the UN Population Fund invited PCI to propose an E-E project in Tanzania. The country had a total fertility rate of 7.2 children per woman, with fewer than half of school-aged children in school, and a per capita income of less than $100. HIV/AIDS was spreading rapidly. There was no television. Radio Tanzania had rudimentary equipment with a signal that did not reach the entire country. Radio Tanzania had never produced a scripted drama, and the notion of E-E was foreign.

PCI met with representatives of five government ministries, five UN agencies, and six NGOs (nongovernment organizations). After a vigorous discussion, they said, "Let's go." In February 1993, my PCI colleague, Bill Ryerson, Dr. Peter W. Vaughan, and Professor Everett M. Rogers from the University of New Mexico traveled to Dar es Salaam to help plan the research design to be utilized to evaluate the effects of *Twende na Wakati* (Let's Go with the Times) so that we could isolate the effects of the radio soap opera from everything else going on in Tanzania to promote family planning and HIV/AIDS prevention. We needed a treatment area and a control area (the latter would not receive the broadcasts). We went to Broadcast House in Dar es Salaam to meet with the Director of Radio Tanzania, Nkwabe Ngwanakilalla. All broadcasts originated in Broadcast House and were conveyed to the nation by seven repeater stations, except daily from 4:00 p.m. until 7:00 p.m., when the radio station in Dodoma cut away from the national network and broadcast local music programming. Radio Tanzania agreed to broadcast *Twende na Wakati* from 6:30 p.m. to 7:00 p.m. Thus the Dodoma area, with a population of 4.5 million people, became the control area for broadcasts of the radio soap opera from 1993 to 1995, after which *Twende na Wakati* was broadcast everywhere in Tanzania.

Rogers and Vaughan obtained research funding from the Rockefeller Foundation and the UNFPA (United Nations Population Fund), through the University of New Mexico. With the cooperation of POFLEP (Population Family Life Education Program), a Tanzanian research center, they conducted a yearly 3,000-person survey, beginning with a prebroadcast baseline survey in July 1993. Ongoing focus group interviews provided a rich information flow to the program's scriptwriters. Clinic intake data were collected from 79 health clinics as to how new clinic enrollees were motivated to adopt family planning methods. Letters to the radio program were analyzed for content and, of course, answered. Tom Kazungu, a Kenyan who had been trained by Miguel Sabido in Mexico City, worked with young scriptwriters from the drama department at the University of Dar es Salaam.

By 1993 *Twende na Wakati* was the most popular radio program in Tanzania, with 57% of the adult population listening. The effects of the E-E radio soap opera were determined by Professors Rogers and Vaughan at the University of New Mexico, working with POFLEP. About 23% of the adult population living in the treatment (broadcast) area adopted a family planning method, and more adopted an effective method of HIV/AIDS prevention from 1993 to 1995. From 1995 to 1997, after the broadcasts of *Twende na Wakati* also began in the Dodoma control area, similar results occurred there (Rogers et al., 1999; Vaughan & Rogers, 2000; Vaughan, Rogers, Singhal, & Swalehe 2000; Singhal & Rogers, 1999).

These results were spectacular, almost too strong to believe, but the evidence was quite convincing given that contemporaneous changes (such as from the National AIDS Control Programme) were removed by the experimental design. The Tanzania Project provided such convincing evidence of the strong effects of E-E that later projects have not found it worthwhile to include a control group in their research designs.

St. Lucia

One day, two unusual men from the Rare Center for Tropical Ecology virtually burst into my New York office. They had a major project in St. Lucia, a small island nation in the Caribbean, aimed at saving the islands' tropical rain forest and a unique inhabitant, a magnificent parrot existing only in St. Lucia. Their job was hopeless unless the St. Lucian population could be motivated to be responsible and reduce family size. The St. Lucia parrot's eggs were believed to be an aphrodisiac and were being consumed by the island's burgeoning population.

The St. Lucia Project centered on an E-E radio soap opera, *Apwe Plezi* (After the Pleasure Comes the Pain), which was very popular, and which scholars found had strong effects on behavior change (Vaughan, Regis, & St. Catherine, 2000). Presently this E-E intervention is being extended to other nations in the Caribbean.

India and Pakistan

Through initiatives by PCI and the Commonwealth Broadcasting Union, planning began (1) with the Director–General of All India Radio (AIR) to mount a Hindi-language radio serial in the high-population growth Hindi Belt of Northern India, and (2) with the Director–General of the Pakistan Broadcasting Corporation (PBC) to mount an E-E program that would be relevant to the varied cultures of that country.

India broadcast a year-long, successful radio soap opera entitled *Tinka Tinka Sukh* (Happiness Lies in Small Pleasures) in 1996-1997. Key to its effectiveness were (1) Shashi Kant Kapoor, then Director–General of All India Radio, and now PCI's Country Director in India, and (2) Ms. Usha Bhasin, an extraordinary executive producer at All India Radio (and now at Doordarshan). Dr. Arvind Singhal at Ohio University collaborated with the Center for Media Studies (CMS), headquartered in New Delhi, in an evaluation of the effects of *Tinka Tinka Sukh* (Singhal & Rogers, 1999; Law & Singhal, 1999; Papa et al., 2000). This program was then translated into four other South Indian languages.

Pakistan was a challenge. During development of the radio program, PBC went through several changes of its director–general. Given Pakistan's language and cultural diversity, the E-E serial drama was broadcast in Urdu, and then was translated into the languages and cultures of the Punjab (Punjabi), Sindh (Sindhi), Balluchistan (Balochi), and the Northwest Territories (Pushtu).

Later Projects

In Mexico, during the mid-1990s, Miguel Sabido produced a powerful telenovela focused on the problem of street children, *Los Hijos de Nadie* (Children of Nobody). This project involved Televisa and UNICEF. The epilogues at the end of each episode were given by actual street children in Mexico City.

In Tanzania, *Twende na Wakati* was originally scheduled to run only to 1997. However, the evaluation of this intervention in 1997 was so positive that UNFPA renewed the broadcasts for four more years. That period is now also finished, but the radio program is deemed too important to Tanzania's development for it to end. In 2002, *Twende na Wakati* was still on the air.

UNFPA's Diane Langston, who initiated the Project in Tanzania, asked PCI to explore a similar intervention in Ethiopia, arguably the most needy country in East Africa. However, the Ethiopian Project had still not jelled when I turned over control at PCI to my successor. In 1998 when I retired as President and CEO of PCI, Bill Ryerson, PCI Executive Vice President, resigned and moved on to founding Population Media Center (PMC) in order to increase the size of the groups using Sabido's E-E methodology. The project has been initiated in Ethiopia with the financial support of the Packard Foundation and the assistance of Tom Kazungu from Kenya and Ramadan M. A. Swahele, who was trained by Everett M. Rogers at the University of New Mexico and in Tanzania (see the William Ryerson and Negussie Teffera chapter in this volume).

I am immensely proud that the E-E approach continues to spread around the world, and that when Miguel Sabido's methodology is harnessed in an effective manner, it contributes to meaningful social change.

LESSONS LEARNED

1. If properly designed and implemented, the mass media can convey the essential information messages to help carry out a national development policy in population, HIV/AIDS control, female equality, and protection of the environment.

2. The goal of such a mass media E-E effort is to achieve widespread change in behaviors that lead to development in a nation.

3. To achieve such massive behavior change, a methodology that informs and motivates mainly by stimulating interpersonal communication among peers is needed. Many development program leaders rely on exposure to messages to reach their objectives. However, these messages seldom lead to the magnitude of changed behavior that is required to solve a social problem.

4. The E-E methodology has been demonstrated to be effective. E-E was designed by Miguel Sabido, and is based on relevant social science theory, such as Bandura's social modeling theory. E-E methodology demands adequate funding, competent management, formative and summative research, and the best creative talent in production, particularly in scriptwriting.

5. Extensive research on the effects of dozens of E-E projects over the past 25 years established that this methodology is transferable and effective in achieving behavior change.

6. An E-E project requires a basis in cultural values and must have a moral foundation in national and international documents, such as the final document from the 1994 Cairo United Nations International Conference on Population and Development, which was ratified by every nation. The E-E methodology cannot be utilized to promote inappropriate educational values in a nation.

When I began work in the field of population communications one-third of a century ago, a paucity of mass media effort existed. The world's total fertility rate was well over twice what it is now. In one generation, the average number of children per woman declined from more than 6 to the current 2.8. It continues to decline.

Here then is an overview of the "decades of discovery" that occurred. Much has been learned; much accomplished. There is yet much to be done.

REFERENCES

Law, S., & Singhal, A. (1999). Efficacy in letter-writing to an entertainment-education radio serial. *Gazette, 61*(5), 355–372.

Papa, M. J., Singhal, A., Law, S., Sood, S., Rogers, E. M., & Shefner, C. L. (2000). Entertainment-education and social change: An analysis of parasocial interaction, social learning, collective efficacy, and paradoxical communication. *Journal of Communication, 50*(4), 31–55.

Risopatron, F., & Spain, P. L. (1980). Reaching the poor: Human sexuality education in Costa Rica. *Journal of Communication, 30*, 81–89.

Rogers, E. M., Vaughan, P. W., Swalehe, R. M. A., Rao, N., Svenkerud, P., & Sood, S. (1999). Effects of an entertainment-education radio soap opera on family planning in Tanzania. *Studies in Family Planning, 30*(3), 193–211.

Singhal, A., Ren, L., & Zhang, J. (1999). *Audience Interpretations of Baixing, an Entertainment-Education Television Serial in China.* New York: Population Communications International.

2. HISTORY OF ENTERTAINMENT-EDUCATION

Singhal, A., & Rogers, E. M. (1989). *India's information revolution*. Thousand Oaks, CA: Sage.

Singhal, A., & Rogers, E. M. (1999). *Entertainment-education: A communication strategy for social change*. Mahwah, NJ: Lawrence Erlbaum Associates.

Vaughan, P. W., Regis, A., & St. Catherine, E. (2000). Effects of an entertainment-education radio soap opera on family planning and HIV prevention in St. Lucia. *International Family Planning Perspectives, 26*(4), 148–157.

Vaughan, P. W., & Rogers, E. M. (2000). A staged model of communication effects: Evidence from an entertainment-education radio soap opera in Tanzania. *Journal of Health Communication, 5*(2), 203–227.

Vaughan, P. W., Rogers, E. M., Singhal, A., & Swalehe, R. M. A. (2000). Entertainment-education and HIV/AIDS prevention: A field experiment in Tanzania. *Journal of Health Communication, 5* (Supplement), 81–100.

Wang, M., & Singhal, A. (1992). *Ke Wang*, a Chinese television soap opera with a message. *Gazette, 49*(3), 177–192.

3

Entertainment-Education as a Public Health Intervention[1]

Phyllis Tilson Piotrow
Esta de Fossard
John Hopkins Bloomberg School of Public Health

Since 1982 the Johns Hopkins University's Center for Communication Programs assisted in some 125 entertainment-education productions worldwide designed to improve public health. Almost all major projects include both explicit health advice and implicit efforts to influence the broader social norms that help determine individual health behavior, such as the treatment of girls and women, distribution of wealth, inequities in access to health care, and environmental protection. Entertainment-education serial dramas proved especially effective in changing knowledge, attitudes, behavior, and norms because they evoke emotions, create role models, stimulate discussion among listeners and viewers, and show the ultimate consequences of both healthy and unhealthy behavior to large, attentive audiences.

"I don't know what to do. I have kept him hidden in my house, doctor. He has AIDS." Wiping the tears from her eyes, the Bangladeshi village wife leads Dr. Jalal to the bed of her emaciated spouse.

---

[1]The authors gratefully acknowledge the support of the United States Agency for International Development (USAID) for much of the funding that made possible the programs reviewed here. Ameena Batada as research assistant; Kathy Wolfe as chapter coordinator; Mark Beisser as graphic designer; and Ann Schmidt as typist, provided valuable assistance.

"Have you come to watch me die?" he asks desperately. "They treat me like an animal, as if I were a cat or dog."

"That is intolerable," replied Dr. Jalal firmly. "We must hate the disease, not the patient. AIDS is very dangerous but people do not get infected by touching." And he placed his hand gently on the thin arm.

"Oh," the sick man replied, "You have laid your hand upon me. At last someone has touched me. Now I realize that I am not an animal. I am a human being after all."

This poignant scene from the Bangladesh television serial *Shabuj Chhaya* captures, almost like a religious parable, an important HIV/AIDS message: Care for the sick, do not shun or stigmatize them. In one 3-minute sequence, this episode illustrates the multifaceted power of entertainment-education (E-E) to convey a specific health message, to evoke a powerful emotional response, and to create a lasting impression that can change viewers' behavior.

The thirteen 30-minute episodes of *Shabuj Chhaya*, aired in 2000, end on another meaningful social note skillfully scripted by Dr. Hamayun Ahmed, noted Bangladeshi writer and producer of the television series. The sympathetic medical doctor tells a dedicated young female health worker from the village, "I have discovered that you are very talented and have learned to read and write all on your own. Why don't you take qualifying exams to advance your own education and career?"

His encouragement, so unlike the malicious gossip that some male villagers have spread about the attractive young woman who aspires to become a professional health worker, moves her deeply. "Yes, doctor," she whispers, "I promise I will." (See photo 3.1 for the public response to the show.)

Shabuj Chhaya, like most of the 50 radio and television serial E-E dramas that Johns Hopkins University's Center for Communication Programs

PHOTO 3.1. The Bangladesh serial drama, *Shabuj Chhaya*, attracted more than 600,000 letters. (CREDIT : BCCP, Courtesy of Photoshare)

(JHU/CCP) assisted in developing countries, conveys multiple health messages: Space and/or limit your family, breastfeed exclusively for six months, recognize danger signs of pregnancy, avoid risky sexual behavior, wash your hands before eating, keep your fingernails short and clean and many more. JHU/CCP strategic communication programs, often built around E-E formats, stress social issues, such as inequities between men and women, rich and poor; the value of girls' education; respect for women as health professionals; child abuse; and the need for community participation in local governance as well as in decentralized health programs. Because health practices and social norms are so closely related, E-E public health interventions often need to address both.

The present chapter summarizes the experience of JHU/CCP in developing or assisting with E-E programs in over 40 countries (Coleman & Meyer, 1990; JHU/CCP, 1998a; NEEF & JHU, 2001; Pelsinsky, 1997). The JHU team, working with talented colleagues overseas, and with support from the United States Agency for International Development (USAID) and other donors, learned a great deal about audiences, health behaviors in communities, E-E content, format, production processes, impact, and evaluation. This chapter discusses some of the major issues and lessons learned, and particularly, the crucial relationship between individual behavior and social norms addressed through entertainment.

USES OF ENTERTAINMENT-EDUCATION

JHU/CCP assisted about 125 E-E programs over the last 20 years (Table 3.1). Songs and music videos were among the first health interventions: National

TABLE 3.1
Entertainment-Education Programs Supported by the Johns Hopkins
University's Center for Communication Programs, 1986 to 2002, by Type
and Region

Region	Serial Dramas		Films and Videos	Songs	Variety Shows	Distance Learning
	Radio	Television				
Africa	18	9	14	8	8	4
Asia	3	7	14	3	1	3
Latin America	3	3	2	7	3	1
Near East	0	4	5	0	1	0
Europe/Eurasia	0	0	3	0	0	0
Totals	24	23	38	18	13	8

Note. These categories are not always clear cut. Some films and videos have been shown serially on television. Variety shows often include serial drama episodes. Songs were incorporated in other productions as well as in separate music videos. Learning programs for service providers were incorporated in various media formats. This classification is based on the principal purpose of each production and avoids double-counting.

and international hits by Tatiana and Johnny in Mexico and in Latin America (*Cuando Estemos Juntos* and *Detente*) (Kincaid, Jara, Coleman, & Segura, 1988); then Lea Salonga and Menudo in the Philippines (*I Still Believe* and *That Situation*, 1988) (Rimon et al., 1994); and King Sunny Adé and Onyeka Onwenu in Nigeria (*Wait for Me* and *Choices*, 1989) (Emah, 1993; JHU/CCP, 1990; Obadina, 1991). These music videos focused on avoiding unwanted pregnancies by delaying sexual activity or, in Nigeria, by planning future child-bearing. More than a dozen other songs have since been developed, mostly in Africa—Burkina Faso, Cameroon, Ghana, Madagascar, Nigeria, Philippines, Tanzania, and Uganda, among others. Several, like *Wake Up Africa* in Francophone Africa, deal with HIV/AIDS and have regional appeal. Some are an integral part of national and regional campaigns like the *Africa Alive* concert series. In Latin America and the Caribbean (Ecuador, Haiti, and Nicaragua) and through a collaborative effort with UNESCO, JHU helped produce songs and music videos that focused on children and adolescents and that included environment issues. Not counting many other songs that were part of larger campaigns, JHU/CCP helped to develop at least 18 popular E-E songs with some health or social messages.

As Table 3.1 shows, E-E comes in many different sizes and shapes. Single films and videos have been important in Asia and Africa where they are shown from video vans as well as on national media. Variety shows are increasingly popular as a means to engage youth directly in content and production (Kiragu, Sienche, Obwaka, Odallo, & Barth, 1998). Television and radio spots now often include E-E through short narrative or familiar characters (Kincaid et al., 1996; Underwood, 2001). Locally, street theatre, community radio, indigenous storytellers, drama contests, and community rallies with local performers incorporate and/or adapt national E-E productions (Valente, Poppe, Alva, de Briceño, & Cases, 1995). Ghana's "Stop AIDS, Love Life" campaign is an example (see photo 3.2).

A unique and innovative form of E-E, pioneered by JHU, supported by ministries of health, and documented as effective in Nepal, is E-E as a component of distance learning for health and community workers (Storey, Boulay, Karchi, Heckert, & Karmacharya, 1999; Boulay, Storey, & Sood, 2002). Radio dramas that incorporate technical health, communication, and community mobilization skills reached thousands of otherwise hard-to-reach health workers in Bangladesh, Indonesia, Nepal, Ghana, Guinea, Haiti, Senegal, and Zambia. In Nepal, one radio serial drama for villagers (*Cut Your Coat According to Your Cloth*) and another for health providers (*Service Brings Rewards*), both written and produced by a well-known Nepali writer, Kuber Gartaula, attracted combined villager and provider audiences and contributed to more spousal discussion, better quality counseling in clinics, and, indirectly, to greater contraceptive use (Storey et al., 1999; Boulay et al., 2002). Client-provider interaction was much improved when both clients and providers listened to the radio programs.

PHOTO 3.2. Community performances and street theater are important E-E components of Ghana's "Stop AIDS, Love Life" campaign. (CREDIT: CCP, Courtesy of Photoshare)

Of all the various formats for E-E programs which JHU/CCP adapted, developed, tested, or contributed to, serial drama—on television where possible, or on radio when access and language are limited, proved to be a highly effective format to promote long-term changes in health behavior and to influence the social norms that can reinforce such changes. JHU/CCP has been involved to some extent in about 50 serial dramas. Approximately half of these were on radio and half on television, primarily in Africa and Asia. Most showed measurable changes in knowledge, attitudes, perceptions of others' attitudes (community norms), and, in many cases, action. These dramas stimulated interpersonal discussion about these issues which often lead to action. (Boulay et al., 2002; Kincaid, Figueroa, Underwood, & Storey, 1999; Lozare et al., 1993). A metaanalysis of the impact of JHU health campaigns (most of which included E-E) suggested that the effects are comparable to various health campaigns in the United States; on average, the number of individuals who adopted the desired behavior change increased by about 7 percentage points and the number of exposed persons who adopted the behavior increased by 12 percentage points (Snyder et al., 1999; Snyder, Diop-Sidibé, & Badione, 2002).

CHALLENGES OF ENTERTAINMENT-EDUCATION

Presenting health messages in an E-E serial drama format raises real challenges, especially when these health messages are specific or technical. For example, some of the early radio serial dramas and videos/films in The Gambia, Ghana, Kenya, Nigeria, and Zimbabwe conveyed messages about the health risks and especially the economic burdens of large, closely-spaced families (Piotrow et al., 1990; Piotrow et al., 1992; Valente, Lettenmaier, Kim, & Dibba, 1993; Valente, Lettenmaier, Kim, Glass, & Dibba, 1994). These programs promoted child spacing and often referred to specific contraceptive methods such as the pill or IUD. But these interventions usually conformed closely to existing social norms, showing that husbands, not wives, made the final decisions and that wives were pleased and compliant. These interventions were far more engaging than previous direct admonitions like "Go to the family planning clinic." But the early E-E programs were not subtle. They rarely focused on character development or suspenseful narrative and often relied on slapstick humor, as in Nigeria, or on sharp stereotypical contrasts between the wise father who spaced his family and prospered versus the foolish father with many children who could not pay for food, school fees, or his wife's health needs (JHU/CCP, 1991a).

As audiences became accustomed to more sophisticated entertainment, it became clear that E-E programs promoting healthy behavior needed to be fine-tuned. Major health problems, such as high infant and maternal mortality, spread of the HIV/AIDS epidemic, and medical and moral problems of abortion, were excellent material for drama. JHU/CCP identified at least seven major challenges in using E-E to transmit specific health advice.

1. **Too much education and not enough entertainment.** Lecturing about good health practices in E-E dramas may sound artificial and unwelcome, especially to those who turn to the media to escape real-life problems. The early Indonesian radio serials, for example, were not popular with young couples who found them pedantic and preachy (Piet, 1981; SRI-Nielsen, 1997). In Nicaragua, when a radio serial drama was pretested, listeners were bored by frequent lectures on breastfeeding from a medical doctor. These lectures were deleted. Dialogues between a village health promoter and a mother experienced in breastfeeding were substituted. Educational messages could not just be inserted like extra courses in a meal but rather needed to be incorporated subtly in the main dishes, like well-chosen spices (Ainslie, 2002).

2. **Too much entertainment and not enough education.** Highly dramatic productions designed to appeal to commercial entertainment audiences may lose sight of the health message. In the Philippine film *Mumbaki*, for example, which was designed to encourage Filipino doctors to serve in rural areas, audience attention was distracted from the family planning/health messages by the excitement of a romantic rivalry and violent tribal conflicts. Although the film, produced and partially funded by a commercial firm, won multiple local awards, donors were critical (JHU/CCP, 1999). Reconciling

donor interest in strong health messages and producer interest in artistic and commercial appeal creates tension in many E-E programs. It is probably the most important single problem that E-E faces. The best way to deal with this problem is by maintaining close contact with donors and encouraging producers to develop a clear design document and to follow it carefully.

3. **Poor quality entertainment.** Characters, plots, and dialogue that are not credible will not attract listeners or viewers and will not influence behavior. Training in basic skills of drama development was a necessary first step and is usually included in preliminary planning for a JHU/CCP E-E series or drama.

4. **No credible urgency.** Most unhealthy behavior does not have an immediate impact. Poor nutrition, large families, risk-taking in sexual behavior, smoking, drinking, and poor hygiene pose long-term health risks, rather than sudden catastrophe. Dramatic entertainment can make these risks seem more immediate and serious, but this effect requires skillful scripting. For example, in the Uganda television series *Centre 4*, market day turned into a stampede for the latrines after shoppers helped themselves to fruit from a seller whose unclean habits contaminated his product.

5. **Routine recommendations.** Specific preventive health measures are often not dramatic—taking a daily contraceptive pill, eating a healthy diet, or breastfeeding. In the Uganda television program, *Time to Care: A Question of Children*, the mother throws her daughter-in-law's pills in the fire—a vivid visual image. The misunderstandings that ensue help to emphasize the need to take a pill each day in order to prevent unwanted pregnancy (Keller, 1997; Kiingi, 1998; Wendo, 1998).

6. **No immediate personal relevance.** Those not directly, immediately, and personally threatened by a particular health problem tend to ignore E-E messages about it. Husbands often are relatively casual about dangers that their wives face in pregnancy and delivery. Many young men and women are in denial with respect to their risk of contracting HIV/AIDS. Films like the Safe Motherhood trilogy in Indonesia and *The Merchant's Daughter* in Morocco focus especially on how men suffer when the health of their wives or daughters is neglected. To capture men's attention, the Indonesian film *Flowers for Nur* was designed as a murder mystery opening with a fight between two men over their relationship with Nur, a conflict in which one was killed (JHU/CCP, 1997b).

7. **Controversies based on culture and tradition.** In reproductive health, cultural sensitivities loom large, first in depicting problems such as STDs, HIV/AIDS, unwanted pregnancy, abortion, and, paradoxically, even more in proposing solutions such as contraceptive or condom use. While dramas and other fictional programs are probably less vulnerable to censorship and retraction than explicit television spots, they often must rely on an indirect approach to avoid political repercussions. One device used in the

PHOTO 3.3. In Egypt's television drama series *And the Nile Flows On*, a young religious leader helps other men understand the need for child spacing. (CREDIT: CCP, Courtesy of Photoshare)

Bangladeshi series *Ey Megh, Eyi Roudro* and in the Egyptian serial *And the Nile Flows On* (see photo 3.3) was for a religious leader to defend use of contraceptives. Explicit advice that might not have been allowed on the air from a lay person or even a health care provider is acceptable from an *imam*.

THE IMPORTANCE OF SOCIAL NORMS

JHU/CCP and major donors for E-E programs such as USAID recognize that a unique advantage of E-E, especially of serial dramas with multiple subplots, is their ability to link health issues with related social behaviors and in the long run to change social norms (Kaiser Family Foundation, 1996; Kincaid, 1993).

The main social norm that affects reproductive health is related to *gender*. The inferior status of women takes such forms as the lack of equal decision-making power in the family, a prevailing preference for male children (which contributes substantially to higher desired fertility and family size), dowry payments in some countries, property ownership and inheritance laws that deprive women of their own or family resources, lack of education, limited access to health care, and inadequate nutrition. Women have little ability to control their own lives from childhood through marriage, reproductive years, and economic livelihood to widowhood and death.

The theme of women's rights and roles has been prominent in JHU/CCP-assisted E-E health programs. Notable examples are a Pakistani television serial drama *Aahat* (1991) (JHU/CCP, 1994; Lozare et al., 1993) and the video *Ek Hi Raasta* (1992) (JHU/CCP, 1995), still vividly remembered by Pakistanis and individuals in other Muslim countries. *Aahat*, a six-episode 60-minute serial, depicted a young urban couple with four closely spaced daughters.

The husband and mother-in-law want to keep trying for a son; the weakened young wife wants to educate her daughters. Their maid servant chooses a dangerous abortion to cope with a large family and an abusive husband. Produced by a leading Pakistani woman director, Sahira Kazmi, and scripted by popular woman screen-writer Huseena Moin, *Aahat* was aired nationally in 1991 and was viewed in Pakistan by 17 to 20 million viewers, about 75% of the intended audience (Lozare et al., 1993). The key messages of gender preference, need for birth spacing, and the importance of husband-wife communication were well understood by viewers. Strong approval of family planning increased from 65% at baseline to 75% after viewing. Some 12% reported that the television program led them to take action to space their children. Between 1990 and 1994, contraceptive prevalence among married women of reproductive age in Pakistan rose from 12% to 18%, a change probably influenced to some degree by this television drama. Today, people who watched this television show as children can repeat the plot and remember its strong emotional impact.

Pressure on young women to be sexually active is an important issue. Lily, a character in a 1998 Peruvian television serial drama, *Time for Love*, first thinks she is not normal because she is not ready for sexual relations with her eager boyfriend. After refusing him, she finds another boy who is more understanding. Her friend, Andrea, follows a different course, as the excerpt in the box shows (see photo 3.4).

A *Time for Love* May Also Mean a Time for Decisions

In this Peruvian television drama, a young man comes to recognize that he also has a responsibility for unplanned pregnancy.

Andrea: I just took a pregnancy test and it came out positive.

Renzo: What are we going to do?

Andrea: I don't know, Renzo. I don't know what we could do.

Renzo: Well, you have to think of something! You're responsible for this!

Andrea: Why me? We're both responsible. What we did, we did together.

Renzo: Okay, but you're the woman and you have to take care of yourself.

Andrea: You're the man and that doesn't change a thing.

Renzo: Well, you're the one that's pregnant. You should have been more careful.

Andrea: What's wrong with you? You know perfectly well that you could have also been more careful. We made a mistake but we have to face it together. Please don't leave me alone. Please!

Renzo: Come here. Forgive me. I'm very scared. I don't know what I'm saying. I love you and we're going to get through this together.

PHOTO 3.4.   Young actors in Peru's *Time for Love* series depict the consequences of careless love versus concern for partners. (CREDIT: BELL SOTTO,
Courtesy of Photoshare.)

ADDRESSING POVERTY

Another social issue in most developing-country E-E dramas is poverty, and
the massive handicaps that face poor families seeking adequate health care.
Six Indonesian films/videos, including both the Equatorial Trilogy on Population and Environment, and the Safe Motherhood films, take place in settings
where women and their families are struggling to survive in the face of rural
economic losses, urban pollution, or a lack of economic opportunity, especially for women (JHU/CCP et al., 1995; Storey, Berutu, & Dutjuk, 1996). The
Indonesian film directed by Arifin Noer, *Tasi, Oh Tasi* is the story of a girl
forced by impoverishment to leave her fishing village for the city, where, vulnerable and without access to reproductive health knowledge and services,
she becomes pregnant. She then must cope as a single parent, alone. She
turns to prostitution. In the Nicaraguan drama *A Secret in the Village*, Yadira
overcomes her poverty with the assistance of friends by setting up her own
business, making tacos, and selling them at a bus stop.

   Whether the subject is the life of street children in Brazil, wives in Nepal,
desperate single women in Ethiopia who give up their illegitimate children, or

men living with HIV/AIDS in Africa, poverty defines and restricts individuals' lives. A lack of funds for medicines and school fees and disrespectful treatment by health professionals create multiple problems for poor families, lower castes, women, and indigenous peoples. JHU/CCP-assisted E-E dramas depict these social inequities as part of the basic setting for characters and narrative. Even when the specific message is health promotion or HIV/AIDS prevention, the underlying themes of gender discrimination and poverty are present and add emotional intensity to the drama. The episode described in the box below is from the first-ever radio E-E drama in Ethiopia.

The Journey of Life: Will It Be a Tragedy for this Ethiopian Family?

Azeb tells her friend, "My husband told me he took children for adoption. He said rich people are waiting to adopt healthy little boys. But he lied. He sold the boy that he did not know was my son to a beggar trader—to be blinded."

"No, no," her friend insisted. "This has not happened yet. We must stop this hideous plan. I cannot believe your husband would do this—to your own birth child."

"We can't," Azeb wailed. "My husband is an important man. He would not want to learn that years ago I was raped—I was just a servant—I had a child—and now my child is going to be blinded and sold as a beggar. Oh my friend, what am I going to do?"

Azeb struggles with the shame of her rape, as her husband misunderstands her anguish and seeks distraction with a prostitute. Then both face the threat of HIV/AIDS from careless infidelity. This 26-part radio serial drama, aired in 2002, revealed the potential tragedy when women are unable to protect themselves or provide for their children. Then men, women, and children all become victims of careless or coercive sex (Ferrara et al., 2002).

Other social norms addressed in various dramas include:

• An increasing emphasis on the independent role of youth and the need for young people to take a more active role in educating one another and in protecting themselves from sexual risk-taking. The youth variety shows designed and implemented in large part by young males and females in Bolivia, Jordan, Kenya, Namibia, Nicaragua, Nigeria, Tanzania, and Zimbabwe with help from Johns Hopkins University are examples (Anonymous, 1996b; JHU/CCP, 1997a; JHU/CCP, 1998b; Kim, Kols, Nyakauru, Marangwanda, & Chibatamoto, 2001; Palmer, 2002; Piotrow & Rimon, 1995).
• Links between population growth, environmental degradation, and deteriorating community and individual health. *Arcandina*, the prize-winning children's serial in Ecuador, written and directed by María Elena Ordoñez, is an educational variety show modeled on *Sesame Street*. Focused on

population and environment, *Arcandina* illustrated both the newly proactive role of youth and the links between health, hygiene, environment, and conservation (Aguilar, 2002).

• Community participation in governance and especially in advocacy and management for decentralized local health facilities. E-E dramas can present positive models on how to strengthen links between a local health center and the community, how to set priorities and advocate for local health care, and how to expand health coverage cost-effectively. Two Zambian radio distance education programs for Neighborhood Health Committee members, *Our Neighborhood* and *Community Health with Sister Evelina*, are entertaining as well as educational with a focus on health, including simple explanations of the Essential Basic Care Package, and on social issues like community mobilization. In one episode, for example, villagers track the source of children's sudden illness to polluted water and join forces to dig a safe new village well (db Studios, 2002).

LINKING HEALTH WITH SOCIAL ISSUES

There are multiple advantages of linking health promotion to social norms (Elkamel, 1995). These combinations attract larger audiences and allies through interest in a broader issue. Women and some men respond to shows with gender messages, while environmental activists respond to conservation messages, like the U.S. National Wildlife Federation, which cited *Arcandina* as the best international population/environment program. These combinations establish a setting or context that resonates with other people facing similar problems. For example, impoverished urban migrants in the Turkish serial *Sparrows Don't Migrate* and rural migrants in the Nepali serial *Cut Your Coat According to Your Cloth* face problems with which many listeners identify. Migration, they find, may not put food on the table or make life easier for large families.

Programs that link health and social issues can strengthen and sustain commitment to an issue that extends beyond specific fictional characters, however compelling. They can position the desired intervention, such as family planning, firmly in the context of other desired objectives. An effective drama can move health behavior issues out of the realm of purely individual actions and into the realm of social norms and policies to enable and reinforce those behaviors. For example, raising the legal age of marriage to discourage too-early childbearing was a major theme in the Egyptian television E-E serial, *And the Nile Flows On*, produced by the Egyptian State Information Service under Nabil Osman (Underwood, Kemprecos, Jabre, Wafai, 1994; Robinson & Lewis, 2002), and in the 2002 Nigerian variety show *Listen Up*.

Existing social norms, such as gender, environmental protection, and disparities in wealth, are highly controversial. Efforts to change these social problems may stimulate stronger opposition to the health measures. Critics in Zambia took messages off the air that advised girls to insist on condom use; the resulting controversy and debate sparked more attention than the original television spots had. Social or environmental issues that can be vividly presented, such as polluted water in the Indonesian film *The Lost Child* or the densely packed slums in the Guatemalan film *The Girl Who Saw the World from Above*, may distract attention from specific health behaviors like family planning.

ADVANTAGES OF SERIAL DRAMAS

Serial dramas continuing for several months or years are an extremely powerful form of E-E that can influence both specific health behaviors and related social norms. Why? (1) Serial dramas capture the attention and the emotions of the audience, (2) serial dramas provide repetition and continuity, allowing audiences to identify more and more closely over time with the fictional characters, their problems, and their social environment, (3) serial dramas allow time for characters to develop a change in behavior slowly, with hesitations and setbacks as occur in real life, (4) serial dramas have various subplots that can introduce different issues in a logical and credible way through different characters, a key characteristic of conventional soap operas, (5) serial dramas can build a realistic social context that will mirror society and create multiple opportunities to present a social issue in various forms, and (6) serial dramas probably offer the best opportunity to realize fully the nine P's that JHU/CCP uses to encapsulate the potential power of E-E (as the box below shows). Serial dramas can present different perspectives and stimulate audience questioning that can lead both to individual health behavior and to changing social norms (Coleman & Meyer, 1990; JHU/CCP, 1997b; Figueroa, Kincaid, Rani, & Lewis' 2002; Kincaid, 1993; Kincaid, 2002; NEEF & JHU, 2001; Nariman, 1993; Piotrow, Kincaid, Rimon, & Rinehart, 1997; Singhal & Rogers, 1999; Sabido, 1981).

The Nine Ps of Entertainment-Education

The entertainment-education approach, or "Enter–Educate," or E-E, is an effective way to promote healthy behavior because it is:

Pervasive: Everywhere, from street theatre to national television, from songs and dances to community radio, entertainment is there, with some kind of message.

Popular: People like entertainment, seek it out, and enjoy it.

Passionate: Entertainment stimulates the emotions, so people remember, talk to others, and are more inclined to take action.

Personal: People identify with dramatic characters as if they were personal friends.

Participatory: People participate by singing, dancing, and talking about entertaining characters, stories, and activities.

Persuasive: People can be persuaded to identify with role models, and then see the consequences of sensible or foolish behavior and imitate what works.

Practical: Entertainment infrastructures and performers are already in place and always look for good dramatic themes.

Profitable: Good E-E helps pay its own way and generates sponsorship, collateral promotions, and, sometimes profit.

Proven effective: Messages from entertainment can change the way people think, feel, and behave, as research has shown.

Source: Piotrow et al. (1997).

How to Link Health With Social Issues

How can health and social issues best be linked in E-E formats so that both messages strengthen each another, instead of competing? Five elements are necessary for a successful serial drama that links health messages and social change effectively.

1. **Creative ability** to produce first-rate entertainment that engages the audience and reflects audience interests.
2. **Technical knowledge** of the health problem and of those actions that can realistically be applied to improve it.
3. **On-site familiarity** with the intended audiences, their prevailing health practices, their rationale for these practices, and incentives or barriers to change.
4. **Cultural sensitivity** to the social norms that underlie specific behaviors.
5. **Time and patience** to bring different skills and knowledge together harmoniously in a coherent plan that all E-E players can understand and follow.

Creative Ability.   Scripting, producing, and acting may be learned skills, but talent is also essential. The best way to locate such talent—which exists in every country—is not through formal contests but more often through informal inquiries in the entertainment industry, personal interviews, exercises following a brief orientation workshop, and sometimes small financial incentives (Rimon et al., 1994). A commitment to E-E and especially to the specific health and social issues involved is illustrated by producers and directors like Carola Prudencio (Bolivia), María Elena Ordoñez (Ecuador), Nabil Osman (Egypt), Norma Guadamos (Nicaragua), Reuben Vysokolan (Paraguay), Gartaula (Nepal), Humayan Ahmed (Bangladesh), Teguh Karya (Indonesia), Slamet Rahardjo Djarot (Indonesia), Arifin Noer (Indonesia), and Jujur Pranato (Indonesia). Sometimes senior practitioners with established reputations are less committed to an issue like gender equity than women or newcomers starting their careers. Creative team members must be able to create characters that live, breathe, talk, struggle, suffer, and succeed in a way that holds audience attention and evokes a strong emotional response as well as an understanding of the health issues. They must be able to generate and resolve credible conflicts among characters, especially conflicts over health behavior (Kincaid, 2002).

Technical Knowledge.   In-depth technical knowledge of family planning, HIV/AIDS prevention, safe motherhood, or clean water can help give accurate answers to hard questions. "What do I do if I miss two pills, nurse?" "My friend got pregnant when her boyfriend's condom broke. What can I do to make sure that does not happen to me?" "How can I have a safe delivery if the clinic is 10 kilometers away?" "How can I be sure a blood transfusion is safe?" "If I am HIV+, how can I feed my baby?" JHU/CCP E-E interventions depend heavily on national ministries of health and local medical experts to help develop the messages. International experts meet with scriptwriters at the start in order to provide technical assistance. Transmitting that information without jargon in a way that families can understand is key.

Familiarity with Practices in the Field.   Knowing current health practices is crucial. Unless scriptwriters really understand what is already happening, they cannot suggest realistic changes. Promoting packaged salt or sugar fortified with micronutrients for oral rehydration may make sense technically, but it did not work well in Zambia where most families could not afford to buy the packages.

To find out what intended audiences see as their major health problems requires substantial formative research, which is essential in developing language, visual images, and persuasive messages. Not only the content, but also the format for E-E health programs, will differ for different people.

Cultural Sensitivity.   A sense of what is acceptable is essential even when an E-E program seeks to shift cultural norms. In Kenya in the 1980s, a television show in which a young girl slapped an older man trying to seduce her was not acceptable. The program was taken off the air (Usiniharakishe, 1986). In Zambia in 2002, an E-E spot in which girls (rather than boys) talked about condoms for protection was not initially acceptable. It was taken off the air, but then, after protests from young people, it was re-broadcast, a signal of change in the culture. Three recent shows—*Jante Chai, Janate Chai* (Bangladesh), *Listen Up* (Nigeria), and *The Suzie and Shafa Show* (Namibia)—all emphasize that girls can refuse sex, negotiate with partners, and insist on protecting themselves, even in male-dominated societies.

Time and Patience. Successful E-E dramas are as much a process as a product. Two detailed manuals by Esta de Fossard, *How To Write a Radio Serial Drama for Social Development: A Script Writer's Manual* (1996) and *How To Design and Produce Radio Serial Drama for Social Development: A Program Manager's Guide* (1998), spell out the steps required. The design process outlined in these guides includes three key elements: the design team, the design workshop, and the design document. As described by de Fossard: "The design document is the end result of the work done by the design team—a group of advisors, such as media specialists, content advisors, and writers—during the design workshop. The design workshop is a designated period of time (usually five working days) in which the team meets and works together to compile the design document. The design document is the blueprint that presents, in written form, the details required by all those involved in the writing, reviewing, production, and evaluation of the serial drama" (de Fossard, 1996). A 26-episode radio serial drama typically requires at least six months to design, script, review, and produce.

To ensure a large audience, E-E benefits greatly from a conspicuous launch with national leaders and entertainment stars. In Nigeria, for example, the *Listen Up!* youth program was launched through community rallies in all the broadcast districts. In Bangladesh, the television serial, *Shabuj Shathi* (which means "Evergreen Friend") featuring a dedicated village health worker, was launched with a 3-mile parade of local luminaries and village field workers carrying green umbrellas through the streets of Dhaka. This launch was part of a campaign centering on a television serial drama (Hasan, 2001; Kincaid, 1999; Talukdar & Hasan, 2001; Whitney, Kincaid, & de Fossard, 1999).

As part of the overall E-E process, evaluation research is important (Hornik, 2002). JHU evaluations have gained in quality and sophistication over the last decade and now include panel surveys, structural equation modeling, and propensity score analysis, as well as standard multivariate analysis. The cost of these evaluations ranges from 5% to 20% of the total budget. In addition, formative research is an essential component of an effective E-E intervention.

Early evaluations measured such changes as self-reported attitude change after listening to Tatiana's and Johnny's songs (Kincaid et al., 1988) or clinic attendance in Nigeria following an E-E program (Piotrow et al., 1990). More recent evaluations measured the impact of mass media and interpersonal communication on knowledge, attitudes, and behavior (Valente et al., 1996; Valente & Saba, 1998), dose-response effects (Jato et al., 1999), changes in perceptions of community norms (Kincaid, 1999), impact of social networks (Kincaid, 2000), increased spousal discussion (Boulay et al., 2002; Kim & Marangwanda, 1997), changes in ideation (Kincaid, 2000), and causal pathways to behavior change stimulated by the emotions in E-E or other forms of communication (Kincaid, 2002). Evaluations are now also addressing cost-effectiveness (Robinson & Lewis, 2002) and the impact of E-E on social change and the process followed by communities to achieve it (Figueroa, Kincaid, Rani, & Lewis, 2002).

CONCLUSIONS AND LESSONS LEARNED

More than two decades of experience with the E-E strategy suggest that in order to be maximally effective:

1. E-E should be of high quality, comparable to commercial material, and should resonate emotionally with the intended audience. Needed is a realistic setting, engaging characters, a compelling story, popular music, and in many cases audience participation. These require a talented and well-trained team of researchers, writers, producers, and actors.

2. E-E should weave health messages naturally, gradually, and subtly into plot, songs, character, and message development rather than inserting health lectures arbitrarily into a program.

3. E-E should be research-based, relying on understanding the audience and situation, health data, and behavior change models and theories, and using qualitative and quantitative methods.

4. E-E should be a sustained and continuing presence, preferably an ongoing series so that audiences can identify closely with the characters and the community and their continuing trials, tribulations, and occasional triumphs, while moving gradually and logically to behavior change.

5. E-E should be part of a broader strategic health program that not only presents specific individual health behaviors but also attempts to establish social norms (or remove constraints) to ensure continuation of the new behavior.

6. E-E, as part of a broader program, should include multiple activities and spin-offs, such as live performances, songs, storybooks, community and celebrity participation, Internet link-ups, print materials, and orchestrated media coverage. Thus, an E-E intervention should be part of a comprehensive campaign.

The health communication team at Johns Hopkins University has found that effective E-E must combine business and technology, commitment and talent, participation and leadership, and above all art and science. To influence behavior and to change social norms, E-E can be a powerful force. As Aristotle pointed out centuries ago, the way people learn is by watching and imitating. As he noted in *Poetics*, "It is natural for people to delight in watching works of art that are realistic representations of life for this is how we learn." In his words, "To be learning something is the greatest of pleasures not only to the philosopher but also to the rest of mankind.... The reason for the delight is that one is at the same time learning—gathering the meaning of things" (Aristotle, 1941). This combination of delight and learning is an apt description. It offers a time-tested model and a worthy goal for E-E today.

REFERENCES

Aguilar, M. (2002). *Arcandina: Beyond television to advocacy, capacity building, and community mobilization.* Unpublished Manuscript, Baltimore, MD: Johns Hopkins University, Center for Communication Programs.

Anonymous (1996b). *Rompiendo tabues por television: "Dialogo al desnudo"* [Breaking taboos on television: "Open dialogue"]. *Opciones, 1*(1 Suppl), 3.

Aristotle (1941). Poetics. In McKeon, R. Ed. *The basic works of Aristotle.* New York: Random House.

Bandura, A. (1986). *Social foundations of thought and action.* Englewood Cliffs, NJ: Prentice-Hall.

Boulay, M., Storey, J. D., & Sood, S. (2002). Indirect exposure to a family planning mass media campaign in Nepal. *Journal of Health Communication,* VII(5), 379–399.

Coleman, P. L., & Meyer, R. C. (1990). *Entertainment for social change.* Proceedings of the Enter-Educate Conference. Baltimore, MD: Johns Hopkins University, Center for Communication Programs.

db Studios Limited (2002). *Community health with Sister Evelina: Production House Report.* Lusaka, Zambia: Zambia Integrated Health Programme, Central Board of Health USAID.

De Fossard, E. (1996). *How to write a radio serial drama for social development: A script writer's manual.* Baltimore, MD: Johns Hopkins School of Public Health, Center for Communication Programs.

De Fossard, E. (1998). *How to design and produce radio serial drama for social development: A program manager's guide.* Baltimore, MD: Johns Hopkins School of Public Health, Center for Communication Programs.

Elkamel, F. (1995). The use of television series in health education. *Health Education Research, 10*(2), 225-32.

Emah, E. (1993). Singing about family planning. *Nigeria's Population,* Oct-Dec, 38.

Ferrara, M., Jerato, K., & Witte, Kim (2002). *A case study of Journey of Life: A process evaluation of a radio serial drama.* Baltimore, MD: Johns Hopkins University, Center for Communication Programs. Unpublished report.

Figueroa, M. E., Kincaid, D. L., Rani, M., & Lewis, G. (2002). *Communication for social change: A framework for measuring the process and its outcomes.* New York: Rockefeller Foundation and Johns Hopkins University, Center for Communication Programs.

Hasan, K. (2001). *Shabuj Chhaya audience evaluation survey 2000*. Dhaka, Bangladesh: ORG-MARG QUEST, Social Research Division. Unpublished report.

Hornik, R. (Ed.) (2002). *Public health communication: Evidence for behavior change*. Mahwah, NJ: Lawrence Erlbaum Associates.

Jato, M. N., Simbakalia, C., Tarasevich, J. M., Awasum, D. N., Kihinga, C. N. B., & Ngirwamungu, E. (1999). The impact of multimedia family planning promotion on the contraceptive behavior of women in Tanzania. *International Family Planning Perspectives, 25*(2), 60–67.

Johns Hopkins University, Center for Communication Programs (1990). *Using television to influence family planning behavior: The experience in urban Nigeria with "In a Lighter Mood"*. Baltimore, MD. Final report.

Johns Hopkins University, Center for Communication Programs (1991a). *Television and family planning practices in urban Nigeria II*. Baltimore, MD. Final report.

Johns Hopkins University, Center for Communication Programs (1994). *Production of the social drama Aahat*. Baltimore, MD. Final report.

Johns Hopkins University, Center for Communication Programs. (1997a). *A dialogue with young people through radio. The youth variety show*. Baltimore, MD. Unpublished report.

Johns Hopkins University, Center for Communication Programs (1997b). *Reaching men worldwide: Lessons learned from family planning and communication projects, 1986–1996*. Working Paper No. 3. Baltimore, MD.

Johns Hopkins University, Center for Communication Programs (1998a). *A report on the Second International Conference on Entertainment-Education and Social Change*. May 7–10. Baltimore, MD.

Johns Hopkins University, Center for Communication Programs (1998b). Advocacy and mass media: A winning combination for Kenyan youth. *Communication Impact, 2*, 1–2.

Johns Hopkins University, Center for Communication Programs (1998c). Distance education works: Improves quality of care by stimulating client demand and provider skills. *Communication Impact, 1*, 1–2.

Johns Hopkins University, Center for Communication Programs (1999). Doctors-to-the-Barrios Film Project, "Mumbaki". Baltimore, MD. Final report.

Johns Hopkins University, Center for Communication Programs (1999). Uganda communication campaigns spur integrated health programs. *Communication Impact!* No. 6. Baltimore, MD.

Johns Hopkins University, Center for Communication Programs (2001). Nicaraguan youth begin to play it safe. *Communication Impact!* No. 12. Baltimore, MD.

Johns Hopkins University, Center for Communication Programs & Film Makers (1995). *Pakistan TV Docu-Drama—Ek Hi Raasta (The Only Way)*. Baltimore, MD. Final report.

Johns Hopkins University, Center for Communication Programs & Television Republic Indonesia & Survey Research Indonesia. (1995). *Production and broadcast of TV dramas*. Baltimore, MD. Final report.

Johns Hopkins University, Center for Communication Programs & Gambia Family Planning Association (1992). *A final survey of family planning knowledge, attitudes, and practice in Brikama, The Gambia*. Baltimore, MD. Unpublished report.

Kaiser Family Foundation (1996). *The uses of mainstream media to encourage social responsibility: The international experience*. Report prepared by Advocates for Youth.

Keller, S. (1997). Media can contribute to better health. *Network, 17*(3), 29–31.

Kiingi, L. R. (1998). Evaluation of the video *Time to Care: The dilemma*. Report prepared for the Delivery of Improved Services for Health (DISH) Project.

Kim, Y. M., Kols, A., Nyakauru, R., Marangwanda, C., & Chibatamoto, P. (2001). Promoting sexual responsibility among young people in Zimbabwe. *International Family Planning Perspectives, 27*(1), 11–19.

Kim, Y. M., & Marangwanda, C. (1997). Stimulating men's support for long-term contraception: A campaign in Zimbabwe. *Journal of Health Communication 2*, 271–297.

Kincaid, D. L. (1993). *Using television dramas to accelerate social change: The enter-educate approach to family planning promotion in Turkey, Pakistan, and Egypt.* Paper presented at the International Communication Association, Washington, DC.

Kincaid, D. L. (1999). *Impact of the Sabuj Sathi television drama of Bangladesh: Key findings.* Baltimore, MD: Johns Hopkins University, Center for Communication Programs. Unpublished report.

Kincaid, D. L. (2000). Social networks, ideation, and contraceptive behavior in Bangladesh: A longitudinal analysis. *Social Science & Medicine, 50,* 215-231.

Kincaid, D. L., (2002). Drama, emotion, and cultural convergence. *Communication Theory, 12*(2), 136-152.

Kincaid, D. L., Figueroa, M. E., Underwood, C. R., & Storey, J. D. (1999). *Attitude, ideation, and contraceptive behavior: The relationship observed in five countries.* Paper presented at Population Association of America, New York.

Kincaid, D. L., Jara, J. R., Coleman, P. L., & Segura, F. (1988). *Getting the message: The Communication for Young People Project* (Special Study No. 56). Washington, DC: U.S. Agency for International Development.

Kincaid, D. L., Merritt, A. P., Nickerson, L., Buffington, S. D., de Castro, M. P., & de Castro, B. M. (1996). Impact of a mass media vasectomy promotion campaign in Brazil. *International Family Planning Perspectives, 12* (4): 169-175.

Kincaid, D. L., Yun, S. H., Piotrow, P. T., & Yaser, Y. (1992). Turkey's mass media family planning campaign. In T. E. Backer & E. M. Rogers (Eds.), *Organizational aspects of health communication campaigns: What works?* Thousand Oaks, CA: Sage.

Kiragu, K., Sienche, C., Obwaka, E., Odallo, D., & Barth, S. (1998). *Adolescent reproductive health needs in Kenya: A communication response-Evaluation of the Kenya youth initiatives project.* Baltimore, MD: Johns Hopkins School of Public Health, Center for Communication Programs. Unpublished report.

Lozare, B. V., Hess, R., Yun, S. H., Gill-Bailey, A., Valmadrid, C., Livesay, A., Khan, S. R., & Siddiqui, N. (1993). *Husband-wife communication and family planning: Impact of a national television drama.* Paper presented at the American Public Health Association, San Francisco.

Nariman, H. (1993). *Soap operas for social change: Toward a methodology for entertainment-education television.* Westport, CT: Praeger.

NEEF & Johns Hopkins University, Center for Communication Programs (2001). Think big, start small, act now. In *Proceedings of the Third International Entertainment-Education Conference for Social Change, Arnhem/Amsterdam, September 17-22, 2000.* pp. 23-24. Amsterdam, Netherlands.

Obadina, E. (1991). "Pop" wins over Nigerians to family planning. *People, 18*(2), 29-30.

Palmer, A. (2002). *Reaching youth worldwide: Johns Hopkins Center for Communication Programs, 1995-2000.* Working Paper No. 6. Baltimore, MD: Johns Hopkins University, Center for Communication Programs.

Pelsinsky, N. (1997). *Enter-educate materials.* Baltimore, MD: Johns Hopkins University, Center for Communication Programs.

Piet, D. (1981). *Grains of sand in the sea.* Washington, DC: Population Reference Bureau, Cycle Communications.

Piotrow, P. T., Kincaid, D. L., Hindin, M. J., Lettenmaier, C. L., Kuseka, I., Silberman, T., Zinanga, A., Chikara F., Adamchak, D. J., Mbizvo M. T., Lynn, W., Kumah, O. M., & Kim, Y. M. (1992). Changing men's attitudes and behavior: The Zimbabwe Male Motivation Project. *Studies in Family Planning, 23*(6), 365-375.

Piotrow, P. T., Kincaid, D. L., Rimon, II, J. G., & Rinehart, W. E. (1997). *Health communication: Lessons from family planning and reproductive health.* Westport, CT: Praeger.

Piotrow, P. T., Rimon, J. G. II, Winnard K., Kincaid, D. L., Huntington, D., & Convisser, J. (1990).

Mass media family planning promotion in three Nigerian cities. *Studies in Family Planning, 21*(5), 265–274.

Piotrow, P. T., & Rimon, J. G. II. (1995). "Enter–educate": Reaching youth with messages of sexual responsibility. *Planned Parenthood Challenges, 1,* 41–5.

Rimon, J. G. II, Treiman, K. A., Kincaid, D. L. Silayan-Go, A., Camacho-Reyes, M. S., Abejuela, R. M., & Coleman , P. L. (1994). Promoting sexual responsibility in the Philippines through music: An enter–educate approach. Occasional Paper Series No. 3. Baltimore, MD: Johns Hopkins University Center for Communication Programs.

Robinson, W., & Lewis, G. (2003). Cost-effectiveness analysis of behavior change interventions: A proposed new approach and an application to Egypt. *Journal of Biosocial Science.* In press.

Sabido, M. (1981). *Towards the social use of soap operas: Mexico's experience with the reinforcement of social values through TV soap operas.* Paper presented at the International Institute of Communications, Strasbourg, France.

Singhal, A., & Rogers, E. M. (1999). *Entertainment-education: A communication strategy for social change.* Mahwah NJ: Lawrence Erlbaum Associates.

Snyder, L. B., Hamilton, M. A., Mitchell, E. W., Kiwanuka-Tondo, J., Fleming-Milici, F., & Proctor, D. (1999). The effectiveness of mediated health communication campaigns: Meta-analysis of differences in adoption, prevention, and cessation behavior campaigns. In Corvetu, R., & Bryant J., (Eds.). *Meta-analysis of media effects.* Mahwah, NJ: Lawrence Erlbaum Associates.

Snyder, L. B., Diop-Sidibé, N., & Badione, L. A., (2002). *Preliminary metaanalysis of the impact of JHU/CCP family planning campaigns.* Baltimore, MD: Johns Hopkins Center for Communication Programs.

SRI-Nielsen (1997). *Topline findings of a programme evaluation study [Grains of sand radio serial].* Jakarta, Indonesia.

Storey, J. D., Berutu, H. M., & Dutjuk, F. (1996). Evaluation of the *Alang Alang* mobil van program, 1996, *Topline Report.* Djakarta, Indonesia: Ministry of Population, BKKBN, PENMOT.

Storey, J. D., Boulay, M., Karchi, Y., Heckert, K., & Karmacharya, D. M. (1999). Impact of the integrated radio communication project in Nepal, 1994-1997. *Journal of Health Communication, 4,* 271-294.

Storey, J. D., & Boulay, M. (2001). *Improving family planning use and quality of services in Nepal through the entertainment-education strategy.* Field Report No. 12. Baltimore, MD: Johns Hopkins School of Public Health, Population Communication Services.

Talukdar, R. B., & Hasan, K. (2001). *Shabuj Chhata image study: Customer perception.* Dhaka, Bangladesh: Center for Communication Programs.

Underwood, C., Kemprecos, L. F., Jabre, B., & Wafai, M. (1994). *"And the Nile Flows On": The impact of a serial drama in Egypt.* Baltimore, MD: Johns Hopkins University, Center for Communication Programs. Project report.

Underwood, C. (2001). *Impact of the HEART campaign: Findings from the youth surveys in Zambia 1999 & 2000.* Baltimore, MD: Johns Hopkins School of Public Health, Center for Communication Programs.

Usiniharakishe—A show of rare educational value. (1986, October 23). *Daily Nation* (Kenya), News Analysis column.

Valente, T. W. (2002). *Evaluating health promotion programs.* New York: Oxford University Press.

Valente, T. W., Lettenmaier, C., Kim, Y. M., & Dibba, Y. (1993). *Final report of the new acceptors survey phase of The Gambia "Fakube Jarra" campaign, January-August, 1991.* Unpublished Report No. 27.

Valente, T. W., Kim Y. M., Lettenmaier, C., Glass, W., & Dibba, Y. (1994). Radio promotion of family planning in The Gambia. *International Family Planning Perspectives, 20,* 96-100.

Valente, T. W., Poppe, P. R., Alva, M. E., de Briceño, R. V., & Cases, D. (1995). Street theater as a tool to reduce family planning misinformation. *International Quarterly of Community Health Education, 15*(3), 279–289.

Valente, T. W., Saba, W. P., Merritt, A. P., Fryer, M. L., Forbes, T., Perez, A., & Beltran, L. R. (1996). *Reproductive health is in your hands: Impact of the Bolivia nation reproductive health program campaign. IEC Field Report No. 4.* Baltimore, MD: The Johns Hopkins School of Public Health, Center for Communication Programs.

Valente, T.W., & Saba, W. P. (1998). Mass media and interpersonal influence in a reproductive health communication campaign in Bolivia. *Communication Research, 25*(1), 96–124.

Valente, T. W., & Bharath, U. (1999). An evaluation of the use of drama to communicate HIV/AIDS information. *AIDS Education and Prevention, 11,* 203–211.

Wendo, C. (1998). *Safe motherhood film launched.* PopLine Reproductive Health Database No. PIP 158789.

Whitney, E., Kincaid. D. L, & de Fossard, E. (1999). Bangladesh TV serial promotes integrated services. *Communication Impact, 7.* Baltimore, MD: Johns Hopkins University, Center for Communication Programs.

4

The Origins
of Entertainment-Education

Miguel Sabido
Nuevo Sol Productions

EDITORS' INTRODUCTION

The basic idea of entertainment-education was developed by Miguel Sabido by integrating his theory of the tone with theoretical elements adapted from Albert Bandura, Eric Bentley, Carl Jung, and Paul MacLean. The evolution of the theoretical basis for entertainment-education has been partially told by Televisa's Institute for Communication Research (1981), Nariman (1993), Singhal and Obregon (1999), and Singhal and Rogers (1999). Here, for the first time, Miguel Sabido (Photo 4.1) tells his personal story of the beginnings and development of entertainment-education, drawing from his recent book on this topic (Sabido, 2002).

When people ask me what I am, I tell them that I am a hands-on communication theoretician. In addition to being a communication theoretician, I produce and direct movies, plays, and radio and television dramas. A practical and theoretical approach to human communication gave birth to various methodologies sustained by a theoretical framework. One methodology, which I originally called "entertainment with proven social benefit," was then translated as "entertainment-education," a concept that is now being used around the world.

61

PHOTO 4.1.   Miguel Sabido being interviewed by a reporter about his tonal
theory in Mexico City in September 2002. (*Source*: Population Media Center.
Used with permission.)

BEGINNINGS

My thinking about what later became entertainment-education started in
1957, when I was directing a college theater play at UNAM (the National Autonomous University of Mexico). I observed a young actress, Martha Zavaleta.
When she was playing the role of an old madame, she had a higher vibration
in her lower body. However, this vibration changed when the same actress
played the part of a young girl in the same play. The first vibration produced an
obscene tone, while the second vibration created a charming tone. I then noticed this phenomenon in other actors. Acting meant changing energy within
the body to portray convincingly a symbol depicted by an actor/actress.

Thrilled by this discovery of vibration and tone, I started to experiment
with various techniques so that the college actors I was directing changed
their energies from one place to another in their bodies. The success of
this effort prompted development of a methodology of stage directing. This
methodology integrated the main acting theories (1) of Stanislavsky, with an
emphasis on emotion memory, (2) of Diderot, with focus on an intellectual
control over the reality on stage, and (3) of Grotowsky, who tried to reach
the innermost regions of the actor. My theater professor at UNAM, Luisa
Josefina Hernandez, was an important influence on my thinking at this time.

She insisted that I use a theoretical framework for each drama that I produced (Singhal & Obregon, 1999).

I then noticed that in every human communication event a tone, similar to the one generated by actors on stage, was created. What is this tone? I could feel it, and I could manipulate the scenes in a play by asking the actors to change the locus of their energies, but I could not explain why this produced a change in the scene and in the reactions of the theater audience. My puzzle about tone led me in 1967 to conduct a series of communication studies sponsored by the then Director of the Mexican Institute of Social Security, Ricardo García Sainz. We began by researching the tone of comics, which included very violent pictures. These still pictures showed the energy location of different individuals, and we could study them thoroughly. We then conducted an experiment on conveying information from the Institute to its audience. I wrote three stories inserting informational cues into very intense melodrama. The readers of these three comics perceived the intellectual messages and changed their behavior in dealing with the Institute. This communication effort was a great success! But I still could not define "tone."

Four years later, in 1971, I applied my budding communication thoery of the tone to television soap operas. I submitted a proposal for a commercial *telenovela* (television soap opera) for social change/benefit. By this time, I had located ten points in the body, which, when energized, would change the tone of acting. These points, which I called nodes, where located in three acting zones: the head, the neck and chest, and the lower part of the trunk (the colon, the pubic area, and the sphincter). This classification, although rudimentary, was useful in establishing a theoretical framework that helped produce the effects to be achieved by a telenovela. Audience ratings provided quantitative data about the degree to which a telenovela attracted an audience (an essential for commercial television). I used qualitative research (focus group interviews and in-depth panel interviews) to measure whether audience individuals laughed, cried, and had fun at appropriate times during the broadcast of the telenovela.

Emilio Azcarraga Milmo, the CEO of Televisa (the Mexican television corporation), let me research the social uses of commercial television, based on my research on the tone. I began to use the telenovela format as the backbone of my methodology for several reasons.

1. The emotional tone of this format produces an identification which can be used to teach the television audience a desired social behavior, such as adult literacy, family planning, or to fight against poverty. Continued exposure to the basic message is important: day after day, week after week, month after month.

2. In contrast to the North American soap opera, the Latin American telenovela has a definite beginning, middle, and ending, and thus provides an

opportunity to tie-in, and expand, the needed infrastructure services, such as family planning clinic services.

3. The telenovela format allows connecting the audience with the infrastructure services in short epilogues at the end of every episode, in order to convey relevant information.

4. Since the telenovela format is a reflection on what is good and bad in society, it is easy to add characters for identification by audience individuals and groups, so they can learn social behavior change without harming audience ratings.

I designed, cowrote with Celia Alcantara (the author of *Simplemente María*), and directed the commercial telenovela *Ven Conmigo*, which was produced by my sister, Irene Sabido. It earned audience ratings of 32 points (comparable or higher than other *telenovelas* then broadcast by Televisa), and influenced almost a million adults to enroll in literacy classes.

Emilio Azacarraga of Televisa referred David Poindexter, then Director of the Population Communications Center, to me in order to create a mass media campaign to combat unwanted population growth in Mexico in 1977. An entertainment-education telenovela, *Acompáñame*, about reducing family size, broadcast on Televisa, had important effects in decreasing the population growth rate in Mexico. Poindexter, convinced of my approach to entertainment-education, then spread my E-E methodology around the world (see the David Poindexter chapter in this volume). Also important during these years was contact with Patrick Coleman of Johns Hopkins University, who adapted and applied my entertainment-education approach to popular music in Latin America, then in the Philippines, and in other nations, and to radio and television soap operas (see the Phyllis T. Piotrow chapter in this volume).

Meanwhile, my theoretical work on tone and its application to entertainment-education continued. From 1975 to 1982 I produced a total of seven E-E telenovelas, which were broadcast by Televisa. All were ratings successes, and led to major changes in human behavior. The soap operas were intended to promote enrollment in adult literacy classes, the adoption of family planning methods, and such other prosocial issues as female equality and the rights of women. I began to increasingly connect my theory of the tone with several other theories (which are reviewed in a later section of this chapter), one of which was MacLean's theory of the triune brain.

MACLEAN'S THEORY OF THE TRIUNE BRAIN

Although my methodology worked well in practice, I still did not know why changing energy from one node to another brought about a change in tone. David Poindexter took me to visit Dr. Paul MacLean at the University of

Virginia, who provided me with an explanation for my observations. According to MacLean (1973), the human brain is composed of three parts. MacLean called the ancient part the "reptile brain." Its nerve connections are found in the central nervous system at the junction of the medulla oblongata, the cerebellum, and the spinal chord. This part of the brain, the reptilian complex, is responsible for the motion behavior of the body: breathing, heart beat, digestion. In the course of human evolution, a second brain was born: The limbic or emotional or mammalian brain, bequeathed to us by our mammal forefathers. It is responsible for emotions. The third brain, the neo-cortex, is integrated with the left and right hemispheres linked by the corpus callosum. This brain allows us to perform functions such as analysis, generalization, induction, and deduction.

When energy goes to the reptilian brain, we are blind victims of our drives, our instincts. When energy goes to the emotional circuits of the mammalian brain, we are moved to identify with a figure (like a telenovela character) that we believe is similar to us, and we react emotionally. When energy goes to our third brain (neo-cortex), we process reality in an intellectual, calculating way.

NODES

Nodes are defined as conglomerates of nerve patterns, veins, and arteries in which energy transduction is concentrated, which, when emitted as flow, can be tuned in by other human beings to create a "drive," an emotional or intellectual response. Here we classify certain of the most important nodes in terms of the triune brain categories (reptilian, limbic, and intellectual).

Reptilian Nodes

"**Drive**" **nodes** correspond to the reptilian brain, and deal with basic motions.

1. **The node of implacability** is located in the base of the nape. The ice-cold look by an actor is similar to that of a reptile's eyes. The node of implacability was used with mastery by Marlon Brando in *The Godfather*, creating a terrifying tone. It is found in the ruling organs of the reptile brain, medulla oblongata, and spinal chord. The medulla is used to encode functions as important as breathing, heart rate, and bowel activities. The node of implacability is a protagonist structure in the survival of the human vibration unit. It regulates the setting of patterns that activate specialized organs in the transduction of vital flows that the unit tunes in from its environment: lungs (air), stomach (food), and heart (oxygen). These are the bases for the megapatterns known as drives. The node of implacability is remote and totally deprived of

human commitment. It is extremely effective on television screens due to the terrifying attraction it creates in the viewer.

2. A second "drive" node is **fleeing**, which is found in the pit of the stomach. This node was used by actress Janet Leigh in the famous shower scene in the movie *Psycho*. It provokes a tone of terror.

3. The node of **intraspecific aggression** is used by violent heroes, such as played by Arnold Swartzenegger or Sylvester Stallone in numerous Hollywood movies.

4. Another node, **sex**, centers around the sexual organs involved in mating, and, when energized, produces a sexual tone. Remember the hips of Marilyn Monroe?

5. The node of **limits** is found at the sphincter. It feeds energy to all the other nodes, or when used by itself, it results in a tone of mysticism.

Limbic Nodes

The **emotional nodes** correspond to the limbic or mammal brain formed by the hippocampus, the hypophysis, and the amygdala, which, when correctly vibrating, can provoke an emotional vibration in the receiver

1. The **emotional head node**, below the eyes, is conveyed when the head vibrates, turning it into an important energy emitter which can change the amplitude, longitude, and frequency of the eyes, which are decoded by the viewer as very emotional. Actress Meryl Streep uses the emotional head node with mastery.
2. The **glottis node** is located above the glottis, and is helpful in creating a very emotional tone that is ideal for soap opera melodramas. Actor Russell Crowe in *Gladiator* used this node.
3. The **philanthropy node** is located at the base of the neck and enormously intensifies emotion. It can cause sympathy or pity. It is absolutely essential for the methodology of entertainment-education since it vicariously provides target audiences with positive reinforcement for the socially proper behavior represented by the educational value of a telenovela. Russell Crowe used this node in *A Beautiful Mind*.
4. The **dignified chest node** is in the center of the chest, and generates a painful and dignified tone.
5. The **painful node** lies in the connection between the armpits. It provokes brutal, emotional, but not physical, pain. It can result in a "chemistry" between actors.

Intellectual Nodes

The **intellectual node** is found in the higher part of the head, behind and above the eyes. When actors concentrate energy in this region, an intellectual tone is given to communication. It changes the wavelength of the eyes, and it can organize intellectual flows and project them through the eyes, body language, and voice pitch. The queen of this node was Rosalind Russell in her motion pictures, especially *Women*.

When a director knows what kind of tone can be developed by his/her actors using which nodes, he/she can use this theoretical framework, and arrange other elements of the flow in a telenovela, such as music, sets, camera movements, plot, props, and costumes. This approach allows the reinforcement of a social value in a commercial television soap opera without harming audience ratings.

FLOW

A human communication code consists of the ordering of flow-encoded vibrations to produce an effect on the reptilian, limbic, and intellectual patterns. All of our lives, we live immersed in a sea of flows. We let some flows come into our system, and keep others out. I define flows as a set of vibrations consciously organized and aimed at producing an effect on one or more human beings.

The foundational idea of entertainment-education is that flows can be enriched. The underlying notion is to use methodologies to enrich the flows with elements that deliver intellectual information, reinforce socially useful values, and display identification processes to a viewer, without breaking away from the tonal parameters of the format of the telenovela.

WHAT IS TONE?

Tone means tension. Muscular tone is the degree of tension that a muscle has. In my theory of the tone, fundamental is the degree of tension and distension (vibration) provoked by the flow in the pattern repertoire formed by the nerve circuits of the receivers.

Tone is the essence of human communication. One cannot classify tones or measure them in a precise way. There is no tone-meter. However, by observing and analyzing tonal groups formed by individuals who decode flows in a similar manner, we can gradually gain a more accurate idea of the functioning of tones in human communication.

A tonal group in an audience is formed by two or more human vibrating units that grant the flow format a similar tone. Tones, as perceived subjectively by two or more individuals, will never be identical, since no repertoire of human nervous patterns combining the pulsional, emotional, and intellectual is identical. But individuals who perceive tones similarly can be grouped into tonal groups.

INTEGRATION WITH OTHER THEORIES

In addition to MacLean's theory of the triune brain, my work to develop an entertainment-education methodology also benefited from Bandura's social learning theory, Bentley's dramatic theory, and Jung's theory of the unconscious.

Bandura's Social Learning Theory

The social learning theory of the famous social psychologist, Dr. Albert Bandura (1976), was called to my attention by Dr. Christina Covarrubias, who was conducting research on the effects of my telenovelas in the mid-1970s. Bandura's theory matched with my theory of the tone. I traveled to Stanford University in order to meet with Dr. Bandura, and incorporated key elements of social learning theory into my work. I was then able to develop the methodology now known as entertainment-education.

Gradually, the idea developed that television soap operas, based on a theoretical foundation of entertainment-education, including aspects of my theory of tone and social learning theory, could result in positive social behavior to solve important social problems such as population growth, extreme poverty, desertification, and so forth. An example is my family planning telenovela *Acompáñame* (Come Along with Me), which after its broadcast in 1977–1978 led to a drop in Mexico's population growth rate from 3.7 to 2.4 over a five-year period. Many other population programs were underway in Mexico at the same time, but most experts believe that the entertainment-education soap opera played an important role in this major demographic change, often called "the Mexican demographic miracle."

As explained in detail later, the idea of positive, negative, and transitional role-models in entertainment-education soap operas was based on Bandura's social learning theory, as was the emphasis on *self-efficacy*, defined as the degree to which an individual believes that he/she can control future situations (see the Albert Bandura chapter in this volume). A soap opera character that performed a positive behavior (consistent with the educational value of the soap opera) was rewarded in the storyline with beneficial outcomes. Thus self-efficacy in performing the behavior was encouraged on the part of audience members.

Bentley's Dramatic Theory

My theoretical work on entertainment-education was inspired by Aristotle's (1961) *Poetics*, which I read as a teenager, and also by Professor Eric Bentley's (1967) theory of five theater genres: Tragedy, comedy, tragicomedy, farce, and melodrama. Bentley is a faculty member at Columbia University in New York.

His book, *The Life of Drama*, helped me understand how his dramatic theory could be incorporated in entertainment-education.

Jung's Theory of Archetypes

I was also influenced by Carl Jung's (1958; 1970) theory of the unconscious, including archetypes, and stereotypes. Soap opera characters that imitate a myth represent archetypes, while characters that imitate life represent stereotypes. This classification, based on Jung's approach, was important in designing the characters for entertainment-education telenovelas.

APPLYING ENTERTAINMENT-EDUCATION THEORY TO TELEVISION SOAP OPERAS

Television soap operas are extremely popular throughout Latin America, and, increasingly, around the world. The typical telenovela (that is not an entertainment-education soap opera) in Latin America follows a scheme consisting of the following elements.

1. A remote past that occurred 20 to 30 years earlier and which gives an origin to a social and family status quo, which is apparently very sound but actually is very fragile and full of secrets from the remote past.
2. This status quo is shattered by a trigger event like a wedding, an assassination, or some other unexpected event.
3. A disorderly process is unleashed in which the protagonist (usually a woman) suffers, at least, three major changes of fortune (this is the main plot).
4. In order to create more cliff-hanging excitement (every telenovela needs approximately 600 cliff-hangers distributed across its 150 one-hour chapters/episodes), a second plot with a second protagonist (relatively less important) is created. A series of characters, confidants, traitors, minor victims, squealers, and so forth are interwoven in the two plots.
5. If the relationship of the nodes of protagonists and antagonists of the two or more plots creates a tension or tone, the audience will affiliate with the daily vibrations offered by the telenovela and its ratings will increase. The same effect may result with secondary characters. If the audience vibrates with them, the producer asks the scriptwriter to extend their roles. The secondary plot changes during the broadcast period, while the original structure of the telenovela remains.
6. The protagonists and antagonists fight a final combat in which the former will win and re-establish a new social and family order.

The characters who form part of this dramatic mimesis are (1) protagonists, those who suffer the dramatic action and represent the value system that the audience shares, (2) antagonists, those who cause the dramatic action and represent the axiological system that the audience rejects, (3) those who are fought for by antagonists and protagonists (almost always handsome men), and (4) the satellites or observers of this dramatic action who hesitate between the two value system.

When I applied Bandura's theory of social learning to this scheme for the usual Latin American telenovela, I decided:

1. To convert the satellite characters into representatives of the target audiences to whom we wanted to teach the socially useful educational content of the E-E message.
2. To achieve identification processes on the part of members of the target audiences for the E-E telenovela. A tonal subgroup within the total audience who daily watch the telenovela is thus formed.
3. To design positive and negative reinforcements for each target audience, so that positive role models for the educational value (for example, small family size) are encouraged, and negative role models are punished for their bad behavior.
4. To display to target individuals the process of heightened self-efficacy regarding the behavior related to the educational value (Bandura, 1997).
5. To provide intellectual information for finding the infrastructure services to increase self-efficacy, and to gain access to socially proper behavior. For instance, in *Ven Conmigo* (Come with Me), my E-E telenovela promoting adult literacy in Mexico in 1974, an older illiterate man was shown how to feel comfortable in an adult literacy class (Televisa's Institute for Communication Research, 1981; Singhal & Rogers, 1999). This television soap opera also showed audience members how to obtain free training booklets that they needed for participation in the adult literacy classes.

This entertainment-education methodology developed during the mid-1970s in Mexico required a great deal of planning in advance of the first broadcast. The educational value(s) of a telenovela had to be designed in great detail, by specifying each of the exact behavior changes that the intervention was to bring about. For example, we might decide that female children should be valued equally with male children. Then the characters, plot, and other details of the soap opera were designed toward conveying this value, and changing audience behavior accordingly. So an entertainment-education soap opera requires several months more planning than does the usual entertainment-only television soap opera.

The Role of Communication Research

Dr. Covarrubias and Dr. Ruben Jara conducted evaluation research in Mexico that demonstrated it was possible to use E-E telenovelas for social benefit without harming audience ratings or advertising sales (Nariman, 1993). Communication research, from the time of the first E-E telenovela in Mexico in 1975–1976, played a key role in the effective use of my E-E theory, and led to important adjustments in the model. The importance of formative and summative research has fortunately spread, as part of the E-E strategy, throughout the world. During the late 1970s I served as Televisa's Vice-President for Research, and as Director of the Institute for Communication Research, which pioneered in evaluating the effects of the seven E-E telenovelas in Mexico that I directed.

For example, the Institute's research on *Ven Conmigo*, the first of the seven E-E telenovelas, involved gathering data from a panel of 600 adults in Mexico City. They were personally interviewed each month during the year of the broadcasts. Dr. Covarrubias directed this investigation. The main point here is that the development of my theory of tones and its integration with other theories into the entertainment-education methodology took place hand-in-hand with research.

LESSONS LEARNED

The following tentative conclusions are draw from my personal experience with E-E telenovelas in Mexico, and with their counterparts in India, China, and other nations where I trained communication professionals in entertainment-education methodology and/or provided advice on various E-E interventions. Much of this work was in collaboration with Population Communication International and its former president, David Poindexter.

1. Intellectual material can be added to an emotional flow without disturbing the tonal parameter of the flow.

Telenovelas that traditionally have an emotional vibration flow can be supplemented with information bits so that an audience individual behaves in a socially desirable manner, such as by visiting a family planning clinic, enrolling in an adult literacy class, or sending a girl child to school. These informational bits need not hamper the emotional nature of a telenovela. Television ratings do not suffer from the educational content of an E-E telenovela (Nariman, 1993). E-E soap operas, when broadcast by commercial television or radio networks, earn audience ratings that are comparable with educational-only soap operas. This conclusion has been thoroughly proven around the world (Singhal & Rogers, 1999).

2. Emotional stimuli can be added to mainly intellectual flow without losing its cognitive coherence.

Vibrating intellectual patterns with stimuli that make emotional patterns vibrate helps an emotional tonal audience segment process an intellectual message. An example is the emotional music and the identifying messages of popular telenovela idols in E-E soap operas that teach individuals how to plan their families, adopt contraceptive methods, and space their children. This intellectual information, when enriched by emotional stimuli, results in an easier incorporation of the former into the emotional repertoires of the audience.

3. It is possible to add "drive" stimuli to a basically intellectual flow so that a "drive" audience segment (a tonal group) tunes in and the flow vibrates the "drive" patterns.

4. It is possible to add "drive" and emotional bits to an intellectual flow.

5. It is possible to intensify the emotional nature of basically emotional flows that are processed by emotional tonal audience segments in a way so that they have a more intense tone for the members of these audience groups, who thus become a more defined tonal group.

6. It is possible to intensify the "drive" factors in "drive" flows processed by "drive" tonal groups in the audience, so as to obtain a more intense tone in the members of that audience segment.

7. It is possible to intensify intellectual stimuli in a basically intellectual flow.

8. It is possible to intensify the "drive" and emotional stimuli in a flow encoded with intellectual rigor.

9. It is possible to display emotional and "drive" factors in the same flow with very little intellectual content.

10. It is possible to display "drive," intellectual, and emotional factors in the same flow in an independent manner, but still part of the flow, for example, one after the other.

I recently used this combination to create a tonal Internet communication, *Stories of Guilt*, which used newspaper headlines on neo-Nazism, the AIDS pandemic, and warfare in the Middle East. These headlines are followed by a very emotional dramatization for seven or eight minutes on each social problem. Then hyperlinks lead to six chat rooms where the individual is offered intellectual possibilities to discuss each social problem, learn possible solutions, and gain further background information. A mailing list can be accessed to form volunteer networks and to engage in other actions.

11. It is possible to locate and analyze flows displaying intellectual, emotional, and "drive" factors in perfect balance.

These 11 propositions necessarily vary in the degree to which evidence is available to support them. Some of the propositions are very well supported by evidence from research, while others are merely hypotheses at the present time.

CONCLUSIONS

It is possible to analyze most human communication processes with the concept of tone and to purposefully change flows to achieve a beneficial effect on individual behavior change and the welfare of society. The present chapter, however, mainly deals with entertainment-education, which is a unique form of communication in several respects. Many E-E interventions purposefully arrange the elements of flow in order to make an audience vibrate in the frontal intellectual lobe, or in the emotional throat, or in the pubic "drive" area. The E-E professional communicator becomes an arranger of tone elements in order to produce vibration repertoires that are reptilian, emotional, and/or intellectual. Communication research is one essential component of entertainment-education, helping increase its effectiveness by providing useful information about the audience, including its constituent tonal groups.

I believe that widespread application of the entertainment-education strategy can lead to important social changes in the world.

1. The major problems of mankind can only be solved if the large masses of population in developing countries behave in a socially useful manner, such as by planning their families, continuing studying, starting a family business, adopting preventive medicine, systematically reforesting and recovering ecological niches, etc. These prosocial behaviors can be learned by the large masses of people in developing countries if the tones with which they interact in reality are incorporated into the formats of popular mass communication media, which permit large audiences to tune them in and process the flow in these formats.

2. Problems such as poverty, runaway population growth, and ecological destruction, which can never be solved by mere presidential decrees, governmental orders, or by today's concept of charity, could then be ameliorated.

3. In most developing countries, the television soap opera is the media format with the largest number of audience members, and thus is the format with the greatest capacity to create tonal groups in society. Every telenovela is a basic reflection about good and evil, since its characters are usually divided into two categories with very different, and often antagonistic, standards. For this reason, most telenovelas are melodramas with the ability to provoke identification and de-identification processes with role models by audience individuals.

4. The extraordinary ability of the flow factors in the television soap opera format to trigger a vibration in the emotional patterns of the audience permits creation of huge emotional tonal groups that are voluntarily exposed for months to the vibrations of the flow. This exposure results in a daily strengthening of their emotional patterns regarding the educational values in an E-E intervention.

5. The basic telenovela format can be enriched in an entertainment-education approach so that new elements can be added, such as an "epilogue" (in which an emotional authority figure offers positive and negative reinforcements to the target audience and adds the necessary information on how to use the infrastructure). Today, epilogues are used in E-E interventions throughout the world.

Entertainment-education methodology fits naturally with the television soap opera, which can provide the backbone for a multimedia campaign (radio, television, brochures, posters, interpersonal communication, and audience groups) to change society in order to improve it.

REFERENCES

Aristotle (1961). *Poetics*. Translated by S. H. Butcher. New York: Hill and Wang.

Bandura, A. (1977). *Social learning theory*. Englewood Cliffs, NJ: Prentice-Hall.

Bandura, A. (1997). *Self-efficacy: The exercise of control*. New York: Freeman.

Bentley, E. (1967). *The life of drama*. New York: Atheneum.

Jung, C. G. (1958). *Psychology and religion*. Translated by R. F. C. Hall. New York: Pantheon Books.

Jung, C. G. (1970). *Archetypes and the collective unconscious*. Buenos Aires: Editorial Paidos.

MacLean, P. D. (1973). A triune concept of the brain and behavior, including psychology of memory, sleep, and dreaming. In V. A. Kral et al. (Eds.). *Proceedings of the Ontario Mental Health Foundation Meeting at Queen's University*. Toronto: University of Toronto Press.

Nariman, H. (1993). *Soap operas for social change*. Westport, CT: Praeger.

Sabido, M. (2002). *The tone, theoretical occurrences, and potential adventures, and entertainment with social benefit*. Mexico City: National Autonomous University of Mexico Press.

Singhal, A., & Obregon, R. (1999). Social uses of commercial soap operas: A conversation with Miguel Sabido. *Journal of Development Communication, 10*, 68–77.

Singhal, A., & Rogers, E. M. (1999). *Entertainment-education: A communication strategy for social change*. Mahwah, NJ: Lawrence Erlbaum Associates.

Televisa's Institute for Communication Research (1981). *Toward the social use of soap operas*. Paper presented at the International Institute of Communication, Strassburg, France.

5

Social Cognitive Theory for Personal and Social Change by Enabling Media[1]

Albert Bandura
Stanford University

EDITORS' INTRODUCTION

Albert Bandura is a leading proponent of social cognitive theory, and his work has directly influenced the development of the entertainment-education strategy. After receiving his doctoral degree from the University of Iowa in 1953, he joined the faculty at Stanford University where he has spent his entire career. His initial research centered on the prominent role of social modeling in human thought, affect, and action. The extraordinary advances in the technology of communications have made modeling a key vehicle in the diffusion of ideas, values, and styles of behavior. Another major focus of Bandura's work concerns the human capacity for self-directedness, which added to our understanding of how people exercise influence over their own motivation and behavior through self-regulative mechanisms. His most recent research is adding new insights on how

[1]Preparation of this chapter was supported by grants from the Grant Foundation and the Spenser Foundation. The present chapter is a revision of one published in P. Schmuck, & W. Schultz (Eds.). *The psychology of sustainable development* (pp. 209-238). Dordrecht, The Netherlands: Kluwer.

people's beliefs in their efficacy to exercise control over events that affect their lives contribute importantly to their attainments, resilience in the face of adversity, and psychological well-being. These different lines of research address fundamental issues concerning the nature of human agency.

Social cognitive theory provides an agentic conceptual framework within which to analyze the determinants and psychosocial mechanisms through which symbolic communication promotes personal and social changes (Bandura, 1986, 2001a). To be an agent is to influence intentionally one's own functioning, and life circumstances. In this transactional view of self and society, people are producers as well as products of their social environment. By selecting and altering their social environment, they have a hand in shaping the course that their lives take.

Human adaptation and change are, of course, rooted in social systems. Therefore, personal agency operates within a broad network of sociostructural influences. Social structures embody rules, resources, and social sanctions designed to organize, guide, and regulate human affairs. These social systems are created, implemented, and altered by human activity. In this dynamic interplay, personal agency and social structure operate as interdependent determinants in an integrated causal structure rather than as a disembodied duality (Bandura, 1997; Giddens, 1984). The present chapter presents the core features of social cognitive theory for effecting personal and social change by mass communication.

Three major components in social cognitive theory promote psychosocial changes via symbolic communication (Bandura, 2001b). The first component is a **theoretical model** that specifies the determinants of psychosocial change and the mechanisms through which they produce their effects. This knowledge provides the guiding principles. The second component is a **translational and implementational model** that converts theoretical principles into an innovative operational model by specifying the content, strategies of change, and their mode of implementation. The third component is a **social diffusion model** on how to promote the adoption of psychosocial programs in diverse cultural milieus. Functional adaptations of the programs are made to different cultural circumstances that provide enabling guidance and enlist the necessary resources to achieve success.

DUAL PATH OF INFLUENCE

In fostering large-scale changes, communication systems operate through two pathways (Fig. 5.1). In the direct pathway, communication media promote changes by informing, enabling, motivating, and guiding audience individuals. In the socially-mediated pathway, media influences are used to link participants to social networks and community settings. These places provide

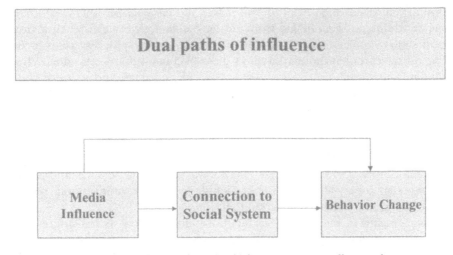

FIG. 5.1.   Paths of influences through which communication affect psycho-social changes both directly and via a socially mediated pathway by linking viewers to social networks and community settings.

continued personalized guidance, as well as natural incentives and social supports for desired changes. The major share of behavioral and valuational changes are promoted within these social milieus. People are socially situated in interpersonal networks. For example, programs aimed at stemming a nation's burgeoning population growth link viewers to family planning services. Programs designed to raise the status of women link viewers to women's support groups. At a more informal level, media influences lead viewers to discuss and negotiate matters of import with others in their lives. In the informal mode of social mediation, the media set in motion transactional experiences that further shape the course of change. Socially mediated influences can have stronger impacts than direct media influence.

SOCIAL COGNITIVE THEORETICAL MODEL

The present section summarizes the tenets of social cognitive theory that provide guidelines for constructing effective media production. A comprehensive theory of human behavior must explain how people acquire attitudes, values, styles of behavior, and how they motivate and regulate their level of functioning.

There are two basic modes of learning. People learn through the direct experience of rewarding and punishing effects of actions, and through the power of social modeling. Trial-and-error learning is not only tedious but hazardous when errors produce costly or injurious consequences. This process is short cut by learning from the successes and mistakes of others. Another major advantage of modeling through the media is that it can reach a vast population simultaneously in widely dispersed locales. Video systems feeding off telecommunications satellites have become a dominant vehicle for disseminating symbolic environments. New ideas, values, and styles of conduct are now being rapidly diffused worldwide in ways that foster a globally distributed consciousness (Bandura, 2002).

Social Modeling

Modeling influences serve diverse functions in promoting personal and social change (Bandura, 1986, 1997). They include instructive, motivational, social prompting, and social construction functions.

With regard to the instructive function, models serve as transmitters of knowledge, values, cognitive skills, and new styles of behavior. Observers also acquire emotional proclivities toward people, places, and objects through modeled emotional experiences. Observers learn to fear that which frightened or injured models, to dislike what repulsed them, and to like what gratified them. Self-debilitating fears and inhibitions can be eliminated by modeling that depicts effective coping strategies and instills a sense of coping efficacy.

The motivational function operates through the depicted benefits and detriments of modeled courses of action. Seeing others gain desired outcomes by their actions can create outcome expectancies that serve as positive motivators. Observed punishing outcomes can create negative outcome expectancies that function as disincentives for similar courses of action. The behavior of others also serves as social prompts that activate, channel, and support modeled styles of behavior. The types of models who predominate in a social milieu determine which human qualities are promoted from among many possible alternatives.

Televised portrayals of human nature, social roles, power relations, and the norms and structure of society shape the public consciousness (Gerbner, Gross, Morgan, Signorielli, & Shanaham, 2002). Media representations gain influence because people's social constructions of reality depend heavily on what they see, hear, and read rather than on what they experience directly.

It is one thing to learn new styles of behavior. It is another to put them into practice, especially in the face of impediments. Several motivators provide support for adopting new forms of behavior.

Perceived Self-Efficacy

Among the mechanisms of self-influence, none is more central or pervasive than beliefs in one's efficacy to exercise control over one's functioning and events that affect one's life. This core belief system is the foundation of human motivation and accomplishments (Bandura, 1997). Whatever course one takes, there are always dissuading difficulties. Unless people believe they can produce desired effects by their actions, they have little incentive to act or to persevere in the face of difficulties. Whatever other factors serve as guides and motivators, they are rooted in the core belief that one has the power to effect changes by one's actions.

Human well-being and attainments require an optimistic and resilient sense of efficacy because usual daily realities are strewn with difficulties. They are full of frustrations, conflicts, impediments, inequities, adversities, failures, and setbacks. These are the price of progress. People must have a strong belief in their own efficacy in order to sustain the perseverant effort needed to succeed. The functional belief system combines realism about tough odds, but optimism that one can beat these odds through self-development and perseverant effort.

People's beliefs in their efficacy can be developed in four ways: (1) through mastery experiences, (2) social modeling, (3) social persuasion, and (4) construal of physical and emotional states. The most effective way of instilling a strong sense of efficacy is through mastery experiences. Successes build a robust efficacy. Failures undermine it, especially in early phases of efficacy development. If people experience only easy successes, they come to expect quick results and are easily discouraged by failure. Resilient efficacy requires experience in overcoming obstacles through perseverant effort. Resilience is also built by training in how to manage failure so it becomes informative rather than demoralizing.

The second way to develop a sense of efficacy is by social modeling. Models are a source of inspiration, competencies, and motivation. Seeing people similar to oneself succeed by perseverant effort raises observers' beliefs in their own abilities. The failures of others can instill self-doubts about one's own ability to master similar challenges.

Social persuasion is a third mode of influence. Realistic boosts in efficacy can lead people to exert greater effort, which increases their chances of success. But effective efficacy builders do more than convey positive appraisals. They structure situations for others in ways that bring success and avoid placing them prematurely in situations where they are likely to fail. They measure success by self-improvement rather than by triumphs over others. Pep talks without enabling guidance achieve little.

People also rely partly on their physical and emotional states in judging their efficacy. They read their emotional arousal and tension as signs of personal vulnerability. In activities involving strength and stamina, people interpret their fatigue, aches, and pains as indicators of low physical efficacy. Mood also affects how people judge their efficacy. Positive mood enhances a sense of efficacy, while despondent mood diminishes it. The fourth way of modifying efficacy beliefs is to reduce people's stress and depression, build their physical strength, and change misinterpretations of their physical states.

Efficacy beliefs regulate human functioning through four major processes: cognitive, motivational, emotional, and decisional. Perceived self-efficacy occupies a pivotal role in causal structures of social cognitive theory because efficacy beliefs affect human functioning not only in their own right, but through their impact on other determinants (Bandura, 1997).

Such beliefs influence whether people think pessimistically or optimistically, or in a self-enhancing or self-hindering way. Efficacy beliefs play a central role in the self-regulation of motivation through goal challenges and outcome expectations. It is partly on the basis of efficacy beliefs that people choose what challenges to undertake, how much effort to expend in the endeavor, how long to persevere in the face of obstacles and failures, and whether failures are motivating or demoralizing. The likelihood that people will act on the outcomes that they expect prospective behaviors to produce depends on their beliefs about whether or not they can produce the required performances. In the affective domain, a strong sense of coping efficacy reduces vulnerability to stress and depression in taxing situations and strengthens resiliency to adversity.

Efficacy beliefs also play a key role in shaping the courses that lives take by influencing the types of activities and environments that people choose. Any factor that influences choice behavior can profoundly affect the direction of personal development. Social influences operating in chosen environments continue to promote certain competencies, values, and interests long after the decisional determinant has rendered its inaugurating effect. Thus, by choosing and shaping their environments, people can have a hand in what they become.

Collective Efficacy

Many of the challenges of life involve common problems that require people to work together with a collective voice to change their lives for the better. Social cognitive theory extends the conception of human agency to collective agency (Bandura, 2000). The strength of families, communities, school systems, business organizations, social institutions, and even nations lies partly in people's sense of collective efficacy that they can solve the problems they face and improve their lives through unified effort. People's shared belief in their collective power to realize the futures they seek is a key ingredient of collective agency.

Efforts at social change typically challenge power relations and entrenched societal practices. Successes do not come easy. To change their lives for the better, people have to struggle against dated traditions and normative constraints. For example, managing sexual and reproductive life requires managing emotionally charged relationships embedded in power relations (Bandura, 1994). In societies with gendered power imbalances, women who want to reduce child bearing have difficulty talking to their husbands about contraceptive methods. The challenge is to enable women to discuss family planning and to provide them with the social support to do so. However, the major burden for contraception should not fall solely on women.

Efforts at change must address sociocultural norms and practices at the social system level. Because of the centrality of perceived efficacy in people's lives, media programs help to raise people's beliefs that they can have a hand in bringing about changes in their lives. For example, in applications of a radio drama in Tanzania, many women believed they had no control over family size. It was predetermined divinely, by fate, or by forces beyond their control. The radio drama raised their perceived efficacy to manage their reproductive life through family planning (Rogers, Vaughan, Swalehe, Rao, Svenkerud, & Sood, 1999).

People must be prepared for the obstacles they will encounter by modeling prototypic problem situations and effective ways of overcoming them. There are several ways of building resilience to impediments through social modeling. People are taught how to manage setbacks by modeling how to recover from failed attempts. They are shown how to enlist guidance and social support for personal change from self-help groups and other agencies in their localities. Seeing others similar to themselves succeed through perseverant efforts also boosts staying power in the face of obstacles.

Goals and Aspirations

People motivate themselves and guide their behavior by the goals, aspirations, and challenges that they set for themselves (Bandura, 1986; Locke & Latham, 1990). Long-term goals set the course of personal change but they are too far removed to overrule competing current influences on behavior. Short-term goals motivate and provide direction for one's efforts in the here and now for incremental change. Goals have little impact unless they are translated into explicit plans and strategies for realizing them. Media programs, therefore, model how to translate a vision of a desired future into a set of achievable subgoals.

Outcome Expectations

Human motivation and behavior are also affected by the outcomes that people expect their actions to produce. Outcome expectations can take three major forms. One set of outcomes includes the material, pleasurable, and aversive effects that the behavior produces. Behavior is also partly regulated by the social reactions it evokes. The social approval and disapproval that the behavior produces is the second major class of outcomes. People adopt personal standards and regulate their behavior by their self-evaluative reactions. They take actions that give them self-satisfaction and self-worth, and refrain from behaving in ways that breed self-dissatisfaction.

Perceived Facilitators and Impediments

Personal and social change would be easy if there were no impediments to surmount. The facilitators and obstacles that people see to changing their behavior are another influential determinant. Some of the impediments are personal ones that undermine efforts at change, such as profound self-doubts that one's efforts would make a difference. Other impediments are situational and structural. Beliefs of personal efficacy affect how formidable these impediments appear.

People who have a resilient sense of efficacy identify ways to overcome obstacles to change. Those who distrust their efficacy view impediments as insurmountable and are easily convinced of the futility of effort. They quickly abort their efforts when they run into difficulties, should they try. Efforts at socially oriented changes are designed to enhance the enabling aspects of social systems and to reduce the impeding aspects.

TRANSLATIONAL
AND IMPLEMENTATIONAL MODEL

The sociocognitive model for promoting society-wide changes, which has now been adopted worldwide, was pioneered by Miguel Sabido (1981) (Photo 5.1). This model uses long-running entertainment-education serial dramas with concurrent plots as the principal vehicle of change. The episodes depict in captivating drama the daily lives of people, some of whom are on adverse life-course trajectories, while others model resiliently effective ways to improve their quality of life. Hundreds of episodes get viewers deeply emotionally engaged in, and identified with, the modeled characterizations that provide enabling guides and incentives for personal and social change. The construction of the dramatic serials draws on the basic principles of social cognitive theory presented earlier.

Differential Modeling

Three types of modeling influences are used in the entertainment-education approach: Positive, negative, and transitional. To take advantage of the attractable and aspirational value of prestigeful modeling, culturally admired

PHOTO 5.1.   Miguel Sabido and Albert Bandura discuss social cognitive theory and its applications in entertainment-education programs at the University of Southern California in 2001. (*Source*: Miguel Sabido. Used with permission.)

television models are selected to exhibit the beneficial styles of behavior. Social attraction increases the impact of modeling influences.

Characters representing relevant segments of the viewing population are shown adopting the beneficial attitudes and behavior patterns. Seeing people similar to themselves change their lives for the better not only conveys strategies for how to do it, but raises television viewers' sense of efficacy that they too can succeed. Viewers come to admire, and are inspired by, characters in their likenesses who struggle with difficult obstacles and eventually overcome them.

The episodes include positive models portraying beneficial lifestyles. Other characters personify negative models exhibiting detrimental views and lifestyles. Transitional models are shown transforming their lives by moving from uncertainty or discarding adverse styles of behavior in favor of beneficial ones. Differential modeling contrasts the personal and social effects of different lifestyles. Viewers are especially prone to draw inspiration from, and identify with, transforming models by seeing them surmount similar adverse life circumstances.

Vicarious Motivators

Another feature of the dramatic productions enlists vicarious motivators for change. The personal and social benefits of the favorable practices, and the costs of the detrimental ones, are vividly portrayed. Depicted beneficial outcomes instill outcome expectations that serve as positive incentives for change.

Showing models discarding subservient roles and challenging inequitable, dated norms requires depiction of some negative reactions to reflect the social reality. These discordant episodes serve to model effective strategies for managing such events successfully, so that viewers come to believe that they can improve the quality of their lives by similar means used perseverantly. Many efficacy-enhancing elements are incorporated in the transactional episodes. For example, in reducing gender inequities, occasional references to accomplished women worldwide working to raise the status of women provide a source of inspiration and support.

In cultures where women are massively subjugated, changing entrenched cultural norms is a slow, gradual process. When large power differentials exist in gender relations, the modeled strategies must be judicious rather than blatantly confrontational which, in real life, can be risky. Male models personifying understanding and support of equitable normative practices can help to mitigate antagonistic social counteractions.

Attentional Involvement

Melodramatic embellishments and emotive music give dramatic intensity to episodes to ensure the viewers' attentional involvement and a high level of viewing. Continued engrossment in a broadcast enhances its impacts.

Symbolic Coding Aids

Still another feature is designed to increase the memorability of the modeled values and social practices. Epilogues summarizing the modeled messages are added to aid the symbolic coding of information for memory representation (see the chapter by Miguel Sabido in this volume).

Environmental Support

It is of limited value to motivate people to change if they are not provided with appropriate resources and environmental supports to realize those changes. Enlisting and creating environmental support is an additional and especially helpful feature for promoting the social changes encouraged by the dramas.

In the monitoring feature of entertainment-education methodology, once a media program is aired, its producers monitor how audience individuals perceive the characters and the dramatized options and consequences. Corrective changes are made, if necessary, in the intervention. Negative modeling must be structured with special care because some audience individuals who subscribe to cultural stereotypes may side with the negative stereotype being modeled (Brown & Cody, 1991). Such unintended effects can be minimized by accenting the adverse consequences of the detrimental life style, and by having the negative models begin to express self-doubt about their life view and behavior.

SOCIAL DIFFUSION MODEL

Effective psychosocial models of change usually have limited social impacts because of inadequate systems for their social diffusion. As a result, society does not profit from successful interventions for social change. Lack of expertise and resources in host countries further undermine perceived efficacy to produce long-running serials that can capture and hold public attention, and change behavior.

Population Communications International (PCI) and the Population Media Center (PMC) remove this impediment by serving as the mechanisms for diffusing globally the use of televised dramas to enhance the quality of family life, to promote gender equality, HIV prevention, and family planning (Ryerson, 1994, 1999). These two nonprofit organizations raise funds from various sources to cover production costs. Social cognitive theory (Bandura, 1986), communication theory (Rogers, 1995; Singhal & Rogers, 1999), and dramatic theory (Sabido, 2002) provide the generic principles of change. But their implementation in serial dramas requires functional adaptations to different cultural milieus.

These dramatic serials are created only on invitation by countries seeking help with intractable social problems. The Centers provide a nation's scriptwriters, producers, and actors with the technical assistance to construct dramas tailored to the societal problems, aspirations, and normative practices of the host country. This creative process involves a close collaborative partnership with local production teams aimed at enabling people to improve their life circumstances. To ensure sustainability of these productions, PCI or PMC workshops equip local partners with the skills to produce engrossing broadcasts for social change on their own.

These socially enabling dramas are not soap operas in which a wide array of characters are endlessly entangled in social conflicts and moral predicaments laced with interpersonal treachery. Nor are they superficial media campaigns marketing quick fixes to intractable social problems. Rather, the sociocognitive genre dramatizes the everyday social problems with which people struggle, models suitable solutions, and provides people with incentives, support, and strategies for bettering their lives. In audience surveys, viewers report the many ways in which the characters in the dramas touch their personal lives. Functional relevance makes these serials immensely popular.

Long-running plot development fosters growing valuation of beneficial styles of behavior and devaluation of detrimental ones. In short, both genres involve storytelling, but they tell entirely different types of stories, serving markedly different purposes. To misconstrue the proactive enabling genre as an ordinary soap opera trivializes its markedly different structure and function.

The sociocognitive dramatizations using Sabido's approach are not aimed at simply changing attitudes, which often bear a weak relationship to behavior. When self-interest conflicts with personal attitudes, people readily find reasons to act in ways that belie their professed attitudes or to justify exemptions to them. As previously noted, the enabling dramatizations serve more powerful functions. They inform, enable, guide, and motivate people to effect changes in their lives. The dramatizations further assist people in their efforts at personal and social change by linking them to enabling and supportive sub-communities and beneficial human services.

These serial dramas are also not "family planning" interventions foisted on the women of poor nations by powerful outsiders. The dramatic productions address the problem of mounting population growth and possible solutions in broader human terms. In many societies women are treated more like property than as persons, denied equitable access to education, forced into prearranged marriages, and granted little say in their reproductive lives. Therefore, one of the central themes in the dramatizations is aimed at raising the status of women so they have equitable access to educational and social opportunities, have a voice in family decisions about child bearing, and serve as active partners in their familial and social lives. This theme involves raising men's understanding of the legitimacy of women making decisions regarding their reproductive health and family life. Moreover, the engrossing programs serve as an excellent vehicle for modeling a variety of functional life skills woven into familial and social transactions.

PCI and PMC serve as the vehicle for social diffusion and also promote cooperation and collaboration among nongovernmental organizations worldwide that are concerned with population growth, environmental and health problems, and human rights. Such alliances increase the chances of success by mobilizing and focusing people's efforts to improve the quality of life for themselves and their children. In addition, PCI and PMC work with professionals in the entertainment industry to heighten their sensitivity to ethnic stereotyping, human rights, health, population growth and environmental degradation in their media productions and to include themes related to these issues in the story lines they create for various types of fictional dramas (see the chapters by David Poindexter and by William Ryerson and Negussie Teffera in this volume).

Cultural and Value Analyses

As is true of any intervention, the use of communication to foster personal and social change raises ethical issues. Ethical evaluations will depend on who selects the types of changes to be promoted, the agents of change, the means used, and the choice and voluntariness of exposure to the influence. Extensive cultural and value analyses are conducted before dramas are developed and implemented. In this formative phase, focus groups, representing various constituencies in the society, identify problems of major concern to them and the obstacles they face. These data provide the culturally relevant information for developing realistic characters and engrossing functional plot lines. The host country production team, drawing on a wide variety of sources, including public health, religious organizations, women's groups, and other constituencies, identity unique cultural values and itemize the types of changes the dramatizations should encourage. Once a program is aired, producers monitor how viewers perceive the characters, with whom they are identifying, and the dramatized options for corrective changes if necessary.

Value disputes are often fueled by wrangling over stereotypes infused with emotive surplus meanings rather than deliberating about changes in real-life terms. The value issues are, therefore, cast in concrete terms of detriments and benefits of particular lifestyles. For example, initial religious and political opposition in Mexico to Miguel Sabido's serials promoting "family planning" turned to support when the nature of the social changes were presented concretely in a value matrix. The tangible values embody respect for human dignity and equitable familial, social, health, and educational opportunities that support common human aspirations. These dramatizations are thus grounded in the internationally endorsed human values codified in United Nations covenants and resolutions. The dramatized options and consequences enable people to make informed choices to improve their lives.

GLOBAL APPLICATIONS OF THE SOCIOCOGNITIVE MODEL

The present chapter thus far has centered on the basic tenets of social cognitive theory and their social applications via translational and social diffusion models. The sections that follow illustrate concretely how these guiding principles have been applied world-wide to alleviate some of the most urgent social problems.

Different indicators are used to gauge the effectiveness of this model. In applications designed to bring down the population growth rate (Rogers et al., 1999), the indices include changes in family size preferences, prevalence of contraceptive use, and reduction in fertility rates. The direct impact of televised influences is affected by level of self-exposure to the modeled values and social practices. Viewership surveys, therefore, assess the reach of the programs, how often people are exposed to them, and how these programs affect viewers at a personal level. The socially mediated impact is measured in terms of the frequency with which people talk about the educational content modeled in the media dramatizations. These types of data permit more refined analyses of impacts as a function of level of self-exposure and social transactions that help to promote desired personal and social change.

As previously noted, serial dramas try to improve people's lives in a variety of ways. These broader social indices of impact include changes in people's sense of efficacy to manage and improve their lives, support of gender equality in opportunities for social and education growth, spousal abuse, health promotion, protection against HIV/AIDS infection, and environmental conservation practices. Some of the themes are unique to a given society, such as attacking the practice of dowry and arranged marriages in which women have no say in their choice of husband.

The outcomes selected for assessment represent the different spheres in which people seek to improve their lives. These socially important assessments need to be supplemented with measurements of the key psychosocial factors through which media influences affect personal and social change. As shown earlier, these sociocognitve factors include people's efficacy beliefs that they can effect changes in their lives by individual and collective action; the goals and aspirations they set for themselves; the material, social, and self-evaluative outcomes they expect their efforts to produce; and the social facilitators and impediments they see to improving the quality of their lives and shaping the social future. Assessment of these key determinants provides guides for the needed adjustments in the dramatizations to enhance their impact.

Promoting National Literacy

Miguel Sabido (1981) first devised the essential elements and structure of the sociocognitive model in a television serial designed to promote enrollment in a national literacy program in Mexico. Literacy is, of course, a key element in personal and national development. He faced the challenge of using commercial television in the public interest without forfeiting viewership.

To reduce widespread illiteracy, the Mexican government launched a national self-instruction program. People who were skilled at reading were urged to organize small self-study groups in which they would teach others how to read with instructional materials (a literacy manual) specifically developed for this purpose. The national appeal produced a disappointing social response, however. So Sabido created a year-long television serial with daily episodes to reach, enable, and motivate people with problems of illiteracy. The main story line in the dramatic series centered on the engaging and informative experiences of one self-instruction group. The implementation model involved creative translation of social cognitive theory into practice. The most popular soap opera performer was cast in the role of the literate model, to take advantage of prestigeful modeling. To enhance the impact of modeling through perceived similarity, she recruits a cast of characters who represent the different segments of the population with problems of illiteracy. Showing people similar to themselves mastering linguistic skills helped persuade viewers that they too possess the capabilities to master the skills that were being modeled. The name of the telenovela, *Ven Conmigo* (Come With Me) portrayed collective mastery of competencies and the accompanying benefits.

A prior interview survey revealed several personal demotivating barriers that dissuaded people from enrolling in the national program for adult literacy. Many believed that they lacked the capabilities to master such a complex skill. Others believed that reading skills could be acquired only when one is young. Still others felt that they were unworthy of having an educated person devote their time to help them. These self-handicapping misbeliefs were modeled by the actors and corrected by the television instructor as she persuaded them that they possessed the capabilities to succeed. The Mexican telenovela included humor, conflict, and engrossing discussions of the subjects being read. The episodes showed the models struggling in the initial phases of learning, and then gaining progressive mastery and self-pride in their accomplishments.

To provide vicarious motivators to pursue the self-education program, the dramatic series depicted the substantial benefits of literacy both for personal development and for national efficacy and pride. Melodramatic embellishments and emotive music gave dramatic intensity to the television episodes to ensure high involvement of the viewers.

Epilogues were used to increase memorability of the modeled messages. To facilitate media-promoted changes, all the instructional material (the manual) was provided by the governmental educational agency. In addition, the series often used real-life settings showing the actors obtaining the instructional material from an actual distribution center, and eventually graduating in a ceremony for actual enrollees in the adult literacy classes. Epilogues also informed the viewers of the national self-instruction program and encouraged them to take advantage of it. What a powerful motivator it turned out to be! On the day after an epilogue urged viewers to enroll in the literacy program, about 25,000 people descended on the distribution center in downtown Mexico

City to obtain their reading materials! The resulting traffic jam tied up vehicles for many hours.

Millions of viewers watched this serial drama faithfully. Compared to non-viewers, viewers of the dramatic series were much more informed about the national literacy program and expressed more positive attitudes about helping one another to learn. The rate of enrollment in the program was 99,000 in the year before the televised series, but shot up abruptly to 900,000 during the year of the broadcasts.

As people develop a sense of efficacy and competencies that enable them to exercise more control over their lives, they serve as models, inspiration, and even as tutors for others in the circles in which they move. This concomitant socially mediated influence can vastly multiply the impact of televised modeling. In the year following *Ven Conmigo*, another 400,000 people enrolled in the self-study literacy program. Through the socially mediated path of influence, televised modeling can set in motion an ever-widening, reverberating process of social change.

Environmental Sustainability by Stemming Population Growth

Soaring population growth is destroying the ecosystems that sustain life, degrading the quality of life, and draining resources needed for national development. Underdeveloped nations are doubling their populations at an accelerating rate. Through a global effort, numerous socially enabling dramas are now being widely used in Africa, Asia, and Latin America to stem the tide of population growth. The host countries that sought help are struggling with widespread poverty and are on a trajectory of doubling their populations over a relatively short period. Burgeoning demographic forces overwhelm efforts at social and economic development.

Unless people see family planning methods as improving their welfare, they have little incentive to adopt them. Sabido developed a series of dramas to reduce the population growth rate in Mexico (Sabido, 1981). Through modeling with accompanying outcomes, the dramas portrayed the process as well as the personal, social, and economic benefits of family planning. The positive family life of a smaller-sized family, whose wife worked in a family planning clinic, was contrasted with that of a married sister overburdened with a huge family and accompanying impoverishment and misery.

Much of the drama of *Acompaname* (Accompany Me) focused on the married daughter from the large family, who was beginning to experience severe marital conflicts and distress over her rapidly expanding family. She served as the transitional model, living in her parents' home, a despairingly crowded and impoverished environment. In dramatic scenes she expresses emotionally her desire for a voice in her family life, to cease having unwanted babies, and to break the cycle of poverty that condemned her family to an inner-city slum with inability to care adequately for her children. She turns to her aunt for help, which serves as the vehicle for modeling a great deal of information about how to manage marital discord and machismo behavior, how to deal with male resistance to contraception and family planning, how to communicate openly in the family, and how to escape the many problems caused by a family overburdened with children.

As the drama unfolds, the young couple is shown gaining control over their family life and enjoying the accruing benefits with the help of a family planning clinic. A priest occasionally appeared in the drama, emphasizing the need for responsible family planning by limiting the number of offspring to those the family can afford to raise adequately. At the end of episodes, viewers were informed in epilogues about existing family planning services to facilitate media-promoted behavior changes.

Compared to nonviewers, heavy viewers of the dramatic serial in Mexico were more likely to link lower childbearing with social, economic, and psychological benefits. They also developed a more positive attitude towards helping others plan their family (Sabido, 1981). Records of family planning clinics revealed a 32% increase in the number of new contraceptive users over the number for the previous year before the series was televised. People reported that the television portrayal served as the impetus for consulting the health clinics. National sales of contraceptives rose from 4% and 7% in the preceding two baseline years, to 23% in the year the television program was broadcast.

Generalization Through Functional Adaptations

Applications of the generic model in India and Kenya illustrate its generalizability through functional tailoring to diverse cultural practices. Efforts to bring down the rate of population growth must address not only the strategies and benefits of family planning, but also the role and status of women in societies in which they are treated as subservient. In some societies, the equity problems stem from machismo dominance; in others, from marriage and pregnancy at the onset of puberty with no say in the choice of husband or the number and spacing of children; and in still others from dispossession by polygamous marriages. In some societies, women are subjugated to the point where they are repeatedly beaten and are not even allowed to turn on a family radio.

The television program in India, *Hum Log* (We People), was designed to raise the status of women, as well as to promote a smaller family norm. It addressed a variety of themes about family life in the context of broader social norms and practices (Singhal & Rogers, 1999). Subthemes devoted particular attention to family harmony amidst differences among family members, elevation of the status of women in family social and economic life, educational opportunities and career options for women, son preference and gender bias in child rearing, the detriments of dowry, choice in spouse selection, teenage marriage and parenthood, spousal abuse, family planning to limit family size, youth delinquency, and community development. Some of the characters personified positive role models for gender equality; others were proponents of the traditional subservient role for women. Still others were transitional models. A famous Indian film actor reinforced the modeled messages in epilogues.

The melodramatic series was immensely popular in India, enjoying top viewership on television, and a massive outpouring of letters in the hundreds of thousands from viewers offering advice and support to the characters. A random sample of 1,100 viewers reported that they had learned from the television program that women should have equal opportunities and a say in decisions that affect their lives, that programs advancing the welfare of women should be encouraged, that cultural diversity should be respected, and that family size should be limited. The more aware viewers were of the messages being modeled, the greater was their support of women's freedom of choice in matters that affected them and of planning for small families (Brown & Cody, 1991; Singhal & Rogers, 1999).

Intensive interviews with village inhabitants revealed that the dramatizations spark serious public discussions about the broadcast themes concerning child marriages, dowry, education of girls, benefits of small families, and other social issues (Papa, et al., 2000). These social transactions went beyond talk to collective community action aimed at changing inequitable normative practices and improving the future. Indeed, one village sent to the broadcaster a large poster letter signed by its inhabitants stating that they would work to eradicate the practice of dowry and child marriages (both illegal in India, but widespread). The enrollment of girls in elementary schools rose from 10% to 38% in one year of the broadcasts.

Many impediments exist to sociocultural change, but their force weakens over time as new ideas gain support and collective benefits outweigh the social costs of dated institutional arrangements. In another Indian village young boys and girls created a self-help action group to promote the changes modeled in the serial drama (Law & Singhal, 1999). These system-level effects illustrate how dramas that address the social problems that people face in enabling ways can spawn the development of collective efficacy.

A story line in a Kenya radio drama revolved around the inheritance of land and the impoverishing effect of large families. The serial drama, broadcast via radio in order to reach rural people, was the most popular program on the air. Contraceptive use increased by 58% and desired family size declined by 24%.

Quantitative analyses, including multiple controls for possible determinants, revealed that the mass media were a major contributor to Kenya's declining birthrate per woman and the reduction in the rate of population growth (Westoff & Rodriguez, 1995).

China, the most populous nation in the world, faces a projected doubling of its current population to the two billion mark in about 70 years. This enormous population growth will have devastating effects on ecological systems. The Chinese one-child policy heightens the traditional cultural preferences for sons. The drama, *Baixing* (Ordinary People), addresses the discriminatory gender bias in Chinese society and fosters psychosocial changes to supplant coercive institutional controls on fertility with voluntary adoption of contraceptive practices and a preference for small families. The television drama graphically portrays the tragedy and injustice of social practices that force women into arranged marriages they do not want and into bearing baby girls that spouses do not want. Viewers are inspired and strengthened by the determination and courage of female characters who challenge the subordinate status of women, and who strive to change detrimental cultural practices. The gender inequity themes seek to raise the valuation of women and expand enabling opportunities for them to become active participants in the social and economic life of Chinese society.

The diverse applications of the sociocognitive model have yielded uniform research findings. The dramatic serials are an extraordinarily effective vehicle for reaching vast numbers of people over a prolonged period. Viewers get deeply involved in the lives of the televised characters. Airing of the televised serials is followed by preference for smaller families and adoption of contraceptive methods. The strength of the social impact increases as a function of level of exposure to the broadcasts (the dose effects). The more that people watch the media program, the more they talk about the educational issues that are aired, the more supportive they are of gender equality, the higher their perceived efficacy to regulate their reproductive behavior, and the more likely they are to adopt contraceptive methods.

Control on Other Independent Variables

Research by Westoff and Rodriguez (1995) shows that the conditional relationship is not an artifact due to more advantaged and efficacious individuals being heavier television viewers. The impact of media exposure on adoption and consistent use of new methods of contraception remained after controlling for life-cycle status, number of wives and children, and a host of socioeconomic factors such as ethnicity, religion, education, occupation, and urban-rural residence. Internal analyses of survey data revealed that the media influence was a major factor in raising motivation to limit fertility and to adopt contraception practices.

In Tanzania, containing seven regions with separate broadcasting trans-mitters, the radio drama was aired in six regions with the other major region serving as a control. Compared to the control region, the radio dramatizations raised viewers' perceived efficacy to determine their family size, decreased their desired number of children, increased the ideal age of marriage for women, increased approval of family planning methods, stimulated spousal communication about family size, and increased use of family planning ser-vices and adoption of contraceptive methods (Rogers et al., 1999). The impact on family planning was replicated (after 1995) when the serial was later broad-cast in the control region. As in the Kenya research, the more often people listened to the radio broadcasts, the more that married women talked to their spouses about family planning and the higher their rate of adoption of contra-ceptive methods. These diverse effects remained after multiple controls for a host of other potential determinants. The fertility rate declined more in the 2-year period of the serial dramas than in the previous 30 years without any change in socioeconomic conditions and little change in death rate (Vaughan, 2003).

Some of the radio episodes targeted sexual practices that risk infection with the AIDS virus. Compared to residents in the control region, those in the broadcast regions increased belief in their personal risk of HIV infection through unprotected sexual behavior, talked more about HIV infection, re-duced their number of sexual partners, and increased condom use (Vaughan, Rogers, & Swalehe, 1995; Vaughan, Rogers, Singhal, & Swalehe, 2000). The number of condoms distributed annually by the National AIDS Control Program in Tanzania remained low in the control region, increased substan-tially in the broadcast regions, and increased significantly in the control region after exposure to the radio broadcasts. Perceived self-efficacy emerged as a significant predictor of reproductive behavior and risky sexual practices.

SUSTAINABILITY BY MODIFICATION
OF CONSUMMATORY LIFESTYLES

The present chapter focused on environmental conservation and sustainabil-ity through population stabilization. The fundings from many cross-cultural applications attest to the generalizability of the generic model with appro-priate functional adaptations. It lends itself readily to other types of lifestyle changes, such as environmental conservation and consummatory practices to promote environmental sustainability. For example, an Indian serial centered on preserving the environment motivated villagers to take collective action to improve sanitation, reduce potential health hazards, adopt fuel conservation practices to reduce pollution, and to launch a tree-planting campaign (Papa et al., 2000). Moreover, villagers persuaded other villages to institute similar environmental practices.

If people are to make decisions supportive of sustained development, they need to be informed of the ecological costs of their consummatory practices and enabled and motivated to turn enlightened concern into constructive courses of action. This change is best achieved through multiple modes of communication (Singhal & Rogers, 1999). Many lifelong consummatory habits are formed during childhood years. It is easier to prevent wasteful practices than to try to change them after they have become deeply entrenched as part of a lifestyle.

To address the environmental problems created by over-consumption, PCI produced a video, *The Cost of Cool*, for distribution to schools that focused on the buying habits of teenagers (PCI, 2000). It tracks the ecological costs of the manufacture of everyday items such as T-shirts and sneakers. Providing teenagers with sound information helped them make informed choices in their buying habits. As one viewer put it, "I'll never look at a T-shirt in the same way." Popular entertainment, using formats such as music concerts, recordings, and videos, provide another vehicle for reaching youth populations, with themes addressing critical social issues, substance abuse, violence, teen sexuality, and gender equality. The impact of these complimentary approaches requires systematic evaluation. The increasing magnitude of the environmental problem calls for multifaceted efforts to alter behavioral practices that degrade the ecological supports of life.

In sum, the research cited here provides convergent evidence from diverse methodologies, multiple controls for a host of other potential determinants, multifaceted forms of assessments, diverse cultural milieus, adaptational themes, and domains of functioning. The findings attest to the social utility of the sociocognitive communication model for effecting personal and social change grounded in internationally endorsed human values with sensitive adaptations to cultural diversity. People enjoy the benefits left by those before them who collectively fought for social reforms that improved their lives. Their own collective efficacy will shape how future generations live their lives. The times call for social initiatives that enable people to play a part through their collective voice in bettering the human condition.

REFERENCES

Bandura, A. (1986). *Social foundations of thought and action: A social cognitive theory.* Englewood Cliffs, NJ: Prentice-Hall.

Bandura, A. (1994). Social cognitive theory and exercise of control over HIV infection. In R. DiClemente and J. Peterson (Eds.), *Preventing AIDS: Theories and methods of behavioral interventions* (pp. 25–59). New York: Plenum.

Bandura, A. (1997). *Self-efficacy: The exercise of control.* New York: Freeman.

Bandura, A. (2000). Exercise of human agency through collective efficacy. *Current Directions in Psychological Science, 9,* 75–78.

Bandura, A. (2001a). Social cognitive theory: An agentic perspective. *Annual Review of Psychology, 52*, 1–26.

Bandura, A. (2001b). Social cognitive theory of mass communications. In J. Bryant, & D. Zillman (Eds.), *Media effects: Advances in theory and research* (2nd ed.), (pp. 121–153). Mahwah, NJ: Lawrence Erlbaum Associates.

Bandura, A. (2002). Growing primacy of human agency in adaptation and change in the electronic era. *European Psychologist, 7*, 2–16.

Brown, W. J., & Cody, M. J. (1991). Effects of a prosocial television soap opera in promoting women's status. *Human Communication Research, 18*, 114–142.

Gerbner, G., Gross, L., Morgan, M., Signorielli, & Shanaham, J. (2002). Growing up with television: cultivation perspective. In J. Bryant & D. Zillman (Eds.), *Media effects: Advances in theory and research*, (2nd ed.) (pp. 43–67). Mahwah, NJ: Lawrence Erlbaum Associates.

Giddens, A. (1984). *The constitution of society: Outline of the theory of structuration*. Berkeley: University of California Press.

Law, S., & Singhal, A. (1999). Efficacy in letter-writing to an entertainment-education radio serial. *Gazette, 61*, 355–372.

Locke, E. A., & Latham, G. P. (1990). *A theory of goal setting and task performance*. Englewood Cliffs, NJ: Prentice-Hall.

Papa, M. J., Singhal, A., Law, S., Pant, S., Sood, S., Rogers, E. M., & Shefner-Rogers, C. L. (2000). Entertainment-education and social change: An analysis of parasocial interaction, social learning, collective efficacy, and paradoxical communication. *Journal of Communication, 50*, 31–55.

PCI (2000). *Fifteenth anniversary*. New York: Population Communications International.

Rogers, E. M. (1995). *Diffusion of innovations* (4th ed.). New York: Free Press.

Rogers, E. M, Vaughan, P. W., Swalehe, R. M. A., Rao, N., Svenkerud, P., & Sood, S. (1999). Effects of an entertainment-education radio soap opera on family planning behavior in Tanzania. *Studies in Family Planning, 30*, 1193–1211.

Ryerson, W. N. (1994). Population communications international: Its role in family planning soap operas. *Population and Environment: A Journal of Interdisciplinary Studies, 15*, 255–264.

Ryerson, W. N. (1999). *Population Media Center*. Shelburne, Vermont.

Sabido, M. (1981). *Towards the social use of soap operas*. Mexico City, Mexico: Institute for Communication Research.

Sabido, M. (2002). *El tono* (The Tone). Mexico City: Universidad Nacional Autonoma de Mexico.

Singhal, A., & Rogers. E. M. (1999). *Entertainment-education: A communication strategy for social change*. Mahwah, NJ: Lawrence Erlbaum Associates.

Vaughan, P. W. (2003). The onset of fertility transition in Tanzania during the 1990's: The role of two entertainment-education radio dramas. Submitted for publication.

Vaughan, P. W., Rogers, E. M., & Swalehe, R. M. A. (1995). *The effects of "Twende Na Wakati," an entertainment-education radio soap opera for family planning and HIV/AIDS prevention in Tanzania*. Unpublished manuscript, Albuquerque, University of New Mexico.

Vaughan, P. W., Rogers, E. M., Singhal, A., & Swalehe, R. M. (2000). Entertainment-education and HIV/AIDS prevention: A field experiment in Tanzania. *Journal of Health Communication, 5*, 81–100.

Westoff, C. F., & Rodriguez, G. (1995). The mass media and family planning in Kenya. *International Family Planning Perspectives, 21*, 26–31.

6

Celebrity Identification in Entertainment-Education

William J. Brown
Benson P. Fraser
Regent University

The proliferation of entertainment media worldwide in recent decades has made celebrities powerful agents of social change. The extensive reach of entertainment media expanded the influence of celebrities across socioeconomic, political, and cultural boundaries (Brown & Singhal, 1999). Although a number of scholars addressed the influence of celebrities on culture from an historical-critical perspective (Boorstin, 1961; Braudy, 1986; Gamson, 1994), very few communication theorists and researchers systematically explored the effects of celebrities on individual and social values, beliefs, and behavior.

Consider these examples of celebrity influence:

- In one episode of the American television serial *Happy Days*, the very popular Fonzi, played by Henry Winkler, decides to get a library card. During the several days that followed the program, libraries across the United States were flooded with requests for library cards from children and teenagers who followed Fonzi's example (Brown, 1992).
- In the Indian soap opera *Hum Log* (We People), the well-known and highly respected film star, Ashok Kumar, gave short epilogues at the end of each television episode, highlighting what viewers could learn from the story. Kumar received 60 to 70 viewer letters each day at his personal

residence, many testifying to the changes audience individuals had made in response to his epilogues (Singhal & Rogers, 1999).

- In Nigeria, two of the nation's most famous singers, King Sunny Ade and Onyeka Onwenu, released two hit songs and accompanying music videos, "Choices" and "Wait for Me," to promote sexual responsibility. Use of contraceptives increased from 16% to 26% among the target audience (aged 15 to 35) during the music campaign (Kincaid, Rimon, Piotrow, & Coleman 1992).

These three examples illustrate the tremendous influence that popular media stars can have on people's behavior. The purpose of this chapter is to discuss the powerful role that celebrities have in today's society. Second, we present a theoretical framework for understanding how celebrities promote social change through audience identification. Third, we provide specific examples of how celebrities have been instrumental in promoting educational messages. Finally, we discuss the implications of employing celebrities as social change agents within the context of an overall entertainment-education (E-E) strategy.

THE ROLE OF CELEBRITIES IN TODAY'S SOCIETY

During the past 40 years, several scholars observed that the role of traditional heroes has been replaced in many cultures by celebrities (Boorstin, 1961; Braudy, 1986; Campbell, 1988; Gamson, 1994). This change is especially pronounced in cultures where the mass media have proliferated. Boorstin (1961) defined a celebrity as a person who is known for being known. When Andy Warhol predicted that everyone would be famous for 15 minutes, he recognized the power of mediated visual images to thrust people into the public spotlight. Those who wield the greatest social influence today are often not traditional heroes such as political, religious, and military leaders. Instead of modeling local heroes and family members, people now model celebrities such as rock musicians, film or television stars, NASCAR drivers, WWF (World Wrestling Federation) wrestlers, athletes, hip-hop artists, fashion models, and more.

Consider the story of Rudy Boesch, a popular contestant on the CBS television program *Survivor* during its debut in the spring of 2000. The 72-year-old Boesch was a Navy enlisted man for 45 years, becoming a distinguished officer of the original SEAL (Sea-Air-Land) Team 2. He completed dozens of missions in Vietnam, earning a Bronze Star for his valor (Adel, 2000). Although Rudy was a hero to those who personally knew him, it was his participation on the television program *Survivor* that gave him national recognition. When Rudy returned to his home in Virginia Beach, Virginia, after the television show was taped, The *Virginian-Pilot* proclaimed, "Hometown fans get a chance to honor their hero" (Bonko, 2000). A large celebration was prepared for Rudy with extensive media coverage to commemorate his making the final group of four *Survivor* contestants. Virginia Beach Mayor Meyera Oberndorf proclaimed a "Rudy Boesch Day." Rudy, overwhelmed, remarked "Now I know how Elvis felt" (Sinha, 2000).

Celebrities who are prominently featured in entertainment programs become role models for audience members. Bill Cosby modeled the life of a morally responsible and faithful husband and father on *The Bill Cosby Show*, which affected how Blacks viewed their own families (Cummings, 1988). Celebrities can become the champions of prosocial behavior (Bouman, 1998), providing audience members with examples of how to think and act and teaching them what consequences will likely follow prosocial and antisocial behavior (see the Albert Bandura chapter in this volume). Popular celebrities in developing countries have attracted strong emotional reactions through culturally appropriate televised drama, raising audience members' concerns about key issues such as health practices (Kincaid, 2002).

Some celebrities achieve greatness, others are "created" by the media, and others, like John F. Kennedy, Jr. and Prince Harry, are born celebrities (Brown, Fraser, & Bocarnea, 2001). For many of these (for example, JFK, Jr., Princess Diana, Lou Gehrig, Joe DiMaggio, Marilyn Monroe, James Dean, Buddy Holly, Elivs Presley, Dale Earhardt), dying through accident or disease resulted in profound expressions of grief and affection (Brown, Basil, & Bocarnea, 1998).

Celebrity Endorsements

The increased exposure to celebrities through both news and entertainment provided advertisers with a powerful means of persuasion. Salaries and endorsement contracts for entertainers have risen dramatically during the past decade. At age 24, Tiger Woods signed a five-year endorsement contract with Nike for $100 million, spurring some financial analysts to predict that Woods would become sports' first $1 billion man (Ferguson, 2000).

Advertising research indicates celebrities can effectively promote product sales by creating more consumer awareness and favorable attitudes toward the products they endorse (Atkin & Block, 1983; Friedman & Friedman, 1979; Freiden, 1984; Kamins, 1990; Tripp, Jensen, & Carlson, 1994). Marketing studies documented the persuasive influences of celebrities such as actor Al Pacino (Friedman, Termini, & Washington, 1977), singer and songwriter Johnny Cash (Kamins, Brand, Hoeke, & Moe, 1989), and actress Mary Tyler Moore (Friedman et al., 1979) for a variety of products. By seeking to match endorsers' public exposure, attributes, and lifestyle with the type of product or service being promoted, celebrities have been shown to be effective influencers of purchasing behavior (Erdogen, Baker, & Tagg, 2001; O'Mahony & Meenaghan, 1997/98; Till & Busler, 2000).

Corporations that employ celebrities as spokespersons also tend to increase their profits (Agrawal & Kamakura, 1995; Mathur, Mathur, & Rangan, 1997). Celebrity endorsers are perceived as more trustworthy and competent as compared to noncelebrities, enhancing product image and increasing product use (Atkin et al., 1983).

During the past decade, advertisers have turned to dead celebrities to promote product sales (Goldman, 1994; Miller, 1993). Albert Einstein, W. C. Fields, Marilyn Monroe, James Dean, Steve McQueen, John Wayne, Humphrey Bogart, Louis Armstrong, Groucho Marx, James Cagney, Greta Garbo, and Babe Ruth have all sold products after their death. Unlike living celebrities, they do not get themselves into trouble, a major concern of companies who hire celebrities to endorse their products.

Celebrity Causes

Celebrities are not only able to promote the sale of products through their endorsements, they are also able to influence social beliefs and behavior such as HIV prevention (Brown, 1991; Brown & Basil, 1995), adult literacy (Singhal, Obregon, & Rogers, 1994), concern for spousal abuse (Brown, Duane, & Fraser, 1997), child abuse awareness (Brown, Basil, & Bocarnea, 1999), sexual responsibility (Kincaid, D. L., Jara, R., Coleman, P., & Segura, F. 1988; Rimon, 1989), and eliminating land mines (Payne, 2000). Many celebrities have taken on the role of chief spokesperson for specific health issues. Notable celebrities and their causes include Jerry Lewis for Muscular Dystrophy, Elizabeth Taylor and Earvin "Magic" Johnson for HIV/AIDS prevention, Sally Struthers for child hunger and malnutrition, Christopher Reeve for neurological research, and Michael J. Fox for Parkinson's disease. A celebrity can become so closely identified with a disease that the person and disease can become synonymous, such as Lou Gehrig and Amytrophic Lateral Sclerosis (ALS).

Colon cancer took center stage when Katie Couric televised her colonoscopy live before millions of viewers. Children's literacy has become a popular cause among dozens of celebrities, including entertainers Susan Sarandon, Billy Crystal, Dolly Parton, Oprah Winfrey, and Rosie O'Donnell; and sports stars Michelle Kwan, Reggie Miller, and Shaquille O'Neal (Towell, 2001).

These examples show that exposure to celebrities through expanding entertainment media is increasing mass audience's access to celebrities, thus extending their social influence. Even fictitious characters such as Harry Potter, Buffy the vampire slayer, Zena, Felicity, and Ali McBeal can be promoters of social change. Both profit and nonprofit organizations recognized the changing role of celebrities within society. Celebrities often become role models and are emulated by large numbers of people who identify with them across socio-cultural, political, and economic boundaries. Few studies, however, provide a theoretical explanation for understanding how people become involved with celebrities (see Sood, 2002) or why people role model the celebrities with whom they identify.

Overall, current literature that addresses the persuasive influence of celebrities fails to achieve two goals: (1) it does not provide an adequate theory of celebrity identification, and (2) it does not focus on articulating the fundamental processes important to celebrity identification.

IDENTIFICATION AS A SOCIAL CHANGE PROCESS

Identification is a fundamental process of social change that has been discussed by several important theorists and social scientists. Johnson, Johnson, and Heimberg (1999) traced the concept of identification to Freud and Lasswell. Eighty years ago, Freud (1922) defined identification as "the earliest expression of an emotional tie with another person." Lasswell (1965) also used this concept, referring to mass identifications such as nationalism. Lasswell's work clearly influenced the study of identification in organizations (Cheney, 1983; Cheney & Tompkins, 1987; Johnson et al., 1999), as has the work of Kenneth Burke, who wrote extensively about the concept of identification (Burke, 1969).

According to Burke (1969), identification occurs when one individual shares the interests of another individual or believes that he or she shares the interests of another. Burke noted that two individuals could be joined and still be distinct. In a pragmatic sense, identification is simply the common ground held by people in communication (Rosenfeld, 1969). Although Burke focused on the efforts of speakers to identify with their intended audiences, identification is also a way in which an audience member can say to a communicator, "I am like you" or "I have the same interests as you" (Cheney, 1983).

The most extensive research on identification is found in the work of Herbert Kelman, a Harvard University psychologist and communication scholar who studied persuasion from a social scientific perspective. Kelman's (1961) seminal paper on identification was part of an early draft of a book that was awarded the SocioPsychological Prize of the American Association for the Advancement of Science in 1956.

Kelman viewed identification as a process of persuasion. He sought to build a theoretical framework for understanding public opinion formation and for making predictions of behavior change. Kelman's theory of social influence encouraged scholars to focus on "determinants of opinion formation and opinion change" (1961). He theorized that if we understood the determinants of opinions and opinion change, we can predict behavioral outcomes.

PHOTO 6.1.   Robert Lopez, more commonly known as "El Vez," interacts with
his fans at an Elvis concert. Lopez' performances of Elvis for the Latino community include songs about immigration rights, achieving the Hispanic American
dream, sexual responsibility, and staying out of gangs. (*Source*: Photograph by
Mitzi L. Gates Bowdler. Used by permission.)

Kelman (1958) proposed three processes of social influence in which a
person adopts the behavior of another individual because of an actual or perceived relationship with that person: Compliance, identification, and internalization. Two means of identification include: (1) "classical identification,"
defined as "attempts to be like or actually be the other person," which is illustrated by the many thousands of Elvis Presley impersonators (Photo 6.1)
who seek to "be like" Elvis (Fraser & Brown, 2002) or the Michael Jordan
fans who want to "be like Mike;" and (2) "reciprocal role identification," in
which "the roles of two parties are defined with reference to one another"
(Kelman, 1961), such as in the case of a soap opera character and his or
her fans. Both soap opera stars and viewers understand their respective roles
in this relationship, played out in soap opera magazines and on soap opera
Web sites.

In classical identification, one person takes on the identity of another person; but in reciprocal role relationships, one person is "empathetically reacting in terms of the other person's expectations, feelings or, needs" (Kelman, 1961). Identification differs from compliance because in the identification process, the individual actually believes in the values, beliefs, and behaviors that he or she adopts from another person. In the compliance process, the individual only displays the appropriate values, beliefs, and behaviors to obtain a favorable reaction from another person or group he or she wishes to please (Kelman, 1958).

A closely related process to identification is parasocial interaction, which occurs when media consumers form pseudo-relationships with both real people and fictitious characters to which they are repeatedly exposed through the media. Horton and Wohl (1956) observed that television viewers commonly form personal bonds with news anchors, soap opera stars, talk-show hosts, and sit-com characters. They referred to the objects of these parasocial relationships as "media persona." Numerous studies affirm that television facilitates the development of psychological and emotional attachments between media stars and their audience members (Levy, 1979; Rubin & McHugh, 1987; Rubin & Perse, 1987; Rubin, Perse, & Powell, 1985; Shefner-Rogers, Rogers, & Singhal, 1998).

Sood (2002) conceptualized parasocial interaction and identification as closely related types of audience involvement. She regards parasocial interaction as affective, cognitive, and behavioral forms of interaction with television characters. Identification is a form of "referential-affective audience involvement" in which television viewers relate to real people such as news anchors, reality show participants, or quiz shows (similarity identification); or relate to fictional characters such as those in soap operas situation comedies, and serial dramas (wishful identification). As with many other descriptions of these two forms of involvement, Sood does not provide a clear theoretical distinction between audience parasocial interaction and audience identification. Both processes seem to overlap and both have affective, cognitive, and behavioral dimensions.

Brown and his colleagues (Brown et al., 1995; Brown et al., 2002; Brown et al., 1997) extended the concept of parasocial interaction beyond the medium of television. They show that media consumers form psychological bonds with athletes, musicians, and other celebrities through a variety of mediated and interpersonal communication networks. For example, Elvis Presley fans developed strong parasocial relationships with him through listening to his music, attending his concerts, attending Elvis festivals, visiting Graceland (his home in Nashville, TN), and acquiring Elvis memorabilia (Fraser et al., 2002).

Although parasocial interaction and identification are closely related processes of audience involvement, there are important distinctions. Developing a relationship with another person and wanting to be like that other person are two different matters. Many people in the media are known very well but not necessarily emulated. A popular celebrity like Elizabeth Taylor, for example, may win the love, affection, and personal attention of many people who have no desire to become involved in HIV/AIDS prevention.

Identification is a more powerful effect than parasocial interaction. A person who identifies with a celebrity attempts to adopt his or her values, beliefs, and behavior. Thus media consumers may adopt the clothing style, manner of speaking, and lifestyle of their favorite celebrity. In extreme cases, some fans identify so closely with a celebrity that they may merge their personal identify with that of a celebrity. While parasocial interaction theory has been applied by mass communication scholars as a measure of audience involvement, comparatively little attention has been given to the study of identification.

One advantage of studying identification is that it extends beyond the attitude-change theories used in communication research to study of celebrity influence. These theories include the persuasion theory developed by Hovland and his associates (Hovland, Lumsdaine, & Sheffield, 1949; Hovland, Janis, & Kelley, 1953), social comparison theory (Festinger, 1954), and the principle of social proof (Cialdini, 1985), attribution theory (Heider, 1958; Kelley, 1973), the social adaptation perspective (Kahle & Homer, 1985; Kamins et al., 1989), McGuire's (2001) hierarchy-of-effects model, and Petty and Cacioppo's (1986) elaboration likelihood model. All these approaches focus on cognitive processes that lead to attitude and behavior change.

However, these theories or models overemphasize the power of cognition and underestimate the power of emotion in promoting long-term behavior change. That is, they do not particularly capture the passionate feelings some individuals have for particular celebrities, producing in some cases enduring changes in peoples' lives—for years people have been, and continue to be, affected by celebrities now long gone—Kurt Cobain, Elvis, JFK, and so forth. Although message sources are likely to influence cognition, media effects research during the past two decades indicates relatively enduring behavior changes may result from the emotional bonds that media audiences form with media personalities such as soap opera characters, rock musicians, and athletic stars (Brown et al., 1995; Japhet, 1999; Nariman, 1993; Sabido, 1989; Shefner-Rogers et al., 1998; Singhal et al., 1994). For example, one Elvis fan underwent plastic surgery so that his facial appearance more closely reflected Elvis (Fraser & Brown, 2002).

THEORETICAL FRAMEWORK
FOR CELEBRITY IDENTIFICATION

Parasocial interaction theory and a theory of identification can be integrated to provide a theoretical framework for understanding the persuasive influences of celebrities. Parasocial interaction theory provides insight into how audience members establish seemingly interpersonal relationships with celebrities, and identification explains how these relationships can change values, beliefs, and behavior of audience individuals. The process of identification, when extended into the realm of the mass media, provides an appropriate theoretical basis for assessing the role of celebrities in E-E campaigns. Kelman's (1958) concept of identification implies behavior change, in that one person "takes on" or "adopts" the behavior of another person. In the case of celebrity identification, the vast majority of people have very little in common with celebrities, whose income, work, and lifestyle are commonly unique or eccentric (Alberoni, 1972; Dyer, 1991). Rather, the vast majority of people want to be like certain celebrities and emulate a representation of their perceived image.

Based on the works of various theorists who have wrestled with the concept of identification, we define celebrity identification as the process by which audience members seek to adopt the values, beliefs, or behavior of well-known public figures or popular media characters in order to emulate their perceived image or accentuate their parasocial relationship with the celebrity. This definition, drawing on the work of the theorists previously discussed, implies that a parasocial relationship, a perceived personal relationship between a media persona and an audience member, is a predictor of celebrity identification.

Dimensions of Celebrity Identification

How does celebrity identification takes place? Utilizing an astronomy metaphor, most celebrities are generally conceived more as novas (stars that burn brightly but then burn out) than as the guiding lights in age-old constellations. A few celebrities demonstrate amazing longevity and thus extend themselves into the realm of what we refer to as icons. Icons are popular figures whose renown transcends the constraints of space and time. Political and social leaders such as Abraham Lincoln, Martin Luther King, Jr., Mohandas Gandhi, Adolf Hitler, Joseph Stalin, and Winston Churchill are examples of icons. One-time film and television stars, whose names have been forgotten over time, are examples of short-term celebrities, which we define as stars. Thus, longevity is a continuum on which stars and icons fall at opposite ends.

A second dimension of celebrity identification is the degree to which individuals identify with celebrities as positive or negative. Positive role models include famous people like Martin Luther King, Jr. and Amelia Earhart, or current athletes like baseball stars Barry Bonds and Sammy Sosa. Negative role models are those whose behavior the majority of the public regards as antisocial, such as athletes like Mike Tyson and Tanya Harding, or, in an extreme sense, mass murderers like Charles Manson and Pol Pot.

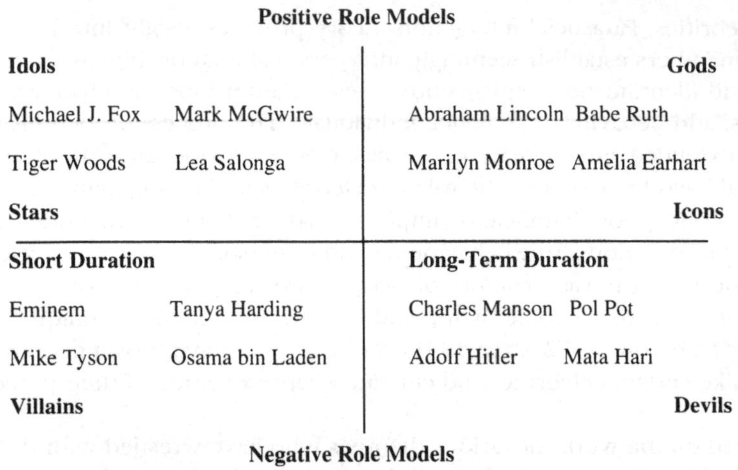

Positive Role Models

Idols		Gods
Michael J. Fox Mark McGwire		Abraham Lincoln Babe Ruth
Tiger Woods Lea Salonga		Marilyn Monroe Amelia Earhart
Stars		**Icons**
Short Duration		**Long-Term Duration**
Eminem Tanya Harding		Charles Manson Pol Pot
Mike Tyson Osama bin Laden		Adolf Hitler Mata Hari
Villains		**Devils**

Negative Role Models

FIG. 6.1.   Two-dimensional celebrity profile.

By combining these two dimensions, four types of celebrities are identified (Fig. 6.1). Long-term positive role models are defined as gods, and long-term negative role models are defined as devils. Short-term positive role models are defined as idols, and short-term negative role models are defined as villains. It is important to note that the difference between those perceived as positive role models and those perceived as negative role models is culturally defined. Some individuals may consider Eminem to be an idol rather than a villain, just as neo-Nazis regard Hitler as a god rather than a devil. We provide illustrations of celebrities (predominantly from the United States) in Fig. 6.1 who are idols, villains, gods, and devils. This matrix is dynamic, in that our perceptions of idols and villains may change over time. Conceptions of gods and devils change more slowly, and may be collectively derived over many decades.

Antecedents and Consequences of Identification

Kelman (1961) discussed the need to provide theoretical constructs that explain (1) antecedent variables to identification, and (2) consequences of identification. We view identification as a process of social change that represents what McGuire (2001) referred to as a higher-order effect in his persuasion model.

Knowledge of a celebrity is a necessary but insufficient condition for parasocial interaction with that celebrity. Parasocial interaction with a celebrity follows media exposure and may lead to identification, making it a necessary but insufficient condition for celebrity identification. Thus, knowing

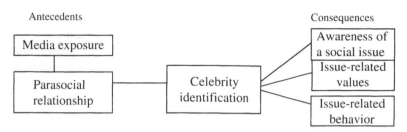

FIG. 6.2.   Antecedents to, and consequences of, celebrity identification.

Larry King as a talented, successful talk show host may or may not lead people to like him, and those who like Larry King may or may not identify with him. Based on previous research (Basil, 1996; Brown et al., 1995), a theoretical framework for studying celebrity influence is formulated in Fig. 6.2. This model shows that the influence of celebrities begins with audience exposure to them, predominantly through the mass media, although small segments of the population may be exposed to celebrities through non-mediated interaction. Media exposure then leads certain individuals into parasocial relationship with celebrities. There may be a small segment of the audience that develops parasocial relationships with celebrities through attending celebrity events (for example, conferences, sporting events, concerts, performances, fundraisers, and festivals). Celebrity identification then leads to changes in audience members' awareness, values, and behavior as they relate to a social issue addressed by the celebrity.

We prefer to look at the links between celebrity identification and values (Rokeach, 1973) because values are more enduring, and possibly more directly linked to behaviors, than are attitudes. However, a number of individuals in society are so strongly influenced by a celebrity that the individuals select to engage in certain behaviors that reflect the values of the celebrity with whom they identify. Twenty-five years after Elvis' death, many of his fan club members give to charity because they remember Elvis' generosity and continue the charitable work that he started, thus continuing a particular legacy. Admirers and worshippers of famous people who have died do charitable works (Mother Teresa), imagine a world at peace (John Lennon), and fight for a safe environment (Princess Diana).

The theoretical framework for studying celebrity identification illustrated in Figs. 6.1 and 6.2 leads us to certain propositions.

1. Media exposure to celebrities leads to parasocial interaction with them.
2. Parasocial interaction with celebrities leads to celebrity identification.
3. Celebrity identification leads to changes in issue-related awareness, values, and behavior consistent with those of the celebrity.

4. People will develop stronger identification with positive celebrity role models than they will with negative celebrity role models.
5. Greater identification with a celebrity will produce greater audience awareness of the social issues, products, and causes associated with that celebrity.
6. Greater identification with a celebrity will produce greater adoption of values and beliefs consistent with those advocated or modeled by the celebrity.
7. Greater identification with a celebrity will produce greater adoption of behavior consistent with that advocated or modeled by the celebrity.

FEATURING CELEBRITIES IN ENTERTAINMENT-EDUCATION

Celebrities are often vital components of E-E campaigns. Since the objective of the E-E communication strategy is to increase knowledge of a personal or social need, influence attitudes, or change overt behavior through entertainment (Singhal & Rogers, 1999), it makes sense to employ celebrities in this task. Preliminary research suggests that E-E may be more effective when celebrities are strategically used within the overall E-E campaign (see Singhal & Rogers [1999] for many examples).

When India launched its first E-E television serial, *Hum Log*, in 1984, Ashok Kumar, a famous Indian film star, was featured at the end of each program. Kumar encapsulated the lesson of each *Hum Log* episode in the epilogue. *Hum Log* was part of a coordinated effort to increase the status of women and to promote family planning in India (Singhal & Rogers, 1988). Viewers of the program referred to specific epilogues they had viewed when sharing their value, belief, and behavior changes in thousands of letters written to Kumar (Singhal & Rogers, 1999).

In Mexico, two popular teenage entertainers, Tatiana and Johnny, promoted sexual responsibility among teenagers through recorded songs and music videos. Their celebrity status no doubt contributed to the high audience ratings generated by their E-E productions.

In partnership with Johns Hopkins University's Population Communication Services, the Philippines Population Center Foundation launched a national sexual responsibility campaign in 1987, featuring Lea Salonga, a 16-year-old popular singer, and the rock music group Menudo. The first song they performed in concert promoting sexually responsible behavior, "That Situation," hit number one on the music charts in Manila and Cebu City within a month of its release (Rimon, 1989). Six months later, Salonga and ex-Menudo singer Charlie Masso performed, "I Still Believe," which also reached number one on the music charts. Both songs popularized by famous entertainers positively influenced Filipino teenagers' knowledge, attitudes, and behaviors associated with sexual responsibility (Kincaid, Coleman, Rimon, & Silayan-Go, 1991; Silayan-Go, 1990).

In the United States, celebrities were instrumental in a number of communication campaigns. One example is the designated driver campaign incepted by the Harvard School of Public Health in 1988. The focus of the campaign was to promote the social norm that drivers should abstain from alcohol (Winsten, 1994). By lobbying Hollywood celebrities, the national campaign, valued at over $100 million dollars, placed designated driver messages in more than 160 entertainment programs (Winsten & DeJong, 2001). The adoption of the designated driver practice was successfully diffused through entertainment, especially among males in the United States (DeJong & Winsten, 1990).

Some celebrities become central to communication campaigns through their own personal tragedies or battles with disease, as in the case of basketball player Earvin "Magic" Johnson, professional actor Michael J. Fox, and cyclist Lance Armstrong. When Johnson learned he had contracted HIV in 1991, he held a news conference and immediately offered himself as a spokesperson for HIV/AIDS prevention. Johnson's announcement diffused rapidly, immediately raising HIV/AIDS awareness among heterosexuals (Dearing & Rogers, 1996; Basil & Brown, 1994) and promoting changes in HIV-related attitudes, beliefs, and sexual behavior (Brown et al., 1995). A year later, Johnson produced and distributed a rap video, "Time Out: Truth about HIV, AIDS, and YOU," with friend Arsenio Hall, featuring several other celebrities. The video, distributed by national video chains such as Blockbuster, communicated with millions of fans how to avoid HIV/AIDS infection (Singhal & Rogers, 2003).

Extensive media coverage has been given to Michael J. Fox's battle with Parkinson's disease. Fox was struck with the disease in the prime of his acting career, reducing his workload dramatically and leading to him leaving the popular television program in which he starred. Fox appeared before the U.S. Congress in 2001 to advocate stem cell research in order to accelerate finding a medical cure for his disease.

Professional cyclist Lance Armstrong was diagnosed with testicular cancer in October 1996 and given only a 20% chance of survival by his doctors. Armstrong not only made a remarkable recovery, he went on to win the Tour de France for several consecutive years in a row. The event is one of the most physically demanding sports. Armstrong has been a popular motivational speaker, helping other cancer victims to courageously fight the disease.

These examples demonstrate the important role that celebrities can play in social and health-related campaigns. In a media-saturated cultural environment, the competition for attention is intense. Celebrities receive instant public recognition and their activities are covered extensively by the news media. Michael J. Fox's recent testimony before the U.S. Congress to discuss the use of fetal tissue for Parkinson's disease research provides an example.

Fox put a young face on what was traditionally viewed as a disease affecting older people. Fox indicated that he was receiving e-mail from people with Parkinson's disease who identified it to their coworkers as the "Michael J. Fox Disease" (Duff, Dunlap, & Herb, 2000). His retirement announcement as a television actor clearly attracted considerable media attention to Parkinson's disease.

Based on the results of numerous E-E campaigns that feature celebrities, we present two additional propositions.

1. Communication campaigns that employ positive celebrity role models as spokespersons for a specific issue will produce stronger audience changes in awareness, values, and behavior associated with the campaign than will communication campaigns that use noncelebrity spokespersons.
2. Communication campaigns that use an E-E approach and that feature a celebrity spokesperson will produce stronger audience changes in awareness, values, and behavior associated with the campaign than will communication campaigns that (1) only use an E-E approach, or (2) only use a celebrity spokesperson.

IMPLICATIONS AND CONCLUSIONS

The obvious benefits gained by featuring celebrities in E-E messages also have some disadvantages. Although some celebrities volunteer their time, the services of those who do not may be expensive. Many celebrities earn more income from advertising than from their principal profession. The celebrity brokering business is lucrative for both the living and the dead. Elvis Presley's beneficiaries made $35 million and John Lennon's beneficiaries made $20 million in the year 2000 (Fong & Lau, 2001). Hiring a celebrity for a single day can cost in excess of $100,000.

A second challenge to employing celebrities is that some campaign planners and educators may find it difficult to work with celebrities because they are unfamiliar with the entertainment culture (Bouman, 1998). Simple contracts for the services of a celebrity can be 30 to 40 pages in length, specifying dressing room accommodations, use of hair and make-up stylists, hotel room services, types of foods and beverages that must be available, the position and type of production lights, and a host of other demands that can be a nightmare to negotiate and satisfy.

Once celebrities do become central to E-E messages, a dramatic change in the celebrity's life, or worse, a moral failure, can become a substantial detriment. The unplanned pregnancy of a teenage girl by a Latin American singer Johnny (Singhal & Rogers, 1999), and of a soap opera character intended to role model family planning (Brown & Cody, 1991), mitigated the effects of the intended educational messages.

Research on strategic use of celebrities to promote social change through E-E messages is in its relative infancy. Recent theory-building efforts—like Sood (2002) and Papa et al. (2000)—on the affective-referential and cognitive-critical dimensions of audience involvement include Tufte's research on audience sense-making of entertainment programs (see Thomas Tufte's chapter in this volume); McCutcheon, Lange, and Houran's (2002) work on celebrity worship, and the present authors' work study of celebrity identification (Fraser et al., 2002), suggest directions for future research. Determining the kinds of people most likely to be influenced by celebrities, the degree to which celebrities should make more direct versus subtler persuasive appeals, and the specific situations in which celebrities will have their greatest effect are in need of systematic study. In addition, more precise measuring instruments are needed to accurately assess individuals' cognitive and affective ties to celebrities, and the behavioral changes that result from these ties.

The ability of popular celebrities like "Magic" Johnson and Elizabeth Taylor to promote HIV/AIDS prevention, or actress Mary Tyler Moore and 1999 Miss America Nicole Johnson to promote diabetes research, or entertainer Jerry Lewis' long-term efforts concerning Muscular Dystrophy, illustrates the important role that celebrities can play in promoting E-E messages. Although villains and devils can certainly attract media attention, E-E planners should focus on searching for positive celebrity role models to support their E-E goals.

The advantages of using celebrities for entertainment-education outweigh potential pitfalls. Here we presented how celebrity influence works within highly mediated cultures like the United States. The conceptual variables, theoretical framework, and propositions presented here should be operationalized and tested in future studies of E-E. Vibrant discussion and diligent research on the identification process should yield valuable knowledge that will improve the effectiveness of the E-E communication strategy.

REFERENCES

Adel, D. (2000, September 1). One for the money. *Entertainment Weekly*, 30–37.

Agrawal, J., & Kamakura, W. A. (1995). The economic worth of celebrity endorsers. *Journal of Advertising Research, 23*, 57–61.

Alberoni, F. (1972). The powerless 'elite': Theory and sociological research on the phenomenon of the stars. In Denis McQuail (Ed.), *Sociology of mass communications* (pp. 75–89). Harmondsworth, England: Penguin.

Atkin, C., & Block, M. (1983). Effectiveness of celebrity endorsers. *Journal of Advertising Research, 23*, 57–61.

Basil, M. D. (1996). Identification as a mediator of celebrity effects. *Journal of Broadcasting & Electronic Media, 40*, 478–495.

Basil, M. D., & Brown, W. J. (1994). Interpersonal communication and news diffusion: A study of "Magic" Johnson's announcement. *Journalism Quarterly, 71*(2), 305–320.

Bonko, L. (2000, August 29). Rudy has eye on space. *The Virginian-Pilot*, pp. E1–E2.

Boorstin, D. J. (1961). *The image: A guide to pseudo-events in America.* New York: Harper & Row.

Bouman, M. P. A. (1998). *The turtle and the peacock: Collaboration for prosocial change.* Wageningen, The Netherlands: Wageningen Agricultural University.

Braudy, L. (1986). *The frenzy of renown.* New York: Oxford University Press.

Brown, W. J. (1991). An AIDS prevention campaign: Effects on attitudes, beliefs, and communication behavior. *American Behavioral Scientist, 34*(6), 666–687.

Brown, W. J. (1992). The use of entertainment television programs for promoting prosocial messages. *Howard Journal of Communications, 3*(3,4), 253–266.

Brown, W. J., & Basil, M. D. (1995). Media celebrities and public health: Responses to "Magic" Johnson's HIV disclosure and its impact on AIDS risk and high-risk behaviors. *Health Communication, 7*, 345–371.

Brown, W. J., Basil, M. D., & Bocarnea, M. C. (1998, July). *Responding to the death of Princess Diana: Audience involvement with an international celebrity.* Paper presented at the International Communication Association, Jerusalem.

Brown, W. J., Basil, M. D., & Bocarnea, M. C. (1999, in press). The Influence of famous athletes on public health issues: Mark McGwire, child abuse prevention, and androstenedione. *Journal of Health Communication, 7.*

Brown, W. J., & Cody, M. J. (1991). Effects of an Indian television soap opera in promoting women's status. *Human Communication Research, 18*(1), 114–142.

Brown, W. J., Duane, J. J., & Fraser, B. P. (1997). Media coverage and public opinion of the O. J. Simpson trial: Implications for the criminal justice system. *Communication Law and Policy, 2*(2), 261–287.

Brown, W. J., Fraser, B. P., & Bocarnea, M. C. (2001, May). *Identification with mass mediated celebrities: Remembering John F. Kennedy, Jr.* Paper presented at the International Communication Association, Washington, DC.

Brown, W. J., & Singhal, A. (1999). Entertainment-education strategies for social change. In D. P. Demers and K. Viswanath (Eds.), *Mass media, social control and social change* (pp. 263–280). Ames, Iowa: Iowa State University Press.

Burke, K. (1969). *A rhetoric of motives.* Berkeley, CA: University of California Press.

Campbell, J. (1988). *The power of myth.* New York: Doubleday.

Cheney, G. (1983). On the various and changing meanings of organizational membership: A field study of organizational identification. *Communication Monographs, 50*, 342–362.

Cheney, G., & Tompkins, P. K. (1987). Coming to terms with organizational identification and commitment. *Central States Speech Journal, 28*, 1–15.

Cialdini, R. B. (1985). *Influence: Science and practice.* Glenview, IL: Scott, Foresman.

Cummings, M. S. (1988). The changing image of the Black family on television. *Journal of Popular Culture, 22*(2), 75–85.

Dearing, J. W., & Rogers, E. M. (1996). *Agenda-setting.* Thousand Oaks, CA: Sage Publications.

DeJong, W., & Winsten, J. A. (1990). *The Harvard Alcohol Project: A demonstration project to promote the use of the "designated driver."* In M. B. Perrine (Ed.), *Proceedings of the 11th International Conference on Alcohol, Drugs, and Traffic Safety* (pp. 456–460). Chicago: National Safety Council.

Duff, D., Dunlap, J., & Herb, R. (2000, August 17). *The fox and the hound: Celebrity and disease.* Unpublished manuscript, Virginia Beach, VA: Regent University, School of Communication and the Arts.

Dyer, R. (1991). A 'star is born' and the construction of authenticity. In C. Glendale (Ed.), *Stardom: Industry of desire* (pp. 132–140). London: Routledge.

Erdogan, B. F., Baker, M. J., & Tagg, S. (2001). Selecting celebrity endorsers: The practitioner's perspective. *Journal of Advertising Research, 41*, 39-48.

Ferguson, D. (2000, September 15). Tiger Close to $100 million Nike deal. *The Associated Press.*

Festinger, L. (1954). A theory of social comparison processes. *Human Relations, 7*, 117-140.

Fong, M., & Lau, D. (2001, February 28). Earnings from the crypt. Retrieved from http://www.forbes.com/2001/02/28/crypt.html

Fraser, B. P., & Brown, W. J. (2002). Media, celebrities, and social influence: Identification with Elvis Presley. *Mass Communication and Society, 5*, 185-208.

Freiden, J. B. (1984). Advertising spokesperson effects: An examination of endorser type and gender on two audiences. *Journal of Advertising Research, 24*(5), 33-41.

Freud, S. (1922). *Group psychology and the analysis of ego.* New York: Norton.

Friedman, H. H., & Friedman, L. (1979). Endorser effectiveness by product type. *Journal of Advertising Research, 18*, 63-71.

Friedman, H. H., Termini, S., & Washington, R. (1977). The effectiveness of advertisements using four types of endorsers. *Journal of Advertising, 6*, 22-24.

Gamson, J. (1994). *Claims to fame: Celebrity in contemporary America.* Berkeley: University of California Press.

Goldman, K. (1994, January 7). Dead celebrities are resurrected pitchmen. *The Wall Street Journal,* p. B-1.

Heider, F. (1958). *The psychology of interpersonal relations.* New York: Wiley.

Horton, D. & Wohl, R. R. (1956). Mass communication and parasocial interaction: Observations on intimacy at a distance. *Psychiatry, 19*, 215-229.

Hovland, C. I., Janis, I. L., & Kelley, H. H. (1953). *Communication and persuasion: Psychological studies of opinion change.* New Haven, CT: Yale University Press.

Hovland, C. I., Lumsdaine, A. A., & Sheffield, F. D. (1949). *Experiments in mass communication: Studies in social psychology in World War II* (Vol. 3). Princeton, NJ: Princeton University Press.

Japhet, G. (1999). *Edutainment: How to make edutainment work for you.* Houghton, South Africa: Soul City.

Johnson, W. L., Johnson, A. M., & Heimberg, F. (1999). A primary and second-order analysis of the organizational identification questionnaire. *Educational and Psychological Measurement, 59*, 159-170.

Kahle, L. R., & Homer, P. M. (1985). Physical attractiveness of the celebrity endorser: A social adaptation perspective. *Journal of Consumer Research, 11*, 954-961.

Kamins, M. A. (1990). An investigation into the 'match-up' hypothesis in celebrity advertising: When beauty may be only skin deep. *Journal of Advertising, 19*, 4-13.

Kamins, M. A., Brand, J. J., Hoeke, S. A., & Moe, J. C. (1989). Two-sided versus one-sided celebrity endorsements: The impact on advertising effectiveness and credibility. *Journal of Advertising, 18*, 4-10.

Kelley, H. H. (1973). The process of causal attribution. *American Psychologist, 28*, 107-128.

Kelman, H. (1958). Compliance, identification, and internalization: Three processes of attitude change. *Journal of Conflict Resolution, 2*, 51-60.

Kelman, H. (1961). Process of opinion change. *Public Opinion Quarterly, 25*, 57-58.

Kincaid, D. L. (2002). Drama, emotion, and cultural convergence. *Communication Theory, 12*, 136-152.

Kincaid, D. L., Coleman, P. L., Rimon J. G., II, & Silayan-Go, A. (1991). *The Philippines Multimedia Campaign for Young People Project: Summary of evaluation results.* Paper presented to the American Public Health Association.

Kincaid, D. L., Jara, R., Coleman, P., & Segura, F. (1988). *Getting the message: The communication for young people project.* Washington DC: U.S. Agency for International Development, AID Evaluation Special Study 56.

Kincaid, D. L., Rimon J. G., II, Piotrow, P. T., & Coleman, P. L. (1992, April–May). *The enter-educate approach: Using entertainment to change health behavior*. Paper presented to the Population Association of America, Denver.

Lasswell, H. D. (1965). *World politics and personal insecurity*. New York: Free Press.

Levy, M. (1979). Watching television news as parasocial interaction. *Journal of Broadcasting, 23*, 69–80.

Mathur, L. K., Mathur, I., & Rangan, N. (1997). The wealth effects associated with a celebrity endorser. *Journal of Advertising Research, 37*, 67–73.

McCutcheon, L. E., Lange, R., & Houran, J. (2002). Conceptualization and measurement of celebrity worship. *British Journal of Psychology, 93*, 67–87.

McGuire, W. J. (2001). Input and output variables currently promising for constructing persuasive communications. In R. E. Rice & C. K. Atkin (Eds.), *Public communication campaigns* (3rd ed.) (pp. 22–48). Thousand Oaks, CA: Sage.

Miller, C. (1993, March 29). Some celebs just now reaching their potential - and they're dead. *Marketing News, 27*(7), pp. 2–4.

Nariman, H. (1993). *Soap operas for social change*. Westport, CT: Praeger.

O'Mahony, S., & Meenaghan, T. (1997/98). The impact of celebrity endorsements on consumers. *Irish Marketing Review, 10*(2), 15–24.

Payne, J. G. (2000). Preface to an era of celebrity and spectacle. In G. Payne (Ed.), *An era of celebrity and spectacle: The global rhetorical phenomenon of the death of Diana, Princess of Wales*. Boston, MA: Emerson College, Center for Ethics in Political and Health Communication.

Petty, R. E., & Cacioppo, J. T. (1986). *Communication and persuasion: Central and peripheral routes to attitude change*. New York: Springer-Verlag.

Rimon, J. G., II. (1989, December). Leveraging messages and corporations: The Philippine experience. *Integration, 22*, 37–44.

Rokeach, M. (1973). *The nature of human values*. New York: Free Press.

Rosenfeld, L. B. (1969). Set theory: Key to understanding of Kenneth Burke's use of the term "identification." *Western Speech, 33*, 175–183.

Rubin, A. M., & Perse, E. M. (1987). Audience activity and soap opera involvement: A uses and gratifications investigation. *Human Communication Research, 14*, 246–268.

Rubin, A. M., Perse, E. M., & Powell, R. A. (1985). Loneliness, parasocial interaction, and local television viewing. *Human Communication Research, 12*, 155–180.

Rubin, R. B., & McHugh, M. P. (1987). Development of parasocial relationships. *Journal of Broadcasting and Electronic Media, 31*, 279–292.

Sabido, M. (1989, March–April). *Soap operas in Mexico*. Paper presented at the Entertainment for Social Change Conference, Los Angeles, University of Southern California, Annenberg School for Communication.

Shefner-Rogers, C. L., Rogers, E. M., & Singhal, A. (1998). Parasocial interaction with the television soap operas 'Simplemente Maria' and 'Oshin.' *Keio Communication Review, 20*, 3–18.

Silayan-Go, A. (1990). Entertainment for change and development: Will it work? In P. L. Coleman & R. C. Meyer (Eds.), *The enter-educate conference: Entertainment for social change* (p. 24). Baltimore, MD: Johns Hopkins University, Center for Communication Programs.

Singhal, A., Obregon, R., & Rogers, E. M. (1994). Reconstructing the story of "Simplemente María," The most popular *telenovela* in Latin America of all time. *Gazette, 54*, 1–15.

Singhal, A., & Rogers, E. M. (1988). Television soap operas for development in India. *Gazette, 41*, 109–126.

Singhal, A., & Rogers, E. M. (1999). *Entertainment-education: A communication strategy for social change*. Mahwah, NJ: Lawrence Erlbaum Associates.

Singhal, A., & Rogers, E. M. (2003). *Combating AIDS: Communication strategies in action*. Thousand Oaks, CA: Sage.

Sinha, V. (2000, August 30). "Rudypalooza!" draws crowd of thousands for homecoming. *The Virginian-Pilot*, pp. A1, A9.

Sood, S. (2002). Audience involvement and entertainment-education. *Communication Theory, 12*, 153-172.

Till, B. D., & Busler, M. (2000). The match-up hypothesis: Physical attractiveness, expertise, and the role of fit on brand attitude, purchase intent, and brand beliefs. *Journal of Advertising, 29*(3), 1-13.

Towell, J. H. (2001). Teaching ideas. *The Reading Teacher, 55*(1), 22-32.

Tripp, C., Jensen, T. D., & Carlson, L. (1994). The effects of multiple product endorsements by celebrities on consumers' attitudes and intentions. *Journal of Consumer Research, 20*, 535-547.

Winsten, J. A. (1994). Promoting designated drivers: The Harvard Alcohol Project. *American Journal of Preventive Medicine, 10*, 11-14.

Winsten, J. A., & DeJong, W. (2001). The designated driver campaign. In R. E. Rice & C. Atkin (Eds.), *Public communication campaigns* (3rd ed., pp. 290-294). Thousand Oaks, CA: Sage.

7

The Theory Behind Entertainment-Education

Suruchi Sood
Johns Hopkins University

Tiffany Menard
Michigan State University

Kim Witte
Johns Hopkins University and Michigan State University

We began our examination of the entertainment-education literature with the assumption that it would be similar in terms of its treatment of theory to other health communication. Typically, health educators or creative talent develop public health communication with little theoretical guidance in the actual message development (Witte, 1996; Nzyuko, 1996). Even when formative research is conducted, little of the information influences the health communication (other than perhaps demographic data). The a priori atheoretical nature of public health communication is contrasted with a wide array of posthoc theoretical explanations for success and failure. It is more difficult to assert any solid claims about health communication successes or failures when the theory is chosen after the messages have been developed.

However, our review of the entertainment-education literature found a theoretically rich body of research. One potential explanation for this difference resides in the origins of each field. Whereas the broader public health communication field started off with scholars evaluating the effects of health communication (after a campaign, for example), the entertainment-education field got its start when the talented television writer and producer Miguel Sabido carefully analyzed what made successful soap operas before developing his own prosocial soap operas. His careful theoretical analysis seems to have set a standard, leading to theoretically rich entertainment-education programs henceforth. The majority of entertainment-education programs are characterized by researchers and creative talent working together to create programs and to explain when and why they work and when and why they fail. Recent books by Piotrow and others (1997), Singhal and Rogers (1999), and others, as well as the proliferation of high-quality doctoral dissertations attempting to generate new entertainment-education theory (for example, Bouman, 1998; Obregon, 1999; Patel, 2002), are cause for celebration in the field.

THE PRESENT RESEARCH

Here we attempt to review the rapidly growing literature on entertainment-education theory, while establishing two parameters for our review. First, to establish a certain level of rigor, we focus on those articles appearing in peer-reviewed journals. Second, we focus on articles about empirically evaluated entertainment-education programs using either qualitative or quantitative data to assess effects. We excluded articles that gave posthoc explanations as to why an entertainment-education program had the effects it did, by scholars who were uninvolved in the original program.

To gather the articles included in the present review, we undertook a complete library (MAGIC, PROQUEST), Internet (Google), and citation index search for the keywords "entertainment-education," "infotainment," "edutainment," and other synonyms (for example, prosocial entertainment, mass media and public health, media and health education, interactive health games, street theater, theater and health, children's television, health and television, health and radio, health soap opera, and so forth). Once all relevant articles were found based on these keyword searches, we conducted additional searches including:

1. Known entertainment-education researchers.
2. Specific entertainment-education programs that were listed in journal articles.
3. Specific countries where entertainment-education programs were known to have taken place.
4. The Web sites of known entertainment-education program funders and developers.
5. The references of all collected articles were scanned for additional works.

Thus, the present review focuses on the empirically based peer-reviewed theoretical research as well as Sabido's initial five theories used to launch the theoretical field of entertainment-education. Two tables are used condense the research in a meaningful way, one on theoretical qualities of the evaluated entertainment-education programs and the other focusing on methodological features of these programs.

THEORETICAL CHARACTERISTICS OF ENTERTAINMENT-EDUCATION PROGRAMS

The theories behind entertainment-education represent diverse disciplinary fields, and range from logical positivistic perspectives to critical theory and humanistic perspectives. Table 7.1 is a description of the theoretical characteristics of peer-reviewed published entertainment-education evaluations, to date, in order of publication date (from the earliest to the latest).

Table 7.1 shows that published evaluations date from around 1990, even for entertainment-education programs that were broadcast earlier. Although many of these entertainment-education programs benefited from a priori theorizing, Table 7.1 shows that a considerable amount of posthoc theoretical explanations were also being generated. For example, *Tinka Tinka Sukh* and *Twende na Wakati* both had multiple studies that reported their effects using different theoretical frameworks (Law & Singhal, 1999; Papa, Singhal, Law, Pant, Sood, Rogers, & Shefner-Rogers, 2000; Rogers, Vaughan, Swalehe, Rao, Svenkerud, & Sood, 1999; Sood, 2002; Vaughan and Rogers, 2000; Vaughan, Rogers, Singhal, & Swalehe, 2000).

As stated previously, entertainment-education theorizing began with Miguel Sabido's analysis of *Simplemente Maria*, a popular Peruvian soap opera that captured the hearts of Peruvians and others. Struck by the degree of prosocial change initiated by the Peruvian soap opera, Sabido studied it for two years to develop a theory for generating successful prosocial soap operas (Singhal & Rogers, 1999). His formula for successful entertainment-education programs included elements from five perspectives: (a) a circular model of communication (Rovigatti, cited in Televisa's Institute of Communication Research, 1981; Singhal & Rogers, 1999), (b) social learning theory (Bandura, 1977), (c) dramatic theory (Bentley, 1967), (d) Jung's theory of the collective unconscious (Jung, 1970), and (e) the concept of the triune brain (Nariman, 1993; Singhal, Rogers, & Brown, 1993). Many of these theories were used by subsequent entertainment-education researchers, especially social learning theory. The predominant theory in virtually all of the E-E projects in Table 7.1 was Bandura's social learning theory (1977), later called social cognitive theory (Bandura, 1986). More recent theorizing focuses on power, the hierarchy-of-effects, diffusion of innovations, theory of planned behavior change, the elaboration likelihood model, and audience involvement/parasocial interaction theories.

TABLE 7.1

Theoretical Characteristics of Selected Entertainment-Education Programs

Authors, Year	Medium	Format	Location	Dates	Theory Used in Design/Evaluation
Brown, 1990 Brown & Cody, 1991	Television	Soap opera	India	1984–1985	Social learning theory (Bandura) Dramatic theory (Bentley) Archetypes of the collective unconscious (Jung) Belief system theory (Rokeach) Theory of tones (Sabido)
Piotrow, Rimon, Winnard, Kincaid, Huntington, & Convisser, 1990	Television, radio, other	Drama series, magazine program	Nigeria	1985–1988	Social learning theory (Bandura)
Piotrow, et al., 1992	Radio, print, interpersonal	Drama series	Zimbabwe	1988–1989	Hierarchy of effects (McGuire) Diffusion of innovations (Rogers)
Singhal, Obregon, & Rogers, 1994	Television	Soap opera "telenovela"	Peru	1969–1971	Social learning theory (Bandura) Dramatic theory (Bentley) Archetypes of the collective unconscious (Jung)
Valente, Kim, Lettenmaier, Glass, & Dibba, 1994	Radio	Drama series	The Gambia (West Africa)	1988, 1990, 1991	Two-step flow (Lazersfeld, Berelson, & Gaudet) Agenda-setting (McCombs & Shaw)
Kim & Marangwanda, 1997	Radio, print, interpersonal	Drama series	Zimbabwe	1993–1994	Diffusion of innovations (Rogers)
Soul City 2001[1] Thomas, Cahill, & Santilli, 1997	Television, radio, print Computer	Drama Interactive game	South Africa New York	1994–ongoing)	Soul City model of behavior change Self-efficacy (Bandura)
Bouman, Maas, & Kok, 1998	Television	Hospital series	The Netherlands	1992–1993	Social learning theory (Bandura) Agenda setting (McCombs & Shaw) Uses and gratifications (Blumler & Katz)

Authors	Medium	Genre	Country	Years	Theories
Kane, Gueye, Speizer, Pacque-Margolis, & Baron, 1998	Television, radio, music	Plays, television spots, recorded songs	Mali	1993	Health belief model (Becker); Theory of reasoned action (Fishbein & Ajzen); Social learning theory (Bandura)
Law & Singhal, 1999	Radio	Drama Series	India	1996–1997	Self-efficacy (Bandura); Collective efficacy (Bandura)
Rogers, Vaughan, Swalehe, Rao, Svenkerud & Sood, 1999	Radio	Soap opera	Tanzania	1993–1995	Social learning theory (Bandura)
Storey, Boulay, Karki, Heckert, & Karmacharya, 1999	Radio	Radio serials	Nepal	1995–1997	Social learning theory (Bandura); Theory of planned behavior (Azjen)
Valente & Bharath, 1999	Community theater	Dramas	India	1993–1995	Diffusion of innovations (Rogers); Hierarchy-of-effects model (McGuire)
Papa, Singhal, Law, Pant, Sood, Rogers, & Shefner-Rogers, 2000	Radio	Drama series	India	1996–1997	Parasocial interaction (Horton & Wohl; Rubin & Perse); Social learning theory (Bandura); Collective efficacy (Bandura); Power (Mumby); Hegemony (Gramsci)
Vaughan & Rogers, 2000	Radio	Soap opera	Tanzania	1993–1995	Hierarchy-of-effects model (McGuire); Stages-of-change (Prochaska); Social learning theory (Bandura); Diffusion of innovations (Rogers); Proposed theory: Six-stage model of communication effects

(Continued)

TABLE 7.1
(Continued)

Authors, Year	Medium	Format	Location	Dates	Theory Used in Design/Evaluation
Kim, Kols, Nyakauru, Marangwanda, & Chibatamoto, 2001	Radio, community media, print, hotline, peers	Variety show	Zimbabwe	1997–1998	Steps to behavior change framework (Piotrow et al.)
Soul City, 2001	Television, radio, print	Youth drama series	South Africa	2000	Soul City model of behavior change
Davenport-Sypher, McKinley, Ventsam, & Valdeavellano, 2002	Radio	Sociodrama, interviews, music, news	Peruvian Amazon	1997–present	Social construction of technology (Slack)
Sharan & Valente, 2002	Radio	Drama serial	Nepal	Began in 1995	Social learning theory (Bandura) Audience involvement Social judgment theory (Sherif, Sherif, & Negarball) Elaboration likelihood model (Petty & Cacioppo) Self-efficacy (Bandura) Collective efficacy (Bandura)
Sood, 2002	Radio	Soap opera	India	1996–1997	
Boulay, Storey, & Sood, in press	Radio, print	Radio serials	Nepal	1995–2001	Two step flow (Lazersfeld, Berelson, & Gaudet)
Gunther & Storey, in press	Radio, print	Radio serials	Nepal	1995–2001	Third Person Effect (Davison) Proposed Model: Indirect Effects Model

Note. ¹Soul City published several empirical articles in a variety of peer-reviewed journals. For the sake of brevity, we present the results from their overall report in this table.

ENTERTAINMENT-EDUCATION THEORIES

Table 7.1 lists the theories and/or theoretical constructs used in the entertainment-education programs of study. The theories fall into seven categories. The majority of entertainment-education effects articles focus on the steps or stages that individuals pass through in the process of adopting and maintaining a new behavior. Other investigations use social psychological theories, in which the expected behavioral outcome is influenced by perceptions and elements of the social environment. The internal processes and workings of the mind are examined in the psychological models. The roles people play and/or the scripts they follow in their lives are examined in drama or role theories. Audience-centered theories focus on "how" entertainment-education programs have their effects. The interplay between society, institutions, and the broader context are the focus in contextual theories. These theories examine how entertainment-education programs interact or influence societies or institutions. Hybrid models combine elements from a variety of theoretical perspectives. These hybrid models are generated by long-term entertainment-education consortia or researchers like the Soul City Institute or Johns Hopkins University's Center for Communication Programs.

Steps/Stages Models

Five steps/stages models include McGuire's (1969) hierarchy-of-effects, the stages-of-change model proposed by DiClemente and Prochaska (1985), steps to behavior change (Piotrow et al., 1997), Rogers' innovations-decision model (1995), and Rovigatti's circular model of communication (Rovigatti, cited in Televisa's Institute of Communication Research, 1981; Singhal & Rogers, 1999).

The hierarchy-of-effects model presents an X-axis comprising several input factors including source, message, channel, and receiver, and a Y-axis consisting of several output factors including the steps an individual must be persuaded to pass through in order to assimilate a desired behavior change (McGuire, 1989). These steps include exposure to the message; attention to the message; interest in, or personal relevance of, the message; understanding of the message; personalizing the behavior to fit the individual's life; accepting the change; remembering the message and continuing to agree with it; being able to think of the message; making decisions based on bringing the message to mind; behaving as decided; receiving (positive) reinforcement for behavior change; and accepting the behavior into the individual's life.

DiClemente and Prochaska's (1985) stages-of-change model suggests that changes in behavior result when individuals move through five distinct stages: Precontemplation, contemplation, preparation, action, and maintenance. Individuals may iterate through the stages in a spiral process before the behavior change becomes a permanent part of their repertoire. Precontemplation is the stage in which individuals do not intend to change their behavior because they are completely unaware or in denial of the behavioral options available to them. Contemplation is the stage in which individuals begin to think about the behavior that is putting them at risk, and begin to think about the need for change. Preparation is the stage in which individuals make a commitment to change and plan how they would make the behavioral change. Action is the stage in which individuals perform the new behavior. Finally, maintenance is the stage in which the new behavior is performed consistently and steps are taken to avoid relapsing into the former risky behaviors.

The steps to behavior change model outlines five steps that individuals go through in order to change their behavior. These steps include: knowledge, attitudes/approval, intention, practice, and advocacy. Piotrow and others (1997) provided indicators from family planning communication to illustrate how these steps work in order to make behavior change possible.

Rogers' (2003) diffusion of innovations theory defines diffusion as the process by which (1) an innovation, (2) is communicated through certain channels, (3) over time, (4) among the members of a social system. The innovation-decision process is the mental process through which an individual (or other decision-making unit) passes from first knowledge of an innovation, to forming an attitude toward the innovation, to a decision to adopt or reject, to implementation of the new idea, and to confirmation of this decision.

The fourth steps/stages model has five distinct steps or stages, but it is a departure from the linear format of the four previous steps/stages models, instead suggesting a circular arrangement of the different aspects of communication. Sabido (inspired by Rovigatti) took the five basic factors in Shannon and Weaver's (1949) communication model (the communicator, message, medium, receiver, and noise) and arranged these factors in a circular model in which factors could interact directly with one another, resulting in communication effects. This novel conceptualization of communication effects allowed Sabido to design complex, multilayered telenovelas.

The stages models play an important role in formative research because they help practitioners define where intended audiences are in the process of change and to design messages to fit specific audience and cultural needs. These models are also useful for providing feedback in the monitoring process, allowing for midcourse corrections in entertainment-education programs. Finally, summative evaluators may find these models useful in that they can map change through the stages resulting from entertainment-education programs (for example, Vaughan & Rogers, 2000).

Social Psychological Theories

The social psychological theories address individuals' psychological beliefs and perceptions about their social environment and include social learning theory (Bandura, 1977), the theory of reasoned action (Fishbein & Ajzen 1975), the theory of planned behavior (Ajzen, 1991), the health belief model (Becker & Rosenstock, 1987), and Rokeach's (1968) belief system theory.

According to social learning theory, self-efficacy, defined as one's beliefs in his or her ability to carry out a certain action, is the driving force for human behavior change. Bandura (1977) explains: "Efficacy expectations are a major determinant of people's choice of activities, how much effort they will expend, and of how long they will sustain effort in dealing with stressful situations" (Bandura, 1977). Outcome expectations (called response efficacy in other models), the other important variable in Bandura's theory, is an individual's belief that a certain behavior will lead to a certain outcome. In an entertainment-education program, soap opera characters "teach" audience members via modeling that they are able to make a recommended response, thereby enhancing self-efficacy perceptions, and that the recommended response works in averting an unwanted outcome, thereby enhancing outcome expectancies.

According to the theory of reasoned action (Fishbein & Ajzen, 1975), a person's behavior is predicted by intentions, which in turn, are predicted by attitudes toward the behavior and by subjective norms. Attitudes are composed of specific beliefs and the evaluation (either positive or negative) of those beliefs. Subjective norms are composed of beliefs about what one believes specific others think about performing a given behavior and one's motivation to comply with those specific others. The more positive the evaluation of behavioral beliefs and the stronger the motivation to comply with perceived norms, the greater the intention to perform a recommended response and the greater the likelihood that the desired behavioral response is actually performed. The theory of planned behavior extends the theory of reasoned action by including the concept of perceived behavioral control as an explanatory variable hypothesized to influence behaviors directly as well as through intentions, in addition to attitudes and subjective norms (Ajzen, 1991). Perceived behavioral control is defined as one's belief about the degree of volitional control s/he has over a given action. One example of the application of the theory of reasoned action (and planned behavior) is evident from the data on the effects of a multimedia entertainment-education campaign in Nepal. The results from this campaign indicate that positive attitudes towards health workers combined with the belief that a majority of community members used family planning (subjective norms) resulted in an intention to adopt family planning by nonusers and actual adoption (behaviors) of family planning among audience members. These intentions and behaviors were in turn influenced by "ever use of family planning" (perceived behavioral control) (Storey et al., 1999).

The health belief model suggests that cues-to-action prompt perceptions of susceptibility to, and severity of, a threat (Becker & Rosenstock, 1987). The perceptions are thought to motivate action. Once an individual is motivated to act, the health belief model hypothesizes that perceptions of the benefits of performing a recommended action are then weighed against the barriers of performing that action. If benefits are perceived to be stronger than barriers, then the advocated health behaviors will be adopted. Perceived barriers to performing an advocated action are the strongest predictor of the lack of positive behavior change (for example, Janz & Becker, 1984).

According to Rokeach's (1968) belief system theory, an individual has many beliefs, some attitudes, and only a limited number of values. Beliefs are the building blocks of attitudes, so an attitude can be comprised of many beliefs, and many attitudes merge to create a value. Changes in beliefs and attitudes may result in short-term behavior change. However, values serve as life-guides and dictate lifelong sets of behaviors. Rokeach suggested that individuals are cognitively aware of the correct way to behave or the end-state they strive for, and that these values underlie an integrated series of behaviors. Values act as "intervening variable[s] that lead to action when activated" (Rokeach, 1973).

These social psychological theories suggest that individual perceptions, beliefs, or values are the driving force of behavior change. They begin to offer explanations for why behaviors may not change in response to an entertainment-education program, as when an individual's beliefs, perceptions, or values are counter to the program's advocated behavior. As is the case with the stages models, this second group of theories/models also serve an important role in formative research, allowing entertainment-education program planners to measure individual levels of perceived threats, attitudes, subjective norms, and values and then comparing these same variables at midterm or at the end of an entertainment-education intervention.

Psychological Models

Cognitive processing models focus on the specific psychological processes individuals undergo when exposed to an entertainment-education program. Here we review social judgment theory (Sherif, Sherif, & Nebergall, 1965), the elaboration likelihood model (Petty & Cacioppo, 1986), and the triune brain perspective (MacLean, 1973). Social judgment theory is based on the concept of latitudes or bandwidths of acceptance or rejection. The theory states that we have certain comfort zones (called latitudes), outside of which we will reject new ideas. The more ego-involved we are with an issue, the narrower our latitude of acceptance and the wider our latitude of rejection. If an entertainment-education program advocates equality of decision-making between men and women, this message may fall within more liberal persons' latitude of acceptance and more conservative persons' latitude of rejection. The key to successfully using social judgment theory in an entertainment-education intervention is to offer messages that suggest small to moderate discrepancies between an audience's initial position (their anchor) and that being advocated. For example, if one's anchor position is that only men should make household decisions, then an intervention can offer a small discrepancy by suggesting that men should make most household decisions but confer with their wives on very large expenses. This small discrepancy may move an audience's beliefs slightly and widen the latitude of acceptance for gender equality.

A second psychological model is the elaboration likelihood model (Petty and Cacioppo, 1986), which suggests two key paths of information processing—the central path and the peripheral path. When people are both motivated to process a message and able to process that message, they will process it centrally, which means they will carefully think about the arguments in the message, elaborate on them, and critically evaluate them. Central processing of messages leads to stable and sustained attitude and behavioral changes. In contrast, when people are either not motivated and/or unable to process a message, they will process it peripherally, which means that they will rely on cues when evaluating arguments in a message. Typical peripheral cues include the use of heuristics, or mental models, such as "If experts say it's good, it must be good" or "If my neighbor breastfeeds her baby, then so should I." Decisions or behavior changes adopted via the peripheral route are unstable and likely to change when a new message is received. Slater and Rouner (2002) extend the traditional elaboration likelihood model by underplaying the distinction between central and peripheral routes of message processing while including engagement (also called absorption or transportation) and identification with characters in an entertainment-education program. According to Slater and Rouner (2002): "Entertainment-education, by blocking counterarguing, provides an extraordinary opportunity to influence individuals who would ordinarily be resistant to persuasion."

A third psychological model, the theory of the triune brain (MacLean, 1973), suggests that individuals process messages cognitively (thinking), affectively (emotional), and animalistically (physical) via three separate brain centers (the neo-cortex, visceral, and reptilian, respectively). MacLean (1973) suggested that the type of processing evoked by a message has a great deal to do with the outcome, such that messages processed via the reptilian portion of our brain trigger basic instinctual urges like hunger, need for sex, or aggressiveness. Messages processed viscerally produce emotional responses. Messages processed in the neo-cortex produce intellectual and thoughtful responses. Sabido adopted McLean's theory and suggested that conventional health education programs failed because they focused on the cognitive processing brain centers only (information dissemination). Therefore, Sabido developed soap operas that prompted intellectual, emotional, and physical responses.

Psychological models offer useful insights into the understanding and processing of entertainment-education programs. For example, they remind us to consider audience predispositions and brain biology as well as how the entertainment-education message might fit into preexisting cognitive schemas. Because of their focus on preexisting beliefs and motivations and abilities, these theories are useful at the formative stage, to assess where audiences are, as well as at the summative stage, to see how messages were processed and what shifts were made.

Drama Theories

The roles that people play and/or the scripts they follow in their daily lives are examined in the drama theories, including Bentley's (1967) dramatic theory, Jung's archetypes of the collective unconscious (1970), and Kincaid's conceptualization of drama theory (2002).

Eric Bentley's dramatic theory (1967) examined five types of drama: Tragedy, comedy, tragicomedy, farce, and melodrama. He explained the structures and effects of each type and provided the framework for creating positive and negative characters and various types of plots. The structure of the melodrama, in particular, caught Miguel Sabido's attention, and was adapted to the case of telenovelas.

Jung's (1970) theory of the collective unconscious was also useful to Sabido. Jung (1970) suggested that there are certain scripts or stories with familiar patterns and characters that people play out throughout history, and that appear in myths, legends, and folktales around the world. These universal scripts or stories are the "archetypes of the collective unconscious" and share universal characters like "prince charming," "the mother," and "the warrior." Jung's theory provides a basis for depicting characters that embody universal psychological and physiological characteristics within common themes in entertainment-education. For example, one of the reasons behind the success of the Peruvian soap opera *Simplemente Maria* was that Maria represented several archetypes, including that of "heroic struggle" that resonates universally (Svenkerud, Rahoi, & Singhal, 1995).

Drama theory, as applied by Kincaid (2002), suggests that individuals go through stages of scene setting, problem build-up, climax, conflict, resolution, and then ultimately, implementation of new collective action. Changes in values, beliefs, and attitudes occur based on emotion and reason (backed by evidence) occurring at the climax stage, where problems have yet to be resolved and conflict is possible. The various stages can occur in different orders and can even be skipped. However, the basic theory suggests that the "essence of drama is confrontation, which generates emotion," which "is the motivational force that drives the action of the characters, leading to conflict and its resolution" (Kincaid, 2002). Kincaid (2002) concluded that "the empathic emotional response in the audience is the motivational force that induces members of the audience to reconceptualize the central problem depicted in the drama and to resolve it in a similar manner in their own lives."

Drama theories offer insight into the creative development of entertainment-education programs. Common legends and folktales occurring within specified cultures can be used to develop powerful, emotionally charged entertainment-education programs that succeed in promoting value, belief, and behavior change.

Audience-Centered Theories

Audience-centered theories examine how audiences interact and react to entertainment-education programs. We review uses and gratifications theory, parasocial interaction, audience involvement, and the two-step flow model.

The uses and gratifications perspective examines "what audiences do with media" instead of "what media do to audiences." This theory suggests that people are active media users who are aware of their needs and use the media to gratify or satisfy these needs. Entertainment-education programs meet some needs triggered by motivations like entertainment (to seek fun, excitement), escapism (to forget about one's worries or problems), information (to learn about the world and others), identity (to find others like oneself to identify with), social interaction (to have topics to talk about or do with others), and so forth. The more that the media program choice meets one's needs, the greater and more enduring the postexposure effects (McQuail, Blumler, & Brown, 1972).

Parasocial interaction, defined as the perceived relationship of friendship or intimacy by an audience member with a remote media persona, is another audience-centered perspective (Blumler & Katz, 1974; Horton & Wohl, 1956). Parasocial interaction has been conceptualized as one measure of analyzing cognitive, affective, and behavioral participation before, during, and after media exposure. Much of the research on parasocial interaction centers on the perceived interpersonal relationship that individuals have with media characters in an entertainment-education program, and how this influences entertainment-education effects. In the radio drama *Tinka Tinka Sukh* from India, the parasocial interaction experienced by many listeners was exemplified by this letter: "Poonam's suicide, Kusum's death at childbirth, Sushma's struggle to stand on her own feet, and Rukhsana's life and problems have shaken up my world and filled my heart with emotions" (Sood, 2002).

Audience involvement, another audience-centered construct, is defined as the degree to which audience members engage in reflection upon, and parasocial interaction with, certain media programs, resulting in overt behavior change. Audience involvement is characterized by two dimensions: (a) affective-referential involvement, and (b) cognitive-critical involvement. Both dimensions rely on reflection, or the degree to which audience members consider a media message and integrate it into their lives. Referential reflection is the degree to which audience members relate a media program to their personal experiences, by indicating "this is exactly what happened to me."

Critical reflection is the degree to which audience members use their own thoughts and imaginations to make sense of a program or message, for example, by suggesting plot changes (Sood, 2002).

The two-step flow model (Lazersfeld, Berleson, & Gaudet, 1968) and its more recent cousin, the indirect-effects model, (Boulay, Storey, & Sood, in press) proposed that mass media only have minimal direct effects on audience members, and that audiences are instead more likely to be influenced by opinion leaders, defined as those individuals in positions of influence and/or decision-making authority in a system. According to the two-step flow model, opinion leaders receive information directly from the media and then pass it on to others. The key to behavior change is interpersonal communication in social networks. Recent research indicates that program evaluations should not only focus on direct exposure to the mass media, but also measure the indirect effects of media exposure disseminated interpersonally to others (Boulay, Storey, & Sood, 2002; Gunther & Storey, in press).

The audience-centered theories described above provide several important concepts that entertainment-education researchers find useful, such as media motivation, need gratification, parasocial interaction, involvement, opinion leadership, indirect effects, and social networks. These concepts allow scholars to examine how audiences use entertainment-education in an intermedia process.

Contextual Theories

Contextual theories represent diverse disciplinary epistemologies and include humanistic and critical perspectives. Included are theories of power (Mumby, 1988), hegemony (Gramsci, in Forgacs, 1989), social constructionism (Davenport-Sypher, McKinley, Ventsam, & Valdeavellano, 2002; Slack, 1989), and agenda-setting (McCombs & Shaw, 1972).

Power is a force that gives one communicator the ability to influence another communicator to take an action, which would not otherwise be taken. Power is not static and operates in the "in-between" spaces in contexts and relationships. Power imbalances can be corrected through empowerment of the unempowered. Empowerment occurs when group members earn their ability to exercise power by becoming expert on the group's task through gathering relevant information, developing alliances, rewarding others for their good work, and demonstrating active involvement in a group. The media are a mechanism to symbolize the power and dominance structure in society or as a force that challenges the existing power/dominance structure.

Hegemony is a Marxist perspective in which the economic and political predominance of one social class over another is examined in terms of the ability of the predominant social class to project its own views as being "common sense" or "natural" to subordinate classes (Gramsci in Forgacs, 1989).

Subordinates willingly and actively consent to the views purported by the predominant class. The role of the media, from this viewpoint, is seen as vital in constructing or opposing this "bourgeois hegemony" and in shifting beliefs, values, and norms. Entertainment-education programs might examine issues of gender equality or civil rights under a hegemonic perspective.

The social constructionism perspective focuses on the construction of meaning within a social context. Meaning and understanding do not lie in an entertainment-education program itself, or in the audience, or in the media through which it is disseminated. Rather, the meanings of messages are derived from the interaction between these three, and within the specific socio cultural environment. Locally situated knowledge, beliefs, and customs are embedded as key parts of entertainment-education efforts. Social constructionism was used to account "for the complexities of interpretation and social change resulting from entertainment-education interventions. The actions and interactions of community members become the focal point for observation and analysis" (Davenport-Sypher et al., 2002).

Agenda-setting theory states that the media determine which issues are important and which issues the public should attend to (Lippman, 1922). Bernard Cohen suggested that the press "may not be successful much of the time in telling people what to think, but it is stunningly successful in telling its readers what to think about" (Cohen, 1963). Early work on agenda-setting viewed the media as an independent variable that predicted which issues the public thinks about. Recently, agenda-setting has been considered a dependent variable, as in "Who sets the media agenda?" (Dearing & Rogers, 1996). Entertainment-education programs can influence the public agenda by focusing on certain key issues.

The theories based on the sociocultural context provide concepts for entertainment-education scholars such as power, empowerment, hegemony, social interaction, social constructionism, agendas, and media attributes. These theories look upon the media as powerful, and they recognize audience members as key participants in the meaning derived and the behavior change engendered from the entertainment-education process.

Hybrid Models

Many entertainment-education scholars over several years have put together hybrid models that combine elements from various theories. Examples of hybrid models are: Vaughan and Rogers' (2000) six-stage model of communication effects, the Soul City model of behavior change (2000), and the Johns Hopkins University/Center for Communication Programs' (JHU/CCP) ideation theory (Kincaid, 2000a, 2000b).

Vaughan and Rogers (2000) utilized three of the four stages models described previously—McGuire's (1989) hierarchy-of-effects, DiClemente and

Prochaska's stages-of-change (1985), Rogers's (1995) innovation-decision process—and combined these with social learning theory (Bandura, 1977) to create a six-stage model of communication effects. These six stages of behavior change are: (a) precontemplation, (b) contemplation, (c) preparation, (d) validation, (e) action, and (f) maintenance. The model "includes both cognitive and affective processes in the internal state of the individual (primarily the first three stages of the model), and interpersonal communication processes in the external environment of the individual (primarily the latter three stages of the model) . . . exposure [to a message] may promote cognitive, affective, role-modeling, or interpersonal communication processes" (Vaughan & Rogers, 2000). These scholars utilized their hybrid model to evaluate the effects of an E-E radio intervention in Tanzania.

The Soul City model of behavior change draws upon several theoretical traditions in order to assess Soul City, a large multimedia entertainment-education program in South Africa. The model consists of three interrelated components: the individual, the community, and the social/political environment. The individual level includes constructs from stage models (knowledge, approval, attitudes) and social psychological models (barriers, locus of control). The community component incorporates diffusion of innovations theory and social influence (changing norms). The individual and community are thought to be embedded in a larger social and political environment. The Soul City model specifically focuses on advocacy, especially in terms of partnership formation, supportive environments for change, and interpersonal communication (see the Shereen Usdin and others' chapter in this volume).

Ideation theory, as utilized by Lawrence Kincaid and his colleagues at the Johns Hopkins University (Kincaid, 2000a, 2000b), integrates the sociodemographic concept of ideation, defined as the spread of novel or modern ideas so people have new ways of thinking about family planning, with eight behavior change variables: skills, environmental constraints, intention (hypothesized to directly cause behavior change), attitude, perceived social norms, self-image, emotional reaction, and self-efficacy. Kincaid and colleagues argued that ideation occurs through interaction within social networks and that behavior change is the result of the cumulative effect of ideation for each variable listed above (Kincaid, Figueroa, Storey, & Underwood, 2001). Entertainment-education programs should address as many different behavior change variables as possible, in order to effect the maximum amount of behavior change.

The broad array of theoretical perspectives just reviewed stem from wide-ranging philosophical origins and offer much insight into entertainment-education effects and processes. This review suggests that the majority of entertainment-education scholars publishing in peer-reviewed journals are committed to rigorous theory-building. We turn now to a description of entertainment education methods found in peer-reviewed journal articles.

METHODOLOGICAL CHARACTERISTICS OF ENTERTAINMENT-EDUCATION PROGRAMS

Entertainment-education programs are evaluated with both qualitative and quantitative methods. Table 7.2 shows the research design and results from various entertainment-education programs. The majority of published entertainment-education evaluations focus on quantitative surveys, with supplemental information provided by such qualitative techniques as ethnographies, focus group interviews, or observation (Singhal & Rogers, 2002). The current standard for evaluating entertainment-education programs consists of baseline and follow-up surveys, comparing those individuals exposed versus those not exposed to the entertainment-education programs, ideally with a treatment and control group.

Formative Research

A first step in implementing an entertainment-education strategy is formative evaluation, a method of analyzing target audiences to determine their needs, desires, behaviors, and media usage in order to develop understandable, high-quality, culturally appropriate characters and storylines. Formative research results allow entertainment-education program designers to make changes in content, refine program materials, receive feedback from audience members, test theoretical components, and to clarify messages. Entertainment-education researchers and program designers use such formative research methods as surveys, focus group interviews, analyses of demographic/health data, collaborative workshops, field observation, and pilot testing with a sample of the target audience. Davenport-Sypher and others (2002) described the innovative use of *promotoras* to develop *Bienvenida Salud!*, an entertainment-education radio intervention in the Peruvian Amazon. Community members elected promotoras, who then assisted in the development of culturally appropriate radio scripts that properly addressed community needs. Participatory formative evaluation methods, such as these, appear to be the wave of the future for entertainment-education.

Measuring Exposure

Prior to measuring audience effects, most researchers investigate audience exposure to determine whether or not the program actually reached the target audience, and if so, through what channel. Exposure is considered both a dependent and an independent variable in entertainment-education evaluation studies. The most common approach to measuring exposure in the studies reviewed was to ask respondents to self-report their degree of exposure:

TABLE 7.2

Methodological Characteristics of Selected Entertainment-Education Programs

Author, Year	Formative Evaluation	Design/Type of Data	Exposure Measurement	Results, Implications, Recommendations
Brown, 1990	Not mentioned in the article	Survey interviews (N = 1,170)	Self-report survey items	1. Viewers' affective involvement with a message can induce changes in beliefs. 2. Exposure to entertainment-education program might result in dependency on television.
Piotrow, Rimon, Winnard, Kincaid, Huntington, & Convisser, 1990	Focus group discussions Pretesting initial episodes	Service statistics Source-of-referral from clinic records Survey interviews	Self-report survey items	1. Substantial and immediate increases in family planning acceptors occurred concurrently with the intervention. 2. Impact can be attributed to (1) audience analysis and pretesting, (2) close links between media, broadcasters, and health care providers, (3) entertainment value, and (4) the use of positive and negative role models.
Brown & Cody, 1991	Not mentioned in the article	Survey questionnaire (N = 1,170)	Self-report survey items Audience ratings	1. Exposure to entertainment-education program might result in dependency on television. 2. One of the first entertainment-education evaluations to show population-level effects on behavior.
Piotrow et al., 1992	Focus group discussions Needs assessment using Demographic Health Survey (DHS) Data	Baseline and follow-up surveys (N = 534 and 229, respectively)	Self-report survey items	1. The radio drama component was the most effective medium in providing new information and stimulating change. 2. Multimedia campaigns can influence male awareness, attitudes toward decision-making, and family planning practice.

134

Bouman & Wieberdink, 1993	Pretesting episodes	Pretesting results Random sample survey (panel design)	Self reported survey items Audience ratings	1. Hardly any changes in knowledge, attitude, and practice concerning smoking and diet were found. 2. It was very difficult to write an effective series on heart health due to differing views and standards and cultural issues. 3. Emphasis should be placed on script sponsoring of heart health messages in already successful series.
Singhal, Obregon, & Rogers, 1994	Needs assessment among intended audience	Personal interviews Archival review Videotaped episodes In-depth focus group discussions	Audience ratings	1. Increased audience enrollment in literacy classes and sewing classes. 2. Formulation of the E-E strategy that has been used in other countries. 3. Success can be attributed to a good production team, appropriate timing, superb actors, viewer involvement, novelty effect, great exposure, and culturally shareable nature.
Valente, Kim, Lettenmaier, Glass, & Dibba, 1994	Small district-level surveys Focus group discussions	Baseline/follow-up surveys (N = 397) Client interviews Listening group interviews	Self-report survey items	1. The campaign encouraged interpersonal communication and motivated viewers to visit family planning clinics. 2. Exposure to the radio program was positively related to knowledge, attitudes, and practice of family planning. 3. The program was able to reach uneducated listeners, thus it had an empowering influence on women.

(Continued)

TABLE 7.2
(Continued)

Author, Year	Formative Evaluation	Design/Type of Data	Exposure Measurement	Results, Implications, Recommendations
Valente, Poppe, Alva, DeBriceno, & Cases, 1995	Pretesting Secondary analysis of demographic data.	One-group pretest-posttest interviews (N = 85 audience members)	Estimates obtained by counselors present at most dramas and follow-up discussions	1. Exposure reduced misinformation about family planning especially among women and those with higher education. 2. Street theater is a cost-effective, entertaining medium for providing public support, and offers a chance for the public to provide feedback and discussion.
Yoder, Hornik, & Chirwa, 1996	Focus group discussions Pretesting	Baseline and follow-up surveys (N = 1,613 & 1,682, respectively)	Self-report survey items	1. Exposure to the program increased levels of family conversations about AIDS. 2. It is realistic to expect quality production value, characters that are similar to audience members, and message clarity.
Kim & Marangwanda, 1997	Needs assessment using DHS data	Baseline/follow-up surveys (N = 1,019 & 1,016, respectively) Service statistics Client exit interviews	Self-report survey items	1. The campaign encouraged partner communication, changed attitudes, and increased approval for family planning. 2. Radio based entertainment-education is an excellent source of family planning information for men. 3. Further research is needed to examine the long-term impact of multiple rounds of male motivational campaigns.
Thomas, Cahill, & Santill, 1997	Observations Focus group discussions Pilot testing	"Proof of concept" Pretest and posttest	Player data and audio responses recorded by each player	1. Most users took negotiation tasks seriously and took advantage of the opportunity to practice their skills. 2. Computer technology offers promise for extending the reach of health education programs in a cost-effective manner.

Bouman, Maas, & Kok, 1998	None	Post-test with nonequivalent groups Panel discussion	National Broadcasting Foundation analysis	1. The majority of the respondents saw both the stories and doctors' advice as realistic. 2. The series set an agenda for social discourse, and elicited a high amount of interpersonal communication. 3. Future research combining audience survey research with ethnographic and cultural studies would be of interest.
Kane, Gueye, Speizer, Pacque-Margolis, & Baron, 1998	Needs assessment using DHS data	Pre and posttest quasi-experimental Survey	Self-report survey items	1. The campaign had both positive and significant impact on contraceptive use among men and women. 2. A campaign utilizing traditional theater, local languages and familiar settings appears to be an effective way of linking, traditional values and practices with acceptance of new ideas related to family planning.
Jato, Simbakalia, Tarasevich, Awasum, Kihinga, & Ngirwamungu, 1999	Not mentioned in the article	Survey interviews Secondary data analysis of the Tanzania DHS (N = 4,225 women)	Self-report survey items	1. Contraceptive acceptance increased dramatically after exposure to various campaign activities. 2. Contraceptive knowledge and use were closely associated with exposure to media messages about family planning. 3. Additional research is needed to determine how to meet women's information needs most efficiently and effectively.

(Continued)

TABLE 7.2
(Continued)

Author, Year	Formative Evaluation	Design/Type of Data	Exposure Measurement	Results, Implications, Recommendations
Law & Singhal, 1999	Not mentioned in the article	Content analysis of letters (N = 237)	Exposure not measured (data collected from letter writers)	1. New knowledge was the most direct observable impact on self-efficacy. 2. In addition to raising individual self-efficacy, the program stimulated collective efficacy in dealing with social issues at the group, community level.
Rogers, Vaughan, Swalehe, Rao, Svenkerud, & Sood, 1999	Workshop to develop a values grid, which formed the basis of the storyline	Field experiment Pre and post design Independent sources for verification via DHS	Self-reported survey items	1. The program had measurable effects on contraceptive adoption. 2. Client flow data indicates increases in both new and continuing users. The program was the source of referral for a quarter of the new clients. 3. Exposure increased self-efficacy with respect to family size, ideal age at marriage, and current family planning use.
Storey, Boulay, Karki, Heckert, & Karmacharya, 1999	Media needs research Focus groups Secondary analysis of government health data Baseline survey	Survey interviews (panel design) Sentinel health post data	Self-report survey items	1. Four attitudinal factors associated intent to use and actual use: personal image of contraceptive users, health workers behavior, gender bias, and family well-being. 2. The program had a significant impact on modern family planning method use, primarily through interpersonal communication with health workers and one's spouse, and normative support for family planning use.

Valente & Bharath, 1999	Baseline research Field testing for effectiveness	Pre/post-drama interviews (N = 93) Comparison group Postdrama-only interviews (N = 99)	Exposure not measured (data collected from audience members attending performance)	1. Mass media were the most reported source of awareness about AIDS by respondents. 2. Knowledge and self-reported attitudes improved as a result of seeing the drama. 3. Future research should explore the cost effectiveness of community drama, whether it motivates behavior change, and how its influence varies across and within cultures.
Papa, Singhal, Law, Pant, Sood, Rogers, & Shefner-Rogers, 2000	Not mentioned in the article	Observational case study In-depth and focus group interviews Survey interviews Content analysis of episodes	Self-reported survey items Observation data	1. The program led to socially desirable effects in the village community. 2. Behavior change can be facilitated by parasocial relationships between audience members and characters. 3. Interpersonal conversations can lead to collective efficacy and community action when individuals believe that collective efforts can solve social problems.
Vaughan & Rogers, 2000	Development of a values grid to determine educational values	Personal interviews at baseline (1993) and each year after for four years in treatment and comparison areas	Exposure measure—not specified	1. Reasons for strong program effects include: messages that were emotional, motivational, and emphasized positive consequences of new behavior. 2. Entertainment-education programs help stimulate interpersonal communication by providing audiences homophilous role models for behavior change. They impact all the stages of behavior change from precontemplation to action.

(Continued)

TABLE 7.2
(Continued)

Author, Year	Formative Evaluation	Design/Type of Data	Exposure Measurement	Results, Implications, Recommendations
Kim, Kols, Nyakauru, Marngwanda, & Chibatamoto, 2001	Involvement of intended audience in program planning Local management committees at each site	Quasi-experimental design Baseline and follow-up surveys (N = 1,426 and 1400, respectively) Survey of radio listeners (N = 700)	Self-report survey items	1. Use of modern contraceptives increased significantly in campaign sites between surveys. 2. The campaign's biggest effect was to convince sexually experienced young people to stick to one partner. 3. The use of multiple channels of communication contributed to the campaign's impact. 4. Future campaigns need to directly address gender inequities that underlie risky sexual decisions by young people.
Soul City, 2001	Literature and press review Expert workshops Focus group and in-depth interviews Field observations Pretesting scripts	Longitudinal panel design national survey National qualitative impact assessment Sentinel site interviews Partnership evaluation Monitoring of national media Cost-effectiveness study	Self-reported survey items	1. Soul City played a role in the implementation of the Domestic Violence Act. 2. Women exposed to the intervention were empowered to negotiate both relationships and safe sex. 3. Exposure was associated with improved knowledge, interpersonal communication, subjective social norms, and intention to participate in community actions across Soul City themes.
Soul City, 2001	Literature and press review Expert workshops Focus group and in-depth interviews Pretesting scripts	Ethnographic studies utilizing in-depth interviews observation and group discussions National surveys	Audience ratings Observations Self reported survey items	1. Exposure to Soul Buddyz facilitates discussion of its topics. 2. Parents exposed to the program were more likely to have more positive attitudes related to respect for children than parents not exposed to the program.

			3. *Soul Buddyz* impacted almost all teachers interviewed in some way, including equipping them to discuss sensitive issues with children, better understanding of children, knowledge of the Child Line number, and more.
Davenport-Sypher, McKinley, Ventsam, & Valdeavellano, 2002	Promotoras (women and girls) are elected by the community to assist in program development	Survey interviews Focus groups discussions Participant observations	Self-report survey items
			1. Listening was communal and interactive in an area that is typically segregated.
			2. Producers regard the radio show as only one part of a long-term approach to community empowerment.
			3. Future research should examine how entertainment-education can sustain social change.
Sharan & Valente, 2002	Media needs research Focus groups Secondary analysis of DHS Baseline survey	Longitudinal panel design survey interviews in three waves (N = 1,442 women total)	Self-report survey item
			1. Over time, there was an increase in joint (spousal) family planning decision-making.
			2. The radio program was more effective in altering the attitudes of the younger segment, whose reproductive decisions will contribute most to future fertility growth.
			3. Research on the role of ethnicity and cultural factors that impact spousal communication is needed.

(Continued)

141

TABLE 7.2
(Continued)

Author, Year	Formative Evaluation	Design/Type of Data	Exposure Measurement	Results, Implications, Recommendations
Sood, 2002	Not mentioned in the article	Self-administered questionnaire among randomly selected registered listeners	Self-report survey items	1. Audience involvement is a multidimensional construct. 2. Audience involvement had a positive impact on self-efficacy and collective efficacy.
Boulay, Storey, & Sood, 2002	Focus groups Secondary analysis of government health data and DHS data. Baseline survey	Sociometric survey In-depth interviews	Self-report survey items, measuring both direct and indirect exposure	1. The effect of indirect exposure on extending the reach of mass media messages is substantial. 2. Indirect exposure is associated with higher contraceptive use. 3. Membership in community groups has an impact on exposure in two ways; first members were more likely to report hearing the program and second community groups appeared to increase indirect exposure to the program.
Gunther & Storey, in press	Focus groups Secondary analysis of government health data Baseline survey	Survey questionnaire Clinic based monitoring of interactions	Self-report survey items Observation data	1. Presumed influence is based on subjective perceptions and more likely driven by mass media than actual experience. 2. Assumptions of mass media influence may explain many outcomes, further tests of the influence of presumed influence are called for.

"Did you listen to the radio yesterday?" "Have you heard anything on the radio about health or family planning in the past eight months?" "Have you heard specific messages about X on the radio?" (Storey et al., 1999). Self-reports have limitations and risk of social desirability effects, where respondents tell an interviewer what they think the interviewer wants to hear (instead of the truth).

Other researchers used proxy variables highly correlated with exposure as estimates of actual exposure, such as audience ratings (Bouman & Wieberdink, 1993), sociometric network data to map both direct and indirect exposure to entertainment-education program messages (Boulay et al., 2002), longitudinal research (using panel surveys) in order to accurately estimate exposure (Storey et al., 1999). One scholar counted crowds at a live entertainment-education event, street theater (Valente, Poppe, Alva, De Briceno, & Cases, 1995).

Characters

Most entertainment-education evaluation studies use audience feedback and measures of involvement and parasocial interaction to analyze the appropriateness, similarity, and likeability of entertainment-education characters. Then they examine how these qualities are associated with the behavior change of audience individuals. Audience feedback regarding Egypt's *Alam Simsim* provided producers with valuable information about the public's receptivity to the program and its characters: "I love Khakha and Filfil very much," "I am 16 years old and I watch *Alam Simsim*. It is very interesting. Also, the characters are fabulous, especially Filfil," and, "My daughter is two years old and she loves your program very much" (USAID Egypt, 2002). Measures of parasocial interaction and audience involvement help to determine specific effects of the characters on behavior change. For example, Sood (2002) measured audience involvement using a 30-item scale that included statements such as, "You felt that your favorite characters were like people you know."

FUTURE DIRECTIONS FOR ENTERTAINMENT-EDUCATION THEORETICAL RESEARCH

The majority of published evaluations of entertainment-education programs use logical positivist perspectives, focus on the individual, employ survey methodologies, and utilize cognitive-rational social psychological or stage theories (Singhal & Rogers, 2002). Additional research is needed on the role of the community, the policy environment, and/or the environmental infrastructure, on E-E effects. Individual-level survey methodologies appear to be the bread and butter of many entertainment-education evaluations, because producers, funders, and policy-makers want to know what percentage of persons changed their behavior. However, it would be useful for the development of a more powerful entertainment-education theory to supplement these methods, perspectives, and foci with alternative research methods.

The exploration of several key concepts could add much to E-E theorizing. One such concept is collective efficacy, defined as "people's beliefs in their joint capabilities to forge divergent self-interests into a shared agenda, to enlist supporters and resources for collective action, to devise effective strategies and to execute them successfully, and to withstand forcible opposition and discouraging setbacks" (Bandura, 1995). Recent theorizing, based on research concerning entertainment-education effects in Indian villages, suggests that community-level variables such as collective efficacy may explain more behavior change than individual-level variables (Papa et al., 2000; see Arvind Singhal and others' chapter on the Indian radio soap opera *Taru* in this volume).

Another rarely examined but important E-E concept is affect. Kincaid (2002) concluded that there was a paucity of "emotions" in communication theory in general and specifically in evaluations of entertainment-education programs. Affect is a generic term for a range of feelings and emotions. Affect can be conceptualized as residing within a person, or it can be conceived of as the emotional valence of a message (Monahan, 1995). Affective responses are primary—they occur before, and influence subsequent, cognitive processing (Murphy, 1990; Murphy & Zajonc, 1993).

The concept of empowerment is becoming the focus of much recent work by entertainment-education researchers (see Arvind Singhal's chapter on participatory theater in this volume). The Freirean empowerment–education framework insists that learners should be involved in: (a) defining and naming their own problems, (b) critically examining these problems and their root causes, (c) creating a vision of a healthier community, and (d) developing social action strategies necessary to overcome limits and achieve their goals (Wallerstein & Bernstein, 1994). Entertainment-education programs are inherently designed to be empowering in that they allow audience individuals to witness their own problems and compare them with the problems that the E-E characters face. As the suggestions for improving conditions and the actions taken to improve these conditions unfold within an entertainment-education story, audiences can be motivated to initiate changes in their own social conditions. Theoretical insights into how people make sense of their lives within their specific cultures, contexts, and relationships are needed (Dervin, 1990; Figueroa et al., 2002).

Entertainment-education theorizing displays great diversity, while based on a solid foundation. Although the entertainment-education field is much younger than health communication or health psychology, it is in some ways further ahead theoretically. We need to understand the dynamics of power, poverty, and health and how an entertainment-education program may influence these dynamics. Methodologies that assess effects at the community or policy level may offer new support or disconfirmation of key entertainment-education findings.

REFERENCES

Ajzen, I. (1991). The theory of planned behavior. *Organizational Behavior and Human Decision Processes, 50,* 179–211.

Armstrong, S. (1997). Soul City. *World Health, 50*(6), 24–25.

Bandura, A. (1977). *Social learning theory.* Englewood Cliffs, NJ: Prentice-Hall.

Bandura, A. (1986). *Social foundations of thought and action: A social cognitive theory.* Englewood Cliffs, NJ: Prentice-Hall.

Bandura. A. (1995). Exercise of personal and collective efficacy. In A. Bandura (Ed.), *Self-efficacy in changing societies* (pp. 1–45). New York: Cambridge University Press.

Bandura, A. (1997). *Self-efficacy: The essence of control.* New York: Freeman Press.

Becker, M. H., & Rosenstock, I. M. (1987). Comparing social learning theory and the health belief model. In W. B. Ward (Ed.), *Advances in health education and promotion, Volume 2* (pp. 245–249). Greenwich, CT: JAI.

Bentley, E. (1967). *The life of drama.* New York: Atheneum.

Blumler J. G., & E. Katz (1974). *The uses of mass communication.* Thousand Oaks, CA: Sage.

Boulay, M., Storey, J. D., and Sood, S. (2002). Indirect exposure to a family planning mass media campaign in Nepal. *Journal of Health Communication, 7,* 379–399.

Bouman, M., Maas, L., & Kok, G. (1998). Health education in television entertainment-Medisch Centrum West: A Dutch drama serial. *Health Education Research, 13*(4), 503–518.

Bouman, M. P. A. (1998). *The turtle and the peacock: Collaboration for prosocial change.* Wageningen, The Netherlands: Wageningen Agricultural University.

Bouman, M. P. A., & Wieberdink, M. S. C. (1993). *Villa Borghese*: A soap series on heart health. *Canadian Journal of Cardiology, 9* (Supplement D), 145D–146D.

Brown, W. (1990). Prosocial effects of entertainment television in India. *Asian Journal of Communication, 1*(1), 113–135.

Brown, W. J. & Cody, M. J. (1991). Effects of a prosocial television soap opera in promoting women's status. *Human Communication Research, 18*(1), 114–142.

Cohen, Bernard (1963). *The press and foreign policy.* Princeton, NJ: Princeton University Press.

Dauchez, P. (2002). Useful theatre in Mali. *Communication processes. 2: Defiance and dominance.* Retrieved July 15, 2002, from http://www.iias.nl/host/ccrss/cp/cp2/cp2-Useful.html

Davenport-Sypher, B., McKinley, M., Ventsam, S., & Valdeavellano, E. E.(2002). Fostering reproductive health through entertainment-education in the Peruvian Amazon: The social construction of *Bienvenida Salud! Communication Theory, 12*(2), 192–205.

Dearing, J. W., & Rogers, E. M. (1996). *Agenda-setting.* Thousand Oaks, CA: Sage.

Dervin, B. (1990). Audience as listener and learner, teacher and confidante: The sense making approach. In R. E. Rice and C. K. Atkin (Eds.), *Public communication campaigns* (pp. 67–86). Thousand Oaks, CA: Sage.

DiClemente, C. C., & Prochaska, J. O. (1985). Processes and stages of change: Coping and competence in smoking behavior change. In S. Shiffman & T. A. Willis (Eds.), *Coping and substance abuse* (pp. 319–334). San Diego, CA: Academic Press.

Figueroa, M. E.; Kincaid, D. L., Rani, M., & Lewis, G. (2002). *Communication for social change: An integrated model for measuring the process and its outcomes.* Communication for Social Change Working Paper Series. Retrieved September 23, 2002, http://www.comminit.com/stcfscindicators/sld-5997.html

Fishbein, M., & Ajzen, I. (1975). *Belief, attitude, intention, and behavior: An introduction to theory and research.* Reading, MA: Addison-Wesley.

Fishbein, M., Bandura, A., Triandis, H. C., Kanfer, F. H., Becker, M. H., & Middlestadt, S. E. (1991). *Factors influencing behavior and behavior change: Final report of the theorists' workshop.* Washington, DC: National Institutes of Mental Health.

Fishbein, M., Triandis, H. C., Kanfer, E. H., Becker, M. H., Middlestadt, S. E., & Eichler, A. (2000). Factors influencing behavior and behavior change. In A. S. Baum, T. A. Revenson, & J. E. Singer (Eds.), *Handbook of health psychology.* Mahwah, NJ: Lawrence Erlbaum Associates.

Forgacs, D. (Ed.) (1989). *An Antonio Gramsci reader: Selected writings, 1916-1935.* New York: Schocken.

Goldstein, S., Anderson, A., Usdin, S., & Japhet, G. (2001). *Soul Buddyz:* A children's rights mass media campaign in South Africa. *Health and Human Rights, 5*(2), pp. 163-173.

Gunther, A. and Storey, J. D. (2002, in press). The influence of presumed influence. *Journal of Communication.*

Horton D., & Wohl R. (1956). Mass communication and para-social interaction: Observation on intimacy at a distance. *Psychiatry, 19*(3), 188-211.

Janz, N., & Becker, M. (1984). The health belief model: A decade later. *Health Education Quarterly, 11,* 1-47.

Jato, M. N., Simbakalia, C., Tarasevich, J. M., Awasum, D. N., Kihinga, C. N. B., & Ngirwamungu, E. (1999). The impact of multimedia family planning promotion on the contraceptive behavior of women in Tanzania. *International Family Planning Perspectives, 25*(2), 60-67.

Jung, C. G. (1970) *Archetypes and the collective unconscious.* Buenos Aires: Ed. Paidos.

Kane, T. T., Gueye, M., Speizer, I., Pacque-Margolis, S., & Baron, D. (1998). The impact of a family planning multimedia campaign in Bamako, Mali. *Studies in Family Planning, 29* (3), 309-323.

Kim, Y. M., Kols, A., Nyakauru, R., Marangwanda, C., and Chibatamoto, P. (2001). Promoting sexual responsibility among young people in Zimbabwe. *International Family Planning Perspectives, 27*(1), 11-19.

Kim, Y. M., & Marangwanda, C. (1997). Stimulating men's support for long-term contraception: A campaign in Zimbabwe. *Journal of Health Communication, 2,* 271-297.

Kincaid, D. L. (2000a). Mass media, ideation, and contraceptive behavior: A longitudinal analysis of contraceptive change in the Philippines. *Communication Research 27*(6):723-63.

Kincaid, D. L. (2000b). Social networks, ideation, and contraceptive behavior in Bangladesh: A longitudinal analysis. *Social Science & Medicine, 50,* 215-231.

Kincaid, D. L. (2002). Drama, emotion, and cultural convergence. *Communication Theory, 12*(2), 136-152.

Kincaid, D. L., Figueroa, M. E., Storey, D., & Underwood, C. (1999). *Ideation and contraceptive behavior: The relationship observed in five countries.* Paper presented at the Population Association of America, New York.

Kincaid, D. L., Figueroa, M. E., Storey, D., & Underwood, C. (2001). *Communication, ideation, and contraceptive use: The relationships observed in five countries.* Baltimore, MD: Johns Hopkins University's Center for Communication Programs.

Law, S., & Singhal, A. (1999). Efficacy in letter-writing to an entertainment-education radio serial. *Gazette, 61*(5), 355-372.

Lazarsfeld, P., Berleson, B., & Gaudet, H. (1968). *The people's choice: How the voter makes up his mind in a presidential campaign.* New York: Columbia University Press.

Lippman, W. (1922). *Public opinion.* New York: Harcourt Brace.

MacLean, P. D. (1973). *A triune concept of the brain and behavior.* Toronto, Canada: University of Toronto Press.

McCombs, M., and Shaw, D. (1972). The agenda-setting function of mass media. *Public Opinion Quarterly, 36,* 176-185.

McGuire, W. J. (1969). Attitudes and attitude change. In G. Lindsey & E. Aronson (Eds.), *Handbook of social psychology* (Vol. 2). Reading, MA: Addison-Wesley.

McGuire, W. J. (1989). Theoretical foundations of campaigns. In R. E. Rice and C. K. Atkin (Eds.), *Public communication campaigns*. Thousand Oaks, CA: Sage.

McQuail, D., Blumler J., & Brown R. (1972). The television audience: A revised perspective. In D. McQuail (Ed.): *Sociology of mass communication*. London: Longman.

Monahan, J. L. (1995). Using positive affect when designing health messages. In E. Maibach & R. L. Parrott (Eds.), *Designing health messages: Approaches from communication theory and public health practice* (pp. 81–98). Thousand Oaks, CA: Sage.

Mumby, D. K. (1988). *Communication and power in organizations: Discourse, ideology and domination*. Norwood, NJ: Ablex.

Murphy, S. T. (1990). *The primacy of affect: Evidence and extension*. Ph.D. dissertation, Ann Arbor, MI: University of Michigan.

Murphy, S. T., & Zajonc, R. B. (1993). Affect, cognition, and awareness: Affective priming with suboptimal and optimal stimulus. *Journal of Personality and Social Psychology, 64*(5), 723–739.

Nariman, H. (1993). *Soap operas for social change*. Westport, CT: Praeger.

Nzyuko, S. (1996). Does research have any role in information/education/communication Programs In Africa? An insider's view. *Journal of Health Communication, 1*,(2), 227–235.

Obregon, R. (1999). *Colombian telenovelas and public health messages: A focus on HIV/AIDS and sexuality issues*. College Park, PA: Pennsylvania State University. *Dissertation Abstracts: AAT 9960642*.

Papa, M., Singhal, A., Law, S., Pant, S., Sood, S., Rogers, E. M., and Shefner-Rogers, C. (2000) Entertainment-education and social change: An analysis of parasocial interaction, social learning and paradoxical communication. *Journal of Communication, 50*(4), 31–55.

Patel, D. S. (2002). *Changing health knowledge, attitudes, and behavioral intentions: An analysis of how much educational content should be inserted into an entertainment-education program*. Ph.D. dissertation. East Lansing: MI. Michigan State University.

Petty, R. E., & Cacioppo, J. T. (1986). *Communication and persuasion: Central and peripheral routes to attitude change*. New York: Springer-Verlag.

Piotrow, P. T., Kincaid, D. L., Hindin, M. J., Lettenmaier, C. L., Kuseka, I., Silberman, T., Zinanga, A., Chikara, F., Adamchak, D. J., Mbizvo, M. T., Lynn, W., Kumah, O. M., & Kim, Y. M. (1992). Changing men's attitudes and behavior: The Zimbabwe Male Motivation Project. *Studies in Family Planning, 23*(6), 365–375.

Piotrow, P. T. Kincaid, D. L., Rimon J. G., II, Rinehart, W. (1997). *Health communications: Lessons from family planning and reproductive health*. Westport, CT: Praeger.

Piotrow, P. T., Rimon, J. G., Winnard, K., Kincaid, D. L., Huntington, D., & Convisser, J. (1990). Mass media family planning promotion in three Nigerian cities. *Studies in Family Planning, 21*(5), 265–274.

Rogers, E. M. (2003). *Diffusion of Innovations*. (5th ed.). New York: Free Press.

Rogers, E. M., Vaughan, P. W., Swalehe, R. M. A., Rao, N., Svenkerud, P., & Sood, S. (1999). Effects of an entertainment-education radio soap opera on family planning behavior in Tanzania. *Studies in Family Planning, 30*(3), 193–211.

Rokeach, M. (1968). *Beliefs, attitudes, and values*. San Francisco: Jossey-Bass.

Rokeach, M. (1973). *The nature of human values*. New York: Free Press.

Rubin, A. M., & Perse, E. M. (1987). Audience activity and soap opera involvement: A uses and effects investigation. *Human Communication Research, 14*,(2), 246–268.

Sabido, M. (1989). *Soap operas in Mexico*. Paper presented at the Entertainment for Social Change Conference. Los Angeles, CA: Annenberg School for Communication, University of Southern California.

Shannon, C. E., & Weaver, W. (1949). *The mathematical theory of communication.* Urbana, IL: University of Illinois Press.

Sharan, M. & Valente, T. W. (2002). Spousal communication and family planning adoption: Effects of a radio drama serial in Nepal. *International Family Planning Perspectives, 28*(1), 16–25.

Sherif, M., Sherif, K., & Nebergall, R. (1965). *Attitude and attitude change: The social judgment-involvement approach.* Philadelphia: Saunders.

Singhal, A., Obregon, R., & Rogers, E. M. (1994). Reconstructing the story of *Simplemente Maria,* the most popular telenovela in Latin America of all time. *Gazette, 54*(1), 1–15.

Singhal, A. & Rogers, E. M. (1999). *Entertainment-education: A communication strategy for social change.* Mahwah, NJ: Lawrence Erlbaum Associates.

Singhal, A., & Rogers, E. M. (2002). A theoretical agenda for entertainment-education. *Communication Theory, 12,* 117–135.

Singhal, A., Rogers, E. M., & Brown, W. J. (1993). Harnessing the potential of entertainment-education telenovelas. *Gazette, 51*(1), 1–18.

Slack, J. O. (1989). Contextualizing technology. In B. Dervin, L. Grossberg, B. J. O'Keefe, & E. Wartella (Eds.), *Rethinking communication: Paradigm exemplars* (pp. 329–345). Thousand Oaks, CA: Sage.

Slater, M. D., & Rouner, D. (2002). Entertainment-education and elaboration likelihood: Understanding the rocessing of narrative persuasion. *Communication Theory, 12*(2), 173–191.

Sood, S. (2002). Audience involvement and entertainment-education. *Communication Theory, 12,*(2), 153–172.

Sood, S., & Rogers, E. M. (2000). Dimensions of intense parasocial interaction by letter-writers to a popular entertainment-education soap opera in India. *Journal of Broadcasting and Electronic Media, 44*(3), 386–414.

Soul City Model of Behavior Change (2002). http://www.soulcity.org.za/

Soul City. (2001). *Soul Buddyz:* Evaluation design. *Soul City.* Retrieved July 30, 2002, from http://soulcity.org.za/Buddyz%20evaluation%20design.htm

Soul City (2001a). *Soul Buddyz* evaluation-illustrative results. *The Communication Initiative.* Retrieved July 30, 2002, from http://www.comminit.com/stbuddyzeval/sld-4657.html

Soul City (2001b). Soul City 4 evaluation: Illustrative results. *Soul City.* Retrieved July 30, 2002, from http://www.soulcity.org.za

Soul City (2001c). Soul City 4 evaluation methodology—Volume 1. *Soul City.* Retrieved July 30th, 2002, from http://www.soulcity.org.za

Sthapitanonda, P. (1995). *Entertainment-education across cultures: A study of the effects of the 'Karate Kids' AIDS film in Thailand.* (Doctoral dissertation, Ohio University, 1990). *Dissertation Abstracts AAT 9614314.*

Storey, D., Boulay, M., Karki, Y., Heckert, K., & Karmacharya, D. M. (1999). Impact of the Integrated Radio Communication Project in Nepal, 1994–1997. *Journal of Health Communication, 4,* 271–294.

Svenkerud, P., Rahoi, R., & Singhal, A. (1995). Incorporating ambiguity and archetypes in entertainment-education programming: Lessons learned from *Oshin. Gazette, 55,* 147–168.

Televisa's Institute for Communication Research (1981). *Toward the use of soap operas.* Paper presented at the International Institute of Communication, Strasbourg, France.

Thomas, R., Cahill, J., & Santilli, L. (1997). Using an interactive computer game to increase skill and self-efficacy regarding safer sex negotiation: Field test results. *Health Education and Behavior, 24*(1), 71–86.

USAID Egypt. (2002). *Alam Simsim* has unprecedented reach. USAID Egypt News. Retrieved June 5, 2002, from http://www.usaid-eg.org/detail.asp?id=54&news=1

Usdin, S., Christofides, N., Malepe, L., & Maker, A. (2000). The value of advocacy in promoting social change: Implementing the new Domestic Violence Act in South Africa. *Reproductive Health Matters, 8*(16), 55–65.

Valente, T. W., & Bharath, U. (1999). An evaluation of the use of drama to communicate HIV/AIDS information. *AIDS Education and Prevention, 11*(3), 203-211.

Valente, T. W., Kim, Y. M., Lettenmaier, C., Glass, W., & Dibba, Y. (1994). Radio promotion of family planning in The Gambia. *International Family Planning Perspectives, 20*(3), 96-100.

Valente, T. W., Poppe, P. R., Alva, M. E., De Briceno, R. V., & Cases, D. (1995). Street theater as a tool to reduce family planning misinformation. *International Quarterly of Community Health Education, 15*(3), 279-289.

Vaughan, P. W., & Rogers, E. M. (2000). A staged model of communication effects: Evidence from an entertainment-education radio soap opera in Tanzania. *Journal of Health Communication, 5*, 203-227.

Vaughan, P. W., Rogers, E. M., Singhal, A., & Swalehe, R. M. (2000). Entertainment-education and HIV/AIDS prevention: A field experiment in Tanzania. *Journal of Health Communication, 5*, 81-100.

Wallerstein, N., & Bernstein, E. (1994). Introduction to community empowerment, participatory education, and health. *Health Education Quarterly, 21*(2), 141-148.

Witte, K. (1996). Notes from the field: Does publishing in academic journals make a difference? *Journal of Health Communication, 1*, 221-226.

Yoder, P. S., Hornik, R., & Chirwa, B. C. (1996). Evaluating the program effects of a radio drama about AIDS in Zambia. *Studies in Family Planning, 27*(4), 188-204.

II

Research and
Implementation

8

No Short Cuts in Entertainment-Education: Designing *Soul City* Step-by-Step[1]

Shereen Usdin
Soul City Institute of Health and Development

Arvind Singhal
Ohio University

Thuli Shongwe, Sue Goldstein, and Agnes Shabalala
Soul City Institute of Health and Development

EDITORS' INTRODUCTION

The authors are employees of the Soul City Institute of Health and Development Communication in South Africa except for Dr. Arvind Singhal of Ohio University. Singhal served on the research advisory committee to Soul City IV, the subject of the present chapter.

"I saw it on the telly [television] and it was an eye opener.... We Black people have this tendency that when we have problems at home we hide them.... A woman who is being abused by her husband won't tell anyone.... What Soul City has done is to show us that if a woman is being abused physically and emotionally, she should report that.... And if you see someone in the street being beaten, you are not supposed to keep quiet ... Like in Soul City when Matlakala was being abused, the community kept quiet until she was

---

[1] The present chapter draws upon Usdin et al. (2000); and Singhal et al. (in press).

hurt and admitted at the hospital. . . . One nurse was angry because her hus-
band was there when Matlakala was beaten. . . . He heard when she screamed
and did nothing to help. Then the next time when the beating happened, they
started hitting tins and made lots of noise and that stopped the fight."
—A woman viewer of *Soul City IV* from Mamelodi
Township in South Africa.

In 1999, in the fourth *Soul City* entertainment-education television series (referred to hereafter as *Soul City IV*) in South Africa, a new collective behavior was modeled to portray how neighbors might intervene in a domestic violence situation. The prevailing cultural norm in South Africa was for neighbors, even if they wished to help an abused woman, not to intervene in such a situation. Wife (or partner) abuse was seen as a private matter, carried out in a private space, with curtains drawn and behind closed doors (Singhal & Rogers, 2003).

In the *Soul City IV* series, neighbors collectively decide to break the ongoing cycle of spousal abuse in a neighboring home. When the next wife-beating episode occurred, they gathered around the abuser's residence and collectively banged pots and pans, censuring the abuser's actions (Photo 8.1). This prime-time entertainment-education episode, which earned one of the highest audience ratings in South Africa in 1999, demonstrated the

PHOTO 8.1.   Neighbors collectively bang pots and pans to protest Thabang's abuse of Matlakala. (*Source*: Soul City Institute of Health and Development Communication. Used with permission.)

importance of creatively modeling collective efficacy in order to energize neighbors, who, for social and cultural reasons, felt previously inefficacious. After this episode was broadcast, pot banging to stop partner abuse was reported in several locations in South Africa. Patrons of a local pub in Thembisa Township in South Africa exhibited a variation of this practice: They collectively banged bottles in the bar when a man physically abused his girlfriend (Soul City, 2000).

The purpose of this chapter is to describe the step-by-step process of designing the *Soul City IV* domestic violence campaign, including aspects of message design, social mobilization, and advocacy. The chapter discusses in detail the formative research and design inputs for the domestic violence storyline, including the pot-banging episode in which neighbors collectively protest a wife-beating situation, modeling a novel way of breaking the cycle of domestic violence. Decisions taken about the delineation of characters, plot, and situations are discussed against the backdrop of cultural and social norms in South Africa. Finally, an assessment is provided of the impact of the *Soul City IV* campaign on domestic violence in South Africa.

Soul City: An Ongoing Multimedia Intervention in South Africa

The Soul City Institute for Health and Development Communication (or Soul City, in short) is a nongovernmental organization based in Johannesburg, South Africa. Soul City was established in 1992 to harness the power of mass media for health and development in South Africa.

South Africa faces enormous health and development challenges: An estimated 20% of South Africans (some 4.2 million people) are HIV positive. For children under five years of age, the largest single cause of death is diarrhea. Mainly a legacy of apartheid, this dismal health record existed despite a highly developed mass media system in South Africa: Some 98% of South Africans access radio, 65% access television, and over 40% access newspapers and magazines.

The bedrock of Soul City's health promotion strategy is entertainment-education (also called "edutainment"), defined as the process of purposely designing and implementing a media message to both entertain and educate, in order to increase audience members' knowledge about an issue, create favorable attitudes, shift social norms, and change the overt behavior of individuals and communities (Singhal & Rogers, 1999; Singhal & Rogers, 2002). In the realm of entertainment-education programming, Soul City pioneered several new directions, including the strategy of having an "on-going" multimedia vehicle to address high priority national health issues. Each year a series of mass media interventions are implemented, including the flagship *Soul City*, a 13-part prime-time television drama series broadcast on South Africa's most popular television channel, a 60-episode prime-time radio drama series broadcast in nine South African languages, covering all regional stations, and some 2.5 million health education booklets, designed around the popularity of the TV series' characters, which are serialized by 11 major newspapers and distributed nationally.

Each year, after the television and radio series are broadcast, several campaign activities are implemented to keep people talking about Soul City and the issues it covers. Such initiatives include the "Soul City Search for Stars" (to recruit talent for next year's television series), and the "Soul City Health Care Worker of the Year" (to recognize outstanding grassroots community workers). The ability of the Soul City Project (including its various media components) to attract advertising revenue allows an unusual opportunity to recover the costs of media production.

The first *Soul City* series (in 1994) focused on maternal and child health, and HIV prevention. The second *Soul City* series (in 1996) focused on HIV prevention, housing and land reform, and tuberculosis and tobacco control. The third *Soul City* series (in 1997) dealt with HIV prevention, alcohol abuse, energy conservation, and violence prevention. The fourth *Soul City* series (in 1999) focused primarily on violence against women, youth sexuality and AIDS, hypertension, personal finance, and small business development. While a fifth and a sixth *Soul City* series were implemented in 2001 and 2002, respectively, the present chapter focuses primarily on the fourth series.

THE FORMATIVE RESEARCH PROCESS
FOR *SOUL CITY IV*

As with all Soul City media materials, extensive formative research was conducted to design the fourth series. *Soul City IV*'s 18-month formative research process included (1) stakeholder consultations, (2) literature reviews, (3) case studies of abused women and abusers, (4) general audience research, and (5) workshops with the National Network on Violence against Women (NNVAW). *Soul City IV* extended the core edutainment vehicle to include a partnership with the NNVAW, a coalition of over 1,500 activists and community organizations in South Africa (Usdin et al., 2000).

Three members of NNVAW, Mpho Thekiso, Lisa Vetten and David Bohlale, worked closely with Soul City in developing the domestic violence series. Vetten's extensive experience in working with abused women, and Bohlale's experience as a male gender activist, brought important perspectives to the project, while Thekiso was critical in mobilizing NNVAW members. Incorporating the "male" perspective was essential to engage men in the audience, as opposed to alienating them. Mmatshilo Motsei, an outspoken survivor of domestic violence in South Africa, also worked closely with the team, providing invaluable inputs in developing the fourth series. The storyline was also extensively workshopped with a group of men (many ex-abusers) working in an organization aimed at transforming other male abusers.

Stakeholder consultations involved in-depth interviews with government and civil society officials who were involved in addressing gender-based violence in South Africa. Stakeholders were concerned that when the *Soul City IV* series motivated abused women to take action, it could place them at increased risk for harm. So the need to establish a "safety net" to assist abused women was broached. The idea to establish a toll-free telephone helpline for women experiencing domestic violence emerged from these consultations. The helpline was advertised in all campaign materials and activities.

An extensive literature review helped situate the *Soul City IV* series in a human rights framework, focusing on the rights of battered women and of their children. It highlighted the adverse impacts of domestic violence on abused women, and on the children who witnessed the violence. It noted that patriarchal attitudes endorsing gender violence were handed down intergenerationally. Male children were socialized by their fathers to believe that they were the "captains of the ship," while female children were socialized by their mothers "to endure."

The literature review revealed that while abused women showed a strong desire to seek recourse from the law, various structural barriers prevented them from seeking help, stemming from the indifference of health workers, the police, and the judiciary. So it was decided to depict the reality of police indifference and apathy to domestic violence situations while at the same time role modeling how health workers, the police, and judges should behave in handling such cases. It was clear from the formative research that the police, health workers, and magistrates needed to be trained to better handle cases of gender-based violence. Accordingly, excerpted clips from *Soul City IV* were used to develop training materials for health workers, police, and the judiciary.

The literature review highlighted the important role that society plays in perpetuating domestic violence, which is widely perceived as a "private affair." This attitude, pervasive among members of the general audience in South Africa, as well as among health workers, police, and judiciary, perpetuated widespread tolerance of domestic violence. It was decided to focus the *Soul City* series on shifting social norms away from tolerating domestic violence. Community action was the way to accomplish this goal.

The NNVAW compiled eight detailed case studies of abused women in South Africa. Further, four focus groups interviews, and four in-depth interviews were conducted with abused women. Their narratives brought realism to the storyline. Another focus group was conducted with male perpetrators. Additionally, four focus groups interviews were conducted with the general public, from both urban and rural areas.

Translating Formative Research Findings

The composite picture that emerged from this formative research process was that gender inequality lies at the heart of domestic violence. Women are expected to tolerate abuse, and men believe they have the right to discipline their partners who are "disobedient." The practice of *lobola* (or "bride price") allowed men to view their spouses as personal property and to abuse them at will. Women were expected to make their marriages work whatever the cost. Domestic violence was culturally tolerated. Women were resigned to accept domestic violence as their lot in life, as something inevitable.

The next step was to translate these formative research insights into clear message briefs for the *Soul City IV* scriptwriters, producers, and directors. A workshop was held with NNVAW members, representing all provinces of South Africa. Consensus was reached on key message issues. It was decided that the television series would be combined with an advocacy campaign to tackle structural barriers that stopped women from seeking help. The message brief was then presented, and discussed intensively in a workshop with the creative team. Mmatshilo Motsei, a survivor of gender violence, attended this workshop, and shared her poignant story. The scriptwriters were then in a workshop with Men for Change, a men's organization that works to reduce domestic violence. The organization includes several men who previously abused their partners. The creative team also watched a number of feature films on domestic violence, immersing themselves in the subject matter.

Scriptwriting

An extensive process of scriptwriting ensued. Story outlines were developed, and developed into scripts. These draft storylines were discussed by audience groups in both rural and urban South Africa. Their feedback, together with that from NNVAW members, was incorporated into new drafts of the scripts. Care was taken to ensure that domestic violence was well integrated into the drama, and that the situations resonated with the audiences' experiences.

Many alterations to the storyline were made. For example, group feedback on the early scripts indicated that Thabang, the perpetrator-protagonist of domestic violence, was portrayed as "too monstrous." Male audience members distanced themselves from Thabang's behavior, perceiving him as a "sick beast." Thabang's behavior was toned down to depict the abuser as a respected person. Also, the domestic violence storyline, initially planned for the first episode, was shifted to the fourth episode, to allow audiences to first see Thabang's "nicer" side, and also to show his family in happier times. This adjustment was important to convey the cycle of abuse in which women remain trapped: They hope that their happy times will return.

Further, in their enthusiasm to convey the intergenerational pattern of domestic violence, the scriptwriters initially created a highly dysfunctional family. Pretesting showed that audience members saw Thabang's behavior as genetically determined, rather than as the result of negative socialization. The storyline was altered to emphasize that violence usually plays out in families perceived to be "normal." NNVAW members also felt that Nonceba, a friend of Matlakala, the abused woman, was "too prescriptive," when, for example, she said: "I can't allow you to go back." Nonceba's dialogue was modified to support Matlakala to make her own decisions, as opposed to disempowering her by making decisions for her.

The creative process culminated in a rigorous translation process which brought together grassroots activists, community actors, cast members, former abusers, and members of the Soul City team to brainstorm dialogue that would resonate with intended audiences. The presence of Thuli Shongwe, a senior researcher at Soul City, was instrumental in enhancing this creative process. Shongwe grew up in Alexandra Township on the outskirts of Johannesburg, surrounded by domestic violence. She was also immersed in the formative research process and brought feeling and authenticity to the dialogues.

During the formative research, respondents often used the word *ukunyamezela* (a Zulu word meaning "to endure") to describe what society expects of women who find themselves in abusive relationships. This word denoted the deep sense of resignation and utter helplessness that characterized women's perceptions of abuse as "their lot in life." Women spoke of no choice but to endure an abusive relationship, describing it "as a cross that they must bear." These words and phrases were creatively woven into the characters' dialogues, eliciting a strong sense of audience identification. For instance, Sister Bettina, when advising Matlakala to take charge of her life, turned a popular Zulu expression, "*Uhlale phezu kwamalahle evutha*" ("You must sit on top of hot coals"), on its head to convey that "you can't sit on a hot stove, and pretend you are not burning." Dialogues were thus often taken directly from the interview transcripts, and embelished to stimulate audience reflection. For example, to challenge the commonly held belief that if a man does not beat his wife, he does not love her, Nonceba tells Matlakala: "Thabang should love you with his heart, not his fists." The use of such local colloquialisms, metaphors, and proverbs helped amplify audience engagement with the series' narrative.

The 18-month long formative research process led to the creation of the following domestic violence storyline for the *Soul City IV* series.

How Domestic Violence Showed Up on Soul City's Radar

Note: This story of how the issue of domestic violence got onto Soul City's "radar" was gleaned during an in-depth interview with Dr. Shereen Usdin, conducted by Arvind Singhal in Johannesburg in August 2002. It was during Singhal's visit to South Africa in July–August 2002 that most of the present chapter was cowritten by Usdin and Singhal, in collaboration with other colleagues at Soul City.

Often, issues and individuals intersect in unplanned ways, and through chance, circumstance, and design, new possibilities emerge. In a modest way, that is how the issue of domestic violence got onto Soul City's "radar."

Dr. Shereen Usdin, Program Manager for the *Soul City IV* series, saw first-hand the impact of domestic violence while training as a medical doctor in the mid-1980s at the Chris Hani Baragwanath Hospital in Soweto. Usdin saw hundreds of cases of battered women with black eyes, bone fractures, miscarriages, stab wounds, and gun shots. The battered women were clinically treated for their physical condition, and then sent home to confront the same dangerous conditions that put them in the hospital in the first place.

A decade later, while earning her MPH degree at Harvard University, Usdin discovered strong parallels in the work of Professor Deborah Prothrow-Stith, a medical doctor who was patching up injured gang members in inner-city neighborhoods, and discharging them back into the same violent environment they came from. When patients threaten suicide, it is considered medical negligence to discharge them back into their stressful environment. This concern prompted Prothrow-Stith to advocate for greater health sector involvement in the prevention of gang violence. For Usdin, this was a Eureka moment. Domestic violence has direct health consequences, and the health sector, as the first port of call for many battered women, has an important responsibility to intervene.

Subsequently, Usdin became an avid reader of literature on domestic violence as a public health issue. Upon return to South Africa, Usdin argued for including domestic violence as a key theme for the *Soul City IV* series.[2]

THE DOMESTIC VIOLENCE STORYLINE

Set in Soul City, a fictional Black township in South Africa, the domestic violence storyline of *Soul City IV* centers around Matlakala, a worker at Masakhane Clinic. Matlakala is married to Thabang Seriti, a respected schoolteacher in the Soul City High School. Thabang has two children from his previous marriage, Bheki and Thembi, and a little girl, Mapaseka, with Matlakala. In the first few episodes, the Seritis seem like a happy family. However, that changes, one day, when Matlakala returns home late from work, and Thabang is furious with her for neglecting family chores. The situation escalates and Thabang knocks Matlakala to the ground (Photo 8.2). The next morning, Thabang tries to make up by helping with household chores. Matlakala forgives Thabang, and the couple seems happy. Nonceba, a friend and Matlakala's coworker, sees her facial bruises and expresses concern. Matlakala tries to cover up by saying that she fell down, but Nonceba suspects that domestic violence was the cause.

---

[2]The theme of domestic violence also fulfilled Soul City's criteria for inclusion: It represented a health issue of national priority.

PHOTO 8.2. An altercation between Thabang and Matlakala which escalates into physical abuse of Matlakala. (*Source*: Soul City Institute of Health and Development Communication. Used with permission.)

Matlakala finds excuses for Thabang's violent behavior. Perhaps he is under financial pressure. One day, Thabang overhears Matlakala telling her father on the phone about the beatings. Thabang is furious: "It's between you and me, Matlakala; it is nobody else's business." Bheki and Thembi are terrified to see Thabang's rage. When Bheki tries to stop Thabang from beating Matlakala, Thabang tells Bheki the man of the house must always be "captain of the ship." Meanwhile, Thembi tells Matlakala that Thabang used to beat her mother. When Matlakala shares this information with her mother, she tells Matlakala to make her marriage work, especially as Thabang's family paid lobola ("bride price") for her.

Matlakala's life experiences a turning point when a white woman, also a victim of domestic violence, is brought to Masakhane Clinic in critical condition. Listening to her tragic story, Matlakala recognizes the strong parallels in her own life: repeated apologies in the ongoing cycle of domestic violence, and the escalation of physical violence over time. When the woman dies, Matlakala knows she could be next.

Matlakala moves into her parent's home, refusing to return until Thabang's family and her family discuss his violent behavior. She wants Thabang to promise—in front of both families—never to hurt her again. When Thabang's father learns of Matlakala's stance, he is furious. He tells Thabang that

Matlakala must be disciplined "according to tradition." A family meeting is held, in the presence of a community elder, who is also the local priest. Matlakala's father takes a strong stand against domestic violence, while Thabang's father emphasizes that cultural tradition dictates that Matlakala be subservient. The community elder challenges the Seriti family's view that culture, or tradition, condones domestic violence. He emphasizes that according to traditional culture, a man who beats his wife is a coward. Thabang apologizes, and Matlakala reluctantly agrees to return.

One day, Matlakala's friends, Ali and Vusi, while walking by the Seriti home, overhear a terrible fight. Thabang refuses to help with baby Masapeka, saying "It is not a man's job." When Matlakala disagrees, Thabang accuses her of disrespect, and beats her violently. She is hospitalized. Ali wanted to intervene but Vusi tells him that "what happens between a man and his wife is none of our business." Matlakala's neighbors, Mandla and Ivy, also overhear the violence, but do nothing. It is, after all, a "private matter."

In the hospital, Matlakala says she has been mugged, but the doctor suspects domestic violence. He tells her about local women's organizations where she can get help, and gives her the toll-free telephone number for the Stop Woman Abuse helpline. Nonceba and Sister Bettina, a nurse at the Masakhane Clinic, encourage Matlakala to seek help. Matlakala telephones the helpline and is referred to a local women's organization. Phumzile, the counselor, tells her about the new Domestic Violence Act (DVA) and how to get a Protection Order.

After being discharged from the hospital, Matlakala returns to her parents home, where an enraged Thabang confronts her. When Matlakala refuses to return home, Thabang threatens to hit her. Matlakala's father calls the police, who arrive but do nothing, saying: "It's another family dispute." Later that evening, at the local community-policing forum, Matlakala and her father confront the neighbors and the police about their inaction. The police captain is angry. He tells the gathering that the new DVA makes it incumbent upon the police to intervene in a domestic violence situation. Later, at the police station, the captain berates the errant cops for their inaction. Meanwhile, Matlakala gets a Protection Order (PO) against Thabang. To Thabang's great embarrassment, the court official serves the PO to him at school, in front of the school principal.

One day, believing that Thabang is in school, Matlakala visits Thembi and Bheki. Thabang follows Matlakala and asks her to return home. When she refuses, he starts beating her. This time, they act. They come out of their homes with pots and pans, and bang them in front of Thabang's home. By making a loud noise, they make it clear to Thabang that they disapprove of his violent behavior, and assure Matlakala that they support her. The police arrive and arrest Thabang, who is charged with breaking the court's Protection Order. Matlakala is examined by a doctor who fills in a medical form. The doctor explains that the medical form can serve as evidence in court. Matlakala goes to the police station to charge Thabang with assault. The court hears her case, and Matlakala's neighbors testify in her favor. Thabang's ex-wife, Nomsa, also testifies against Thabang's long-standing pattern of abusive behavior. Thabang is finally found guilty of assault and of violating a Protection Order.

In prison, Thabang meets Jabu, who runs a support group for abusive men. But Thabang is not interested. However, when his son, Bheki, shows signs of violent behavior, Thabang relents. In a poignant scene, when Thabang confronts his son about his errant ways, Bheki accuses Thabang of teaching him violence. This revelation represents a turning point for Thabang. In prison, he reflects upon the consequences of his abusive behavior. He seeks the help of Jabu's support group. Meanwhile, Matlakala emerges empowered from her marital ordeal. She has overcome.

Why Pot Banging?

Note: The story of how "pot banging" became the medium of protesting domestic violence in the *Soul City IV* series was also gleaned during an in-depth interview with Dr. Shereen Usdin, conducted by Arvind Singhal in Johannesburg in August 2002.

In 1995 during her MPH (Masters in Public Health) studies at Harvard, *Soul City IV* program manager, Dr. Shereen Usdin, read a World Bank Report on *Violence Against Women: The Hidden Health Burden* in which Lori Heise and others (1994) documented various community responses to domestic violence. In certain Latin American countries, neighbors banged pots and blew whistles outside the house of the abuser to indicate their disapproval, preventing further harm to the woman.

Two years later, while Usdin interviewed a battered woman in a Cape Town shelter (as part of the formative research for *Soul City IV*), the Latin American story suddenly resurfaced. Usdin heard the woman describe the moment when she walked away from her abusive relationship, closing the door of her home. She said what was most difficult for her was to say goodbye to her kitchen. She described her kitchen as a "safe place" where her husband never entered. There she could be "free" with her friends and she had some measure of control. She recalled her "gleaming pots and pans."

For Usdin, this posed a poignant question: Weren't the pots and pans that the woman recalled with pride really symbols of her oppression? If so, could these symbols of her oppression be turned into instruments of her liberation? Accordingly, in *Soul City IV*, the community's disapproval of domestic violence in their neighborhood was expressed through collective pot-banging outside the home of the abuser, protecting the woman from further harm. Pots and pans, symbols of a woman's oppression, were turned into agents of her liberation.

DECISIONS ABOUT THE CHARACTERS

The female and male protagonist, as well as other key characters in the domestic violence storyline, were chosen carefully, given that three *Soul City* series had been broadcast previously, and it was vital to maintain character consistency from one series to the next.

Selecting Matlakala as the woman protagonist involved a series of careful decisions. Various established characters in *Soul City* series I to III were considered for this role, including the well-loved Sister Bettina, the nurse at Masakane Clinic. However, she was unsuitable because her husband, Vusi, was by now established as a positive male role model. Matlakala was most suitable, as she was single in *Soul City* series I to III, which afforded an opportunity in *Soul City IV* for her to marry Thabang, a newly introduced character. Further, she was perceived by audience members as likeable, happy, and self-confident. Likeability was important to ensure that audience members would not automatically find reasons to blame her for the abuse she faced. Her state of happiness and self-confidence allowed *Soul City IV* to depict the debilitating impacts of domestic violence on a battered woman, leading to depression, plummeting self-esteem, and despair.

The turning point in Matlakala's life comes when she sees her own plight reflected in the story of the white woman dying at Masakhane Clinic. Whether the dying woman should be black or white was in itself a carefully thought-out decision. Formative research suggested that domestic violence was perceived mainly as a problem in the black community, despite strong evidence that this social ill cut across racial lines in South Africa. The initial idea for the story was to show the parallel experiences of two abused women—one black, one white. However, in order not to dilute the emotional engagement of audience members with two competing protagonists, the choice was made to primarily focus on the experience of Matlakala, a black woman.[3]

However, to ensure that audience members did not mistake the domestic violence issue as an issue confined to black women, an abused white woman was deliberately introduced in *Soul City IV*. Rushed into the Masakhane's Clinic's emergency room in critical condition after being stabbed and beaten by her violent boyfriend, she survives long enough to tell the story of her abuse. She described to Matlakala the "classic" cycle of domestic violence, from the honeymoon phase with her boyfriend, to tension build-up, to explosion and battering, to his apology, and then the start of another honeymoon period (Photo 8.3). By hearing the white woman's story, including the escalating levels of violence in her relationship—from abusive words, to fists, to sticks, to bottles—Matlakala realized what lay in store for her. Through this

---

[3]The focus on Matlakala's experience was consistent with Soul City's primary viewership in South Africa, which is predominantly black (about 90% of the total audience).

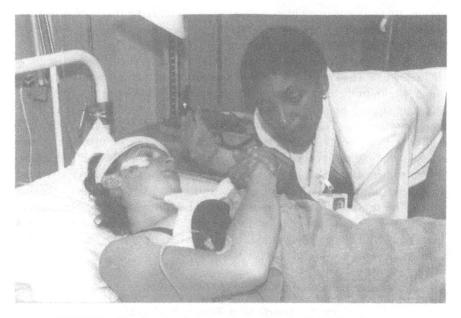

PHOTO 8.3.   Upon hearing the battered woman's story, Matlakala realizes what lies in store for her in the future. (*Source*: Soul City Institute of Health and Development Communication. Used with permission.)

encounter, Matlakala considers the possibility of leaving her long-standing abusive relationship with Thabang.

As a newly introduced character, Thabang, the male protagonist for domestic violence, was to embody the traits of an abuser as identified in formative research. Many battered women felt that their community and family members did not believe that they were being abused, and that their respected, likeable husbands were incapable of such behavior. Thabang was portrayed as a respected, middle-class teacher, who was perceived as "Mr. Nice Guy." Being middle-class was important to convey that domestic violence cuts across economic strata, and is not exclusively a behavior of the poorer socioeconomic class. Formative research pointed to the importance of Thabang being cast as a nonZulu, one of the many other cultural groups in South Africa. A prevailing stereotype is that Zulu men tend to be strong-headed, violent, and warrior-like, and therefore more likely to be wife-beaters. So he was given a seSotho (another cultural group) name: "Thabang Seriti." Thabang spoke in the seSotho language, in order to convey that abusers do not hail from any one specific cultural group.

Formative research directly influenced how Thabang's character would evolve, especially whether or not he would mend his violent ways. Discussions with a group of men, including former abusers, who conduct men-to-men outreach programs to discourage gender-based violence, highlighted reasons that motivate men to stop abuse: a brush with the law, public humiliation, the loss of a job as the result of violence, fear of arrest, fear of losing one's family, and the debilitating psycho-social impacts of violence on children.

How did *Soul City IV* incorporate these learnings in shaping Thabang's character? As Thabang's abuse of Matlakala escalated, he was humiliated publicly both in the neighborhood where he lived, and also at his workplace. The pot-banging, for instance, was consciously crafted to represent a public embarrassment for Thabang in his neighborhood. The DVA court order was also purposely served to Thabang at his workplace, in the presence of the school principal. Ultimately, Thabang was arrested, losing his job and family. What finally made Thabang turn, however, was when Bheki, his teenage son, directly attributed his violent behavior in school to what he learned from his father. The traumatic psycho-social impact on children was further emphasized in *Soul City IV* through Bheki's deteriorating school performance, and heart-rendering scenes of fear and insecurity when he and his sister, Thembi, witness Thabang's abuse of Matlakala.

Patrick Molefe Shai: Reel or Real Life?

The character of the abusive husband, Thabang Seriti, was played by the well-known South African actor, Patrick Molefe Shai. After *Soul City IV* went on the air, Shai disclosed in a radio interview that he abused his wife in real life, and that acting in the television series had been gut-wrenching for him. Encouraged by Soul City, Shai spoke out against domestic violence on the national media, and appeared in community events organized by the NNVAW to coincide with the television series' broadcast. He continues to do so.

As a celebrity, Shai painted a powerful picture of a man who had moved from being a violent husband to one who respected his wife. Here Shai described in his own words, how his "reel" and "real" life intersected:

"I have been an actor for 27 years, playing a variety of roles with distinction, and honored with four Best Actor Awards. When playing an abusive husband in the *Soul City IV* series, I experienced first-hand the pain and scars I was inflicting on my wife and children.

The events of filming that day are deeply etched in my mind. I was beating my coactress and as she screamed, her face was transformed into my wife's face. Her pleading sounded just like my wife's and the screams of the children actors became those of my children. Mixed emotions swelled inside me. The performance was too real.

I shouted 'Cut!' Then I ran outside and cried. I have never experienced so much pain while performing a character. But this was not just another performance. I had a rare opportunity to see myself in a state of anger. Only this time, I could control my anger.

What really pained me that day was the realization that inflicting violence is a choice. When I fought with my wife, bringing her pain and fear, I did not

make the right choice. I now know that violence with women is wrong. Thanks
to Soul City, today I am a crusader against domestic violence."
    Yours truly,
    For all the victims of domestic violence,
    Patrick Molefe Shai

DECISIONS ABOUT SITUATIONS

The design of *Soul City IV* involved countless decisions, based on formative
research results, about how to address cultural and social norms related to
gender socialization in South Africa. These decisions were then translated
into delineating specific situations in the *Soul City IV* storyline.

For instance, the popular Zulu saying "*umuzi ngumuzi ngomfazi*" (literally "A home is a home because of a woman") embodies the social pressure
on abused women to stay with the abuser no matter how harmful the home
may be to them. A woman is expected to endure abuse without complaint.
Religious and cultural norms dictate that "It is her duty to make the marriage
work," and coping with an abusive husband "is a cross that she must silently
bear."

The social practice of lobola, the bride price paid (in cash and/or kind)
by the groom's family to the bride's family, entraps the woman in an abusive
relationship. Lobola is perceived as conferring "ownership" of the woman by
the man and his family, exemplified by the Zulu saying "*Ingcwaba lomuntu
wesifazane lilapho endele khona*," which means "The grave of a woman is
with her in-laws." There exists no respite for a woman; she is trapped until
her death. By "owning" the woman, a man has "license" to discipline her
when she disobeys him. Also, the patriarchal mindset "*ga go poo pedi mo
Sakeng*" (a seSotho proverb meaning "Two bulls can't stay in the same *kraal*")
specifies the woman's subservient position in the home.

How were these cultural norms addressed in *Soul City IV* in the context
of Thabang's abuse of Matlakala? Frustrated by Thabang's recurring abuse,
and subsequent hollow apologies, Matlakala insists on a meeting between
both families, mediated by a community elder, a priest. Formative research
suggested that family mediation represents the first step in addressing marital
discord. The presence of the community elder represented a credible voice
that could articulate an alternative conception of culture. Combining the
role of the community elder with a priest helped in countering the negative
socializing aspects of religion.

In the conflictual family mediation, Thabang's father repeatedly blames
Matlakala's behaviors as the cause of domestic violence, accusing her of not
playing the role of a dutiful, obedient spouse, despite the payment of lobola
to her family. The respected priest challenges Thabang and his father (and

thereby the audience members) to examine the practice of lobola in another light. He explains that the purpose of lobola is to cement the relationship between the bride and groom's family, and is a way for "the groom to thank the bride's family for having given birth to the woman he loves." The dialogues and exchanges between the two families and the elder were generously laced with proverbs, metaphors, and local colloquial sayings (such as "A home is a home because of a woman") to evoke audience identification with long-standing cultural traditions, stimulating reflection on their current relevance.

During the course of the mediation meeting, Matlakala's mother undergoes a major shift in her own thinking about whether or not Matlakala should continue to "bear the burden of her cross." Prior to the meeting, she espoused the traditional line, pressuring Matlakala to *Ukunyamezela* ("endure"). As the meeting progressed, she begins to realize the injustice meted out to her daughter by Thabang's family, reconsiders her interpretation of lobola, and is convinced that prevailing cultural practices should not justify women's

PHOTO 8.4.   Intergenerational socialization of domestic violence as Thabang tells his son Bheki that a man must always be the "captain of his ship." (*Source*: Soul City Institute of Health and Development Communication. Used with permission.)

oppression. She clearly sees the harmful impact of patriarchal beliefs on Thabang, realizing the harm that she did to Matlakala by perpetuating her subservience.

This perpetuation of "harmful" intergenerational gender socialization, from father to son and mother to daughter, is carefully portrayed in an intense scene between Thabang and his son, Bheki, after Thabang violently abuses Matlakala. Distraught by the incident, a traumatized Bheki leaves the room, only to be accosted by Thabang outside their house. Thabang reprimands Bheki for crying (men don't cry), advising him that one day, when he grows up, he will understand that a man must always be "the captain of his ship" (Photo 8.4).

ADVOCACY AND SOCIAL MOBILIZATION

The *Soul City IV* series was conceived as an integrated health promotion intervention. As noted previously, formative research showed the need to address domestic violence intersectorally, including removal of structural barriers, especially the indifference of the police and judiciary, which discouraged abused women from pressing charges. In early episodes, when the police were called to attend to Thabang's violent behavior with Matlakala, they trivialized the situation: "We have far more important matters to attend to."

Soul City and the NNVAW formulated an advocacy campaign to complement the fourth television series, focusing on expediting the implementation of the Domestic Violence Act (DVA). While the law had recently been passed in South Africa, its implementation was inordinately delayed. This legislation aimed to break the barrier of police indifference by holding the police accountable for responding to domestic violence. Failure to assist abused women could lead to disciplinary action, including suspension or dismissal. So in later episodes, the indifferent police were taken to task for ignoring the tenets of the DVA.

Advocacy activities included direct lobbying of the government and media advocacy (to generate maximum coverage in the news media), combined with social mobilization in the form of community mass meetings and public marches (Usdin et al., 2000). The advocacy campaign, ran contemporaneously with the *Soul City IV* series in late 1999. Various community events were held to protest the silence on domestic violence and to pressure the government to implement the DVA. *Soul City IV* actors, including Patrick Molefe Shai, who played Thabang, actively participated in these community events. Many events coincided with the broadcast of certain highly emotional episodes, especially the one broadcast during the week of National Women's Day. Episodes were shown on huge screens at some of these mass meetings.

Numerous excuses were given by the government for tardiness in implementing the DVA. Resources were lacking to train health workers, the police, and the magistrates in the new DVA. The Soul City-NNVAW partnership assisted the South African government in raising funds to expedite police and judicial training in the DVA. NNVAW activists addressed the South African Parliament, pressuring legislators to act. Also, each episode of the *Soul City IV* series ended with a slide that announced that the DVA would be implemented shortly. This message put pressure on the government to speedily implement the act.

Designing *Soul City IV* to Facilitate Training

As noted previously, formative research identified the urgent need to train police, health workers, and magistrates in domestic violence issues, including gender sensitization, and the tenets of the new Domestic Violence Act (DVA). Training of lay counselors in domestic violence was also identified as important.

Segments of *Soul City IV* series were developed which could later be edited onto a videotape for training purposes. For example, when a battered Matlakala is in the hospital, the attending doctor role models how health workers can sensitively inquire whether or not domestic violence was involved. The scene depicted the important role that health workers, who often represent the first port of call for abused women, can play in breaking the cycle of domestic abuse. The doctor gives Matlakala the toll-free telephone number for the helpline, thus connecting her with available services.

Similarly, the story of *Soul City IV* was designed to be useful for police training. Initially, the police are portrayed as indifferent. When called to assist Matlakala, they refuse to help, and trivialize domestic violence by dismissing it as a private affair. Their police captain takes them to task, explaining that they have contravened the new Domestic Violence Act, which mandates the police to respond or face disciplinary action.

Similarly, the scene in which Matlakala visits a counselor was designed with later training in mind. In fact, the originally scripted scene was refilmed because it showed an unsympathetic counselor sitting across the desk from an abused Matlakala. The newer version was more compassionate, with both the counselor and Matlakala sitting next to each other. This scene modeled how counselors should listen to abused women in a nonjudgmental and nonprescriptive manner, and help them make appropriate decisions for themselves.

IMPACTS OF *SOUL CITY IV*

The impacts of the *Soul City IV* multimedia series and the Soul City-NNVAW partnership were independently evaluated through a variety of quantitative and qualitative methods: A before-after national sample survey, a community-based study of two sentinel sites, ethnographic observations, semistructured interviews, focus group and in-depth interviews, local and national media monitoring, document review, and secondary analysis of existing data bases.[4] This triangulated approach to data collection was designed to assess the impacts of *Soul City IV* at the level of the individual, community, and society.

Soul City IV reached an estimated 16.2 million people in South Africa through radio, television, and print, achieving a 79% penetration among its target audience, including a 62% penetration among rural audiences. The television series achieved top audience ratings (it was consistently in the top three rated television programs in South Africa), winning six coveted Avanti Awards, including the prize for South Africa's Best Television Drama.

An analysis of the quantitative data showed that those exposed to *Soul City IV* were significantly more likely to say that domestic violence is not a "private affair," and that abused women should not "put up with it," compared to those not exposed to the Soul City series (Singhal et al., in press). As a woman viewer from Umlazi Township noted: "[Soul City] has opened our eyes as women, we know now that if we are being abused we don't have to keep quiet about that. We should report it, and there are steps to follow if we want to report the abuse." Exposure to the series was also associated with shifts in audience members' subjective norms about domestic violence.

Audience members with higher levels of exposure to *Soul City IV* were more likely to recognize ill-treatment as "abuse," more likely to disclose abusive experiences, and more likely to reflect on how to stop abusive behaviors. Qualitative insights, such as the following statement from a married man in a rural area, provided additional support for such a claim:

> "Since I have started watching Soul City I have realized that I am an abuser. . . . I have tried to change and it's not that easy. . . . Because I have that picture of abuse in my mind whenever I think of doing it, I stop. It's quite tough to make that conscious decision but you have to stick to it and as time goes by it will be easy just to talk about your problem without even resorting to violence."

---

[4]Several studies were conduced of the *Soul City IV* series, which are available from the Soul City Institute of Health and Development Communication, Parkstown, South Africa. They include (1) Samuels, T., Mollentz, J., Olusanya, R., Claassens, M., Braehmenr, S., & Kimmie, Z. *An evaluation of Soul City 4*. Community Agency for Social Enquiry (CASE), October, 2000; (2) *Soul City Series 4—Qualitative impact assessment*; data collection and data processing by Social Surveys, under supervision of K. Hall and K. Daniels; Audience Reception Analysis by Esca Scheepers; and Violence Against Women analysis by Esca Scheepers and K. Daniels, October, 2000; (3) *Soul City Series 4—Qualitative impact assessment*; data collection and data processing by Social Surveys, under supervision of K. Hall and K. Daniels; analysis by Esca Scheepers, October, 2000; (4) *Impact evaluation of Soul City in partnership with the NNVAW*, researched for Soul City by Women's Health Project, N. Christofides, January, 2001; and (5) *Impact of the Soul City/NNVAW partnership on policy implementation at a provincial government level*, researched for Soul City by Strategy and Tactics, M. J. Smith, January, 2001.

An analysis of qualitative data suggested that *Soul City IV*'s audience members identified with role models in the television series (such as Matlakala), and felt empowered to address the abuse they faced in their daily lives. As one woman noted:

"I used to suffer just like Matlakala. He would come home drunk and I would be harassed, kicked out of the house.... Then one day *Soul City* came along...I liked that they were talking about woman abuse.... I called my husband in while it was still on air. He listened the first time and said nothing. The second time he asked me why are they having a program like this? I said to him it's because they know that men are abusing their wives.... I am tired of you coming home drunk and beating me, so I want you to hear for yourself what you are doing to me. I want you to listen very well so that when we go to the authorities you should remember that I have tried to make you to understand what you are doing to me. He then asked if it truly is like this, and I said yes. He thought about that for quite some time.... Then one day he came home and told me that he wanted to change. Today he talks to me freely and my child knows his father, before he did not because he knew the one who used to only fight. I really never thought it could be like this."

Quantitative data showed that the *Soul City IV* series stimulated public discussion and dialogue on domestic violence. Some 36% of the audience members talked to someone about domestic violence in the period during and shortly after exposure to the series. Overall, the research shows that the *Soul City IV* campaign can be credited with enhancing audience members' self and collective efficacy, and for creating a supportive environment for individuals and communities to take action.

Those exposed to the *Soul City IV* campaign were more likely to tell the abused person about the telephone helpline, and more willing to call the police in the event of someone being abused. Quantitative data show that *Soul City IV* influenced audience members to help other abused women, as well as to help themselves. Some 14% of the respondents said that they did something to stop domestic violence in their lives, or in the lives of someone close to them, in the period shortly after the *Soul City* series was broadcast.

Survey results showed that those exposed to the various mass media elements of the *Soul City IV* series were more willing to stand outside the house of an abuser and bang pots (Fig. 8.1). Several reports of pot or bottle banging were noted in various communities. Some 4% of the respondents said they had made a noise in public to protest against domestic violence.

Further, the Soul City-NNVAW partnership was highly effective in raising audience members' knowledge and awareness of organizations working to stop domestic violence, and in enhancing access to local support services through the telephone helpline. Some 39% of the survey respondents knew about the helpline. Among those who knew, 16% of the women and 13%

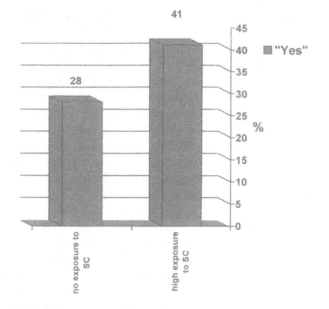

FIG. 8.1. Those exposed to the *Soul City* series were more likely to bang pots to protest domestic violence

of the men had saved the telephone number for future use. Four percent of those who knew about the helpline had called the helpline at least once.

Social mobilization at the grassroots level through the NNVAW network and the media advocacy campaign elements contributed to the implementation of the Domestic Violence Act. As a female viewer in KwaMhlanga stated: "Soul City influenced us to organize the citizen's march, emotions were high." A representative of the South African Police Service noted: "There were pressures [to implement the DVA]. . . from occasions where people held marches and stuff like that."

Soul City IV mobilized communities to take action. For example, in Mamelodi Township, close to Pretoria, a group of women protestors marched to the court where a man was on trial for battering his wife to death, and shouted "Thabang, Thabang" (the name of the wife-beater in the Soul City *IV* storyline). A few weeks previously, these women actively participated in the woman's funeral, covering her grave with soil—an activity that is usually conducted by men.

CONCLUSIONS

The *Soul City IV* series exemplifies the step-by-step process of designing, developing, and implementing an entertainment-education campaign on domestic violence, in partnership with a grassroots organization, the National Network of Violence Against Women (NNVAW). The campaign was comprehensively integrated with advocacy and social mobilization activities to influence individual, community, and social norms on domestic abuse, as well as to influence the socio-political environment through policy change.

Theoretically, the *Soul City IV* campaign highlighted the importance of modeling new sociocultural realities in entertainment-education television—as exemplified by the depiction of collective pot banging to stop domestic abuse. The campaign also emphasized the importance of modeling both self-efficacy and collective efficacy so that individuals and communities could be empowered to break the silence on domestic violence, question prevailing attitudes, and take action to change social norms.

The bedrock of the *Soul City IV* domestic violence campaign was an 18-month formative research process which included stakeholder consultations, literature reviews, case studies of abused women and abusers, target audience research, and workshops with the NNVAW. The formative research helped shaped the domestic violence storyline, including the pot-banging episode in which neighbors, who previously felt inefficacious, collectively protest a wife-beating situation, thus modeling a novel way of breaking the cycle of domestic violence.

Impact data from the 1999 *Soul City IV* campaign suggest the potential of entertainment-education programs, enhanced through formative research, social mobilization, and advocacy, to impact individual, community, and societal changes.

The impacts of *Soul City IV* continued in 2003, some three years after its broadcast. The series shifted attitudes and social norms, creating a climate less tolerant of domestic violence. The national toll-free telephone helpline, established to provide a safety net for abused women, continues to operate. The training packages continue to be used to change the attitudes and behaviors of the police, judiciary, health workers, and lay counselors. The DVA is in place and organizations within the NNVAW are currently involved in monitoring its implementation.

This chapter points to the advantages of analyzing in detail a single episode (or several related episodes) of an entertainment-education program in order to understand the rigor and the many steps involved in producing effective entertainment-education. Data gathering from both message designers and the audience of an E-E program provides a holistic understanding of how the process of message design (and its subsequent production) impacts message reception.

Finally, a key lesson from the *Soul City IV* domestic violence campaign is that in order to be effective, entertainment-education must be designed with the active involvement of those most affected.

REFERENCES

Heise, L., Pitanguy, J., & Germain, A. (1994). *Violence against women: The hidden health burden.* Discussion Paper 255. Washington DC: World Bank.

Singhal, A., & Rogers, E. M. (1999). *Entertainment-education: A communication strategy for social change.* Mahwah, NJ: Lawrence Erlbaum Associates.

Singhal, A., & Rogers, E. M. (2002). A theoretical agenda for entertainment-education. *Communication Theory, 12*(2), 117–135.

Singhal, A., & Rogers, E. M. (2003). *Combating AIDS: Communication strategies in action.* Thousand Oaks: Sage.

Singhal, A., Usdin, S., Scheepers, E., Goldstein, S., and Japhet, G. (in press). Harnessing the entertainment-education strategy in Africa: The Soul City intervention in South Africa. In Charles Okigbo (Ed.), *Development and communication in Africa.* Boston, MA: Rowman and Littlefield.

Soul City (2000, September). *The evaluation of Soul City 4: Methodology and top-line results.* Paper presented at the Third International Entertainment-Education Conference for Social Change, Arnhem, The Netherlands.

Usdin, S., Christofides, N., Malepe, L, & Maker, A. (2000). The value of advocacy in promoting social change: Implementing the new Domestic Violence Act in South Africa. *Reproductive Health Matters, 8*(16), 55–64.

9

Organizing a Comprehensive National Plan for Entertainment-Education in Ethiopia

William N. Ryerson
Population Media Center

Negussie Teffera
Population Media Center-Ethiopia

EDITORS' INTRODUCTION

William Ryerson has a 32-year history of work in reproductive health, including 17 years of experience adapting the Sabido methodology for entertainment-education communication to various cultural settings. Previously, as Executive Vice President of Population Communications International, Ryerson designed and implemented projects in a number of countries, including Tanzania, China, Brazil, and India. Here, with his colleague, Dr. Negussie Teffera, he discusses the organization of an Ethiopian E-E campaign.

Plans for the wedding and reception have moved forward, and invitations have been sent out based on the assurance of the leading shop owner that he will supply all of the food needed for several hundred guests. But Zinabu, the truck driver bringing those supplies, is now a day late. He invited the known drug dealer, Damite, to come with him on this trip. Where are they? A phone call hints that there's been some terrible tragedy on the highway.

Meanwhile, Wubalem is fighting a death sentence imposed by the court. Her lawyer explained that she acted in self-defense when she hit the homeowner of the house where she was a maid with a bottle, killing him, as he attempted to rape her. Will her sentence be commuted? If you speak Amharic and live in Ethiopia, stay tuned and you will find out.

In the meantime, the Oromiffa-speaking population of Ethiopia is listening to the exploits of Abba Bullo, a man in the rural village of Ganda Oda, who has two wives and a mistress, plus eight children. He sees his eight children solely as his property, to do with as he wishes, and he wants to have more. But his wife, Kume, defied him, and sent one of his daughters to school. Now the daughter is late in coming home. He knew that educating his daughters was a bad idea, and he is furious with both his wife and his missing daughter. How will he react when he finds out that two men hidden along the road abducted his daughter? Will he attempt to rescue his daughter, or let the men keep her? In his region of Ethiopia, 80% of marriages take place through abduction.

The drama in these and other characters' lives keep millions of Ethiopian audience members coming back week after week to find out what happens next. Certain key characters will evolve into positive role models for a wide range of social and health issues that affect the status of women and the reproductive health of the population of Ethiopia.

Combined with traveling stage plays, videos, writing contests for poetry and short stories, and the training of journalists, the Population Media Center in Ethiopia is pursuing its "Whole Society Strategy" to maximize attitudinal and behavioral changes among the population regarding the goals set by the Ethiopian government for family planning, AIDS prevention, and related issues.

THE WHOLE SOCIETY STRATEGY

Because of strong evidence of their effectiveness, social-content dramas are a centerpiece of the strategy for behavior change in many countries. Nevertheless, changes in such taboo and tradition-bound issues as sexuality do not occur rapidly. One advantage of using entertainment-education dramas, as opposed to documentaries or single–episodes dramas, is that they allow time for an audience to form emotional bonds with the characters, and allow characters to evolve in their behavior with regard to educational issues.

The Whole Society Strategy involves using several media formats to send mutually reinforcing messages that deal with deeply held beliefs about women's roles, about the desirability of children, about relations between men and women, and about taboos. Whether it is male dominance in romance and sex, or the desirability of sons, or the blessing of children, the messages are carried and reinforced in a range of media, from comic books to radio to religious sermons to television news to movies. Key elements of the Whole Society Strategy include: (1) segmentation research to identify audience segments and the media formats consumed by each; (2) research to identify media formats that can leverage other media to stimulate cross-segment reinforcement; (3) multiple media formats to address critical cohorts; (4) ongoing research to fine-tune campaign operations; and (5) collaboration with government and NGO activities through partnerships.

Population Media Center (PMC) focused efforts in Ethiopia on the Miguel Sabido methodology of entertainment-education broadcast dramas, which has been found to have strong behavioral change effects in other countries, such as Kenya, Tanzania, and India (Singhal & Rogers, 1999; Rogers, Vaughan, Swalehe, Rao, Svenkerud, & Sood, 1999; Vaughan, Rogers, Singhal, & Swalehe, 2000).

ETHIOPIA

With a population of 69 million, Ethiopia is the third most populous country in Africa. Ethiopia's annual population growth rate of more than 3% and a total fertility rate of more than 6 children per woman (Central Statistical Authority, 2000) are recognized as an obstacle to fulfilling national development goals. The infant mortality rate of 110 per 1,000 live births and maternal mortality of 1000 per 100,000 live births are among the highest in the world (Ministry of Health, 1998). Ethiopia is a high priority area for population programs and reproductive health services. The government adopted an explicit population policy with the aim of decreasing the total fertility rate of six children per women to four by increasing the contraceptive prevalence rate from the current 8% to 44% by the year 2015 (National Office of Population, 1993).

Ethiopia is a complex society with a long, turbulent history of intergroup relations and exchange. Most people in Ethiopia are either Christians or Moslems, and these religions cross ethnic boundaries. Although the main dialects are Amharic, Oromiffa, and Tigrigna, there are at least 76 other dialects spoken in the country (Ethiopian Science and Technology Commission, 1985).

Ethiopia is one of the poorest countries of the world, with (1) a per capita income of US $120 in 1998; (2) a life expectancy of 48 years for males and 51 years for females, with falling life expectancy by 2005 because of AIDS-related deaths; (3) an illiteracy rate of 62% (males) and 77% (females) (the highest in Africa); (4) a net enrollment in primary education of only 30% of school-aged children; and (5) an estimated three million individuals infected with the HIV virus and an HIV/AIDS seroprevalence of rate 7.3% among the adult population (Central Statistical Authority, 2000; Sisay, 2001; Population Media Center, 2001a; 2001b).

The ethnic cultures of Ethiopia are interwoven with myths, superstitions, and conceptions of humankind, including its psychic and sexual life, that sometimes contradict basic findings of science. Women and children suffer the effects of harmful traditional practices, such as nutritional taboos, genital mutilation, and early marriage or marriage by abduction (National Committee on Traditional Practices of Ethiopia, 1998; Ethiopian Science and Technology Commission, 1985).

Women's health in Ethiopia is undermined by a combination of social, cultural, and economic factors that determine their low status in society. Early marriage is one of the causes of low female participation in modern sector employment (National Committee on Traditional Practices of Ethiopia, 1998; Seyoum, 1990; Seyoum & Tesfaye, 1996). In rural areas, and to a lesser extent in urban settings, traditional value systems have imposed, and continue to impose, unbearable burdens on Ethiopian women. In Ethiopia, awareness of family planning is around 80%, but its practice is less than 10%. Millions of women of fertile age are not using a family planning method even though they do not wish to get pregnant. Half say they intend to use a family planning method sometime soon (Central Statistical Authority, 2000; National Office of Population, 2000; Ministry of Health and National Office of Population, 2000; Johns Hopkins University and National Office of Population, 2001; Packard Foundation, 2000 & 2001).

GETTING STARTED

In Ethiopia, as in much of Africa, broadcasting is essentially controlled by the government. The vast majority of radio listeners and television viewers are exposed to government broadcasting stations. In September 1999, Tom Kazungu, an entertainment-education expert from Kenya, David Poindexter, former President of Population Communications International, and Bill Ryerson, President of PMC, visited Addis Ababa for discussions with government officials regarding a possible project. David Poindexter previously knew Dr. Negussie Teffera, then the director of the government's National Office of Population. As the person responsible for developing Ethiopia's population policy and overseeing its implementation, Negussie advised on how to proceed in implementing a communication intervention for Ethiopia.

The Population Media Center team identified key issues for a potential project in Ethiopia, which included reducing ideal family size, increasing the ideal age of marriage and childbearing, enhancing understanding of the relative safety of contraceptives compared to early and repeated childbearing, overcoming fears of infidelity resulting from family planning use, increasing belief in the appropriateness of determining the number of one's children, enhancing public acceptance of employment for women outside the home, promoting education for girls, and promoting gender equity and elevation of female status.

During the initial visit and in two subsequent visits in 2000, PMC representatives met with the Ministry of Health, the HIV/AIDS Council Secretariat, the UN Population Fund, the World Health Organization, UNICEF, UNAIDS, the Family Guidance Association of Ethiopia, the Organization for Social Services for AIDS, USAID, the Norwegian Embassy, the Swedish Embassy, the David and Lucile Packard Foundation, the World Bank, and a number of private business leaders and reproductive health researchers. The Ethiopia project described in this chapter grew out of these discussions.

IMPLEMENTING THE
ENTERTAINMENT-EDUCATION STRATEGY

Radio Ethiopia is the only nationwide broadcaster that reaches a majority of the population. Television only reaches 4% of the population in this poor country (Negussie, 1990; Population Media Center, 2000b). In Ethiopia, we started with the idea of applying the Sabido methodology of long-running entertainment-education melodramas, which sparked initial interest by many stakeholders. The writing and production of the Amharic and Oromiffa-language serials began in early 2002. Save the Children-U.S. contracted with Population Media Center to create a spin-off, 24-episode melodrama on cassettes, using characters who would be of particular interest to truck drivers and to commercial sex workers, with particular focus on preventing the further transmission of HIV/AIDS. The cassettes are distributed to truck drivers as they travel between the port in Djibouti and Addis Ababa. Truck drivers play a particularly key role in HIV/AIDS transmission in Africa.

PMC also formed a partnership with CARE–Ethiopia that provided support for the Oromiffa-language radio serial, while helping to promote reproductive health services of CARE in Oromia. Other spin-offs of the broadcast soap opera are possible, including comic books featuring the key characters, training cassettes for health care workers using clips from episodes in which characters who are health care providers are involved, as well as derivative products that may reinforce popularity of the program, such as dolls, caps, and T-shirts. PMC submitted a proposal to fund a multimedia arts program, which was funded by the David and Lucile Packard Foundation, in which creative artists produce various art forms about population-related issues in Ethiopia.

For budgetary reasons, Population Media Center decided to limit the Oromiffa language program to one episode per week (with a repeat broadcast), plus the two episodes per week in Amharic. Population Media Center approached possible donors, arguing that short-term, inexpensive projects would not likely cause the attitudinal and behavioral effects regarding reproductive health that were desired. We used evidence gathered in the 1993–1997 Tanzania project to show that a long-term strategy can yield important behavior change effects (Rogers, Vaughan, Swalehe, Rao, Svenkerud, & Sood, 1999; Vaughan et al., 2000). Before PMC's first visit to Ethiopia in 1999, we identified foundations, like the David and Lucile Packard Foundation, that had indicated that Ethiopia was a priority country. We met with the staff of the Packard Foundation's population department to discuss their possible interest in the Ethiopia project. During our initial visit to Ethiopia, we met with various funders that were identified by our country host as possible supporters, and from them we identified still more prospective funders.

During our initial country visit in 1999, we learned that Dr. Negussie was planning for early retirement from government service. We asked him to lead the project in Ethiopia, and he agreed, starting in early 2000. PMC informed the Packard Foundation and other donors operating in Ethiopia that the project would be in competent hands. The Packard Foundation responded with a three-year grant in April, 2000, and PMC undertook the process of registration with the government. The early commitment by the Packard Foundation assured potential donors that PMC's project in Ethiopia was likely to succeed. Indeed, Albert Bandura's social learning theory (see Chapter 5) applies to philanthropic behavior, as it does to other activities. Role modeling by prestigious donors is important in convincing others to jump on the bandwagon.

Full-time program coordinators with radio broadcasting experience in theatrical arts and scriptwriters with a specialization in population and HIV/AIDS were recruited through newspaper advertisements. A full-time researcher with a master's degree from the London School of Hygiene and a background in medical demography was also employed, in addition to eight scriptwriters for the Amharic radio program and six scriptwriters for the Oromiffa radio program.

PLANNING WORKSHOPS

The Ethiopia Project was designed to support the national efforts (1) to fight the HIV/AIDS epidemic, and (2) to promote family planning adoption. In 2000, PMC held two workshops to plan the proposed radio dramas. The first workshop, for senior program producers, writers, researchers, and media managers, raised participants' awareness of how a research-based entertainment-education program could bring about behavioral changes in reproductive health, including HIV/AIDS avoidance. The principles of behavior change communication and the methodology for formative research were discussed. A second workshop for stakeholders focused on the effectiveness of research-based media programs using the entertainment-education strategy. Participants included government and non-governmental organizations involved in

IEC activities and professionals in theatre arts and media communication (Population Media Center, 2000a).

An Advisory Committee was selected to provide guidance to the project and to ensure coordination with health service providers. A Technical Committee was chosen to review each script for medical and health accuracy.

FORMATIVE RESEARCH

Formative research was used to design the Ethiopia Project by (1) defining the target audiences, (2) understanding the knowledge, attitudes and practices of the target audiences, and (3) ensuring that the issues were dealt with in a culturally relevant and appropriate manner. The primary audience for the formative research findings was the creative team of writers and producers of the radio programs (Population Media Center, 2000b).

The audience must be able to identify with the media characters. They should say, "I know that character; he or she is just like my neighbor." The circumstances of the characters must also seem familiar to audience members, who should be able to say, "That happened to my brother."

The values to be emphasized directly stemmed from the national constitution, laws, and policies of the country, including the United Nations agreements to which the country is a signatory. For example, Ethiopia guarantees the right of all people to be educated. However, formative research indicated that many girls have been denied an education. Therefore, two values were consistently emphasized in the radio programs: (1) the positive value that "It is good to educate your daughters," and (2) the negative value "It is bad to not educate your daughters."

Five discrete methods were used to carry out the formative research in Ethiopia:

1.   Interviews with experts in the fields of (a) family planning; (b) sexually transmitted diseases; (c) status of women; (d) culture; and (e) environment.

2.   A literature review of all relevant studies, which led to a report that was understandable by the nontechnically trained creative team.

3.   Some 34 focus group discussions were conducted by a local agency, Birhan Research (Photo 9.1). Excerpts from the discussions were useful in writing the scripts, and the audiotapes were useful for the writers and producers to get a sense of how individuals sound when they talk about certain subjects.

4.   A total of 1,020 personal interviews were conducted with a sample of people from different regions, urban and rural, and men and women of different ages and marital status. This included issues related to the influence of the culture on sexual and reproductive decision-making, feelings of self-efficacy with regard to these issues, insight into the interpersonal dynamics

PHOTO 9.1.   Focus group research for the E-E radio serial, *Dhimbiba*, being conducted in Ethiopia by Birhan Research for the Population Media Center. (*Source*: Population Media Center.)

of married couples, and other issues. A research agency was commissioned to design the interview questionnaire, using examples from other countries as a starting point and adapting them to the specific cultures of Ethiopia.

5.   The producers and writers visited rural villages in order to get a sense of what life is like in those settings, to record village sounds, to learn what topics people discuss, and to obtain a sense of what the clinics and other health/social services are like. The Ethiopia project also gathered Ethiopian proverbs that reflect negative attitudes towards women and children, which are used by scriptwriters as a source of material in the E-E dramas.

TRAINING WORKSHOPS

Training was provided to the production and writing team both at home and abroad. Two radio producers were sent to Kenya for a two-week training course in studio management and production techniques. In 2001–2002, five weeks of training was provided for playwrights and scriptwriters in Ethiopia to acquaint them with the Sabido methodology for entertainment-education. Trainers included Miguel Sabido; Tom Kazungu, the first person in Africa and the first person in radio to use the Sabido methodology in a radio program that he produced in Kenya; Rose Haji, the producer of the Tanzanian radio drama that was studied for its effects on family planning use and AIDS avoidance in the 1990s; Ramadhan Swalehe, who led the research center in Tanzania that gathered the survey data; Virginia Carter, former head of drama for Norman Lear's "All in the Family," "Maude," and "The Jeffersons"; and David Poindexter, a 30-year veteran of promoting entertainment-education programs worldwide.

PRODUCTION OF THE ENTERTAINMENT-EDUCATION RADIO DRAMAS

The soap opera design used in the Ethiopia project is similar to the design used for entertainment-education radio dramas in Kenya and Tanzania. These differed from Miguel Sabido's television dramas which focused on one educational issue. African soap operas blend several related issues into one serial drama. In Africa, it is difficult to address the adoption of family planning or HIVAIDS prevention without simultaneously addressing the status of women. In each country where Sabido's E-E methodology is applied, his model is adapted to the cultural setting of that country.

OBJECTIVES

Three specific objectives were to be pursued in the Ethiopia project. First, we intended to change behavior among the target audience regarding HIV/AIDS and use of family planning through the production of research-based radio E-E dramas and other communication activities. Second, we sought to enhance the creativity and communication skills of the writers and media practitioners in order to enable them to address reproductive health and HIV/AIDS issues effectively. Third, we conducted media communication and audience research activities for effective selection and use of media channels.

The Ethiopia project's programs are based on Miguel Sabido's E-E methodology, and are broadcast in two major Ethiopian languages (Amharic and Oromiffa). The target population in Amhara, Oromia, and Addis Ababa Regions comprises nearly 75% of the Ethiopian population.

The Ethiopia Project will (1) produce 312 serial drama episodes in Amharic and transmit them over Radio Ethiopia twice a week, and repeat them on FM radio, (2) produce 156 serial drama episodes in Oromiffa and transmit them over Radio Ethiopia once a week, with a repeat on another day on Radio Ehiopia, (3) produce 24 episodes of an Amharic audio serial drama targeting long-distance truck drivers and sex workers along the Addis Ababa-Djibouti travel corridor (Photo 9.2).

Stage Dramas

In Ethiopia, mobile stage dramas reach millions of people in indoor and outdoor settings, such as schools, colleges, churches, stadiums, and market places. Two stage dramas were produced in the first year of the project, based on the best selected scripts. Stage dramas are inexpensive and are seen as credible by the traditional elements of society. They can attract attention and stimulate thinking if situations are effectively dramatized. Stage dramas were

PHOTO 9.2.   Abdulnasser Hajihassen, producer of the Oromiffa language E-E
radio soap opera, recording an episode of *Dhimbiba* in a studio in Addis Ababa.
(*Source*: Population Media Center.)

instrumental in bringing about desired changes in audience behavior concerning reproductive health and HIV/AIDS issues (Singhal & Rogers, 2003).
The stage dramas reinforce the radio messages.

Video Production

The Ethiopia project includes a plan for the production of two video documentaries focusing on population, reproductive health, and HIV/AIDS. Some
250 copies of each will be distributed to schools, anti-AIDS clubs, colleges,
training centers, and workshops.

Poems and Short Stories

Poems and short stories are popular and much loved by Ethiopians. Poems
greatly contributed to the life of Ethiopians. It is common to listen to impressive and instantly created poem recitals in public places. In 2003, the project
held poem and short story writing contests, and the winning poems and short
stories were recited over radio and television and in public meeting places and
schools. They were also printed in daily newspapers and in selected monthly
magazines. The plan is to organize a second poetry and short story contest at
the national level, focusing on HIV/AIDS and reproductive health.

Capacity Building Through Training

An assessment of social-content media and theatrical activities in Ethiopia
showed that most media practitioners, playwrights, and artists needed training both in their professional fields and in reproductive health (Population

Media Center, 2000b; Negussie, 1988; National Office of Population, 2000; Colle & Ostman, 1998). In 2003, potential trainees (experts in media and theatrical arts, journalists, amateur and professional artists) from Amhara, Oromia, and Addis Ababa Regions were invited to participate. Two workshops of ten days each were organized, and action plans for future activities were developed. With some technical support, the newly trained journalists, playwrights, and artists will design similar programs in their respective areas for achieving specific reproductive health behavior goals. In total, the project provides training for 30 media practitioners in basic communication skills and reproductive health and HIV/AIDS issues. It will also train 30 drama scriptwriters and producers of serial drama production, using the entertainment-education strategy.

Launching the Serial Dramas

Launching the radio dramas included a colorful ceremony in mid-2002, which was attended by ministers and other high-ranking officials, and representatives of government and nongovernmental organizations. Special T-shirts and leaflets that displayed the titles of the serial dramas were distributed to participants. The title of the Amharic drama is *Yeken Kignit* (Looking Over One's Daily Life) and that of the Oromiffa drama is *Dhimbiba* (Getting the Best Out of Life). The Amharic program is broadcast Sunday evenings at 8:30 p.m. and Wednesday evenings at 9:15 p.m. on Radio Ethiopia. The Amharic program is repeated on FM radio on Mondays and Thursdays at 3:00 p.m. The Oromiffa program is broadcast on Sundays at 6:30 p.m. on Radio Ethiopia and repeated on Wednesdays.

Working With Save the Children USA

At the request of Save the Children USA, PMC is presently working on an audio cassette serial drama for addressing HIV/AIDS issues along the Addis Ababa-Djibouti corridor. The target audience is over 10,000 truck drivers and their assistants and commercial sex workers working in the corridor. A rapid assessment was conducted, and the results were used by the scriptwriters, who personally observed all the focus group discussions. In 2003, PMC produced 24 half-hour episodes and distributed the cassettes to truck drivers and to commercial sex workers. Additional episodes are being developed.

Working With UNDP

At the request of the UN Development Program (UNDP) office in Ethiopia, PMC provided advice on various aspects of HIV/AIDS prevention communication. PMC also assisted in organizing a workshop, "Media Coalition for

Fighting HIV/AIDS in Ethiopia." PMC and UNDP have also agreed that PMC will conduct both media research and HIV/AIDS prevention communication training.

Working With IPAS Ethiopia

PMC has also been asked by the IPAS Ethiopia office to assist in producing a video, poster, and flyer on aspects of unsafe abortion and unwanted pregnancy in Ethiopia. A memorandum of understanding has been signed, and work is in progress.

Working With the World Bank

PMC assisted the World Bank group working with the National HIV/AIDS Council Secretariat in developing an HIV/AIDS prevention communication and advocacy strategy plan. In addition, PMC, in collaboration with other governmental, nongovernmental, and UN agencies, developed criteria for the selection of HIV/AIDS-related communication projects.

MONITORING AND EVALUATION

The Ethiopia project developed a comprehensive monitoring and evaluation system as an integral part of the project design. The plan consists of different activities that can be implemented in collaboration with concerned agencies. Evaluation of listening groups, listeners' letters, script analyses, and data on client numbers is conducted on an ongoing basis. Focus group discussions are conducted quarterly. Large-scale surveys are analyzed pre- and post-broadcast.

The Ethiopia project formed listening groups of households of the Amharic and Oromiffa speaking population to monitor listener perceptions of the radio serial dramas. These listening groups comment on each radio episode in order to enable project managers to assess audience reactions and provide feedback to the scriptwriters. Sample listener letters are chosen randomly from over 200 received daily in order to gauge audience reactions. Audience concerns will be continuously included in the story line.

Focus group discussions are conducted quarterly throughout the radio dramas' broadcast period in order to monitor listeners' responses. Focus group guides were developed to ask about listeners' perceptions of characters, story lines, and educational issues.

Isolating the Effects From Other Activities

The principal source about the radio programs' effects are pre- and post-intervention surveys that are conducted by personal interviews. A preintervention survey was conducted in May 2002. A postintervention survey will be conducted at the end of the broadcast period with a representative sample of the sexually active population.

Data on Client Numbers

In addition to the pre- and post-broadcast surveys of listeners and nonlisteners, PMC asked 48 health service agencies to participate in gathering information on why people seek reproductive health services. Data include the number of clients seeking services before, during, and after the radio dramas are broadcast. Open-ended questions are asked as to why individuals seek health service, and whether a client listened to one of the radio serial dramas. Statistical analyses will be conducted by Earl Babbie and Nancy Luke, sociologists with expertise in evaluation research. The formative research and prepost surveys are overseen by Dr. Assefa Hailemariam of Birhan Research, in Addis Ababa. The initial data shows, as of June 2003, 35% of new clients seeking reproductive health services have heard one or both of PMC's radio serial dramas.

LESSONS LEARNED

1. The Ethiopia Project uses both formative and summative research to ensure that this entertainment-education intervention is culturally appropriate, to ensure that the enthusiasm for the project by donors and stakeholders is fulfilled, and to determine the effectiveness of the Sabido entertainment-education methodology in changing attitudes and behavior.

2. All relevant leaders in the host country for an E-E project should be involved early and consistently in the process of conceiving, designing, implementing, and evaluating an E-E intervention.

3. The expertise of the research team helps ensure that the evaluation strategy meets internationally recognized standards for scholarly research on program effectiveness.

Thus the Ethiopia project represents a combination of outsiders and insiders to the system, building on the unique contributions of each.

REFERENCES

Central Statistical Authority (2000). *Ethiopia demographic and health survey*. Addis Ababa.
Colle, R. D., & Ostman, R. E. (Eds.) (1998). *Information, education, and communication in reproductive health for Ethiopia*. Ithaca, New York: Cornell University, Department of Communication, in collaboration with the National Office of Population and UNFPA, Addis Ababa.

Ethiopian Science and Technology Commission (ESTC) (1985). *Pilot study on some of the origins and sources of traditional religions and scientific beliefs and practices of some Ethiopian nationalities.* Addis Ababa: Ethiopian Science and Technology Commission.

Johns Hopkins University Center for Communication Programs and National Office of Population (JHU & NOP) (2001). *Ethiopia reproductive health communication project: Family planning and HIV/AIDS prevention formative and baseline study.* Baltimore, MD: Johns Hopkins University, Center for Communication Programs.

Ministry of Health (1998). *Reproductive health needs assessment report.* Addis Ababa.

Ministry of Health and National Office of Population (MOH & NOP) (2000). *Rapid assessment on knowledge, attitude and practices related to reproductive health in Ethiopia.* Addis Ababa.

National Committee on Traditional Practices of Ethiopia (NCTPE) (1998). *Baseline survey on harmful traditional practices in Ethiopia.* Addis Ababa.

National Office of Population (NOP) (1993). National population policy of Ethiopia. Addis Ababa: Office of the Prime Minister.

National Office of Population (NOP) (2000). *National population information, education, and communication and advocacy strategy (2000-2005).* Addis Ababa.

Negussie, T. (1988). *The role of mass communications in social and economic development in some developing countries: The case of Ethiopia.* Unpublished Ph.D. Thesis, Cardiff, Wales: University of Wales.

Negussie, T. (1990). Population information, education, and communication activities in Ethiopia: A short survey. *Population and Development Bulletin, 1*(2), 49-61.

Packard Foundation (2000). *Reproductive health/family planning and HIV/AIDS: Knowledge, attitude, behavior, and services in three zones in the Amhara Regional State.* Addis Ababa.

Packard Foundation (2001). *A study of reproductive health issues and knowledge, attitude and practice of family planning methods, Oromia Regional State, Ethiopia.* Addis Ababa.

Population Media Center (2000a). *Proceedings of the stakeholders' workshop on the role of the media entertainment-education strategies for addressing population and HIV/AIDS issues in Ethiopia.* Addis Ababa.

Population Media Center (2000b). *Summary report on the assessment of radio and TV entertainment-education programs in Ethiopia.* Addis Ababa.

Population Media Center (2001a). *Findings from the literature review on POP/IEC and RH/FP issues including HIV/AIDS in Ethiopia.* Addis Ababa.

Population Media Center (2001b). *Findings of formative research to develop a radio serial drama for HIV/AIDS prevention and RH/FP services utilization.* Addis Ababa.

Rogers, E. M., Vaughan, P. W., Swalehe, R. M., Rao, N., Svenkerud, P., & Sood, S. (1999). Effects of an entertainment-education radio soap opera on family planning behavior in Tanzania. *Studies in Family Planning, 30,* 193-211.

Seyoum G. S. (1990). Social structure and fertility in Addis Ababa. *Population and Development Bulletin, 1*(2), 18-32.

Seyoum, G. S., & Tesfaye, A. (1996). *The social and cultural correlates of family planning and fertility related behavior in Ethiopia.* Addis Ababa: National Office of Population.

Singhal, A., & Rogers, E. M. (1999). *Entertainment-education: A communication strategy for social change.* Mahwah, NJ: Lawrence Erlbaum Associates.

Singhal, A., & Rogers, E. M. (2003). *Combating AIDS: Communication strategies in action.* Thousand Oaks, CA: Sage.

Sisay, W., (2001). The demographic dimensions of poverty. *Population and Development, 7*(1), 12-18.

Vaughan, P. W., Rogers, E. M., Singhal, A., & Swalehe, R. M. (2000). Entertainment-education and HIV/AIDS prevention: A field experiment in Tanzania. *Journal of Health Communication, 5,* 81-100.

10

Evolution of an E-E
Research Agenda

Bradley S. Greenberg
Michigan State University

Charles T. Salmon
Michigan State University

Dhaval Patel
UNICEF, New York

Vicki Beck
*University of Southern
California*

Galen Cole
*Centers for Disease Control
and Prevention*

A lead character on a TV series particularly popular with adult males was diagnosed with prostate cancer. For 12 episodes, that storyline on *NYPD Blue* was blended among the series' typical stories. The character progressed through symptoms, diagnosis, prognosis, surgery, complications, and recovery. Viewers could learn about PSA testing, incontinence, pain, erectile dystunction, and the value of talking with others. Because social researchers were not involved in the development of that storyline, however, an opportunity for concurrent entertainment-education (E-E) research was lost.

Entertainment-education has emerged and is recognized as a major tool for social change throughout the world. Personnel resources, line-item budget allocations, and mission statements have been committed to E-E by dozens of domestic organizations with dedicated public service objectives. An E-E program was established at the Centers for Disease Control and Prevention (CDC) in 1998, based partly on the recommendations of an expert panel of communication scholars and media industry executives convened four years earlier (Salmon, 1994). Recent activities include programmatic efforts by the CDC to suggest and counsel on crosscutting public health topics for storylines in daytime television soap operas and primetime dramas (Beck, 2000). Similar efforts have been made by the White House Office of National Drug Control

Policy to influence drug storylines in primetime television series (Schlosser, 1998) and by the Kaiser Family Foundation to promote and study health messages aired on popular television shows (Brodie et al. 2001). In 1998 the White House launched a major antidrug campaign with E-E components. In 2001 Congress funded CDC to develop a media campaign with E-E components targeted at the physical activity and nutrition of young people.

While support for E-E activities is growing in the United States, the commitment in international venues has been much more intensive. The potential social outcomes of media messages designed to impact family planning, gender discrimination, adult literacy, and child welfare behaviors have been examined in some 200 E-E campaigns in over 50 countries (Bouman,1999; Singhal & Brown, 1997; see Piotrow and de Fossard's chapter in the present volume).

The premise for these efforts is that receivers will benefit because they learn a new idea, think differently about some idea, or behave differently as a result of their exposure, especially because the message was embedded in an entertaining context. To that end, organizations engaged in E-E activities are pointed to the direct and/or indirect influence of media content designed to reach targeted audiences with specific messages. The two primary means for doing so are either by self-creation and distribution of that content, as is most common in international E-E efforts, or by attempts to influence others who are responsible for that creation and distribution, the most common U.S. approach. The latter efforts put considerable pressure on media professionals to distinguish more legitimate requests for inclusion from less legitimate, typically more commercial attempts at seeking limited media time and space.

Within this framework for E-E, there has been little domestic research that focuses on E-E outcomes, and few attempts at a comprehensive research agenda. This chapter identifies issues that are fundamental in advancing theory and research on E-E and presents recommendations from an expert panel convened in May 2000 to establish an E-E research agenda for the CDC. We explore four interrelated, building-block questions:

1. What are the parameters of E-E?
2. What fundamental conceptual and strategic issues should be studied?
3. How should E-E evaluation efforts proceed?
4. What is a reasonable research agenda for E-E?

THE PARAMETERS OF E-E

The parameters of E-E appear rather limitless, which no doubt constitutes a tribute to the considerable potential of this communication strategy. But it also creates a particular challenge for social scientists of communication behavior.

Just within the considerable set of U.S. E-E activities and programs, on which this chapter focuses, one can find reference to such disparate elements as:

1. A brief reference to a morning-after drug in a prime-time television series (Brodie et al., 2001).
2. Background posters hanging on the walls of sets for television sit-coms and dramas, touting the Designated Driver concept (Winsten, 1994).
3. An assortment of prenatal care messages in a daytime soap opera (Greenberg & Busselle, 1996).
4. A systematic portrayal, over a period of several months, of a character dying of cancer (Sharf & Freimuth, 1993; Sharf, Freimuth, Greenspon, & Plotnick, 1996).
5. An entire television series, *Sesame Street*, that was broadcast for many years (Cook et al., 1975).

The cornucopia of what is defined as E-E reflects different media, different genres within media, different message lengths and strategies, different production techniques and philosophies, and different distribution schedules, among other variations. This lack of conceptual clarity is an inevitable artifact of history and culture. As previous scholars noted, the use of entertainment to educate in the form of modeling behaviors and imparting values deemed "prosocial" is not new, but rather is rooted in the ancient art of storytelling (Brown & Singhal, 1999). Greek theatre, epic poems, anthems, and childhood fables of disparate oral cultures constitute some of the earliest uses of this communications practice, albeit somewhat different from the use of E-E in feature-length films and TV series (Singhal & Rogers, 1999). Different cultures operating under different sets of political and economic constraints approached E-E quite differently.

In developing countries, television is viewed as an essential tool for modernization. There, the predominant approach to E-E has been for industry insiders to adopt the philosophy and techniques of Miguel Sabido (Nariman, 1993) and create longstanding, commercially successful and scientifically based broadcast series designed expressly to educate the population about social problems, but to do so in an entertaining and engaging fashion. In the United States, the main focus of the present chapter, the predominant E-E approach instead has been for industry outsiders to work with producers of existing commercial programs designed expressly for entertainment (Montgomery, 1989). In this context, they attempt, through lobbying and influence efforts, to introduce educational content in the form of dialogue, background visuals, and story ideas. Obviously there are exceptions to this rough-hewn dichotomy, but the point is that what is labeled E-E in developing countries is often quite different in scope, function, and form from its counterpart in the United States and other developed nations, thereby muddying the conceptual waters.

Definitions of E-E each emphasize a somewhat different facet of the concept. In its most basic conceptualization, E-E is "putting educational content into entertainment media messages" (Singhal, 1990), a definition that portrays E-E in its most common form in developed countries: (1) as a strategic communication process, (2) initiated by a partner interested in educating by capitalizing on the popularity of entertainment (Bouman, 1999; Piotrow, Meyer, & Zulu, 1992). Other conceptualizations portray E-E as content rather than process: "A performance which captures the interest or attention of an individual, giving them pleasure, amusement, or gratification while simultaneously helping the individual to develop a skill to achieve a particular end by boosting his or her mental, moral or physical powers" (Nariman, 1993).

Some conceptualizations emphasize a single level of analysis, such as that proposed by Singhal and Rogers (1999): "Entertainment-education is the process of purposely designing and implementing a media message both to entertain and to educate, in order to increase audience members' knowledge about an educational issue, create favorable attitudes, and change overt behaviors." More recently, scholars argued for expanding the level of analyses to include changes in individuals, families, communities, organizations, and/or a society as a whole (Papa, Singhal, Law, Pant, Sood, Rogers, & Shefner-Rogers, 2000; Singhal & Rogers, 2002).

Other scholars offered further distinctions. Piotrow (1990) and Brown (1991), for example, emphasized an economic facet by defining E-E as an opportunity for an instructional message to pay for itself while fulfilling commercial and social interests. Murdoch (1980), among others, described E-E as an informal educational process directed primarily at youthful audiences to teach moral and ethical behavior through stories. Singhal and Rogers (2002) posited that E-E is ". . . not a theory of communication, but rather a strategy. . . ."

The rise of E-E in the United States is decidedly a phenomenon of the late twentieth century, resulting largely from several factors, such as disappointment with the performance of traditional media campaigns to elicit behavior change (Freudenberg et al., 1995). In many campaigns, an entertainment component has either been ill conceived or merely a single strategy not linked to some broader intervention (Singhal et al., 1999). These shortcomings may have resulted in audiences avoiding or ignoring educational messages. In contrast, E-E offers an engaging portrayal of an issue, provides a viewer with characters with whom he or she can readily identify, and generally heightens a viewer's involvement with an issue through his or her orientation to a favorite character.

A second factor has been the conspicuous presence of such "antisocial" content as tobacco, alcohol, and violence in U.S. entertainment programming. This phenomenon has been labeled "entertainment degradation" to refer to the glorification of unhealthy behaviors in attempts to increase their appeal (Singhal et al., 1999). Research evidence supports the notion that exposure to such antisocial messages induces changes in attitudes and behavior (Bushman & Huesman, 2001). As a result, advocates of "prosocial" content have used E-E to essentially fight fire with fire, offering viewers a more balanced perspective with regard to the portrayal of healthy and unhealthy behaviors.

A third factor, especially in societies with strong commercial media systems, is that audience perceptual defenses are triggered by blatant attempts at persuasion via public service advertising, Web banner ads, or advocacy pamphlets. A television viewer, for example, is conditioned to expect these persuasion attempts at regular intervals throughout the day. E-E is thought to circumvent these defenses through its seamless integration of information and diversion.

A fourth factor is that E-E has the potential to provide a far more comprehensive treatment of an issue than could otherwise be afforded in a 30- or 60-second public service ad. For example, season-long episodes devoted to a health topic can do much more than can a single 60-minute episode. The advantage of this factor is that viewers can be presented with specific behaviors to adopt and specific action steps to take.

TOWARD A RESEARCH AGENDA

A prime benefit of E-E's evolving definition is its ability to pose new questions, the answers to which expand the E-E paradigm. Here, we wish to identify an exemplary subset of researchable issues suggested by the existing framework and by the extant research based on it. We first identify the basis on which we choose such issues, i.e., the evaluative criteria used to establish a research agenda.

To ensure that E-E research moves ahead in a systematic way, E-E evaluators and researchers should make explicit, before evaluating a program, the theoretical or conceptual underpinnings of the programming (Chen & Rossi, 1983; Patton, 1986; Torvatn, 1999; Cole, 1999). Those who wish to use E-E as an intervention must a priori develop a "logic model" or "theory of action" (Patton, 1986; Weiss, 1995) that carefully explicates how the message is designed to impact the audience. Without knowing the preconceived relationship between an E-E program's delivery and its effects, it is difficult to determine whether the program was delivered as planned and whether or not it produced intended effects (Chen, 1990; Weiss, 1995; Worthen, 1996; Cole, 1999). Furthermore, when there is no explicit link between programmatic activities and their intended effects on the problem(s) targeted by the E-E program, information generated by the evaluation is of little value in improving the program (Patton, 1986; Chapel & Cotton, 1996). Likewise, when successes or failures cannot be attributed to individual E-E program components, it is nearly impossible to project the results of the evaluation to other program efforts or to know which parts made a difference and which components did not (Chen, 1990; Weiss, 1996; Cole, 1999). This last point is particularly important if one wants to enhance aspects of the E-E program that work and/or improve or eliminate components that do not work.

Provus (1971) asserted that if a program is successful others will want to copy it. Therefore it is important to know the exact recipe of the programmatic activities so that it can be reproduced. In short, without the benefit of a clearly articulated plan for how a program is supposed to work, one cannot ascertain whether it did work, and why it did or did not produce the intended benefits (Weiss, 1996).

Reproduction is key in the primary theoretical framework that has been used for E-E. Bandura's social cognitive theory (Bandura, 1977) stated that we learn behaviors, attitudes, and beliefs by observing models. Those outcomes are enhanced primarily when the models are rewarded for what they do, when they are attractive, and when the receiver identifies with the model. In parallel fashion, these outcomes are minimized by unattractive models who exhibit undesirable behaviors for which they are not rewarded or even punished. These elements lead to greater reproduction or avoidance of what the model does and says.

With this reasoning and given our preferred focus on elements of communication theory, we will exemplify this phase of evolving a research agenda by focusing on message components that are generic to content development in most E-E plans. Here, we elaborate on questions of the E-E diet, amount, order of presentation, repetition, and spread. We choose these elements because E-E practitioners working in a competitive media environment have little if any control over them. That condition enhances the need to consider their implications for the development of sound E-E strategies as opportunities increase for partnerships with media producers to develop content for entertainment programming. We also acknowledge that by examining them one at a time, we overlook the fact that the outcome of any recipe is an interaction of the ingredients, rather than just a summation. Determining effects without regard for how the components work together and/or disaggregating message components to a level that allows meaningful, unambiguous differentiation among them are competing concerns. Here are examples of problematic E-E message characteristics that require a sounder conceptual and empirical base.

1. *The diet issue.* Historically, the organizational goal of public service agencies involved in E-E efforts has been to use entertainment to enhance education, not the other way around. The diet question focuses on what portion of each "E" is necessary and beneficial. Is the menu to be designed to favor the education or the entertainment component? Does a 50/50 split, or some other ratio between the two ingredients, maximize the desired outcome? Excessive entertainment may dilute the educational component.

A parallel concern is that excessive educational information could result in bored receivers, or outright rejection of a message that runs counter to current beliefs or practices. A precise answer is unlikely, but parameters within which an effective E-E diet may be prescribed would seem to be a reasonable expectation.

Moreover, the dichotomy in "E" and "E" implied by the way we framed this issue might be offset by considering whether a more seamless integration of the two is possible.

2. *The amount issue.* Perhaps the largest amount of health content on a prime-time commercial television series in the United States was the year-long ovarian cancer storyline on *Thirtysomething* (Sharf, Freimuth, Greenspon, & Plotnick, 1996). Their follow-up study determined that 79% of the viewers interviewed believed they had learned something and 40% had taken a health-related action based on their viewing. Such opportunities are rare if one is working with commercial broadcasters. Nonetheless, if one were to carry a health issue/theme throughout an entire episode, more positive responses would be anticipated than if there were only a few references to the issue. But the nature of the relationship between the size or length of the dose and its outcome is unclear.

When change agents have control of message content—as is not the case with commercial television shows—they must decide how big a message should be constructed. The tendency to want as much (or as big) as we can get, has yet to be validated in outcome measures. However, message size must be linked to message goals, and the small steps or changes that are typically sought in E-E efforts should be calibrated with message size.

3. *The order of presentation issue.* Attention to locating the strongest position of the entertainment component, relative to that of the educational message, is absent from past literature. Should we lead with the entertainment? There is reason to believe, from the distraction literature, that using entertainment initially might serve the dual purposes of generating interest and moving the receiver to a less defensive posture (Festinger & Maccoby, 1964; Petty, Wells & Brock, 1976). "Off-guard" may be preferred to "en-garde" with social messages that prescribe the need for changing behavior. On the other hand, primacy advocates argue that the best opportunity for behavior change consists of a first impression (Eagly & Chaiken, 1993), although we wish to gain attention and avoid boring the receiver. That stance leads to dissension as to whether the first impression we wish to have is as an entertainer or a teacher. Perhaps we should close with the educational message, such as in an epilogue. Research on recency suggests that, in the absence of an adjacent opposing view, the best bet for message recall is if it is the last item to which audience individuals are exposed, or the last item they recall (Eagly & Chaiken, 1993). Then, there is the opportunity to blend the two "E's" throughout the message. Here, frequent shifts between entertainment and education elements may confuse some receivers or may maintain a higher

level of interest in the educational message when preceded and followed by entertaining content. Ways of smoothing "E" and "E" into a virtually indistinguishable order are worthy of study.

4. *The repetition issue.* A general communication maxim is that repetition is good, at least up to a certain point. Ascertaining that point is an empirical question in E-E programs. Some E-E insertions occur but once, others many times. If we can assume that message quality is high and that message size is reasonable, then we posit that repetition would be positively related to E-E effects. How can a message be repeated before tedium or even revulsion sets in?

Commercial advertising research shows the potential for "boomerang" effects from excessive repetition (Pechmann & Stewart, 1988). Too much repetition is likely to increase rejection, or to have the audience "tune out" the message. Repetition, with variation, is possible. Variation, however, produces a new set of issues. Is the variation to be in the education component, the entertainment component, or both?

5. *The spread issue.* In 1998 a lead character on *NYPD Blue* was diagnosed with prostate cancer. The storyline continued for 12 episodes, sometimes in a single scene and sometimes across several scenes in an episode. The educational content dealt with diagnostic procedures, treatment options, potential complications, surgery, postsurgery complications, and recovery, within the context of two or three other storylines in each episode. If the writers had condensed this E-E material into a couple of episodes, then perhaps the audience would not be as emotionally or cognitively involved. Spreading the issue over time, as in real life, sustained the storyline's realism. This decision to carry one health story over that length of time was viewed by tens of millions of Americans.

The strategic question is the relative distribution of information over time. One can choose to provide small or large doses of education over short or lengthy periods of time. Will the audience have consistent exposure if the content is over an extended period? How much of the education should be redundant?

Other issues can be addressed if E-E is to continue to mature as a communication strategy. For example, *genre* comparisons, e.g., humor versus adventure stories, *mode* comparisons, e.g., audio versus written, *format* comparisons, e.g., text versus graphics, and *source* comparisons, e.g., the relative credibility of different spokespersons, would lead us in new directions.

A CONTINUING RESEARCH AGENDA FOR E-E

A research framework that encompasses E-E was delineated recently when the CDC convened a panel of 14 mass communication researchers in May 2000

(Salmon, 2001).[1] The specific intent of this meeting was to accommodate E-E issues that are specific to a domestic United States context, in contrast to the bulk of the research findings in other country settings.

How does E-E originating in the U.S. differ from that in Latin America, Africa, and Asia?

1. E-E efforts in the United States exist in a competitive environment. Anti-obesity health messages may be offset by junk food advertising. Delay of the onset of smoking or sexual activity may be offset by advertising messages and by the frequent portrayal of these activities as benign or socially beneficial in popular television shows and movies. Antianorexia themes may be diminished by media emphasis on ultraskinny models in both television programs and commercials. Thus, audiences are likely to receive a barrage of competing messages on many health issues, with offsetting outcomes.

2. The cluttered U.S. media environment makes it more difficult to pinpoint the source or locus of a behavior change. Tracing outcome responses to specific messages likely requires more intensive research methodologies than have typically been implemented in the past.

3. Today's media environment in the United States is more diversified, as well as more competitive. E-E effectiveness can be enhanced through a multimedia approach, although this increases costs. For example, efforts to place single educational messages in entertainment television shows can be accompanied by offering viewers a telephone number to call, or a Web site for additional information, or a chat room. E-E efforts directed at children can include comic books, videos, and games.

4. Supplementing a multimedia approach or a single medium approach to E-E is the need to consider the benefit of interpersonal communication. Although Singhal & Rogers (2002) constrain E-E to "media messages" in their conceptual definition, E-E media messages often activate interpersonal channels (Valente, Kim, Lettenmaier, Glass, & Dibba, 1994). For example, child viewers of *Sesame Street* learned more and gained more social skills when parents actively participated in the learning process (Lesser, 1974). Teachers as well can be stimulated to encourage students' efforts initially obtained through media experiences, inside or outside of the classroom.

5. The Internet is a major candidate for future E-E efforts, but it has not been in the past. Because the Internet requires more involvement from its users, users in turn may give it greater attention and credence. E-E on the Internet can take the forms of interactive games, videos, music, and chat

---

[1]Participants in the 2000 CDC E-E conference included Alison Alexander, Vicki Beck, Sholly Fisch, Deborah Glik, Bradley Greenberg, Robert Hornik, Glen Nowak, James Potter, Donald Roberts, Everett M. Rogers, Charles Salmon, John Sherry, Dorothy Singer, Monique Ward, Ellen Wartella, and Barbara Wilson.

rooms, among others, all of which can be (and have been) infused with social issues. For example, puzzle fans may find themselves interactively or individually piecing together an interesting puzzle whose outcome is an osteoporosis message. Teenage music fans may be encouraged to interactively create lyrics that encourage hygiene and to share their effort karaoke-style in a chat room. Other newer media, e.g., direct satellite transmission and interactive books and toys, also merit consideration in E-E planning efforts. The Internet has been utilized to convey E-E *telenovelas* about breast cancer screening to Hispanic women (see the chapter by Everett M. Rogers in this volume).

The desired outcomes of E-E interventions should be specified and more rigorous evaluations should be encouraged than currently exist in United States settings (Salmon, 2001). What are the critical differences between those overseas settings where E-E has been extensively implemented versus the United States?

1. In Latin America, Africa, and Asia, less media competition exists for the minds of the audience than in the United States.
2. A national government often is the dominant, and sometimes the only, media provider. There is often a close working relationship between a national government and media systems in pursuing agreed-upon social goals. This collaborative role is not the standard in the United States, where the media's watchdog role is more emphatic and where the government and E-E efforts are often at odds with the media, e.g., media depictions of such health behaviors as smoking and sexual activity. In this context, media creators are more likely to keep E-E consultants at arm's length.
3. The target recipients are typically the poorest and neediest segment of the population. In a commercial media system, this audience is least desirable, as the system's goal is to deliver potential buyers to advertisers.
4. Exposure to antagonistic messages is more easily contained, banned, or altogether absent. Such a compelling advantage does not exist in the United States.

An E-E international conference in the Netherlands (Fokkens & Jacoby, 2001) verified the need for more systematic evaluations of the impact of E-E. The following examples are illustrative:

Case #1. The theme of a movie called *Yellow Card* was teenage pregnancy in Africa. A young man impregnates one girl while falling in love with another. In the preproduction process, formative research with focus group interviews required one year and preceded script writing. Then, the rough-cut of the film was shown to about 1,000 young people, often leading to further revisions. The conference presenter told the assemblage, "Unfortunately, there was no money left for evaluation research" (Fokkens & Jacoby, 2001). In other words, whether the film influenced any young person in Africa was unknown.

Case #2. A controversial antismoking campaign was implemented in the Netherlands in 1998. It was based on formative research showing that young people perceive smoking to be cool and tough. So the E-E planners showed young nonsmokers doing activities with a tough edge. For example, in one spot, a male adolescent was working in a restaurant. He responds to a belligerent female customer's request for apple juice by urinating into a glass and serving it to her, while uttering, "Here's your apple juice," followed by, "but I don't smoke." After two years of broadcasting this spot, the conference presenter said that impact evidence from this intervention was yet to be obtained (Fokkens et al., 2001).

A U.S. television series *Gideon's Crossing*, debuted in the 2000 season. It was a medical show set in an urban hospital and it aired an episode that dealt with cancer. Assume that some health agency helped develop the script and believed that an adequate evaluation would demonstrate the merits of the E-E intervention.

Following is a set of dynamic outcome variables, stripped of their health content, so that they can be generalized to a broad range of social outcomes:

1. Determine if the specific information in the message is salient enough to be recalled with, or without, prompting (this taps the relative importance of the information to the audience).
2. Determine if the issue related to the specific information has a high priority (e.g., is it now more central to the personal and/or public agenda of the recipient).
3. Assess the credibility of the information received.
4. Assess the credibility of the information source.
5. Find out if the viewer is better informed than prior to exposure.
6. Determine if the message stimulated or strengthened interest in the issue presented.
7. Evaluate any possible change in attitude toward the issue.
8. Determine if any subsequent behavior occurred as a result of the message.

THE 2000 CDC CONFERENCE
ON ENTERTAINMENT-EDUCATION

This framework of outcomes outlines the research agenda developed during the May 2000 CDC conference. The purpose of the conference was to "propose a meaningful and practical research agenda, wherein health issues are the central content areas and positive health effects are the goals" (Salmon,

2001). The original 63 research questions were prioritized into five major research topics.

The research area designated to be of highest priority was that which would "identify and systematically study factors that can potentially mitigate or enhance the magnitude of E-E effects and effectiveness" (Salmon, 2001). Example questions include:

1. What levels and types of exposure to E-E content are necessary for the adoption of prosocial behavior?
2. Under what conditions are unintended effects of E-E most likely to occur?
3. What effect does postviewing discussion have on adoption of prosocial practices?
4. Can E-E effects be enhanced through such Internet features as chat rooms?
5. How can E-E be used to influence social norms?

The second research priority was that of "describing the . . . information environment in terms of the nature and frequency of E-E content appearing in entertainment programming" (Salmon, 2001).

1. In what ways are the educational issues of interest portrayed in entertainment programming?
2. What specific theories are most applicable to developing E-E messages?
3. What educational issues are being depicted over time, and with what frequency?
4. What are different ways in which characters can be shown to cope with health problems, and which are most effective in terms of role modeling?
5. What are the most common ways in which E-E messages are embedded in entertainment programming?

A third research priority was the expressed need "to develop an enhanced understanding of the audiences for E-E programs, particularly children and youth" (Salmon, 2001).

1. What types of television characters are considered credible sources of information?
2. How can youth be targeted through E-E messages?
3. What media do children and youth use for entertainment, and what opportunities for synergy exist (between, for example, the Internet and television)?
4. What are the various issue concerns of most adults, youths, and children?

"A fourth genre of research is needed to focus on descriptive research about the entertainment industry itself, the interface between the scientific community, and the entertainment creative process," and understanding industry needs for information and receptivity to E-E partnerships (Salmon, 2001).

1. What do writers/producers want from information resources, and in what form?
2. What are effective ways of motivating writers/producers to address specific issues?
3. What sources do writers/producers currently use to obtain expert advice and/or accurate information?
4. What issues and concerns are currently on the agenda of writers/producers?

A final priority was organization-centered applied research to evaluate the effectiveness of an organization's E-E efforts.

1. What are the most appropriate outcome measures to use in evaluating the effectiveness of an organization's E-E efforts?
2. How can an organization most effectively frame educational issues to producers of media content?
3. What specific methodologies and/or research methods are most appropriate for assessing the impact of an organization's E-E efforts?
4. How can an organization measure the extent to which its E-E efforts have directly enhanced the visibility of the organization's initiatives?

CONCLUSIONS

The primary focus of this chapter was to establish a research agenda for E-E scholarship. Important ethical considerations are involved in the conduct of research on E-E strategies. Two questions illustrate these salient concerns:

1. What public policy concerns arise from efforts by government agencies to use E-E to influence American citizens, e.g., through drug storylines in prime-time television?
2. What are the ethical implications of government agencies using E-E to promote one value-laden solution over another, e.g., condoms versus abstinence as a means of controlling HIV/AIDS among teenagers?

An elementary principle is that blending entertainment content with educational content makes the latter more palatable and more effective, and does not detract noticeably from the former. Research has yet to determine if the entertainment content is enhanced by the presence of education.

This chapter proposes a stringent basis for belief in E-E as an important and potentially necessary strategy for promoting social issues like health. That basis resides in the need to provide stronger scientific evidence for all major phases of E-E efforts. Strategic decisions as to how to describe target audiences, to assess their current values and beliefs, and to design the messages, the forms of distribution, the choice of sources, etc., characterize the input phases in developing an integrative marketing communication approach. In other words, under what conditions can E-E efforts be maximized? At the same time, these decisions bridge directly to the outcome phase—just what it is that the campaign seeks to yield? Only through systematic and rigorous research can such decisions be grounded increasingly on strong evidence rather than on folklore or assertions. Only then can the scientific community provide sound advice about E-E proposals.

In addition, there is no systematic monitoring of the health content available in these channels. If your message stresses a healthy lifestyle, you need to know what others are saying about a healthy lifestyle, as well as how still others may be depicting an unhealthy, but attractive lifestyle.

Much research on the effects of mass communication in communication-based interventions predates the Internet, 100+ channel television systems, and other new communication technologies. These developments are not yet of concern in the implementation of the E-E strategy in many parts of the world, but they are very important in understanding the context of E-E efforts in the United States. A superabundance of health messages are available: health television channels, fiction and nonfiction medical shows on television, and thousands of health information Web sites. Competition for the finite time and attention of the U.S. audience escalates when these various types of health communication are combined.

REFERENCES

Bandura, A. (1977). *Social learning theory*. Englewood Cliffs, NJ: Prentice-Hall.

Beck, V. (2000, November). *Tune in for Health: Entertainment-education for reaching audiences at risk*. Paper presented at the American Public Health Association, Boston.

Bouman (1999). *The turtle and the peacock: Collaboration for prosocial change*. Wageningen, The Netherlands: Wageningen Agricultural University.

Brodie, M., Foehr, U., Rideout, V., Baer, N., Miller, C., Flournoy, R., & Altman, D. (2001). Communicating health information through the entertainment media. *Health Affairs, 20*(1), 192–199.

Brown, W. J. (1991). Prosocial effects of entertainment television in India. *Asian Journal of Communication, 1*(1), 113–135.

Brown, W. J., & Singhal, A. (1999). Entertainment-education media strategies for social change: Promises and problems (pp. 263–280). In D. Demers & K. Vishwanath (Eds.), *Mass media, social control, and social change*. Ames, Iowa: Iowa State University Press.

Bushman, B. J., & Huesmann, L. R. (2001). Effects of televised violence on aggression. In D. Singer & J. Singer (Eds.), *Handbook of children and the media* (pp. 223–254). Thousand Oaks, CA: Sage.

Chapel, T., & Cotton, D. (1996). *Introduction to program evaluation: A guide for planning and policy practitioners*. Prepared for the Office of Program Planning and Evaluation. Atlanta, GA: Centers for Disease Control and Prevention.

Chen, H. T. (1990). *Theory-driven evaluations*. Thousand Oaks, CA: Sage.

Chen, H. T., & Rossi, P. H. (1983). Evaluating with sense: The theory-driven approach. *Evaluation Review, 7*(3), 283–302.

Cole, G. (1999). Advancing the development and application of theory-based evaluation in the practice of public health. *American Journal of Evaluation, 20*(3), 453–470.

Cook, T. D., Appleton, H., Conner, R. F., Shaffer, A., Tamkin, G., & Weber, S. J. (1975). *Sesame Street revisited*. New York: Russell Sage Foundation.

Eagly, A. H., & Chaiken, S. (1993). *The psychology of attitudes*. Fort Worth, TX: Harcourt Brace Jovanovich.

Festinger, L., & Maccoby, N. (1964). On resistance to persuasive communications. *Journal of Abnormal and Social Psychology, 68*, 359–366.

Fokkens, P., & Jacoby, R. (2001). The entertainment-education 2000 event magazine (On-line). The International Entertainment-Education 2000 Conference, Amsterdam, The Netherlands. Available: www.entertainment-education.nl.

Freudenberg, N., Eng, E., Flay, B., Parcel, G., Rogers, T., & Wallerstein, N. (1995). Strengthening individual and community capacity to prevent disease and promote health: In search of relevant theories and principles. *Health Education Quarterly, 22*, 290–306.

Greenberg, B. S., & Busselle, R. (1996). Soap operas and sexual activity: A decade later. *Journal of Communication, 46*(4), 153–160.

Lesser, G. S. (1974). *Children and television: A lesson from Sesame Street*. New York: Random House.

Montgomery, K. C. (1989). *Target prime time*. New York: Oxford University Press.

Murdoch, G. (1980). Radical drama, radical theater. *Media, Culture, & Society, 2*, 151–168.

Nariman, H. N. (1993). *Soap operas for social change*. Westport, CT: Praeger Press.

Papa, M., Singhal, A., Law, W., Pant, S., Sood, S., Rogers, E. M., & Shefner-Rogers, C. L. (2000). Entertainment-education and social change: An analysis of parasocial interaction, social learning, collective efficacy, and paradoxical communication. *Journal of Communication, 50*(4), 31–55.

Patton, M. Q. (1986). *Utilization-focused research* (2nd ed.). Thousand Oaks, CA: Sage.

Pechmann, C., & Stewart, D. W. (1988). A critical review of wearin and wearout. *Current Issues and Research in Advertising, 11*, 285–330.

Petty, R. E., Wells, G. L., & Brock, T. C. (1976). Distraction can enhance or reduce yielding to propaganda: Thought disruption versus effort justification. *Journal of Personality and Social Psychology, 34*(5), 874–884.

Piotrow, P. T. (1990). Principles of good health communication. In P. L. Coleman & R. C. Meyer (Eds.), *Proceedings from the Enter-Educate Conference: Entertainment for Social Change* (pp. 13–14). Baltimore, MD: Johns Hopkins University, Population Communication Services.

Piotrow, P. T., Meyer, R. C., & Zulu, B. A. (1992). AIDS and mass persuasion. In J. Mann, D. J. M. Tarantola, & T. W. Netter (Eds.), *AIDS in the world* (pp. 733–759). Cambridge, MA: Harvard University Press.

Provus, M. M. (1971). *Discrepancy evaluation: For educational program improvement*. Berkley, CA: McCutchan.

Rogers, E. M., Vaughan, P. W., Swalehe, R. M. A., Rao, N., Svenkerud, P., & Sood, S. (1999). Effects of an entertainment-education radio soap opera on family planning behavior in Tanzania. *Studies in Family Planning, 30*(3), 193–211.

Salmon, C. T. (1994, February). *Using entertainment-education to research a generation at risk. Summary report from a conference meeting sponsored by the U. S. Centers for Disease Control and Prevention*. Atlanta, GA: CDC.

Salmon, C. T. (2001). *Setting a research agenda for entertainment-education*. Proceedings from the conference meeting of the Centers for Disease Control and Prevention, Atlanta, GA.

Schlosser, J. (1998). Drug czar praises TV. *Broadcasting & Cable, 128*(46), 89.

Sharf, B. F., & Freimuth, V. S. (1993). The construction of illness on entertainment television: Coping with cancer on *thirtysomething*. *Health Communication, 5*(3), 141–160.

Sharf, B. F., Freimuth, V. S., Greenspon, P, & Plotnick, C. (1996). Confronting cancer on *thirtysomething*: Audience response to health content on entertainment television. *Journal of Health Communication, 1*, 157–172.

Singhal, A. (1990). *Entertainment-education communication strategies for development*. Unpublished doctoral dissertation, Los Angeles, CA: University of Southern California.

Singhal, A., & Brown, W. J. (1997, May). *Entertainment-education and social change: Past, present and future*. Paper presented at the Second International Conference on Entertainment-Education and Social Change, Athens, OH.

Singhal, A., & Rogers, E. M. (1999). *Entertainment-education: A communication strategy for social change*. Mahwah, NJ: Lawrence Erlbaum Associates.

Singhal, A., & Rogers, E. M. (2002). A theoretical agenda for entertainment-education. *Communication Theory, 12*(2) 117–135.

Torvatn, H. (1999). Logic models: A tool for telling your program's performance story. *Evaluation and Program Planning, 22*, 73–82.

Valente, T. W., Kim, Y. M., Lettenmaier, C., Glass, W., & Dibba, Y. (1994). Radio promotion of family planning in The Gambia. *International Family Planning Perspective, 20*, 96–100.

Weiss, C. H. (1995). Nothing as practical as good theory: Exploring theory-based evaluation for comprehensive community initiatives for children and families. In J. P. Connell, A. C. Kubisch, L. B. Schorr, & C. H. Weiss (Eds.), *New approaches to evaluating community initiatives: Concepts, methods, and contexts* (pp. 65–92). Queenstown, MD: Aspen Institute.

Weiss, C. H. (1996). Excerpts from evaluation research: Methods of assessing program effectiveness. *Evaluation Practice, 17*(2), 173–175.

Winsten J. A. (1994). Promoting designated drivers: The Harvard Alcohol Project. *American Journal of Preventive Health, 10*(3), 11–14.

Worthen, B. R. (1996). Editors note: The origins of theory-based evaluation. *Evaluation Practice, 17*(2), 169–171.

11

Working With Daytime and Prime-Time Television Shows in the United States to Promote Health

Vicki Beck

The Norman Lear Center
USC Annenberg School for Communication

Health themes in television shows have generated no lack of successful programs and characters in white jackets, e.g., *Dr. Kildaire; Ben Casey; Marcus Welby M.D.; Dr. Quinn, Medicine Woman; ER; Chicago Hope; LA Doctors; Providence; Presidio Med;* and more. Nonmedical daytime and prime-time shows in the United States have also produced a steady diet of public health topics and characters. Many resulted in long-running storylines with major characters who encounter unintended pregnancy (*Maude*), cancer (*thirtysomething*), mental health issues (*LA Law*), transplantation (*NYPD Blue*), teenage drug and alcohol abuse (*7th Heaven*), safe sex/avoiding pregnancy (*Felicity, Dawson's Creek*), violence against women (*Beverly Hills 90210*), heart disease (*Any Day Now*), diabetes (*The Young & The Restless*), breast cancer (*One Life to Live*), HIV/AIDS (*The Bold & The Beautiful*), and more.

The inclusion of health stories in popular television shows adds drama and suspense. Health experts would also like to ensure that viewers learn accurate and useful health information by viewing these programs, and, ideally, take a constructive step in disease prevention and health promotion. A growing number of organizations in the United States hope to adapt lessons learned by the global E-E community, and to apply these in the United States. Further, these organizations are attempting to evaluate E-E interventions more proactively than earlier efforts, which captured viewer responses well after the story line ended (Sharf & Freimuth, 1993; Sharf, Freimuth, Greenspon, & Plotnick, 1996).

The present chapter reviews recent successful E-E interventions in popular American television dramas in order to show the kinds of influences that E-E programs can achieve. Specifically, the history of the development of an E-E program for public health is traced, including recommendations by expert panels, audience research with viewer surveys, a proposed E-E research agenda, outreach to television shows, and the emergence of a growing collaboration of health experts with the Hollywood creative community. The chapter concludes with lessons learned and future priorities for E-E programs in the United States.

INFORMING AND MOTIVATING VIEWERS
ABOUT HEALTH

The U.S. daytime drama *The Bold and the Beautiful* (*B&B*) is possibly the most-watched television show in the world. Produced in Los Angeles, California by CBS Entertainment, this program has an estimated 300 million viewers in 110 countries (Bell-Phillip Television Productions, 2002), including Egypt, India, Bangladesh, China, Russia, the Philippines, Kenya, Uganda, and South Africa. The show first aired in 1987, and in 2002 was the number two rated daytime drama in the United States (Dawidziak, 2002).

While this popular soap opera features mostly made-for-television American characters, it dishes up universal themes of romantically entangled lives with daily life-and-death dilemmas, including health issues that are familiar to mass media audiences around the world. Anecdotal reports from Africa indicate that some viewers travel from distant places and many gather in neighborhoods or villages to watch the show on a single television set. Health officials in Eastern Cape Province, South Africa report that no meetings are scheduled and that crime decreases throughout the Township during the time when the program airs (O'Leary, 2002).

When the executive producer of *The Bold and the Beautiful* took an interest in the global AIDS epidemic in the summer of 2001, he turned to the Centers for Disease Control and Prevention (CDC) to assist with a storyline. The CDC is the federal agency charged with the prevention and control of disease, injury, and disability in the United States, and is frequently asked to intervene in major epidemics around the globe. The CDC also works with writers and producers of Hollywood television shows to encourage accurate depictions of health issues. CDC staff met with a producer from the television show about two months before this request, to offer expert assistance on health storylines, to provide tip sheets on public health topics, and to brief the producer on women's health issues for possible character and story development.

Two behavioral scientists from CDC's HIV/AIDS program were identified to provide expert information for the HIV storyline. The first expert advised on the accuracy of an evolving script that focused on a young man, Tony, who would be diagnosed with HIV that he contracted from a former partner. Many of the issues in the storyline were also being studied at the CDC and addressed in national education and communication campaigns—for example, HIV testing, partner notification, stigma, and living with HIV/AIDS. When the television story led to the adoption of a young child orphaned by AIDS, the second CDC expert joined the advisory team to consult on orphanages in Africa.

Tony's HIV

On August 3, 2001 the HIV/AIDS storyline was introduced on CBS-Television in the United States. Viewers learned, along with Tony, that he was HIV positive (Photo 11.1). As part of the collaboration with CDC, the network agreed to produce a public service announcement (PSA). The actor who played Tony encouraged viewers to call the CDC's national, toll-free, 800-hotline-number if they wanted more information on HIV/AIDS. The PSA aired a second time

PHOTO 11.1. The doctor tells Tony his HIV test showed that he is HIV-positive. (*Source*: Photograph by John Paschal/JPI. Used with permission.)

PHOTO 11.2. Tony discusses his HIV status with his fiancé Kristin in the AIDS storyline on *The Bold & the Beautiful*. (*Source*: Photograph by John Paschal/JPI. Used with permission.)

ten days later when the character, Tony, divulged his HIV status to his fiancé in the television show (Photo 11.2). The result was an overwhelming number of calls to the CDC-sponsored hotline within a few minutes of the broadcast. Phones were jammed and operators were unable to respond to all of the callers. The second PSA resulted in the largest spike of callers during that calendar year (Kennedy, O'Leary, Beck, Pollard, & Simpson, 2002).

The Bold & the Beautiful storyline offers an important example of audience impact, i.e., information-seeking behavior that was the direct result of an E-E effort fueled by an executive producer's desire to inform his audience about a critical public health issue (Photo 11.3). The call levels for the *B&B* time slots were more than 1,000 calls higher than the next highest levels for those two days (Kennedy et al., 2002). When hotline responses were compared to responses for other television broadcasts of the hotline number during 2001, including its broadcast during an MTV special on AIDS, call volume was still substantially higher following the *B&B* storyline. This example shows that information-seeking can be substantially stimulated when a health message is tied to an ongoing storyline.

Breast Cancer on *The Young and the Restless*

Additional data on viewers who call information hotlines were collected in July 2002. These callers responded to a PSA for cancer information that aired

PHOTO 11.3. Tony and Kristin marry and visit an orphanage in Africa where they adopt a young child, Zende, whose mother died of AIDS. (*Source*: Photograph by Aaron Montgomery/JPI. Used with permission.)

on the daytime drama, *The Young & the Restless* (*Y&R*). Ashley, a major character on the show, was diagnosed with, and treated for, breast cancer. The storyline appealed to viewers' emotions through a melodramatic treatment that allowed them to hear about the diagnosis when the character (Ashley) with whom they identified, heard it. The educational messages embedded in the script addressed screening, diagnosis, and treatment for breast cancer. The PSA produced in conjunction with the storyline included a toll-free number for the Cancer Information Service (CIS) sponsored by the National Cancer Institute.

As a result of the PSA, 211 interviews were completed with viewers who called the toll-free number. The daytime drama callers were somewhat different from regular callers to the CIS hotline (Davis & Bright, 2002). Callers stimulated by the television show were twice as likely to be members of the general public (62% versus 30%) and to be from a minority group (18% versus 9% were Hispanic, and 21% versus 9% were African American) than regular callers to the Cancer Information Service. In addition, callers were more likely to be interested in learning about cancer prevention and risk (15% versus 6%) and cancer screening (11% versus 7%); and less likely than regular callers to be interested in cancer treatment (14% versus 30%). These findings provide further evidence that a PSA linked to a health-related storyline can stimulate hard-to-reach audiences to call for preventive health information.

Health Effects of Primetime Television

Primetime television shows can have an even greater impact on regular viewers (Beck & Pollard, 2001; Brodie, Foehr, Rideout, Baer, Miller, Flournoy, & Altman, 2001; Keller & Brown, 2002; Sharf et al., 1993; Sharf et al., 1996). Primetime television shows are half-hour or hour-long dramas and comedies that air between 8 and 11 p.m. in the United States and draw much larger audiences than do daytime dramas (about 50 million regular viewers as compared to about 19 million regular viewers for daytime dramas).

A top-rated television prime-time drama, *ER*, about a busy Chicago hospital's emergency room, educates viewers each week about health topics. A series of telephone surveys conducted before and after an episode that included a message about emergency contraception revealed a substantial increase in the number of regular *ER* viewers who could accurately define emergency contraception and explain how to access it should a need for it arise (Brodie et al., 2001).

A second survey resulted in similar findings about an *ER* storyline on human papillomavirus (HPV) in which a teenage girl is diagnosed with this sexually transmitted disease. After the show, many more viewers knew about the silent nature of HPV and its link to cervical cancer (Brodie et al., 2001). Several years earlier, Sharf et al. (1993) and Sharf et al. (1996) found that young women who routinely watched *thirtysomething* were emotionally and cognitively influenced by a cancer storyline on this show. This study was conducted after the show was canceled, but strong effects were demonstrated.

Since many television programs in the U.S. routinely incorporate health-related facts and dramatic storylines on a wide range of topics (i.e., HIV/AIDS, safer sex, cancer, alcohol abuse, and cardiovascular disease), E-E approaches with writers and producers can be used for reaching audiences with accurate health information. Both government and nongovernment organizations are increasing efforts to work with popular entertainment media to reach a wide audience, many of whom may have less access to health care, pay less attention to print and broadcast health news, and have more difficulty understanding what they read.

AN ENTERTAINMENT-EDUCATION PROGRAM FOR PUBLIC HEALTH

The proliferation of health content and its popularity in entertainment television shows appears to be growing in recent years, and Hollywood's need for health experts to consult on television scripts may be growing as well. Writers call on medical experts when they are unable to find what they need online, or when the storyline requires very detailed diagnostic and treatment information. Public health experts stand ready to help with information about prevention. At the CDC, health communication specialists employ multiple channels and formats to reach audience segments most affected by health issues. While the goals of entertainment and public health are not always compatible, there is a genuine interest among many writers to use accurate health information. If writers are interested in educating their audience, or building drama and conflict, they can easily weave health information and issues into scripts in an unobtrusive manner that supports the storyline.

In the United States, the entertainment industry is a business driven by bottom-line considerations and an artistic medium protected by law. Writers and producers make decisions about direction and content of storylines and have the final say about what is included in the script. The role of public health in this process is most aptly described as a resource role. In this capacity, health experts provide technical assistance and educate creative staff about health issues, but they are not considered part of the creative team nor do they have a role in determining what material is used or not used in the storyline.

Dr. Jeffrey Koplan, a leader in health sciences at Emory University in Atlanta and a past CDC director, was a young disease investigator with the Los Angeles County Department of Health Services in the early 1970s when he consulted on a television pilot (a new television show). To his surprise, some of his comments were not taken seriously. Like many others who have served as technical consultants, Dr. Koplan learned early in his career that Hollywood is in the entertainment business first, and health communication second (Beck, 2000).

As director of the CDC, Dr. Koplan recognized the potential of Hollywood to educate the public about health issues. He met with writers and producers of *ER* and *The West Wing*, and with leaders of Hollywood guilds and studios who were involved in a wide range of television projects (Stolberg, 2001). The meetings fostered dialogue about critical public health issues and resulted in new storylines on these topics.

For decades, television and film producers, writers, and studio executives have called upon the CDC and other government agencies to help them with health storylines and screenplays. Many make visits to the agencies to interview researchers. Frequently, Hollywood writers explore new concepts for television shows or films about disease detectives, scientists, and modern medical research and therapies.

Two TV pilots on the CDC's elite training program for new disease detectives (the Epidemic Intelligence Service, or EIS) failed to be picked up for the 2002–2003 TV season. One script was not produced, and the other was produced, but not picked up for the fall season.

In the past decade, several public health organizations have successfully promoted important health topics and prevention information to TV scriptwriters, resulting in storylines or mentions in television shows. Examples are reproductive health messages (Brodie et al., 2001); immunization messages (Glik, Berkanovic, Stone, Ibarra, Jones, Rosen, Schriebman, Minassian, & Richardes, 1998); designated driver messages (Winsten & DeJong, 2001); and antidrug messages (Office of the National Drug Control Policy, 2000). All demonstrated the potential of E-E to convey health information to mass media audiences.

Given the ever-present role of television as a health educator in the early 1990s and the growing concern over youth health risk with HIV, in 1994 the HIV/AIDS Program at CDC convened a group of communication experts to consider a more proactive, coordinated role for the CDC to work with the entertainment industry in order to reach diverse audiences with disease prevention information. This activity laid the foundation for what would become a national E-E program for public health.

THE CDC ENTERTAINMENT-EDUCATION PROGRAM

In February 1994 approximately 30 experts from communication, public health, advocacy, and entertainment organizations gathered with CDC staff in Atlanta to consider CDC's role in E-E for HIV/AIDS. At that time, international research projects had demonstrated the impacts of health messages in radio and television E-E soap operas (Singhal & Rogers 1999). In the United States, the Harvard Alcohol Project had demonstrated the effectiveness of working with the Hollywood entertainment industry to convey messages about designated drivers in television shows (Winsten & DeJong, 2001). And the long-running television show *Sesame Street* had educated preschool children about social and cognitive skills in the United States and abroad (Bogatz & Ball, 1971; Children's Television Workshop, 1988).

The purpose of the HIV/AIDS conference was described in the follow-up report (Salmon, 1994):

> The primary goal of the conference was to provide CDC with specific recommendations regarding the propriety, potential costs and benefits, and feasibility of engaging in proactive collaboration with entertainment industries. The conference concentrated on HIV/AIDS issues to maintain focus, though the application of entertainment-education to broader public health concerns was considered as well.

The panel of invited experts recommended supporting the establishment of an E-E function at CDC (Salmon, 1994):

> There is overwhelming and enthusiastic support for designating a CDC unit to serve as a liaison with, and a scientific resource for, the entertainment industry. This unit should be proactive rather than only reactive, and should strive to

create a structured, systematic, and sustained working relationship with producers of entertainment programming based upon a solid foundation of public health research, epidemiological expertise, and field experience.

Suggestions for developing the effort were not limited to HIV/AIDS. The panelists encouraged the CDC to provide resources to the Hollywood industry on a wide range of health issues. Specific recommendations were detailed under four general headings: public policy considerations, audience effects, staff roles, and the liaison function.

Following the conference, the HIV/AIDS program launched a social marketing campaign, the Prevention Marketing Initiative, with national efforts and five local demonstration projects (Kennedy, 2000; Strand, Rosenbaum, Hanlon & Jimerson, 2000). Activities included the production of an MTV special on HIV/AIDS for the network's youth audience. At the local level, a radio soap opera was produced by teens in Nashville to promote HIV prevention among African American youth (Duke, 1998). The radio program was successfully replicated in three other cities and developed in Spanish for Hispanic youth (Davis, 2002).

By 1998 an E-E pilot project was established in the CDC Director's Office of Communication to support the agency's health communication campaigns targeted to diverse audiences at risk for preventable disease and injury. Formative audience research and segmentation, use of marketing databases, and a wide range of outreach efforts were integrated into communication campaign efforts across health issues (Freimuth, Linnan, & Potter, 2001; Parvanta & Freimuth, 2000).

By 2000 a second expert panel was convened and a second report identified research gaps in evaluating the effects of E-E on audiences in the United States. University-based communication scholars reviewed the literature and proposed a research agenda "wherein health issues were the central content areas and positive health effects were the goals" (Salmon, 2000; also see the chapter by Bradley Greenberg and others in this volume).

The CDC sought to understand what U.S. audiences were learning about health from entertainment television shows. Formative audience research revealed what was commonly reported in media stories—that television is a very important source of health information for most Americans (Malone, 2002).

THE HEALTHSTYLES SURVEY

The Healthstyles Survey is a proprietary database product developed by Porter Novelli, a social marketing and public relations firm based in Washington, DC. The sample is drawn from the DDB Needham Lifestyles survey which bases its sample on seven U.S. Census Bureau characteristics, considered by most market research experts to create a sample that best represents the U.S. population (Maibach, Maxfield, Ladin, & Slater, 1996). One section of the survey asks questions about television viewing habits and learning from, and acting on, health information in entertainment television shows, i.e., daytime and primetime dramas.

The CDC analyzed data from the 1999 survey ($N = 2,636$) and the 2000 survey ($N = 2,353$) to describe audience characteristics for daytime television and prime-time viewers. The vast majority of regular viewers (who watch daytime or prime-time shows two or more times a week) consider television their main source of health information (Beck & Pollard, 2001; Pollard & Beck, 2000).

Daytime drama viewers (nearly one out of five respondents) reported television as their main source of health information more often than prime-time viewers (about one-half of all respondents). Nearly half of all regular television viewers reported they learned about health from television shows. Up to one-half of the viewers took some action as a result, with African American women more likely than others to take action after they heard about a health topic on a television entertainment show. Interpersonal discussion is one important outcome of viewing health information on television shows. Many Healthstyles respondents who were regular viewers said they discussed the health topics with others, and some took action to prevent the problem, told someone else to do something, called for further information, or visited a medical doctor or health clinic.

Minority women in the United States represent individuals with a disproportionate burden of disease and injury. Social modeling theory (Bandura, 1986) suggests that viewers (i.e., minority women) may be more likely to respond and to model behavior with positive outcomes when they identify with characters in a television show. They may also be more likely to avoid risky behavior when negative outcomes are shown.

Minority audiences frequently fail to take advantage of resources and infrastructure available to them (Baezconde-Garbanati, Portillo, & Garbanati, 1999), suggesting that extra efforts are critical to reinforce their attention to health information. When a health storyline airs on network television, E-E organizations may have an opportunity to provide the television show with an 800-number or PSA on the same health topic. The cancer storyline on the *The Young & the Restless* showed that responses can be generated from minority audiences in the United States when a toll-free number is linked to a daytime television storyline (Davis & Bright, 2002).

ENTERTAINMENT INDUSTRY RESOURCES

When the CDC's entertainment-education pilot project was established in 1998 as an agency-wide outreach effort, its first objective was to educate

Hollywood writers and producers about public health issues. Credible health materials were provided by the CDC, tailored to the needs of television entertainment writers. Health experts provided technical assistance when a scriptwriter asked for help; public health speakers presented at conferences attended by scriptwriters; and in 2001 the CDC established online health tip sheets that were easy for Hollywood creative personnel to access.

Daytime and primetime scriptwriters in Hollywood adhere to extraordinarily tight deadlines to create television programs that keep audiences coming back for future episodes. Creative and entertaining storylines are primary, and time to research and identify sources for medical and health topics may be very limited. Frequently, this task is assigned to researchers and scriptwriters' assistants who occupy entry-level positions and have little or no background in health. Shows like *ER* generally employ one or more medical or health care professional(s) as writers and continuity staff to advise on the scripts and authenticity of the sets and procedures that are shown, but they are the exception.

A growing number of health advocacy organizations recognize the need for health and medical expertise in Hollywood and promote their topics and offer their health and medical experts to television shows. When asked, most scriptwriters say they prefer a central clearinghouse for health information and access to experts on multiple topics.

The CDC program initiated its process of working with television shows through the development of a liaison unit that scriptwriters could access for resources, and that public health staff could access to reach scriptwriters. Some 60 tip sheets on health subjects were initially developed and combined with other public health materials in a loose-leaf binder for television personnel. Eventually, these materials were put online at a dedicated Web site for writers and producers (http://www.cdc.gov/communication/entertainment_education.htm).

Several television storylines were produced with CDC expertise during the period from 1998 to 2001: Hepatitis C, antibiotic resistance, and vaccine preventable disease *(ER)*; HIV, anthrax, and tuberculosis *(Chicago Hope)*; hepatitis C, flesh-eating bacteria, and chickenpox *(LA Doctors)*; STDs and skin cancer *(Beverly Hills 90210)*; breast cancer *(One Life to Live)*; hospital infection *(General Hospital)*; cardiovascular disease *(Any Day Now)*; and chlamydia *(Sex in the City)*. CDC experts provided briefings for scriptwriters at MTV (violence), NBC Saturday Morning shows (youth risk behavior), *ER* (various health topics), and *Any Day Now* (women's health issues).

In 2001 the CDC recognized the early successes and limitations of the Atlanta-based pilot effort and announced a request for proposals from outside the agency to establish an E-E program for public health. The result was a cooperative agreement partnership with the University of Southern California's Annenberg School for Communication's Norman Lear Center. The Norman

Lear Center offered a Los Angeles base, health communication theory and research expertise, and E-E experience.

COLLABORATIONS AND THEIR RESULTS

In 2002 Hollywood, Health & Society was launched as a USC/CDC collaboration, based in Los Angeles with an impressive advisory board of 35 entertainment, academic, and health leaders. The board is cochaired by: (1) the executive producer of a popular prime-time television show, *Law and Order: SVU*, who is also a former executive producer of *ER*; and (2) the president of the Writers Guild of America West. A new Web site was launched to promote the services of the USC program and the easy links to the CDC Web site, which had been reported as a top source for health information for Hollywood scriptwriters (Duke & Company, 2001; Wilson, 2002).

The USC-based program also established a key alliance with the Writers Guild of America West to host expert panel discussions on public health topics for its members—scriptwriters for motion pictures, broadcast television, cable television, and new technologies. The first panel discussion, which coincided with the launch of the Hollywood, Health & Society Program, addressed bioterrorism and featured CDC experts along with executive producers of prime-time TV shows, *The Agency* and *Law and Order: SVU*. A second panel discussion addressed "*What Are We Doing to Our Kids?*" with youth behavioral and marketing experts and writers from prime-television shows and film, *The Simpsons, The Guardian, Boston Public, Malcolm in the Middle*, and *Blue Crush*.

At the same time, a unique new partnership was forged between the CDC's Office of Women's Health and the American Federation of Television and Radio Executives (AFTRA), which represents actors and other professional performers and broadcasters in television, radio, and other technology formats. Members from the New York, Los Angeles, and San Francisco chapters of AFTRA joined with local health department counterparts to educate their own members and the public about women's health issues (Wilson, 2002). As a result of these first-year efforts, women's health materials were distributed at major events during National Women's Health Week in May, 2002. In addition, women's health topics were featured on television talk shows and news media broadcasts.

One particularly productive collaboration with a prime-time show occurred when a producer from *ER* requested a CDC expert to advise on a storyline about smallpox as a possible bioterrorism threat. This request came a few months after the tragedy of September 11, 2001 and the subsequent anthrax contamination in U.S. postal mail. A medical doctor who was a writer/producer on *ER* was developing the script. It dealt with two young children who became ill after returning from travel to a foreign country with their parents. The family went to the hospital twice before the children were diagnosed with pox-like lesions. The family and emergency room staff exposed to the children were quarantined, and the entire emergency room was placed in a lockdown situation, causing panic and hysteria among other patients who were not allowed to leave. Smallpox and bioterrorism were suspected and tissue samples were sent to the CDC. By the end of the show, smallpox was still not a definitive diagnosis. According to the Neilsen ratings, 27.5 million Americans watched the episode (Harvard School of Public Health, 2002).

The CDC consultant encouraged the *ER* scriptwriters to include the public health procedures that would be observed in a hospital emergency room and provided them with key facts about smallpox. As part of a health education outreach to allay public fear, national public health organizations, including the association of state health officers, launched a media campaign. Background information on smallpox and a list of media spokespersons were distributed to local and national news media to encourage news stories following the television show. As a result, at least 87 broadcast news stories about smallpox aired that day or the following day (VMS Monitoring Report, 2002).

A Harvard School of Public Health survey showed increased knowledge among *ER* viewers about the smallpox vaccine after the episode aired. As a result of the show, a majority of regular viewers (57%) knew it was important to receive the vaccine to prevent the onset of disease after exposure to the virus (Harvard School of Public Health, 2002). Only 39% of viewers knew this information prior to the airing of the smallpox storyline on *ER*.

RECOGNITION OF EXEMPLARY
HEALTH STORYLINES

The Sentinel for Health Award for Daytime Drama (http://www. entertainment.usc.edu/hhs.htm) was established by the CDC in 2000 to recognize "exemplary accomplishments of daytime dramas that inform, educate, and motivate viewers to live safer and healthier lives." The Award acknowledges the power of American soap operas to convey health information to daytime audiences, who are among the most loyal viewers of television shows (Dawidziak, 2002) with strong representation among groups at greatest risk for preventable diseases (Pollard & Beck, 2000).

The annual award event is currently administered by Hollywood, Health & Society in collaboration with the annual Soap Summit conference for daytime network executives, writers, and producers (http://soapsummit.org). This annual event is presented by PCI to highlight relevant health and social issues for potential storyline development. It features public health speakers on topics such as violence against women, STDs, youth risk behavior, obesity, youth violence, body image, women's health issues, tobacco, teenage suicide, and HIV/AIDS.

Judging for the annual award program is conducted in two stages: (1) CDC topic experts review entries for accuracy of depictions; and (2) a panel of experts from entertainment, advocacy, public health, and academia review finalists for potential benefit to the viewing audience and for entertainment value. During the first three years, ten storylines were recognized as finalists: HIV/AIDS, disability, drunk driving, and breast cancer in 2000; fetal alcohol syndrome, HIV/AIDS, teen drug abuse, and diabetes in 2001; and HIV/AIDS and breast cancer in 2002. The winning storylines were breast cancer (2000), diabetes (2001), and HIV/AIDS (2002).

A uterine cancer storyline from 1961–1962 was recognized in 2002 as the first health storyline in daytime drama. It received the first Sentinel for Health Pioneer Award, which was established to recognize storylines that aired before 2000 and that achieved a "first" in daytime drama. In accepting the award, head writer Agnes Nixon reported that she personally received letters from viewers who thanked her for producing the storyline because there was little information about cancer prevention in the entertainment media. Entries to the annual award program have included several letters from viewers reporting on the impact of the storylines. Similar to Healthstyles Survey findings, the letters indicate many viewers called their doctors, discussed the health topic with others, encouraged their friends and family members to seek medical help, and/or visited a health care provider (many obtained a diagnosis) after seeing a character with similar symptoms on the show (Wiard, 2001).

BOX 11.1.   Memorable Quotes from Award Materials, 2001 Sentinel Award winner, The *Young and the Restless*.

A Mother Wrote

Your story line on diabetes couldn't have come at a better time and it really impacted my life in a way I never thought possible . . . My son was diagnosed with diabetes as a college student and spent three days in intensive care at the same time Raul was experiencing it. I would truly like to speak to someone from your show to let them know the relevance of this topic to me and my family. We all had to learn about diabetes just like Raul's family and friends had to learn. My parents took it very hard, but my mom is an avid fan of the *Y&R*, and seeing it played out and listening to everything helped her to come to some sort of terms with it.

A Grandmother Wrote

I would like you to know by watching *Y&R* like I always do, and have been for over 25 years, that it helped me to find out why I have been so sick. So I asked my doc for a test and told him how I was feeling, and I am diabetic. Thanks for putting that on your show. I'm 45 years old and thanks to you I'll be around to see my 3rd grandchild due in January 2002.

A Couple Wrote

This past week we were caring for our friends' children while they were out of the country. Their five-year-old daughter was just not herself. She was craving water all the time and drinking it so fast—as if she inhaled it. My husband tapes Y&R, and he said to me—"Remember Raul?" There were many more symptoms and several visits to the pediatrician before diabetes was diagnosed. One more day and she would have been in a coma. Thanks to Y&R, she is OK. Your story line on diabetes was very educational and very real.

Source: Wiard (June 2001).

Numerous other award programs have recognized film and television portrayals of health and social issues in the United States. Two that have achieved a high degree of participation are the SHINE Awards, for portrayals of sexual health issues (http://www.advocatesforyouth.org/news/events/shine.htm), and the PRISM Awards, for portrayals of substance abuse issues (http://prismawards.com).

CONCLUSIONS

The entertainment-education initiatives described in the present chapter focus primarily on educating script writers and producers of U.S. television shows about critical health and safety issues, providing resources for storyline development, collaborations for expanding this activity within the industry, and recognition of exemplary work. Research and evaluation provide feedback and critique for improvements in the program. The overall goal is that accurate health information finds its way into television scripts so that viewers become aware of health issues and what they can do to improve and protect their own health. An anticipated outcome is behavioral responses that support healthier lifestyles and disease and injury prevention.

Hollywood, Health & Society is not an advocacy organization that focuses on single issues, and is not a paid media campaign that purchases advertising or message placement. The focus of the Hollywood, Health & Society program funded by CDC is to provide a range of health resources for entertainment writers and producers in the form of credible experts and information.

Some important lessons learned in the early development of E-E for U.S. television programs include:

1. E-E professionals, who appreciate the Hollywood entertainment industry as a business and understand the process of script writing and

storyline development, are in an advantageous position to work with television creative staff.

2. The opportunity to work with television shows is directly related to the usefulness of health information resources and the responsivenes of staff to provide appropriate health experts and materials in a timely manner.

3. E-E organizations must carefully assess their role as a resource versus critic or watchdog, since the latter can compromise working relationships when a resource organization to the Hollywood industry is perceived as highly critical.

4. E-E evaluation efforts can be achieved through creative partnerships that are responsive to timely field assessments of broadcast storylines.

5. Collaboration among health organizations is a key to building effective outreach efforts for E-E messages.

6. Collaboration with television industry organizations is a key to building credibility, access, and support for E-E efforts in network television in the United States.

With the growth of multicultural audiences in the United States, and the recognized health disparities associated with minorities, strategic E-E efforts will demand more targeted outreach to TV shows that are popular among these audiences, and more research to demonstrate health effects. This approach calls for working with Spanish-language telenovelas that are hugely popular in the United States, and with U.S.-based shows that draw large Hispanic and African American audiences. Writers and producers need current data and education on culturally sensitive issues that impact health status and disease risk among minority groups.

Finally, if E-E programs are to succeed in the long-term, educational efforts should ensure that young filmmakers and television scriptwriters are exposed to health topics and resources during their formative training years. At this time, writers may be more receptive to health issues as topics for dramatic entertainment programming. When they become familiar with issues and resources early on, they are more likely to consider them when they begin working in the industry.

REFERENCES

Baezconde-Garbanati, L., Portillo, C. J., & Garbanati, J. A. (1999). Disparities in health indicators for Latinas in California. *Hispanic Journal of Behavioral Sciences, 21,* 302–329.

Bandura A. (1986) *Social foundations of thought and action: A social cognitive theory.* Englewood Cliffs, NJ: Prentice-Hall.

Beck, V. (2000, May). *Entertainment-education at CDC.* Paper presentation at the CDC Research Conference: Setting A Research Agenda for Entertainment Education. Atlanta.

Beck, V., & Pollard, W. E. (2001, October). *How do regular viewers of prime-time entertainment television shows respond to health information in the shows?* Paper presented at the American Public Health Association. Atlanta.

Bell-Phillip Television Productions (2002, August 13). Countries and territories in which *The Bold and the Beautiful* can be viewed (110). Los Angeles, California.

Bogatz, G. A., & Ball, S. (1971). *The second year of Sesame Street: An evaluation.* Princeton, NJ: Educational Testing Service.

Brodie, M., Foehr, U., Rideout, V., Baer, N., Miller, C., Flournoy, R., & Altman, D. (2001). Communicating health information through the entertainment media: A study of the television drama *ER* lends support to the notion that Americans pick up information while being entertained. *Health Affairs, 20,* 192–199.

Children's Television Workshop (1988). *International adaptations of Sesame Street: Description and evaluation.* New York: Children's Television Workshop.

Davis, J. C. (personal communication August 30, 2002).

Davis, S., & Bright, M. A. (2002, July 31). *Young and Restless* Callers to the National Cancer Institute's Cancer Information Service, July 3–5, 2002. California Branch, Cancer Information Service, National Cancer Institute. [e-mail correspondence].

Dawidziak, M. (2002, September 1). Think daytime soaps are on the bubble? Maybe yes, maybe no, TV experts say. *Television Week, San Diego Union-Tribune,* 6–7.

Duke, M. (1998, January 27). Radio soap opera gives teenagers a dose of HIV reality. *Nashville Banner,* A-19.

Duke, W. E., & Company (2001). *Final report to the Robert Wood Johnson Foundation: Entertainment & health planning project.* Pacific Palisades, California.

Freimuth, V., Linnan, H. W., & Potter, P. (2001). Communicating the threat of emerging infections to the public. *Emerging Infectious Diseases, 6,* 337–347.

Glik, D., Berkanovic, E., Stone, K., Ibarra, L., Jones, M. C., Rosen, B., Schriebman, Gordon, L., Minassian, L., & Richardes, D. (1998). Health education goes Hollywood: Working with prime-time and daytime entertainment television for immunization promotion. *Journal of Health Communication, 3,* 263–282.

Harvard School of Public Health (2002, June 13). Press Release: After *ER* smallpox episode, fewer *ER* viewers report they would go to emergency room if they had symptoms of the disease: Viewers more likely to know about the smallpox vaccine. Boston, Massachusetts.

Keller, S. N., & Brown, J. D. (2002). Media interventions to promote responsible sexual behavior. *Journal of Sex Research, 39,* 68.

Kennedy, M. G., (2000). Special Issue on PMI: Introduction and Overview. *Social Marketing Quarterly, 6,* 5–11.

Kennedy, M. G., O'Leary, A., Beck, V., Pollard, W. E., & Simpson, P. (2002). Increases in calls to the CDC National STD and AIDS Hotline following AIDS-related episodes in a soap opera. *Journal of Communication,* in press. Atlanta, GA: CDC.

Maibach, E., Maxfield, A., Ladin, K., & Slater, M. (1996). Translating health psychology into effective health communication: The American Healthstyles Audience Segmentation Project. *Journal of Health Psychology, 1,* 261–277.

Malone, M. E. (2002, March 12). Health Section: TV remains dominant source for Americans on medical information. *Boston Globe,* C1.

Office of the National Drug Control Policy (2000, July). *Media campaign update fact sheets: Entertainment industry outreach.* Washington, DC.

O'Leary, A. (personal communication July 17, 2002).

Parvanta, C. F., & Freimuth, V. (2000). Health communication at the Centers for Disease Control and Prevention. *American Journal of Health Behavior, 24*(1), 18–25.

Pollard, W. E., & Beck, V. (2000, November). *Audience analysis research for developing entertainment-education outreach: Soap opera audiences and health information.* Paper presented at the American Public Health Association. Boston.

Salmon, C. T. (1994, February). *CDC Conference Summary report: Using entertainment-education to reach a generation at risk.* Atlanta, Georgia: CDC.

Salmon, C. T. (2000, May). *CDC Conference Summary report: Setting a research agenda for entertainment-education.* Available online at http://www.cdc.gov/communication/eersrch.htm.

Sharf, B. F., & Freimuth, V. S. (1993). The construction of illness on entertainment television: Coping with cancer on *thirtysomething. Health Communication, 5,* 141-160.

Sharf, B. F., Freimuth, V. S., Greenspon, P., & Plotnick, C. (1996). Confronting cancer on *thirtysomething*: Audience response to health content on entertainment television. *Journal of Health Communication, 1,* 157-172.

Singhal, A., & Rogers, E. (1999). *Entertainment-education: A communication strategy for social change.* Mahwah, N.J.: Lawrence Erlbaum Associates.

Stolberg, S. G. (2001, June 26). Science Times: CDC plays script doctor to spread its message. *The New York Times,* D1-2.

Strand, J., Rosenbaum, J., Hanlon, E., & Jimerson, A. (2000). The PMI local site demonstration project: Lessons in technical assistance. *Social Marketing Quarterly, 6,* 13-22.

VMS Monitoring Report (2002). Small Pox 5/16 to 5/17.

Wiard, N. (2001, June). "Raul's Diabetes," entry for *The Young and the Restless,* Sentinel for Health Award for Daytime Drama, Los Angeles, University of Southern California, Hollywood, Health and Society.

Wilson, K. E. (2002, November). *An evaluation of the CDC Resource Book for TV Writers and Producers.* Presented at the American Public Health Association Annual Meeting, Philadelphia, PA.

Winsten, J. A., & DeJong, W. (2001). The designated driver campaign. In R. E. Rice and C. K. Atkin (Eds.) *Public communication campaigns* (3rd ed) (290-294). Thousand Oaks, CA: Sage.

12

Entertainment-Education Television Drama in the Netherlands

Martine Bouman
Netherlands Entertainment-Education Foundation

In fall 2001 the weekly Dutch television drama series *Costa*! was broadcast on Monday evenings during prime-time (9:30 p.m. to 10:15 p.m.). On screen the setting is a beach club in Salau, on the Spanish Costa del Sol. People are sitting on the terraces that line the beach, enjoying themselves in the morning sun. Frida, played by the hottest Dutch actress Katja Schuurman, is walking to her apartment after an early morning stroll. Inside, her promiscuous roommate Agnetha, depicted by the tall blonde Froukje de Both, kisses her previous night's lover goodbye. As Frida comes in, Agnetha, barely dressed in a white bathrobe, falls back in the bed. "This is the way I like' em best," she sighs, "No strings attached, no address, no other details, I don't even recall his name!" Frida, with her exotic looks is certainly the most wanted "catch" of the series, but every now and then cutely shows her caring side, obviously has reservations. "I don't want to interfere in your love life," Frida muses, "But there's something to say about the dangers of your behavior." "Dangers?" Agnetha snaps back, "You needn't bother, I always make love double Dutch!" At Frida's apalled "Double Dutch?" she responds: "Yes, of course: I always use a condom, and I take the pill as well. Double protection, so nothing can happen to me!"

PHOTO 12.1.   Maarten, played by Hugo Haenen, and Laura, played by Linda de Wolf, two central characters in the Dutch television series *Villa Borghese*. (*Source*: Netherlands Heart Foundation.)

In fall 1992 the weekly Dutch drama series *Villa Borghese* was broadcast on Thursday evenings, in prime-time (8:25 p.m. to 9:15 p.m.). The setting is the lavishly decorated interior of Villa Borghese, a health farm somewhere at the Dutch countryside. The camera shows the room of young consultant Maarten, played by a Dutch Adonis, Hugo Haenen, as he puts his laptop computer away and closes the curtains. In the semidarkness the door opens and his new love interest, *Villa Borghese*'s dietician Laura, played by beautiful, black-haired Linda de Wolf, comes in, dressed in nothing more than an oversized silk shirt (Photo 12.1). As they kiss, she almost immediately pushes him away: "I can smell you picked up smoking again! Why?" Maarten clumsily replies: "I'm so sorry. I think it's the stress. I'm really trying to quit." He convinces her of his good intentions, and together they fall in bed, where she starts to undress him.

The Costa! Cast

Katja Schuurman and Froukje de Both are two of the three sexy actresses that made the Dutch television drama series *Costa!* so popular (Georgina Verbaan is the third) (Photo 12.2). The title of the television series refers to the name of the beach club Costa! on the Spanish Costa del Sol, where youngsters have a good time, drink, flirt, and hang around the beach. This television series (and its predecessor, the movie *Costa!*) is broadcast in the Netherlands in prime-time and attracts high viewer rates among youngsters. The scene described, and others, were coached by Stichting Soa Bestrijding, the Dutch Foundation Against Sexually Transmitted Diseases. By using popular media, Stichting Soa Bestrijding wants to influence the norms and values of Dutch youngsters regarding safe sex. Eight out of ten episodes contained safe sex messages, varying from incidentally showing a condom to explicitly discussing safe sex practices. A formal contract was signed and 22,500 Euros (approximately U.S. $22,500) were paid by Stichting Soa Bestrijding to EndeMol Netherland, the producer of the television series, to write the specific storylines.

PHOTO 12.2. The cast of *Costa!* (Left: Katja Schuurman; middle: Georgina Verbaan; right: Froukje de Both) (*Source*: Studio Kroon. Photograph by Ray Christian. Used with permision.)

RISE OF THE E-E STRATEGY IN THE NETHERLANDS

These scenes are examples of an entertainment-education (E-E) television intervention in the Netherlands.[1] The scenes about safe sex in *Costa!* were

---

[1] Other examples of Dutch E-E television interventions in the late 1980s and early 1990s are the comedy series *Familie Oudenrijn*, the *Way of Life Show*, docu-drama *Twaalf Steden, Dertien*

the result of in-script-participation initiated by Stichting Soa Bestrijding, the Dutch Foundation Against Sexually Transmitted Diseases. *Villa Borghese* was a coproduction, purposively designed and implemented to promote a healthy lifestyle, initiated by the Netherlands Heart Foundation.

Twenty years ago, such E-E interventions as *Costa!* and *Villa Borghese* would not have been possible in the Netherlands. At that time, collaborating with scriptwriters of popular television programs was problematic, because national health organizations had strong reservations about using a popular medium like a tabloid, a gossip magazine, a soap opera, or other drama series to communicate serious health messages. Apart from their unfamiliarity with popular culture, health organizations feared losing their respectable image.

Then, the climate for using entertainment television for health communication purposes changed. Especially the issue of health inequalities and the urgent need to develop new health communication methods played a major role in the rise of E-E in the Netherlands. Health communication professionals knew that, if the attention of the target audience were to be caught and held, especially if the audience is not spontaneously interested in health messages, it is no longer sufficient to rely solely on the rationality of the message. More emotionally appealing and popular communication methods must be brought into play. The E-E strategy aims at being more compatible with the lifestyles and culture of audiences who lack a "reading culture" and make less use of print media and more use of television. E-E television is based on popular culture, is more people-oriented (human interest) than object-oriented, and resembles a parochial network in the sense that it is a main source of inspiration and information, and encourages conversations with family, friends, and neighbors.

An important step in the history of E-E in the Netherlands was the start of an experimental project, Health Education and Drama, in 1990. The Netherlands Heart Foundation, in collaboration with the Dutch Health Education Center, developed this project. The aim of the project was to investigate whether television drama could be a useful health communication method to reach lower socioeconomic audiences and to map the conditions for effective collaboration between media-, subject-, and health-communication specialists, in the production of television programs for health communication purposes (Bouman & Wieberdink, 1993). The question of the right balance of education and entertainment, and collaboration with the media industry, was of much interest. In order to gain insight in these matters, an E-E intervention, the drama series *Villa Borghese*, was designed and implemented to promote a healthy lifestyle.

Ongelukken, the comedy series *Oppassen*, the hospital dramaseries *Medisch Centrum West*, and the game and talk show *Op leven en Dood*.

Villa Borghese

The title of the 13 episodes series *Villa Borghese* refers to a fictitious health farm in Holland, including a restaurant, swimming pool, and fitness centre. In this setting, opportunities were offered to come to terms with the importance of exercise, diet, not smoking, and dealing sensibly with stress. The aim of the series was to move social norms in the direction of a healthy lifestyle. The main characters in the series, primarily staff and costomers at the health farm who represented positive health behavior, had to be on the "winning side" and to be attractive to imitate.

This television series was designed as part of the Project on Health Education and Drama, initiated by the Netherlands Heart Foundation. The 13-episode series (50 minutes each) was broadcast in 1991 on Thursday evenings in primetime by AVRO, a public broadcasting organization, and produced by René Stokvis Productions.

The total cost of the series was 1,180,000 Euros (U.S. $1,180,000). The Netherlands Heart Foundation and the Dutch Prevention Fund contributed 295,000 Euros each (50%). The other half was paid by the AVRO.

This experiment with *Villa Borghese* provided understandings of the collaboration involved in an E-E coproduction (Bouman, 1999, 2002; Bouman & Van Woerkum, 1998; Bouman & Wieberdink, 1993; Wieberdink, 1992; Zandvliet, 1998). The lessons learned served as input to other television projects, such as the hospital drama series *Medisch Centrum West* in 1992–1994 (Bouman, Maas, & Kok, 1998) and, more recently, the drama series *Costa!* in 2001 (Van Empelen & Kok, 2002).

The rise of the E-E strategy in the Netherlands was also facilitated by changes in the media landscape. The Netherlands, as most countries in Western Europe, originally had a strong public broadcasting system, based on the National Media Act. The start of commercial broadcasting in the late 1980s, however, drastically influenced the field of television. Presently, public and commercial television channels coexist in the Netherlands. Media regulations have become less strict and allow government-related organizations (such as a ministry or a national health organization) under certain conditions to sign coproduction contracts with broadcasting organizations. Also, due to the strong competition for viewers between public and commercial broadcasting organizations, public broadcasting organizations have shifted their programming towards more and lighter entertainment. This shift provides more room for the design and implementation of E-E programs for social change.

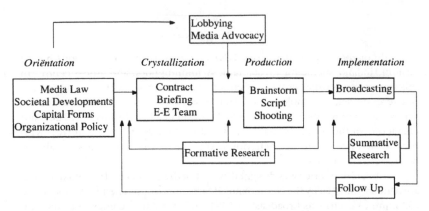

FIG. 12.1.   Stages of collaboration in entertainment-education. *Source*: Bouman (1999).

BEYOND ENTERTAINMENT

The E-E strategy is defined as "the process of purposively designing and implementing a mediating communication form with the potential of entertaining and educating people, in order to enhance and facilitate different stages of prosocial (behavior) change" (Bouman, 1999). An essential element in this definition is constituted by the words "purposively designing and implementing." The storylines about safe sex in *Costa!* and about smoking in *Villa Borghese* did not occur by accident. They resulted from planned collaboration between professionals from the television and health communication field. An essential in the E-E definition is goal-setting: "To enhance and facilitate different stages of prosocial (behavior) change." An E-E program goes beyond just entertainment. Its ultimate purpose is to contribute to the process of social change in health, environment, racial tolerance, etc. The intervention needs to be thoroughly planned. Different stages in collaboration demand different inputs from the partners (Figure 12.1). The design and implementation of the program need to be based on a multidisciplinary theoretical framework, as well as formative and summative research.

E-E PARTNERSHIP ARRANGEMENTS

E-E is a field of scholarly analysis, but its professional practice is strongly linked to the entertainment industry. This "marriage" between communication scholars and television professionals offers a challenge: How can both collaborate in entertainment projects without short-changing the other party? As in every partnership, commitment is required. Four types of E-E partnership arrangements are distinguished: (1) E-E lobbying, (2) E-E in-script participation, (3) E-E coproduction, and (4) E-E production (Bouman, 1999,

2002).[2] These partnership arrangements can be seen as a continuum with lobbying at one extreme and independent production at the other. In practice, an independent E-E production hardly exists and will therefore not be discussed here.

Health organizations or prosocial-issue groups can try to frame their lobbying request in such a way that media partners feel that there is something for them to gain. In the United States, a long line of Hollywood lobbyists and advocacy groups provide incentives, facts, expertise, support, and awards for storylines (Shefner & Rogers, 1992; Cantor, 1979; Montgomery, 1989). In the Netherlands these specific media lobbying organizations do not exist as such, although we see tendencies that point in that direction.[3] Of course health organizations try to increase their influence by establishing personal networks with members of the media community, but there is no formally organized E-E lobby movement in the Netherlands.[4] In the case of E-E lobbying, it is extremely important to find out what the norms, values, and rules of

---

[2]E-E lobbying is defined as "a strategy of prosocial organizations to put informal or formal pressure on broadcasting organizations or independent producers to deal with prosocial communication in their entertainment programs." E-E in-script participation is defined as "a formal transaction between a prosocial organization and a broadcasting organization or independent producer to use an already existing entertainment program as a carrier of prosocial communication." An example of this type of E-E collaboration in the Netherlands is the dramaseries *Costa!*. E-E coproduction is defined as "a formal transaction between a prosocial organization and a broadcasting organization or independent producer to design, produce and broadcast a new entertainment program for prosocial communication purposes." In this E-E partnership arrangement, entertainment television programs are especially designed for prosocial communication purposes. An example of this type of E-E collaboration in the Netherlands is the dramaseries *Villa Borghese*. E-E production is defined as "an initiative of a prosocial organization to act as an independent producer and design and produce one's own entertainment program for prosocial purposes and 'sell' it to a broadcasting organization."

[3]Such as Landelijk Bureau Leeftijdsdiscriminatie (age and elderly issues); E-quality (gender and ethnic issues); Stichting Omroep Allochtonen (ethnic issues) and Bureau Beeldvorming NOS, at present called 'Meer van Anders' (a lobbying organization about gender and ethnic issues within the television world itself).

[4]A possible explanation might be the fact that the broadcasting system in the United States is commercial in origin. Economic forces determine what kinds of television programs will be made. When groups are discriminated against (black, elderly, women, disabled), grassroots organizations advocate for proper media coverage. In the Netherlands, however, the different political and religious parties used to have their own broadcasting organizations and channels. These were, and still are, financially supported by members' and subscribers' fees. This so-called "pillarized" system makes it more possible for many voices in society to speak and be heard. The need for grass roots movements to protest and lobby for causes is therefore less important, although founding a new public broadcasting channel by an interest group is not very easy and requires a lot of effort. In the Netherlands, in the last few years several interest groups (new age groups, homosexuals, elderly) tried to attain the status of a public broadcasting organization, such as: Omroep 2000, Zender 7; Ommekeer; Radio Vitaal; Morgana; Charisma TV; and GTV. These initiatives were not successful however, and the necessary number of subscribers/members was not achieved.

the game are in the media world. Because there is no formalized agreement to collaborate; one is dependent on the goodwill of the other party.

As explained earlier, purposively designing and implementing an E-E program requires strategic planning. When health organizations want an E-E television program to be part of an integrated health campaign, they cannot rely on E-E lobbying. One way to be sure of the commitment of broadcasting companies is to pursue a more formal partnership arrangement: E-E in-script participation or E-E co-production. In these arrangements, health organizations establish a collaborative contract with their entertainment industry partner and pay a certain amount of "capital" to have their prosocial issue dealt with in the scripts of popular television programs. In the case of an in-script participation such as *Costa!* the program already exists and the scriptwriter has already put his or her own professional mark on the program. In an E-E co-production arrangement, new entertainment television programs are created and especially designed for prosocial communication purposes, as in *Villa Borghese*.

STEERING POWER

Obviously, the collaborative basis for the parties involved is quite different in these four partnership arrangements. Most steering power can be expected in the E-E coproduction arrangement, less in E-E in-script participation, and least in E-E lobbying. It would seem logical, therefore, to strive for the E-E coproduction arrangement, but both partnership arrangements have their own pros and cons. *Villa Borghese*, based on a coproduction arrangement, and *Costa!*, based on an in-script-participation, illustrate these advantages and disadvantages.

As a new series *Villa Borghese* had to establish its popularity and create rapport with the audience. It was difficult to gain high viewer ratings. *Villa Borghese* attracted 650,000 viewers, almost half of what was hoped for (Bouman & Wieberdink, 1993; ResCon, 1992a).

An advantage for *Costa!* was that the television series had no need to establish itself as a new genre (as *Villa Borghese* did). *Villa Borghese* was designed to propagate a healthy lifestyle, a genre with no precedent at that time in the Netherlands. The Stichting Soa Bestrijding could ride on the popularity of *Costa!* (the movie) and the already high viewer ratings of its television sequel.

A too-blatant selling of the educational message in E-E is ineffective. In the preparation stage of *Villa Borghese*, there was much discussion with the designated writers about the script and how the health messages should be incorporated. Issues such as a low-fat diet, dealing sensibly with stress, not smoking, and regular exercise were found to be very difficult for the scriptwriters to dramatize. The result was withdrawal by the first team of Dutch scriptwriters after almost a year of working together on the production.

They took the copyright of the series with them, including the title and the original setting of the series, namely *Sport Centrum Van Houten*. Due to time constraints, a second team of scriptwriters was hired in the UK. These writers were experienced professionals in BBC drama. They designed a new setting for the television series, a beauty farm. This hiring of English professionals, however, added an extra handicap to the E-E project as the scripts needed to be translated to Dutch and a special dialogue coach was needed during the shooting of the episodes. In *Villa Borghese* the planning schedule for the design and implementation of the drama series was one and a half years. Near the end of the collaboration, it suffered from time and energy constraints.

The way the health message was incorporated in *Villa Borghese* proved to be overly didactic. The storyline lacked suspense and developed too slowly (Bouman & Wieberdink, 1993; ResCon, 1992b). Apart from a lack of experience in designing E-E drama, this problem was due to the fact that the funding agencies (The Netherlands Heart Foundation and the Netherlands Prevention Fund) wanted to see "value for money." There were only 13 episodes, so the educational content was brought into play too quickly, although the health professionals and the media producers thought that the television series should provide entertaining drama first. *Villa Borghese* suffered from these imbalances. Alarmed by low viewer ratings and based on feedback from a viewers' panel, the scriptwriter and producer tried to create greater suspense by having one of the main characters hospitalized and die from a sudden heart attack. But these events appeared too late in the day. Due to low viewer ratings, the broadcasting organization cancelled the series.

Writing sex storylines for *Costa!* was not too difficult for the scriptwriters, because it was a "sexy" subject. The setting of a beach resort made it easy to introduce and show safe sex practices. However, some poor handling of the safer sex issue occurred. One of the main characters, for example, shaves off his pubic hair in a desperate attempt to get rid of newly acquired crab lice. This event lacked the consent of the Stichting Soa Bestrijding, as shaving is far from a solution to the lice problem. Because of the in-script-participation arrangement, Stichting Soa Bestrijding only had a say over the specific script parts that they had agreed upon, and not over the rest of the script. In some scenes the scriptwriters exaggerated and stereotyped sexual activities of youngsters in the television series. This problem could have been prevented by a coproduction partnership, as in *Villa Borghese* where the steering power of health experts was far greater.

IS IT ENTERTAINMENT-EDUCATION?

In a strict sense, one could claim that the E-E strategy can only be applied in co-production arrangements where television programs are new and purposively designed in order to meet the E-E criteria. These criteria imply the use of a theoretical framework and use of formative and summative research. In this sense, the storylines of *Costa!* miss the E-E boat (as do many other European and U.S. in-script-participation productions). Stichting Soa Bestrijding established the collaboration with EndeMol, the production company, when the design process was already in full progress. Most of the scripts of *Costa!* were already prepared and only short dialogues and scenes could still be inserted. The main characters were selected and no formative research on safer sex practices was conducted.

Nevertheless, Stichting Soa Bestrijding chose to collaborate. They briefed the scriptwriter team about the safer sex issues involved, and checked the storylines in the script. The rationale for their quick decision was the complete lack of any safer sex element in the predecessor of the television series, *Costa!* the movie (with one million young viewers in the three Benelux countries, it was considered a Dutch box-office hit). Stichting Soa Bestrijding proactively established contact with the makers of *Costa!* the television series. This pragmatic stance is understandable and realistic. They knew they were jumping on a fast train. In order to obtain insight into the impact of the safer sex storylines, Stichting Soa Bestrijding organized focus group interviews with youngsters aged 13–19 during and after broadcasts of the episodes. These qualitative data served as formative research for making a second series.

In Western countries there are hardly any E-E drama series designed in the strict sense of the definition of entertainment-education, because most of them are based on an in-script participation arrangement. The level of influence that health communication professionals can have in the E-E design process is directly related to the type of partnership arrangements. The highest influence is in an E-E coproduction arrangement. In *Villa Borghese*, the series could be designed according to behavior change theories (social learning, self-efficacy theory, parasocial interaction), because it was part of the agreement that health communication professionals would be involved in the design and implementation process. *Villa Borghese* can be regarded as the first Dutch drama series that explicitly put Miguel Sabido's E-E methodology to a test.

THEORETICAL DESIGN

The essence of the E-E strategy is to use television characters as role models for prosocial behavior. According to Sabido's methodology of E-E soap operas, there are three types of role models: (1) those that support the prosocial behavior (positive role models), (2) those that reject it (negative role models), and (3) those that doubtfully, but gradually change their opinion in favor of the prosocial behavior (these are transitional models) (Nariman, 1993). In *Villa Borghese*, Laura, a dietician and staff member at the health farm, represented a positive role model. Maarten, a young consultant and a visitor at the health farm who was struggling with his unhealthy habits (smoking, junk food, and stress), symbolized a transitional role model. Luciano, the five-star cook of *Villa Borghese* who takes bribes from rich clientèle for cooking high-fat meals, represented a negative role model. Maarten adopts a healthier lifestyle during the soap opera series. He and Laura start a romance, while Luciano dies from a sudden heart attack.

In order to monitor audience reactions to the storyline and characters, a panel of 23 viewers were followed during broadcasting of the drama series *Villa Borghese*. It showed that Maarten, who was intended to be a transitional role model, was evaluated by the panel members as a positive role model! Initially members of the audience panel liked him because he was good-looking and a hard-working man; later they liked him because he adopted a healthier lifestyle and for his support to the management of the health farm. Luciano was evaluated by the audience as a positive role model in the beginning and negative at the end of the television series. Laura was regarded as a positive role model during the entire series. When the actors and actresses of *Villa Borghese* were typecast, some were hesitant about being involved in a "health education" series. They were afraid to be labelled as a "health freak," which might damage their career. Their contracts contained a clause that did not allow them to play an opposite character in another television series (e.g., Laura could not play a drunken mother).

In *Villa Borghese*, credibility was meant to play an important role in the modelling process. The main characters were paramedical professionals and staff members of the health farm. Members of the audience panel indicated that they thought visiting a health farm was a rather exaggerated way to improve one's health. The original script called for the fancy health farm to be taken over by its staff members and transformed into a public health center during its second broadcasting season. Due to low ratings, however, the series was not continued.

People's trust in statements by film and television celebrities played an important role in the series *Costa!* In the Double Dutch scene, admired celebrity actress Katja Schuurman plays the caring person who warns her friend about the risks of her promiscuous behavior. The characters in *Costa!* were already identified and selected. It was therefore not possible to create positive, negative, and transitional role models. The scriptwriter himself allocated the storylines to the actors/actresses in a way that he found logical. Some safer sex messages, for example, were attributed to the actress Georgina Verbaan, who played a naïve and clumsy young woman. No one on the audience panel identified with her. She was certainly not a positive role model. Typecasting her for delivering safer sex messages proved to be a wrong choice.

The information provided in the television series *Villa Borghese* was too general and perhaps even too trivial (ResCon, 1992a). The series dealt with the importance of a healthy lifestyle and its essential aspects in a rather general way and paid considerable attention to emphasizing the effectiveness of health behavior change, highlighting the extent to which certain habits such as not smoking, a low-fat diet, and sufficient exercise have a positive influence on health. Self-efficacy, the extent to which people think that they have the skills to change their behavior, and imparting the skills to handle different situations (like smoking and eating), seems to offer a better option for changing behavior than emphasising the damaging effects of these behaviors for health.

The television program should show the desired health behavior by the characters and depict how ordinary people deal with health dilemmas in their everyday life, instead of having them say what the audience ought to do. Nariman (1993) remarked, "It is important to note that entertainment-education soap operas address their objectives by associating them with pre-existing human values and dramatizing how specific characters learn to more fully actualize these values in their lives by practicing the prosocial behavior."

THE CREATIVE DESIGN PROCESS

In an E-E collaboration there is always tension between following systematic plans, as health communication professionals are trained to do, and following creative impulses, as television professionals are trained to do (Runco & Albert, 1990; van Woerkum, 1981, 1987). Especially in a coproduction arrangement where all partners work closely together, these differences come to the fore. A health communication professional stated, "Brainstorming for television professionals often means creating all kinds of ideas and acting out every wild fantasy, although there is a limited budget that allows for only so much of the expressed ideas. Then we have to sober them up and calculate the possibilities. Often enough it appears that some of the ideas are not at all feasible, for example, that the actors they had in mind were not available" (Bouman, 1999). Health communication professionals often become annoyed (although some are also thrilled) with how television professionals indulge in fantasies and how they let their imagination run wild.

Health communication professionals feel the urge to pull the creative team back to earth. The crucial question for television professionals is how to visualize ideas and thoughts (a dominant right brain mode of thinking; see Sperry in Edwards, 1986). Health communication professionals ask such questions as "Is what is said logical and true? Can this message cause a prosocial effect?" (a dominant left brain mode of thinking; see Sperry in Edwards, 1986). A television professional said about health communication professionals in this regard, "From start to finish, they are busy guaranteeing that their facts and figures will be taken into account. If I do that, I would have no room left for intuition, for big strokes. These big strokes may not be precisely right, but they do guide my thinking" (Bouman, 1999). This television professional claimed, "In a certain stage, I want to be free to do what I think best. If there are tight agreements about certain messages, then I still want to initiate the propositions. You can agree or not agree, but don't follow me around all the time. It is a completely different way of thinking" (Bouman, 1999).

Creative professionals claim that they need freedom in order to create work with "a spirit" (Bouman, 1999). A television professional said, "For a writer it is very important to be able to produce from his own creativity, that the product bears his own special signature. If he does just what he is called for, because it's just another assignment, you always get a product without a spirit or soul" (Bouman, 1999).

These interview fragments bring up the question of who is in charge of the creative process, given the fact that an E-E television program has to reconcile the goals and aims of both professions (educational and creative). A theoretical perspective about stages of creativity was developed in the early 1960s by the American psychologist Jacob Getzels. Getzels distinguished five stages of creativity: first insight, saturation, incubation, ah-ha!, and verification (Edwards, 1986).

When we combine Getzel's insight in the stages of creativity with Sperry's different (left and right) modes of thinking, we may elucidate the respective roles that health communication and television professionals play in the stages of collaboration in an E-E television program (Fig. 12.2). The role of health communication professionals, as representatives of the left brain mode of

First Insight	Saturation	Incubation	Ah-Ha!	Verification
R	L	R	R	L

L-mode	R-mode
Verbal	Nonverbal
Syntactical	Perceptual
Linear	Global
Sequential	Simultaneous
Analytic	Synthetic
Logical	Intuitive
Symbolic	Concrete
Temporal	Nontemporal
Digital	Spatial

FIG. 12.2.   Five stages of creativity. (*Source*: Bouman 1999, after Getzel's conception of Creativity and Sperry's theory of the functioning of the left and right brain hemisphere, in Edwards 1986.)

thinking, are especially important in the saturation and verification stages. The role of television professionals, as representatives of the right brain mode of thinking, is important in the incubation and illumination stages. Either television professionals or health communication professionals can develop the first insight.

Television professionals preferred to get as much information as possible at the saturation stage, and then to be left alone at the incubation stage. Health communication professionals who did not interfere with this right-mode thinking process of television professionals were regarded by them as relatively good collaboration partners.

IMPLEMENTATION

Both health communication and television professionals want a television program with high entertainment value and high viewer ratings. These are cooperative motives, but the two sets of actors diverge in interest and become competitive when it comes to the ultimate goal (Pruitt & Carnevale, 1993). Health communication professionals want to influence the audience's knowledge, attitude, and behavior, while television professionals want to entertain the audience and satisfy commercial sponsor-revenue ambitions as well as their professional standards. Win-win situations are defined as agreements in which both parties accomplish their major goals. In a negotiation context, according to Pruitt and Carnevale (1993), there are four possible outcomes: Victory for one party, compromise, win-win agreement, and nonagreement. What conditions need to be met to satisfy both partners about the collaboration process in E-E?

Health communication professionals usually have scientific training in which matters of objective information, truth, balancing of values, and standardized protocols and procedures are important. Television professionals have professional training in which creativity, originality, spontaneity, and authorship are important. On commencing their E-E collaboration, both sets of professionals enter the process with their own professional standards and frames of reference. Earlier research (Bouman, 1999) showed that these two frames of reference (and perceptions of reality) often conflict in the daily practice of producing an E-E program. Health communication professionals specify their aims and goals by means of a thorough and often detailed briefing, based on their frame of reference. After the briefing and the discussion with the television professionals, the latter also start to work on the project from their own frame of reference. During the actual production stage, the conflict becomes more evident. While both professionals think they are doing a good job, each is questioned and criticized by the other because the production process does not evolve in the direction that the other wants.

A reference frame for conflict is fought out at the production level, on the work floor. Recognizing this potential conflict, both professionals invest time in socializing with each other in order to influence the decisions that are made. But the production of the television program takes place in the domain of the television professionals, so ultimately their frame of reference proves to be more decisive. Health communication professionals, more often than television professionals, reframe their issues. During the collaboration process, and especially at the production stage, they are confronted with controversies that are based on different perceptions of reality. Because of the deadline structure of television, which requires quick and decisive answers when problems arise, there is not much time for reflection. This results most of the time in accepting the television professionals' frame of reference. Health communication professionals only in rare cases succeed in having television professionals accept their frame of reference.

Television professionals almost always succeed in bending the reframing process into their direction (situation 2 in Fig. 12.3). When a conflict of frames of reference exists, the E-E collaboration ultimately leads to victory for the entertainment partner over the education partner.

Can the different frames of reference be reconciled in a balanced E-E product? Bourdieu (1993; 1998) stated that the field that is most subject to the demands of the market will dominate the market orientation of other fields. Other fields can either submit to this domination or try to capitalize their own forms of capital in a way that aims to rebalance the power structure. One form of power, other than economic, that health organizations used in their contact with media professionals is their monopoly on legitimate information (that is, expertise).

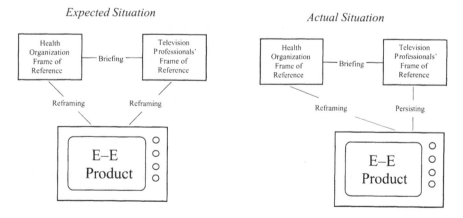

FIG. 12.3.   Symmetry and asymmetry of power in entertainment-education.
Source: Bouman (1999).

According to Bourdieu, every field wants to protect and accumulate its different forms of capital. The accumulation of capital by the television professionals is a certain threat to the health communication field, and vice versa. By collaborating with television professionals in entertainment genres, health professionals risk losing their respectable image (in their field of health communication). An elitist ivory tower position must be surrendered in order to collaborate with television professionals. The reverse is also true. Television professionals collaborating with health communication professionals may become "too didactic" in the eyes of their entertainment colleagues, and lose their credibility and respect in the television entertainment world.

Health organizations that want to collaborate with television professionals need to develop a proactive media policy in which specific choices for television partners, television genres, and approaches in television programs are carefully and consciously made beforehand. On the other hand, television organizations that want to collaborate with health organizations must be willing to reframe their frame of reference and to invest in the creation of common ground. In order to create a joint frame of reference, an E-E workshop for the members of the E-E team and other relevant stakeholders should be a standard procedure that initiates every E-E collaboration. In the crystallization stage of the *Villa Borghese* project, a briefing retreat was organized for the collaboration partners. The principles of E-E were sketched out, and the aim and target groups for the television series were outlined.

E-E television programs are designed in a high-risk context. Criteria that normally apply for purely educational or purely entertainment television formats do not fit with the criteria for E-E genres. Therefore E-E television programs should be perceived as a new genre, and as such should be accepted and acknowledged in both the television and the health communication field.

LESSONS LEARNED

Since the first E-E projects such as *Villa Borghese* were launched in the Netherlands in the early 1990s, several important lessons have been learned. Health communication professionals are better equipped now to deal with the tensions and challenges in an E-E television project.

1. In an E-E television project, it is important that both the health organization and the television organization delegate professionals who are capable of dealing with the intrinsic tensions of combining entertainment and education and differences in work culture. Health communication professionals, among other things, should invest more time in watching different genres of television as part of their professional schooling in order to become more television literate.

2. In order for both health communication and television professionals to become skilled collaboration partners, the integration of E-E teaching modules in present teaching institutes and departments in the field of television and health communication is an important next step. E-E has gradually become part of the professional discourse of Dutch health communication scholars and researchers. Health organizations in the Netherlands use popular media in their campaigns; doctoral and masters communication students write theses on the E-E strategy, and guest lectures and workshops are organized as part of professional schooling activities. Although there are media entertainment departments in Dutch universities, a specific E-E curriculum is still missing. To contribute to the above, the Netherlands E-E Foundation (NEEF) was founded in 1998 to stimulate E-E research and to create a platform for E-E professionals.

The Third International E-E 2000 Conference was held in the Netherlands. This Conference led to the E-E 2000 Declaration (NEEF and JHU/CCP, 2001).[5] NEEF designed an E-E handbook on a CD-Rom for students and practitioners, funded by the Dutch Health Research and Development Council. At present NEEF conducts a research and implementation project *Gezondheid in Beeld* (an analysis of Dutch soap operas and their portrayal of sexual health issues), funded by the Dutch Health Research and Development Council. This project features close collaboration between researchers, health communicators, and the media industry.

3. Future E-E television drama could be more successful if time were invested in the crystallization stage to create mutual understanding and a joint frame of reference between television professionals and health communication professionals. When the actual production process starts, there is no time for such relationship-building.

The present chapter illustrated some of the do's and don'ts of E-E television projects with examples from the Dutch drama-series *Villa Borghese* and *Costa!* Hopefully these insights will contribute to further the collaboration that is fundamental to effective entertainment-education.

REFERENCES

Bouman, M. P. A. (1999). *The Turtle and the peacock: Collaboration for prosocial change: The E-E strategy on television.* Wageningen, Netherlands: Wageningen Agricultural University.
Bouman, M. P. A. (2002). Turtles and peacocks: Collaboration in entertainment-education television. *Communication Theory, 12*(2), 225–244.
Bouman, M. P. A., Maas, L., & Kok, G. J. (1998). Health education in television entertainment: A Dutch drama serial. *Health Education Research, 13*(4), 503–518.

---

[5]For the digital conference report, see http://www.entertainment-education.nl and http://www.jhuccp.org.

Bouman, M. P. A., & Wieberdink E. A. M. (1993). *Villa Borghese*: A soapseries on heart health. *Canadian Journal of Cardiology, 9* (Suppl.D), 145D–146D.

Bouman, M. P. A., & Woerkum, C. van. (1998, July). *Television entertainment for health: Collaboration aspects of the design process.* Paper presented to the International Communication Association, Jerusalem.

Bourdieu, P. (1993). *The field of cultural production: Essays on art and literature.* Cambridge, England: Polity Press.

Bourdieu, P. (1998). *Over televisie.* Amsterdam: Boom.

Cantor, M. G. (1979). The politics of popular drama. *Communication Research, 6*(4), 387–406.

Edwards, B. (1986). *Drawing on the artist within.* New York: Fireside Book, Simon & Schuster, Inc.

Montgomery, K. C. (1989). *Target primetime: Advocacy groups and the struggle over entertainment television.* New York: Oxford University Press.

NEEF and Jhu/CCP (2001). Proceedings of the Third International Entertainment-Education Conference, for Social Change. Arnham/Amsterdam, September 17–22, 2000, Netherlands 423.

Nariman, H. N. (1993). *Soap operas for social change: Toward a methodology for entertainment-education television.* Westport, CT: Praeger Publishers.

Pruitt, D. G., & Carnevale P. J. (1993). *Negotiation in social conflict.* Buckingham, England: Open University Press.

ResCon (1992a). *Dramaserie Villa Borghese: Resultaten van een effectmeting.* Den Haag, The Netherlands: Nederlandse Hartstichting.

ResCon (1992b). *Dramaserie Villa Borghese: Resultaten van een kwalitatief onderzoek.* Den Haag, The Netherlands: Nederlandse Hartstichting.

Runco, M. A., & Albert, R. S. (Eds.) (1990). *Theories of creativity.* Thousand Oaks, CA: Sage.

Shefner, C. L., & Rogers E. M. (1992, May). *Hollywood lobbyists: How social causes get into network television.* Paper presented at the International Communication Association Conference, Miami.

Van Empelen, P., & Kok, G. (2002) *Costa!: Een soap als medium om jongeren voor te lichten over SOA.* Research report Capaciteitsgroep Experimentele Psychologie, Universiteit Maastricht, Maastricht, The Netherlands.

Wieberdink, E. A. M. (1992). *'Villa Borghese': Een verslag van de ervaringen en resultaten van het project 'GVO en Drama'.* Utrecht, The Netherlands: Landelijk Centrum GVO.

Woerkum, C. M. J. van (1981). Planmatigheid versus creativiteit. *Massacommunicatie, 9*(1/2), 48–59.

Woerkum, C. M. J. van (1987). *Massamediale voorlichting: Een werkplan* (2nd ed.). Meppel/Amsterdam: Boom.

Zandvliet, A. (1998). De popularisering van een gezonde leefstijl. Een casestudie van de produktie van een 'soap' in de gezondheidsvoorlichting. In P. Schedler and F. Glastra, *Voorlichting in veldtheorethisch perspectief* (pp. 69–85). Deventer, The Netherlands: Lemma BV.

13

Entertainment-Education Programs of the BBC and BBC World Service Trust

Michael J. Cody
Sangeeta Fernandes
Holley Wilkin
University of Southern California

Mark Fowler, a popular character on *EastEnders*, contracted HIV when he was a young, drug-taking rebel. Later, as an adult, he stopped taking his combination pills because he could no longer cope with the side effects. He subsequently contracted pneumonia so severe he fell into a coma. Emotions ran high as *EastEnders'* viewers watched as his mother maintained a constant vigil, but they had to wait for the following weeks' episodes to see if Mark lived or died. Mark survived and is later reintroduced to his girlfriend from his rebel days, who was now dying from AIDS. He visited her in the hospice, and married her before she died.

This storyline provided amble opportunity to educate the public about HIV, how it is contracted, how to cope with it, and the importance of social support structures and medical assistance at lives' end. It is one of many examples of the use of E-E by the British Broadcasting Corporation (BBC), a leader in the effective use of radio and television to educate and inform through both educational programs and E-E programs. In this chapter we will briefly overview several of the important E-E programs created and aired by the BBC. We will start, however, by discussing the unique history of the BBC.

THE BRITISH BROADCASTING CORPORATION

The British Broadcasting Corporation (BBC) began in the 1920s as a radio company, and later emerged as the world's first public television system. Unlike the development of the broadcast industry in the United States of America, the BBC was created under a Royal Charter to provide a free service to the public, with the objectives to "inform, educate, and entertain" by providing quality, realistic, programming serving the interests and needs of the general public. These important developments are chronicled on the BBC Web site, and in the BBC Charter:

> In the view of the wide spread interest which is taken by Our Peoples in broadcasting services and of the great value of such services as means of disseminating information, education and entertainment, We believe it to be in the interests of the Our Peoples . . . that there should be an independent corporation which should continue to provide broadcasting services. . . . We deem it desirable that the Service should continue to be developed and exploited to the best advantage and in the national interest. (http://www.bbc.co.uk/thenandnow/educate_home.shtml)

Important features of the Charter include the fact that the BBC is a corporation operating 'independent' of government, providing a quality service that furthers the national interest, through "information, education, and entertainment." The Charter was renewed, most recently in 1996, confirming its "editorial independence" until 2006 when the Charter will undoubtedly be renewed again (see: http://www.bbc.co.uk/info/bbc/charter.shtml).

One of the first to recognize the role of broadcasting to do more than entertain was the BBC's first Director–General, Lord John Reith, who wrote, in 1924:

> I think it will be admitted by all that to have exploited so great a scientific invention for the purpose and pursuit of entertainment alone would have been a prostitution of its powers and an insult to the character and intelligence of the people. (http://www.bbc.co.uk/thenandnow/educate_home.shtml)

Lord Reith placed great emphasis on using radio, and later television, to educate and inform the public, and his legacy is still felt at the BBC. In the 1930s BBC school broadcasts were heard in over 8,000 schools. In 1951 *The Archers* (a radio dramatic serial) was launched to educate the British on agricultural innovations and livestock health issues, after Britain endured shortages during World War II; it became one of the most popular, long-lived, and enduring radio programs in the world. Another triumph occurred in 1971, with the launch of The Open University. It is today the UK's largest university, with over

200,000 students and customers (http://www.open2.net/). The BBC educational programs in general encompass a wide variety of issues, and programs such as *BBC Nature* and *BBC Knowledge* provide "new ways to learn as you watch" (http://www.bbc.co.uk/thenandnow/educate_home.shtml).

With its Royal Charter, the BBC operates with considerable autonomy, free of political interference, funded by collecting a licensing fee on each television set owned and operated in the UK, roughly $150 USD a year. The BBC was thus free to air programs "associated with high quality output in the areas of original and classic drama and serials, light entertainment, comedy, documentary and, outside broadcasts, and sports coverage" (Phillip Drummond, personal communication, March, 12, 2002). Today, however, public debate rages between "elitists" advocating high culture and "populists" seeking more pure entertainment (including some soap operas). Consequently, the BBC has to balance "quality programming" serving the public interests for both elitists and populists.

THE THREAT OF COMMERCIAL TELEVISION

In 1955 commercial television was introduced in the United Kingdom under the independent television network ITV, providing competition for the UK audience and forcing the BBC to pay attention, eventually, to "ratings." ITV attracted many viewers with the creation of shows such as *Coronation Street*, a popular soap opera featuring an urban working class community set around Manchester, in the traditionally industrial North West of England, which premiered in the early 1960s. By the 1980s the BBC was beginning to struggle to keep viewers, as *Coronation Street* reigned supreme in popularity. The BBC "realized that they needed to find some new popular programmes in order to bring the viewers back to the BBC" (Brake, 1994, p. 7). Due to its original Charter, however, the BBC confronted a difficult dilemma: to compete for audience ratings while simultaneously providing quality programming that serve the public's interest.

To tackle this dilemma, the BBC turned to producer Julia Smith and script editor Tony Holland, who provided the creative force to launch a new soap opera (Smith & Holland, 1987). The two are responsible for the birth of *EastEnders*, a soap opera about a community of working class Londoners living in the East End. *EastEnders* became one of the BBC's "most consistently popular shows since its launch" (Brake, 1994, p. 7), and *EastEnders* soon rose to challenge *Coronation Street* for audience share (Middleham & Wober, 1997). Week by week, the two soap operas competed for top ratings. The BBC has also added a number of medical dramas (*Casualty*, *Doctors*) that achieve both high ratings and maintain quality programming. The BBC also featured a number of important health-related storylines, although from time to time questions arise as to whether the health information on *Casualty* is accurate and fully presented (also see next section of this chapter).

A critically important step was taken in 1999 when the BBC World Service Trust was created as an independent charity within the BBC World Service to promote development through the innovative use of media in developing countries and in countries in transition (see mission statement at: www.bbc.co.uk/worldservice/us/trust/index.shtml). The newly established BBC World Service Trust exists to mobilize the increasingly powerful voice of the media, so that it can play its part as a catalyst for social change. The Trust was set up to focus education, training, health, and development activities in one unit, drawing on the expertise within Bush House (the BBC's main office in London) and the BBC as a whole. Its key role is to use media to promote development and to build media expertise in developing countries. The Trust relies on radio, television, and integrated programs to tackle important social problems, including leprosy (detailed later in this chapter, and: www.bbc.co.uk/worldservice/us/trust/index.shtml).

THE BBC SOAP OPERAS AND OTHER PROGRAMS

According to Buckingham (1987), Crayford, Hooper, and Evans (1997), and Smith and Holland (1987), British soaps often represent realistic representations of working class individuals and their problems: "British soap opera has been a mirror to many contemporary social themes over the past 15 years ... help[ing] make soap opera one of the many ways by which people now normalize their lives" (Crayford et al., 1997, p. 1649). The emphasis on realistic representations of working class individuals dates at least to the world's longest-running soap opera, the radio dramatic serial, *The Archers*, featuring the lives of a fictitious farming family, the Archers. This dramatic radio serial uses a formula of humor, character development, and conflict to introduce information about modern farming practices to listeners, devoting 60% of content to entertainment and 40% to education (see Singhal & Rogers [1999] for an overview of the program). *The Archers* maintains a devoted following on BBC Radio 4, especially in rural sections of the United Kingdom. *The Archers* Web site provides access to programs that listeners have missed, quizzes, and fun activities, and archived stories from years gone by. The program ceased to include educational materials on farming in the 1970s, but the Archer family and new members to the cast continue to raise a number of more universal social and health issues relevant to more urban audiences, such as alcohol abuse (see, for more details: http://www.bbc.co.uk/radio4/archers/index.shtml). One important element of the Archers' success, however, is that it demonstrated early that a particular formula of drama, humor, and education proved successful in educating listeners, giving credibility to an E-E format in the UK which was not documented in the United States during the 1950s and 1960s.

The *EastEnders*

Later, during the 1980s television shows such as *Coronation Street* and *East-Enders* emerged as exemplars of the "slice of reality" that is so characteristic of British soaps. In the case of *EastEnders*, people live in small apartments in terraced houses and meet each other at such places as a pub, the Queen Vic, the street market, the café, or the Laundromat. This small setting coupled with a close-knit community provides ample opportunity for scriptwriters to raise a number of issues (Middleham & Wober, 1997). The producers consider the show to be in the "social realist tradition," and emphasize that each show features "everyday life" and its problems, and life as it unfolds in the "inner city today" (Middleham & Wober, 1997, p. 531). The characters on the program are ethnically diverse, so as to provide a realistic representation of the actual population in London's East End.

EastEnders garnered a huge following among the UK public because viewers identified with characters and with the problems they confronted in everyday life, like unemployment, family conflict, alcohol abuse, and much more. Once characters were developed and defined, and understood as certain "archetypes" with articulated goals, storylines were written to include how a variety of rebels, rivals, or antagonists would pursue their goals and block others from achieving their goals. Many of the scenes in the program focus on confronting and solving problems, and on conflict between characters. Viewers tune in for the suspense, drama, and conflict. Of course, strategically placed cliff hangers would keep viewers emotionally involved (see the story of Mark Fowler, below). Emphasis is placed first on "entertainment," with educational elements interlaced unobtrusively with the plots. As is the case in the typical E-E program, these prosocial storylines operate to increase interpersonal conversations among viewers about the programs, and to increase information-seeking behavior. The programs direct viewers to toll-free numbers or to the BBCi Web site for additional information.

Social issues were raised the first year that *EastEnders* aired (Brake, 1994), and have continued for over 17 years since. In the first year, Michelle Fowler struggled to cope with being a pregnant schoolgirl, raising issues about abortion and underage sex (and, as the audience soon found out, with a much older man). A favorite character, Mark Fowler, was tempted to experiment with drugs and joined a racist organization. Meanwhile, Angie Watts, who operated the local pub, was convicted of drinking and driving, which forced her (and viewers) to confront the reality of alcohol abuse and addiction.

EastEnders' insistence on producing a "slice of life" soap led to a diverse range of important issues addressed over the years, including stories about homosexuals, rape, unemployment, racial prejudice, single-parent families, teenage pregnancy, prostitution, arranged marriages, attempted suicide, drug problems, alcoholism, generational conflicts, extramarital affairs and marital dissolution, sexism, urban deprivation, problems with pregnancies/breast feeding, domestic abuse, safety hazards, the importance of learning new skills, and mental breakdown.

In fact, a visit to the Web site (www.bbc.co.uk/eastenders/helpindex.shtml) reveals how many health-related storylines and organizations are provided to the interested viewer. In January of 2003 these include bereavement, road safety, and domestic violence, all featured in recent episodes of the program. In another recent storyline, the show employed the expertise of a professional advisor in order to ensure a realistic portrayal of a schizophrenic character. In 1997, Dr. Reveley, a psychiatrist and professional advisor to the National Schizophrenia Fellowship, was asked to advise the show on a story line concerning Joe Wickles, a teenager who battled psychotic depression and was diagnosed with schizophrenia. *EastEnders* succeeded in providing fairly accurate information about the stigma of schizophrenia, with Reveley's advice (Reveley, 1997). The storyline won a mental health award, and a toll-free number and Web address were included in a subsequent episode. A large number of viewers called the number seeking additional information (Lougrhan, 2001). The inclusion of a hotline number in conjunction with soap opera storylines has illustrated that E-E storylines increase interest in learning more about specific health issues. Hardyman and Leydon (2002) found an increase in "worried well" callers to a cancer hotline during and after a Coronation Street storyline in which a popular character was diagnosed with, and died quickly of, cervical cancer.

Arguably one of the most memorable storylines on *EastEnders* featured Mark Fowler. When viewers first met Mark, he was a sulky, rebellious teenager. He ran away from home when he was 17, got involved in drugs and ended up in a detention center for burglary. When he came home he was 22, and had discovered that he had contracted HIV. As a rule he has been healthy, but a pneumonia scare was a reminder of the dangers of the virus with which he continues to live. This pneumonia scare truly caught the attention of the *EastEnder* viewers (see Box 13.1). Considerable sympathy has been expressed for Mark who was reunited with Gill, the girlfriend from his wild years, from whom he contracted HIV. By this time, however, she had developed full-blown AIDS. Mark married a very sick Gill, who died the next day. One can imagine during Mark's pneumonia and Gill's death that viewers would have had the same intense emotional and psychological experiences that viewers shared with the television character "Nancy" on the American program *thirtysomething*, when she coped with cancer (see Sharf & Freimuth, 1993;

Sharf, Freimuth, Greenspon, & Plotnick, 1996), presumably causing feelings of empathy, sympathy, mental rehearsals of what viewers would say or do if such events happened to them, interpersonal conversations with other viewers, an interest in learning more about the HIV virus, and intentions to avoid the virus.

BOX 13.1. HIV Cliff Hanger for *EastEnders*

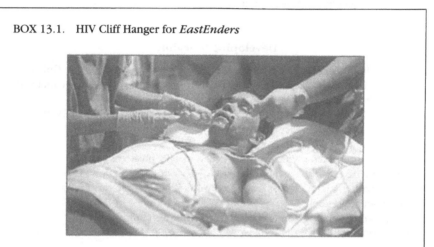

Mark Fowler's condition is critical after contracting pneumonia. (*Source:* BBC used with permission)

Emotions will be running high in *EastEnders* next week as Mark Fowler—played by Todd Carty—lies critical in hospital with pneumonia. In Monday night's episode, fans of the BBC soap will see Mark fighting for his life as the illness makes him progressively weaker and unable to breathe.

At his bedside, his mother Pauline Fowler, played by Wendy Richards, will keep a constant vigil after being told that the next 24 hours will decide whether her son lives or dies.

Mark—who is HIV positive but not taking his prescribed drugs—was last seen in Thursday night's episode collapsing onto the floor of his kitchen.

'Progressive illness'

Over the last few weeks, he has been complaining of feeling unwell. A spokeswoman for the program said: "HIV is a progressive illness and Mark is experiencing what other sufferers go through as the disease takes its toll.

"The reason this attack of pneumonia is so severe is that Mark has not been taking his combination pills.

"He recently decided to stop taking them because he could not cope with the side-effects."

Also watching anxiously for signs of improvement will be Mark's friend Lisa Shaw, played by Lucy Benjamin.

Market trader Mark collapsed after a tearful scene with former flatmate Lisa as he begged her not to leave him to live with Melanie Healy, played by Tamzin Outhwaite.

In a previous episode, Mark had told Lisa—who is the girlfriend of Phil Mitchell, played by Steve McFadden—that he was in love with her. But, she eventually decided to move out after relations between them had become increasingly strained.

Developing Storyline

Mark is thought to have contracted the HIV virus from his first wife Gill who was infected by a drug dealing ex-boyfriend. Gill died the day after she married Mark in hospital.

Over the past few years, Mark has been shown coping with his HIV. He has managed to keep it under control with various different drugs and received regular counseling to help combat the illness.

Since his character Mark was diagnosed as HIV positive, a number of storylines have been written around the issue. Most notably, Mark was seen having to deal with a wide range of reactions to his illness, some hostile, from other Albert Square residents.

Adapted from: http://news.bbc.co.uk/1/hi/entertainment/603548.stm. First posted on the BBC website Friday, 14 January, 2000, 15:18 GMT

Using Web sites

Many television programs in the UK use web sites to reach viewers. The Web site for *Hollyoaks* and other programs on Channel 4, the UK's second independent TV channel, recently celebrated the fact that more than 10 million people visited the site during a single month, November 2002 (http://www.merseytv.com/default.asp?loc=pressrelease&pressID=68). The Web site (http://www.hollyoaks.com) links the Web surfer directly to "Chloe's Clinic" (one of the options on the search category) for help with specific health or social issues featured in the program. During December of 2002 and January of 2003, information focused on the pros and cons of getting an abortion, paralleling a dilemma faced by a character named Becca on the program. External links to independent Web sites were included (e.g., http://www.abortion-help.co.uk). In September of 2002 the site focused on issues of alcoholism and literacy, which were raised in the television program.

On the other hand, the Web site for *Coronation Street* (http://www. coronationstreet.co.uk/index.xml) provides no direct links to health or social issues. A search on "health" on the Web site results in a separate page listing 10 links to nutrition, weight loss, exercise, etc., with no mention of a character on the program or a storyline. This is unfortunate, since it is preferable for viewers who are interested in a particular issue affecting a character they like on a program to easily locate relevant helpful information on the Web site. The BBC programs and web sites do in fact serve the public more fully than do programs on ITV.

Medical programs have become popular in recent years, and programs like *Casualty* and *Doctors* also address health and social issues, much like medical dramas in the United States and the Netherlands (see the chapters in the present volume by Vicki Beck and by Martine Bouman). On the main Web page for *Casualty* (http://www.bbc.co.uk/casualty/), one can click on the "Advice" tag and go directly to issues addressed recently in the program. In December 2002 and January 2003 the topics (and appropriate links to additional sites) included matters of confidentiality, testicular cancer, anaphylaxis, dysmorphia, and retinitis pigmentosa. One Web site for *Doctors* incorporates a "Diagnosis of the Day" tag, which changes every three to seven days, depending on the content of the show (http://www.bbc.co.uk/puresoap/ storyupdates/doctors.shtml?20021115). Stories featured on both the program and the Web site included alcohol abuse, cardiomyopathy, dementia, Huntington's disease, and post-traumatic stress disorder.

Using Multiple Media

The fact that the BBC controls television, radio, video production, and publishing provides power and enables the BBC to exploit all media in concert in order to tackle any number of specific issues more fully. The BBC has campaigns like "Fighting Fat, Fighting Fit," and "Hitting Home," a campaign on domestic violence which began in February of 2003. The "Fighting Fat, Fighting Fit" campaign was the largest health education campaign ever undertaken by the BBC, and involved programming on BBC channels One and Two, BBC Radio 2, and local radio programs (Miles, Rapoport, Wardle, Afuape, & Duman, 2001; Wardle, Rapoport, Miles, Afuape, & Duman, 2001). It was launched on a major show called *Weight of the Nation*, and was sustained with three additional programs, *Fat Free*, *Fat Files*, and *Body Spies*. Viewers also registered to join the program, and both a book and video were sold. *Fat Free* was a six-part documentary that followed how five people lost weight over a six-month period. *Fat Files* was a trilogy broadcast later in the evening featuring the science of obesity. *Body Spies* was broadcast on weekday afternoons and was aimed at smokers, viewers who eat and drink too much, and was comprised of viewers who represented "lifestyle challenges" (Wardle et al., 2001). *Body Spies* featured individuals from the program traveling the UK and spying on those who had registered with the program to lose weight, revealing to viewers, family, and friends what the individuals were doing correctly (or not).

While much of the programming in this campaign was educational in nature, standard E-E theories of persuasion and behavioral change were clearly relevant: Modeling, social comparison processes, strong, multiple arguments, gain-framed messages, suspense, conflict, and humor were integral to the broadcasts. The campaign was successful in altering the eating habits and lifestyles of women (aged 26 and older), while men and viewers younger than 25 were largely unaffected (Miles et al., 2001; Wardle et al., 2001). The most obese viewers did not sustain behavioral changes over the five-month period assessed (Miles et al., 2001). Nonetheless, the campaign had an important and sustained impact on a sizeable portion of the viewing public, with a number of women consuming more fruits and vegetables, fewer starchy foods, fewer snacks, exercising more, and losing weight.

The BBC now plans to tackle the problem of domestic violence, using multiple programs and media (see Box 13.2). It relies on several of its highly popular soaps (*EastEnders*, *Casualty*), documentaries, and specials on television, multiple radio broadcasts, partnerships with local media, and an available infrastructure in place for viewers to take action (Helpline and Web site).

BOX 13.2.   BBC Press Release(12.12.02)

***Hitting Home*—a BBC campaign tackling domestic violence head-on**
- Every minute in the UK, the police receive a call from the public asking for assistance in a domestic violence situation.
- One in five young men and one in ten young women think that abuse or violence against women is acceptable.
- Domestic violence accounts for almost a quarter (23%) of all violent crime.
- One in four women will experience domestic violence at some time in their life.

These facts are shocking but they do reveal that for many people in the UK domestic violence is a fact of life.

In February 2003, the BBC tackles this subject in *Hitting Home*—a season of bold and inspiring programmes across TV, radio and online.

Working closely with the relevant agencies, *Hitting Home* examines mental and physical abuse in relationships highlighting that this is an issue that can affect anyone, no matter what their age, gender, or social status.

Many victims dare not speak out, and many perpetrators don't acknowledge their behavior or don't know where to go for help.

The campaign helps break the taboos and myths surrounding domestic violence.

Hitting Home features in prime-time and daytime BBC ONE programming, storylines in *Casualty* and *Neighbors*, a powerful intimate documentary,

Dangerous Love: Tales of Domestic Violence, an *Eastenders* special and a *Panorama* report.

CBBC shows a specially written drama and *Newsround* feature; Radio 1, Radio 2, Radio 4, the Asian Network, 1Xtra, and BBC Local Radio are tailoring programs in support.

Plus, there will be a BBC THREE documentary, *Storyville* on BBC FOUR, and films on all channels.

With real-life stories, expert advice, and celebrity testimony, *Hitting Home* tackles the themes of physical and emotional abuse.

Further support and advice will be available through a freephone advice line —08000934934—and an extensive web site—www.bbc.co.uk/hittinghome. (Both will go live on 4 February).

Contributor, actor David Soul, comments: "There's no excuse, there are consequences. The hardest part is to look at oneself and to those that you love and that you've hurt. We live with the guilt or shame."

Source: http://www.bbc.co.uk/pressoffice/pressreleases/stories/2002/12_december/12/hitting_home.shtml

THE BBC WORLD SERVICE TRUST

The BBC World Service is one of the most credible and respected broadcast agencies in the world. Each year more individuals tune in to BBC World Service radio broadcasts, with an estimated audience in 2000 of some 153 million. Housed within the BBC World Service is a separate, independent charity, the BBC World Service Trust, which has become a recognized leader of radio and television programs advocating respect for individual rights and respect for diversity, globally (see http://www.bbc.co.uk/worldservice/us/trust/index.shtml).

Most of BBC World Service Trust (WST) programs are educationally oriented, such as teaching radio listeners in Somalia how to read, and teaching journalism in Nigeria. WST also features programs in different countries on sex and reproductive health, and features different programs in different countries on tobacco (such as *Tobacco on Trial*). WST is attempting to build an infrastructure within various countries so that the producers and writers in those countries can launch and maintain educational and E-E programs independent of the BBC or other external agencies.

Several E-E programs launched by the BBC WST are highlighted here, because they demonstrate the power of E-E interventions, as well as how the Trust achieves its mission. These include *The Combat against Leprosy*, *The Prevention of Blinding Trachoma*, and *Pine Street* (a radio soap in Albania tackling issues of violence, corruption, and intolerance).

Another recent E-E project, *The National AIDS Control Program*, was launched in July 2002 and the evaluation report is due in July of 2003 (see: http://www.comminit.com/pdskdv32002/sld-4338.html).

Combating Leprosy

Box 13.3 provides an overview of the leprosy campaign launched in India, as summarized on the Communication Initiative web site (http://www.comminit.com/stbbcleprosy/sld-4027.html). This campaign sought two goals: to persuade people to seek treatment and to reduce the stigma associated with leprosy. The Trust devoted 1.1 million pounds (1.77 million USD) for the campaign, which focused on five Indian states where most leprosy cases are located. This campaign cured 176,000 cases of leprosy.

BOX 13.3.   BBC World Trust Leprosy Project—India

BBC WST & Doordarshan Leprosy Project in India Since 1983, leprosy has been simply and quickly curable with MultiDrug Therapy, and since 1995 the drugs have been available free of charge to every patient in the world. The biggest remaining barrier to eliminating the disease is ignorance and stigma: people do not know the drugs are available, and people are afraid to seek treatment. The BBC World Service Trust developed and implemented a campaign in India to address this. The 16-month project began in September 1999 and focused on the 5 states in India where leprosy is endemic. Funding was provided by the UK government's Department for International Development. In accordance with the Trust's philosophy of working in partnership with national broadcasters in developing countries, all programming was created by Doordarshan TV and All-India Radio.

PROGRAM OVERVIEW

The campaign underlined the fact that leprosy is totally curable and that drugs are available free throughout India. It also emphasized that leprosy is not spread by touch and that leprosy patients should not be excluded from society.

TV—A total of 25 advertising spots and 12 campaign dramas in Hindi, Bengali, and Oriya were produced for the campaign. With constant repetition, they accounted for more than 45 hours of TV. Among the formats used to carry the messages were Hindi film romances, rural folk operas, famous Hindu fables, domestic dramas, and comedies.

Radio—A total of 213 radio programs were broadcast more than 6,000 times. Thirty-six radio advertising spots were made in three languages: Hindi, Bengali and Oriya. They were then "transcreated" into 18 local dialects for broadcast by AIR substations, making 136 spots altogether. There were also 12 musical dramas made in main languages and dialects and an eight-part radio serial and 41 radio call-in shows.

Community—1,700 live theatre performances in villages, small towns, and urban slums throughout the project's five focus states to widen the reach of the campaign messages with approximately 500,000 people attending and participating. Performances were based on popular-entertainment forms, including folksongs, magic shows, and drama.

Posters—offered basic information about leprosy symptoms and treatment and stressed the importance of community care and support for people with leprosy. 85,000 produced and displayed. Showed a real-life young woman who had overcome leprosy thanks to the support of her friend. 'If there's friendship, this is it,' said the text.

Videos—2,700 "video van" screenings featuring the most popular TV spots and dramas produced under the BBC-Doordarshan partnership.

Press Relations—press conferences in the capitals of the five target states. More than 95 articles appeared in the regional English and vernacular press. Two-day press workshops on leprosy were held in Bihar, Madhya Pradesh, and Orissa.

Film—A 10-minute feature film on a leprosy theme screened in cinemas in Hindi-speaking states.

IMPACT

Media Reach—campaign reached 59% of respondents, equivalent to 283 million people.

Misconceptions—equivalent of 178 million people persuaded to reject [the] belief that leprosy is hereditary and the equivalent of 120 million people corrected their understanding that that leprosy is communicable by touch.

Curability & Communicability—The percentage of the total population who believe leprosy is transmitted by touch fell from 52% to 37% to 27%. The percentage believing that leprosy patients receiving treatment are infectious fell from 25% to 20% to 12%. The percentage who regard leprosy as curable rose from 84% to 88% to 91% of the population (99% of those exposed to the campaign regarded leprosy as curable, compared to 79% of people who had not seen the campaign.

Symptoms—awareness of loss of sensation as a possible symptom was already high (65%) and rose to 72%, then 80%. Awareness of pale reddish patches as a possible symptom remained level at 86%. Awareness of nonitchy patches as a possible symptom rose from 37% to 53% to 55%.

Awareness—Awareness of the modern cure for leprosy: Control Group Villages: 56%; Village with Live Drama Shows—82%. Rural Awareness of a modern leprosy cure free of cost: Exposed to the poster—89% No exposure—20%.

Stigma—Percentage of people claiming they would be willing to sit by the side of a leprosy patient: Control Group Villages—64%; Village with Live Drama Shows—74%. Percentage of people claiming they would be willing to eat food served by a leprosy patient rose from 32% [baseline—November 1999] to 50% [September 2000].

Source: http://www.comminit.com/drum_beat_133.html

Evaluation reports conducted by the ORG Centre for Social Research in New Delhi demonstrated that exposure to radio and television programs significantly affected public beliefs about leprosy and tolerance for those afflicted. However, live performances and posters also were effective. Approximately 500,000 people attended at least one of the 1,700 performances conducted in various dialects. Research demonstrated that those who viewed live drama shows in villages were more aware of modern cures (82%) and voiced tolerance for sitting next to a leprosy patient (74%) relative to those not exposed to village shows (56% and 64%, respectively). Some 89% of those exposed to one of the 85,000 posters knew that the cure for leprosy was free, compared to only 20% not exposed to posters. The appeal used in the posters, and in the videos, featured a real-life young woman who had overcome leprosy due to the support of her friend, "If there's friendship, this is it."

Other E-E Interventions

A different approach was used to combat leprosy in Nepal. The Nepalese Comedians Fight Leprosy Campaign relied on two famous Nepalese comedians, and saturated radio and television airwaves with spots and dramas based on comedy and music. The media campaign lasted for 30 days, and was followed by a weeklong outreach campaign conducted by health workers. The results were impressive: 100,000 people reported for diagnosis, and 11,700 people were treated for leprosy. The level of stigma (measured in terms of people who would refuse to sit next to a patient with a leprosy deformity) fell by 25% (http://www.comminit.com/drum_beat_67.html).

Box 13.4 provides information about the project combating trachoma that involve the BBC World Service Trust and the International Trachoma Initiative in Ghana, Egypt, Nepal, and Niger utilizing radio, print materials, theatre, posters, and music (http://www.bbc.co.uk/worldservice/us/trust/020306_trachoma.shtml). A video van was purchased in order to promote trachoma control in Ethiopia (http://www.trachoma.org/home.asp). In Tanzania a village-level campaign on prevention of blindness utilized street theatre, posters, and "health animators" (entertainers with health messages), colored flip charts, children's songs and music, and messages played on cassette players. Independent audience research showed that peoples' understanding of how to prevent trachoma increased by 150%. A national radio campaign was launched in the second phase of this project, and a 60-minute drama has been produced in Swahili for village screening (http://www.comminit.com/pdsBBCWST/sld-2285.html).

BOX 13.4.   Prevention of Blinding Trachoma

Trachoma is the world's leading cause of preventable blindness. Almost 6 million people are blind worldwide due to the disease and almost 10% of the world's population are at risk of blindness or severe visual impairment if the disease is not controlled.

The Campaign

In 2001 the BBC World Service Trust organized a health communication campaign to support the elimination of blinding trachoma in Ghana. The campaign was implemented with the support of the International Trachoma Initiative (ITI), in partnership with national radio broadcasters. Following the success of this project, the Trust was awarded further funds by ITI to conduct simultaneous campaigns in Ethiopia, Nepal, and Niger from late 2001. Trachoma is endemic throughout Ethiopia and Niger, and it persists in areas of Nepal. The programme focuses mainly on rural areas where the disease is more prevalent and where previous treatment strategies have been not sufficiently effective.

The Disease

Trachoma usually begins in early childhood, but does not cause blindness until much later in life as repeated infections cause inflammation and scarring on the inside of the eyelid. The disease is spread easily from person to person, by hands, on clothing, or by flies. Repeated infections can eventually cause blindness—but this stage does not occur until adulthood, when people who should be in their most productive years find themselves unable to earn a living for their families.

The disease is however both treatable and preventable. The Trust's focus is on the prevention of the disease, hence the main aims of the campaign are to promote face washing among children, to improve household and community sanitation and hygiene, and to increase health education.

A Multimedia Campaign

The campaign combines mass media, as well as community media and print materials, to raise awareness of trachoma and its prevention. The levels of television penetration in the campaign countries are quite low so the Trust is concentrating its efforts on radio, working together with local broadcasters to produce a broad array of radio spots, jingles, minidramas, and educational features and interviews. The stations have donated air-time in exchange for onsite technical and production training by experienced BBC staff. In addition, the Trust is developing print media materials such as posters and flipcharts and organizing community media events such as video screenings and street theatre.

Source: http://www.bbc.co.uk/worldservice/us/trust/020306_trachoma.shtml

In 1999 WST launched a radio soap opera in Albania in order to increase awareness and debate of social issues among Albanians. The program features stories on human rights, domestic violence, corruption, blood feuds, tolerance, and much more. As is often the case with an effective E-E program, a sizeable portion of the public tunes in to the program, which prompts interpersonal conversation and debate, individuals learn by listening and debating, and the radio performers have reached celebrity status in Albania (see, for more details: http://www.comminit.com/pdsBBCWST/sld-2286.html, http://www.comminit.com/pds9-00/sld-1325.html).

An important feature of the Albanian Project is that most Western agencies turned their backs on Albania, although there are tremendous needs to be met. Albania was isolated from much of the world for more than 40 years, when the brutal Stalinist leader Enver Hoxha controlled virtually every aspect of a citizen's life. This isolation ended in 1990 but the nation's infrastructure was in shambles and citizens were unfamiliar with modern business practices, democracy, and capitalism. Many citizens voted for the first time in 1992. Corruption was rampant; riots and looting occurred when a pyramid scheme collapsed in 1997, bringing down the government. Its citizens looted armories, criminal organizations smuggled girls to Italy for prostitution (among other criminal acts), and a half million ethnic Albanians escaped NATO bombing in Yugoslavia in 1999 by literally walking to Albania from Yugoslavia, worsening an already dismal economic situation. The WST first became involved with the issue of Albanian refugees, and then launched the radio soap opera in 1999.

Clearly, the urgent need in 1999–2000 was to provide information to citizens; and the WST was successful in doing so: "It's made a great impact," says Rupert Wolfe Murray, Deputy Director of IRC, one of the largest NGOs in the country. "The soap opera is addressing issues of real concern in this country, but in an imaginative and creative way. It's done a lot to fill the information vacuum and put across solid well researched facts to the listeners" (http://www.comminit.com/pdsBBCWST/sld-2286.html).

CONCLUSIONS

The BBC is unique in its position as a noncommercial broadcast and publishing corporation operating independently of government and focused on serving in the public interest. From its earliest days the BBC sought to inform, educate, and entertain, but within certain limitations. While certain comedies (i.e., *Absolutely Fabulous*) depict questionable behaviors (alcohol, cigarette, and drug use), they portray people and lifestyles that are markedly "British" and use satire effectively. Our point here, however, is that many BBC programs do far more than purely entertain. This is true of BBC soap operas, its educational programs, its news programs, and documentaries. As an institution the BBC routinely incorporates health or social issue stories into programs, and helpful, relevant information about the issue of the week is often located on BBCi. From the standpoint of effectively changing and sustaining behavioral changes, the BBC is capable of organizing campaigns utilizing soap operas, documentaries, news programs, films, printed materials, radio, and the Internet to tackle obesity, domestic violence, and more. Finally, the BBC WST emerged as an effective advocate of both educational and E-E programming around the world, advocating individual rights, tolerance, and health.

However, there are two problems with the available literature on E-E programs in the UK. First, despite the fact that soap operas and medical shows like *EastEnders*, *Casualty*, *Doctors*, and *Hollyoaks* raise social and health issues, and companion materials are available online, there is little evidence-based research on who is motivated to seek the materials and act on them. No research articles in peer-review journals have appeared on the relative effectiveness of storylines on AIDS, cancer, and heart problems featured on British soap operas. In comparison, extensive research was conducted in the United States (Alcalay, Alvarado, Balcazar, Newman, & Huerta, 1999; Brodie, Foehr, Rideout, Baer, Miller, Flournoy & Altman, 2001; Keller & Brown, 2002; Kennedy, O'Leary, Beck, Pollard, & Simpson, 2002; Lalonde, Rabinowitz, Shefshy & Washienko, 1997; Sharf & Freimuth, 1993; Sharf, Freimuth, Greenspon, & Plotnick, 1996; Winsten & DeJong, 2001), in the Netherlands (see Martine Bouman's chapter in this volume), or in South Africa (see the chapters by Shereen Usdin and colleagues, and by Suruchi Sood and colleagues). The BBC is obliged to produce and broadcast quality programs, but while its obligation is to provide quality programming, this obligation does not extend to demonstrating that it is specifically effective in promoting health or healthy lifestyles. Second, there has been little discussion of utilizing theory or of advancing new theory in the BBC E-E programs (see Singhal & Rogers, 2002). Nonetheless, no other agency in the world has used E-E programming so consistently and extensively as the BBC.

AUTHORS' NOTE

The authors thank Meg Quinn and Natalia Olenicoff for helping research, and watching episodes of, *EastEnders* and *Coronation Street*, when enrolled in the Semester Abroad London Program offered by the University of Southern California, in Spring 2002. We also thank Richard Hodkinson, our local Brit, and Phillip Drummond, our favorite Scot, for helpful comments on the content of this chapter and for general background information on the BBC.

REFERENCES

Alcalay, R., Alvarado, M., Balcazar, H., Newman, E., & Huerta, E. (1999). *Salud para su corazon*: A community-based Latino cardiovascular disease prevention and outreach model. *Journal of Community Health, 24*, 359–379.

Brake, C. (1994). *EastEnders: The first 10 years*. London: Parkwest Publishers.

Brodie, M., Foehr, U., Rideout, V., Baer, N., Miller, C., Flournoy, R., & Altman, D. (2001). Communicating health information through the entertainment media: A study of the Television drama *ER* lends support to the notion that Americans pick up information while being entertained. *Health Affairs, 20*, 192-199.

Buckingham, D. (1987). *Public secrets: EastEnders and its audience*. London: British Film Institute.

Crayford, T., Hooper, R. & Evans. S. (1997). "Death rates of characters in soap operas on British television: Is a government health warning required?" *British Medical Journal, 315*, 1649-1652.

Drummond, Phillip, personal communication, March 12, 2002.

Hardyman, R., & Leydon, G. (2002, March). Popular media as a means of increasing public awareness of health issues: The case of cancer. Paper presented to the British Sociological Association, Leicester, England. Also available online (as power point presentation): http://www.cancerbacup.org.uk

Jackson, A. (1997). Let the media work for you, not against you. *British Medical Journal, 314*, 526.

Keller, S. N., & Brown, J. D. (2002). Media interventions to promote responsible sexual behavior. *Journal of Sex Research, 39*, 68.

Kennedy, M. G., O'Leary, A., Beck, V., Pollard, W. E., & Simpson, P. (2002). Increases in calls to the CDC National STD and AIDS Hotline following AIDS-related episodes in a soap opera. Unpublished paper, Center for Disease Control and Prevention, Atlanta, Georgia.

Lalonde, B., Rabinowitz, P., Shefshy, M. L., & Washienko, K. (1997). *La esperanza del Valle*: Alcohol prevention novellas for Hispanic youth and their families. *Health Education and Behavior, 24*, 587-602.

Lougrhan, G. (2001, July 22). You don't have to be mad to be British. . . . Retrieval on September 26, 2002, from http://www.Nationaudio.com.

Middleham, G. & Wober, J. M. (1997). An anatomy of appreciation and of viewing amongst a group of fans of the serial *EastEnders*. *Journal of Broadcasting & Electronic Media, 41*, 530-547.

Miles, A., Rapoport, L., Wardle, J., Afuape, T., & Duman, M. (2001). Using the mass-media to target obesity: An analysis of the characteristics and reported behaviour change of participants in the BBC's 'Fighting Fat, Fighting Fit' campaign. *Health Education Research, 16*, 357-372.

Reveley, A. (1997). Soap tackles stigma of schizophrenia. *British Medical Journal, 314*, 1560.

Sharf, B. F., & Freimuth, V. S. (1993). The construction of illness on entertainment television: Coping with cancer on *thirtysomething*. *Health Communication, 5*, 141-160.

Sharf, B. F., Freimuth, V. S., Greenspon, P., & Plotnick, C. (1996). Confronting cancer on *thirtysomething*: Audience response to health content on entertainment Television. *Journal of Health Communication, 1*, 157-172.

Singhal, A. & Rogers, E. M. (1999). *Entertainment-education: A communication strategy for social change*. Mahwah, NJ: Lawrence Erlbaum Associates.

Singhal, A., & Rogers, E. M. (2002). A theoretical agenda for entertainment-education. *Communication Theory, 12*, 117-135.

Smith, J., & Holland, T. (1987). *The EastEnders: The inside story*. London: BBC Publishing.

Wardle, J., Rapoport, L., Miles, A., Afuape, T. & Duman, M. (2001). Mass education for obesity prevention: The penetration of the BBC's 'Fighting Fat, Fighting Fit' campaign. *Health Education Research, 16*, 343-355.

Winsten, J. A., & DeJong, W. (2001). The Designated Driver Campaign. In R. E. Rice and C. K. Atkin (Eds.) *Public communication campaigns* (3rd ed.) (290-294). Thousand Oaks, CA: Sage.

14

Social Merchandizing in Brazilian Telenovelas

Antonio C. La Pastina
Texas A&M University

Dhaval S. Patel
UNICEF, New York

Marcio Schiavo
Communicarte and Gama Filho University

"When God created the world, he did not give land to anyone because all that are born here are his sons. But only those that make the land productive deserve it. The best fertilizer is the sweat of those who work on the land."
    —Benedito Rui Barbosa, 1997 (translated by the first author).[1]

"I believe the telenovela already fulfilled its mission; it preached the message of peace in the land. At the same time, it showed that the issue is serious and must be resolved."
    —Benedito Rui Barbosa, 1997 (translated by the first author).[2]

Entertainment-education (E-E) is increasingly utilized as a strategy throughout the world to promote prosocial behaviors in health, international development, and gender equality. Although E-E efforts can be traced to the 1950s and 1960s (Sherry, 1997), the rate at which academic institutions, governmental agencies, and nonpolitical groups create, implement, and evaluate

---

[1] Voice over and an intertitle in the last episode of *O Rei do Gado* (The Cattle King) (Silva, 1997, p. 2).

[2] Cited in Castro (1997, p. 7).

261

E-E interventions soared, especially in the past three decades. By 2002 an estimated 200 E-E interventions had been implemented in more than 50 countries (Bouman, 1999; see Phyllis T. Piotrow and Esta de Fossard's chapter in this volume).

Regardless of the setting, a common goal of these E-E programs is to entertain and educate audiences in order to catalyze social change in a socially desirable manner. However, the mechanisms for implementing and delivering E-E messages to various audiences differ, thereby allowing scholars and practitioners to compare and contrast different kinds of E-E programs (Singhal & Rogers, 1999). For example, some organizations have used serialized radio and television drama programs predominately to target individuals and to change their health practices in countries such as India (Sood & Rogers, 1996), the Philippines (Kincaid, Coleman, Rimon, & Silayan-Go, 1991), and Nigeria (Piotrow, Rimon, Winnard, Kincaid, Huntington, & Convisser, 1990). On the other hand, Soul City, a nongovernmental organization in South Africa that uses the synergistic power of multimedia channels, employs a comprehensive, socioecological approach (Japhet & Goldstein, 1997). In Brazil, E-E strategies have many similarities to these and other attempts, but they have developed into a unique strategy locally labeled as "social merchandizing" (SM).

SOCIAL MERCHANDIZING

Social merchandizing is a type of marketing that uses the Brazilian *telenovela* (BT), or serialized television drama, to sell, not products, but awareness of issues deemed important by writers and network executives. Just as commercial marketers work with network broadcasters to insert product images (i.e., product placement) into Brazilian television programming to sell products and to make a profit (La Pastina, 2001; Melo, 1989), social merchandizers and scriptwriters also place "products" into Brazilian telenovelas. The difference is that these products are prosocial messages rather than commercial items. Only recently, Brazilian writers such as Benedito Rui Barbosa, who wrote some of the most successful telenovelas in the 1990s, acknowledged that they see the Brazilian telenovela and social merchandizing as a genre, and as a strategy for promoting social and political views in an intended manner (Hamburger, 1999; La Pastina, 1999; La Pastina, Straubhaar, & Almeida, 1999).

In order to gain an appreciation for social merchandizing and the Brazilian telenovela and to comprehend how they are similar and different from other E-E strategies, this chapter begins by detailing the development of the Brazilian telenovela. Then, the current state of social merchandizing is explicated, and finally the lessons learned from the Brazilian E-E framework are offered in order to understand how it may be replicated in other parts of the world.

THE BRAZILIAN TELENOVELA

Distinct from U.S. soap operas, Latin American, and Brazilian telenovelas in particular, are broadcast daily in primetime: They "have very definitive endings that permit narrative closure," normally after 180 to 200 episodes depending on their popularity, and are designed to attract a wide viewing audience of men, women, and children (Lopez, 1991 p. 600). Telenovela narratives are dominated by a few leading characters and rely on class conflict and the promotion of social mobility (Mazziotti, 1993). First introduced into Brazilian society during the early 1950s and modeled after the Latin American prototype, telenovelas evolved into a distinctive genre.

In 1986 *Variety* defined the Latin American telenovela as a popular art form as distinctive and filled with conventions as the Western produced in the United States (Telenovela is something else, 1986). Telenovelas and soap operas have common roots, but over time they have developed as distinct genres. In Latin American production centers, these distinctions have been emphasized, creating particularities in themes, narrative style, and production values. For Lopez (1995), the Mexican telenovelas are weepers, ahistorical telenovelas with no context provided. Colombian telenovelas are more comedic and ironic with a greater concern for context. Venezuelan telenovelas are more emotional, but they do not have the baroqueness of Mexican narratives. Brazilian telenovelas are the most realistic with historically based narratives that have a clear temporal and spatial contextualization.

Several writers claim that the landmark telenovela that started the redefinition of the genre in Brazil was *Beto Rockfeller* aired by Tupy Network in 1968–1969 (Lopez, 1995; Mattelart & Mattelart, 1990; Mazziotti, 1993; Ortiz, Borelli & Ramos, 1988; Straubhaar, 1982). *Beto Rockfeller* was the story of a lower-middle-class young man who sold shoes for a living. Using his charm and wit, he began to socialize with the upper-class while pretending to be a millionaire. *Beto Rockfeller* escaped the traditional mold of the genre, presenting a telenovela in which the artificial melodramatic attitudes were abandoned and a more contemporary setting and a colloquial speech pattern were adopted. The telenovela achieved very high audience ratings and led the network to stretch it to its limits. Instead of the usual six to eight months, *Beto Rockfeller* was broadcast for almost 13 months (Fernandes, 1994).

The success of that telenovela demonstrated to scriptwriters, producers, and network executives that the Brazilian telenovela could move away from the traditional Latin American telenovela model. Not only was the use of the language altered, but *Beto Rockerfeller* was a harbinger, foreshadowing the changes in the history of the Brazilian telenovela: TV Globo and social merchandizing, both of which further widened the gap between the Latin American *telenovela* and the Brazilian telenovela. Not only would the language of the Brazilian telenovela continue to evolve, but the dramatic structure, narrative strategies, and production values also would get over-hauled by Brazil's immense Globo Network.

Over the last five decades, Brazilian audiences have become accustomed to telenovelas. Watching telenovelas has become an integral part of the daily routine for millions of Brazilians who lack economic and social capital to engage in alternative forms of entertainment. The high audience ratings attest to the popularity of the genre, but the success of fashion trends started by telenovela characters, the discussion of topics raised by the telenovelas, and the blending of fiction and reality in Brazilian daily life (Guillermoprieto, 1994) attest to the viability of the genre as a social, economic, and political force in Brazil.

TELEVISION GLOBO NETWORK

The 1965 creation of Globo, presently the largest television broadcast net-work in Brazil, stimulated the evolution of the Brazilian telenovela into its present-day form. With the success of *Beto Rockerfeller*, Globo decided to champion its style in future telenovelas by introducing three modifications: (1) investing heavily in production value through the use of new technolo-gies, (2) increasing the use of external shoots, which involve moving the cameras outside the studios and filming on the streets, a practice still avoided by most U.S. soap operas and Mexican telenovelas due to higher costs, and (3) a sole reliance on scripts produced by Brazilian writers with a marked focus on modern urban spaces and current social issues. These changes did not happen overnight, nor were they totally planned, but rather they evolved as the result of a series of structural factors in a particular histor-ical moment in Brazilian life. For a discussion of the historical evolution of Globo and the telenovela genre, see Harold (1988), Hernandez (2001), Mattos (1980; 2000), McAnany (1984), Sinclair (1996), and Straubhaar (1982; 1996).

In the last three decades Globo, supported by the Brazilian military regime (Mattos, 2000), became the leading television network in the nation, barely allowing competing networks to attract a fraction of the total audience.[3] Because of Globo's dominance in telenovela production and audience ratings,

---

[3]Presently, besides Globo, there are six other national networks: SBT, Bandeirantes, Record, Gazeta, CNT, and the Educational Channels. The first television network in Brazil, Tupy, was closed in 1980, and its stations licensed to two groups: SBT and Manchete. Manchete later closed and its stations became part of the CNT Network. Excelsior, another important network in the early decades of Brazilian television, was closed by the dictatorship in the early 1970s.

popularity, and reach, this chapter focuses on TV Globo when discussing Brazilian telenovelas and social merchandizing.[4] According to Fadul, McAnany, and Morales (1996), telenovelas produced in this period, especially in the 1970s and 1980s, were centered predominately in Rio de Janeiro and dealt with an urban, middle-class lifestyle portrayed in a dramatic but entertaining manner with high production values, which the network promoted as the "Globo Pattern of Quality" (*Padrão Globo de Qualidade*) (Mattos, 2000; Straubhaar, 1982).

Because of the military regime's censorship policies during the 1970s, writers worked under the careful eye of the military in the theater and movie industries. However, some found employment in Globo television, a media space in which, even if censored, allowed stretching the limits of what was acceptable in the repressive atmosphere. For example, seasoned writer Benedito Rui Barbosa's first rural telenovela, which aired in 1971–1972, was also the first Brazilian telenovela to use the genre for educational purposes. In *Meu Pedacinho de Chão* (My Own Little Piece of Land), he "placed on the screen a land conflict in which the daughter of the landowner used guns to help the invaders. The [military] censors came with their scissors and cut twelve scenes" (Um autor com..., 1996). *Meu Pedacinho de Chão*, coproduced by TV Cultura, the public television station in the state of São Paulo, had some scenes censored, but most of the prosocial messages were left intact (such as rural life problems, hygiene promotion, and agricultural information) (Fernandes, 1994). During this period, scriptwriters and Globo were clearly forced to work in tandem with the military regime to promote the nationalization of the culture (Mattos, 1980).

Beginning in the mid-1980s, the political *abertura* (opening), which involved the transition of power from the military to a civilian government in 1990, allowed Brazilian telenovela writers to increase the visibility of their social agendas by including national social and political debates in their narratives. In other words, Globo's telenovelas were transformed, shifting from entertainment containing limited, and sometimes censored, socioeducational material to entertainment with a strong prosocial agenda. Globo openly provided writers with a platform to delve into issues of social and political significance (e.g., elections, strikes, corruption), which under the military's gaze could not be openly discussed. Writers developed more melodramatic, dynamic narratives that showed the local, current, and daily struggles of Brazilian society. Their telenovelas did not break completely with their melodramatic roots but rather incorporated a national voice by introducing a

---

[4]From 1970 to 1995 Globo produced 167 telenovelas. It is the largest telenovela producer in Brazil (Fadul & McAnany, 1998), followed by TV Tupy, which ceased to exist in 1980. Tupy was the first station in Brazil and remained the leading network until the late 1960s and early 1970s when it lost its audience to Globo.

popular language and using colloquialisms and characters rooted in the daily life of the Brazilian metropolis.

Globo and other smaller television networks, as well as producers and scriptwriters, increased Brazilian telenovela revenues and profits by placing products and services in the narrative (i.e., household goods, sports cars, and industrial services). However, Globo and Brazilian *telenovela* writers realized that by including socioeducational issues they could sell not just tangible goods, but messages with community and societal implications. Intentionally or not, Globo transformed the Brazilian telenovela from a purely entertainment genre that evolved away from the mainstream Latin American telenovela model into a forum for the discussion of Brazilian reality. In the process, social merchandizing became established as a feature of 1990s Brazilian television.

THE CURRENT STATE OF SOCIAL MERCHANDIZING

Globo's success began to raise attention not only in Brazil but in other parts of the world. During the early 1990s international development organizations, such as Population Communication International (PCI), began to forge relationships with Globo to develop a systematic, sustainable strategy for the insertion of prosocial issues that also would be economically feasible for the television network. Although Globo, along with scriptwriters, already had begun to develop telenovelas with some educational messages, the network needed to be sure that prosocial telenovelas would continue to be profitable. As a result, Globo looked to the principles of commercial marketing that it had been using for numerous years to sell products.

In Brazil, product placement, called "merchandising," is an important source of funding for Globo's telenovelas. Commercial merchandizing is a media strategy consisting of the promotion of products and/or services in attempts to influence the buying habits of consumers and audiences (La Pastina, 2001). By inserting products (i.e., product placement) into the script of a telenovela, the actors/characters become sales representatives, in a matter of speaking, for the products. There are similar examples in the movie industry, which has taken a similar approach with certain films. When Pierce Brosnan, a British actor who portrays the charismatic spy James Bond, drives a BMW automobile that is technologically modified for the purposes of tracking down the enemy in a Bond film, the producers are working with BMW advertisers to raise consumer awareness about the automobile in hopes of promoting sales. Scriptwriters creatively inserted the product, the BMW auto, naturally into the film's storyline without disrupting the narrative or drama.

Using commercial marketing and product placement as a foundation, social merchandizing efforts replaced tangible, commercial products with social and educational messages. The strategy began to receive attention by Globo, writers, producers, nongovernmental groups and the news media, beginning in the mid-1990s, as a viable means of promoting social change (Apolinário, 1996; Guerini, 1996; Firme, 1994). Unlike commercial product placements, which are mostly defined by the network's marketing and advertising departments with minor consultation with the telenovela writer, early social issue insertions were generally based on the writers' personal agenda. As long as the telenovela was profitable and sustained viewer ratings, scriptwriters were not typically told what prosocial issues to include, thereby giving them the freedom to insert or sell issues that were of concern to them. Issues ranged from missing children (Gloria Perez's *Explode Coração*, 1995), to racial equality and homosexual relationships (Silvio de Abreu's *Próxima Vítima*, 1994), to land reform and political integrity (Benedito Rui Barbosa's *O Rei do Gado*, 1996–1997).

More recently, Globo, development organizations, and scriptwriters worked collectively to create intentional, programmatic agendas that dictate the type of prosocial issues inserted into the narrative. Lobbying efforts by different organizations (i.e., Population Communications International, Communicarte, Fiocruz, etc.) helped prompt TV Globo to adopt an official position supporting the inclusion of socioeducational messages in its telenovelas. For example, Globo Network hired a consultant to help promote prosocial insertions, and Globo is working with Fiocruz Fundação Oswaldo Cruz, a Brazilian health research center, to map illnesses in Brazil that could be combated through telenovela initiatives (Apolinário, 1996).

SOCIAL MERCHANDIZING
PROSOCIAL THEMES

Benedito Rui Barbosa, a veteran scriptwriter, believes that telenovelas are privileged sites in which to discuss the problems and conflicts of a nation and to promote awareness, and ultimately change, in many diverse issues ("Um autor com . . . ," 1996, p. 122–123). In order to understand what problems have been targeted in Brazilian telenovelas through the SM strategy, Communicarte, a social marketing consulting office in Brazil, monitored Globo's telenovelas since 1995 to determine the type of socioeducational issues inserted in the texts. Here we discuss four telenovelas aired in 2000, the types of prosocial scenes found in them, and we analyze the types of representation of two.[5]

---

[5]In 1999 Comunicarte monitored seven telenovelas, but in 2000 the number dropped to four due to the broadcasting of four historical telenovelas by Globo: *Forca de um Desejo*, *Esplendor*, *Terra Nostra*, and *O Cravo e a Rosa*. These telenovelas attempted to present factual information about historic occurrences, making it difficult to include contemporary social issues.

The four telenovelas were *Malhação* (a late afternoon teenage soap opera), *Vila Madalena* and *Uga Uga* (two evening comedies), and *Laços de Família* (a prime-time drama).[6]

Communicarte researchers identified 580 social merchandizing scenes in the four shows. In this chapter, a scene with a social merchandising theme does not refer to a single occurrence in the narrative, like a punctual image of a product or a single mention of an issue, but rather, these 580 insertions are scenes with social merchandising content that occurred during the length of the telenovela. So a scene can be a short interaction between a couple of characters or as complex as a subplot within the narrative that might last for several episodes. The four telenovelas discussed here, *Malhação, Vila Madalena, Uga Uga,* and *Laços de Família* contained 364, 69, 72, and 93 social insertions, respectively. When the different SM scenes were examined, Comunicarte researchers developed five categories to classify the types of insertions: (1) social issues, (2) sexuality, (3) drug abuse and prevention, (4) reproductive health, and (5) gender relations (Comunicarte, 2001).

First, 344 SM segments dealt with social issues: (1) teen initiatives (teenagers as leaders and actors promoting the collective social good); (2) environmental protection; (3) public sanitation; (4) adoption and children's rights to a family; (5) problems with the health system; (6) promotion of basic education; (7) transit education; (8) divorce; (9) the rights of people living with HIV and AIDS patients; and (10) discrimination against marginalized groups such as blacks, homosexuals, bisexuals, and slum dwellers.

The second thematic group was sexuality. Ninety-six insertions included messages about teenage sexuality, practicing a healthy sexual life during different phases of one's life, STD/HIV prevention, sexual fantasies, sexual harassment, and sexual dysfunctions with an emphasis on impotence and temporary erectile dysfunction.

Third, the four telenovelas contained 51 SM scenes related to drug abuse and prevention. The problems attacked include the consumption of tobacco products, alcoholic beverages, steroids, and medications without prescription. Additionally, experimentation with alcoholic beverages and tobacco was discouraged in the dramas.

The fourth category dealt with reproductive health, for which 47 insertions were created by Globo and the scriptwriters of the four telenovelas. Specifically, the SM messages addressed myths about menstruation, sexual impotency, prejudices regarding STD/AIDS, necessary care during pregnancy, social and psychological implications of unwanted pregnancies, and the legal procedures for abortions in Brazil.

---

[6]*Malhação* is a term for exercising to tone one's body. *Vila Madalena* is the name of a trendy neighborhood in São Paulo. *Uga Uga* is an onomatopoeia used in Brazil to refer to vocal utterances by prehistorical men. It was used in this telenovela to represent males' inability to communicate emotionally. "*Laços de Família*" means family ties.

Finally, 42 insertions focused on gender relations, with the main issues being raising awareness about the professional training of women, male responsibilities during adolescence (regarding sexual practices), female labor, unfair household labor division when both spouses work outside the house but the woman is responsible for all household chores, and prejudices about romantic relationships that included members of different age groups, especially when the woman is the older partner (Communicarte, 2001).

The different SM issues and thematic categories illustrate the range of prosocial issues concerning telenovela writers and producers. In order to better visualize how these themes were inserted into the Brazilian telenovelas, aspects of two of the telenovelas studied by Communicarte (2001), *Malhação* and *Laços de Família*, are dissected in detail.

MALHAÇÃO

Malhação, following a soap opera format, has been broadcast in Brazil since 1995. While the show has changed substantially during this period, it has retained its focus on a teen audience. Initially the drama was located in an exercise club, but in the last two years its primary setting moved to a precollege prep school with a clearly defined youth audience.[7] As a long-lasting Brazilian soap opera, this program acquired a reputation among youngsters throughout the nation for providing not only entertainment but also a way to stay abreast of the latest slang and fashion trends in Rio de Janeiro, a major urban center and a recurrent set for most telenovelas. Research with adolescents watching the program indicated that the teenagers' engagement with the drama provided them with a source of pleasure and a forum to obtain information perceived as vital (i.e., new word usage, exercise trends, dating norms in urban centers, and fashion) (La Pastina, 1999; Miranda-Ribeiro, 1997). Additionally, the SM content of the telenovela become an important venue for teens to discuss safer sex and their sexuality along with larger social problems.

In 2000 this late afternoon show reached audience ratings of 34 points, which was unparalleled in previous years.[8] The newer version of this television program may have contributed to its higher ratings. The language became more dynamic and representative of diverse segments of youth culture. Additionally, because the drama expanded its setting from a gym to a school, and incorporated the home and the streets, the telenovela created new locations

---

[7]In Brazil, most students intending to enter college attend a preparatory course (3, 6, or 12 months long). These are privately run courses that prepare students for the universities entrance exams.

[8]Each ratings point corresponds to 1 million viewers as measured by IBOPE, the Brazilian Institute of Public Opinion.

TABLE 14.1
Social Merchandising in *Malhação* in 2000 (N = 346)

Topic	Number of Insertions
Social questions	216
Gender relations	12
Drug abuse	36
Sexuality	54
Reproductive health	28
Total	346

that allowed for more prosocial issues. Table 14.1 shows that most SM insertions were about social issues (n = 216), while the remaining prosocial scenes focused on gender relations (n = 12), drug abuse (n = 36), sexuality (n = 54), and reproductive health (n = 28).

Two socioeducational examples from *Malhação* episodes in 2000 speak to the strength of social merchandizing. For several weeks, the show attempted to promote voluntary assistance to low-income schools, with two of the main characters promoting a campaign to increase collaboration between students and teachers to change the quality of public education. Their actions in the drama reinforced the idea that all youngsters have the right to an education, while underscoring the social and structural problems affecting the educational system in Brazil.

Another important storyline focused on youth sexuality, specifically addressing unplanned pregnancies among teenagers. A teen couple gave birth to an unplanned baby who was not wanted. Because the mother in the television program had to quit school and stay at home with the child, while the father tried to get into a university, this pregnancy in the melodramatic, entertaining narrative showed viewers implications of an unplanned birth. Within the narrative, discussions erupted about the practice of mutually pleasurable, responsible sex, the risks of unprotected sexual behavior (i.e., pregnancy, STD/AIDS), the use of contraceptives, a woman's right to her body (i.e., abortion for undesired pregnancies and access to abortion), and male responsibilities.

LAÇOS DE FAMÍLIA

Manoel Carlos, the scriptwriter for Globo's *Laços de Família*, dealt with health issues in most of his telenovelas. Central characters in his melodramas dealt with breast cancer, handicap mobility, lung diseases, etc. *Laços de Família*, a prime-time drama, was no exception.

TABLE 14.2
Social Merchandising in *Laços de Família* in 2000 (N = 93)

Topic	Number of Insertions
Social questions	50
Gender relations	14
Drug abuse	00
Sexuality	14
Reproductive health	15
Total	93

Table 14.2 shows the type and number of SM health issues inserted in the telenovela. *Laços de Família* used humor to provide accurate information about sexual impotence and its therapy, as well as leukemia. At one point, the line between fiction and reality blur when many of the telenovela's actors went to a Christmas party at the Brazilian National Institutes of Cancer, where they interacted with children suffering from leukemia. Because the show and its characters/actors traveled outside the traditional broadcasting boundaries, an increase in bone marrow donations was observed in Brazil (Communicarte Marketing Social, 2001).

TV GLOBO'S BROADCASTING TIME-SLOT STRUCTURE

Beyond the SM issues inserted in the Brazilian telenovelas, another important aspect of Globo Network strengthens the social merchandizing approach in Brazil. The success of SM on Globo is partially due to: (1) the strategic use of different time-slots to target specific audience segments during primetime, and (2) collaboration between scriptwriters who have their own social agenda and specialized merchandising writers who are attuned to time and audience. From 5 p.m. to 10 p.m. daily, Globo attempts to attract a particular audience with a specific telenovela slotted in a particular timeframe. Due to Globo's audience segmentation process, the merchandizing writers who know the language and trends of a particular audience are charged with producing insertions for the time-slot that targets that specific audience. Therefore, an organic, cultural relationship exists between the prosocial messages within the narrative, the scriptwriters, and the social merchandizers.

Different time-slots at TV Globo are central to the success of the social merchandising approach (Table 14.3). Regardless of the Brazilian telenovela's ever-changing nature, Globo maintained the same broadcast schedule for many years, consisting of four or five main serialized programs starting in the afternoon and ending late in the evening (5 p.m. to 10 p.m. usually). The

TABLE 14.3
Telenovelas on Globo Network.

Time-slot	Target Audience	General Format	Aired in 2000
5 pm	Teens	Teen-oriented drama-comedy set in a school; centers on discussion of sexuality and youth behavior	*Malhação* since 1995
6 pm	Women (housewives); children; teens; retired people	Family melodrama; some literary historical dramas adapted from Brazilian classics	*Força de um Desejo*
7 pm	Broad audience base, but greater focus remains on women, teens and children	Romantic comedy	*Vila Madalena* and *Uga Uga*
8:30 pm	Broadest audience base, normally the highest ratings for the whole evening	Contemporary dramas with a tradition to incorporate social or political issues	*Laços de Família*
10:30 pm	Mature audience	Highly polished miniseries (5–30 episodes) normally adapting contemporary or classic literary Brazilian texts	

five o'clock slot is typically aimed at teenagers and issues relevant to them. For example, *Malhação* is broadcast since 1995 in the late afternoon. Because of its long run, this program has been well-suited to include the largest number of social merchandising insertions. Next, Globo at 6 p.m. broadcasts a highly melodramatic telenovela, often a literary adaptation. The target group for this time-slot is older than the 5:00 o'clock show, comprised of the elderly, housewives, and children. After a 15-minute local newscast, Globo at seven o'clock goes back to a younger but more mature audience, 18-to-34-year-olds. Frequently, the telenovela during this time slot includes a storyline and issues that appeal to teens and children as well, and the program is normally a comedy set in an urban location or occasionally on an exotic beach. From 8 to 8:30 p.m., the network broadcasts the national news, with Globo's star prime time show following immediately. Because this time-slot attracts the largest and most diverse audience, Globo actors, writers, directors, and producers invest a great deal more time, energy, and money there, as compared to other telenovelas. The SM themes tend to be more complex, hovering between melodramatic and serious storylines containing layers of social and political insertions. The remaining late evening slots are filled, from 9:30 p.m. to 10:30 p.m., with one-hour shows with audience profiles varying according to the program, which can range from comedy shows to news magazines, and, from 10:30 p.m. to 11:30 p.m., adaptations of contemporary and classical Brazilian literature with higher production values and shorter duration (five to thirty episodes), which normally appeal to more mature audiences.

LESSONS LEARNED

Since social merchandising in telenovelas is Brazil's answer to educating audiences while entertaining them, scholars and practitioners can learn much about this unique E-E approach in hopes of improving the strategy and possibly applying it to other nations. Although Brazilian telenovela's social merchandising has similarities with other E-E strategies, a number of differences exist, which can best be understood in light of their unique characteristics, strengths, and limitations.

Production Process

Unlike other global E-E television and radio shows that are produced in a linear fashion, where the entire storyline is written months before it is broadcast, Brazilian telenovelas are created in a cyclical, continuous manner with ongoing external, diverse inputs from organizations, the government, and the audience. Brazilian writers, producers, and directors are writing and shooting upcoming episodes for a telenovela only a few weeks before they are broadcast. This process allows for last-minute changes, can reflect new social trends, and can include up-to-the-minute political events. The storyline in Brazilian telenovelas and SM are constantly evolving due to community input primarily through audience ratings and focus group interviews. According to Mattelart and Mattelart (1990), Brazilian telenovelas are an "open genre" where telenovela creators receive input from viewers and fans, theatrical productions, advertisers, the elite, the popular press, institutional networks, marketing research firms, and other social forces in the society such as the Catholic Church, the government, and activist groups (Hamburger, 1993).

An example can be seen during Manoel Carlos's telenovela, *Laços de Família*. After the drama's broadcasts began, Carlos met with Brazilian First Lady Ruth Cardoso. She asked him to include her main social initiative, *communidade solidária* (solidarity community), a program designed to promote volunteerism to deal with social issues in the nation. A few days later, Carlos inserted Mrs. Cardoso's volunteer organization into the storyline. Clearly, Carlos, Globo, and the telenovela were "open" enough to include in the narrative an unplanned event of current relevance to Brazil.

The dynamic nature of Brazilian telenovelas and SM, as well as the organizational culture at Globo create continuously changing television programs that are dependent on audience input, thereby allowing for prosocial messages to be shaped and reshaped to achieve greater effectiveness.

Multiple Approach

The Brazilian telenovelas/SM approach is different from other E-E interventions due to their relationship with TV Globo. Throughout the network's history, it has maintained a multicontinuous broadcast of dramas throughout the day. For more than 30 years, Globo aired telenovelas six days a week throughout the year, creating a media space that tackles different socioeducational issues for multiple audiences. This model has both strengths and disadvantages, when compared to E-E programs elsewhere.

On one hand, Globo's multiissue, multiaudience, multidrama format ensures that most of the viewing audience can be reached through some telenovela during each day. Many E-E interventions address only one issue for a specific audience throughout its broadcast, not reaching other segments of the viewing public because storylines, characters, and messages were not created with nontarget groups in mind. Globo and social merchandizing seem to have a solution to this concern because audiences are exposed to prosocial telenovelas, messages, and characters that create a strong sense of identification. Moreover, even when a telenovela ends and the drama is off the air, the actors often are in another program. The use of the same actors in different shows forces audiences to deal with the new prosocial issues in the new drama and potentially deal with the older messages associated with characters that the current actors portrayed in previous telenovelas. In this manner, Brazilian telenovelas and social merchandizing engage audiences through character association with old and new prosocial insertions, even though the new telenovela may not contain any of the previous socioeducational messages.

On the other hand, the continuity of shows, messages, and actors may offer drawbacks. Because audiences are exposed to many social merchandizing insertions, the natural cross-fertilization of information between storylines in different time-slots, as well as consecutively over the years, may become cognitively burdensome and boring to the point that viewers do not spend adequate time understanding, interpreting, and questioning the messages (Patel, 2002). Due to the overabundance of educational information in the multitude of telenovelas, individuals may watch and superficially analyze the prosocial messages that are most relevant to them.

Organic Nature

Currently, many E-E projects in the world are developed, funded, and evaluated by individuals who are not from the country for which the intervention is designed. While these E-E planners and implementers consult with local people for advice, much of the efforts are undertaken by external organizations. Social merchandising as practiced in Brazil by the Globo network is a strictly Brazilian activity. Brazilian telenovelas and SM are a byproduct of a home-grown, organic process that originates from years of historical, structural, organizational, and motivational influences, and social changes. The long history of telenovelas in Brazil, which now includes a very contemporary slant, is far from the traditional, melodramatic model found in other Latin American countries.

The historical development of Brazilian telenovelas, its relationship to the dictatorship in its early stages, and the semimonopoly with which Globo network operated over several decades created forces difficult to replicate in other parts of the world. The organic nature of telenovelas as a response to historical forces provides a strong connection between the genre and the audiences that grow up with it. This strength can also become a hindrance in limiting the level of insertions and the malleability of writers to collaborate, since it is mostly on a voluntary basis and relies on the authors' interest in the topic and willingness to incorporate it into the narrative.

Intentionality

An additionally unique factor about social merchandizing in Brazil, as compared to other E-E strategies, is the degree to which telenovelas are intentionally constructed (and by whom) for purposes of prosocial awareness and social change. Although TV Globo does get some concerted input from international development organizations, community leaders, and the Brazilian government, the television network allows scriptwriters a high level of independence with regard to what type, and how much, of the storyline is dedicated to social merchandizing. Because of this freedom, many script writers look to their personal agendas as a guide for the socioeducational content in their telenovelas. If audience ratings remain high, the melodramatic structure of the program stays intact and Globo does not interfere with the writer's organic drama production.

This approach is far different from E-E programs in many other nations that are characterized by conscious, top-down decision-makers and funders who consciously set public agendas by telling producers, scriptwriters, and directors what type of messages, narratives, and characters need to be created for an E-E intervention. The primary advantage of the level and type of intentionality rests in the writers' vision that the socioeducational insertions, in most cases, are to be a natural, coherent part of the plot line from the beginning, rather than an afterthought. Brazilian scriptwriters include issues that they perceive to be central to the development of their characters and consequently critical to the melodramatic narrative. Because SM insertions are not the driving force behind the narrative, as may be the case with top-down agendas set by network executives or external organizations, Brazilian scriptwriters have more flexibility to develop plot lines based on the intentional input of the audience and the writer's personal ideas.

Evaluation

Social merchandizing in Brazil is unusual because no collective, large-scale evaluations have been conducted to date that examine the effectiveness of this placement strategy used in Brazilian telenovelas. No definitive data are available currently that speak to the efficacy of social merchandizing insertions nor is research found on the number and type of prosocial messages included in telenovelas. Only since 1995 has an effort been made to track prosocial insertions in all of Globo's telenovelas by Comunicarte, the social marketing office in Rio de Janeiro that has worked with Globo to increase writers' awareness of the potential of using telenovelas to promote social change.

Although television has an enormous potential to disseminate information and influence social change, much is still unknown about how and why the social merchandizing process and Brazilian telenovelas can, and do, have an impact in a traditional society (Kottak, 1991). Unlike most other E-E campaigns, a lack of evaluative research on Brazil's SM strategies points out limitations and raises questions. For example, why are impact and outcome evaluations not valued in Brazil, whereas formative and process evaluations (during the design and broadcast phases) are so emphasized? What are monies from Globo, international organizations, and governemental agencies really funding production versus evaluation? How can social merchandizers and scriptwriters continue to insert prosocial messages without research that lends support to SM's credibility and effectiveness? If evaluative research does exist, why is it not regularly published and disseminated as in other E-E programs? Do Brazilian telenovelas and SM lead to long-term behavioral and cultural changes? Because of a dearth of replies to these questions, which have been answered to some extent in other E-E settings, future telenovelas in Brazil utilizing the SM approach should consider conducting evaluative studies for self-improvement.

Recommendations

What can E-E designers, scholars, funders, and evaluators learn from Brazil's E-E framework if they want to replicate certain parts of the strategy elsewhere?

1.   Future E-E interventions must incorporate prosocial insertions organically into a telenovela's narrative, since poorly produced sequences hinder the flow of the narrative and consequently limit the audience. Brazil has shown that these messages need to be associated with the storyline, but connecting

them to the broader, current, social, and political reality of society may make them more effective.

2. An important element of the long-term use of media for social change in the developing world should be to boost the media infrastructure and production abilities to promote the development and utilization of local media products that could incorporate E-E messages. Audiences prefer locally produced television programs because they address the viewers' sensibilities, history, style of humor, and sense of place. Promoting local infrastructure and working with scriptwriters and producers to have locally relevant social issues incorporated in their television programs. In the long run, this strategy might prove to be effective in developing writers' and producers' sensibilities to the role of media in social change.

3. Instead of using a single shot approach, E-E efforts in other nations should strongly consider adopting a continuous flow of television programs that allow the local media to become a part of the daily life of the audience, as is the case in Brazil. This continual process may increase the audience's ability to interpret messages, bolster the possibilities of reaching a broader audience, and create more venues to include different E-E messages.

4. Media producers, network executives, and E-E scriptwriters must incorporate prosocial messages based on the local flavor of their community. The success of SM in Brazil stems from the personal agenda of writers, the willingness of Globo to listen to the lobbying attempts of religious organizations, political groups, external development agencies, and the general audience. By placing the responsibility for disseminating prosocial ideas upon themselves through homegrown production and local input, rather than externally, they have created a unique, effective strategy in one country, which warrants the attention of other E-E interventions.

The practice of social marketing in Brazilian telenovelas may not be easily replicable in other national contexts due to the specific political, economic, social and cultural structures that allowed for the genre to develop in the particular direction that it did in Brazil. Social merchandizing in Brazil provides an alternative model that the field of E-E can consider when designing, implementing, and evaluating future campaigns for behavior change.

REFERENCES

Apolinário, S. (1996). Globo quer marketing social em todas as novelas. *O Estado de São Paulo*, T9.

Bouman, M. P. A. (1999). *The turtle and the peacock: Collaboration for prosocial change.* Wageningen, The Netherlands: Wageningen Agricultural University

Castro, D. (1997). Autor de novela diz sofrer ameaças. *Folha de São Paulo*, Tvfolha: 7.

Communicarte Marketing Social (2001). Merchandising Social, Informe Annual. Rio de Janeiro, Comunicarte.

Fadul, A., & McAnany, E. (1998, July). *As temáticas socio-demográficas na telenovela brasileira (Rede Globo, 1970-1995)*. Paper presented at the conference on Social Impacts of Telenovelas in Brazil, Tiradentes, Minas Gerais.

Fadul, A., McAnany E., & Morales, O. (1996). *Telenovela and demography in Brazil*. Paper presented at the International Association for Mass Communication Research, Sydney, Australia.

Fernandes, I. (1994). *Telenovela Brasileira: Memória*. São Paulo: Editora Brasiliense.

Firme, M. (1994). Sexo, ética e folhetim. *Jornal do Brasil: TV Section*, 16.

Guerini, E. (1996). Merchandising social invade o horário nobre. *Folha de São Paulo, TV Folha*, 4-5.

Guillermoprieto, A. (1994). Rio, 1993. *In the heart that bleeds, Latin America now*. New York: Vintage.

Hamburger, E. I. (1993). Telenovelas in Brazil and the "feminization" of the gaze. Unpublished manuscript. São Paulo, Brazil.

Hamburger, E. I. (1999). *Politics and intimacy in Brazilian telenovelas*. Unpublished doctoral dissertation, Chicago: University of Chicago, Department of Anthropology.

Harold, C. M. (1988). The "Brazilianization" of Brazilian television: A critical review. *Studies in Latin American Popular Culture*, 7, 41-57.

Hernandez, O. (2001). *Global love: Telenovelas in transnational times*. Unpublished doctoral dissertation. Austin, TX: University of Texas at Austin.

Japhet, G., & Goldstein, S. (1997). Soul City experience. *Integration*, 53, 10-11.

Kincaid, D. L., Coleman, P. L., Rimon J. G. II, & Silayan-Go, A. (1991, November). *The Philippines multimedia campaign for young people project: Summary of evaluation result*. Paper presented at the American Public Health Association, Atlanta.

Kottak, C. (1991). Television's impact on values and local life in Brazil. *Journal of Communication*, 41(1): 70-87.

La Pastina, A. (1999). *The telenovela way of knowledge: An ethnographic reception study among rural viewers in Brazil*. Unpublished doctoral dissertation. Austin, TX: University of Texas at Austin.

La Pastina, A. (2001). Product placement in Brazilian prime-time television: The case of a telenovela reception. *Journal of Broadcasting & Electronic Media*, 45, 541-557.

La Pastina, A. C., Straubhaar, J. D., & Almeida, H. B. (1999, May). *Producers, audiences and the limits of social marketing on television: The Case of O Rei do Gado, a telenovela about land reform in Brazil*. Paper presented at the International Communication Association, San Francisco.

Lopez, A. (1991). The melodrama in Latin America: Films, telenovelas, and the currency of a popular form. In M. Landy (Ed.), *Imitations of life: A reader on film and television melodrama* (pp. 596-606). Detroit: Wayne State University Press.

Lopez, A. M. (1995). Our welcomed guests: Telenovelas in Latin America. In R. Allen (Ed.), *To be continued... Soap operas around the world*. (pp. 256-275). New York: Routledge.

Mattelart, M., & Mattelart, A. (1990). *The carnival of images: Brazilian television fiction*. New York: Bergin and Garvey.

Mattos, S. (1980). *The impact of the 1964 revolution on Brazilian Television*. San Antonio, TX: V. Klingensmith.

Mattos, S. (2000). *A televisão no Brasil: 50 anos de história (1950-2000)*. Salvador, Bahia, Brazil: Editora Pas.

Mazziotti, N. (1993). El estado de las investigaciones sobre telenovela lationoamericana. *Revista de Ciencias de la Informacion*, 8, 45-59.

McAnany, E. G. (1984). The logic of culture industries in Latin America: The television industry in Brazil. In V. Mosco & J. Wasko (Eds.), *The critical communications review: Volume II changing patterns of communication control* (pp. 185–210) Norwood, N.J.: Ablex.

Melo, E. G. d. C. (1989). *Telenovela* and merchandising: The structure of television production in Brazil. Unpublished master's thesis, Austin, TX: University of Texas at Austin. Department of Radio-TV-Film.

Miranda-Ribeiro, P. (1997). Telenovela and the sexuality transition among teenagers in Brazil. Unpublished doctoral dissertation, Austin, TX: University of Texas at Austin.

Ortiz, R., Borelli, S., & Ramos, R. (1988). *Telenovela: História e producão*. São Paulo: Brasiliense.

Patel, D. S. (2002). *Changing health knowledge, attitudes, and behavioral intentions: An analysis of how much educational content should be inserted into an entertainment-education program.* Unpublished doctoral dissertation, East Lansing, MI: Michigan State University.

Piotrow, P. T., Rimon J.G., II, Winnard, L., Kincaid, D. L., Huntington, D., & Convisser, J. (1990). Mass media family planning promotion in three Nigerian cities. *Studies in Family Planning, 21,* 265–273.

Sherry, J. (1997). Prosocial soap operas for development: A review of research and theory. *Journal of International Communication, 4,* 75–101.

Silva, F. (1997). *O Rei do Gado* redime pais inexistente. *Folha de SãoPaulo—TV Folha*. São Paulo: 2.

Sinclair, J. (1996). Mexico, Brazil, and the Latin World. In J. Sinclair, E. Jacka, & S. Cunningham (Eds.), *New patterns in global television: peripheral vision* (pp. 33–66). New York: Oxford University Press.

Singhal, A., & Rogers, E. M. (1999). *Entertainment-education: A communication strategy for social change.* Mahwah, NJ: Lawrence Erlbaum Associates.

Sood, S., & Rogers, E. M. (1996, November). *Parasocial interaction by letter-writers to an entertainment-education soap opera in India.* Paper presented at the Speech Communication Association, San Diego.

Straubhaar, J. D. (1982). The development of the telenovela as the preeminent form of popular culture in Brazil. *Studies in Latin American Popular Culture, 1,* 138–150.

Straubhaar, J. D. (1996). The electronic media in Brazil. In R. Cole (Ed.), *Communication in Latin America: Journalism, mass media, and society* (pp. 217–243). Wilmington, DE: Scholarly Resources.

Telenovela is something else. *Variety* (1986, March 12) p. 142. Um autor com vontade de escrwer. (August 6, 1996). Veja, 122–123.

15

Delivering Entertainment-Education Health Messages Through the Internet to Hard-to-Reach U.S. Audiences in the Southwest

Everett M. Rogers
University of New Mexico

Meet the Montoyas is a series of six entertainment-education *fotonovelas* produced by the New Mexico Department of Health's Diabetes Control Program. Each fotonovela tells, in still photos and bubbletext (something like comic books), how the Montoyas, a fictional Hispanic family in New Mexico, deal with the onset of diabetes on the part of the head of the Montoya family. These entertainment-education fotonovelas, available in both English and Spanish, were distributed to the public through health clinics and by other means, but they reached only a small portion of the intended audience. Then *Meet the Montoyas* was placed on the La Plaza Telecommunity's Web site in 1998 by the Diabetes Wellness Project, a Federally funded health intervention in Taos County, NM. Community outreach trainers employed by the Project taught people how to use computers and the Internet, and guided them to *Meet the Montoyas* on the Web site (Photo 15.1). La Plaza Telecommunity is a local intranet, established in the early 1990s to provide access to the people of Taos County (who have the lowest per capita income of any county in New Mexico, which has one of the lowest per capita incomes of the 50 states).

Internet communication technology today provides a promising means of reaching low-income, underserved populations in order to decrease the burden of diabetes, cancer, and other illnesses. For example, consider an E-E

PHOTO 15.1.   A community outreach trainer from the La Plaza Telecommunity demonstrates computer and Internet use to an elderly Hispanic woman in Taos County, NM on his laptop computer, by showing her *Meet the Montoyas,* a *fotonovela* on diabetes. (*Source:* Personal files of the author.)

narrative about breast cancer screening, intended to change the behavior of older Hispanic women.

Rosa and Mammography Screening

Rosa is a 50-year old Hispanic woman whose mother died of breast cancer, as did more recently an aunt. Her friends urge Rosa to get her first mammogram, but she is terrified of doing so, and repeats traditional, fatalistic rationales for not doing so (she is a transitional role-model). Her friends (they are positive role-models) counter these arguments for the educational issue of mammography screening. Rosa has a cousin (a negative role-model) who is also at risk, and who supports her in her reluctance. Rosa then encounters problems of how to get to the breast cancer screening facility, and money to pay for the screening, and some family resistance, and starts to give up, despite her friends' prompting. Her friends finally help her through these problems, and they agree to go together for mammograms. To Rosa's relief, her mammogram is negative. But a small node is seen on the breast of one of her friends. Her friends rally to help the friend with her family responsibilities while she undergoes treatment. The treatment is successful, due to early intervention. Meanwhile, the negative role-model cousin is diagnosed with advanced breast cancer. She needs a radical mastectomy and chemotherapy, but the prognosis is not optimistic. The friends decide to make their mammogram visit together on a regular basis.

If the entertainment-education narrative in the above box were delivered to its target audience via the Internet, it would reach many more people than if it were made available through print fotonovelas or by other channels. Further, the Internet is an interactive medium, allowing for questions from members of the target audience to actors in the fotonovela. Here we see how the Internet allows particular health messages to reach specialized audiences in the United States and elsewhere.

The objective of the present chapter is to explore how the Internet can be utilized to deliver E-E health messages to low-income minorities in the Southwestern United States. We use breast cancer screening as an example in this chapter.

POTENTIAL OF THE INTERNET FOR E-E

In 2002 about 71% of all adult Americans were using the Internet. This inter-active communication technology was diffusing to older individuals of lower socioeconomic status, with fewer years of formal education, and to those of minority affiliation. These newer Internet users, who tend to be underserved by most health programs and who may be at-risk for illnesses such as cancer, represent an important potential audience for health prevention messages.

Entertainment-education (E-E) is defined as the intentional placement of educational content in entertainment. E-E based behavior change interventions can be highly effective, especially with audiences who may have limited literacy, who may not be initially very motivated to process a message, or who may be initially resistant to the message (Singhal & Rogers, 1999, 2002; Slater, 1997; Slater & Rouner, 2002). However, most past E-E health interventions were confined to radio and television broadcasts, and there have been few efforts to date to use the Internet in combination with the entertainment-education strategy.

Highly interactive, Web-based entertainment-education interventions with, or without, interactive epilogues can be designed to deliver fotonovelas like the story of Rosa (see box). The entertainment-education strategy fits well with the popularity of television soap operas (telenovelas) with an intended audience of Hispanic people in the Southwestern United States, and offers the potential for reaching individuals who are current and possible future adopters of the Internet.

EFFECTS OF THE
ENTERTAINMENT-EDUCATION STRATEGY

The E-E strategy has been utilized in over 200 health intervention programs in 50 countries in Latin America, Africa, and Asia over the past 25 years, dealing with such educational issues as HIV/AIDS prevention, family planning, environmental health, teenage pregnancy prevention, and gender equality. Evaluation research indicates that if these E-E interventions are implemented properly, relatively strong effects on knowledge gain, attitude change, and behavior change result (Singhal & Rogers, 1999; Piotrow, Kincaid, Rimon, & Rinehart, 1997). These strong effects of E-E health interventions, many in the form of radio or television soap operas, are the result of the E-E strategy's (1) sound basis in Bandura's (1977; 1997) social learning/social cognitive theory as well as its consistency with other major theories of behavior change (Slater & Rouner, 2002; Slater, in press; Singhal & Rogers, 2002), (2) popularity, particularly with socioeconomically disadvantaged audiences, and (3) a high degree of involvement of audience individuals and the stimulation of interpersonal discussion with peers about the educational content, after exposure to the E-E messages (Table 15.1).

Despite the positive results of E-E interventions on health behavior change in developing countries, the E-E strategy has not been utilized widely to date (1) in the United States, or (2) for cancer prevention (Singhal & Rogers, 1999), although several Hollywood soap operas have used cancer-related entertainment episodes, such as Vicki's breast cancer on ABC's *One Life to Live*, which won a CDC Sentinel for Health Award for Daytime Drama in 2000, and a 1990 cancer event on ABC's *thirtysomething* (this event was found to have measurable effects, such as stimulating peer discussion about cancer (Sharf, Freimuth, Greebspon, & Plotnick, 1996). The Centers for Disease Control and Prevention (CDC) collaborates with the Hollywood creative community in incorporating health issues in soap operas and other television shows,

TABLE 15.1
Effects of Selected E-E Health Interventions on Behavior Change

Intervention	Country	Strength of Effects	Author(s)
1. Telenovelas for family planning, adult literacy, and gender equality	Mexico	Strong	Nariman (1993)
2. TV soap opera for family planning and gender equality	India	Fairly strong	Singhal & Rogers (1989)
3. TV soap opera for family planning	Nigeria	Strong	Piotrow et al. (1990)
4. TV soap opera for family planning	Turkey	Strong	Kincaid et al. (1993)
5. Radio soap opera for family planning	The Gambia	Strong	Valente et al. (1994)

like *The Bold and the Beautiful* and *The Young and the Restless*, which are broadcast in the United States and in some 110 other countries around the world. Tony, a character in the *The Bold and the Beautiful*, learns that he is HIV-positive, discloses his status to his fiancé, Kristin, and they decide to marry. On their honeymoon in Africa, they decide to adopt an AIDS orphan. This entertainment-education approach to HIV/AIDS was awarded the CDC's Sentinel for Health Award for Daytime Drama in 2002. The way in which television viewers in India perceive of these health issues in Hollywood soap operas is currently being investigated by Arvind Singhal and Everett M. Rogers, in collaboration with Population Communications International (PCI), the Norman Leer Center at the University of Southern California, and the CDC.

E-E interventions offer an opportunity to test communication and social psychological theories of behavior change in real-life settings. Bandura's (1977; 1997) social learning/social cognition theory provides a basis for the design of positive, negative, and transitional role-models in E-E interventions, and for encouraging self-efficacy in audience individuals in adopting preventive health behaviors. E-E interventions are typically narratives, which, as Green and Brock (2000) demonstrated experimentally, can "transport" (that is, involve) audience individuals into the story, so that behavior change is facilitated. A narrative can transport an individual to another time and place by moving him/her into an imagined situation. Narratives, as in E-E approaches, are stories that raise unanswered questions, present unresolved conflicts, and depict not yet completed activity. Hence, narrative approaches to behavior change are highly involving of audience individuals (Green & Brock, 2000). Such audience involvement facilitates peer discussion about the narrative, which leads to behavior change.

Theory development and laboratory-based experimental research efforts examine the persuasive effects of narratives on health-related attitudes and behavior (Slater, in press). For example, an experimental study suggested that narrative elements were effective in influencing the beliefs of audience members who are resistant to a health prevention message, while quantitative scientific evidence was not effective (Slater & Rouner, 1996). Another study suggested that embedding persuasive health messages in a narrative story line nearly eliminated counterarguing, even among potentially resistant audience members (Slater, 1997).

Today the Internet offers a potential communication channel for health-oriented E-E interventions. More than two-thirds of the U.S. population currently use the Internet, and further diffusion is proceeding at a rapid rate (Cole, Suman, Schramm, van Bel, Lunn, Maguire, Hansen, Singh, Aquino, & Lebo, 2000; Pew Internet Survey, 2002). Some 52 million Americans sought health information on the Internet. As Internet access increases, delivery of E-E interventions for cancer prevention or some other health issue offers a promising opportunity and challenge. Few health interventions systematically employ the E-E approach via the Internet, despite the potential of the Internet for communicating health information (Chamberlain, 1996; Eysenbach, 2000; Fotheringham, Owies, Leslie, & Owen, 2000). An interactive soap opera Web site to promote knowledge of breast cancer screening among Hispanic women was found to have beneficial effects on intentions (Jibaja, Kingery, Noff, Smith, Bowman, & Holcomb, 2000), but it did not fully utilize the E-E approach, such as the use of positive, negative, and transitional role-models, inclusion of interactive epilogues, and it was not based on Bandura's social learning/social cognitive theory.

DIFFUSION OF THE INTERNET AND THE DIGITAL DIVIDE

More than two-thirds of U.S. adults have used the Internet, with a major increase in the past two years (Cole et al., 2000; Hindman, 2000; Miller, 2001; Pew Internet Survey, 2002). Compared to users, nonusers of the Internet are characterized by lower socioeconomic status, less education, and older age, and are more likely to be members of minority populations.

The digital divide is the gap that exists between individuals advantaged by the Internet and those individuals relatively disadvantaged by the Internet (Colby, 2001; Rogers, 2001). Public policies have been pursued in the United States to close this digital divide, and there is some evidence that the digital divide may be narrowing. Spooner, Rainie, Fox, Harrigan, and Lenhart (2000) reported that the racial gap between African Americans and European Americans is closing in recent years, although opposite evidence has also been reported (Hoffman & Novak, 1998; McConnaughey, Everette, Reynolds, & Lader, 1999). Miller (2001) analyzed data from seven national surveys from 1983 to 1999 to show that the gaps in Internet access were not widening over time.

Rogers (2001) identified three strategies to bridge the digital divide: (1) promote and utilize public access centers (Lentz, Straubhaar, La Pastina, Main, & Taylor, 2000; Buller, Woodall, Rogers, Woodall, Zimmerman, Slater, Pepper, Bartlett, Hines, Unger, Hau, & LeBlanc, 2001b), (2) fit Internet/Web content to the particular needs of new and future Internet users (Bier, Gallo, Nucklos, Sherblom, & Pennick, 1998; Slater, Zimmerman, Tipton, Halverson, Kean, & Rost, 1994; Zarcadoolas, Blanco, Pleasant, & Boyer, 2000; Buller, Woodall, Hall, Borland, Ax, Brown, & Hines, 2001a; Buller et al., 2001b; Berland, Elliott, Morales, Algazy, Kravitz, Broder, Kanouse, Munoz, Puyol, Lara, Watkins, Yang, & McGlynn, 2001; Zimmerman, Akerelrea, Buller, & LeBlanc, in press), and (3) provide new means of accessing the Internet, such as wireless devices, palm pilots, and cellular telephones (Rogers, 2003).

The present author reanalyzed data from two Pew Internet national surveys (N = 6,036) conducted in March/April, 2000 in order to identify the characteristics of new Internet users (who were 17% of the total sample, who adopted Internet use in the six months prior to the surveys). These new adopters included a larger percentage of Hispanics (9.4%) than did earlier adopters of the Internet (7.4%). Nevertheless, Hispanics (12% of the total U.S. population) are still underrepresented among all Internet users. New users were characterized by less formal education, lower socioeconomic status, and somewhat lower incomes, compared to previous users of the Internet.

Hispanic women have a relatively high degree of parasocial interaction with media personalities, such as television soap opera actors. Frequent advertisements on Univisíon, the leading Spanish-language television network in the United States, invite viewers of entertainment telenovelas to contact soap opera stars via the Internet (this new service is particularly popular with older Hispanic women). Several million Spanish-language viewers in the United States over the past few years have contacted Univisíon's telenovela Web sites in order to interact with soap opera stars. The content of such interaction is not health-related, but it could be.

APPROPRIATE WEB CONTENT
FOR NEW INTERNET USERS

A decade or so in the future, almost all Americans may be using the Internet, and the current access-divide may almost disappear (Rogers, 2001). This access-divide, however, may be replaced by other demographically based "divides," as less-educated, lower socioeconomic status, seniors, and minorities, who are the new Internet users of today, will experience difficulties in using the Internet in order to obtain health information. A likely long-term divide is due to cultural and stylistic mismatches between existing Web sites versus the needs and expectations of new users of the Internet (Barnhardt, 2000; Berland et al., 2001). Research suggests that much Web content is inappropriate for new users because it is written at too high a level of readability, is too highly text-based and has relatively few graphics, and the content often has limited relevance for new Internet users (Barnhardt, 2000). The health information that people want from the Web is difficult to access because of the overwhelming volume of information and its inconsistent organization, and because current search strategies are inadequate.

The need for improved readability of health Web sites is particularly important today, given that new Internet users are characterized by lower levels of formal education. A sample of health-related Web sites was found to require an average of 13.2 years of education for users to understand their contents, with more than half of the Web sites requiring a college education for readability (Berland et al., 2001). Clearly, this high level of written content of Web sites is inappropriate for new users of the Internet, many of whom, research shows, are reading at, or below, the eighth-grade level. The high degree of frustration felt by many currently new Internet users is suggested by the 13% of users who have discontinued use of the Internet.

Many print health communication messages are written at much too high a level of difficulty for most consumers, particularly the approximately one-third of the U.S. population with low levels of health literacy, and for the population for whom information has been translated from English to Spanish (Berland et al., 2001). Health literacy is the degree to which individuals have the capacity to obtain, process, and understand basic health information and services needed to make appropriate health decisions (Rogers, Ratzan, & Payne, 2001). For example, Jackson, Davis, Bairnsfather, George, Crouch, and Gault (1991) found that 275 patient brochures utilized in seven outpatient clinics were written at a reading level of 12.4 years of education, far above the 5.4 years of formal education that the clinic patients actually possessed. Four consent forms were written at a level (measured by standard readability indexes) requiring a readability level of 22.5 years of education! Williams, Counselman, and Caggiano (1996) found that only 45% of the patients in an urban hospital were able to read that hospital's emergency room discharge instructions. Similar findings have been reported in many other studies of health literacy (Rogers, Ratzan, & Payne, 2001; Kalichman, Benotsch, Suarez, Catz, & Miller, 2000).

Alternatives to written health messages can be utilized, such as patient videodiscs like *The Story of María* (Sweeney & Gulino, 1998), a patient video on colon cancer screening (Meade, McKinney, & Barnas, 1994), a soap opera-style video on mammography screening (Davis, Berkel, Arnold, Nandy, Jackson, & Murphy, 1998), or fotonovelas (Paskett, Tatum, Wilson, Dignan, & Velez, 1996; Jibaja et al., 2000). A Web-based E-E fotonovela intervention for mammography screening would seem to offer an effective means to reach women with relatively low levels of health literacy.

HEALTH INFORMATION NEEDS
OF INTERNET USERS

New users of the Internet in recent years tend to have relatively stronger needs for health information, including cancer prevention information, and to have more serious health problems (Eng, Maxfield, Deering, Ratzan, & Gustafson, 1998). Several investigations (O'Connor & Johnson, 2000; Barnhart, 2000; Eng & Gustafson, 1999) show that large numbers of Americans today seek health information from the Internet. For example, a national survey of 6,413

Internet users found that 63% said they went online for health/medical information (Fox & Rainie, 2000). "Breast cancer is one of the most common health-related search topics among users of the Internet" (Meric, Bernstam, Mirza, Hunt, Ames, Ross, Kuerer, Pollack, Musen, & Singletary, 2002, p. 579).

However, research (Biermann, Golladay, Greenfield, & Baker, 1999; Evans, 2001; Eysenbach & Diepgen, 1998; Fotheringham, Owies, Leslie, & Owen, 2000; Patrick, Robinson, Alemi, & Eng, 1999; Rice & Katz, 2001; Silberg, Lundberg, & Musacchio, 1997; Winkler, Flanagin, Chi-Lum, White, Andrews, Kennett, DeAngelis, & Musacchio, 2000; Weisbord, Soule, & Kimmel, 1997) also shows that certain of the health information on the Internet is of dubious scientific accuracy and may be perceived by Internet users as having low credibility (Cole et al., 2000; Flanagin & Metzger, 2000). Some 86% of Internet users seeking health/medical information online were concerned about unreliable information (Fox & Rainie, 2000). The Internet is problematic for members of the public who are unable to distinguish between scientifically proven versus bogus health information (Gustafson, Robinson, Ansley, Adler, & Brennan, 1998). The World Wide Web in 1996 contained approximately 200,000 documents about cancer, including a Web site for the sale of shark cartilage as a cancer cure (Keoun, 1996). Because the Internet is a highly decentralized network, there is little gatekeeping of Web content.

On the other hand, many high-quality health Web sites sponsored by government agencies and by nonprofit organizations are available via the Internet. Investigations (Eng, Maxfield, Deering, Ratzan, & Gustafson, 1998) indicate that information about breast cancer prevention, presented in a culturally appropriate manner through computer interactivity, is readily accepted by older, diverse populations, once they have learned the basic skills of using the human/computer interface such as a touch screen or mouse (Slater et al., 1994). Breast cancer screening messages presented in a soap opera format are particularly well accepted (Jibaja et al., 2000).

BREAST CANCER AND MAMMOGRAPHY SCREENING

Breast cancer is the leading type of cancer among women in the United States, with over 75% of breast cancers diagnosed in women aged 50 or over. Although Hispanic women are not at greater risk for breast cancer than nonHispanic women, they are more likely to die from this disease (Ramirez, McAlister, Gallion, Ramirez, Garza, Stamm, de la Torre, & Chalela, 1995), mainly because of late detection (Richardson, Marks, Solis, Collins, Birba, & Hisserich, 1987). The survival rate for women whose cancer is detected early, when it is localized, is estimated at 97%. However, the rate drops to 76% when the cancer has spread regionally, and for women with distant metastases the rate is only 21% (American Cancer Society, 1998).

A major explanation for late-stage diagnosis is underutilization of breast cancer screening (Richardson et al., 1987), which is an important problem for Hispanic women. The most effective method for early detection of breast cancer among older women, including Hispanic women, is mammography (Tabar & Dean, 1987). An analysis of available randomized controlled trials found that mammography reduced breast cancer mortality by about 30% for women in their 50s, and by about 17% for women in their 40s (IOM Committee on Communication, 2002).

Past research shows that effective inreach and outreach activities can increase mammography screening rates by about 20% (Yabroff, O'Malley, Mangan, & Mandelblatt, 2001; IOM Committee on Communication, 2002). Past research with Hispanic women (for example, Coe, Hartman, Castro, Campbell, Mayer, & Elder, 1994) suggests a wide "KAP-gap" (Knowledge, Attitudes, Practice), that is, a difference between knowledge of a preventive health action like mammography screening versus its proper practice. Past investigations (Rogers, Vaughan, Swalehe, Rao, Svenkerud, & Sood, 1999; Singhal & Rogers, 1999, 2003) show that E-E is uniquely capable of moving individuals from high levels of knowledge and favorable intentions, to effective practice of a preventive health action.

Cultural and social cofactors are among the most important variables to consider in designing E-E interventions to increase mammography breast cancer screening behavior among Hispanic women. Hispanic women have different beliefs about breast cancer screening than do nonHispanic women (Hubell, Mishra, Chavez, & Valdez, 1995). Some Hispanics hold traditional cultural health beliefs that discourage preventive health behaviors such as breast cancer screening. For example, Hispanic women tend to believe that breast cancer is an illness that inevitably causes death, even if treatment is received. Salazar (1996) found that Hispanic women fear the diagnosis of breast cancer because many believe that breast cancer is fatal. Hispanic women who hold this fatalistic belief are less likely to believe that breast cancer screening is efficacious.

REACHING HISPANIC PEOPLE IN THE SOUTHWEST WITH INTERNET HEALTH MESSAGES

Several past studies demonstrate that Internet-delivered health messages have potential for changing the behavior of Hispanic people. For example, the effects of an interactive, multimedia CD-ROM on breast cancer prevention were evaluated by Slater and others (1994). The 32 respondents were Hispanic,

African American, Native American, and Anglo low-income women averaging 48 years of age. The use-session of each participant was videotaped, so that problems in computer and program use that the individual experienced could later be coded and analyzed. Almost all of the Hispanic women learned how to navigate the computer-based system, in order to access cancer-prevention information.

A four-year research project supported by the National Cancer Institute (NCI) is currently investigating the Internet as a means of changing the cancer-prevention nutrition behavior of low-income Hispanic, Anglo, and Native American people in the Upper Rio Grande Valley of New Mexico and Colorado. This research project began in Taos County, NM and has expanded to six counties in northern New Mexico and southern Colorado (Buller et al., 2001b). One important lesson learned from this investigation is that considerable time and effort are required to design, develop, and test for usability Web-based materials for preventive health behavior change (Zimmerman et al., in press). Similar experience has been reported by other scholars using focus group interviews and other formative research methods in the design of an interactive Web intervention, and by designers of E-E health interventions (Singhal & Rogers, 1999). The nutrition Web site is being tested during 2002–2003 with local Anglo, Hispanic, and Native American adults in a randomized pretest/posttest controlled experiment. Individuals are recruited to participate in the trial of the Web site by community outreach trainers and by opinion leaders. The participants are randomly assigned to interact with the nutrition Web site immediately versus after a six months' period.

Communication scholars are also conducting an NCI-supported research project to design and evaluate a Web-based smoking prevention and cessation program for Hispanic and Anglo middle-school students, entitled Considerthis.org. Extensive efforts since 1997 were required to design and create this highly interactive, entertaining intervention through a formative research process (Buller et al., 2001a; Hall, Ax, Brown, Buller, Woodall, & Borland, 2002). Production challenges included determining the minimum technology requirements, authoring dynamic Web pages, and programming content modules. The Considerthis.org Web site features six 50-minute modules on media literacy, interpersonal relationship and communication skills, stress management, the biological effects of tobacco, decision-making skills, values clarification, and resistance skills. The content in these modules is tailored to the specific smoking experience of individual users. The feasibility and effectiveness of the Considerthis.org Web site is currently being tested in a randomized controlled trial with over 1,000 students in 20 middle schools in Denver, Albuquerque, and Tucson.

Learning how to use a computer and the Internet/Web is not an insurmountable barrier for diverse populations with low levels of income and formal education (Bier et al., 1998; Gallo & Horton, 1994; Zarcadoolas, Blanco, Pleasant, & Boyer, 2000; Debowski, Wood, & Bandura, 2001; Weinberg,

Schmale, Uken, & Wessel, 1996). Studies of Internet-delivered health communication in the Southwestern United States suggest the potential of the Internet and the World Wide Web. However, none of these investigations used the E-E strategy.

INVESTIGATING INTERNET-DELIVERED E-E
FOR BREAST CANCER SCREENING

The present author and his colleagues proposed an Internet-delivered E-E intervention that utilizes a narrative approach, as story-telling narratives are a customary style of communication for older Hispanic women. As Cole (1997, p. 346) stated: "Narrative must be authentic with respect to the lives, culture, plights, and language of the populations for whom the materials are designed." The E-E Web sites of study will use a fotonovela approach with interactive epilogues. These epilogues in the two E-E Web site interventions bridge the gap between the fictional world of the E-E story and the real world in which audience members live. Each episode of a typical entertainment-education soap opera ends with a brief epilogue that (1) summarizes the main educational points of the episode, and (2) provides a bridge to its application in the lives of audience members. Past research shows that an individual who is familiar, credible, and trusted by audience members is most effective in delivering these epilogues. Many audience members display a strong desire to interact directly with the characters and producers of E-E dramas. For example, an E-E television soap opera in India, *Hum Log*, received 400,000 letters from viewers, many indicating a high degree of parasocial interaction with the actors and/or the epilogue-giver (Sood & Rogers, 2000).

Epilogues are believed to increase the likelihood that lessons from the E-E narrative will be incorporated into the beliefs and overt behaviors of audience individuals (Singhal & Rogers, 1999). The one previous Internet-delivered narrative intervention for breast cancer screening (Jibaja et al., 2000) did not include epilogues. Moreover, none of the previous E-E interventions for other health behaviors evaluated the effects of including epilogues in a randomized controlled trial (Singhal & Rogers, 1999). Similarly, no previous research examined the social psychological mechanisms through which such epilogues increase the impact of E-E interventions on health behavior change. In the epilogues of study, E-E actors will talk with audience members and respond to specific common questions and concerns about breast cancer screening. The proposed research will evaluate the effects of (1) an E-E fotonovela with interactive epilogues, in comparison (2) to the fotonovela with epilogues that are not interactive, and (3) a didactic Web site which represent the "usual and customary" control condition. This didactic Web site will contain basic breast cancer screening information, but it will not be presented using the E-E strategy.

Our culturally appropriate E-E formats are expected to increase parasocial interaction (the degree to which an individual perceives that he/she has a personal relationship with a media personality [Alperstein, 1991; Singhal & Rogers, 1999, 2002; Sood & Rogers, 2000]), and involvement (the degree to which an individual feels herself/himself to be a participant in a media message), which should lead to more mammography screening behavior (Kirby, Ureda, Rose, & Hussey, 1998; Sood & Rogers, 2000; Singhal & Rogers, 1999, 2002). Likewise, the degree to which computer-based communication is perceived as similar to the characteristics of face-to-face interaction (Burgoon, Bengtsson, Bonito, Ramirez, Dunbar, & Miczo, 2001; Rafaeli, 1988; Ha & James, 1998; Rogers, 1986; Walther, 1996) should be increased by individuals' vicarious involvement with the characters portrayed in the E-E Web sites.

Data on respondents' adoption of mammography will be determined in a six months' follow-up survey interview, after these older Hispanic women participated in one of the three interventions. In a debriefing at the end of the experimental session (which will be conducted in community centers in Hispanic urban neighborhoods in Denver and Albuquerque), participants will be offered help in making an appointment for mammography screening. Participants will be provided with a coupon at the end of the experimental session and asked to present this coupon to their health/medical provider should they visit the provider in the next six months. The coupon will contain a message to the provider that asks them to mail it back to the project research staff, reporting whether or not the participant had a mammogram. This coupon will provide a validity check on self-report data, which will be gathered in follow-up interviews.

CONCLUSIONS

This chapter argued that the entertainment-education strategy can be utilized in fotonovelas that are delivered via the Internet to specialized population segments, such as Hispanic people in the Southwestern United States. As the rate of adoption of the Internet, presently at more than two-thirds of the U.S. adult population, increasingly reaches lower-income, less-educated individuals with the greatest health needs, the potential of this interactive communication technology deserves investigation.

The approach described here, which has been demonstrated in several projects currently underway and planned, is to create E-E health interventions in the form of fotonovelas, with and without interactive epilogues, which are then tested in randomized controlled trials. For instance, older Hispanic women can be recruited to local telecenters in their community where they are taught to use computers and the Internet, and then participate with an E-E Web site for mammography screening. If the E-E intervention is found to be effective, it can then be made publicly available through the Internet.

Most past research on the E-E strategy has been conducted by means of audience surveys, and only occasionally in field experiments. The research approach described in the present chapter uses randomized controlled trials, which may provide improved understanding of E-E effects, and of the process through which such effects occur.

The following lessons learned are derived from previous investigations of Internet-delivered health communication.

1. *Considerable time, resources, and expertise are required to design and create Web sites to convey health messages.*
2. *Internet-based health messages are highly involving of audience individuals, due to the highly interactive nature of computer-based technologies.*
3. *While Internet-delivered health communication interventions would seem to fit naturally with the entertainment-education strategy, this combination remains an untested potential.*

REFERENCES

Alperstein, N. M. (1991). Imaginary social relationships with celebrities in television commercials. *Journal of Broadcasting and Electronic Media, 35*, 43–58.

American Cancer Society (1998). *Breast cancer facts and figures*. Atlanta: American Cancer Society, Report.

Bandura, A. (1977). *Social learning theory*. New York: Prentice Hall.

Bandura, A. (1997). *Self-efficacy: The exercise of control*. New York: Freeman.

Barnhardt, J. M. (2000). Health education and the digital divide: Building bridges and filling chasms. *Health Education Research, 15*(5), 527–531.

Berland, G. K., Elliot, M. N. Morales, L. S., Algazy, J. I,. Kravitz, R. L., Broder, M. S., Kanouse, D. E., Munoz, J. A., Puyol, J-A, Lara, M, Watkins, K. E., Yang, H., & McGlynn, E. A. (2001). Health information on the Internet: Accessibility, quality, and readability in English and Spanish, *JAMA, 285*(20), 2612–2621.

Bier, M., Gallo, M., Nucklos, E., Sherblom, S., & Pennick, M. (1998). Personal empowerment in the study of home Internet use by low-income families. *Journal of Research on Computing in Education, 30*(2), 107–121.

Biermann, J. S., Golladay, G. J., Greenfield, M. V. H., & Baker, L. H. (1999). Evaluation of cancer information on the Internet. *Cancer, 86*(3), 381–390.

Buller, D. B., Woodall, W. G., Hall, J. R., Borland, R., Ax, B., Brown, M., & Hines, J. M. (2001a). A Web-based smoking cessation and prevention program for children aged 12 to 15. In R. E. Rice & C. K. Atkin (Eds.), *Public communication campaigns* (3rd ed., pp. 357–372). Thousand Oaks, CA: Sage.

Buller, D. B., Woodall, W. G., Rogers, E. M., Woodall, P. B., Zimmerman, D., Slater, M., Pepper, J., Bartlett, K., Hines, J., Unger, E., Hau, B., & LeBlanc, M. M. (2001b). Formative research activities to provide Web-based nutrition information to adults in the Upper Rio Grande Valley. *Family and Community Health, 24*(3), 1-12.

Burgoon, J. K., Bengtsson, B., Bonito, J. A., Ramirez, A., Dunbar, N. E., & Miczo, N. (2001). *Testing the interactivity model: Communication processes, partner assignments, and the quality of collaborative work.* Unpublished paper. Tucson, AZ: University of Arizona, Department of Management Information Systems.

Chamberlain, M. A. (1996). Health communication: Making the most of new media technology: An international overview. *Journal of Health Communication, 1*, 43-50.

Coe, K., Hartman, M. P., Castro, F. G., Campbell, N., Mayer, J. A., & Elder, J. P. (1994). Breast self-examination: Knowledge and practices of Hispanic women in two Southwestern metropolitan areas. *Journal of Community Health, 19*(6), 433-448.

Colby, D. (2001). Conceptualizing the 'Digital Divide': Closing the 'gap' by creating a postmodern network that distributes the productive power of speech. *Communication, Law, & Policy, 6*, 123-173.

Cole H. P. (1997). Stories to live by: A narrative approach to health behavior research and injury prevention. In D. S. Gochman (Ed.), *Handbook of health behavior research IV* (pp. 325-349). New York: Plenum Press.

Cole, J. I., Suman, M., Schramm, P., van Bel, D., Lunn, B., Maguire, P., Hansen, K., Singh, R., Aquino, J. S., & Lebo, H. (2000). *The UCLA Internet Report: Surveying the digital future.* Los Angeles, CA: UCLA Center for Communication Policy.

Davis, T. C., Berkel, H. L., Arnold, C. L., Nandy, I., Jackson, R. H., & Murphy, P. W. (1998). Intervention to increase mammography utilization in a public hospital. *Journal of General Internal Medicine, 13*, 230-233.

Debowski, S., Wood, R., & Bandura, A. (2001). *Impact of guided exploration and enactive exploration on self-regulating mechanisms, and information acquisition through electronic search.* Unpublished paper, Murdoch, Australia: Department of Commerce, Murdoch University.

Eng, T. R. & Gustafson, D. H. (1999). *Wired for health and well-being: The emergence of interactive health communication.* Washington, DC: Office of Public Health and Science, U.S. Department of Health and Human Services, Report.

Eng, T. R., Maxfield, A., Deering, M. J., Ratzan, S. C., & Gustafson, D. H. (1998). Access to health information and support: A public highway or a private road? *JAMA, 280*, 1371-1375.

Evans, W. (2001). Mapping mainstream and fringe medicine on the Internet. *Science Communication, 22*, 292-299.

Eysenbach, G. (2000). Consumer health informatics. *British Medical Journal, 320*, 1713-1716.

Eysenbach, A. J., & Diepgen, T. L. (1998). Toward quality management of medical information on the Internet: Evaluation, labeling, and filtering of information. *British Medical Journal, 317*, 1496-1502.

Flanagin, A. J., & Metzger, M. J. (2000). Perceptions of Internet information credibility. *Journalism and Mass Communication Quarterly, 77*(3), 515-540.

Fotheringham, M. J., Owies, D., Leslie, E., & Owen, N. (2000). Interactive health communication in preventive medicine: Internet-based strategies in teaching and research. *American Journal of Preventive Medicine, 19*(2), 113-120.

Fox, S., & Rainie, L. (2000). *The online health care revolution: How the Web helps Americans take better care of themselves.* Washington, DC, Pew Internet & American Life Project.

Gallo, M. A., & Horton, P. B. (1994). Assessing the effect on high school teachers of direct and unrestricted access to the Internet: A case study of an East Central Florida high school. *Educational Technology Research and Development, 42*(4), 17-39.

Green, M. C., & Brock, T. C. (2000). The role of transportation in the persuasiveness of public narratives. *Journal of Personality and Social Psychology, 79*(5), 701-721.

Gustafson, G. H., Robinson. T. N., Ansley, D., Adler. L., & Brennan, P. F. (1998). Consumers and evaluation of interactive health communication applications. *American Journal of Preventive Medicine, 16*(1), 23–29.

Ha, L., & James, E. L. (1998). Interactivity reexamined: A baseline analysis of early business Web sites. *Journal of Broadcasting & Electronic Media, 42*(2), 457–474.

Hall, J. R., Ax, B., Brown, M., Buller, D. B., Woodall, W. G., & Borland, R. (2002). Challenges to producing and implementing the Considerthis.org Web-based smoking prevention and cessation program. *Electronic Journal of Communication*.

Hindman, D. B. (2000). The rural-urban digital divide. *Journalism and Mass Communication Quarterly, 77*(3), 549–560.

Hoffman, D. L., & Novak, T. P. (1998). Bridging the racial divide on the Internet, *Science, 280,* 390–391.

Hubell, F. A., Mishra, S. I., Chavez, L. R., & Valdez. R. B. (1995). Cultural beliefs about breast and cervical cancer among Latinas and Anglo women. *Journal of General Internal Medicine, 10* (Supplement), 121–128.

Institute of Medicine Committee on Communication for Behavior Change in the 21st Century (2002). *Speaking of health: Assessing health communication strategies for diverse populations.* Washington, DC: National Academy Press.

Jackson, R. H., Davis, T. C., Bairnsfather, L. E., George. R. B., Crouch, M. A., & Gault, H. (1991). Patient reading ability: An overlooked problem in health care. *Southern Medical Journal, 84*(10), 1172–1175.

Jibaja, M. J., Kingery, P., Noff, N. E., Smith, Q., Bowman, J., & Holcomb, J. R. (2000). Tailored, interactive soap operas for breast cancer education of high-risk Hispanic women. *Journal of Cancer Education, 15*(4), 237–243.

Kalichman, S. C., Benotsch, E., Suarez, T., Catz, S., & Miller, J. (2000). Health literacy and health-related knowledge among persons living with HIV/AIDS. *American Journal of Preventive Medicine, 18*(4), 325–331.

Keoun, B. (1996). Cancer patients find quackery on the Web. *Journal of the National Cancer Institute, 88,* 1263–1265.

Kincaid, D. L., Yun, S. H., Piotrow, P. T., & Yasser, Y. (1993). Turkey's mass media family planning campaign. In T. E. Backer & E. M. Rogers (Eds.), *Organizational aspects of health communication campaigns: What works?*(pp. 68–92). Thousand Oaks, CA: Sage.

Kirby, S. D., Ureda, J. R., Rose, R. L., & Hussey, J. (1998). Peripheral cues and involvement level: Influences on acceptance of a mammography message. *Journal of Health Communication, 3,* 119–135.

Lentz, B., Straubhaar, J., LaPastina, A., Main, S., & Taylor. J. (2000, May). *Structuring access: The role of public access centers in the 'Digital Divide'.* Paper presented at the International Communication Association, Acapulco.

McConnaughey, J., Everette, J. D., Reynolds, T., & Lader, W. (Eds.) (1999). *Falling through the Net: Defining the digital divide.* Washington, DC: U.S. Department of Commerce, National Telecommunications and Information Administration, Report.

Meade, C. D., McKinney, W. P., & Barnas, G. F. (1994). Educating patients with limited literacy skills: The effectiveness of printed and videotaped materials about colon cancer. *American Journal of Public Health, 84,* 119–120.

Meric, F., Bernstam, E. V., Mirza, N. Q., Hunt, K. K., Ames, F. C., Ross, M. I., Kuerer, H. M., Pollack, R. E., Musen, M. A., & Singletary, S. E. (2002). Breast cancer on the World Wide Web: Cross-sectional survey of quality of information and popularity of Web sites. *British Medical Journal, 324,* 577–581.

Miller, J. D. (2001). Who is using the Web for science and health information? *Science Communication, 22*(3), 256–273.

Nariman, H. (1996). *Soap operas for social change.* Westport, CT: Praeger.

O'Connor, J. B., & Johnson, J. F. (2000). Use of the Web for medical information by a gastroenterology clinic population. *JAMA, 284*(15), 1962-1964.

Paskett, E. D., Tatum, C., Wilson, A., Dignan, M., & Velez, R. (1996). Use of a photoessay to teach low-income African American women about mammography. *Journal of Cancer Education, 11*, 216-220.

Patrick, K., Robinson, T. N., Alemi, F., & Eng, T. R. (1999). Policy issues relevant to evaluation of interactive health communication applications. *American Journal of Preventive Medicine, 16*(1), 35-42.

Pew Internet & American Life Survey (2002). Getting serious online. Washington, DC: Pew Research Center, Report 55.

Piotrow, P. T., Kincaid, D. L., Rimon, J., & Rinehart, W. (1997). *Health communication: Lessons from family planning and reproductive health*. Westport, CT: Praeger.

Piotrow, P. T., Rimon, J., Winnard, K., Kincaid, D. L., Huntington, D. L., & Convisser, J. (1990). Mass media family planning promotion in three Nigerian cities. *Studies in Family Planning, 21*(5), 265-273.

Rafaeli, S. (1988). Interactivity: From new media to communication. *Sage Annual Review of Communication Research, 16*, 110-134.

Ramirez, A. G., McAlister, A., Gallion, K. J., Ramirez, V., Garza, I. R., Stamm, K., de la Torre, J., & Chalela, P. (1995). Community level cancer control in a Texas barrio: Part I: Theoretical basis, implementation, and process evaluation. *Journal of the National Cancer Institute Monographs, 18*, 117-122.

Rice, R. E., & Katz, J. (Eds.) (2001). *The Internet and health communication*. Thousand Oaks, CA: Sage.

Richardson, J. L., Langholz, B., Bernstein, L., Burciaga, K. D. & Ross, R. K. (1992). Stage and delay in breast cancer diagnosis by race, socioeconomic status, age, and year. *British Journal of Cancer, 65*, 922-926.

Richardson, J. L., Marks, G., Solis, J. M., Collins, L. M., Birba, L, & Hisserich, J. C. (1987). Frequency and advocacy of breast cancer screening among elderly Hispanic women. *Preventive Medicine, 16*, 761-774.

Rogers, E. M. (1986). *Communication technology: The new media in society*. New York: Free Press.

Rogers, E. M. (2001). The digital divide. *Convergence, 7*(4), 96-111.

Rogers, E. M. (2003). *Diffusion of innovations*, Fifth Edition. New York: Free Press.

Rogers, E. M., Ratzan, S. C., & Payne, J. G. (2001). Health literacy. *American Behavioral Scientist, 44*(12), 2172-2195.

Rogers, E. M., Vaughan, P. W., Swalehe, R. M. A., Rao, N., Svenkerud, P., & Sood, S. (1999). Effects of an entertainment-education radio soap opera on family planning behavior in Tanzania. *Studies in Family Planning, 30*(3), 193-211.

Salazar, M. K. (1996). Hispanic women's beliefs about breast cancer and mammography. *Cancer Nursing, 19*(6), 437-446.

Sharf, B. F., Freimuth, V. S., Greebspon, P., & Plotnick, C. (1996). Confronting cancer on *thirtysomething*: Audience response to health content entertainment television. *Journal of Health Communication, 1*, 157-176.

Silberg, W. M., Lundberg, G. D., & Musacchio, R. A. (1997). Assessing, controlling, and assuring the quality of medical information on the Internet: *Caveat lector et viewor*—Let the reader and buyer beware. *JAMA, 277*, 1244-1245.

Singhal, A., & Rogers, E. M. (1989). *India's information revolution*. Thousand Oaks, CA: Sage.

Singhal, A. & Rogers, E. M. (1999). *Entertainment-education: A communication strategy for social change*. Mahwah, NJ: Lawrence Erlbaum Associates.

Singhal, A., & Rogers, E. M. (2002). A theoretical agenda for entertainment-education. *Communication Theory, 12*(2), 117-135.

Singhal, A., & Rogers, E. M. (2003). *Combating AIDS: Communication strategies in action.* Thousand Oaks, CA: Sage.

Slater, M. (1997). Persuasion processes across receiver goals and message genres. *Communication Theory, 7,* 125–148.

Slater, M., & Rouner, D. (1996). Value affirmation and value protective processing of alcohol education messages that include statistics and anecdotes. *Communication Research, 23,* 210–235.

Slater, M., & Rouner, D. (2002). Entertainment-education and elaboration likelihood: Understanding the processing of narratives persuasion. *Communication Theory, 12*(2), 173–187.

Slater, M. (in press). Entertainment-education and the persuasive impact of narratives. In Brock, T., Strange, J. J., & Green, M. C. (Eds), *Narrative impact: Social and cognitive foundations.* Mahwah, NJ: Lawrence Erlbaum Associates.

Slater, M. D., Zimmerman, D. E., Tipton, M. L., Halverson, H., Kean, T., & Rost, J. D. (1994). Delivering health information to the disadvantaged: Assessing a hypertext approach. *Hypermedia, 6*(2), 67–86.

Sood, S. & Rogers, E. M. (2000). Dimensions of parasocial interaction by letter-writers to a popular entertainment-education soap opera in India. *Journal of Broadcasting & Electronic Media, 44*(3), 386–414.

Spooner, T., Rainie, L., Fox, S., Harrigan, J., & Lenhart, A. (2000). *African-Americans and the Internet: Narrowing the gap.* Washington, DC: Pew Internet and American Life Project, Report 25.

Sweeney, M. A., & Gulino, C. (1988). Interactive video in health care: Blending patient care, computer technology, and research results. *Journal of Biocommunication, 15,* 6–11.

Tabar, L., & Dean, P. (1987). The control of breast cancer through mammography screening: What is the evidence? In E. Sickles (Ed.), *Radiological clinicians of North America* (pp. 993–1005). Philadelphia: Saunders.

Valente, T. W., Kim, Y. M., Lettermaier, S., Glass, W., & Dibba, Y. (1994). Radio promotion of family planning in The Gambia. *International Family Planning Perspectives, 20,* 96–100.

Walther, J. B. (1996). Computer-mediated communication: Impersonal, interpersonal, and hypersonal interaction. *Communication Research, 23,* 3–43.

Weinberg, N., Schmale, J., Uken, J., & Wessel, K. (1996). Online help: Cancer patients participate in a computer-mediated support group. *Health Social Work, 21*(1), 24–29.

Weisbord, S. D., Soule, J. B., & Kimmel, P. L. (1997). Poison online: Acute renal failure caused by oil of wormwood purchased through the Internet. *New England Journal of Medicine, 337,* 825–827.

Williams, D. M., Counselman, F. L., & Caggiano, C. D. (1996). Emergency department discharge instructions and patient literacy: A problem of disparity. *American Journal of Emergency Medicine, 14,* 19–22.

Winkler, M. A., Flanagin, A., Chi-Lum, B., White, J., Andrews, K., Kennett, R. L., DeAngelis, C. D., & Musacchio, R. A. (2000). Guidelines for medical and health information sites on the Internet: Principles governing AMA Web sites. *JAMA, 283,* 1600–1606.

Yabroff, K. R., O'Malley, A., Mangan, P., & Mandelblatt, J. (2001). Inreach and outreach interventions to improve mammography use. *Journal of the American Medical Women's Association, 56,* 166–173.

Zarcadoolas, C., Blanco, M., Pleasant, A., & Boyer, J. F. (2000). *Unweaving the Web: An exploratory study of low-literate adults' navigation skills on the World Wide Web.* Unpublished paper, Providence, RI: Brown University, Center for Environmental Studies.

Zimmerman, D. E., Akerelrea, C. A., Buller, D. B., & LeBlanc, M. (in press). Integrating usability testing into the development of a 5 a Day nutrition Web site for at-risk populations in the American Southwest. *Journal of Health Psychology.*

III

Entertainment-Education Interventions and Their Outcomes

III

16

Entertainment-Education in the Middle East: Lessons From the Egyptian Oral Rehydration Therapy Campaign[1]

Rasha A. Abdulla
University of Miami

In 1983, Egypt launched an oral rehydration therapy (ORT) campaign in answer to an urgent need to cut down on the rate of infant mortality caused by diarrheal-related diseases. Two years after it started, the *British Medical Journal*, 1985, p. 1249) described the Egyptian campaign as "what may be the world's most successful health education program."

At that time, diarrheal-related diseases were responsible for more than 30% of infant mortalities worldwide (World Health Organization, 2002). In Egypt, the infant mortality rate for children under two was about 140 per thousand (El Mougi & El Tohamy, 1983; United Nations Children's Fund, 1987). Diarrheal-related illnesses, especially dehydration, accounted for more than half of the child mortality cases in Egypt (Kreuger, 1983; Gabr, 1983). The objective of the campaign was to decrease this rate by 25% in its first five years (Stone, 1983; Bartholet, 1986).

The Egyptian campaign proved to be very successful. Only two years after it started, awareness levels of ORT reached 90%, and usage rates reached 70%. As a result, infant mortality rates dropped in half. When the ORT campaign

---

[1]Correspondence regarding this chapter should be addressed to Rasha A. Abdulla at rabdulla7@netscape.net.

ended in 1991, awareness levels were close to 100% with a 96% usage rate. Infant mortality rates declined by 70% (Charnock, 1985; El Kamel, 1985; White, 1991).

This chapter analyzes the Egyptian ORT campaign, focusing on its entertainment-education (E-E) components, and the factors that led to its success in the Egyptian cultural context. We review development communication and E-E in Egypt, and then proceed to examine the details of the ORT campaign in terms of its theory-based E-E components as well as its successful implementation. We conclude with some practical E-E lessons for development communication campaigns.

AN OVERVIEW
OF ENTERTAINMENT-EDUCATION IN EGYPT

Egypt has a reputation in the Arab world as a leader in the development and production of media content. Cairo, the nation's capital, is known as the "Hollywood of the Middle East." As the leading and the most sophisticated television program and cinema producer in the region, Egyptian programs and movies are exported to most Arab countries and are a main component of all Arab media channels. The Egyptian dialect of spoken, colloquial Arabic is the most widely understood in the Arab world, a direct result of Arabs growing up with Egyptian programs, music, and drama (Boyd, 1999; Center for Development Communication, 1989; Harris, 1993). According to Boyd (1999):

> When Egypt started a television service, the country was able to undertake a massive artistic effort. Its well-developed film industry and tradition of live theater provided what almost all other counties in the Arab world lacked: performers as well as personnel to operate the complicated equipment and to produce programs. Ironically, even after the March 1979 Egyptian-Israeli peace treaty that resulted in agreements by Arab ministries of information to boycott Egyptian media, Egyptian films, videotapes, and artists still dominated Arab television. (p. 16)

The concept of development communication and education through entertainment has existed in Egypt since the media were introduced, which may be one advantage of having a government-owned and operated media system. At the time when television was new, the government policy was to make it available to as many people as possible. Television set prices were subsidized, and the government made thousands available free of charge for installation in different cultural centers and cooperative units in rural and urban areas (Boyd, 1999). Development and education became part of the culture of television viewing in Egypt.

Television viewing is a reality in all Arab countries—rich and poor alike—for even the poorer countries, such as Egypt, the Sudan, and Yemen, realize that this visual medium is an important political and development tool.... Parents moreover believe that television is a way in which their children's education, and possibly their view of the world, can be broadened.... Among the lower classes, television set ownership is more than a status symbol: It is a means of family entertainment within what is believed to be a better education for children, if only by giving them a view of the world (Boyd, 1999, p. 6, 8, 52).

E-E Television in Egypt

When television was introduced in Egypt in 1960, it was encouraged by the government (as radio and cinema had been previously) to produce prosocial "drama and programs with a message" that would benefit Egyptian and Arab audiences. Such programming ranged from educational programs to subtle E-E drama and soap operas. Early on, "educational programs aimed at promoting economic and social development targeted different segments of the population, such as housewives, peasants, factory workers, and policemen, with information on health care, literacy, and ways to enhance agricultural or industrial production" (Diase, 1993). *The Secret of Production* was probably the first educational program targeting factory workers. It was followed by a series of literacy programs that still run today, as Egypt continues to try to reduce adult illiteracy rates, estimated in 2000 at 45% (UNDP, 2002). Educational programs for different school years are also a constant on Egyptian television (and now an even bigger dose of such programs run on a special Educational Channel, one of eight Nile Television Thematic Channels), and so are different health programs.

Egyptian audiences, especially those of the middle and lower socioeconomic classes, expect to find something educational or some sort of "advice" in most Egyptian serials and soap operas, which have a very wide viewership (Diase, 1993). In this historically oral society, lower classes with little, if any, formal education "appreciate television as an important source of both entertainment *and* education" (Diase, 1993). Egyptian serials often try to satisfy these audiences. Most of the social drama presented on Egyptian (and eventually Arab) television attempts to enrich its audiences through social learning. The learning ranges from the more common handling of social situations and family affairs to the more E-E oriented serials, series, or television spots that are specifically designed to promote particular prosocial issues.

One example of such E-E oriented drama is a series named *Secret of the Land*. Targeting peasants and farmers with information about agriculture and irrigation, *Secret of the Land* started airing twice a week in 1989 (Diase, 1993). Funded by the United States Agency for International Development (USAID), the L.E. 2.15 million budget (about U.S. $900,000 in 1989, or about $390,000 in 2003) was intended to fund 28 episodes. However, the Egyptian

Radio and Television Union (ERTU) offered to broadcast the show for free, and the stars of the show all volunteered their pay. The budget was therefore used to produce 65 episodes (El Kassaby, 1993). These episodes are still rerun today on Egyptian and Arab television stations. The show followed a sitcom format, featuring a funny, but not-too-well-educated peasant, whose not-too-smart agricultural decisions and day-to-day actions in the field are humorously critiqued and reformed by more experienced peasants, including the *Omda* (mayor of the village) and an agricultural engineer. By frequently showing the older and wiser farmers consulting with government-appointed agricultural experts who are available to them free of charge, the television series also indirectly served to increase the experts' credibility among the farmers. The show was so successful and had such a wide viewership that well-renowned stars sought to participate in it, although it is the only show in the history of Egyptian and Arab television that does not feature its stars' names. Based on the selfless request of the participating stars, the opening and closing captions read, "Starring: Stars who love Egypt."

After the success of *Secret of the Land*, another purely E-E series was produced named *The Family House*. Funded by the Ford Foundation, the International Development Research Centre (IDRC), and Johns Hopkins University's Center for Communication Programs (JHU/CCP), *The Family House* was produced in 1992 by the Egyptian Center for Development Communication (CDC) to promote health messages about drug addiction, HIV/AIDS prevention, child spacing, home accidents, and general hygiene and sanitation. Following the format of regular Egyptian series, *The Family House* was composed of 15 episodes of 45 minutes each, aired during the evening prime-time hours, when an estimated 90% of Egypt's population (52 million at that time) were watching. The successful series, which starred some of Egypt's most renowned talent, was sold to other Arab countries and shown on their television screens as well (CDC, 1989; Diase, 1993; Harris, 1993).

According to Farag El Kamel, Executive Director of the CDC, the secret behind the success of this and other Egyptian E-E series is the emphasis given to audience research and pretesting. As "people here [in Egypt] actually expect to learn something from the show," the CDC researchers interviewed groups of 200 people in Egypt, Morocco, and Jordan before the production of *The Family House* to determine what they wanted in the television show. Through these interviews, issues such as child spacing and general household hygiene were brought to the attention of the television producers, and were consequently integrated into the show (Harris, 1993).

E-E Television Spots

Series or serials are not the only form of E-E drama that has been produced in Egypt. Several campaigns of one- to three-minute television spots were launched on family planning, garbage disposal, *bilharzias* (snail fever), healthy eating habits, hygiene, and sanitation. These spots all featured (1) well-known Egyptian actors and actresses, (2) humorous or down-to-earth, non-preaching language, and (3) catchy jingles and/or slogans.

An example of one popular E-E spot campaign in Egypt is a family planning campaign known as the *Ana Zannana* (I am Grouchy) campaign, after the name of its lead character, Zannana. This campaign included 15 television spots, each with a clear, separate message about family planning and child spacing. The lead character, Zannana, was played by one of Egypt's leading female comedians. Different spots were aired an average of five times a day, starting in 1988. Each spot aired more than 100 times over the campaign's first year. A typical spot in the *Ana Zannana* campaign featured Zannana, who is always humorously grouchy, relentlessly pushing her daughter to have another baby, or giving her bad advice about family planning. Through humorous, witty dialogue, the daughter and/or her husband would explain to Zannana why her advice was not such a good idea, often referring to medical sources and/or government family planning centers.

The campaign was very successful. An evaluation survey by Wafai & Associates included personal interviews with 1,797 Egyptian men and women. All respondents indicated that they had seen at least one *Ana Zannana* spot. Almost all (99%) said that they understood the messages, and 70% recalled at least one message (cited in *Lights! Camera! Action!*, 1989).

THE EGYPTIAN ORT CAMPAIGN

The Egyptian ORT campaign had the same format as the *Ana Zannana* television spot campaign. The ORT campaign was initiated by the government of Egypt in 1983, as part of the National Control of Diarrheal Diseases Project (NCDDP). It continued for eight years, until 1991.

All around the world in the early 1980s, some 5 million children under five were dying each year from diarrheal-related diseases, especially dehydration (WHO, 2002). In Egypt, in 1983, the number of children under two years of age who were dying from diarrhea was estimated at 130,000 per year, an infant mortality rate of 140 per thousand (El Mougi & El Tohamy, 1983; UNICEF, 1987). Diarrheal-related illnesses, especially dehydration, were the most common diseases affecting Egyptian infants, accounting for more than half of all child mortality cases in the country (Kreuger, 1983; Gabr, 1983). The objective of the NCDDP was to decrease the infant mortality rate resulting from diarrheal-related diseases, especially dehydration, by 25% during its first five years (Stone, 1983; Bartholet, 1986).

The NCDDP campaign was mounted by the Egyptian Ministry of Health and Population (MOHP). An estimated budget of $50 million was designated for the project, of which USAID contributed $26 million. UNICEF and the WHO supplied technical and material assistance.

The NCDDP was comprised of five major units. The Marketing and Mass Education Unit had the task of designing the right communication messages and delivering them through appropriate communication channels to the selected target populations. The Research and Evaluation Unit supplied much-needed quantitative and qualitative research, and developed a total evaluation framework for the project. The Training Unit managed the practical training of doctors, nurses, and pharmacists in rehydration centers. The Production and Distribution Unit monitored the production of the oral rehydration salts (ORS) and other medical solutions. The fifth unit was comprised of 26 governorate coordinators, who acted as liaisons for Egypt's 26 governorates (El Sayyad, 1983). We focus in the present chapter primarily on the Marketing and Mass Education, and the Research and Evaluation units in an attempt to analyze and evaluate NCDDP's communication strategy.

What Is ORT?

Dehydration occurs when continued diarrhea causes rapid depletion of water and sodium in the human body. Dehydration can be treated by administering ORS, a sodium and glucose solution. This therapy was developed by medi-cal research institutions in Bangladesh and India in the mid-1970s. Glucose accelerates the absorption of the sodium solute in the small intestines, thus causing the body to rehydrate. ORS is simply a mixture of salt, sugar, and water, ingredients that are readily available in every household. Since the WHO adopted ORS in 1978 as its primary tool to fight diarrhea, the world-wide mortality rate for children suffering from acute diarrhea has fallen from 5 million to 1.3 million deaths per year.[2] ORT gives the dehydrated child ORS plus food (WHO, 2002).

The ORT Campaign E-E Strategy

The high infant mortality rate in Egypt prior to the initiation of the NCDDP was not due to a lack of scientific knowledge or to the unavailability of medical care. Actually, ORS was available to the public free of charge through UNICEF long before the present project was launched. However, it was never used on a wide scale. As Jerry Russell, UNICEF program advisor, put it, "Children

---

[2]On May 8, 2002, WHO released a new, improved formula for ORS that it asserts will save more millions of lives and reduce the severity of illness of children under five, who are suffering from acute diarrhea. WHO said the new formula for ORS will reduce the severity of diarrhea and vomiting, the need for hospitalization, the use of costly intravenous fluid treatment, and the overall length of illness (WHO, 2002).

were dying and the sachets were not being used—they were piling up in warehouses" (Charnock, 1985). The problem was a lack of awareness and delivery of the scientific knowledge available, as well as faulty and outdated practices by parents and medical personnel. The scientific revolution that came about with the use of ORT as a cure for dehydration had not yet reached many medical practitioners in Egypt, who still followed the old methods of treating dehydration and diarrhea with antibiotics and starvation for the dehydrated child (El Mougi & El Tohamy, 1983).

ORT Target Audience

The communication strategy of the Egyptian ORT campaign was therefore established with two target audiences in mind: (1) all mothers of children under five, and (2) other specific target groups who deal directly or indirectly with parents of a dehydrated child, including health care personnel, pharmacists, mass media reporters, and decision-makers. The objective of the campaign was to teach, persuade, and change the behavior of these two target audiences regarding the management of diarrhea and dehydration (El Kamel, 1983).

Information needed to reach these two target audiences was classified into three types of knowledge: (1) awareness-knowledge, (2) how-to knowledge, and (3) principles knowledge. Awareness-knowledge included such information as the fact that diarrhea could lead to more serious diseases like dehydration (or, in Arabic, *gafaf*), which could lead to the death of the child; that there are different kinds of *gafaf*; that *gafaf* is easier to treat in its early stages; that most cases of *gafaf* could be treated by the mother at home and only critical cases need hospitalization; and that the symptoms of *gafaf* are vomiting, sunken eyes, dry skin, loss of appetite, and general weakness (Abdulla, 1993).

How-to knowledge included information on avoiding the complications of diarrhea, by giving the child plenty of fluids, food and/or breast milk; and for parents of children who have *gafaf*, information on the need to administer ORS (*mahloul mo'alget el gafaf*, or simply *el mahloul*), how to get ORS, the right way of mixing the solution, and the correct dosage to give the child (Abdulla, 1993).

Principles knowledge included basic health information on what diarrhea is, its causes, and the fact that the mother's first priority should be to prevent dehydration rather than to stop diarrhea (Abdulla, 1993).

Preliminary Research

The ORT campaign laid heavy emphasis on scientific research. Before the mass media campaign started, formative research determined the most suitable sachet size and package design for ORS. The UNICEF sachets that were available at the time contained 20 grams of ORS each. The sachet contents were to be dissolved in a one-liter container, to be consumed by the child over a period of eight hours. The Research and Evaluation Unit of the NCDDP conducted research on containers in the Egyptian home, especially in rural areas. They found that very few homes had a clean one-liter bottle available. The most common container in the Egyptian home was an empty soft drink bottle, a 200-milliliter container. Research was conducted on the bacterial count in the ORS solution over time. The UNICEF sachets, after a few hours, had a bacterial count of undesirable levels. It was therefore concluded that the most convenient size for the ORS sachet is 5 grams, to be dissolved in 200 milliliters of water, and consumed by the child in one and a half hours. The containers would be readily available (or at least easily obtained) in every Egyptian home, and the bacterial count of the solution would not increase much since the solution is consumed in much less time than was the case with the UNICEF 20-gram sachets (S. Nasser, personal communication, August 3, 2002).[3]

Research was also conducted that involved typical Egyptian mothers in the choice of the product name, and the Arabic word for dehydration (*gafaf*), which was non-existent before NCDDP. Mothers were also involved in choosing the logo of the project, which shows a mother holding her baby and spoon-feeding ORS to the baby (Fig. 16.1). The logo implies the mother's love and care for the child. The logo was featured on all ORT products and publications, as well as in all campaign advertisements and at all health centers and ORT clinics. Research later showed that the ORT logo had at one point become "the most recognized advertising symbol in Egypt" (Business Alliance for International Economic Development [BAIEC], 2002, p. III 14).

The product itself, ORS, was readily available to the public in a very affordable way. The price of ORS was only 90 pts per pack (about 40 cents U.S. in 1983, or 16 cents in 2003). A pack contains 10 sachets, three of which are usually sufficient for treating a dehydrated child. A child's life could be saved for only 27 pts (about 12 cents in 1983, or less than 5 cents in 2003), which is affordable even for low socioeconomic classes. Furthermore, ORS is available free of charge at any of the 3,000 government ORT centers throughout Egypt.

Singhal and Rogers (2002) discussed three types of resistance that face an E-E campaign: (1) message production, (2) message environment, and (3) message reception. The ORT campaign in Egypt faced none of these. The campaign had the support of the national government, medical personnel, and the public, which was a very important factor in its success. For example, the government waived the ban on advertising of drugs on Egyptian television in the case of ORT. There were no competing or contradicting messages to the medical and health information provided in the television spots. Furthermore,

---

[3] Dr. Shafika Nasser was the head of the Research and Evaluation Unit of the NCDDP. She is also a professor of Public Health and Nutrition at Cairo University's Faculty of Medicine.

FIG. 16.1. The logo of the Egyptian ORT campaign was chosen based on input from the target audience. (*Source*: Egyptian Ministry of Health and Population.)

the campaign did not contradict, in any way, with any religious or social norms that could have impeded its reception. On the contrary, there was a thirst for this kind of information among the audience, especially mothers, as they realized its importance to the health and well-being, indeed to the survival, of their children. Thus the campaign capitalized on the affective and emotional aspects of the issue, which, according to Singhal and Rogers (2002), can be very effective in motivating the practice of prosocial health habits and behaviors.

ORT Communication Channels

The various channels of communication used were based on audience research dealing with the characteristics of the target audiences. Before the mass media campaign started, the project ensured that appropriate medical personnel were properly trained, that specialized medical centers were established and provided with medical supplies and educational materials, and that the ORS itself was readily available (S. Nasser, personal communication, August 3, 2002). For doctors, nurses, pharmacists, and other educated segments of the audience, training programs were established along with the production of booklets, pamphlets, and educational audio and video tapes. Several national and regional conferences on ORT were organized. One accomplishment of the campaign was to eliminate differences in treatment among medical professionals. This consensus facilitated communication later on to the public as the message was direct, concise, and, most importantly, consistent. Research showed that the main target audience for the ORT campaign was 80% illiterate and living in rural areas. Therefore, reliance on print media was excluded. Television and radio, along with interpersonal communication, were the main channels used in this health campaign (El Kamel, 1983).

Audience research about the main target audience's media habits indicated strong preference for watching television drama (series and movies), and low exposure to talk shows and health programs. Radio listening habits followed a similar pattern. Moreover, television drama was highly favored across socioeconomic classes. ORT communication messages should therefore be (1) in the form of drama, and (2) aired before, during, or immediately after television series or movies. The message content and design were simple and nontechnical, using colloquial, Egyptian Arabic, and using terms and descriptions of diarrhea used by the average and the below-average mother (El Kamel & Hirschhorn, 1984). The spots portrayed mothers as "caring, loving, and smart, and certainly not as negligible or ignorant. In communicating with doctors and other 'elite' target groups, the theme [of the messages] was the scientific or medical 'revolution' resulting from ORT" (El Kamel, 1983). Research showed that 90% of Egyptians have access to television (El Kamel, 1983).

Pilot Testing

Pilot studies took place in Alexandria, Egypt, for three months (August–October, 1983) and on a national level for two months (January–February, 1984) to test the efficiency of sample 30-second and one-minute television spots that were produced for the campaign by the Egyptian CDC. The spots first featured Foad El Mohandis, a veteran actor (who starred in many children's programs), comedian, and social commentator. El Mohandis was also invited to medical centers to meet with mothers in person to find out more about their concerns, and to deliver an informal medical lecture, prepared by NCDDP medical personnel (S. Nasser, personal communication, August 3, 2002). El Mohandis proved to be a popular figure with mothers. Evaluation research at the end of 1984 showed that awareness of ORT increased from 2% to 60%, with 40% of the sample having already used ORT, compared to only 1% before the campaign started less than a year earlier (Fig. 16.2). Television proved to be a successful medium, with over 58% of the sample citing it as their source of information about ORT (El Kamel & Hirschhorn, 1984).

Research, however, also showed ample room for improvement. Some dissatisfaction with Foad El Mohandis surfaced, as a non-medical male, and also

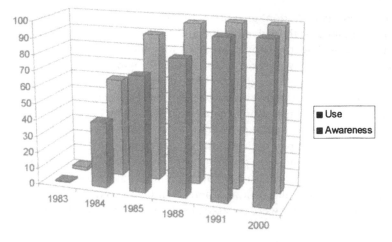

FIG. 16.2.   Percentage of ORT awareness and use in Egypt 1983–2000. (*Source*: Compiled from Charnock (1985); El Kamel (1985); El Kamel & El Tohamy (1988); El Kamel & Hirschhorn (1984); UNDP (2002); UNICEF (2002); White (1991).)

a comedian. Mothers, while thrilled to meet a celebrity, were more interested in the celebrity factor than in the medical information. They were excited to meet El Mohandis, but they did not learn enough from him. He was therefore replaced with Karima Mokhtar, a well-respected Egyptian actress. Mokhtar is another popular star of numerous Egyptian soap operas and dramas. Moreover, she is known for appearing as the wise, loving, and tender mother, and therefore seemed to be a perfect fit for the ORT campaign. Research later showed that she was extremely credible with mothers and successful in delivering the ORT messages.

ORT Communication Messages

The ORT campaign used 15 one-minute spots to convey its messages. Each spot mainly featured a baby suffering from diarrhea or dehydration, with Mokhtar either taking care of the baby, or advising the baby's mother on how to take care of the baby. The three types of ORT knowledge (discussed above) were delivered through the television spots. The language used was easy and non-technical, and the tone was non-preachy, loving, and motherly. Each spot would show how to prepare and administer ORS, explaining and showing, for example, that the 200 milliliters of water needed to mix with one ORS sachet is the standard size of a small soft drink bottle. Each spot ended with the same catchy, educational jingle that helped mothers remember what to do. A literal translation of the lyrics of the jingle would be:

To prevent dehydration, give the baby ORS
In 200 milliliters, then give the baby food
And, God willing, the baby will have a long life
Why would we have any fears? As I was just saying
To prevent dehydration, give the baby ORS.

The jingle was repeated in a loop over and over at the end of each television spot, and the catchy tune soon became popular among Egyptians. The phrase "Give the baby ORS," in Arabic, *"Edilo mahloul,"* soon became part of the everyday culture in Egypt, coming to mean something like, "Don't worry, there is a solution" or "Things are going to be all right." It was not uncommon to hear youth in different parts of Egypt, across various socioeconomic classes, jokingly or seriously telling one another, "Don't worry. *Edilo mahloul"* to symbolically mean that they were capable of solving whatever problem they faced.

Institutional and Interpersonal Communication

The ORT campaign used a combination of communication channels. For the main target audience, it used mass media, primarily television. Institutional and interpersonal communication came into play through a multitude of training programs and conventions for health professionals and medical personnel. Interpersonal communication took place particularly in rural areas and villages through a project called "depot-holders." Depot-holders were leading members of the rural community, who were carefully identified and recruited to keep a supply of ORS at their homes. They were ready, willing, and able to provide ORS to any villager who needed it, and to offer help and guidance on fighting dehydration.

The idea was first tried in the rural area of Sohag Governorate in Upper Egypt in summer 1984. Research showed that depot-holders increased awareness by 18% (Loza, 1985). In 1985, the depot-holders system was implemented in five other rural governorates in Upper and Lower Egypt, covering a total population of 794,000 rural inhabitants in 213 villages. During their first four months of service, depot-holders saved the lives of an estimated 28,000 diarrheal-sick children. They also trained and coordinated efforts among 71 physicians and 170 nurses in rural areas. Infant and child mortality rates in rural areas decreased substantially, compared to one year earlier. There was a 37% reduction in mortality rates for infants under one year, and a 54% reduction for one to four-year olds. Moreover, depot-holders helped promote further trust in the formal medical establishment regarding ORT (Abdel Aziz & Loza, 1986).

Singhal and Rogers (1999) argued that an E-E effort is more successful when it is complemented by other messages "to form an integrated communication campaign" (p. 209). The ORT televised messages were supported by the efforts of medical personnel and depot-holders throughout Egypt. Furthermore, educational posters and pamphlets were printed to supplement the campaign. Given the high illiteracy rates among the main intended audience, all printed matter featured detailed illustrations of the steps required to prepare ORS. The ORT logo was featured on all publications, and posters at medical centers and clinics also indicated the presence of a qualified ORT health care personnel or depot-holder.

Evaluation Research

Evaluation research was conducted throughout the campaign, including large-scale national surveys of mothers and physicians, as well as records of ORS sales and the distribution of free ORS packets. By the end of 1985, ORS packet consumption increased from 6 million to 24 million units. Awareness levels increased to 90% throughout Egypt, with over 70% using ORT (Charnock, 1985). Infant mortality rates were cut to almost half (El Kamel, 1985). By 1988, awareness levels reached 98% and usage, 82%. ORS consumption increased to 35 million units. Eighty percent of those interviewed reported television spots as their primary source of information (El Kamel & El Tohamy, 1988). Infant mortality rates decreased to only 50 per thousand (Miller, 1989). By the end of the project in 1991, almost all mothers (more than 99%) knew about ORT, with a usage rate of 96%. Infant mortality rates were estimated at 45 per thousand, a reduction of almost 70% of what it was before the ORT campaign. The campaign is estimated to have saved the lives of more than 100,000 children in its first two years, and many more hundreds of thousands since then (*BMJ*, 1985; White, 1991).

In 1991, the NCDDP and its media campaign, as a national health care project of a specific time period, came to an end. However, the medical care and the educational efforts aimed at saving Egyptian children's lives continued as the Egyptian Diarrheal Diseases Control Program. This ongoing program is part of the Maternity and Childhood Care Sector of the Egyptian Ministry of Health and Population. The monitoring and evaluation research established by the NCDDP on diarrheal-related diseases and ORT use is still carried out today as part of the Egyptian Demographic and Health Survey (EDHS), a major, large-scale census survey, whose results are published every four years (S. Nasser, personal communication, August 3, 2002). The latest available figures indicate that infant mortality rates are still dropping. Infant mortality rates in 2000 were 37 per thousand, and 43 per thousand for children under five (United Nations Development Programme, 2002) (Fig. 16.3). The rate for infant mortality as a result of diarrheal-related diseases was 4.7 per thousand, a 94% reduction from 1983, when the NCDDP started. For children under five, the rate is 0.27 per thousand, a reduction of 93% since 1983 (Ministry of Health and Population, 2002) (Fig. 16.4). ORT usage rate remains at over 96% (UNICEF, 2002).

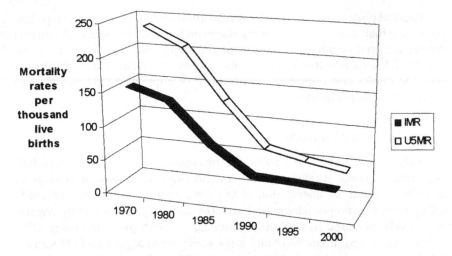

FIG. 16.3.   Infant and under five mortality rates in Egypt, 1970–2000. (*Source*:
Compiled from BAIED (2002); UNDP (2002); United Nations Economic Com-
mission for Africa [ECA] (2002); UNICEF (1987, 2002); USAID (2000); World
Health Organization Statistical Information System [WHOSIS] (2002).)

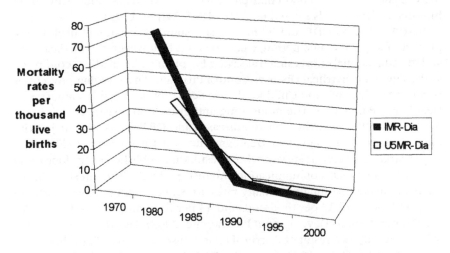

FIG. 16.4.   Infant and under five mortality rates as a result of diarrheal-related
diseases in Egypt, 1970–2000. (*Source*: Compiled from BAIED (2002); UNDP
(2002); ECA (2002); UNICEF (1987, 2002); USAID (2000); WHOSIS (2002).)

THE ORT CAMPAIGN
AND COMMUNICATION THEORY

Just as the success of the ORT campaign rested on formative research, the success of the project also was based on communication theory. The campaign was based on several theories of development communication: (1) social marketing, (2) diffusion of innovations, and (3) social learning theory.

Social Marketing

Social marketing was defined by Kotler (1975) as:

> The design, implementation, and control of programs seeking to increase the acceptability of a social idea or practice in a target group(s). It utilizes concepts of market segmentation, consumer research, idea configuration, communication, facilitation, incentives, and exchange theory to maximize target group response (cited in Solomon, 1989, p. 87).

Social marketing is concerned with how to sell concepts such as brotherhood in the same way commercial products, such as soap, are sold. Borrowing from the concepts of commercial marketing, social marketing directs its efforts towards the hardest-to-reach and least affluent groups, thus helping to narrow the knowledge gap about a particular topic, so that those with initially higher knowledge levels do not achieve proportionately even higher levels than those with initially lower levels of knowledge (Rogers, 1995; Solomon, 1989).

The effective application of the principles of social marketing in the Egyptian ORT campaign was a factor in its success. Market segmentation was determined in a concise manner. The characteristics and media habits of the two main target audiences were determined through vigorous research, and separate media strategies and channels were used with each target audience. The message was consistent, and took different formats according to the specific segment of the audience that was targeted. The main character featured in the television spots was a credible, motherly figure, and one that made sense in the local culture. Finally, the packaging and the price of the product (ORS) were appropriate for the intended audiences.

Evaluation and monitoring through rigorous research continued through all phases of the ORT campaign, thus providing media experts with valuable feedback for their planning.

Diffusion of Innovations

The ORT campaign was also designed with the principles of the diffusion of innovations in mind. Rogers (1995) defined diffusion as "the process by which an innovation is communicated through certain channels over time among the members of a social system" (p. 5). Diffusion can lead to social change. "When new ideas are invented, diffused, and are adopted or rejected, leading to certain consequences, social change occurs" (Rogers, 1995, p. 6).

Rogers (1995) discussed four major elements in diffusion theory: (1) the innovation, (2) the communication channels, (3) time, and (4) the social system. He argued that the innovation does not have to be really "new" in an absolute sense. Rather, it is the perceived newness of the innovation by the potential adopter that matters. "If the idea seems new to the individual, it is an innovation" (p. 11). This perceived newness applies to ORT, for although it was available prior to the campaign, almost nobody was using it.

The characteristics of the innovation, according to Rogers (1995), begin with its having a relative advantage (or benefit) for the user, as well as compatibility with existing social and religious values, and with the needs of potential adopters. Moreover, an idea will be more easily adopted if it is simple to understand, available for trial, and observable, having visible results. ORT has an obvious user benefit of saving children's lives. It does not contradict social or religious values. It is easy to obtain and use, and its effect is relatively easy to observe. ORT was therefore ideal for adoption in terms of its perceived attributes as an innovation.

Communication channels are the means through which the potential adopters of an innovation get to know about the new idea. Various channels of communication can be used simultaneously to communicate an idea. As Hancock (1980) put it, "Communication is a concept elastic enough to include interpersonal, institutional, and mass communication forms" (p. 11). Rogers (1995) argued that mass media channels are most effective in creating awareness-knowledge, whereas interpersonal communication, face-to-face exchange between two or more individuals, is more effective in persuading individuals, especially early adopters, to adopt an innovation. The variety of communication channels used in the ORT campaign in Egypt helped establish its success. While television was most successful in creating awareness of the therapy and its usage, interpersonal communication through the depot-holders (who represented local influentials in this campaign) helped spread the ORT message and the technical training and know-how in rural areas.

The social system was defined by Rogers (1995) as "a set of interrelated units that are engaged in joint problem-solving to accomplish a common goal. The members or units of a social system may be individuals, informal groups, organizations, and/or subsystems" (p. 23). By eliminating inconsistencies in ORT usage and treatment styles, all parties involved in conveying the campaign message, through interpersonal communication and/or the mass media, spoke with a consistent voice. Such consensus eliminated confusion among audience members, and provided greater credibility to the message and to the health providers who disseminated the ORS packets. With the government backing up the campaign and providing ORS and medical training free of charge, all components of the social system worked in unity to achieve the campaign goals.

Social Learning Theory

The Egyptian ORT campaign was also based on Albert Bandura's social learning theory. This social psychological approach argues that learning takes place through observational modeling, that is, through watching other people act in a particular situation and modeling one's own behavior after what one has observed (see Albert Bandura's chapter in this volume). Social learning is particularly effective through mass media channels, and especially when the observed behavior is reinforced with a reward (Bandura, 1977, 1994). ORT potential users learned about the therapy by watching Karima Mokhtar's television spots, and, for some, by observing depot-holders' attitudes and the way they handled diarrhea and dehydration. The reward, better health for children, was perceived by the audience as precious and worthwhile. The target population simply modeled their behavior regarding ORT after what they observed, and started to act similarly.

The two-step flow of communication was also utilized in the ORT campaign. This model advocates the power of interpersonal relationships in affecting people's behavior change. Communication messages flowing through the mass media have their greatest effects on a particular segment of society. These opinion leaders then serve to spread the message to the less active segments of the social system. Audiences are affected by their ties with other individuals in the way they interpret and, more importantly, act on a mass-mediated communication message (Katz & Lazarsfeld, 1955; Lazarsfeld, Berelson, & Gaudet, 1948). Depot-holders provided these interpersonal links, and helped further spread and give credibility to the message of the ORT campaign.

The ORT campaign managed to avoid the threat posed by the knowledge gap hypothesis, which proposes that an increase in knowledge levels is relatively greater among the higher socioeconomic and more educated segments of a target audience (Tichenor, Donohue, & Olien, 1970). Instead, the campaign served as a gap-leveler, particularly reaching less affluent members of the audience.

LESSONS LEARNED

Several factors contributed to the stunning success of the Egyptian ORT campaign as an E-E effort. The following factors are prerequisites for an effective E-E intervention:

1. The ORT campaign realized the importance of communication theory as a base for its planning and implementation.
2. The Egyptian ORT campaign relied heavily on scientific research every step of the way. Extensive pretesting and pilot studies were carried out in the initial stages of the project. Regular monitoring and evaluation surveys were conducted annually.
3. The ORT campaign kept its target audiences in mind at all times, and had a sound knowledge of their media habits.
4. The use of drama and music facilitated the absorption and recall of the ORT messages.
5. Communication channels were chosen appropriately, and the messages were designed to suit the intended audiences, especially the less affluent and the lower socioeconomic and less-educated classes.
6. The use of interpersonal communication channels and depot-holders helped to further integrate the ORT message for the rural and less-educated segments of the audience.
7. The message design, treatment, and presentation were appropriately targeted, simple, consistent, and focused. The message was presented in non-technical, colloquial Arabic.
8. The ORT campaign featured a main character that made motherly sense in the Egyptian local culture, and whom the rural, lower socioeconomic classes could relate to, identify with, and trust.
9. The ORT campaign was concerned with an important health issue that addressed a thirst for information. The audience recognized their need for information about ORT, and knew it was for their own good.
10. The product, ORS, was of obvious benefit to the users, had high levels of compatibility, triability, and observability, and was simple to understand and use.
11. Lack of resistance to the campaign messages was enhanced by the fact that the messages did not contradict social or religious values.
12. Involving the audience through formative research in choosing a logo for the campaign and the Arabic words for ORS and dehydration helped common people relate to the ORT campaign, and further decreased any potential resistance to the messages.
13. ORS packets were readily available for free or at a very low price, making the treatment affordable even for the very low socioeconomic classes.
14. The availability of well-trained ORT medical personnel and health center staffs, who had one consistent message to deliver, made it easier for audiences to seek help and to trust the medical establishment with regards to ORT.

The Egyptian ORT campaign succeeded in saving the lives of hundreds of thousands of infants and children, making it one of the most successful health programs in the world. It resulted in a substantial reduction in infant and child mortality rates as a result of diarrheal-related diseases in Egypt: a 94% reduction for children under two, and a 93% reduction for children under five. The Egyptian ORT campaign is yet another example of the potential prosocial effects of the media, when a well-designed and researched E-E intervention is carried out.

REFERENCES

Abdel Aziz, G., & Loza, S. (1986). Experiment in using community residents to distribute ORS reduces child deaths and improves link between community and formal health facilities. *Diarrheal Control Newsletter, 5*, 8-10.

Abdulla, R. (1993). *The National Control of Diarrheal Diseases Project (NCDDP): 1983-1991.* Unpublished term paper. Cairo, Egypt: American University in Cairo.

Bandura, A. (1977). *Social learning theory.* Englewood Cliffs, NJ: Prentice-Hall.

Bandura, A. (1994). Social cognitive theory of mass communication. In J. Bryant & D. Zillmann (Eds.), *Media effects: Advances in theory and research* (pp. 61-90). Hillsdale, NJ: Lawrence Erlbaum Associates.

Bartholet, J. (1986, October 12). TV campaign injects a health-care serum into Egypt. *Chicago Tribune,* p. 9.

Boyd, D. (1999). *Broadcasting in the Arab world: A survey of the electronic media in the Middle East* (3rd ed.). Ames, IA: Iowa State University Press.

British Medical Journal (1985, November 2). Egypt's triumph with oral rehydration, *291,* 1249.

Business Alliance for International Economic Development (2002, March). *Protecting America's future: The role of foreign assistance.* Retrieved August 5, 2002, from http://www.fintrac.com/alliance/chapter-3.pdf

Center for Development Communication (1989). *The Family House: A public health soap opera.* Proposal submitted to the Center for Communication Programs, Johns Hopkins University, Baltimore, MD.

Charnock, A. (1985, December). Simple solution saves lives. *The Middle East,* 54.

Diase, M. (1993). *Serials are mostly entertainment, but Egyptians like to learn from them.* Paper presented at the International Communication Association, Washington, DC.

El Kamel, F. (1983). *The National Control of Diarrheal Diseases Project: The communication strategy.* Paper presented to the National Control of Diarrheal Disease Project, Cairo, Egypt.

El Kamel, F. (1985). *How the Egypt ORT campaign succeeded.* Paper presented at the International Conference on Oral Rehydration Therapy (ICORT II), Washington, DC.

El Kamel, F., & El Tohamy, A. (1988). The media and ORT—even more to come. *Diarrheal Control Newsletter, 7,* 17-18.

El Kamel, F., & Hirschhorn, N. (1984). *Thirst for information: Development communication in oral rehydration therapy and family planning.* Paper presented at the National Control of Diarrheal Disease Project, Cairo, Egypt.

El Kassaby, S. (1993). *Secret of the Land episodes: Analysis of television development agricultural campaign* [Abstract]. Unpublished term paper. Cairo, Egypt: American University in Cairo.

El Mougi, M., & El Tohamy, K. (1983). Changing pattern of attitudes towards management of acute diarrhea. *Diarrheal Control Newsletter, 1,* 8-9.

El Sayyad, L. M. (1983). The national campaign to promote oral rehydration in Egypt. *Diarrheal Control Newsletter, 1,* 12.

Gabr, M. (1983). Malnutrition and diarrheal diseases. *Diarrheal Control Newsletter, 1,* 3-4.

Harris, C. (1993, January). Health: The soap opera version. *International Development Research Centre Reports*, 24–25.

Hancock, A. (1980). *Planning for development: An operational framework*. Paris: UNESCO.

Katz, E., & Lazarsfeld, P. (1955). *Personal influence: The part played by people in the flow of mass communications*. New York: Free Press.

Kotler, P. (1975). *Marketing for nonprofit organizations*. Englewood Cliffs, NJ: Prentice-Hall.

Kreuger, U. (1983). UNICEF support of Egypt's National Control of Diarrheal Diseases Project. *Diarrheal Control Newsletter, 1*, 3.

Lazarsfeld, P., Berelson, B., & Gaudet, H. (1948). *The people's choice: How the voter makes up his mind in a Presidential election*. New York: Columbia University Press.

"Lights! Camera! Action! Promoting family planning with TV, video, and film" (1989, December). *Population Reports J, 38*.

Loza, S. (1985). Mothers learn more and diarrhea mortality rates go down when neighbors distribute ORS. *Diarrheal Control Newsletter, 4*, 12–13.

Miller, P. (1989). The impact of NCDDP on infant and childhood mortality. *Diarrheal Control Newsletter, 9*, 1–6.

Ministry of Health and Population (MOHP) (2002). *Infant mortality rates in Egypt*. Retrieved August 1, 2002, from http://www.mohp.gov.eg/Sec/HealthData/HMHC5.asp

Rogers, E. M. (1995). *Diffusion of innovations* (4th ed.). New York: Free Press.

Singhal, A., & Rogers, E. M. (1999). *Entertainment-education: A communication strategy for social change*. Mahwah, NJ: Lawrence Erlbaum Associates.

Singhal, A., & Rogers, E. M. (2002). A theoretical agenda for entertainment-education. *Communication Theory, 12*(2), 117–135.

Solomon, D. (1989). A social marketing perspective on communication campaigns. In R. E. Rice & C. Atkin (Eds.), *Public Communication Campaigns* (2nd ed.) (pp. 87–123). Thousand Oaks, CA: Sage.

Stone, M. P. (1983). USAID role in National Control of Diarrheal Diseases Project. *Diarrheal Control Newsletter, 1*, 2.

Tichenor, P. J., Donohue, G., & Olien, C. (1970). Mass media flow and differential growth in knowledge. *Public Opinion Quarterly, 34*, 159–170.

United Nations Children's Fund (1987). *The state of the world's children 1987*. New York: Oxford University Press.

United Nations Children's Fund (2002). *The state of the world's children 2002*. New York: Oxford University Press.

United Nations Development Programme (2002). *Human development report 2002: Deepening democracy in a fragmented world*. New York: Oxford University Press.

United Nations Economic Commission for Africa (2002). *Infant mortality rates of Northern African countries, 1950–2050*. Retrieved August 3, 2002, from http://www.un.org/Depts/eca/divis/fssd/nafmort.htm

The United States Agency for International Development (2000). *Congressional presentation: Egypt*. Retrieved August 3, 2002, from http://www.usaid.gov/pubs/cp2000/ane/egypt.html

White, M. (1991). NCDDP: The completion of an initial phase. *Diarrheal Control Newsletter, 13*, 1.

World Health Organization. (2002, May 8). *New formula for oral rehydration salts will save millions of lives*. Retrieved June 8, 2002, from http://www.who.int/inf/en/pr-2002-35.html

World Health Organization Statistical Information System (2002). *Selected indicators for Egypt*. Retrieved August 3, 2002, from http://www3.who.int/whosis/country/indicators.cfm?country=EGY&language=english

17

The Turkish Family Health and Planning Foundation's Entertainment-Education Campaign[1]

Yaşar Yaşer

Turkish Family Health and Planning Foundation

The Turkish Family Health and Planning Foundation (TFHPF) is a private, nonprofit organization established in 1985 by eminent industrialists, businessmen, and scientists under the leadership of a Turkish businessman, Vehbi Koç. The purpose of the Foundation is to improve and expand family planning and health services in Turkey. In 1988, this Foundation was the first organization in Turkey to pioneer the use of a mass media campaign to inform the public about the population problem. It included the design, pretesting, and production of experimental radio and television dramas, comedy spots, and serials. It was designed as a comprehensive campaign based on appropriate research, audience segmentation, and adequate testing of media materials. Ten different educational spots were launched in October 1988. The campaign activities included a national population awareness symposium, a television serial, a television documentary, two television films, 10 radio spots, an educational videocassette, 2,000 copies of two different family planning posters, 5,000 calendars, and 200,000 copies of family planning method-specific brochures.

[1]The present author acknowledges the collaboration of the Center for Communication Programs at Johns Hopkins University for their important role in the Turkish Family Planning campaign, which is reported in greater detail in Kincaid, Yun, Piotrow, and Yaser (1993).

Here I discuss how the campaign unfolded and its outcomes. The focus is on the goals of the campaign, the strategy that was designed, and how both formative research and theory (social marketing) were used in designing the campaign. I then discuss how the campaign was implemented, its evaluation, and how aspects of the campaign are used currently.

CAMPAIGN OBJECTIVES

The national multimedia family planning campaign was designed to promote the concept of family planning, modern contraceptive methods, and the availability of family planning service facilities. Contraceptive behavioral change was a long-range objective. The TFHPF focused on the following short-term campaign objectives:

1. To promote the general concept of "family planning" as a substitute for the narrow concept of "birth control."
2. To increase women's awareness of modern contraceptive methods and their availability throughout Turkey.
3. To promote discussion between spouses about family planning and family size.
4. To generate broad support for the family planning campaign and family planning in general in the Turkish government and among other key opinion leaders and decision-makers.

TFHPF undertook research, planning, and production in late 1987 and 1988. The intensive media campaign period began in October 1988 followed by evaluation research in early 1989.

The first step in planning the campaign involved using formative research to learn more about people's knowledge, attitudes, and practices regarding family planning. In mid-1987, a prominent advertising firm, Ajans Ada, conducted 30 focus group interviews with 180 women from seven provinces throughout Turkey. They also conducted four focus group interviews with 30 men.

Formative Research Used in Designing the Campaign Strategy

A. Focus Group Interview Results

Many Turkish women want fewer children. Lack of adequate family planning information and services are the most frequently cited obstacles to family planning practice, along with the husband's opposition.

Regardless of differences in background characteristics such as urban/rural, educated/uneducated, working/nonworking, and Eastern/Western Turkey, most women said that if family planning services were readily available they would make use of them.

In general, women's knowledge about family planning is limited and misinformation about modern methods is widespread.

Religious and ethical views are not major obstacles to women's practice of family planning. Generally, women who want to use family planning methods overlook religious concerns.

B. Survey Results

1. While 60–70% of women are literate, fewer than 30% read a newspaper daily.
2. About 85% of women listen to their own or someone else's radio for an average of slightly more than one hour daily.
3. Nearly all (93%) women watch their own or someone else's television set for an average of more than three hours daily.
4. Women usually obtain family planning information from nonprofessional sources (friends and neighbors) rather than from health professionals, perhaps accounting for misinformation.
5. Women strongly approve of family planning communication and think that information should be more widely disseminated.
6. Women living in the more developed Marmara and Central Regions of Turkey are better educated, more knowledgeable about family planning, and more likely to use contraception.
7. Education is highly correlated with knowledge of family planning and with use of contraception.

CAMPAIGN STRATEGY

TFHP decided that this first national family planning campaign should reach a broad, general audience. Thus the campaign was targeted at married women aged 15–44 and, to a lesser degree, men from both urban and rural areas. Opinion leaders and decision-makers constituted a third target audience, since their support was crucial to the family planning program. As a result of formative research, 10 themes were developed for use in each of the mass media messages: (1) it is bad to have more children than you can care for; (2) take precautions to avoid unwanted pregnancy; (3) modern, reliable, and safe family planning methods are available at clinics; (4) the term "family planning" means having only as many children as you want and spacing them out (family planning leads to a healthy mother, healthy children, and a happy home);

(5) proper child spacing is important to the health of the mother and child; (6) A small family is a happy family; (7) family planning is a man's responsibility; (8) Islam supports family planning; (9) consult with health workers for advice; and, (10) Turkey's rapid population growth hampers its socioeconomic development.

Based on these results, THFPF considered additional messages to provide information about specific modern family planning methods. However, Turkish Radio and Television (TRT) would not approve references to specific family planning methods because they felt the audience might find such material offensive. The strategy, therefore, was (1) to stick to the 10 major themes in the first media campaign, and (2) to demonstrate by means of evaluation research that Turkish people appreciate family planning information in the media, and would not be offended by more explicit messages.

MEDIA REACH AND MEDIA MIX

The fact that television and radio had such extensive reach in Turkey made it feasible to concentrate the campaign on broadcast media. It was decided to make the campaign's message as appealing as possible. Thus, extensive use was made of humor, music, and emotional drama in realistic interpersonal situations. Humorous interviews with typical Turkish characters were turned into short television spots for television. One of Turkey's leading comedians, Ugur Yücel, was featured in the spots. A television entertainment-education (E-E) serial dramatized the hardships of a migrant family with six children living in a squatter slum of Istanbul. Well-known actors played the leading role. Perihan Savaş, one of Turkey's most popular actresses, starred in a feature television drama about an urban professional woman faced with an unwanted pregnancy. Production standards for this television drama were as high as for commercial television and radio productions.

A next step was to select an appropriate media mix. Given the high impact of television and the target audience's broad exposure to this medium, television played the central role in the campaign. All 10 messages were delivered through television spots, dramas, and programs. Radio and print media were used to support broadcast media. Special events were important means for reaching opinion leaders and decision-makers.

Rather than disseminate all 10 messages at the same time over a three-month period, particular types of messages were released in phases in order to maximize their impacts on the intended audience. The first phase of the campaign focused on national opinion leaders, some of whom would publicly criticize the media campaign if not given orientation and preparation prior to the broadcast of family planning messages. A next step was to distribute print materials to public and private family planning distribution points.

Complementary print messages were made available for health service providers to use before demand for their services increased. The print materials also prepared service providers for the television and radio broadcast phases of the media campaign. A 30-minute educational video about family planning was distributed to the Ministry of Health, THFPH, and other health facilities to show to clients and to use in training courses.

A middle phase of the campaign consisted of a one-minute television feature drama, eight short radio dramas, five short educational television spots, and five humorous television spots, repeatedly shown on television to reach the largest possible audience. Each short spot was followed by a common "tag" message which reinforced the key themes of the campaign: Practice family planning for a happy, healthy family; modern, safe, and reliable family planning methods are available; and visit your local health clinic for more information and services. In a third phase of the campaign, a powerful, emotional three-part television drama was broadcast. This television series was designed (1) to create audience awareness of such problems as difficulties in raising and educating large families in modern society, unwanted pregnancies, induced abortion, and so forth, and (2) to motivate audience members to seek information about family planning services.

In a final phase of the campaign, TFHPF's IEC director appeared on television to officially close the campaign and to thank all of the organizations that contributed to the campaign and the audience.

CAMPAIGN EFFECTS

Sparrows Don't Migrate, a three-part television drama, was the story of a family with six children living in a squatters' slum in Istanbul. Family planning themes were interwoven as mother and daughter both experienced unplanned pregnancies. Other television dramas were produced and broadcast, such as *But Mother. . .*, and a 26-minute documentary called *A Child Is Crying There*. *Hope Was Always There* was a three-part television series starring a rural midwife. The series was very popular. It enhanced the image and promoted the work of trained midwives who provide substantial health, family planning, and maternal and child health services throughout rural Turkey. The director of this program, Ms. Bilge Olgaç, participated in this media campaign as a woman dealing with women's issues.

The filming was done in a village in eastern Turkey, 1,000 miles away from Istanbul. It took three months before Ms. Olgac reached the town in which she would do the filming because she made 12 stops on the way, visiting villages, and talking with villagers, their midwives, and nurses in the villages to make her movie coincide with reality. She learned about the problems and

PHOTO 17.1. Ömer and his large family in the Turkish Family Planning film
Berdel. (*Source:* Turkish Family Health and Planning Foundation.)

hardships that these midwives and villagers were living before she started
work on the script, which made the movie very realistic. The enthusiastic
woman's direct involvement in this venture made people appreciate the movie
even more. The film was requested by many women's organizations in Turkey
for several years after the media campaign. In Manisa, a city in Central-West
Turkey, campaign materials were used on Women's Day on March 8, 1996
and also in training seminars for "Educating the Local Media on Reproductive
Health" in Adana, Urfa, Diyarbakr, Trabzon in 1997–1999. The materials are
currently used in the continuation of the project in two towns in eastern
Turkey.

A 90-minute movie entitled *Berdel* was produced by the Foundation in
1990. This film was directed by Atif Yulmaz and starred Türkan Şoray and Tarik
Akan, the most popular movie stars in Turkey. The film won six international
awards including the Europe Cinema 1991 Fellini Award (Best Film of Europe
Award). The message of the film was that men should value their girl children
and should not seek younger wives in disregard of the feelings of their older
wives in order to have sons (Photo 17.1). Other awards were the 41st Berlin
International Film Festival (1991), Golden Palm Award in the 12th Mostra De

Valencia Cinema Del Mediterrani (1991), and the Population Institute's 1991 Global Media Award for Best TV Film (1991).

Praise for *Berdel*

David Stratton of *Variety* movie magazine wrote: "*Berdel*, one of the best pictures unveiled in the Berlin Film Festival's Panaroma section, is a simple but emotionally devastating indictment of arcane customs persistent in some rural areas of Turkey. This production of Turkey's Family Health and Planning Foundation has a message to get across, but the film's director makes his point without undue propaganda."

Ömer loves his wife, who has given him five daughters, but his macho image demands a son. When another baby girl is born, he reluctantly decides he must get a new wife, but since he can't afford a dowry, he decides to follow an age-old custom and exchange his eldest daughter Beyaz for a wife. The film's director tells this sad little story without fuss, moving the narrative along briskly. As lives are destroyed because of Omer's pride in insisting that he have a son, emotions in the film are very strong."

Source: Variety (1991).

Entertainment can catch the attention of a large audience, while education can at the same time transmit important social values. The multimedia campaign, the films, *Berdel*, and the story of the rural midwife influenced a number of other organizations to undertake similar activities throughout the world.

Evaluation research demonstrated that:

1. At least 80% of the Turkish population was exposed to one or more of the campaign messages.
2. More than 70% approved of the content of the campaign messages.
3. More than 60% of husbands and wives discussed family planning issues with each another as a result of the campaign.
4. Pre- and post-surveys identified about 350,000 new users of modern contraceptive methods, particularly the intra-uterine device, an effective, long-term, clinic-based method.
5. The campaign was extremely cost-effective. To motivate a modern family planning method user cost less than $1.00 per woman.

Endorsements for the Media Campaign in Turkey

We seem to have allocated an impressive amount of airtime to these family planning campaign programs on radio and TV and I think it is a breakthrough. I am very pleased that TRT was a collaborator in this very unique but very useful campaign. I am doubly happy that a very important issue for the economic and social development of Turkey like family planning, which has, I think, been willfully ignored for many years, is coming to the forefront.

—Adnan Kahveci, Minister of State in charge of TRT

My congratulations to you for this campaign. This, I believe, was the first communication campaign in Turkey of its kind. My Ministry will be very anxious to collaborate with you in every aspect of this problem. The Ministry will be supporting your efforts to the best of its means.

—Nihat Kitapci, Minister of Health (MOH)

The success of the project, I think, mainly stems from its correct approach to family planning. Turkish people are practical and can easily adapt to changes but they have very high ethics and moral values as well.

—Hasan Celal Güzel, Minister of Education.

'Have as many children as you can look after' being the principal slogan of the campaign, I think we are on the right course of action because you cannot bluntly tell people not to have children. It is their human right to have a family. But when you put it mildly like you did in your campaign it becomes inoffensive and more acceptable by people. This campaign will open new doors in the economic and social development of Turkey.

—Nazli Ilcak, Editor of *Bulvar* Newspaper

SOCIAL MARKETING

TFHPF implemented a social marketing program to increase the availability and use of quality, low-cost contraceptives, such as condoms and low-dose pills. A new condom brand, "OK," was developed and Turkish Radio and Television (TRT) aired advertising for this brand. This event was the first time in Turkish television history that advertising was permitted for a specific brand of condom. Three television comedy shows promoted the "OK" condom with sardonic humor that attracted the attention of people.

The partner company in this venture made spot checks through their wholesale and retail system about the increase in "OK" condom sales. Some 63% of the people surveyed said that they switched to "OK" condoms after seeing the humorous ads on television. This use of E-E was based on humor (Ugur Yücel and Ms. Oya Başar, both top comedians in Turkey).

Evaluation of this social marketing intervention indicated:

1. The "OK" condom advertising was remembered by 68% of survey respondents.

2. A substantial increase in sales of low-dose contraceptive pills, healthier for most women to use, occurred as a result of the national campaign. The market share of low-dose pills increased from 50% in 1991 to 61% in 1992,

while the total commercial market for pills increased by 18%. This increase represents more than 50,000 Turkish women using this modern method in less than a year, including success in reaching targeted lower socioeconomic individuals who represent 60% of current pill users in Turkey.

Entertainment-Education opened the way for the social marketing campaigns that would not otherwise have been acceptable.

CONCLUSIONS

The E-E efforts described here were the first such effort ever carried out in Turkey. The campaign might have backfired, but did not because of the use of formative research.

E-E played an important advocacy role in winning over high-level government officials to the concept of family planning. The lack of opposition and high level of public interest in these materials made family planning and the use of mass media for family planning promotion possible and acceptable.

All parts of the media campaign utilized female, talented writers, directors, and producers, giving them an opportunity to highlight women's concerns before the Turkish public in a way that had never been done before.

A first-rate male comedian injected humor and irony into the television series, which made it possible to emphasize sensitive issues more strongly. For example, one television advertisement showed a farmer, dividing up what was once an ample plot of land belonging to his grandfather, to his own children with only enough remaining to put in six flower pots.

REFERENCE

Kincaid, D. L., Yun, S. H., Piotrow, P. T., & Yaser, Y. (1993). Turkey's mass media family planning campaign. In T. E. Backer & E. M. Rogers (Eds.), *Organizational aspects of health communication campaigns: What works?* (pp. 68–92). Thousand Oaks, CA: Sage.

18

Cartoons and Comic Books for Changing Social Norms: *Meena*, the South Asian Girl

Neill McKee
Johns Hopkins University

Mira Aghi
Rachel Carnegie
Consultants

Nuzhat Shahzadi
UNICEF

The purpose of the present chapter is to demonstrate that animated film is an effective entertainment-education (E-E) medium to consider, especially when a regional development theme or problem is being addressed. Animated film and related materials, such as comic books, can address sensitive social and behavioral issues in an effective way if the audience is fully involved in the creative process through extensive formative research. Such tools can be harnessed for social mobilization and changing social norms.

In the past decade *Meena*, a cartoon figure of a young South Asian girl, has become part of the region's culture and a key communication tool in the struggle for girls' rights and gender equity. *Meena* was "born" in Bangladesh in 1991 and spread to India, Pakistan, Nepal, Sri Lanka, the Maldives, Bhutan, and Southeast Asia. The *Meena* stories are an example of an E-E strategy that engages the hearts and minds of people of all ages in important social development issues, such as discrimination in food and domestic workloads, which are common in South Asia, as witnessed in the following quotes from formative research for *Meena*:

> My mother tells me to save the best piéces of meat for my brother.
> —An 11 year-old girl in rural Pakistan

> Yes, boys can fetch water, but in our society they do not do it. This is because of our pride. We want females to do all the household work.
> —A young man, Savar, Bangladesh

THE BIRTH OF *MEENA*

The *Meena* stories were designed to address such traditional attitudes of gender inequality. Below is one example that has been told and retold in families and communities throughout South Asia:

In "Dividing the Mango," Meena picks a juicy mango off the highest branch of a tree. When her mother divides the fruit, she gives the larger share to Meena's brother, Raju. In her disappointment, Meena begins to reflect on how food is unequally distributed between herself and her brother (Photo 18.1). Later, Meena seizes the chance to prove her point. When Raju teases Meena, saying that her work is easy, Meena playfully challenges him to change places for a day. Exhausted by doing his sister's tasks, Raju complains bitterly when his mother gives him Meena's usual small serving at supper. The family has at last come to realize how much work Meena does everyday and to recognize that girls need as much good food as boys. In the end, Raju also offers to help Meena with her chores.

PHOTO 18.1.   Meena notices she gets less food than her brother, Raju, and begins to ask why. (*Source:* UNICEF's Meena Communication Initiative.)

This story proved to be a powerful tool in dealing with gender discrimination, as demonstrated in the following remarks by audience members:

> Since I saw the film, I have become very conscious when I serve food to my daughter.
>
> —A woman in Dhaka, Bangladesh

> The story showed us how we should stay together in harmony . . . share all the household tasks . . . go to school together and take equal food. That is because both boys and girls are growing children."
>
> —A 10-year-old boy, Ghior, Bangladesh

> The act of giving less food to a girl is common practice with our people, but no one has ever shown this as *Meena* has done. She has brought out the issue for us all to discuss. *Meena* addresses many problems. Some issues can be resolved quickly, and others slowly, but we need something like *Meena* as an entry point.
>
> —A female community education worker, Bihar, India

In urban suburbs and slums, in towns and villages, such stories inspire young girls and challenge their brothers, parents, grandparents, and their extended family to rethink their behavior towards girls. The popular theme song of the *Meena* animated film series calls out to the viewer to "Think once again about the girls in your family. What make them happy? What makes them sad? What do they long for in their future lives? Let's give girls a chance to find their dreams."

Meena is grounded in South Asian cultures through extensive formative research, but she was first conceived in Prague. Throughout the Communist period, animated filmmakers in Czechoslovakia kept up the quality of their craft. In March 1990 UNICEF hosted a meeting in Prague on the use of animated film for development communication. Many works were reviewed, including Walt Disney's first attempts to teach people about malaria and population control in the 1950s; *Karate Kid*, on the protection of street children against HIV; and *Prescription for Health*, a Canadian film used throughout the world on the prevention of diarrheal diseases. Famous individuals in the cartoon industry attended the Prague meeting, such as the late Bill Hanna, co-owner of Hanna-Barbera Studios and creator of famous cartoon figures such as *Yogi the Bear*. The late James P. Grant, former Executive Director of UNICEF, challenged Hanna and Neill McKee (coauthor of this chapter), who had just joined UNICEF in Bangladesh, to come up with an animated film project. McKee was stimulated by the opportunity and aware that 1990 was the "Year of the Girl Child" in South Asia, as declared by the South Asian Association for Regional Cooperation (SAARC). McKee awoke the next morning with the figure of a young cartoon girl in his head. So began *Meena's* journey.

From dream to reality, however, meant a great deal of hard work: advocacy, discussions, proposal writing, and fundraising. The production of animated

film is expensive and it was decided that a regional audience was needed to
justify the costs. Keys to success were the backing of a regional management
team and the hiring of consultants to carry out in-depth research with local
communities.

Ten years later, *Meena* is alive and growing, as is suggested from the following quote:

> In Fungling bazaar of Taplejung, 500 people turned out to watch the *Meena*
> video. . . . While we were there, the villagers not only requested us to screen
> the video in the villages [not only in towns], but they also tried to pressurize
> us to do so . . . In Khotang, the police had to be called in to control the crowds
> that had come to the screening.
>
> —Yagya Sharma, journalist, Nepal

The *Meena* cartoon character, like *Donald Duck* or *Mickey Mouse*, does
not change in age or appearance. She remains a nine or ten year old, ready
to enter the lives of young children in South Asia as long as the issues she is
addressing remain current.

BACKGROUND AND RATIONALE

By the end of 1990, the governments of South Asia, realizing that social change
would be a long-term endeavor, declared the 1990s as the "Decade of the Girl
Child." They recognized that special focus was needed to address discrimination against girls and to promote their education, health, and development. In
countries like Bangladesh, India, Nepal, and Pakistan, female children face differential treatment in all spheres of their lives. Deep-rooted traditional beliefs
and practices threaten their protection, survival, and development.

In the 1980s, the governments of South Asia ratified the "Convention to
Eliminate All Forms of Discrimination Against Women" (CEDAW) (United
Nations, 1979) to counter blockages to women's development, such as the
practice of *purdah* that keeps women hidden and excluded from education
and participation. Such formal practices are symptoms of the patriarchal social norms in South Asia that continue to reinforce low expectations from
women and girls, as is evident from the statement below.

> In our family setting girls and women are neglected. We do not give them any
> importance, because we feel that they are useless. We do not have the same
> feelings for boys. We feel that the boys will be able to work and earn money to
> support the family.
>
> —A local leader in Savar, rural Bangladesh

In the early 1990s, all South Asian governments ratified the "Convention of the Rights of the Child" (CRC) (UNICEF, 1990), which contains 54 articles about survival, protection, and development of children that are to be incrementally implemented. *Meena* is founded on a rights-based analysis of the situation of girls in South Asia.

The most fundamental rights of the child are the rights to life and maximum survival and development (Article 6), the rights to health and nutrition, and access to health services, safe water, and sanitation (Article 24). Girls have higher infant and child mortality rates than boys due to lack of access to health care, higher rates of disease, and malnutrition. South Asia is the only region of the world where women do not have a longer life expectancy than men. A number of *Meena* stories directly address this problem, such as "Saving a Life," in which Meena uses her negotiation skills and creative thinking to save a female infant from dehydration and death due to diarrhea (see Chapter 16 by Rasha Abdulla in this volume).

Article 2 of the CRC deals with all forms of social discrimination, including gender. In South Asia, stereotyping and role modeling of girls' behavior and expectations start at a very early age. Girls are often bullied by boys and may suffer physical violence if they resist. Unhealthy superstitions and customs abound, such as isolation and food restrictions at the time of menstruation. Practices of dowry and early marriage continue, and contribute to further gender inequity in health, education, economic activity, and legal assistance in the inheritance of property. The daughter is often seen as "belonging to someone else" since she will soon be married, and the bride is often seen as an "outsider" to the groom's family. Such problems and potential solutions to them are creatively woven into the *Meena* stories.

Article 1 of the CRC defines a child as a person under the age of 18. *Meena* stories promote the idea that children should be allowed to have their childhood, to play, and to develop their social skills (Article 31), rather than being overwhelmed by household chores. Thousands of young girls are employed as housemaids or must seek a livelihood through working in factories, at very low wage levels, where they may be subjected to physical and sexual abuse. The issue of child labor (Article 32) is addressed in "Meena in the City," a story in which Meena is tricked into becoming a housemaid and uses her thinking skills to get out of the situation and makes sure a young maid she has met is allowed to go to school.

The very first *Meena* story, "Count Your Chickens," is an imaginative tale in which Meena demonstrates the need to educate girls when she helps to catch a chicken thief through her self-taught counting skills (Photo 18.2). The CRC states that children have a right to education (Article 28). South Asia has made great strides in the last decade towards increased girls' school enrollment, although girls' dropout rates remain quite high. *Meena* stories not only deal with enrollment in school, they deal with the important issues

PHOTO 18.2. Meena convinces the community about the importance of girls' education by using her counting skills to catch a chicken thief. (*Source:* UNICEF's Meena Communication Initiative.)

of gender sensitivity and quality of education (Article 29), factors which help both girls and boys develop their full potential.

Many other child rights embedded in *Meena* stories are often ignored in South Asia, but are fundamental to the development of the whole child: access to appropriate information (Article 17); respect for the views of the child (Article 12); and freedom of expression (Article 13). In South Asian cultures, the child, especially the girl, does not have a voice and is not recognized as a real person until she "comes of age." *Meena* stories are designed to deal sensitively with these issues instead of coming into direct conflict with traditional beliefs.

CARTOONS AND COMIC BOOKS
FOR SOCIAL CHANGE

The *Meena* communication packages consist of animated films/videos, comic books, discussion guides and posters, and two radio series produced in collaboration with BBC World Service. The core materials are produced in English,

Bangla, Hindi, Nepali, and Urdu, with various materials now available in about 20 other Asian languages. The creators of *Meena* decided that films and videos were needed for wide dissemination of *Meena*'s themes and that animated cartoons would be the "flagship" communication tool. In viewing live-action films, people in multiethnic environments respond to cultural and social cues such as dress, facial features, language and accents, housing, and vegetation that may alienate or distract them. They may be fascinated by what they see, but miss the main message or conclude that the situations posed are "someone else's problem." Through formative research, a set of characters, backgrounds, and storylines can be designed in animated film and comic book formats that strike a common chord across a diverse region (McBean & McKee, 1996).

Another value of animated film and comic books is that very difficult social issues can be portrayed in sensitive, nonthreatening ways, without losing story impact (McBean & McKee, 1996). *Meena* was formulated through formative research over a two-year period—hundreds of focus group discussions and in-depth interviews were carried out on the concepts, characters, images, names, themes, and draft storylines.

CREATIVE DEVELOPMENT AND FORMATIVE RESEARCH PROCESS

The challenge was to create a character that could be universally loved and identified with across the region. Some success is evident below:

It would have been very difficult for us to talk about the rights of girls without the symbol of Meena . . . Meena is something special . . . Every family in India has a Meena.
> —Jayshree, a village teacher from Orissa, India

Meena is like us . . . Meena explains our thoughts in her words. She's from a poor family. She understands our problems and difficulties. She experiences these problems herself.
> —Yasmin, a girl from Dhaka, Bangladesh

Meena is just like us. She solves problems that are just like ours.
> —Rahima, a 13-year-old girl guide from Pakistan

Meena is the story of every house, generally a story we don't speak about. That is why *Meena* is so special and so close to us. Sometimes I feel I am Meena . . . I was always a rebel. *Meena* has validated my feelings that I was right all along. My father insisted that his granddaughter feed her older brother. I opposed it. If I hadn't seen *Meena*, I would have let it pass.
> —Ranjan Singh, a teacher and father from Bihar, India

PHOTO 18.3.   Of the multiple images of South Asian girls that were pretested,
audiences preferred the drawing on the right, which inspired the final image
of Meena. (*Source:* UNICEF's Meena Communication Initiative.)

Girls and their families throughout the South Asian region identify closely
with *Meena* and her experiences. Such identification is founded on a painstak-
ing process of regional consultation and formative research. In 1991, UNICEF
held consultations in Bangladesh, India, Pakistan, and Nepal with key figures
in governments and NGOs, as well as with artists, writers, and other creative talent. This process sifted out the key qualities for *Meena*, to create a
universal, but unique, little girl (Photo 18.3).

It was decided that the motivation for change in attitudes and behavior
towards girls should be positive, building on recognition of girls' potential,
rather than trying to evoke guilt at their ill treatment. The idea of Meena's
parrot was suggested in Pakistan, where in folklore the bird has a reputation for wisdom. This idea was accepted in other countries. A clear sense
of Meena's personal qualities and visual appearance began to emerge when
artists in each country were asked to draw images of a girl, her family, and
a parrot. In some pictures, the girl seemed oppressed, in others, full of
vitality and fun. This later was the image identified as Meena. Different artists
in the region contributed images, such as a playful image of Meena skip-
ping through the fields, while Mithu the parrot flies behind, holding her
braid.

Regional consultation involved identifying different creative talent to work
on the series. The studios of Ram Mohan in Bombay, the leading animator
in India, were selected. Mohan directed production of the first episode of
Meena in Hanna-Barbera's studios in Manila, and thereafter took over the complete process. A creative team worked with Ram Mohan to develop the first
composite images of Meena, based on the many inspirational designs gathered around the region. Meena's appealing face and simple image quickly
emerged. Then, designs were tested and modified until the final version

was established, with Meena wearing a combination of a long shirt (without trousers) from Pakistan and a skirt or dress from other countries. Even the colors of the clothes were selected on the basis of research into their cultural connotations.

A greater challenge was to develop a landscape that could be recognized across a region spanning mountains and flood plains, and deserts and fertile green fields. The creative team wove illustrations of bright green fields with strips of desert beyond, hills, and flat lands. Realism was not lost: frogs lurk in muddy puddles and cow pies, used for fuel, are drying on the wall near Meena's house.

The research process for *Meena's* creation was one of the most extensive exercises in formative research in the history of development communication. Over an 11-year period, hundreds of focus group and in-depth interviews were held with over 10,000 girls and boys, parents, and other community members. Parents can support girls to go to school, but school facilities and good teachers are needed to deliver quality education. Broad involvement of different groups of respondents ensures that multiple perspectives are taken into account to build a consensus of views.

The formative research approach in *Meena* is not regarded merely as a tool for pretesting preconceived concepts and images with the target audience. Before the materials are designed, the researchers go to communities to determine their attitudes and perceptions on each issue. The respondents' stories are then used as inspirational material in the first phase of script writing. The scripts are researched to check comprehension, educational value, cultural appropriateness and acceptability, credibility of the solutions proposed, and entertainment value. At the final stage, visuals from the story are also tested to create new characters and locations.

Meena's development is shown as necessarily linked to that of other people who are important in her life. Other members of her family learn and grow. *Meena* goes beyond describing the status quo to envisage a transformation that has been carefully negotiated for credibility and realism through formative research.

Field testing of the first *Meena* episode in 1992, with 2,500 respondents across the region, established that the film was entertaining but viewed seriously in terms of its ideas about education for girls. People rarely spoke of Meena as an animated, fictional character.

Formative research is used to ascertain that each episode of the *Meena* series maintains the delicate balance and dynamic tension between education and entertainment in stories that appeal to both children and adults. Particular care is needed to prevent the film episodes from becoming overloaded with message content, or, alternatively, to ensure that a serious issue was not treated flippantly. An example from one episode of the value of formative research findings is summarized below (Box 1).

Research on "Dividing the Mango"

This episode of *Meena* is about discrimination in food distribution and work-load between girls and boys (a synopsis of the story was provided at the top of this chapter). Formative research was conducted in India, Pakistan, Bangladesh, and Nepal. Inequitable food distribution is not openly recognized and could provoke audience resistance. Mothers often denied that such practices existed. But reflection on Meena's experiences "unlocked" the issue and enabled moth-ers to acknowledge that food discrimination did exist and to discuss the reasons for it.

Key findings from formative research were that discrimination in food distri-bution was based on both quantity and quality. In poorer areas of South Asia, girls were deprived on both accounts, whereas in richer areas girls received less "quality" food (meat, fish, eggs, and dairy products). Both concepts were incorporated in the film. It was felt that boys "needed" more food because their work is outside and perceived as harder than girls' domestic work. The story-line therefore emphasized both the energy required for girls' work and the fact that boys and girls, as growing children, have an equal need for, and right to, nutritious food.

Meena was made to face problems in controlling the cow, usually tended by her brother. The grandmother originally stated that it was a "tradition" that girls get less food than boys. Since the word "tradition" was often interpreted as something desirable, it was replaced by the expression: "That's the way it is!" Grandmother's attitude to Meena was softened. The mother was originally depicted as unsympathetic to Meena. This depiction was revised to show the mother as amused by Meena's antics and a willing participant in her game, when she gives Raju Meena's usual plate of food.

A series of case studies conducted in Nepal, after the final film had been screened, characterized the responses to "Dividing the Mango." Kanti Acharya, a 17-year-old schoolgirl, compared what she had seen on the screen with her own life. She had already begun raising the issue with her parents: "You don't ask my brother to work and you want me to do all the household work, and yet in the end you scold me if I do poorly in school." Her parents were also reported to be changing. They also want their son to help with work, like Meena's younger brother.

Source: UNICEF (Dec. 2001, p. 7)

USING *MEENA* TO FOSTER SOCIAL CHANGE

Meena was created as a complimentary regional initiative, not as a separate project. *Meena* is comprised of a set of communication tools designed to fit into the programs of many organizations working towards the common goal of empowering girl children. *Meena* stories highlight the moral imperative of fulfilling children's rights, but they also recognize the difficulties of placing such obligations solely on parents' shoulders. How do parents living in absolute poverty fulfill both their sons' and daughters' rights? The *Meena* series aims not to preach about rights, but rather to raise awareness and discussion of the issues and to support communities and families in finding ways to fulfill their children's rights.

Meena was formulated for use in a three-tiered, development communication strategy of advocacy, social mobilization, and behavior change communication. *Meena* is used as an advocacy tool to increase political commitment for changing the situation of girls and women in South Asia. Political commitment involves decisions by leaders to use their power to influence social change, including changes in policies and laws that decrease discrimination against girls and women. For example, policies and laws are needed regarding female abortion and infanticide; putting family life or life skills education in schools; reducing school fees for girls from lower socioeconomic backgrounds and other budgetary provision for their education and access to social services; and enforcement is required on the legal age of sexual consent and marriage, and on laws regarding dowry, or other customs which are detrimental to the development of females.

Meena is also designed to be used as a catalyst for bringing together partners in governments, NGOs, the media, and private sector. Such alliances can work to create an enabling environment, including strengthened education, health, and other social services, microcredit, legal protection systems, and more positive cultural and media influences. The process of establishing such an alliance is called *social mobilization*. However, *Meena* materials are fundamentally designed for behavior change communication, including behavioral development for children and adolescents who have not yet fully formed many behaviors, as well as behavior change for the adults who affect their children's lives by their attitudes and actions. These tools address individual knowledge, attitudes, and practices, as well as social norms that inhibit the development of girls. Figure 18.1 may be useful in conceptualizing the relationship between these various components of strategic communication in *Meena*.

The creators of *Meena* decided that the complexity of factors required for successful behavior change and positive behavior development called for stories that capture the attention of a wide cross-section of the public, beginning with opinion-setters and educators. The stories must be informative as well as provocative to generate audience discussion. They must motivate through their entertainment value, but also be based on formative research into existing value systems. The stories also have to address the life skills and enabling environment factors that are crucial for behavior change.

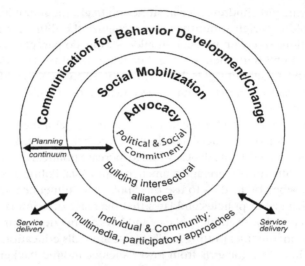

FIG. 18.1. *Strategic Communication Model. Source*: Adapted from McKee, Manoncourt, Chin, & Carnegie (2000, p. 107)

Girls in South Asia are denied vital skills that could help protect them against many threats to their development. These life skills include problem-solving, decision-making, critical thinking, communication, negotiation, coping with emotions and stress, self-assessment, conflict resolution and management, and relationship skills such as empathy (Carnegie & Weisen, 2000).

The planning of *Meena* stories took these elements into account, which helped to foster the emergence of a new model (Fig. 18.2) to guide girls' and women's empowerment, HIV/AIDS prevention, and programs with a strong behavior change component.

Meena's creators believed that only when knowledge of health and social issues is combined with motivation and skills, with full consideration of all environmental barriers and facilitating factors, will girls and women become more equal partners in society. *Meena* has been implemented very widely as a tool for social change by a large number of partners. For example, in Bangladesh, government ministries and NGOs were equal partners in making *Meena* a household name. Since *Meena* was launched, Bangladesh's national television network (BTV) has been screening *Meena* videos in children's programs, as well as on prime-time. The mobile film unit of the Ministry of Information screened *Meena* films to an estimated three million people. The *Meena* radio series was rebroadcast by Radio-Bangladesh several times. *Meena* is popularized throughout Bangladesh through the press, billboards, and folk media. Many *Meena* stories are included in the national formal school curriculum reaching over 30,000 schools in 32 districts. NGOs like the Bangladesh Rural Advancement Committee (BRAC), Grameen Bank, and others continue to

FIG. 18.2.   Behavior Development and Social Change Model. *Source*: McKee et al. (2000, p. 214)

use *Meena*. For instance, *Meena* stories have been included in the curriculum of BRAC's 32,000 community-based, nonformal primary schools since 1997 and its Rural Credit Program continues to screen *Meena* videos to clients. In addition, BRAC is publishing and marketing *Meena* stories.

Meena in Nonformal Schools in Bangladesh

Gono Shaharjjo Sangstha (GSS) has been a pioneer of quality primary education in Bangladesh. GSS's nonformal education program operates over 700 schools for disadvantaged children in rural and urban Bangladesh, including working children. These schools are based in the communities they serve and are established with strong community involvement. They represent an example of quality standards in education that can be achieved through effective training and intensive supervision and support.

GSS introduced the *Meena* comic books into their literacy activities in 1993. GSS staff assisted in the development and translation of these books. GSS follows a child-centered, integrated approach to learning, in which different subjects are linked. *Meena* themes, such as gender equity or early marriage, have been used as a basis in classes three to five, integrating literacy, numeracy, health, and social studies. The aim is to mediate learning through the children's own experiences, relating education to their real lives. *Meena* stories are used to create such links. Children also write essays about, and draw pictures of Meena and themselves, which are made into books for other children to read. The comic books, posters, and videos have been used regularly to stimulate discussion on how Meena's experience relates to the children's lives. Teachers report that this process develops children's critical thinking skills, especially on issues of gender and social discrimination. As one school principal stated: "*Meena* works very well with children. It has really changed their thought and reasoning process."

GSS used the *Meena* videos as a trigger for discussion at monthly meetings with parents. Children are encouraged to take *Meena* comic books home to share with their families. Children prepared dramas, inspired by *Meena* stories, and invited their parents to watch. They used the story, "Count Your Chickens," to encourage their friends to attend school and their parents to attend adult literacy classes. When *Meena* stories are broadcast on television and radio, children also report discussing the issues with their parents.

A teacher in a GSS school noted: "Because of *Meena*, children realize there is no difference between girls and boys. It is helping girls to know their rights. We also show the films to parents to enjoy, and then to discuss about keeping their daughters in school. *Meena* is an excellent tool for raising awareness in our community about the issues of girls."

Source: UNICEF (Dec. 2001, p. 27)

In India, a *Meena* talk show was aired on Doordarshan, the national television network, during prime-time children's viewing hours. On the show, children, parents, and experts from around the country watch a *Meena* film and then discuss the issues raised. India's Ministry of Information and Broadcasting oriented its field publicity units in 31 Indian states and union territories to use *Meena* as a tool to initiate community discussion of issues related to the girl child. About 300,000 Nehru Yuva Youth Clubs at the block and district levels are disseminating *Meena* stories at the community level. In addition, a commercial educational publisher is printing and marketing *Meena* materials in all major Indian languages.

In Pakistan, *Meena* characters have been systematically integrated as a communication resource into different sectors. Meena and her brother are used as "ambassadors" for child rights. For instance, in Baluchistan, *Meena* is the symbol of a movement by the Boy Scouts to get their sisters into school, called "Brothers for *Meena*." UNICEF is developing innovative ways to use *Meena* as a much-needed source of supplementary reading material for primary schools and is integrating *Meena* materials into NGO training, orientation, and awareness raising activities. *Meena* has grown to be very popular, even in the far reaches of the country.

"On Sunday, I was in the Sindhi desert at 45 degrees. We went to this tiny mud hut school, beyond the town of Sehwan, and there was Meena beaming from the walls in four posters. This school was set up by the Sindh Education Foundation. The children said they liked Meena very much and told me two of her stories: "Count Your Chickens" and "Meena's Three Wishes." In this tiny isolated village, there were a couple of television sets run off of car batteries, and they had seen the films on television. It was a great thrill, particularly as I was not there to be shown *Meena* activities. It was just part of children's life and education there. In this village, girls were coming to school for the first time. They were bright-eyed, confident girls. The village had also established a women's literacy center, and the girls told me that when the teacher is away, they go and teach the women. I felt like I had walked into a *Meena* film set! Too hot for Mithu, but some great camels!" (Rachel Carnegie, British Communication Consultant, Trip Report, May 1, 2002).

In Nepal, nationwide *Meena* social mobilization was launched in 1998 and by the end of the year had covered 36 of 75 of Nepal's districts. Unique partnerships have developed between UNICEF, government, mass media, and NGOs in support of the goals of the campaign. *Meena* is used as a key resource in initiating community discussions on child health, development, and gender issues. *Meena* images and messages are painted on three-wheel vehicles in Kathmandu for raising mass awareness of girl child issues.

Sri Lanka, Bhutan, the Maldives, and Vietnam participated in formative research for three new *Meena* stories. Language versioning of some of the materials is being undertaken in these new partner countries and program planning and implementation has begun.

EVALUATION OF *MEENA*

A full impact evaluation of *Meena* is planned. UNICEF commissioned a number of evaluation studies of *Meena* at national or project levels.

1. Bangladesh National Media Survey (UNICEF, Dec. 2001): The 1998 National Media Survey included questions related to *Meena*. Some 44% of urban adult television viewers and 17% of rural adult television viewers remembered seeing *Meena* on television. In addition, 97% of adult respondents who saw *Meena* stated that they liked her "very much." Of Dhaka residents who watch television, more than 50% knew the Meena character and identified the series as "being about 'girls' rights."

2. 1999 *Meena* Baseline Study in Bangladesh (UNICEF, Dec. 2001): This study was conducted to provide a baseline for a new quality education initiative using *Meena*. Awareness of *Meena* by school-going children was 85% for girls and 87% for boys. Of nonschool-going children, 40% of girls and 38% of boys knew about *Meena*. *Meena* is highly popular among both school-going and nonschool-going children, almost all of whom said that they liked *Meena*. Approximately 66% of school-going children and 56% of nonschool-going children perceived Meena as a village girl. Less than one fifth

of children saw Meena as a cartoon character. What children liked most about Meena was her eagerness to learn about new ideas. Identification with Meena's character was quite strong among all interviewed children. A large proportion of parents (85% of females and 80% of males) understood that girls face problems in Bangladesh. Many parents mentioned that *Meena* helped bring about increased gender awareness by highlighting specific problems.

3.   Impact study in Pakistan (*UNICEF, Dec. 2001*): A small impact study was conducted in Pakistan in 1997. Following exposure to *Meena* films, a positive shift in children's attitudes towards being more gender-fair was recorded. After viewing *Meena*, children became much more expressive, imaginative, spontaneous, and bold.

From a child right's perspective, *Meena* can be a strong tool for bringing childhood to a large segment of children, who have been robbed of it. It provides role models to them in indigenous cultural and age-specific contexts. It introduces change in attitudes towards children and gender-related issues.

In 2001 a study was completed (UNICEF, Dec. 2001) to document the multiple ways in which *Meena* has been utilized in South Asia and elsewhere in the world. *Meena* was adapted widely by UNICEF and its partners. Box 3 gives examples of the utilization of *Meena* in a folk media project in India.

"Meena Muppet Roadshow" in Bihar, India

The *Meena* launch in Bihar was marked by the "Meena Muppet Roadshow." This show arose in response to the challenge of taking *Meena* stories to rural areas that are not reached by electronic media. The Roadshow was developed by Gatividhi, a Patna-based theater group, and sponsored by the Indian government's Department of Welfare and UNICEF. The inaugural show in 1998 in Patna was watched by over 2,000 people. Since then, the "Meena Roadshow" has performed hundreds of shows in rural towns and villages in Bihar before thousands of people. The shows are performed with masked actors, including adolescent girls, acting to a prerecorded music track. The plays are based on *Meena* stories, adapted and improvised for each community.

"We can change the dialogue of the play in different places and in different circumstances and can add the needs of local people . . . *Meena's* story is happening in every single house in Bihar. After the show we interview people about their views on children. We later go back to the schools and see the attendance lists" (A Member of the "Meena" Muppet team).

"We have grandmothers come up and say: 'Today we have learned that girls should go to school.' Many say that it is the first time they have recognized that it is a girl's right to go to school" (A Member of the "Meena" Muppet team). *Meena* will not go anywhere uninvited. A local group must host the show. An early invitation came from the oldest school for girls in Patna, Bankipore Girls' School, where 1,500 girls watched the show and afterwards talked animatedly for hours, refusing to go home. The School insisted that the show had to be repeated, as another 1,500 girls wanted to watch it.

In 1999 the Roadshow continued to travel and the original troupe was involved in training other groups. Fourteen more troupes were trained by the end of 1999. The Roadshow received wide coverage in Bihar through the press and radio. The Meena Muppet Troupe also worked in schools in seven districts, training students to perform *Meena* plays. Girls have never before acted or been on stage. *Meena* has also been used in mobilizing teachers in private schools on children's rights. In some cases the Roadshow inspired girls to establish their own *Meena* Clubs in schools.

Source: UNICEF (Dec. 2001, p. 53).

LESSONS LEARNED

Meena has been sustained for over a decade in South Asia and beyond, an achievement by itself for any E-E initiative. A close analysis of experiences from various implementing countries reveals factors that contributed to *Meena*'s success over the years. One is a passionate sense of ownership that has been generated in participating countries from the beginning. *Meena* is the result of wide-scale formative research that involves programmers, researchers, writers, and artists with communities in a true partnership process. People feel *Meena* is from Bangladesh, India, Pakistan, Nepal, Sri Lanka, or the Maldives. *Meena* is the first large cartoon series in South Asian local languages, set in local environments, voicing local concerns, and produced mainly by South Asians.

For the past decade, many of the same people in the core creative team have been guiding *Meena*'s development processes, with new members joining. This team has been the informal custodian of the concepts, characters, images and uses of *Meena*.

Involving top-level policy makers in advocacy events has been a key strategy in garnering political commitment for *Meena*. Strong partnerships have been built with the media to highlight such events. September 24th is now recognized as "Meena Day" in South Asia. High-level advocacy facilitated integration of *Meena* into the development projects and programs of public and civil society sectors. *Meena* has gone much beyond being a regional symbol. The collective activities of *Meena* partners contributed to the general feeling that *Meena* belongs to "everyone" and can be integrated into various, like-minded programs to enhance their development objectives.

What is the future sustainability of *Meena*? As wider ownership evolved and demands for *Meena* escalated, UNICEF began to explore options for *Meena*'s future. In early 2002, a series of meetings were undertaken with partners from the NGOs, such as BRAC and the Grameen Bank; philanthropic trusts in India such as Birla, Tata, Mahendra, and Ambani; and in the private sector, Nokia and Archies Stores, to explore the long-envisaged establishment of an independent foundation for *Meena*. An operational model for a *Meena* Center (UNICEF, May 28, 2002) has been developed and plans are underway for its implementation. It is envisaged that this Center will manage *Meena* production of new products, initiation of new communication and marketing ventures, licensing and coordination of partners, technical support, implementation of guidelines on what *Meena* can and cannot promote, and custodial oversight of copyright to protect the integrity of product development and production processes. *Meena* is a powerful tool through mass media channels and the danger is that she could be used for unauthorized or even antisocial purposes.

Strong ownership by South Asian communities guarantees proper use of *Meena*. Strong emphasis has been placed on facilitated discussions with *Meena* materials at the community level. Communities used *Meena* to reflect on their attitudes, perceptions, and existing practices towards girls, and what could be done to improve their situation. Capacity building of community facilitators has also been emphasized and behavior change and behavior development strategies have strongly focused on interpersonal communication and group approaches.

What general lessons learned from the *Meena* experience might apply to other E-E interventions?

1. *Extensive qualitative and systematic formative evaluation is even more crucial when designing an effective E-E program that will be utilized in a variety of different cultures.*
2. *A cartoon character can provide a positive role model with which people from various regional cultures can identify.*
3. *Communication tools (like an E-E cartoon) can be used by a wide variety of implementing partners thereby galvanizing a process of social mobilization for a common development objective.*

Meena has come to stay in South Asia as long as she is needed to fight for the rights of children. *Meena* is a role model who is challenging while culturally acceptable; a girl who makes audiences laugh and cry.

REFERENCES

Carnegie, R., & Weisen, R. B. (2000). The ability to act: Strengthening people's life skills. In N. McKee, E. Manoncourt, Chin S. Y. & R. Carnegie (Eds.), *Involving people, evolving behaviour* (pp. 121–154). New York: UNICEF, Penang, Malaysia: Southbound.

McKee, N., Manoncourt, E., Chin. S. Y., & Carnegie, R. (Eds.) (2000). *Involving people, evolving behaviour*. New York: UNICEF; Penang, Malaysia: Southbound.

McBean, G., & McKee, N. (1996). The animated film in development communication. In J. Greene & D. Reber (Eds.), *Drawing insight: Communicating development through animation*, (pp. 10–15). New York: UNICEF, Penang, Malaysia: Southbound.

UNICEF (1990). *First call for children: Convention on the rights of the child.* New York: UNICEF.

UNICEF (2002, May 28). A proposal for *Meena's* sustainability, Regional Office for South Asia. Kathmandu, Nepal.

UNICEF (2001, December). *Meeting "Meena": Documentation study on utilisation of MCI.* Kathmandu, Nepal: UNICEF Regional Office for South Asia.

United Nations (1979). *Convention to elimination of all forms of discrimination against women (CEDAW).* New York.

19

Air Cover and Ground Mobilization: Integrating Entertainment-Education Broadcasts With Community Listening and Service Delivery in India[1]

Arvind Singhal
Devendra Sharma
Ohio University

Michael J. Papa
Central Michigan University

Kim Witte
Johns Hopkins University and Michigan State University

"We listen to each episode of Taru. *We then discuss the episode's content in our listeners' club. Through the medium of* Taru, *we are learning lots of new things, and I am trying to incorporate many of them in my life to make it better. After listening to this radio serial, we have taken decisions to wipe*

[1] We thank the following individuals and organizations for their collaboration, support, and conduct of the present research project: David Andrews and Kate Randolph of Population Communications International (PCI), New York; Gopi Gopalakrishnan, Arisingh Dutt, Shejo Bose, Neelam Vachani, Sourov Chowdhury, Pankaj Kumar Singh, Gopa Chatterji, Akhilesh Kumar Sharma, and Sushil Kumar of Janani in Patna, India (some of these individuals have moved from Janani since our collaboration); Karuna Shrivastav, Dr. Alka Kumar, and Kamal Dutt of All India Radio; Pandit Ram Dayal Sharma of Brij Lok Madhuri; Mrs. Usha Bhasin of Doordarshan; P.N. Vasanti, Mumtaz Ahmed, Chetna Verma, Alok Shrivastav, Alee Sinha, and the team of field researchers at the Centre for Media Studies, New Delhi, India. This research was supported by a grant from PCI to Ohio

*out the caste discrimination in our village, teach dalit (lower caste) children,
and to pursue higher education."*
                              —Vandana Kumari, a 17 year-old member of Village Kamtaul's
                              Taru listeners club, Bihar State, India, in a personal interview,
                                                                      September 2, 2002.

The young woman quoted above listens regularly to the radio serial, *Taru*,
broadcast by All India Radio (AIR), the Indian national radio network. Her
father, Shailendra Singh, is a rural health practitioner (RHP) in Kamtaul Village
in Bihar State, and a respected public figure (in summer 2002 he was elected a
Ward Commissioner). Singh's health clinic is called a *Titly* (Butterfly[2]) Center,
and is part of a network of 20,000 rural health practitioners, organized by
Janani, a nongovernmental organization that promotes reproductive health
care services in the poor Indian States of Bihar, Jharkhand, Madhya Pradesh,
and Chattisgarh. These four States have a population of 190 million people;
the highest fertility, infant mortality, and maternal death rates in India; and
the lowest literacy and contraceptive prevalence rates.[3]

In 1999 Shailendra Singh and his wife, Sunita, underwent a three-day course
in reproductive health care, first-aid, maternal and child health, and diagnosis
and treatment of STIs/RTIs (sexually transmitted infections and reproductive
tract infections) at a Janani training facility in Patna. Janani purposely invited
both Singh and his wife for training as most rural Indian woman are embarrassed to seek reproductive health services from a male RHP. Now, with a
trained woman health practitioner Sunita (referred by village women as *Didi*
or "sister"), female villagers could discuss sex, seek prenatal and antenatal
care, and access contraceptives. After registering in Janani's rural health network, Singh's clinic in Kamtaul Village began to stock Janani's branded *Mithun*
("Bull") condoms, *Apsara* ("Angel") oral contraceptive pills, and pregnancy
dipsticks.

In February 2002 Singh and Sunita's health practice in Kamtaul Village
became the center of a novel experiment in entertainment-education radio
broadcasting, when All India Radio, in cooperation with Population Communications International (PCI), New York, broadcast an entertainment-education
radio soap opera *Taru* (the name of the program's female protagonist) in four
Hindi-speaking states: Bihar, Jharkand, Madhya Pradesh, and Chhatisgarh.[4] All

---

University. A version of the present paper was presented to the International Communication
Association, San Diego, 2003.

[2]Rural health practitioners often call on patients in their homes, like a butterfly that goes
from flower to flower. Hence, the label *Titly* (Butterfly) Center.

[3]Together, the States of Bihar and Jharkhand have a population of 102 million, an annual
per capita income of $101 (the lowest of any State in India), a total fertility rate (TFR) of 3.5, a
contraceptive prevalence rate of 24%, and only 32% literacy.

[4]From May 2002 onwards, *Taru* began its year-long broadcasts in the other Hindi-speaking
States of Rajasthan, Uttar Pradesh, Uttaranchal, Himachal Pradesh, Delhi, and Haryana.

India Radio and PCI's ground-based partner in these four Indian states was Janani. Preprogram publicity for *Taru* was conducted on-the-air by All India Radio and, on-the-ground, *Taru* was publicized by Janani's 20,000 strong network of RHPs (like Singh and Sunita), *Taru* posters (Photo 19.1), and over 700 strategically placed wall paintings at major highway intersections (Photo 19.2) (Singhal & Rogers, 2003).

In four villages in Bihar State, selected carefully to fulfill certain criteria (detailed later), folk performances dramatizing the *Taru* storyline were carried out (led by one of the present authors, Sharma) a week prior to the radio serial's broadcasts to prime the message reception environment. Shailendra Singh's Kamtaul Village was one such site for the folk performances. Singh and his wife Sunita spread word-of-mouth messages about the folk performance, encouraging hundreds of people to attend, and awarded transistors (with a sticker of *Taru's* logo) to groups who correctly answered questions based on the folk performance. These groups were then formalized as *Taru* radio listening clubs. Each group received an attractive notebook (with a *Taru* logo), and were encouraged and urged to discuss the social themes addressed in *Taru*, relate them to their personal circumstances, and record any decisions, or actions, they took as a result of being exposed to Taru.

RHP Shailendra Singh's daughter, Vandana, her younger sister, a cousin, and two friends formed the young women's listening club in Kamtaul Village. A *Taru* fever has since raged in the Singh household. Discussions of *Taru* inspired the Singh family to undertake several new initiatives: They stopped a child marriage in Kamtaul Village, launched an adult literacy program for *dalit* (low-caste) village women, and have facilitated the participation of dalits in community events. Further, since *Taru* began broadcasting, Singh's monthly sales of Mithun condoms and Apsara pills have jumped 400%.[5]

What explains such ground-breaking social changes as are occurring in Kamtaul Village? The present chapter argues that synergistic possibilities for social action can emerge when entertainment-education radio broadcasts are strategically integrated with community-based group listening and locally available health care services. Social transformation was catalyzed when (1) All India Radio provided the entertainment-education "air cover" in the form of *Taru*, (2) *Taru* listening groups acted as informal organizing units for social deliberation and local action, and (3) Janani's rural health network provided the ground-based service delivery. Each component complemented the contributions of the other.

In the present chapter we provide a historical background on the *Taru* Project, a description of its on-the-air and on-the-ground components, and the radio serial's storyline. Our methodology for assessing the impacts of

---

[5]In the month of February 2002, when *Taru* began broadcasting, Singh sold 22 pieces of Mithun condoms, seven cycles of Apsara pills, and no pregnancy dipsticks. In August, 2002, Singh sold 90 pieces of Mithun condoms, 30 cycles of Apsara pills, and five pregnancy dipsticks.

PHOTO 19.1.   Shailendra, the rural medical practitioner in Village Kamtaul,
standing next to a *Taru* poster. Shailendra is an avid listener to *Taru*. He inter-
vened in a child marriage in the village, and works tirelessly to remove caste-
based inequities in his village. (*Source*: Personal file of the authors. Photograph
by Arvind Singhal.)

PHOTO 19.2.   A 15 feet by 8 feet wall-painting on the Patna-Muzzafarpur Highway, promoting the broadcasts of *Taru*, and the rural medical practitioner network of Janani. This painting contains the logo for *Taru*, an announcement
about the time and day of broadcast of *Taru*, and the name of the sponsor,
Janani's Titly Center. Some 700 such wall paintings were placed in strategic
locations in Bihar State prior to broadcasting *Taru*. (*Source*: Personal file of
authors. Photograph by Arvind Singhal.)

Taru is described, including the use of video testimony and participatory
photography. We then present the results from our community-based study
in certain select villages of Bihar State, explaining the process through which
community members enact system-level changes as a result of exposure to
Taru. We investigate the power dynamics, the resistances, and the audience members' struggles in the process of media-stimulated change, a process involving parasocial interaction, peer communication, and collective
efficacy.

HISTORICAL BACKGROUND: FROM
TINKA TO *TARU*

The inspiration for the *Taru* Project came from a previous community-based
investigation of the impacts of *Tinka Tinka Sukh* (Happiness Lies in Small
Pleasures), a radio soap opera, in Lutsaan Village of North India. In January
1997, 184 villagers in Lutsaan signed a pledge not to give, or accept, dowry (an
illegal but widespread social practice in India). These villagers also pledged to

not allow child marriages (also an illegal but common practice), and pledged to educate daughters equally with their sons (Papa, Singhal, Law, Pant, Sood, Rogers, and Shefner-Rogers, 2000). The petition, in the form of a colorful 20 by 24 inch poster-letter, was mailed by Lutsaan villagers to All India Radio, which was broadcasting *Tinka Tinka Sukh*. In the radio program, a young women, Poonam, is abused by her husband and his parents for bringing an inadequate dowry, until she commits suicide.

The poster-letter stated: "Listeners of our village [to *Tinka Tinka Sukh*] now actively oppose the practice of dowry—they neither give nor receive dowry." A young tailor in the village was especially influenced by the radio program episodes about dowry and initiated the process of writing the poster-letter among the people in his tailor shop. As a result of the forces set in motion by the tailor, the villagers formed radio listening clubs, planted trees for reforestation, and built pit latrines for improving village sanitation. Girls' enrollment in the village's schools increased from 10% at the time of the radio broadcasts to 38% two years later. Fewer dowry marriages and child marriages occurred in Lutsaan, although these practices did not disappear completely in the village (Papa et al., 2000).

Authors Singhal and Papa (with editor Everett M. Rogers) conducted an in depth case study of the empowerment process in Lutsaan over several years (Singhal & Rogers, 1999; Papa et al., 2000). The Lutsaan case study sug- gested entertainment-education interventions have their strongest effects on audience behavior change when messages stimulate reflection, debate, and interpersonal communication about the educational topic among audience members (Papa et al., 2000), and when services can be delivered locally. These insights from Lutsaan were applied in formulating the *Taru* Project, which included a partnership with a ground-based service delivery organi- zation, Janani; preprogram publicity of *Taru* through Janani's extensive RHP network; and the establishment of listeners' groups to encourage peer-based conversations.

Radio Listening Clubs

The idea of broadcasting to listening groups is not new. In 1956 India was the site of the famous Pune Radio Farm Forum Project, which was a field experiment to evaluate the effects of radio farm forums, each consisting of several dozen villagers who gathered weekly to listen to a half-hour radio program (broadcast by All India Radio) and then to discuss its contents (Kivlin, Roy, Fliegel, & Sen, 1968). The theme of the radio forums was "Listen, Discuss, Act!" One of the radio broadcasts might deal with rodents as a problem. Following discussion of this topic in a radio forum, villagers would mount a rat-control campaign in their community.

The research evaluation showed that the Pune radio farm forums helped to "unify villagers around common decisions and common actions," widening "the influence of the *gram panchayat* [village government] and broadening the scope of its action" (Mathur & Neurath, 1959, p. 101). The farm forums spurred discussions among villagers, leading to decisions about digging wells, adopting purebred bulls and Leghorn chickens, and establishing *balwadis* (children's enrichment centers) (Singhal & Rogers, 2001). At the village level, the radio forums acted like voluntary organizations "whose members were neither appointed by authority nor elected to represent specific group interests," signifying an important experiment in village democracy (Mathur & Neurath, 1959, p. 101). Members voluntarily engaged in village clean-up drives, planting papaya trees, and building pit latrines.

THE *TARU* PROJECT

Taru was a 52-episode entertainment-education radio soap opera, broadcast in India from February 2002 to February 2003. Its purpose was to promote gender equality, small family size, reproductive health, caste and communal harmony, and community development. *Taru* began broadcasting in Bihar, Jharkhand, Madhya Pradesh, and Chattisgarh States in India on February 22, 2002 (and later in the entire Hindi-speaking belt of North India from May 2002). One episode was broadcast each week on Friday at 8:00 p.m., with a repeat broadcast each Sunday at 3:40 p.m. Each episode of *Taru* began with a theme song and a brief summary of the previous episode. Each episode ended with an epilogue that posed a question to the listeners, inviting them to write in their responses to AIR. Half way through the *Taru* broadcasts (in October 2002), Kiran Bedi, a well-known woman police officer in India and a social activist, hosted two interaction programs with *Taru's* listeners, answering questions on the air.

The idea of integrating on-air entertainment-education broadcasts with ground-based listening and service delivery was floated in September 2000, in a New York-based meeting between David Andrews and Kate Randolph of Population Communications International; Gopi Gopalakrishnan, Arisingh Dutt, and Shejo Bose of Janani; and author Singhal of Ohio University.[6] As a first step, PCI hired MODE, an India-based research organization, to conduct a literature review and site-based formative research (in Bihar and Madhya Pradesh States) to distill the educational issues to be addressed in *Taru*. In the next 17 months the *Taru* Project progressed rapidly as roles and responsibilities of the partners were defined.

PCI looked after the overall management of the *Taru* Project: It provided the technical assistance for creating the radio serial, sponsored a visit for half-a-dozen members of All India Radio's creative team to Bihar State to gain

---

[6]PCI President David Andrews and Janani's President Gopi Gopalakrishnan had met a year or two prior to this 2000 meeting, and had discussed possibilities of working together.

familiarity with Janani's program, and hosted a workshop with the AIR creative team to design a blueprint for the radio serial. Ohio University (1) designed the Project's theoretical framework for integrating *Taru's* on-the-air and on-the-ground activities, (2) carried out a pretest of *Taru's* pilot episodes in collaboration with the Centre for Media Studies (CMS), New Delhi, and (3) implemented the summative research evaluation plan (detailed later) for the present project in collaboration with CMS. Janani sponsored the broadcasts of *Taru* in the four states, worked with Ogilvy Outreach, a Bombay-based advertising and PR agency, to develop a logo for *Taru* as well as the preprogram publicity materials (posters, stickers, flyers, and wall paintings), distributed these materials to RHPs, and provided logistical support to (a) Brij Lok Madhuri to conduct the *Taru* folk performances, and (b) to Ohio University and the Centre for Media Studies to conduct the field-based research in Bihar State. All India Radio was responsible for producing the radio serial, broadcasting it, and for inviting and collecting listeners' feedback.

Orchestrating Audiences Through Folk Performances

The ground-based prepublicity for *Taru* included the performance of a folk play, patterned after the storyline of *Taru*. The purpose of these folk performances was to generate buzz about *Taru* prior to its broadcasts, to distribute publicity material, and to establish listening groups. Usually mass media programs face an audience lag, the time needed to build a sizeable and dedicated audience (Singhal & Rogers, 1999). Preprogram publicity and the ground-based orchestration through folk performances helped shorten this audience lag for *Taru*.

Folk performances were conducted in four villages—Kamtaul, Madhopur, Chandrahatti, and Abirpur—each drawing an audience of 600 to 800 people (Photo 19.3). Devendra Sharma⁻ (one of the present authors) scripted the *Taru* folk performance in the *nautanki*[8] genre, using a *nat* and *nati* (male and female narrators) to engage the audiences. A song in the *Alha* folk format introduced the themes and characters of *Taru*. The folk performance was customized to the local Bihar milieu (including use of local colloquial expressions, costumes, and props) in a two-day workshop with members of Rangkarm, a local theater group in Patna. Rangkarm, which included a dozen actors, actresses, and instrumentalists, collaborated with author Sharma, Janani officials, and RHPs to organize and stage the folk performance in the four locations. Audience members were goaded to listen to *Taru* themselves and

---

⁻Sharma is also Creative Director of Brij Lok Madhuri, an organization dedicated to using Indian folk forms for social change.

[8]A popular folk theater form of North India.

PHOTO 19.3. Some 800 people from eight neighboring villages gathered near Abirpur Village to watch a folk performance about *Taru*, prior to the broadcast of the radio soap opera. The purpose of the folk performance was to stimulate interest in listening to *Taru*, to form listening clubs, hand out listeners' diaries to members of the listening clubs, and to distribute *Taru* posters, stickers, and pamphlets to prime message reception. (*Source*: Personal files of authors. Photograph by Devendra Sharma.)

to encourage others to tune in, and the dates and times of broadcasts were repeated several times.

After the performances, four listening groups were formed in each of the four villages, including (1) a young female listener group (Photo 19.4), (2) a young male listener group, (3) an adult female listener group, and (4) a family listener group. Each listening group had six to eight members. Each group received an attractive diary to record their impressions of the radio serial and summarize their conversations, decisions, and actions.

Taru's Story

The story of the radio serial revolves around Taru, a young, educated woman who works in Suhagpur village's Sheetal Center (patterned after Janani's Titly center), an organization that provides reproductive health care services and carries out village self-help activities. Taru is idealistic, intelligent, and polite, and works to empower rural women. Taru is a close friend of Shashikant, who like Taru, is educated, intelligent, and involved in social work at the Sheetal Center. He belongs to a lower caste and is subject to discrimination by the high caste people in the village. Taru likes him for his sincerity, and he, in turn, is supportive of Taru's ameliorative efforts. While there is an undercurrent of romance between the two, they have not yet explicitly expressed it, given that Shashikant is mindful of his lower caste status (Taru belongs to an upper caste family).

Taru's mother, Yashoda, is highly supportive of her daughter, whom she sees as an embodiment of her own unaccomplished dreams. On the other hand, Mangla, Taru's rogue brother, derides Taru's social work, and ridicules her friendship with the lower-caste Shashikant. With the help of Aloni Baba (a village saint) and Guruji (a teacher), Taru and Shashikant fight multiple social evils in a series of intersecting storylines, including preventing a child marriage and encouraging girls to be treated on par with boys.

A subplot involves Naresh, his wife Nirmala, his sister Ranjana, his mother Ramdulari, and his four daughters. Ramdulari insists on a fifth child, arguing for the importance of having a grandson. Nirmala uses contraception to avoid an unwanted pregnancy, and as the story evolves, Ramdulari undergoes a change of heart and starts valuing her granddaughters.

Another subplot involves Neha, a close friend of Taru, who is newly married to Kapileshwar, the son of the local *zamindar* (landlord). Kapileshwar starts out as a controlling husband, restricting Neha's mobility outside of the home. But Neha wants to lead a meaningful life and begins a school for dalit (low-caste) children. Kapileshwar undergoes a change of heart, and becomes highly supportive of Neha's activities, despite criticism from his parents (Table 19.1).

PHOTO 19.4. (Left to right) Usha Kumari, Sunita Kumari, and Kumari Neha, members of the Abirpur young women's listening club, who regularly listen to *Taru* on the transistor radio that they won in the quiz competition following the *Taru* folk performance in their village. (*Source*: Personal files of the authors. Photograph by Arvind Singhal.)

TABLE 19.1
The Main Characters of *Taru*

Name	Characterization
Taru	The lovable young woman protagonist who works at the Sheetal Center, an NGO promoting reproductive health services and self-help activities in the village. While she belongs to an upper caste, she is a very close friend of Shashikant, her colleague, who is of a lower caste. She is a positive role model for gender and caste equality.
Shashikant	The young, dignified, educated male protagonist who works with Taru at the Sheetal Center. Though of a lower caste, he is a staunch supporter of women's rights, and an organizer (with Taru) of village self-help activities.
Neha	Taru's friend and supporter. An educated woman who is married to Kapileshwar, Neha faces resistance from her husband and in-laws for her village-based initiatives, including teaching underprivileged low-caste village children. But she persists and inspires others.
Kapileshwar	Neha's husband. Initially, he played the role of a male chauvinist and a traditional upper caste individual who looked down upon lower-caste people. With time, he begins to support his wife and her initiatives.
Aloni Baba	A respected religious person in the village. He speaks out against social ills, including giving and taking dowry, early marriage of girls, and discrimination between girl and boy children. He supports Taru and Shashikant in their endeavors against child marriage, promotion of small family size norm, and the education of girls.
Guruji	A friend and follower of Aloni Baba. A light-hearted, humorous person who uses the local Bihari dialect to reinforce Aloni Baba's message.
Mangla	Taru's brother, a loud mouth, and a negative role model. He does not like Taru's involvement at the Sheetal Center nor her friendship with the low-caste Shashikant. He is always looking for ways to foment trouble.
Ramdulari	An old traditional village woman, who is Naresh's mother and Nirmala's mother-in-law. She has four granddaughters and initially longs for a grandson. As the story develops, Ramdulari's behavior toward her granddaughters becomes more compassionate and she no longer desires a grandson.
Nirmala	Ramdulari's daughter-in-law, Naresh's wife, and mother of four daughters. She loves her daughters and believes that they are as precious as are boys. She uses contraceptives to avoid becoming pregnant, even though her mother-in-law wants her to have at least one boy.
Phirki Chachi	The middle-aged village gossip and busybody, who incites and creates trouble.
Ranjana	Naresh's sister and Nirmala's sister-in-law. Taru and Shashikant help her to stand on her own feet through self-employment.

RESEARCHING *TARU*

Our research on *Taru* is guided by methodological triangulation, the use of multiple research methods (both quantitative and qualitative) to measure the same phenomenon. While the present chapter relies primarily on data collected from a community case study of Village Abirpur in Vaishali District of Bihar State, and from our observations of Village Kamtaul, Madhopur, and Chandrahatti (where a high degree of field orchestration, including folk performances, was conducted) in Bihar's Muzaffarpur District, other forms of data were collected to deepen our understanding of how *Taru* influenced its audience: (1) personal interviews with key officials involved in the production of *Taru*, including its executive producer, director, and writers; (2) a pre-post random sample survey of 1,500 respondents each, including both listeners and nonlisteners, in a sentinel research site in Begusarai District, Bihar State, India; (3) a pre-during-post, four-group, panel design quasi-experiment study to gauge the additive effects of the influence of (a) field orchestration activities such as folk performances, establishment of listening groups, and diary recordings; (b) preprogram publicity of *Taru* through posters, stickers, and flyers by the RHPs, and (c) reproductive health service delivery through the presence of a Titly Center RHP and his spouse; (4) a content analysis of a sample of listeners' letters in response to *Taru*; (5) a content analysis of the educational themes and character portrayals in the 52 episodes of *Taru*; (6) monthly collection of point-of-referral data on the sales of condoms, pills, and pregnancy dipsticks from Titly Centers in our research sites; and (7) a longitudinal design of five rapid surveys to assess the degree of audience exposure to *Taru*, conducted at two-month intervals during the broadcasts of *Taru*.

Taru's Listenership

Our five rounds of rapid exposure assessment surveys conducted in 2002 suggest that *Taru* is regularly listened to in 10 to 15% of all households in Begusarai District, our sentinel research site in Bihar (Table 19.2). While realizing the problems associated with estimating State-level population estimates from district-level sentinel site sample surveys, an extrapolation of these numbers suggests that *Taru* may have a listenership of between 20 to 25 million people in the four Indian States of Bihar, Madhya Pradesh, Jharkhand, and Chattisgarh, whose combined population is about 190 million people. If these lisenership numbers for *Taru* hold in other Indian States (where *Taru* began broadcasting in May 2002), the listenership of Taru in the entire Hindi-speaking region of North India, which has a total population of 625 million people, may range from 60 to 75 million people.

TABLE 19.2

Longitudinal Assessment Through Four Rapid Random Surveys in Begusarai
District of Bihar State to Gauge (1) Listenership to *Taru*, (2) Listeners'
Perceptions of Similarity of *Taru*'s Characters to Them, and (3) Listeners'
Intentions to Change Their Behaviors as a Result of Listening to *Taru*

Assessment Dimension	Rapid Survey 1* April, 2002 (N = 369)	Rapid Survey 2 June, 2002 (N = 457)	Rapid Survey 3 September, 2002 (N = 521)	Rapid Survey 4 November, 2002 (N = 371)
Percent of *Taru* listeners in surveyed households	15%	10%	12%	13%
Listeners' perceptions of how similar *Taru*'s characters are to them	30%	48%	37%	45%
Liseners' intentions to change their behaviors as a result of listening to *Taru*	61%	80%	50%	83%

*Note. Broadcasts of *Taru* began in late-February 2002 and ended in February 2003. The
rapid surveys were conducted regularly at two-month intervals.

Community Case-Study and Field Observations

In Village Abirbur, CMS researchers and the present authors made eight
rounds of visits in 2002, spending about 40 person days. Another round
of visits, of roughly 20 person days, occurred in early March 2003, soon
after *Taru's* final broadcast. In September 2002, accompanied by author
Singhal, CMS researchers conducted 16 in-depth interviews and three focus
group interviews (with 28 respondents) with *Taru* listeners in Abirpur,
and five in-depth interviews in Village Kamtaul, including RHP Shailendra,
his wife Sunita, and their daughter Vandana. These interviews were audiotaped and transcribed from Hindi into English. Our team members also
investigated examples of individual and social change reported by villagers in
Kamtaul, Madhopur, and Chandrahatti, spending a total of 10 person days in
these sites in 2002. Various techniques of data collection were employed
including participant-observation, note-taking, and photo and video documentation.

Methodological Innovations in *Taru* Project

The *Taru* Project employed various methodological innovations in the conduct of entertainment-education research.

Video Testimony

We conducted video documentation of the *Taru* project, a new methodological approach in entertainment-education. Audiotaped testimonies privilege the spoken and written word but fail to capture the affective, nonverbal, and spatial domains of listeners' responses. For instance, audiotapes, or their transcribed text, cannot capture the emotions of poor *dalit* village women, who, for the first time in their life, are learning to read and write. Nor can textual descriptions fully capture the open-air atmosphere of a village school, or the enthusiasm of the young men and women who established it.

In conceptualizing the *Taru* Project, we envisaged our role (and responsibility) as being more than simply summarizing and interpreting the views of the "others." We provided our respondents a means to speak for themselves, in their own space, accompanied by such emotions as joy, anger, frustration, and resolve. Under the guidance of one of the present authors (Singhal), and the field-based leadership of coauthor (Sharma), 21 oral testimonies of *Taru* listeners were videotaped in Abirpur, Kamtaul, Madhopur, and Chandrahatti villages in December 2002. Some 14 hours of video were recorded, including shots of listeners' group discussions after listening to a *Taru* episode, and activities undertaken (such as the adult literacy program in Kamtaul Village). Careful about not just privileging the voice of men or the social elite, which can happen in E-E program evaluations, our video testimonies consciously focused on the voices of poor women, the most "muted" social group in Bihar.

A paragraph from author Sharma's field notes (of December 15, 2002) during the video documentation process is illustrative: "During our video shoot in Abirpur, Soni, a young girl of 15 years and a member of a *Taru* listener's group invited me hesitantly to her house for a meal. As I went inside, I saw that her mother was cooking on a *chulha* (mud stove). Her house—made of mud, reed, and husk—was in a dilapidated condition. With great courage and resolve, Soni told me (on film) that her father was unemployed and that they could hardly make ends meet.... What struck me most was that even with a large family to look after [Soni has four brothers and sisters], and difficult financial circumstance, Soni and her mother were fiercely proud and dignified. I remember the poignancy of the moment when I shot the interview of Soni's mother in their *aangan* [an open space in the house usually surrounded by rooms], with the burning *chulha* serving as the only source of light, while Soni served dinner to me and her siblings. Soni and her mother said on tape: "When Taru and her mother Yashoda can fight harsh circumstances in the radio serial, why can't we?"

Participatory Photography

To gauge the influence of *Taru* on audience members, we employed participatory photography, drawing inspiration from the work of Paulo Freire (1970) and Augusto Boal (1979), who argued for handing over the means of production to the people. As opposed to asking people questions, and thereby constraining the nature and scope of their word responses, we handed out eight disposable cameras to *Taru* listeners in Abirpur, Kamtaul, Madhopur, and Chandrahatti, and asked them to capture *Taru's* influence on them (or their community) through the language of images.

Our participatory photography method was inspired by a Freirean literacy project in Lima, Peru, which in 1973, asked poor people certain questions in the Spanish language, but requested them to answer them by using pictures. When the question "What is exploitation?" was asked, some people took photos of a landlord, grocer, or a policeman (Boal, 1979, p. 123). One child took a picture of a nail on a wall. It made no sense to adults, but other children were in strong agreement. The ensuing discussions showed that many young boys of that neighborhood worked in the shoe-shine business. Their clients were mainly in the city, not in the barrio where they lived. As their shoe-shine boxes were too heavy for them to carry, these boys rented a nail on a wall (usually in a shop) where they could hang their boxes for the night. To them, that nail on the wall represented "exploitation."

When we asked our *Taru* listeners to "shoot back" (in images) the influence of the radio serial in their lives, we ended up with over 200 photographs.[9] Here we describe a photo from Vandana's camera, the young listener quoted on top of the chapter. The photo shows Vandana (she asked her cousin to take this picture) standing next to a young man of her age (about 17-years-old). When we asked her what the picture signified, she said: "This is my boyfriend, a boy who is a friend. He studies in my high school and we attend the same coaching class. I feel comfortable talking to him and sharing my thoughts with him. I am not shy and timid like other girls of Village Kamtaul, who feel nervous talking to boys. If Taru and Shashikant can be good friends, why can't we?" In the picture, Vandana is donning jeans, an outfit that conservative villagers regard as inappropriate. Also, perhaps for the first time in the history of Kamtaul Village, a young woman invited a young man to stand beside her and pose for a photograph. Vandana gives credit for this confidence to *Taru.*

IMPACT OF *TARU*

Our study of *Tinka Tinka Sukh* in Lutsaan Village (discussed previously) suggested that an entertainment-education program can spark the process of social change by drawing listeners' attention to socially desirable behaviors

---

[9]Author Singhal and Sharma are carrying out an in-depth study of these participatory visual responses.

(Papa et. al, 2000). When listeners develop parasocial relationships with the characters of an E-E program, they may be motivated to consider changes in their own behavior. E-E programs can stimulate peer conversations among listeners, which can create opportunities for collective efficacy to emerge as people consider new patterns of thought and behavior. However, existing power structures resist the process of social change, and people's own thinking is fraught with paradoxes and contradictions as they "negotiate" their actions with their intentions. Was there evidence for these processes in the villages of Bihar, where our present investigation of *Taru* was based?

Parasocial Interaction With *Taru*

Parasocial relationships are the seemingly face-to-face interpersonal relationships which can develop between a viewer and a mass media personality (Horton & Wohl, 1956). The media consumer forms a relationship with a performer that is analogous to the real interpersonal relationships that people have in a primary face-to-face group (Papa et al., 2000; Perse & Rubin, 1989; Rubin & Perse, 1987; Sood & Rogers, 2000). Horton and Wohl (1956) argued that when a parasocial relationship is established, the media consumer appreciates the values and motives of the media character, often viewing him or her as a counselor, comforter, and model. Rubin and Perse (1987) argued that parasocial interaction consists of three audience dimensions: cognitive, affective, and behavioral.

Cognitively oriented parasocial interaction is the degree to which audience members pay careful attention to the characters in a media message and think about its educational content after their exposure (Papa et al., 2000; Sood & Rogers, 2000). Such reflection on the educational themes can help media consumers recognize that they could make different behavioral choices in their personal lives. Bandura's concept of self-efficacy (Bandura, 1997) is linked to behavior change that a person considers and/or enacts. *Self-efficacy* is an individual's perceptions of his/her capacity to deal effectively with a situation, and to control this situation (Bandura, 1995). For example, after receiving messages from an entertainment-education program, is a person persuaded that they have the ability to change their behavior in a socially desirable way?

In Village Kamtaul, RHP Shailendra Singh noted how listening to *Taru* motivated him to intervene in a delicate situation: "We have applied the learnings of *Taru* in real life. Just as Taru and Shashikant prevent a girl child marriage in the radio serial, we also stopped a child marriage from occurring in Kamtaul. We politely said that this was wrong, and concerned people came around and changed their decision" (personal interview, August 19, 2002).

Sunita, Singh's wife, greatly admired Neha, a friend of Taru in the radio serial, who establishes a school to educate dalit (low-caste) children. Sunita

PHOTO 19.5.   Sunita (standing right), the wife of RHP Shailendra Singh, who was inspired by Neha (a friend of Taru) in the radio serial, to begin an adult literacy class for lower-caste women in Kamtaul Village. (*Source*: Personal files of the authors. Photograph by Devendra Sharma.)

launched adult literacy classes for 20 lower caste women in Kamtaul's Harijan Tola (the lower-caste settlement) (Photo 19.5). It is highly uncommon in an Indian rural setting for a high-caste woman to interact with women of lower castes. "If Neha could do it, so could I," Sunita noted.

Ratneshwar, the younger brother of the RHP in Village Madhopur, also wished to start a school but did not feel efficacious to do so. After listening to *Taru* and particularly being influenced by characters like Shashikant, Taru, and Neha, he was able to realize his dreams: "I really enjoy teaching children. After listening to *Taru*, I turned this dream into reality." Ratneshwar's School, which meets in front of the Titly Center, is attended by 25 to 30 children aged 10 to 12 years. Ratneshwar charges a minimum admission fee.

Affectively oriented parasocial interaction is the degree to which an audience member identifies with a particular media character, and believes that his/her interests are joined (Burke, 1945). The stronger the identification, the more likely that character's behavior will affect the audience member. Soni in Village Abirpur exemplified this identification: "I love Taru. She is so nice. I also like Shashikant. When Taru is sad, Shashikant makes her laugh. When

Taru is sad, I am sad. When Mangla asks her to not see Shashikant, and Taru feels bad, I feel bad." Audience members view their favorite characters as close personal friends, and become emotionally upset when certain characters face difficult personal situations.

The affective identification may be so strong that audience members adjust their daily schedules to listen to the radio program to maintain an ongoing relationship with their favorite characters. As Dhurandhar Maharaj, a male listener in Abirpur Village, noted: "Every Friday at 8 p.m. I have to be close to my radio. It's like meeting friends." For some audience members, the identification with a character may be so high that they cannot distinguish the fictional character from the actor. For instance, Kumari Neha, a member of the young women's listener group in Abirpur said: "I wish Taru could come to our village. She is so sweet and polite. If I learn so much from hearing her voice, what will she do to me when I see her in person." Neha identifies so strongly with Taru that she cannot make the distinction between the "reel" Taru and the real Taru.

Behaviorally oriented parasocial interaction is the degree to which individuals overtly react to media characters, for instance, by "talking" to these characters, or by conversing with other audience members about them. Such conversations may influence audience members' thinking about an educational issue and motivate them to change their behavior in a specific way. The centrality of interpersonal or group interaction to behavior change has been documented by various researchers (Auwal & Singhal, 1992; Papa, Auwal, & Singhal, 1995, 1997; Rogers & Kincaid, 1981). The present study, however, draws attention to a specific type of interpersonal communication that creates opportunities for collective efficacy (discussed later in the present chapter).

Katz, Liebes, and Berko (1992) argued that parasocial interaction can prompt referential involvement on the part of audience members. Referential involvement is the degree to which an individual relates a media message to his/her personal experiences (Papa et al., 2000; Sood & Rogers, 2000). Before audience members consider behavior change as a result of observing or listening to a media character, they must be able to relate the experiences of the character to their own personal lives. If a connection cannot be made between the lives of a character and the experiences of an audience member, behavior change would certainly seem less likely for that individual.

Usha Kumari, a college girl in Abirpur, is indebted to *Taru* for making her strong and inspiring her to implement her dreams: "There are many moments when I feel that Taru is directly talking to me. Usually at night. She is telling me 'Usha you can follow your dreams.' I feel she [Taru] is like my elder sister . . . and giving me encouragement. I thank her for being with me" (personal conversation, September 4, 2002). Usha's uncle, Manoj Maharaj, is Abirpur's village RHP and treats villagers for minor ailments. Usha was fascinated by the sight of her uncle giving injections and dreamed that one day she would be able to serve her people's health needs. However, it was difficult to implement as the movement of young, unmarried women is considered inappropriate in her village. Impressed with the boldness of Taru to fight social obstacles, Usha went through an important change in her personal life: "Previously I lacked in self-confidence, but I have slowly gotten out of my shell. I am learning how to administer medication, including injections and saline drips, from my uncle" (personal communication, September 4, 2002). Usha estimated that between June to August, 2002 (a three-month time-period), she administered over 200 injections.

Many young women listeners of *Taru* say they are "transformed." Meenakshi, a 16-year-old listeners' group member in Madhopur, talked "on camera" in front of her parents about the importance of using a condom to protect oneself from HIV infection. She also mentioned that she would encourage her partner to use condoms when appropriate. Meenakshi noted: "I learned this information about HIV/AIDS from the episodes of *Taru*. After listening to these episodes, I took a decision that I will discuss how to protect oneself from AIDS with my friends and family members." Meenakshi's desire to openly discus information on sex-related topics in Madhopur Village is remarkable, given that such topics are taboo.

In sum, exposure to *Taru* led to parasocial interaction between certain audience members and characters in the soap opera. How did these parasocial relationships prompt peer conversations among listeners?

Social Learning Through Peer Conversations

Our data provide numerous examples of how *Taru* stimulated conversations among listeners, creating a social learning environment for social change. Social learning is particularly important in entertainment-education because the intention of E-E message designers is to change audience members' perceptions and behaviors by providing audience members with examples of behaviors that are socially desirable or undesirable (Bandura, 1977, 1997). The characters are designed to be appealing or unappealing to audience members. Involvement with these characters often prompts discussions among audience members concerning the socially desirable behaviors promoted by an entertainment-education program.

Soni Kumari, a member of the young women's listening club in Kamtaul Village, noted: "Almost 50% of the girls in our High School [out of a total of 300] listen to *Taru*. In fact, we have even painted a wall in our school to promote the listening to *Taru*. Every Monday in School, during the break, we meet to discuss the previously broadcast episode." Vandana Kumari, another listening group member, pointed to a specific result that came out of these discussion: "We discussed in school what to do for our friend.... She was only 16 when her parents got her married. She stopped coming to school.

We knew she was staying at home. One day, when we saw her father coming to our school, we spoke to our teacher and asked him to convince her father to not keep his daughter at home. Now she has resumed her classes.... She will continue to study until she goes to her husband's home in a year or two."

Kumari Neha, a listening group member in Abirpur Village, noted: "Our discussions of *Taru* have given us strength and confidence. Now I am not shy of speaking in front of my parents. Taru taught us that one should always speak sweetly and politely. When you mean well, who can oppose you? Even the devil will melt. We have all told our parents that we will like to go to college, and we will not marry in a household which demands dowry" (personal communication, September 5, 2002).

In Kamtaul Village, family-based conversations between RHP Shailendra Singh, his wife Sunita, and their two younger daughters and niece (the latter three are members of the young women's listening club) have led to a debunking of several traditional practices that humiliated lower-caste villagers. For instance, when Vandana's elder sister got married in June 2002 (four months after *Taru* had begun its broadcast), Singh purposely invited the village's "untouchables" to attend the wedding. Some of the lower-caste people helped with the wedding arrangements and some even served drinks to the guests. Singh noted: "Several people refused[10] the drink, but most people accepted. I made sure that the servers were properly groomed and wore clean clothes. For those who confronted me later, I told them that I am a 'doctor' and my profession does not allow me to discriminate" (personal conversation, September 2, 2002).

Audience members can share their similar and different perceptions of the information presented in the media program. They can talk about considering or adopting the socially desirable behaviors that are highlighted in the media program. These interpersonal discussions create a social learning environment in which people learn from one another. Collective efficacy emerges when people share ideas about the social problems facing their system, and discuss ways of confronting resistance to their plans for social change.

Collective Efficacy Stimulated by *Taru*

Our data provided numerous examples of how *Taru* inspired collective efficacy and community action to solve social problems. In Abirpur Village, young female and male members of *Taru* listeners' groups, after seven months of discussion and deliberation, started a school for underprivileged children, inspired by the character of Neha in the radio serial. Some 50 children attend

---

[10]In India, many continue to believe that the touch of an "untouchable" is impure and inauspicious.

this school regularly, which meets six days a week, from 4 to 6 p.m. in the open air, under a tree near the Titly Center. Young women of 15 to 20 years of age teach these children. Young men helped convince the parents to send their children to school and help with the operational logistics. Establishing the school was a collective act of both young men and women in Abirpur. Such mixed-sex collaboration is highly uncommon in Indian villages. As Sunita Kumari noted: "Before listening to *Taru*, we were shy and uncomfortable in talking to boys. Now that we are in a group, we feel comfortable to talk to them, and we do so on an equal footing."

The rise in collective efficacy among young women listeners of *Taru* is reflected by an incident from author Sharma's video documentation visit to Bihar in December 2002. It is not common for young women to interrupt conversations among men, let alone challenge their veracity. During a male group interview, some young men claimed that, inspired by a *Taru* episode which portrayed the ills of substance abuse, they quit the habit of eating *gutkha* (chewing tobacco). But the young women, who overheard their conversation, aggressively challenged their claim: "These boys are lying. A few may have left the habit, but most of them are just saying this in order to gain fame on the video." The act of challenging the boys openly reflects the collective efficacy gained by the young women's listeners' group in Abirpur Village.

Another example from Abirpur Village demonstrates how an individual's rise in self-efficacy can subsequently spur collective action. After listening to *Taru*, Dhurandhar Maharaj, a 17-years-old Hindu male listener, questioned the caste and religion-based discrimination that was prevalent in Abirpur and decided do something about it: "When I heard Mangla [Taru's rogue brother] insult Shashikant for his low-caste, I was furious. Then I realized I myself did not mix with the Muslim students in my class. It took me two to three days to muster enough courage to sit next to Shakeel Anwar, who is Muslim. Now Shakeel is my best friend, and all his friends are my friends" (personal conversation, September 3, 2002). Dhurandhar soon realized that Shakeel's younger sister stopped going to school after the eighth grade. Her parents were reluctant to send her to the neighboring town's school without an escort. Dhurandhar, Shakeel, and their half dozen closest friends discussed this problem, and decided to take turns escorting Shakeel's sister. Once this plan was implemented, six other friends of Shakeel's sister, who also had stopped going to school for a similar reason, resumed their schooling. Dhurandhar noted: "Now they go in a group and it does not even matter if we can't escort them on certain days."

The evidence presented here shows that exposure to *Taru* stimulated interpersonal discussions about educational issues and motivated some listeners to engage in collective action to solve community problems. However, our data suggests, consistent with our previous findings of the effects of *Tinka*

Tinka Sukh in Village Lutsaan, that social change seldom flows directly and immediately from exposure to an entertainment-education media program that prompts parasocial interaction. Instead, audience individuals who are exposed to the program may create a social learning environment in which new behavior options are considered but they discover that change often proceeds in a circuitous manner. What works for a media character may not work so easily in real-life situations in which there is community resistance to new behaviors. Certain community members may develop a sense of collective efficacy in solving a social problem, but the solution they devise may not be effective. Although a person may say that they believe in performing a certain action, these beliefs may not reflect his/her actions.

Nonlinearity of Social Change: Power, Resistance, and Paradoxical Behaviors

Our data provided numerous examples of how existing power structures in the villages can serve as a barrier to social change. Individuals or groups, who wish to undertake a certain ameliorative action, often face resistance from social structures. For instance, in India, caste, gender, and class mediate the extent to which people can overcome restrictions and barriers to progress. Mumby (1997) situated such "power" as neither simply prohibitive nor productive, but recognizes it as simultaneously "enabling and constraining human thought and action" (pp. 357-358). Indeed, a number of scholars have encouraged examining discursive practices of social system members as they resist and subvert the dominant social order (Burrell, 1993; Gramsci, 1971; Mumby, 1997; Papa et al., 2000).

Both in Abirpur and Kamtaul villages, members of the young women's listeners' club criticized the caste bias of their elders, which prevented them from listening to *Taru* with other friends who belonged to another caste. Initially the young girls felt powerless to oppose these parochial traditions, however, soon they devised ways to subvert them. In Kamtaul, the young women agreed to individually hear the *Taru* episodes at home, and then later discuss them during school break. By August 2002, six months after *Taru's* broadcasts began, they felt efficacious enough to openly gather at the local Titly Center, or at someone's home, to listen collectively.

Paradox and contradiction are also an integral part of the process of social change (Papa et al., 2000). Since established patterns of thought and behavior are difficult to change, people often engage in an adjustment process until the new behavior patterns are fully internalized. For instance, Manoj Maharaj, RHP of Abirpur Village, talked at great length about how caste-based discrimination was on the ebb in Abirpur. However, in a casual conversation, Maharaj strongly supported other kinds of discrimination. When author Singhal asked him if

Abirpur Village had any people living with AIDS, he said: "There are two AIDS patients in the neighboring village. And he [despite being the sole health provider in the area], will not touch them."

Gender equality was a prominent theme throughout the episodes of *Taru*. One of the most vocal proponents of this theme in Kamtaul Village was Vandana Kumari, the young women quoted at the beginning of this chapter. When author Sharma met with her in December 2002 and asked her if she would spend her future life tending to the *chulha* (mud stove) (implying she would be a home-maker); she said: "I will not tend to the *chulha*. I will use a gas burner." Although Vandana had internalized perceptions about the importance of women to go to college and forge a career, she did not recognize that her views on using the gas burner versus the *chulha* contradicted this professed support for women as being more than homemakers.[11]

So power, resistance, and paradoxical thinking were apparent in our *Taru* research sites as people struggled with social change. *Taru* played an important role in stimulating these effects. Conversations that support behavior change are important, even if that talk is not always supported by subsequent action. As Rushton (1975, 1976) observed, words alone can exert influence on the behavior of others. Thus, a mother who talks to her daughter about gender equality may influence her daughter to further her formal education, even though the mother still acts under patriarchal dominance. For instance, Neeraj Kumari, a family listeners' group member in Abirpur Village, who plays the role of a traditional *bahu* (daughter-in-law), tending to the needs of her in-laws, husband, and two young children, noted: "My life is the way it is. But my children will marry whom they want . . . we will not give or take dowry." Gudiya, a young listener in Madhopur, said: "I don't know how life will turn out for me, but I will definitely make my daughter like Taru."

CONCLUSIONS

The *Taru* Project is intended to improve access to health services provided by rural medical practitioners in remote areas of Bihar State and to empower radio listeners in small listening groups. Our results suggest that when people organize themselves around a common purpose (in this instance, listening to a radio soap opera), the interactions help stimulate reflection, debate, and action, which may not occur for an individual listener. When individuals organize in small groups to take charge of their lives, they shift community norms, which may make the social change more sustainable.

---

[11]Weick (1979) argued that this type of paradox emerges when a person does not recognize that their ideas within one system (for example, homemaking) contradict his/her ideas within another system, such as gender equality.

In this study, we learned that E-E programs can spark processes of individual and social change through the formation of parasocial relationships between audience members and media characters. Audience members consider changes in their own behavior based on what has worked or not worked for media characters. E-E programs can also initiate a process of social learning as audience members talk among themselves and consider behavior change at the individual and collective level. Some of this social learning may inspire collective action as audience members work together to improve community life (as illustrated by the newly established open-air school in Village Abirpur).

However, individual and social change is rarely a simple, linear process. Audience members may encounter powerful forces of resistance as they attempt to change power dynamics in a community. In addition, attempts to change behavior are often fraught with paradoxes and contradictions that point to the difficulty of altering entrenched actions within complex communities. Despite these difficulties, our findings suggests that synergistic possibilities for social action emerge when entertainment-education broadcasts are integrated with community-based group listening and locally available health care services.

REFERENCES

Auwal, M. A., & Singhal, A. (1992). The diffusion of Grameen Bank in Bangladesh: Lessons learned about alleviating rural poverty. *Knowledge: Creation, Diffusion, Utilization, 14*, 7-28.

Bandura, A. (1977). *Social learning theory*. Englewood Cliffs, NJ: Prentice-Hall.

Bandura, A. (1995). Exercise of personal and collective efficacy in changing societies. In A. Bandura (Ed.), *Self-efficacy in changing societies* (pp. 1-45). New York: Cambridge University Press.

Bandura, A. (1997). *Self-efficacy: The exercise of control*. New York: Freeman.

Boal, A. (1979). *The theatre of the oppressed*. New York: Urizen Books.

Burke, K. (1945). *A grammar of motives*. Berkeley, CA: University of California Press.

Burrell, G. (1993). Eco and the bunnymen. In J. Hassard & M. Parker (Eds.), *Postmodernism and organizations* (pp. 71-82). Newbury Park, CA: Sage.

Freire, P. (1970). *Pedagogy of the oppressed*. NY: Continuum.

Gramsci, A. (1971). *Selections from the prison notebooks* (Q. Hoare & G. Nowell Smith, Trans.). New York: International.

Horton, D., & Wohl, R. R. (1956). Mass communication and parasocial interaction. *Psychiatry, 19*, 215-229.

Katz, E., Liebes, T., & Berko, L. (1992). On commuting between television fiction and real life. *Quarterly Review of Film and Video, 14*, 157-178.

Kivlin, J. E., Roy, P., Fliegel, F. C., & Sen, L. K. (1968). *Communication in India: Experiments in introducing change*. Hyderabad: National Institute of Community Development.

Mathur, J. C., & Neurath, P. (1959). *An Indian experiment in farm radio forums*. Paris: UNESCO.

Mumby, D. K. (1997). The problem of hegemony: Rereading Gramsci for organizational communication studies. *Western Journal of Communication, 61*, 343-375.

Papa, M. J., Auwal, M. A., & Singhal, A. (1995). Dialectic of control and emancipation in organizing for social change: A multitheoretic study of the Grameen Bank in Bangladesh. *Communication Theory, 5*, 189–223.

Papa, M. J., Auwal, M. A., & Singhal, A. (1997). Organizing for social change within concertive control systems: Member identification, empowerment, and the masking of discipline. *Communication Monographs, 64*, 219–250.

Papa, M. J., Singhal, A., Law, S., Pant, S., Sood, S., Rogers, E. M., & Shefner-Rogers, C.L. (2000). Entertainment-education and social change: An analysis of parasocial interaction, social learning, collective efficacy, and paradoxical communication. *Journal of Communication, 50(4)*, 31–55.

Perse, E. M., & Rubin, R. B. (1989). Attribution in social and parasocial relationships. *Communication Research, 16*, 59–77.

Rogers, E. M., & Kincaid, D. L. (1981). *Communication networks: Toward a new paradigm for research*. New York: Free Press.

Rubin, A. M., & Perse, E.M. (1987). Audience activity and soap opera involvement: A uses and effects investigation. *Human Communication Research, 14*, 246–268.

Rushton, J. P. (1975). Generosity in children: Immediate and long-term effects of modeling, preaching, and moral judgment. *Journal of Personality and Social Psychology, 31*, 459–466.

Rushton, J. P. (1976). Socialization and the altruistic behavior of children. *Psychological Bulletin, 83*, 898–913.

Singhal, A., & Rogers, E. M. (1999). *Entertainment-education: A communication strategy for social change*. Mahwah, NJ: Lawrence Erlbaum Associates.

Singhal, A., & Rogers, E. M. (2001). *India's communication revolution: From bullock carts to cyber marts*. Thousand Oaks, CA: Sage.

Singhal, A., & Rogers, E.M. (2003). *Combating AIDS: Communication strategies in action*. Thousand Oaks, CA: Sage.

Sood, S., & Rogers, E. M. (2000). Dimensions of parasocial interaction by letter-writers to a popular entertainment-education soap opera in India. *Journal of Broadcasting and Electronic Media, 44(3)*, 389–414.

Weick, K. (1979). *The social psychology of organizing* (2nd ed.). Reading, MA: Addison-Wesley.

20

Entertainment-Education Through Participatory Theater: Freirean Strategies for Empowering the Oppressed[1]

Arvind Singhal
Ohio University

"I believe that all the truly revolutionary theatrical groups should transfer to the people the means of production in the theater so that the people themselves may utilize them. The theater is a weapon... a weapon of liberation."
—Augusto Boal (1979, p. ix)

"The dramatist should not only offer pleasure but should, besides that, be a teacher of morality and a political advisor."
—Aristophanes (quoted in Boal, 1979, p. xiv)

The present chapter describes participatory theater in South Africa, Brazil, and India as a means of empowering audience individuals to lead social change. The focus on participation by oppressed individuals as a means of organizing for social change was recognized as important by scholars and practitioners of

---

[1] The present chapter draws upon Singhal (2001) and Singhal and Rogers (2003). The author thanks Professor Keyan Tomaselli, Ms. Miranda Young-Jahangeer, and Mr. Mkhonzeni Gumede of the Centre for Cultural and Media Studies, University of Natal, South Africa, for sharing experiences about the Westville's Prison Theater Project in Durban and the DramAidE Project in KwaZulu-Natal Province.

development communication since the 1990s. Here this direction is integrated with the entertainment-education strategy, for the potential benefit of both participatory communication and E-E.

In Westville Prison in Durban, South Africa, a group of Black women inmates—all convicted for murdering their partners—perform an autobiographical play for their fellow prisoners, the prison staff, and representatives of the Justice Department, the South African Gender Commission, and media journalists (Young-Jahangeer, 2002). The protagonist is an "every woman" whose husband abuses her. When she seeks her parent's help, they tell her that her husband's family paid *lobola* (bride price), and that she should put in more effort to make her marriage work. When she goes to the priest, he asks her to kneel down and pray. She goes to the police station to report her abuse. The policeman, who knows her husband from their drinking together at the *shabeen* (local pub), gives him a telephone call. The husband goes to the police station and beats her, while the policemen, silent colluders in the act, look on. Outraged and desperate, the woman hires an assassin to kill her husband. She is convicted for murder and sentenced to life imprisonment.

At the end of the play, the women stand and sing *"emhlabeni sibuthwele ubunzima"*, a traditional Zulu song of endurance. Then, one-by-one, they face the audience to recite gut-wrenching personal testimonies about their physical abuse, psychological torment, and daily victimization. The Westville Prison Theater, a project of the Department of Drama and Performance Studies at the University of Natal, is based upon Paulo Freire's (1970) liberatory pedagogy and Augusto Boal's (1979) Theater of the Oppressed (TO) to empower women who face "quadruple" oppression on account of their gender, race, class, and inmate status (Young-Jahangeer, 2002). Prison Theater is not just defined by the oppressed characteristics of its creators—poor Black women prisoners— but also by the space in which it is enacted: the prison (Barry, 2000). It gives voice to oppressed women inmates who gain in self-confidence, discover the power of social cohesion, and who use theater to question the oppressive structures underlying their present condition.

Through Prison Theater, women inmates make visible the tortuous abuse that motivated their crime, and show the gender insensitivity of the laws under which they were tried and convicted. Prison Theater influenced local police officials, judiciary, and correctional staff to revisit the sentences meted out to women inmates, and to raise awareness about the importance of making South Africa's legal and prison system more gender sensitive. Prison Theater's power lies in its participatory, emotionally engaging, and autobiographical narrative, and in its ability to connect "oppressed" and "oppressive" structures in a nonthreatening manner. Further, Prison Theater embodies a process of participation that is empowering both as a *means* (for the oppressed poor

Black women inmates) and as an *end* (in terms of the structural outcomes that are generated).

Drawing upon the principles embodied in Westville's Prison Theater, the present chapter analyzes participatory communication practices, especially participatory theater, as an alternative application of the entertainment-education strategy. The dialogic pedagogy of the noted Brazilian educator Paulo Friere is discussed, including its application by Augusto Boal in a well-known global movement called the Theater of the Oppressed (TO). TO's techniques of the spect-actor (a spectator-turned-actor), Image Theater, Forum Theater, Invisible Theater, and Legislative Theater are analyzed, followed by a discussion of participatory theater experiences in South Africa, India, and Brazil. Entertainment-education scholarship and practice can benefit by consciously incorporating dialogic, participatory processes in designing, producing, and assessing social change interventions.

PARTICIPATORY COMMUNICATION

The concept of participation is not new. Long before participation was purposefully advocated for social change, people had formed collectivities in order to farm, defend, and even destroy (Singhal, 2001). However, the discourse of participatory communication is relatively new. It gathered momentum in the 1970s, as discontent mounted with top-down and trickle-down communication approaches to social change (Jacobson, 1993; Uphoff, 1985). Participatory communication is defined as a dynamic, interactional, and transformative process of dialogue between people, groups, and institutions that enables people, both individually and collectively, to realize their full potential and be engaged in their own welfare (Singhal, 2001). All participation is communication-driven, but all communication is not participatory (Fraser & Restrepo-Estrada, 1998; White & Nair, 1999). Gumucio Dagron (2001) provided a useful typology to distinguish participatory communication from other communication strategies for social change (Table 20.1).

While participation comes in all shapes and sizes, participatory communication means working with and by the people, as opposed to working on or working for the people. At the risk of oversimplifying, one may contend that there are two major, but interrelated, approaches to participatory communication (Servaes, 1999). The first approach centers on the dialogic pedagogy of the noted Brazilian educator, Paulo Freire. The second approach, often broadly labeled as the participatory community media approach, or the alternative communication approach, centers on the ideas of access, participation, self-determination, and self-management, sharpened during the UNESCO New World Information Order debates of the 1970s. Although both sets of

TABLE 20.1

Participatory Versus Nonparticipatory Communication Strategies

Participatory Communication Strategies	*Versus*	*Nonparticipatory Communication Strategies*
Horizontal lateral communication between participants	Versus	*Vertical* top-down communication from senders to receivers
Process of dialogue and democratic participation	Versus	*Campaign* to mobilize in a short-term without building capacity
Long-term process of sustainable change	Versus	*Short-term* planning and quick-fix solutions
Collective empowerment and decision-making	Versus	*Individual* behavior change
With the community's involvement	Versus	*For* the community
Specific in content, language, and culture	Versus	*Massive* and broad-based
People's needs are the focus	Versus	*Donors' musts* are the focus
Owned by the community	Versus	*Access* determined by social political and economic factors
Consciousness-raising	Versus	*Persuasion* for short-term

Source: Gumucio Dagron (2001)

participative approaches share several commonalties, their arenas of communicative application have been somewhat distinct. For instance, the Freirean theory of dialogic communication is based more on interpersonal and group dialogue in a community setting, and hence, has found more application in the practice of community development, literacy education, participation, and transformation. The participatory community media approach focused on issues of public and community access to appropriate media, participation of people in message design and media production, and selfmanagement of communication enterprises. Its applications are thus more in community radio and television, street theater and folk media, participatory video, and community informatics, Internet, and telecenters.

Human Dignity: The Compass of Participation

For many observers, "participation" and "participatory" make sense as means. That is, with participation, projects and programs become more humane, more effective, and more sustainable (Chambers, 1999, p. 8). For others, participation is an end in itself: A set of desired processes and relationships. Whatever the mix of reasons, a new consensus has put participation at the center stage of social change initiatives during the 1990s.

While there may not be a clean way of resolving the issue of participation as means or ends, the compass of participation rests on preserving and enhancing the dignity of the individual. Nothing is more important to a participant's dignity than having the opportunity to influence his/her own future. As Saul Alinsky (1971, p. 122), an American community organizer and champion of participatory approaches, emphasized: "If you respect the dignity of the individual, you are working with his desires, not yours; his values, not yours; his ways of working and fighting, not yours; his choice of leadership, not yours; his programs, not yours."

Handouts and other forms of charity are anathema to people's participation. The government of Mexico once decided to pay tribute to Mexican mothers. A proclamation was issued that every mother whose sewing machine was being held by the Monte de Piedad (the national pawnshop of Mexico) should have her machine returned as a gift on Mother's day. There was tremendous jubilation after this announcement. Here was an outright gift without any participation on the part of the recipients. Within a few weeks, however, the same numbers of sewing machines were in the national pawn shop (Alinsky, 1971). We conclude, with Saul Alinsky, that one should never do anything for anybody that they can do for themselves.

PAULO FREIRE'S DIALOGIC PEDAGOGY[2]

Born in 1921 in Recife, in Northeastern Brazil, Paulo Freire learned lessons about hunger and desperation as an eight-year old, when his father, a state police official, lost his job. The family savings were soon gone, and other kinship safety nets were exhausted. While his father eventually found a job and Freire's middle-class existence was restored, the powerful childhood lesson from the trauma of living in poverty stayed with Freire for life.

Freire's most important career lesson came in the early 1950s when he was in charge of establishing adult literacy programs in poverty-stricken Northeastern Brazil. During an introductory seminar for illiterate and semiilliterate adults, a wage laborer, who had listened to Freire's presentation on the benefits of learning to read and write, challenged Freire to understand the "world" in which members of the audience were living. Speaking in the local vernacular, the illiterate laborer painted a highly evocative word-picture of the grinding poverty that he and his family endured, of his inability to speak like educated people, and daily struggles with domination and exploitation.

The laborer's moving story, told in his own words, influenced Freire's ideas about what education should and should not be. He realized that an educator's greatest challenge was to understand, appreciate, and respect the knowledge

---

[2]For more on Paulo Freire, see the following Web sites: http://www.paulofreire.org/; http://www.infed.org/thinkers/et-freir.htm; http://wwwvms.utexas.edu/~possible/freire.html; http://nlu.nl.edu/ace/Resources/Documents/FreireIssues.html

PHOTO 20.1.   Brazilian educator Paulo Freire, who developed pedagogical techniques to empower the oppressed. (*Source*: Personal files of the author.)

of people's lived experience as expressed in their vernacular. He also realized that politics and pedagogy were inseparable. With experimentation and experience, Freire's pedagogical methods incorporated ideas on critical reflection, dialogue and participation, autonomy, democracy, problematization, and the crucial connection between theory and practice (Freire, 1998). Freire's empowering aproach was deemed dangerous politically by Brazil's rightwing military regime, which seized control in 1964, and he was exiled for over two decades before returning to São Paulo in the mid-1980s to serve as Secretary of Education for the city of São Paulo (Photo 20.1).

Freire is best known for his classic book, *Pedagogy of the Oppressed* (Freire, 1970) in which he argued that most political, educational, and communication interventions fail because they are designed by technocrats based on their personal views of reality. They seldom take into account the perspectives of those to whom these programs are directed. Freire's dialogic pedagogy emphasized the role of "teacher as learner" and the "learner as teacher," with each learning from the other in a mutually transformative process (Freire & Faundez, 1989). The role of the outside facilitator is one of working with, and not for, the oppressed to organize them in their incessant struggle to regain their humanity (Singhal, 2001). True participation, according to Freire, does not involve a subject-object relationship, but rather a subject-subject relationship.

In Freirean pedagogy, there is no room for teaching "two plus two equals four." Such rote pedagogy, according to Freire, is dehumanizing as it views learners as empty receptacles to be "filled" with expert knowledge. Freire criticized this "banking" mode of education, in which "deposits" are made by experts. The scope of action allowed students (or intended beneficiaries) "extends only as far as receiving, filing, and storing the deposits" (Freire, 1970, p. 58). Instead, Freire advocated problem-posing as a means to represent to people what they know and think, not as a lecture, but as an involving problem. So a lesson on "two plus two" might proceed in the following dialogic manner (Singhal, 2001):

Teacher: How many chickens do you have?
Poor farmer: Two.
Teacher: How many chickens does your neighbor have?
Poor farmer: Two.
Teacher: How many chickens does the landlord have?
Poor farmer: Oh, hundreds!
Teacher: Why does he have hundreds, and you have only two?

So goes the dialogic conversation that over time stimulates a process of critical reflection and awareness ("conscientization") on the part of the poor farmer, creating possibilities of reflective action that did not exist before. Freire emphasized that the themes underlying dialogic pedagogy should resonate with people's experiences and issues of salience to them, as opposed to well-meaning but alienating rhetoric (Freire, 1998). Once the oppressed, both individually and collectively, begin to critically reflect on their social situation, possibilities arise for them to break the "culture of silence" through the articulation of discontent and action.

FREIRE IN PRACTICE: AUGUSTO BOAL'S
THEATER OF THE OPPRESSED[3]

Inspired by the writings and teachings of fellow countryman Paulo Freire, and his own experiences with dramatic performances, Brazilian theater director

---

[3]This section on Augusto Boal's Theater of the Oppressed draws upon the following Web sites: http://www.communityarts.net/readingroom/archive/boalintro.html; http://www.gn.apc.org/resurgence/issues/unwin204.htm; http://www.unomaha.edu/~pto/augusto.htm; http://cid.unomaha.edu/~pto/augusto.htm#bio

PHOTO 20.2. Augusto Boal, founder of the Theater of the Oppressed (TO), which applies Freire's principles to empower the poor, the weak, and the vulnerable. (*Source*: TOPLAB. Photo by Rashid Khoumarlou. Used with permission.)

Augusto Boal developed Theater of the Oppressed (TO), an international movement to use theater as a vehicle of participatory social change. Raised in Rio de Janeiro, Boal studied chemical engineering at Columbia University in New York, before founding the Arena Theater in Saõ Paulo in the mid-1950s (Photo 20.2). TO's techniques—based on Freirean principles of dialogue, interaction, problem-posing, reflection, and conscientization—are designed to activate spectators to take control of situations, rather than passively allowing things to happen to them.

Boal coined the term "spect-actor" for the activated spectator, the audience member who takes part in the action. How did Boal hit upon the idea of a spect-actor? In the late 1950s, when Boal was experimenting with participatory theater, audiences were invited to discuss a play at the end of the performance. In so doing, Boal realized they remained viewers and "reactors." To facilitate audience participation, Boal, in the 1960s, developed a process whereby audience members could stop a performance and suggest different actions for the actors, who would then carry out the audience suggestions. During one such performance, a woman in the audience was so outraged that the actor could not understand her suggestion that she charged onto the stage, and acted out what she meant. For Boal, this defining event marked the birth of the spect-actor (not spectator). From that day, audience members were invited onto the stage. Thus, passive spectators are changed into actors who become transformers of the dramatic action. Spectators delegate no power to the actor (or character) either to act or think in their place (Boal, 1979). Rather, spectators assume a protagonist role, change the dramatic action, try out various solutions, discuss plans for change, and train themselves for social action in the real world.

The Theater of the Oppressed is a form of popular, participatory, and democratic theater of, by, and for people engaged in a struggle for liberation. Drawing upon Freire's principles, Boal's theater is necessarily political. Its main purpose is to make the unequal equal and the unjust just. Boal argued that most people are hesitant to take political action because of "cops in their heads," that is, their fear of oppressors. So Boal developed a series of theatrical "cops-in-the-head" exercises to ferret out internalized oppression (Boal, 1992). Through TO, the "cops in peoples' heads" are identified, and strategies for overcoming these fears are charted.

TO is basically a form of rehearsal theater designed for people who want to learn ways of fighting against oppression in their daily lives. The theatrical act by itself is a conscious intervention, a rehearsal for social action based on a collective analysis of shared problems of oppression (Boal, 1979). Boal hit upon the idea of theater as a rehearsal for action by accident. Once afternoon, in the early 1960s, Boal presented the struggle of Brazilian peasants in a theatrical piece using fake guns as props. When the show ended, the peasants came to Boal and said: "That was a great idea! Where are the rifles?! Let's go! You said that we were going to take over!" (http://www.communityarts.net/readingroom/archive/boalintro.html). They thought Boal was serious about starting a revolution. Boal realized that theater was not only a portrayal of revolution, but also represented a rehearsal for revolution.

PARTICIPATORY THEATRICAL TECHNIQUES

Theater of the Oppressed utilizes the following key forms: (1) Image Theater, (2) Forum Theater, (3) Invisible Theater, and (4) Legislative Theater.

#1. Image Theater

Boal believed that the means of producing theater is the human body, which is the source of sound as well as movement (Boal, 1979). To control the means of theatrical production means to control the human body. Through body control, a spectator (or passive observer) becomes an active protagonist. According to Boal (1979), human beings are so conditioned to expression through words that their bodies' expressive capabilities are underdeveloped. Boal's TO techniques include over 200 exercises and games for participants to get to know their bodies, including their possibilities and limitations (Boal, 1992). Exercises are designed to "undo" the participants' muscular structures, and to raise consciousness about how one's body structure embodies an ideology. For instance, when a peasant is called upon to act as a landlord, or a worker to act as a factory owner, or a woman to act as a policeman, not only do their physical bearings change, but their postures reflect the ideology associated with their new roles.

In Boal's technique of Image Theater, participants are allowed only to use their bodies to portray realities. No words are allowed. Image Theater begins with an arrangement of human bodies on a stage in several poses, with various facial expressions, and using different props in order to denote a certain prevailing reality—for instance, exploitation. Participants are then asked to portray an ideal image by reconfiguring the human bodies, their expressions, and the surrounding props. Finally, participants are challenged to portray a transitional image by once again reconfiguring the human bodies, their expressions, and the props. In essence, participants are challenged to think through how to move from a prevailing reality to an ideal image. Various options are tried, discussed, and refined. Boal argued that the power of Image Theater lies in "making thought visible" (Boal, 1979, p. 137). By avoiding the idiom of language, communicative problems associated with denotative and connotative meanings, and encoding and decoding losses, are overcome.

#2. Forum Theater

Forum Theater is a theatrical game in which a problem is shown in an unsolved form to which the audience is invited to suggest, and act out, solutions (Boal, 1992, p. xxi). Forum Theater begins with the enactment of a scene in which a protagonist (played by an actor) tries, unsuccessfully, to overcome oppression relevant to that particular audience. The joker[4] (master of ceremonies) then invites the spectators to replace the protagonist at any point in the scene where they believe an alternative action could lead to a solution. Anyone can propose a solution, but it must be done on stage. The scene is replayed numerous times with different interventions from different spectators. This

---

[4]The joker is the director/master of ceremonies in a performance. For instance, in Forum Theatre, the joker sets up the rules of the event for the audience, facilitates the spectators' replacement of the protagonist, and sums up the essence of each solution proposed in the interventions. The term derives from the joker (or wild card) in a deck of playing cards. Just as the wild card is not tied to a specific suit or value, neither is the TO joker tied to an allegiance to any one performer, spectator, or interpretation of events.

results in a dialogue about the oppression, an examination of alternatives, and a rehearsal for real solutions (Boal, 1979).

For example, in the early 1970s, in Chimbote, a fishing port in Peru, Boal's technique of Forum Theater was used by workers in a fish meal factory to combat ruthless exploitation by the factory owner. Factory workers, in their role as spect-actors, suggested several solutions to address the oppression. The first suggestion was "Operation Turtle," that is, the workers would slow down their production; the second suggestion was to "speed up," that is, the workers would work faster in order to overload the machinery so that they could rest while it was being fixed; a third suggestion was to bomb the factory; a fourth suggestion was to go on strike (Boal, 1979). The merits of each of these suggestions were discussed, rehearsed, and all were deemed implausible. Finally, someone suggested that the workers should form a union. After a long period of deliberation, including rehearsing the union's role, this suggestion was deemed plausible.

Why were the previous suggestions discarded by the spect-actors? When the suggestion of bombing the factory was discussed, the workers realized that it would destroy their source of work. How would the bomb be manufactured? By whom? When the suggestion about going on strike was discussed, workers realized that the factory owner could easily go to the local town square and recruit other unemployed workers. Forming a workers union to gain collective bargaining power with the factory management provided them with the most appropriate means to achieve their goal.

In Forum Theater no idea is imposed. The audience has an opportunity to try out all their ideas, to rehearse all possibilities, and to verify them in theatrical practice (Boal, 1979). Forum Theater provides a way to examine all possible paths, serving as a rehearsal for practice. In so doing, it evokes the desire on part of spect-actors to practice in reality the act that they rehearsed in theater.

El Extensionista

One of the coeditors of this book (Rogers) participated in a TO play in Mexico City in 1980 presented by *El Teatro Campesino* (Peasant Theater). An agricultural extension agent gradually realizes that the main problem of the village farmers with whom he is assigned to work is not their use of technologies leading to greater cotton production. Instead, the farmers are being underpaid for their production, so that they are unable to get out of debt. The extension agent then helps the farmers organize a cooperative to oppose the wealthy businessmen who are exploiting them. The coop is effective in gaining higher market prices for the poor farmers' cotton, and they begin to attack other pressing problems. The businessmen hire an assassin to murder the extensionista, the agricultural change agent, and plant rumors among the cooperative members.

At this point, the actors on stage halt their performance, sit down at the front of the stage, and ask the audience how they would finish the action. Some audience members voted for realism, insisting that the elites will continue to dominate the poor farmers. But most audience individuals demanded that the farmers, now empowered, would continue to organize against economic domination. Some members from the audience jumped on stage to join the actors in showing this scene. Others in the audience criticized their performance, and demanded further changes. Discussion and participation continued for several hours.

#3. Invisible Theater

Invisible Theater is a rehearsed sequence of events that is enacted in a public, nontheatrical space with the explicit goal of capturing the attention of onlookers who do not know they are watching a planned performance. Its goal is to bring attention to a social problem for the purpose of stimulating public dialogue. Actors take responsibility for the consequences of the "show."

Invisible Theater is both theater and real life, for although rehearsed, it happens in real time and space (Boal, 1979). It can be enacted in a restaurant, on a sidewalk, in a market, on a train, or with a line of people waiting at a bus stop. Invisible theater suddenly erupts in a place where people naturally congregate. For instance, in 1973, in a 400-person restaurant in a well-known hotel in Chiclayo, Peru,[5] a protagonist actor ordered an expensive barbecue of 70 *soles*, loudly complained about its poor quality, and when confronted by the waiter with the bill remarked: "I am going to pay for it, but I am broke. . . . So I will pay for it with labor power" (Boal, 1979, p.145). While the headwaiter was summoned, the rising din of the waiter-protagonist interaction began to catch the attention of patrons sitting in neighboring tables. When the headwaiter arrived, the protagonist offered to pay for the barbecue by working as a garbage thrower. When he asked how much money the garbage thrower in the restaurant made, a fellow actor, sitting at a neighboring table, said: "Seven *soles* per hour." The protagonist then exclaimed: "If I work as a garbage man, I'll have to work ten hours to pay for this barbecue, which took me ten minutes to eat. It can't be! Either you increase the salary of the garbage man, or reduce the price of the barbecue" (Boal, 1979, p. 145). Other actors, sitting in neighboring tables joined in the "public" dialogue, making visible the exploitation of the poor in affluent settings.

In Invisible Theater, while people go about their daily lives, an issue is made into a public scene. Boal knew that while people ordinarily do not want to

---

[5]This Invisible Theater performance was part of a Paulo Freire-inspired literacy program conducted in Peru in the early 1970s.

get involved, they are always looking from the corner of their eye. By seeing a public "spectacle," people are forced to think about it. The onlookers almost always side with the oppressed, not the oppressor (Boal, 1979).

#4. Legislative Theater

Boal, like Freire, was tortured and exiled for his cultural activism by the military dictatorship that governed Brazil for two decades. Both returned to Brazil in 1984 with the return to civil society, and became active in public service: Boal served as Mayor of Rio de Janeiro in the early 1990s, whereas Paulo Freire was the Secretary of Education in the city of Sao Paulo. Boal used theater to assess and solve people's problems. Members of his Center for the Theater of the Oppressed (CTO) went on neighborhood streets, asking people to portray the problems that they wished to change. One change involved getting the telephone booths lowered for disabled individuals.

Boal used theatre as a participatory political tool to make new laws, labeling this technique "Legislative Theater" (Boal, 1998). As Boal (quoted in http://www.gn.apc.org/resurgence/issues/unwin204.htm) noted:

> CTO worked with nineteen groups of oppressed people. They would do plays about social problems, discuss with their own communities, and dialogue with other communities.... Out of these activities many legislative proposals came to my office. We had what we called the metabolizing cell, which was a group of actors and also lawyers. They would transform all the suggestions into proposals for new laws. I would present those proposals in the chamber like any other legislator. But the proposals for legislation would come not out of my head, but from the people.
>
> I presented 42 different proposals for new laws, 13 of which were approved. Thirteen laws that are now in existence in Rio are ones which were proposed by the population.... For instance, in Rio we passed the first Brazilian law to protect witnesses of crimes. It is a very comprehensive law that includes physical protection, includes the transference of witnesses from the place where they live to another place where they are more secure, to be given a new identity during the period of danger.

Boal's Theater of the Oppressed, including its many formats—such as Image Theater, Forum Theater, Invisible Theater, and Legislative Theater, are directly rooted in the pedagogical and political principles espoused by Paulo Freire: The situation lived by the participants should be understood, including its root causes, and changing the situation should follow the precepts of social justice (Freire, 1970). Boal deserves tremendous credit for taking the principles of Friere's dialogic pedagogy, and enhancing it with his own wide-ranging experiences in theater, to create an engaging "poetics of the oppressed." Boal considered Freire to be his supreme teacher.

When Freire died of a heart attack in 1997, Boal said: "I am very sad. I have lost my last father. Now all I have are brothers and sisters" (Boal quoted in http://www.goucher.edu/library/wilpf/boal_bio.htm).

PARTICIPATORY THEATER: SERVING THE OPPRESSED

TO's techniques have been used by thousands of drama troupes over the world, and by community organizers and facilitators as participatory tools for democratizing organizations, analyzing social problems, and transforming reality through direct action.[6] TO's many disciples and variants are known variously as agit prop ("agitation propaganda"), radical, alternative, and people's theater. Well-known examples include the Community Theatre Movement in Nicaragua, which in the 1970s effectively combined elements of theater, music, and dance to raise the political consciousness of *campesinos* (farmers), eventually overthrowing President Anastasia Somoza, Nicaragua's long-ruling dictator. In the Philippines, the People's Theater Network, a grassroots theater movement composed of over 300 regional groups, created a new breed of performing artists: the ATOR, the actor, trainer, organizer, and researcher. In South Africa, Protest Theater by the politically disenfranchised made visible how apartheid victimized Black people (Loots, 1997).

Here we discuss applications of Freire's dialogic pedagogy, Boal's TO techniques, including their home-grown reinventions in three countries, located on three continents: South Africa, India, and Brazil.

Drama AIDS Education in South Africa

DramAidE, short for Drama AIDS Education, is a university-based[7] nongovernmental organization (NGO) that uses Freire's (1970) and Boal's (1979) participatory theatrical methods and other interactive, nonjudgmental, and culturally sensitive educational methodologies to train students, teachers, nurses,

---

[6]In the United States, the Theater of the Oppressed Laboratory (TOPLAB) was founded in New York City in 1990 to provide a forum for the practice, performance, and dissemination of the techniques of TO. TOPLAB conducts on-site training workshops on theater as an organizing tool for activists in neighborhood, labor, peace, human rights, youth, and community-based organizations. Its trainees used interactive theater to analyze and explore solutions to problems of oppression and power that arise in the workplace, school, and community problems connected to AIDS, substance abuse, family violence, homelessness, unemployment, racism, and sexism. TO techniques are also taught at the University of Omaha, at the Headlines Theater in Vancouver, and at the Mandala Center in Seattle, Washington.

[7]DramAidE is a collaborative venture of the University of Zululand and the University of Natal, Durban, South Africa.

caregivers, and members of churches and community-based organizations in HIV/AIDS prevention, care, and support (DramAidE, 2001). It works primarily in KwaZulu-Natal Province of South Africa, where some 35% of people in the age group 15 to 49 are HIV-positive. By 2002 DramAidE initiated participatory plays, workshops, and community events in over 1,000 secondary schools in KwaZulu-Natal Province, using locally expressive forms such as drama, songs, dances, and poems. DramAidE looks at health holistically, promoting among the youth a sense of pride in their bodies, and generating in them a positive self-image, self-esteem, and self-confidence (Dalrymple, 1996).

DramAidE's school-based program involves community education, plus lifeskills education targeted at secondary school students. First a DramAidE team of actor-teachers stages an AIDS play in front of the entire school. The play is followed by an intense, interactive question-and-answer session; and the students and teachers are challenged by DramAidE officials to create plays to reflect their own vulnerability to HIV/AIDS, including ways to prevent it (Dalrymple, 1996). Drama workshops are held for students and teachers that include group discussions, role-playing, and teamwork; as also, self-evaluations of the risk of contracting HIV, and culturally acceptable strategies to address these problems. The DramAidE program culminates with an "Open Day," a community event in which students perform an HIV/AIDS play for their parents, teachers, local leaders, and people living with AIDS (PWAs). In a cultural context where sex is "doable" but "untalkable," and where there is no parent-to-child or teacher-to-student communication about sex, the "Open Day" brings sexual taboos into the open (Dalrymple, 1996). Through the medium of play, students feel free talking about hitherto sensitive topics such as masturbation or *ukusoma* (nonpenetrative "thigh sex"). The HIV/AIDS play is part of an all-day event which includes prayers; speeches by local leaders, headmasters, and headmistresses; and traditional Zulu songs and dances (Photo 20.3).

The goal of the DramAidE intervention in secondary schools of KwaZulu-Natal Province is to create, in a Freirean sense, a generation of "sexual subjects," who can regulate their sexual life, as opposed to being objects of desire and the sexual scripts of others (Paiva, 2000). To create sexual subjects, DramAidE's theater workshops are holistic and participatory, emphasizing improvisations and role plays and allowing participants to rehearse different presentations of the self (Sutherland, 2002). For instance, drawing upon Boal's work, a tableau in a drama workshop may show a picture of a fierce, proud Zulu man holding a stick in his hand (Dalrymple, 1996). Behind him is a woman carrying a heavy load on her head and a baby on her back. Participants are asked to react to the picture, encouraged to change it, and provide reasons for the change. The ensuing discussion, initially, centers on the need for the man to have his hands free to protect his family; however, later the discussion moves to talking about the importance of the couple sharing the

PHOTO 20.3.   Secondary school students in KwaZulu-Natal Province, South
Africa, perform an HIV/AIDS play for other students, parents, teachers, and
community leaders as part of DramAidE project's open day celebrations.
(*Source*: DramAidE. Used with permission.)

burden, including responsibilities for child care. Some participants may suggest that the man and the woman need to walk side-by-side, holding each
other's hand. DramAidE's workshops are designed to stimulate critical thinking among young people, and empower the youth to learn, rehearse, and take
actions to practice healthy behaviors. The gumboot dance, usually done only
by men, is performed by both male and female students during the Open Day
celebrations.

DramAidE's focus is not just on changing individual behavior of students
through participatory theater, but also to influence the existing social norms of
the community about HIV/AIDS, including those of parents, teachers, church
leaders, nurses, caregivers, and local officials. DramAidE's participatory interventions seek to catalyze a social movement of healthy lifestyles, which has
room for both sexual restraint and abstinence, as well as a window to celebrate
sexual healthy passions. Participating schools often initiate, at the encouragement of DramAidE officials, health promotion clubs, which establish programs
for cleaning toilets, disposing of unhygienic waste, and ensuring a clean drinking water supply. Several of these youth-initiated clubs raised their own funds
to purchase toilet paper, disinfectants, and gloves (Sutherland, 2002).

An evaluation of DramAidE's school-based interventions showed that participating students, including members of health promotion clubs, were less

likely to engage in risky sexual behavior, more likely to behave like empowered "subjects" (as opposed to powerless "objects"), and more likely to practice behaviors that reflect gender-role equality (Sutherland, 2002). School
teachers unanimously praised the participatory, experiential, entertaining,
and engaging methodology employed by DramAidE: "DramAidE's approach
is very good because it comes in the form of a game. . . . We as educators are
lacking in using dramatization, plays, and music . . . whereas the learners are
entertained by them" (Sutherland, 2002, p. 34).

Theater for Empowerment in India[8]

Several theater groups in India use participatory approaches to raise consciousness about oppression and to empower the exploited. For instance, the
late Safdar Hashmi's *Jan Natya Manch* (People's Theater Forum) is a street
theater group that conducts plays for the poor who live in urban slums. These
plays include *Gaon Se Shahar Tak* (From Village to City), a story about a small
farmer who lost his land and is forced to become an industrial worker in a
city; *Hatyaare* (Killers) on communalism; *Aurat* (Woman), a play that deals
with bride burning, dowry, and wife-beating; and *Machine* which deals with
capitalist oppression of the working class. During a performance of *Halla
Bol* (Attack), a play about the Indian government's repression of the labor
movement, Hashmi was beaten to death (Bharucha, 1990). Hashmi's life and
his tragic death show the power of participatory theater in challenging the
established order, and in seeking a more just future for the oppressed. It also
shows that such activism often comes with high personal risks.

Another well-known street theater personality in India is Badal Sircar, a
town-planner- turned-activist who pioneered the "Third Theater" movement
in India. Sircar's plays are designed to conscientize an urban audience about
exploitation in rural India, and to empower rural audiences to take more control of their destiny (Dutta, 1983). For instance, Sircar's play *Bhoma* dealt
with the oppressive plight of wood-cutters in the Sundarbans forest region
in Bengal. Like Boal, Sircar's theatrical style debunks the notion of a passive
audience that views and hears from a distance. Instead, the audience's role is
defined by a "stirring within" and "experiencing." Four-way communication
is fostered in Sircar's performances: from performers to spectators, performers to performers, spectators to performers, and from spectators to spectators
(Dutta, 1983).

In India's Tamil Nadu State, Nalamdana (meaning "Are You Well?" in Tamil)
is a street theater group that implements entertainment-education interventions dealing with various aspects of health: HIV/AIDS, maternal and child

---

[8]The section on Badal Sircar draws upon a Web-site on Indian street theater: http://www.
indiaprofile.com/religion-culture/streettheatre.htm

health (MCH), children's rights, suicide prevention, cancer, and women's empowerment (Singhal & Rogers, 2003). A typical Nalamdana presentation takes place in the evening, in the open air of a village square or an urban slum, with several thousand audience members sitting on the ground. The performance takes place on an improvised stage, with blankets and cloths draped as a backdrop. Before the play begins, the actors announce that five individuals will be invited from the audience after the show to answer questions about the educational content. An interactive theatrical performance on HIV/AIDS is followed by questions about the means of HIV transmission. The two-hour show ends with an announcement giving the address and telephone number of nearby HIV testing and counseling centers, and brochures are distributed.

The following day, the Nalamdana actors return to the same location for a series of small group "workshops" about the educational theme of the previous evening's show, in order to obtain feedback from audience members about the drama. Thus the scripts for the Nalamdana shows are continually being rewritten, with inputs from the audience members who participate in the day-after postmortems. The Nalamdana acting troupe members are constantly learning from their audiences about what they like and dislike, and their other reactions to the dramas. The Nalamdana actors say that they see their main role as conducting research, rather than just as acting. The continuing exchange with audience members keeps the acting fresh, and prevents burnout of the actors. Nalamdana prefers street theater to television or film, because this format allows the direct exchange of ideas with audience members. Over the past nine years, Nalamdana estimates that their street theater audiences total over a million people, mainly composed of audiences in urban slums and rural areas, with little formal education (those most in need of Nalamdana's HIV prevention message).

Audience members are highly involved in the street theater. From the stage, the audience looks like "a sea of eyeballs," says R. Jeevanandham, project manager of the Nalamdana group. The actors estimate that their typical drama is about 25% education and 75% entertainment. If Nalamdana goes too heavily on the education side, they lose the involvement of their village audiences.

A scholarly journal article reporting an evaluation of Nalamdana's dramas says that they are particularly effective in correcting misconceptions about HIV/AIDS (Valente & Bharath, 1999). For instance, when a sample of the audience was asked whether mosquito bites could transmit HIV (they cannot), the rate of correct answers increased from 42% at pretest (before the performance) to 98% at posttest. Individuals with the lowest levels of formal education increased their knowledge of HIV transmission the most, as the result of Nalamdana's show. Self-reported attitudes toward people living with HIV/AIDS improved, showing that the Nalamdana drama decreased stigma.

In short, Nalamdana provides an engaging way to behavior change communication about HIV prevention, and reaches those individuals who need it most.

A Pedagogy of Prevention in Brazil

In 1990 Vera Paiva, a psychologist at the University of São Paulo and an expert in HIV/AIDS and gender issues, used Paulo Freire's participatory approach and Pichon Reviere's group process methodology to involve students and teachers in the low-income schools of São Paulo City in HIV/AIDS prevention. Based on a deep understanding of the sociocultural dimension of risk, the goal of the intervention was to create "sexual subjects" (much like the aim of the DramAidE project in South Africa, discussed previously). A sexual subject is one who engages consciously in a negotiated sexual relationship based on cultural norms for gender relations, who was capable of articulating and practicing safe sexual practices with pleasure, in a consensual way, and who is capable of saying "no" to sex.[9]

In collaboration with students, teachers, and community members, Paiva developed a pedagogy of HIV prevention which sought to stimulate collective action and response from those directly affected by HIV, and who live in a vulnerable context (Singhal & Rogers, 2003). Face-to-face group interaction with girls and boys pointed to the importance of understanding the role of sexual subjects in various "sexual scenes," composed of the gender-power relationship between participants, their degree of affective involvement, the nature of the moment, the place, sexual norms in the culture, racial and class mores, and others (Paiva, 1995). Words such as AIDS, *camisinha* ("little shirts" or condoms), and others were decoded, and participants proposed new words and codes for naming the body and gender rules, thus generating new realities.

Paiva employed a variety of creative, engaging, and dramatic techniques to help participants formulate a pedagogy of prevention: group discussions, role-playing, psychodrama, team work, homework, molding flour and salt paste to shape reproductive body parts and genitals, games to make condoms erotic, and art with condoms (to be comfortable in touching them with one's bare hands). To break inhibitions during role-plays, a "pillow" was placed in the middle of the room, symbolizing a sexual "subject." For example, the pillow could represent an "in-the-closet" gay or a lesbian, a virgin schoolgirl, or a bisexual schoolboy. Participants could adopt the pillow to have internal discussions with the subject, experience themselves in the place of the other,

---

[9]Vera Paiva (1995, 2000) also used Freirean methods to launch community and school-based HIV prevention programs in Sao Paulo, Brazil.

or understand their own fantasy. The pillow provided a vehicle to speak out through an imaginary character, while preserving individual privacy (Paiva, 1995).

Group processes showed that sexual inhibitions could be broken in the context of *sacanagem* (sexual mischief), accompanied by exaggerated sexual talk and eroticization of the context (Paiva, 1995). Condoms became easily discussable when both the boy and the girl were ready to "loosen the hinges of the bed," or "turnover the car," while engaging in sex. Thus the pedagogy of prevention was based on an "eroticization" of prevention.

Evaluation of Paiva's project were not based on counting the number of condoms used; but on the progress made by students, teachers, and community members in becoming "sexual subjects." They were collectively empowered to make choices, and to act them out in culturally appropriate ways.

Participatory Mass Media E-E in Brazil

A strong participatory movement in the state of Ceará in Brazil in 1997 brought artists from all walks of life to join hands against AIDS. It illustrates an integration of mass media E-E with participatory approaches. This movement is the brainchild of Ranulfo Cardoso, Jr., who was greatly influenced by Paulo Freire's participatory strategy and by Augusto Boal's Theater of the Oppressed. Beginning in Fortaleza, the capital of Ceará State, and supported by funds from the MacArthur Foundation, the *Bricantes Contra a AIDS* (Street Artists Against AIDS) Project trained hundreds of artists in developing emotionally powerful scripts on HIV prevention, care, and support, and performing them in schools, prisons, and street markets. Cordel, a popular, rhyming, storytelling folk form in Brazil's Northeast, was coopted for this movement. The most effective theater scripts were turned into entertainment-education *radionovelas* (radio soap operas), launching another movement called *Radialistas Contra a AIDS* (Radio Broadcasters Against AIDS). The most popular radio soap opera, *Radionovela da Camisinha* (Radio Soap Opera Condom) is broadcast in Ceará and in other states of Brazil.

Ceará's participatory experiences in using theater, art, and radio to promote HIV prevention and to reduce AIDS-related stigma has spread to artists from eight Brazilian States, including Rio de Janeiro, Bahia, Pernabuco, and others. The use of participatory theater, local folk media forms, and radio, which reaches 90% of the low-income population in Brazil, represents an innovative integration of E-E approaches to HIV prevention (Singhal & Rogers, 2003).

CONCLUSIONS

Most past entertainment-education interventions have utilized mass media vehicles (television, radio, films, video, or comic books) to tackle issues of development and social change. Seldom are such media-centered E-E interventions designed, owned, and operated by the people themselves. E-E programs, like most literacy programs, are designed and implemented by experts for a "target" audience, leaving little room for the dynamic dialogic pedagogy espoused by Paulo Freire and Augusto Boal. The one-way nature of mass media interventions, as also the desire of development officials to reach large audiences, relegates the relatively smaller-reach theater-based interventions to the sidelines of most development programs.

The present chapter argued for more consciously adding participatory theatrical practices to the entertainment-education arsenal. The dialogic pedagogy of Paulo Freire and Augusto Boal's Theater of the Oppressed techniques (for example, the "spect-actor") transform entertainment-education interventions from being a one-way "monologue" into a two-way "dialogue" between audience and actors. Mass media-based E-E initiatives should work hand-in-hand with engaging participatory theater initiatives, each supplementing the other.

As the field of entertainment-education continues to evolve, grow, and reinvent itself, participatory strategies for empowering the underdogs will increasingly find a more central place in the E-E discourse. Perhaps other entertainment-education interventions could incorporate elements of the participatory approaches described in this chapter, moving spectators to become spect-actors.

REFERENCES

Alinsky, S. D. (1971). *Rules for Radicals*. NY: Vintage Books.

Barry, E. M. (2000). Women's prisoners on the cutting edge: Development of the activist prisoners' rights movement. *Journal of Crime, Conflict, and World Order, 27*(3), 22–28.

Bharucha, R. (1990). Letter to the dead. *Theater, 14*, 6–9.

Boal, A. (1979). *The theatre of the oppressed*. New York: Urizen Books.

Boal, A. (1992). *Games for actors and nonactors*. New York: Routledge Press.

Boal, A. (1998). *Legislative theatre*. New York: Routledge Press.

Chambers, R. (1999). Foreword. In S. A. White (Ed.). *The art of facilitating participation* (pp. 8–10). New Delhi: Sage.

Dalrymple, L. (1996). The use of traditional forms in community education. *Africa Media Review, 11*, 75–91.

DramAidE (2001). *Annual report. 2000/2001*. Kwadlangezwa, South Africa: DramAidE Office, University of Zululand.

Dutta, E. (1983). Introduction. In B. Sircar, *Three plays* (pp. 1–4). Calcutta: Seagull Books.

Fraser, C., & Restrepo-Estrada, S. (1998). *Communicating for development: Human change for survival*. New York: I.B.Tauris.

Freire, P. (1970). *Pedagogy of the oppressed*. NY: Continuum.

Freire, P. (1998). *Teachers as cultural workers: Letters to those who dare to teach*. Boulder, CO: Westview Press.

Freire, P., & Faundez, A. (1989). *Learning to question: A pedagogy of liberation*. Geneva; World Council of Churches.

Gumucio Dagron, A. (2001). *Making waves: Stories of participatory communication for social change*. New York: Rockefeller Foundation.

Jacobson, T. L. (1993). A pragmatist account of participatory communication research for national development. *Communication Theory, 3*(3): 214-230.

Loots, L. (1997). Remembering protest theater in South Africa. *Critical Arts, 11*, 142-152.

Paiva, V. (1995). Sexuality, AIDS, and gender norms among Brazilian teenagers. In Han ten Brummelheis and Gilbert Herdt (Eds.), *Culture and sexual risk: Anthropological perspectives on AIDS* (pp. 79-96). Amsterdam, Netherlands: Gordon & Breach.

Paiva, V. (2000). *Fazendo arte com a camisinha: Sexualidades jovens em tempos de AIDS*. São Paulo: Summus Editorial.

Picher, M. (nd). What is the Theater of the Oppressed? http://www.toplab.org/whatis.htm.

Servaes, J. (1999). *Communication for development: One world, multiple cultures*. Cresskill, NJ: Hampton Press.

Singhal, A. (2001). *Facilitating community participation through communication*. New York, NY: UNICEF.

Singhal, A., & Rogers, E. M. (1999). *Entertainment-education: A communication strategy for social change*. Mahwah, NJ: Lawrence Erlbaum Associates.

Singhal, A., & Rogers, E. M. (2003). *Combating AIDS: Communication strategies in action*. Thousand Oaks, CA: Sage.

Sutherland, L. (2002). *DramAidE RBM project: Evaluation report*. Durban, South Africa: DramAidE Office, University of Natal.

Uphoff, N. (1985). Fitting projects to people. In Cernea, M. M. (ED.) (1985). *Putting people first: Sociological variables in rural development* (pp. 369-378). Oxford, UK: Oxford University Press.

White, S. A., & Nair, K. S. (1999). The catalyst communicator: Facilitation without fear. In S. A. White (Ed.) *The art of facilitating participation* (pp. 35-51). New Delhi: Sage.

Young-Jehangeer, M. (2002, May). *Working from the inside/out: Drama as activism in Westville female prison*. Paper presented to the International Conference on Convergence: Technology, Culture, and Social Impacts, University of Natal, Durban, South Africa.

Valente, T. W., & Bharath, U. (1999). An evaluation of the use of drama to communicate HIV/AIDS information. *AIDS Education and Prevention, 11*(3), 203-211.

21

Soap Operas and Sense-Making: Mediations and Audience Ethnography

Thomas Tufte
University of Copenhagen

Theoretical approaches to entertainment-education (E-E) and actual communication strategies using E-E interventions have, in recent years, experienced substantial developments in how scholars and practitioners conceive, design, monitor, and assess E-E (Singhal & Rogers, 2002). The present chapter addresses a particular issue that requires further reflection and conceptual clarification, which is how best to assess E-E interventions. How can we improve our understanding of the audience's sense-making processes? Sense-making is the production of meaning which is articulated by the audience on the basis of their viewing of a specific television program or genre, in this case the viewing of soap operas. How do we identify which social and cultural processes an E-E intervention articulates? How can we improve our measurement of the social and cultural impacts of E-E interventions? A theoretical-methodological approach to the analysis of audience sense-making is proposed, suggesting new ways of evaluating how E-E interventions influence their audiences.

This chapter suggests that the theory of mediation advocated by Colombian scholar Jesus Martin-Barbero (1993; Martin-Barbero & Munoz, 1992) can be used productively to increase understanding of the processes of audience sense-making, and to improve our understanding of the dynamic relationship between media, culture, and everyday life. Martin-Barbero's works help us

399

understand the role of melodrama, soap operas, and entertainment in general in the everyday life of people. Martin-Barbero defined mediation as the articulations between communication practices and social movements and the articulation of different tempos of development with the plurality of cultural matrices (Martin-Barbero, 1993). Mediations are the set of influences that structure, organize, and reorganize the understanding of the reality that an audience lives. Mediation is the process in which sense is made in the communication process. Martin-Barbero's communication analysis becomes less media-centric, placing the media in the broader context of cultural activities. His theory fits with British cultural studies of the past 20 years.

The proposed methodology for evaluating how audiences make sense of E-E programs is audience ethnography. Audience ethnography has developed within the tradition of qualitative audience studies, and has increasingly been used in studies of how audiences make sense of soap operas (Hobson, 1982; Kottak, 1990; La Pastina, 1999; Leal, 1986; Tufte, 1995, 2000). In this chapter, I demonstrate the uses of audience ethnography, drawing upon my study of a popular Brazilian *telenovela, A Rainha do Sucata* (The Rubbish Queen).

E-E AND COMMUNICATION
FOR SOCIAL CHANGE

The field of E-E has undergone significant developments, both in theory and practice, in recent years. A rethinking of the theoretical and methodological basis for E-E strategies is taking place. Key contributions are being added to what hopefully will become a well-founded framework for E-E strategies for social change.

Airhihenbuwa, Makinwa, Frith, and Obregon (1999) proposed a communication-based framework for HIV/AIDS prevention, arguing the need to consider contextual domains when designing and evaluating HIV/AIDS communication interventions: gender, socio-economic status, spirituality, culture, and government policy. These domains are increasingly referred to in the growing international debate about how to design, implement, and evaluate effective E-E interventions. However, the main problem linked to this new UNAIDS communication framework is how to implement it. Obregon and Lyra (2002) noted that the UNAIDS communication framework served the important role of influencing the debate on communication for social change, including debates about E-E strategies, contributing significantly to what today is consensus on the need to consider culture, spirituality, government policies, socioeconomic status, and gender as contextual domains when communicating about HIV/AIDS. This framework was developed through a participatory process involving many practitioners worldwide in regional seminars. Thus the framework reached an important level of consensus among HIV/AIDS prevention professionals.

Singhal and Rogers (1999) presented a range of case studies of E-E programs as a useful summary of this evolving field. They identified future needs for the E-E field, including more scientific research on E-E communication, "to better understand how, why, and when E-E programs are more or less effective" (p. 225). They suggested a five-point research agenda for furthering the field of E-E: (1) attention to variability in E-E interventions; (2) attention to resistances to E-E; (3) attention to the rhetorical, play, and affective aspects of E-E; (4) rethinking previous conceptualizations of behavior change; and, (5) employing methodological pluralism and measurement ingenuity (Singhal & Rogers, 2002).

Singhal and Rogers call for a rethinking of the old conceptualization of behavior change. Audience ethnography, informed by the theory of mediations, is one response to their call for methodological pluralism and more in-depth interventions.

By focusing on how audiences make sense of E-E programs, the present chapter stresses the multiplicity of E-E reception, giving particular attention to what E-E scholars traditionally call "resistance" in E-E reception. Certain audience members identify with negative role models in E-E interventions, in an oppositional reading of the intended E-E message. Stuart Hall's text-audience dynamics identified in his encoding-decoding model (Hall, 1973) emphasized the negotiation process of any encounter between a media text and its intended audience. Hall identified three main forms of reading any media text: (1) the preferred reading, (2) the negotiated reading, and (3) the oppositional reading. Singhal and Rogers (1999) described the oppositional reading of an E-E text, an oppositional reading of what the encoders envisaged, which they call the "Archie Bunker effect" (so named after those highly prejudiced audience members who identified positively with Archie Bunker, a negative role model in the 1970s U.S. television program, *All in the Family*). Reception analysis has shown over the years the diversity of ways in which media texts—be they E-E interventions or others—are understood and appropriated by audience individuals. Following the proposed theory of mediation as a guideline for analysis of sense-making processes, the issue become less to overcome resistances than to understand which mediations influence the sense-making process, and thereby to understand the way in which media texts are incorporated into the social and cultural practices of the audience.

Numerous theories and case studies are proving useful in responding to the call for more research on the rhetorical, play, and affective aspects of E-E. Singhal and Rogers (2002) mentioned that in relation to E-E, communication scholars have "dismissed emotions as unimportant, internal, irrational, uncontrollable, amoral and ahistorical" (p. 126). A growing body of research has over the past two decades increasingly recognized the importance of emotions in audience reception of fiction as it appears on television (1) in Europe (Ang, 1985; Brown, 1994; Brunsdon, 1981; Hobson, 1982; Radway, 1984; Tufte, 1993, 1995, 2000), (2) in Latin America (Alfaro, 1988; Covarrubias, Bautista,

& Uribe, 1994; Fadul, 1993; Fuenzalida, 1997; Grisolli, 1994; Gonzalez, 1998; Jacks, 1999; Leal, 1986; Martin-Barbero, 1993; Martin-Barbero et al., 1992; Maziotti, 1993), and (3) in the United States (Allen, 1985; 1995; Katz & Liebes, 1987; Kottak, 1990; La Pastina, 1999; Press, 1991). However, there has been very little contact between this body of reception analyses and E-E investigation. Only in a few cases have links been established (Fuenzalida, 1992, 1997; also see the chapter by Bradley Greenberg and others in this volume). The challenge lies is bringing insights from how audiences handle melodrama and deal emotionally with a serial drama, in dialogue with the field of E-E research.

Finally, Singhal and Rogers (2002) call for methodological pluralism reflects current trends in newer media and in communication research. Contrary to trends in the 1970s and 1980s, there is today a growing recognition in audience research of the need to move beyond claiming superiority of a certain type of data over another. Thus, the full consequence of Singhal and Rogers (2002) call for methodological pluralism is to develop more integral strategies for how to analyze audience response.

Drawing on the distinction between emic and etic data (Krippendorff, 1980), Stewart and Shamdasani (1990) make a strong point in support of a methodological bridging. Emic data arise in a natural or indigenous form, and are only minimally imposed by the researcher or the research setting. Etic data represent the researcher's imposed view of the situation. Seldom is research purely etic or emic. E-E investigations traditionally used emic data like that from focus group interviews in some formative and summative research, but have rested most evaluations of impacts mainly on etic data, such as from audience surveys or from quantifying qualitative data.

> Neither emic nor etic data are better or worse than the other: They simply differ. Each has its place in social science research: Each complements and serves to compensate for the limitations of the other. Indeed, one way to view social science research is as a process that moves from the emic to the etic and back, in cycle. Phenomena that are not understood well often are studied first with tools that yield more emic data. As a particular phenomenon is understood better and greater theoretical and empirical structure is built around it, tools that yield more etic types of data tend to predominate. As knowledge accumulates, it often becomes apparent that the explanatory structure surrounding a given phenomenon is incomplete. This frequently leads to the need for data that are more emic, and the process continues (Stewart et al., 1990, in Morrison, 2002, p. 28).

The argument for letting a theory of mediations illuminate the forms of data collection, and using audience ethnography as a means to operationalize it, push the emic type of data collection. This chapter argues that more emic data are what is required to advance understanding of how E-E works best in communication for social change.

PARTICIPATION AND COMMUNITY INVOLVEMENT

The resurgence of Freire's dialogical pedagogy as an overriding perspective to communication for social change (Figueroa, Kincaid, Rani, & Lewis, 2001; Huesca, 2001; Tufte, 2000) represents a useful integration of community-based liberating pedagogy and dialogical communication (see Arvind Singhal's chapter in this volume). The Brazilian adult educator and philosopher Paulo Freire had no deep understanding of, or interest in, the mass media, as he made plain in an interview that I conducted with him in 1990 (Tufte, 1990). His main orientation was to face-to-face communication and small-scale group interaction. However, Freire had a clear understanding of the need to deal with the power structures of society, and the need for the underdogs of society to struggle to conquer a space for their critical reflection and dialogue. A previous interview with Freire identified a clear strategic aspect required for social change communication: the need to conquer space; challenge normative, moral, and social borderlines; and to arrange a critical dialogue on pertinent issues as a pathway towards social change (Tufte, Eriksen, Rasmussen, Jensen, & Vistisen 1987). Freire's "conscientization" (consciousness-raising) could be utilized to articulate community involvement in E-E strategies. This pathway offers a means through which E-E interventions increasingly can connect to, and address questions of, power, inequality, and human rights.

A number of recurrent issues have been addressed in recent developments in the field of E-E and communication for social change, although they have not adequately been brought together and reflected upon in an integrated manner. The theory of mediations captures a range of these recent developments in E-E. Such recent developments include:

1. Context: With UNAIDS having taken the lead, increased attention is being given to contextual domains in HIV/AIDS communication, including E-E communication for social change.
2. Emotions: The large body of research on how audiences relate emotionally to soap opera characters, establish parasocial interaction with them, and/or become involved in pleasurable television viewing is becoming linked to the need for E-E research to expand its understanding of these mechanisms. HIV/AIDS communication should not only be about sexual practices but also more broadly conceived, with concern for emotional relationships, identification, love, and sexuality.

3. Participation: With inspiration from Paulo Freire's ideas about dialogue and conscientization, there is a growing recognition of the need to have people define, articulate, and lead their own social change processes.

E-E AND HIV/AIDS

Advances have been achieved in planning, implementing, and evaluating E-E. Many of the advances sought and found have taken place in the context of the HIV/AIDS communication challenge. The Director of the USAID-financed Synergy Project, Barbara O. de Zalduondo, in speaking about communication practices, identified second-generation HIV/AIDS communication as a growing paradigm. This paradigm benefited from previous experiences, and has developed a more sensitive, complex, and nuanced communication response to HIV/AIDS. Zalduondo speaks of how second-generation HIV/AIDS communication is managing to consider prevention and care interaction, avoid stereotypes, be attentive to life cycles, reach and engage men, be sensitive to HIV+ perspectives, and have diverse aims such as changing attitudes and behaviors, combating determinants of risk, and promoting an enabling environment (Zalduondo, 2001).

This positive note on recent achievements came through at the International Roundtable on Communication for Development, hosted by UNFPA in Managua, Nicaragua, in November 2001 (the final declaration is available at: www.comminit.com/roundtable2/index.html). The Roundtable focused on HIV/AIDS communication, with several examples of successful uses of E-E in combating the pandemic. Both South Africa's *Soul City* as well as Nicaragua's *Puntos de Encuentro* were highlighted as best practices. Key achievements that were identified in the field of HIV/AIDS communication included: (1) successfully broadening awareness of HIV/AIDS, (2) increasing knowledge of how HIV/AIDS is contracted, (3) placing HIV/AIDS in the context of human rights, (4) increasing knowledge and demand for effective services, and, (5) mobilizing political support for national HIV/AIDS plans. Unresolved challenges include the fact that people are often treated as objects of change rather than as agents of their own change, and that communication strategies have often focused exclusively on a few individual behaviors rather than also addressing social norms, policies, culture, and supportive environments. Communication strategies convey information from technical experts, rather than sensitively placing accurate information into dialogue and debate.

BRIDGING PARADIGMS?

Several scholars argued the need for bridging communication paradigms in an effort to move beyond the limitations of previous communication practice when wishing to respond to such current development challenges as HIV/AIDS prevention (Morris, 2000; Tufte, 2001; Waisbord, 2001).

New schools of thought are being explored in relation to E-E and communication for social change. Sood (2002) made a recent plea for focusing on the concept of audience involvement in E-E in order to be more sensitive to the needs of the people for whom they are designed. This focus should make it possible "to situate entertainment-education dramas within a Freireian empowerment-education framework" (Sood, 2002, p. 167). Sood outlined the four key phases required for such a process to develop. We need to know how the suggested framework can be put into practice, and how such interventions should be assessed.

Tufte (2002) identified a need to broaden the approaches regarding how to integrally conceive, design, and evaluate E-E interventions. First, we need to develop a social and cultural theory base to better understand the social environments in which people communicate and develop particular behaviors. Second, we need to rely on a theory that can help expand the object of study in these evaluations, moving beyond the narrow text-reader relationship and into studying communication processes in their contexts. Third, we need a methodological approach that can identify, understand, and explore sense-making processes as they occur in everyday lives.

FROM MEDIA TO MEDIATIONS

How do different audiences make sense of E-E interventions? Jesus Martin-Barbero's theory of mediations provides one approach to understand sense-making. We seek to increase E-E scholars' insights into the complexities and subtleties of E-E's sense-making processes by suggesting an analytical approach which offers new strategies to explore how E-E interventions relate to people's sense-making.

The focus is on understanding how media texts (such as soap operas in E-E interventions) interact with, and become part of, social and cultural practices. As Martin-Barbero stated: "Instead of starting our analysis from the logic of production and reception and studying their relationships with the logic of cultural imbrication and conflict, we propose to start with the mediations where the social materialization and the cultural expression of television are delimited and configured" (Martin-Barbero, 1993, p. 215).

The mediations approach springs from the conception of interpretative reading (Sarlo, 1983): "In an interpretative reading, as in consumption, there is not just reproduction but also production, a production which questions the centrality of the dominating text and the message understood as the source of truth which circulates in a process of communication" (Martin-Barbero, 1993, p. 214). The role, meaning, and understanding of the text is negotiated: "The text is no longer the machine which unified heterogeneity, no longer a finished product, but a comprehensive space, crossed by different trajectories of meaning" (Martin-Barbero, 1993, p. 214). This echoes many of the perspectives and findings in European and North American cultural studies.

When communicating about larger issues, for example HIV/AIDS prevention, there is not just a simple message to convey, but a deep social, cultural, and political problem to address, make visible, put on the public agenda, and to promote public and private reflection and action upon. To understand to which degree these objectives are met, the analysis of mediations becomes a particularly useful approach.

Martin-Barbero used Bourdieu's theory of practice to understand how elements of structure are present in the sociocultural activities of people. He furthermore argued that culture should be viewed as a field of struggle (based on Gramsci's hegemony theory). Finally, Giddens' structuration theory is used by Martin-Barbero to introduce the self into reflexive action. An E-E intervention can influence reflexive action and structure, but negotiations in the sense-making process suggest the impossibility of exact control over the communicative process.

What are the mediations of which Martin-Barbero speaks? To achieve an optimal assessment of the impact of an intervention, mediations must be analyzed. Martin-Barbero suggested three spaces of mediations: the daily life of the family (social relationships), social temporality (time/space interaction), and cultural competence (people's habitus) (Martin-Barbero, 1993, pp. 211–224). Understanding the impact of an E-E intervention requires analysis of these spaces of mediations. Drawing on this research protocol set by Martin-Barbero, the Mexican scholar Guillermo Orozco proposed a typology of mediations:

1. Individual mediations come from our individuality as communicative subjects. They are mental schemes with which people perceive, pay attention to, assimilate, process, evaluate, memorize, or express themselves.
2. Institutional mediations are a production of meanings that result from the participation of the individual in the family, school, company, friendship group, neighbors, etc.
3. Mass media mediations are the distinct technologies, languages, and genres of each medium.
4. Situational mediations concern the situation, spaces, and modes of reception.
5. Mediations of reference are located in a certain context or environment (age, gender, ethnicity, class) and thus interact with the communication medium (Orozco,1997; Lopes, 2002, p.11).

The *Soul City 4* television series in South Africa addressed three levels of intervention in their E-E strategy: the individual, the community, and the societal levels, and they achieved certain impacts at each level (Soul City Evaluation, 2001). Reviewing *Soul City 4*'s evaluation from the perspective of mediations, it appears that many of the mediations outlined above have been assessed, although not all (see the Shereen Usdin and others' chapter in this volume). For example, the analysis of the situational mediations was not included in Soul City's evaluations. They are rarely seen in E-E evaluations. Also, the depth of the individual mediations could have been pursued further.

The Brazilian media scholar, Maria Immacolata Lopes, suggested one way of organizing the analyses of mediations, a strategy she applied in a study of how Brazilians make sense of telenovelas (Lopes, 2002, pp. 11–12):

1. The structural dimension of the mediation indicates the level of the structural insertion of the mediation. Lopes (2002) analyzed four levels of telenovela mediations in everyday life: structural (societal), institutional, individual, and technical.
2. The source of the mediation includes the social position of class, family, subjectivity, fiction genre, and format.
3. The loci of mediation is the context of the mediation, whether grand global contexts, the reception context, the production context, or the actual product as a locus of mediation.
4. The discourse in which the mediation is inserted, such as the syntax, semantics, and pragmatic of the mediation.

Lopes and her team of researchers explored four mediations for a telenovela in the lives of four Brazilian families over an eight-month period. Eleven different research methods were used to collect data, from media consumption questionnaires and life-story interviews, to discussion groups and genre interviews.

ANGLO-SAXON TRADITION OF CULTURAL STUDIES

The cultural studies tradition generated insights useful in operationalization of the theory of mediations: (1) recognition of the polysemy of the text (Hall, 1973, 1980); (2) the active reception process (Ang, 1985; Jensen, 1986; Morley, 1980; Radway, 1984); (3) the intertextual relationship of media texts (Fiske, 1987); (4) the forms and uses of soap operas in everyday life (Leal, 1986; La Pastina, 1999; Tufte, 2000); (5) the experiences of pleasure in using and consuming popular cultural genres (Brown, 1994; Hobson, 1982; Radway

1984); (6) gender characteristics in audience reception (Press, 1991; Radway 1984); (7); interpretative communities (Morley, 1986); and (8) social uses of the media (Lull, 1980, 1988, 1990; Press, 1991; Tufte, 2000). These issues help scholars respond to the call for future E-E investigations set forth by Singhal and Rogers (2002).

Cultural studies are primarily studies of mediations and are consistent with Martin-Barbero's theory of mediations. As such, the cultural studies traditions in the Northern Hemisphere converge with Latin American cultural studies. Cultural studies, drawing on social and cultural theory, are useful in broadening the scientific basis of E-E investigations.

Audience ethnography draws on ethnographic methods to study specific social groups that constitute audiences (listeners, viewers, readers, or users). The objective is to explore how these audiences make sense of media texts and/or technologies. Audience ethnography grew out of qualitative audience studies in the 1980s (Jensen, 2002). Audience ethnography helps meet the need for improved analysis of audience sense-making in E-E interventions (Gillespie, 1995; Leal, 1986; Tufte, 2000). Key points to pursue are:

1. To explore the media-audience relationship as a multilateral and multi-dimensional relationship which takes place in the context of multiple mediations.
2. To approach reception analysis as an analysis of a social process, not as an analysis of a particular moment.
3. To view audience reception as a negotiation of encoded meanings by the receptors. Capturing this process of negotiation requires analysis of social interaction, of everyday talk, and analysis of the multiple sites of such negotiations.

TELENOVELAS: TOUCHING EVERYDAY EXPERIENCE

I utilized audience ethnography to analyze audience sense-making in a study of how low-income urban women in Brazil made use of telenovelas (Tufte, 2000). The study was based on a multisited ethnographic field study of 13 women from three different urban sites in Brazil. I studied their everyday life with emphasis on their media uses. Ethnographic techniques applied included participatory observations in homes and neighborhoods, in-depth interviews with the women and their families, field diaries, and photo-ethnography. A limited survey was conducted with 110 women in their neighborhood. I also made a content analysis of a specific telenovela that was popular at the time, *A Rainha do Sucata* (The Rubbish Queen). Furthermore, the study included an analysis of the history of the neighborhoods and the family history of each woman respondent, and finally an analysis of the media history and media development at the national, community, and individual level. I developed and applied a theoretical-methodological framework based on three focus areas and incorporating a range of the mediations identified by Orozco (Tufte, 2000). The three focus areas were: (a) a genre analysis, including the history and development of the genre; (b) an analysis of everyday life, exploring the social order and cultural characteristics of the women; and (c) an analysis of the media flow, including both the social uses of the media and a focused reception analysis of *The Rubbish Queen*.

The Rubbish Queen

The Rubbish Queen, a telenovela of 177 episodes, was launched on April 1, 1990 as part of Rede Globo's 25th anniversary celebrations. Written by Silvio de Abreu, one of Brazil's leading script writers, the telenovela was screened in an ideal time slot at 8:00 pm. Like all telenovelas in Brazil, it was screened daily, six days a week for six months. It had an audience of approximately 70 to 80 million people (ratings of 40 to 50 points).

The Rubbish Queen deals with a poor family who becomes rich by recycling rubbish. Throughout the 1980s social and economic marginalization grew in Brazil, with the consequence that a growing number of people had to survive in the informal economy and in untraditional jobs. In the Brazil of the 1990s the economic crisis was massive and optimism had vanished. Thus, the theme and name of *The Rubbish Queen* fit well with the contemporary reality.

The main conflict involved a confrontation between two women, the nouveau riche Rubbish Queen, Maria do Carmo Pereira (played by Regina Duarte, Brazil's most popular actress) and society woman Laurinha Albuquerque Fiqueroa (played by Gloria Menezes, a renowned actress of theatre and telenovelas). The plot unfolds in São Paulo around the lives of Maria do Carmo and Laurinha, their families, friends, and colleagues. Laurinha and Maria do Carmo have a mutual point of reference in Edu. In addition to being Laurinha's stepson, Edu is Maria do Carmo's old classmate from school. Both women fight ferociously for the good opinion and love of Edu.

One main theme of the narrative is a love story, a rivalry between Laurinha and Maria do Carmo. The other theme is the constant power struggle between two social classes. On one side is the threatened São Paulo elite, the traditional upper class society of coffee barons. They live in their own world, cultivate their European roots and customs, dress in European style, and practice expensive hobbies. On the other side are the nouveaux riche, who have earned, not inherited, money. One of my respondents spoke of the class dimension in *The Rubbish Queen*:

"It was the story about a woman who was very poor. She managed to become 'somebody' in life here, gain status in society because she worked a lot. She began selling old iron and other second-hand materials with her father, until they succeeded in achieving everything they had. She was very sad about her father spending so much money on paying her school fees. She went to school with children from a higher social level, so they made fun of her. They called her the rubbish queen. They bullied her a lot. She kept all this in her mind and sought constantly to rise in life, always upwards in life, and always with this wound in her heart."

Research Findings

The major findings of this investigation include:

1. *Telenovelas* articulate strong emotional engagement and increase audience involvement. Women's interest in the telenovela was spurred by the fact that the drama was about love: "I liked '*Rubbish Queen*' because it was an everyday story—a story which is found in my family and in my friends' families . . . I was able to identify myself with Maria do Carmo [the protagonist of the telenovela] because her life was more or less the same as mine," said Ilda, 41. As Ilda demonstrates, the narrative in general relates to aspects of the everyday of her family and friends, and Maria do Carmo's story relates to her own life. Fuenzalida (1992, p. 8) previously identified that the "testimonial form presents ordinary people as actors and protagonists, and thereby validates audiences' daily life. In this televisual form many people may recognize themselves as actors in their daily story, with actions and circumstances like theirs: It is the true story of most people." Personal discourse, referred to in Ilda's statement, related to her concern for the family and the community to which she belongs, and to a more individualized gender-specific identification with the woman Maria do Carmo. Relevance and recognition established a relation of trust and openness, paving the way for a high degree of involvement by Ilda and other viewers of the telenovela.

When I asked the women respondents *why* they liked a particular telenovela, they said: "Oh, it was full of emotion" (Ana), "The novela moved people a lot" (Clara), and "It was very moving" (Ilda). Ana stated, referring to another telenovela *Pantanal*:

"I liked it, I loved it. It was a great novela. It was a very strong novela, a novela full of emotion. I like it a lot."
Could you perhaps explain me, when you talk about emotion, what do you mean?
"It is something we like, something that makes us feel happy."
What is it in the novela that makes you feel happy?
"When a couple quarrel and then return and settle down peacefully with each other, kissing, hugging, and then they marry. Well, then we feel happy. Or when you are hoping two people get each other."

Most of the women demonstrated a strong identification with the emotional television dramas. They confirm a point made by Fuenzalida (1992), the fundamental emotional relation between media, culture, and everyday life. Thus, the call made by Singhal and Rogers (2002) to give more attention to the rhetorical, play, and affective aspects of E-E connects with such findings. I found that telenovelas often proved more relevant to the Brazilian female audience than did news broadcasts. Fuenzalida (1992) argued that we should take emotion seriously. Telenovelas, due to their widespread popularity in Latin American countries, constitute a much more important and relevant educational instrument than news programs or public service announcements. "The redundancy of the serials makes its attraction rationally inexplicable, but the interest is, precisely, emotional" (Fuenzalida, 1987, p. 25). This perspective also calls for modesty in expectations concerning the impacts of an E-E intervention: "The educational efficiency of the televised messages depends much more on the viewers' perception than on the intentions of the broadcasting station" (Fuenzalida, 1994, p. 15).

2. Telenovelas increase dialogue and debate, and can break the silence around controversial or taboo issues. In Brazil, telenovelas from the late 1980s onwards introduced taboo issues, be it a love affair between a married woman and a priest, or a love affair between two people who later in the story turn out to be brother and sister. Such issues question the norms and values upon which personal relationships in Brazilian society are based, and challenge moral codes. When embedded in identifiable settings and with realistic characters in a telenovela, these issues are not normally rejected but instead get debated by the public. In HIV/AIDS communication, we often need to introduce taboo issues and to break the silence about, and the stigma concerning, people living with HIV.

In my Brazil study, the 6:00 p.m. telenovela *Belly for Hire* (Barriga de Aluguel, Globo 1991) touched upon an unfamiliar topic that became a great talking point in Brazil. *Belly for Hire* is about two young families and their fight over a baby. This telenovela was particularly popular with women who were mothers with young children. The story is about a poor woman who wants to earn money by giving birth to a child to be given to a rich couple, who are unable to have children themselves. Geraldina, a 38-year-old low-income woman, described the story:

"Because they are rich, the couple believe that they can buy everything and do everything [Geraldina's friend Dora interrupts and says: 'Even buy themselves a son']. And she, because she is a poor girl who had never seen so much money in her life, she sees all that money and so agrees to be a surrogate mother. But now, when she has given birth to the child, she realizes what she has got into, and then she refuses to deliver the child."
Why? She will make a lot of money from it?

"No, because on one hand she gives the money back and on the other, there is no sum of money that could make her sell her son."

Geraldina, her friend Dora, and many of the other women in my Brazil study discussed this topic a great deal. Geraldina identified with the dilemma of the surrogate mother, because, as Geraldina said: "Any woman who is a mother can see herself in this woman's place." Dora added: "OK, it was another man's seed, but that does not mean a thing." This topic absorbed them, but they did not imagine it could have really occurred in Brazil: "There have been cases like this, but not here in Brazil, have there, Dora?" (Dora answered: "No").

Themes from a telenovela can start a debate among women audience members. Many other Brazilian telenovelas sparked, and continue to spark, similar debates when raising controversial themes. The state of harmony with which many telenovelas and soap operas begin is challenged by the introduction of taboo issues which challenge the relational structures and moral codes present in an initial state of harmony, but simultaneously may very well become articulators of debate and gossip as Mary Ellen Brown (1994) pointed out. *Belly for Hire* is an example of this stimulation of interpersonal communication.

For purposes of evaluation, this example suggests the need to get as close as possible to identifying the actual talk and gossip about the content of telenovelas, making it possible to assess how the narrative of the E-E text is appropriated by its audience. It can provide valuable insights enabling an improved balance between openness, explicitness, subtleness, humor, etc. in future E-E media texts.

3. Telenovelas socialize viewers to new lifestyles and articulate cultural citizenship. Telenovelas over the years in Brazil served as useful socializers of new lifestyles, particularly for migrants to urban areas. My study revealed the existence of what I called a hybrid sphere of signification, neither public nor private, but very much part of everyday life, geographically placed in the border zone between the privacy of the home and the public sphere of the street. Identifying such contexts of reception permits an improved understanding of processes such as the formation and articulation of identity; the organization of time, space, and social relations in everyday life; how ontological security is produced and; how social norms are affirmed, adapted, and revised.

Despite portraying a material world far from the viewers' own lives, Brazilian telenovelas touch everyday experiences which are highly recognizable for audiences. Telenovelas articulate a sense of social and cultural membership and belonging to communities that are national, gendered, and often across class, counterbalancing the many processes of sociocultural and political-economic marginalization experienced by low-income citizens in Brazil. Thereby, telenovelas become an important way of exercising cultural citizenship in the sense of finding recognition of everyday concerns. Viewers recognize in telenovelas the themes of striving to participate as members of different communities, transforming their use of telenovelas into a process that promotes belongingness and citizenship. Given the massive presence of nationally produced fiction programs in the lives of Brazilians and many other Latin American audiences, and increasingly elsewhere, this genre has an enormous potential for promoting public debates, thus exercising some degree of advocacy, in addition to articulating identities as citizens.

CONCLUSIONS

This chapter provided a perspective on how E-E scholars can view the relation between soap operas and their audiences. We introduced Martin-Barbero's theory of mediations, and proposed audience ethnography as a means of better understanding how soap operas impact individuals' sense-making processes. We emphasized the need among E-E planners and practitioners to analyze the culture and everyday practices of their audiences from the perspective of mediations, suggesting the multipronged typology of mediations set forth by Guillermo Orozco. Brazilian women's uses of telenovelas were used as an illustration.

This chapter challenges the current manner in which many donors, policymakers, and E-E planners conceive and evaluate E-E communication, often conceived as short-term interventions, and evaluated with emphasis on the narrow text-audience relationship. To fully understand, identify, and analyze sense-making processes, a broader perspective is required.

REFERENCES

Airhihenbuwa, C. O., Makinwa, B., Frith, M., & Obregon, R. (Eds.). (1999). *Communications framework for HIV/AIDS: A new direction*, Geneva: UNAIDS.

Alfaro, R. M. (1988). Los usos sociales populares de las telenovelas en el mundo urbano. *Programa Cultura, 2*, 223-259.

Allen, R. (1985). *Speaking of soap operas*. Chapel Hill, NC: University of North Carolina Press.

Allen, R. (Ed.). (1995). *To be continued . . . Soap operas around the world*. London: Routledge.

Ang, I. (1985). *Watching Dallas*. London: Methuen.

Barriga de Aluguel. *Telenovela* screened on Rede Globo in 1991.

Brown, M. E. (1994). *Soap operas and women's talk. The pleasure of resistance*. London: Sage.

Brunsdon, C. (1981). Crossroads: Notes on soap opera. *Screen 22, 4*, 32-37.

Covarrubias, K., Bautista, A., & Uribe, B. A. (1994). *Cuéntame en Qué se Quedó. La telenovela como fenómeno social*. Mexico: Trillas/Felafacs.

Fadul, A. M. (Ed.). (1993). *Serial fiction in TV. The Latin American telenovelas*. Sao Paulo: USP.

Figueroa, M. E., Kincaid, L., Rani, M., & Lewis, G. (2001). *Guidelines for the measurement of process and outcome of social change interventions*. Baltimore, MD: CCP/JHU. Prepared for the Rockefeller Foundation.

Fiske, J. (1987). *Television culture*. London: Methuen.

Fuenzalida, V. (1987). La influencia cultural de la television. *Dialogos 17*, 20-29.

Fuenzalida, V. (1992, November). *TV broadcasting for grassroot development*. Paper presented at the Conference on TV and Video in Latin America. Denmark, Danchurchaid.

Fuenzalida, V. (1994). *La apropriación educativa de la telenovela*. Santiago: CPU.

Fuenzalida, V. (1997). *Television y cultura cotidiana. La influencia social de la TV percibida desde la cultura cotidiana de la audiencia*. Santiago: CPU.

Gillespie, M. (1995). *Television, ethnicity, and cultural change*. London: Routledge.

Gonzalez, J. (Ed.). (1998). *La cofradía de las emociones (in)terminables: Miradas sobre telenovelas en Mexico*. Guadalajara, Mexico: Universidad de Guadalajara.

Grisolli, P. (1994). Drømmefabrikken. *Mediekultur (Special Issue on TV, Culture and Development in Latin America)*, 46-49.

Hall, S. (1980/1973). Encoding-decoding in the television discourse. Birmingham: CCCS. Occasional Paper 7.

Hobson, D. (1982). *Crossroads: The drama of a soap opera*. London: Methuen.

Huesca, R. (2001). Conceptual contributions of new social movements to development communication research. *Communication Theory 11*(4), 415-434.

Jacks, N. (1999). *Querencia. cultura, identidade e mediacao*. Porto Alegre, Brazil: Editora da Universidade.

Jensen, K. B. (1986). *Making sense of the news*. Aarhus, Denmark: Aarhus University Press.

Jensen, K. B. (2002). Media reception: Qualitative traditions. In K. B. Jensen (Ed.), *A handbook of media and communication research: Qualitative and quantitative methodologies*. London: Routledge.

Katz, E., & Liebes, T. (1987). Decoding Dallas. Notes from a cross-cultural study. In H. Newcomb (Ed.), *Television: The critical view* (pp. 419-433). Oxford: Oxford University Press.

Kottak, C. P. (1990). *Prime-time society: An anthropological analysis of television and culture*. Belmont: Wadsworth.

Krippendorff, K. (1980). *Content analysis: An introduction to its methodology*. Thousand Oaks, CA: Sage.

La Pastina, A. (1999). *The telenovela way of knowledge: An ethnographic reception study among rural viewers in Brazil*. Unpublished Ph.D. dissertation, Austin, TX: University of Texas at Austin, Department of Radio-TV-Film.

Leal, O. F. (1986). *A leitura social da novela das oito*. Rio de Janeiro: Vozes.

Lopes M. I .V. de (2002, July). *A methodology for telenovela research*. Paper presented at the IAMCR Conference, Barcelona.

Lull, J. (1980). The social uses of television. *Human Communication Research 6*, 195-209.

Lull, J. (1988). *World families watch television*. Thousand Oaks, CA: Sage.

Lull, J. (1990). *Inside family viewing: Ethnographic research on television audiences*. London: Routledge.

Martin-Barbero, J. (1993). *Communication, culture, and hegemony. From media to mediations*. London: Sage.

Martin-Barbero, J., & Munoz, S. (1992). *Televisión y melodrama*. Bogotá, Colombia: Tercer Mundo Editores.

Maziotti, N. (1993). *El espectáculo de la pasión: Las telenovelas latinoamericanos*. Buenos Aires: Colihue.

Morley, D. (1980). *The 'nationwide' audience*. London: British Film Institute.

Morley, D. (1986). *Family television*. London: Comedia.

Morris, N. (2000, October). *A comparative analysis of the diffusion and participatory models in development communication*. Paper presented at the USAID/Rockefeller Foundation Conference on Realities and New Approaches: Development Communications in the Twenty First Century. Bellagio Study and Conference Center, Italy.

Morrison, D. (2002, July). *The institutional beginnings of focus group research as a way of understanding the audience, and their misuse over time.* Paper presented at the IAMCR Conference, Barcelona.

Obregon, R., & Lyra, P. (2002, July). *HIV/AIDS communication in Latin America: A review of NAP's experiences.* Paper presented at the IAMCR Conference, Barcelona.

Orozco, G. (1997). *La investigación en comunicación desde la perspectiva qualitativa.* México City: IMDEC.

Press, A. (1991). *Women watching television.* Philadelphia: University of Pennsylvania Press.

Radway, J. (1984). *Reading the romance: Women, patriarchy, and popular literature.* London: Verso.

Sarlo, B. (1983). *Lo popular como dimensión: Tópica, retórica y problemática de la recepción.* Unpublished Paper. Buenos Aires.

Singhal, A., & Rogers, E. (1999). *Entertainment-education: A communication strategy for social change.* Mahwah, NJ: Lawrence Erlbaum Associates.

Singhal, A., & Rogers, E. (2002). A theoretical agenda for entertainment-education. *Communication Theory, 12,* 117-135.

Sood, S. (2002). Audience involvement and entertainment-education. *Communication Theory, 12,* 153-172.

Soul City 4: Evaluation. Integrated summary report. (2001, July). Parkstown, South Africa: Soul City.

Stewart, D. W., & Shamdasani, P. N. (1990). *Focus groups: Theory and practice.* Thousand Oaks, CA: Sage.

Tufte, T. (1990, November). *Interview with Paulo Freire.* Unpublished. Sao Paulo, Brazil.

Tufte, T. (1993). Everyday life, women and telenovelas in Brazil. In A. Fadul (Ed.), *Serial fiction in TV: The Latin American telenovelas* (pp. 77-102). Sao Paulo: USP.

Tufte, T. (1995). How do telenovelas serve to articulate hybrid cultures in contemporary Brazil? *Nordicom Review, 2,* 29-36.

Tufte, T. (2000). *Living with the Rubbish Queen: Telenovelas, culture, and modernity.* Luton, England: University of Luton Press.

Tufte, T. (2001). Entertainment-education and participation: Assessing the communication strategy of Soul City. *Journal of International Communication, 7,* 25-51.

Tufte, T. (2002, July). *Edutainment and participation.* Paper presented at the IAMCR Conference, Barcelona.

Tufte, T., Eriksen, A., Rasmussen, F., Jensen, S., & Vistisen, H. (1987, April). *Interview with Paulo Freire.* Unpublished. Sao Paulo, Brazil.

Waisbord, S. (2001, May). *Family tree of theories, methodologies and strategies in develompent communication: Convergences and differences.* Prepared for the Rockefeller Foundation. www.comminit.com/roundtable2/indez.html. Declaration: International Communication for Development Roundtable. Managua, Nicaragua. November, 2001.

Zalduondo, B. O. de (2001, March). *Second generation HIV/AIDS communication: Applying lessons learned.* Presentation to USAID.

22

Entertainment-Education and Participation: Applying Habermas to a Population Program in Nepal

J. Douglas Storey
Johns Hopkins University

Thomas L. Jacobson
University of Buffalo, State University of New York

One conceptual problem associated with analyzing participatory communication for development is lack of a clear definition of participation. Another problem concerns the matter of scale. The participation literature tends to limit itself to processes at the village level, yet certain kinds of social change require the involvement of large-scale organizations and support from the State. The present chapter addresses these conceptual problems using Jurgen Habermas's theory of communicative action with a focus on the concepts of "ideal speech" and the "public sphere." This theory is applied to a case study of a population program in Nepal, coordinated by Johns Hopkins University's Population Communication Services, that centered on entertainment-educational radio and community media. The concepts of ideal speech and the public sphere are illustrated in relation to this program to explicate a definition of participatory communication that provides analytic leverage in relation to both small and large-scale programs and to extend the range of entertainment-education theorizing.

Approaches to the study of development communication evolved over recent decades from an earlier emphasis on the mass media dissemination of messages toward an emphasis on participatory processes of communication, processes that are more dialogical and community oriented (Berrigan, 1979; Lewis, 1993; Servaes, Jacobson, & White, 1996; White, Nair, & Ascroft, 1994). This participatory approach is employed widely enough today that it can no longer be called new. However, it remains somewhat undertheorized and lacks fundamental definition (Huesca, 2002; Jacobson & Servaes, 1999). Some approaches to participation are relatively strategic and the sincerity of intentions to truly involve local people can on occasion be questionable (Diaz-Bordenave, 1994, Mato, 1999). Important questions are: What exactly is participation? What kind of communication characterizes participation?

There is also the matter of scale. The participation literature tends to limit itself to processes at the village level. This restriction is due in part to the community-based scale of many development projects, and perhaps in part to the interpersonal/classroom context addressed in much of Paulo Freire's highly influential work, especially in his earliest books (Freire, 1970; 1973). Some analysts argue that participation is also important at larger scales, such as in the context of social movements (Rahman, 1993; White, 1999). Certain kinds of social change require the involvement of large-scale organizations including bureaucratic institutions. In the case of some health programs where lives are in the balance (for example, HIV/AIDS or maternal mortality prevention), the time required for small scale, intensively participatory approaches becomes a questionable luxury.

Many useful kinds of large-scale change must include large nongovernmental organizations (NGOs), multilateral development agencies, and the national state (Midgley, Hall, Hardiman, & Narine, 1986). Nevertheless, the role of such organizations in participatory change is seldom addressed, and when it is, it is often implied that large-scale programs are inherently antiparticipatory. Although most large-scale programs have in the past not been participatory, one would hope that this could become common. Must development initiatives generated at national and large-scale regional levels necessarily nullify participation as self-determination? Can participation be defined in such a manner that local, regional, and national levels of social organization might be productively coordinated? Are some forms of mass communication, like entertainment-education (Singhal & Rogers, 1999), suited to fostering participation?

We tackle these conceptual problems by proposing that Jurgen Habermas's theory of communicative action offers a promising characterization of participatory communication. The theory's central concepts, including "ideal speech" and the "public sphere," directly address definition and scale. Habermas is explicitly concerned with participation in several ways (Habermas, 1975, p. 137; 1984, p. 115). Although the predominant treatment of

Habermas' work has been theoretical, applied studies have been proposed and conducted (Barry, Stevenson, Britten, Barber, & Bradley, 2001; Forester, 1988, 1992; Hamer, 1998; Pusey, 1991; Webler & Tuler, 2000). The relevance of Habermas' work to development communication has been argued (Gonzalez, 1989; Jacobson & Kolluri, 1999; Servaes, 1989). Furthermore, some forms of entertainment-education, particularly those that engage popular culture and traditional social networks, may in some respects facilitate communicative action (Storey, 1999).

In addition, the theory of communicative action includes a general theory of social and cultural change. We believe that this framework can be used to differentiate at least some desirable forms of cultural change from others that are undesirable (Jacobson, in press). The full scope of the theory is necessary to characterize participatory communication for social change in developing countries. However, we address this larger framework only in passing, choosing for reasons of space to focus on basic definitions and the problem of scale, with some reference to the more general question of sociocultural change.

For over 15 years, Johns Hopkins University's Population Communication Services (JHU/PCS) program, funded by the United States Agency for International Development (USAID), worked with the Government of Nepal (GON), and a variety of development agencies and nongovernmental organizations (NGOs) to address challenges posed by Nepal's population growth rate. The Nepal population program consists of a multifaceted program of activities, ranging from large to small, short-term to long-term. Core elements of this Project are ongoing radio drama serials, folk performances, and cultural celebrations, all forms of entertainment-education. These activities together address issues across levels, from that of individual Nepalese struggling to improve their own, and their family's, health, to that of policy development at the national level. Over these various time frames, and across this range of activities and issues, participation was by design both a core strategy and a primary goal, with entertainment-education used as a means to foster it. The concepts of communicative action and participation are illustrated in relation to these ongoing activities in Nepal.

COMMUNICATIVE ACTION
AND PARTICIPATION

The theory of communicative action is most often discussed in relation to two of its concepts, the ideal speech situation and the theory of the public sphere. We draw attention to Habermas' larger theory of social change and its relevance to the present analysis. Finally, the theory's implications for the study of participatory communication are summarized.

Habermas began his analysis of the public sphere in his doctoral disser-tation published subsequently, and much later, in English as *The Structural Transformation of the Public Sphere* (Habermas, 1989). Here he analyzed the evolution of discussion by private citizens about matters of public im-portance, thus offering a communicative orientation to the analysis of civil society. Civil society provides a foundation for legitimate democratic power not due solely to the institution of private property, notably private ownership of the media, but also because of the essence of the communicative process itself. The theory of the public sphere was elaborated over recent years to in-clude the notion of multiple public spheres (Habermas, 1996, pp. 287–328). It addresses the role of dialog in the creation of decentered identities capable of participation in democratic ethics (Habermas, 1987). It includes a diagnosis of the mechanisms required for public opinion to be fed more meaningfully into the formal deliberations of national political institutions (Habermas, 1996).

The theory of communicative action was developed after Habermas' initial work on the public sphere (Habermas, 1984, 1987). The aim of this work was to provide an account of the universalistic basis of, at one level, free speech. Habermas argued that the desire for free speech is not just an accident of Western society, but is ultimately the expression of a set of reciprocal ex-pectations regarding the validity of communicative utterances presumed in all human communication. Reciprocal expectations concerning the validity claims of truth, appropriateness, and sincerity of statements make commu-nication possible, even deceptive communication (Habermas, 1984). While Habermas recognized that strategic and manipulative forms of communica-tion are common in everyday conversation, he regarded the three validity claims as a pragmatically necessary means for the coordination of human behavior.

Whether behavior coordination involves agreement about the nature of the physical, social, or subjective worlds, the process of communication re-quires that participants presume all three validity claims in all statements. If doubts arise as to a claim's validity, then it can be "thematized," or raised for discussion. The claim is "redeemed," or justified, when agreement on the claim is reached, including agreements to disagree. Good faith action, oriented towards arriving at agreement regarding claims, is "action oriented towards understanding," or "communicative action" strictly speaking. "... I shall speak of communicative action whenever the actions of the agents involved are co-ordinated not through egocentric calculations of success but through acts of reaching understanding" (Habermas, 1984, pp. 285–286).

The "ideal speech situation" represents a counterfactual ideal that is ap-proximated when communicative action is undertaken, regardless of whether thematized claims focus on truth, appropriateness, or sincerity. During com-municative action, participants must be free to "call into question any pro-posal," to "introduce any proposal," and to express any "attitudes, wishes, and needs." There must be a symmetrical distribution of opportunities to contribute to discussion (Habermas, 1990, pp. 88–89). Again, this ideal is neither a transcendental category nor a normative wish, but rather is built into the structure of human behavior.

Different discourses are used in resolving disagreement over different kinds of claims. Behavior coordination takes place in relation to claims about the *physical* world through use of empirical discourse, in reference to factual assessment and ultimately a secular, scientific attitude. Behavior coordination takes place in relation to claims about the *social* world through use of normative discourse, in reference to values. Behavior coordination takes place in relation to claims about the *subjective* world through expressive discourse. The public sphere is a place where all nonspecialized discourse takes place, and where specialized discourses interact when their object domains cross from one social sphere to another.

Ideal speech properly includes argument and persuasion among its repertoire of more specific behaviors (this is not the persuasion in propaganda and in advertising). Habermas sometimes characterizes communicative action as a process through which outcomes are determined by "the force of the better argument" rather than through power. This aspect of the theory represents an alternative to studying persuasion as a strategic form of pursuing ends regardless of the interests of others, and highlights a common aspect of communication (for example, open and honest persuasion) as being commonplace and in no way undesirable. The nature of argument is analyzed at length, differentiating argument in which participants are open to themselves being persuaded, and to reaching mutual understanding, from argument in which there is no intent to reach understanding (Habermas, 1984, pp. 18–42).

The relationship between communicative action, strictly speaking, and the public sphere is therefore key to Habermas' work. The presumptions that underlie interpersonal communication also underlie communication in the public sphere in at least two ways. As noted, their empirical necessity warrants the claim that expectations regarding free speech are not accidental, but are in some respects universalistic (Habermas, 1990). Habermas argued that these expectations are required of democratic governance and of social progress generally. While the former is an empirically based normative claim, the latter is a description of the functions necessary for social reproduction from a systems theory perspective.

Communicative action in the public sphere is necessary for sustained legitimacy of government, the creation and transmission of social norms, and processes related to identity formation. The circumvention of communicative action in the public sphere degrades public belief in the legitimacy of governance and can lead to political apathy (Habermas, 1975). Contrary to the rational actor theory predominant in American political science, citizen belief in governmental legitimacy does not depend on utilitarian calculations regarding the trade-off between effort expended and personal gain. Rather, it depends on the sense that citizens have that their voices will be heard, and their challenges to validity claims recognized, if they choose to make such claims for recognition. Moreover, if deeply normative changes are pressed upon society by historical conditions in the absence of communicative action, as a resource for collective response to these changes, anomie is a likely outcome. If social values change without deliberation, without public consideration of desirable preferences about ways to live, then social norms break down. Not only do politics then seem irrelevant, but social trends begin to separate from family value patterns and hence from the processes of identity formation. Habermas treated this outcome as "colonization of the cultural lifeworld" (Habermas, 1987, pp. 153-199).

This dual connection between communicative action and the public sphere produces the means for analyzing social and cultural change. On one hand, undesirable change, or lifeworld colonization, can be identified in instances where social values change under pressure from forces outside of public deliberation, chiefly the unrestrained force of market priorities and the inappropriate employment of technical expertise in areas where public communicative action is most suitable. On the other hand, a model of desirable social and cultural change can be specified precisely as communicative action in the public sphere about matters of general social and cultural concern. Habermas referred to this process as the "reflexive appropriation of tradition" (Habermas, 1996, p. 493). Cultural change undoubtedly takes place in many respects below the level of conscious reflection, individually and socially. However, in periods of rapid cultural change it is important that changes brought to consciousness be thematized in the public sphere and interpreted by the public. Decisions to abandon or to retain traditions need to be made collectively if they are to continue providing normative frameworks within which social integration and identity formation can be achieved. Market forces and external expertise have roles to play, but these must assist the deliberations made by citizens rather than determine them (Jacobson, 2000).

HABERMAS' THEORY AND PARTICIPATORY COMMUNICATION

What is the relevance of Habermas' theory to the study of participatory communication for social change? First, the conceptual framework of validity claims, reciprocal expectations, and the symmetrical distribution of opportunities to contribute in discussion offer a well-developed specification of participatory communication. Second, the theory of the public sphere links the treatment of communicative action at interpersonal and small group levels to participation at village, district, and national levels. Thus participatory communication at these levels is interconnected. Third, the theory provides a framework within which participation can be related to cultural change.

This approach to participatory communication at least in some respects complements Paulo Freire's work (see Arvind Singhal's chapter in this volume). Parallels between Freire's and Habermas' work have been noted, despite many differences in their aims and conceptual tools (Morrow & Torres, 2002; Pietrykowski, 1996; Ramella & De La Cruz, 2000). The theory of communicative action is intended to be as sensitive to authenticity and empowerment as is Freire's approach, even if it has been developed at a more abstract theoretical level. Both are entirely devoted to democratic processes, even if they have different emphases. Freire's treatment of democracy focuses on the relationship between dialog, self-development, and democratic practice (Freire, 1993, 1996). Habermas' theory has been elaborated in relation to a range of larger social subsystems, such as an analysis of the relationships between cultural plurality and law (Habermas, 1998). "Habermas is particularly interested in the question of translating the theory of practice from the microinteractive level to that of the organization and institutionalization of self-reflection and enlightenment" (Morrow & Torres, 2002, p. 138). Both Habermas and Friere are "modernists" (McLaren & Leonard, 1993, p. 3).

The theory of communicative action can be used to analyze communication for social change programs, including entertainment-education, with regard to their participatory content. We do not wish to assume here that all development programs can be participatory, although perhaps they ought to be.

Participatory communication is defined as communicative action, a process in which participants engage in action oriented to understanding. Action oriented to understanding includes the freedom to "call into question any proposal," to "introduce any proposal," and to express any "attitudes, wishes, and needs." There must be a symmetrical distribution of opportunities to contribute to discussion. This definition of participatory communication can be applied conceptually at multiple scales of social change through its relevance to the idea of the public sphere. Public spheres operate whenever private citizens meet to discuss matters of public importance: in town squares, village meetings, regional media, or in national political forums. If vigorous public spheres are present at any or all of these levels, then even nonparticipatory message programs can be subject to citizen review and criticism. In optimal instances they are part of a social context in which programs are legitimated within the context of representative democratic processes generally.

Health information campaigns are legitimated in this manner as a matter of course in developed countries. Campaigns are in principle, and sometimes in fact, subject to public criticism. The content of such communication campaigns is legitimated with reference to the qualifications of professional organizations employed in message design. Authorization for health campaigns comes from various sources, including State agencies that provide funding. Where private funding is used, authorization also comes from agencies responsible for regulation and oversight.

Entertainment-education programs will be participatory insofar as communicative action involving potential audience members is employed during their design and implementation, and insofar as programs are made subject to meaningful public review and criticism.

NEPAL'S POPULATION PROGRAM

Nepal is the poorest country in Asia after Afghanistan, and one of the poorest in the world (Population Reference Bureau, 2001). It remained largely closed to the world until 1951. Since then the country's population has increased from less than 9 million to 23.5 million. Development advances accompanied this huge increase: The poverty rate dropped from 90% to 50%, and literacy increased from 2% to 40%. Still, 50 out of 1,000 infants die in their first three months and 1 in 45 women die from causes related to childbirth, in part due to high fertility rates (Government of Nepal, Ministry of Health, 2001).

One of the surest ways to reduce both maternal and neonatal mortality is to increase birth intervals and reduce the total number of children that a woman bears by giving her greater control over her fertility. Yet, in 2001 only 39% of married Nepalese between the ages of 15 and 49 used some form of contraception (Government of Nepal, Ministry of Health, 2001).

In the 1980s Nepal's population program emphasized sterilization and was overly coercive. Nepal's population program today emphasizes informed choice and focuses on "unmet need," defined by women themselves: Women who say they want to postpone or avoid childbearing and also report that neither they nor their partner is using contraception are defined as having an unmet need (Robey, Ross & Bhushan, 1996). In Nepal, 28% of married women (over 1 million in number) say they have an unmet need for family planning.

Among the reasons for unmet need in Nepalese families are limited contraceptive supplies, their unreliable distribution, poor communication skills of health workers, lack of public understanding of reproductive and contraceptive biology, opposition from husbands and communities, gender discrimination, high rates of infant mortality, and exaggerated fears of contraceptive side-effects. Nepal's population program today uses a mixed approach designed to help couples consider the many factors involved in making a decision about contraception, while simultaneously trying to create conducive social and service environments. Messages emphasize choosing what is best for one's family; spouses are encouraged to talk to each other about family decisions, including: how many children to have and when; the importance of equally valuing female and male children; the need to provide for the children a couple has; the benefits of a well-planned family for the mother, the children, and the family as a whole; and the use of contraception to help the family achieve its goals. Other efforts seek to improve the quality of the health service delivery system so that it is more responsive to the demands of an increasingly informed public. Efforts of international agencies, Nepal government ministries, nongovernmental organizations, and private companies are joined in a coordinated effort to improve reproductive health.

COMMUNICATIVE ACTION AND NEPAL'S POPULATION PROGRAM

Beginning in 1994 JHU/PCS helped a diverse set of partners to design and implement an integrated communication program centering on entertainment-education: two radio drama serials and various forms of community performance, designed to involve local and national leaders, local beneficiaries, and community groups in building a sustainable family planning program. The Program consists of three kinds of communication activities: (1) training in interpersonal communication and counseling, (2) mass media programs on reproductive health and social change, and (3) mobilizing networks for behavior change, each of which uses entertainment-education to expand and facilitate discourse about health, gender, family well-being, and development.

Interpersonal Communication/Counseling

Formative research showed that poor communication between clients and health workers was a main reason for unmet contraceptive needs. Younger clients were especially reluctant to seek contraceptive services because they anticipated insensitive and impersonal treatment at the hands of health workers. Clients did not feel free to communicate their needs and desires. Aspects of communicative action were fostered at the clinic level by teaching both providers and clients better communication skills through a series of district-level workshops, as well as through two radio drama serials: *Service Brings Reward* (designed primarily for health workers) and *Cut Your Coat According to Your Cloth* (designed primarily for the general public).

Both training approaches modeled counseling principles framed by the Nepalese concept of *Abhibadan* (a form of respectful greeting). Translated roughly to an English acronym as GATHER (Rinehart, Rudy, & Drennan, 1998), the ABHIBADAN acronym reminds health workers to follow specific steps of client-oriented counseling:

- **Greet** clients, expressing respect and friendliness.
- **Ask** the client to put into their own words the choice(s) they are facing, and ask them questions to help them clarify their feelings.
- **Tell** the client about the available options, providing accurate information according to the client's needs.
- **Help** the client think about the possible advantages and disadvantages of each option.
- **Explain** how to carry out their decision.
- **Returns** to the clinic should be encouraged by inviting clients to return if they have questions or concerns.

Workshops and the *Service Brings Reward* radio drama aimed to improve the ability of health providers and their supervisors to communicate with, and counsel, clients effectively. Training materials encouraged service providers to give clients all the information available, pro and con, about options. These materials encouraged health workers to help clients speak freely, ask questions, and make informed choices on their own (Photo 22.1). Health workers are taught that these skills can be applied to other topics besides contraceptive

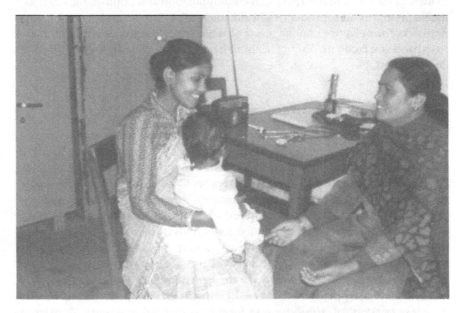

PHOTO 22.1. A female health worker counseling a mother and her child after a medical examination at the Bhaktapur Health Post in Nepal. (*Source*: Photograph by Harvey Nelson. Used with permission.)

use, including child survival, safe motherhood, HIV/AIDS prevention, spousal communication, and others.

The second entertainment-education radio drama serial, *Cut Your Coat According to Your Cloth*, was designed to teach clients how to interact with health workers. The flip side of GATHER/ABHIBADAN for clients was NA-MASKAAR, also a respectful form of greeting in Nepali, which reminded clients how to exercise their right to know, to ask for services and information delivered in an appropriate way, to understand the pros and cons of available options, and to discuss what they have learned with others. By addressing both sides of the client/provider equation, the Nepal Program aimed to improve the quality and symmetry of client-health worker interaction.

The GATHER process teaches an approach similar to communicative action. This interaction teaches both health service workers and clients how to "thematize" and "redeem" validity claims. The distribution of opportunities to contribute through questions and statements of concern is "symmetrical" in spirit. Clients are taught to "raise any proposal" they wish. The Program was explicitly aimed at making client/health worker interaction more egalitarian and symmetrical, and this symmetricality was depicted in the E-E radio drama. This application of the theory of communicative action has been studied in connection with small-scale program evaluation (Jacobson & Kolluri, 1999).

Mass Media

The mass media component of the Nepal population program consisted of two radio serials explicitly designed to foster discourse, expand access to accurate information, and support informed decision-making. Entertainment-education is particularly suited for these purposes because it can foster discourse on a large scale and at many levels (Storey, 1999).

Cut Your Coat According to Your Cloth, a radio drama serial for the general public, began broadcasting in 1996 and continues today. *Cut Your Coat* was designed around the central concept of the "well planned family," and encourages individuals to plan their families to suit their own interests and choices, through family and spousal communication in which choices are jointly determined. It encourages women to express their aspirations and concerns about reproduction and family in a culture that has traditionally offered little opportunity for women to do so, encouraging them to speak openly to "people in authority" (such as health workers and community leaders). Questions aired at the end of each radio episode encourage listeners to comment on the radio program. Listener letters are routinely read on the air during lead-in and lead-out segments of each episode.

Between 1996 and 2000, over 200 episodes were produced, reaching an estimated 8 million men and women of reproductive age. Reinforcing the E-E radio serial are workbooks for newly literate Nepalese, based on stories

PHOTO 22.2.   A listeners' group gathered in Mainapokhar, Nepal, to listen to the radio serial, *Cut Your Coat According to Your Cloth*. (*Source*: Johns Hopkins University's Center for Communication Programs. Photograph by Khemraj Shrestha.)

contained in the radio drama and designed for use in women's literacy programs and community discussion groups.

A second radio program, *Service Brings Rewards*, is a distance-education serial designed for health workers. Like *Cut Your Coat*, it uses a dramatized format to improve service provider counseling skills and workplace morale by reinforcing a sense of professionalism. Like *Cut Your Coat*, the distance education radio serial has been on the air weekly since 1996. It models positive client-provider interactions and portrays health workers as integral members of the community. Research shows that this E-E radio program is also popular among clients (Storey, Boulay, Karki, Heckert, & Karmacharya, 1999).

Both of these media programs were developed through extensive research, needs assessment, consultation, and pretesting among stakeholders and end users. The program received extensive inputs from listener groups in Nepal (Photo 22.2). Teams of program staff regularly visited Nepal villages to conduct community meetings, play segments of the radio serials, and to record feedback from listeners, excerpts of which are routinely aired.

While the radio programs are not dialogical in an interpersonal sense, they foster the testing of validity claims required by communicative action. Various forms of feedback and accountability are available in principle and in practice.

Networks for Behavior Change

In order to further address community-level processes of social change, the Nepal population program worked with the Center for Development and Population Activities (CEDPA) in Nepal and their network of local NGOs to design a series of community-based health activities directly at the grassroots level, many of which used an entertainment-education or a community-celebratory approach. Community events related to reproductive health included National AIDS Day, National Condom Day, and International Women's Day. They aimed to mobilize social networks and peer group influences.

For example, Women's Day activities in 1997 drew over 11,200 marchers, and "Post-Partum Care" theme-oriented materials were distributed by NGOs in over 4,500 villages. Display exhibitions, games, street theater, and song competitions supported women's health, prevention of sexually transmitted diseases, and "well-planned family" themes (Photo 22.3). Activities organized by mothers' clubs, credit-savings groups, and others were linked to E-E radio messages featuring these groups' efforts including child spacing, breast feeding, and women's literacy. Over 60 organizations participated in networking programs at the community level.

PHOTO 22.3. A street theater performance on family planning in Mainapokhar, Nepal, conducted on National Condom Day 2001. (*Source*: Johns Hopkins University's Center for Communication Programs. Photograph by Khemraj Shrestha.)

Some such activities aim to valorize new behavioral options through a combination of education, celebration, and entertainment, but they are not inherently manipulative if their conduct is subject to review under democratic conditions. The Nepal population program is distinctive in the way it attempts, through participatory activities, to go beyond the traditional development model. The Nepal program is an integrated entertainment-education campaign (albeit an imperfect one) for communicative action and informed decision-making.

Participatory communication is both a means to behavior change as well as a desired end-state of its own. The Nepal population program employs mass media, interpersonal communication, and community networks as tools, with the goal of expanding communication opportunities for individuals and social systems so that people are better able to make decisions that affect their lives. The benefits of making family planning decisions in the larger context of individuals' lives are demonstrated. Spousal and family communication are emphasized. In short, the Nepal Program can be considered an integrated entertainment-education campaign (albeit an imperfect one) for communicative action and informed decision-making.

RESEARCH ON PROGRAM IMPACTS

To what extent do clients perceive the Nepal population program as participatory? To what extent are the E-E radio programs perceived as external influences versus as owned by the community? Do Nepalese citizens take part in program activities for the reasons expected by program planners? Is Nepalese democracy strong enough at the local, regional, and national levels to provide the public spheres required for the potential expression of local discontent with population program activities? These questions are key to evaluating the success of the Nepal program's participatory elements from the viewpoint of communicative action.

Voluntary client response may be an indication of the extent to which a program is credible and withstands the test of validity claims. Representative sample surveys conducted in 1994, 1997, and 1999 for the purpose of evaluating the impacts of the E-E radio serials showed more than a 13 percentage point increase in contraceptive use among women, and a 17 percentage point gain among men during this period. While the national contraceptive prevalence rate (CPR) remained steady around 39%, the CPR in the main project areas rose from 36% in 1994 to 49% in 1999 (ten points above the national average). The 1999 CPR among those who reported that they listened to the radio serials was 67% (Storey & Boulay, 2001).

Clients exposed to the radio serials were more proactive in their interactions with health workers, health workers used more positive counseling techniques after listening to their respective radio serial, and both contraceptive adoption and continuation rates increased (indicating that clients' concerns were being addressed) when health workers and clients had been exposed to the radio program (Storey et al., 1999; Storey & Boulay, 2001; Gunther & Storey, 2003; Boulay, Storey, & Sood, 2002).

These evaluation studies of the Nepal population program were designed outside the conceptual framework of communicative action, discussed previously. Nevertheless, they seem to indicate the operation of communicative action in health programs and to suggest how communicative action can be related to prosocial changes. These preliminary data suggest that entertainment-education interventions can serve the interests of families with unmet needs for contraception, and that this intervention is in large part communicative, and hence participatory.

CONCLUSIONS

This chapter addressed two of the problems attending the conduct of participatory communication activities and entertainment-education for development. One is the problem of definition, and the other is the matter of scale. The theory of communicative action brings a useful conceptual framework to analysis of these two problems. We illustrated application of this theory in relation to the activities of the Nepal population program. This application suggests how entertainment-education can facilitate participation and communicative action in concrete ways.

Participatory communication is defined as communicative action at multiple levels. Interaction among service providers and local clients in development projects can be meaningfully analyzed using the framework of ideal speech. Efforts to strengthen democratic processes at both the local and national levels can be analyzed using the concepts of the public sphere and meaningfully facilitated through entertainment-education. Further, the multiple levels of social organization that need to be taken into account in any but the smallest-scale development programs can be conceptualized in relation to one another through the operation of communicative action in different kinds and levels of programs and public spheres. Finally, the standard of communicative action can be used to differentiate cultural change undertaken through collective self-reflection in the public sphere versus change imposed from outside.

Entertainment-education can be used for strategic purposes, in Habermas' sense of nonparticipatory communication. However, in health promotion campaigns in industrialized countries, the idea of mass media health-oriented campaigns cannot be considered illegitimate by their nature. They have valuable, legitimate, and even participatory applications (McKee, 1994; Storey,

1999). We propose to identify when these techniques are used in a participatory fashion and when they are not. The Nepal study suggests that communicative action can help guide analysis of entertainment-education and also the design of programs to maximize participatory opportunities.

REFERENCES

Barry, C. A., Stevenson, F. A., Britten, N., Barber, N., & Bradley, C. P. (2001). Giving voice to the lifeworld. More humane, more effective medical care? A qualitative study of doctor-patient communication in general practice. *Social Science & Medicine, 53* (4), 489–505.

Berrigan, F. (1979). *Community communications: The role of community media in development*. Paris: UNESCO.

Boulay, M., Storey, D., & Sood. S. (2002). Indirect exposure to a family planning mass media campaign in Nepal. *Journal of Health Communication*, 7, 379–399.

Diaz-Bordenave, J. (1994). Participative communication as a part of building the participative society. In S. A. White, K. S. Nair. & J. Ascroft (Eds.), *Participatory communication: Working for change and development* (pp. 35–48). New Delhi: Sage.

Forester, J. (1988). Introduction: The applied turn in contemporary critical theory. In J. Forester (Ed.), *Critical theory and public life* (pp. ix–xix). Cambridge, MA: MIT Press.

Forester, J. (1992). Critical ethnography: On fieldwork in a Habermasian way. In M. Alvesson & H. Wilmott (Eds.), *Critical management studies*. Thousand Oaks, CA: Sage.

Freire, P. (1970). *Pedagogy of the oppressed*. New York: Seabury Press.

Freire, P. (1973). *Education for critical consciousness*. New York: Seabury Press.

Freire, P. (1993). *Pedagogy of the city*. New York: Continuum.

Freire, P. (1996). *Letters to Cristina: Reflections on my life and work*. London: Routledge.

Gonzalez, H. (1989). Interactivity and feedback in Third World development campaigns. *Critical Studies in Mass Communication*. 6, 295–314.

Government of Nepal Ministry of Health (2001). *Nepal demographic and health survey 2001 (NDHS)*. Kathmandu, Nepal: Author.

Gunther, A. & Storey, D. (2003). The influence of presumed influence. *Journal of Communication, 53*(2), 199–215.

Habermas, J. (1975). *Legitimation crisis*. Boston: Beacon Press.

Habermas, J. (1984). *The theory of communicative action, Volume 1: Reason and the rationalization of society*. Boston: Beacon Press.

Habermas, J. (1987). *The theory of communicative action, Volume 2: A critique of functionalist reason*. Boston: Beacon Press.

Habermas, J. (1989). *The structural transformation of the public sphere: An inquiry into a category of bourgeois society*. Cambridge: MIT Press.

Habermas, J. (1990). *Moral consciousness and communicative action*. Cambridge: MIT Press.

Habermas, J. (1996). *Between facts and norms: Contributions to a discourse theory of law and democracy*. Cambridge, MA: MIT Press.

Habermas, J. (1998). Struggles for recognition in the democratic constitutional state. In C. Cronin & P. De Greif (Eds.), *The inclusion of the other: Studies in political theory / Jürgen Habermas* (pp. 203–238). Cambridge. MA: MIT Press.

Hamer, J. H. (1998). The Sidama of Ethiopia and rational communication action in policy and dispute settlement. *Anthropos, 93*, 137–153.

Huesca, R. (2002). Participatory approaches to communication for development. In W. B. Gudykunst & B. Mody (Eds.). *Handbook of international and intercultural communication* (pp. 499–518). Thousand Oaks. CA: Sage.

Jacobson, T. L. (2000). Cultural hybridity and the public sphere. In Wilkins, K. (Ed.), *Redeveloping communication for social change: Theory, practice, and power* (pp. 55–72). New York: Rowman & Littlefield.

Jacobson, T. L. (In Press). *Participatory communication for social change: The relevance of the theory of communicative action. Communication Yearbook 27.* Thousand Oaks, CA: Sage.

Jacobson, T. L., & Kolluri, S. (1999). Participatory communication as communicative action. In T. L. Jacobson & J. Servaes (Eds.), *Theoretical prospects for participatory communication* (pp. 265–280). Cresskill, NJ: Hampton Press.

Jacobson, T. L., & Servaes, J. (Eds.) (1999). *Theoretical prospects for participatory communication.* Cresskill, NJ: Hampton Press.

Lewis, P. (1993). *Alternative media: Linking global and local.* Paris: UNESCO.

Mato, D. (1999). Problems of social participation in "Latin" America in the age of globalization: Theoretical and case-based considerations for practitioners and researchers. In T. L. Jacobson & J. Servaes. (Eds.), *Theoretical prospects for participatory communication* (pp. 51–75). Cresskill, NJ: Hampton Press.

McKee, N. (1994). A community-based learning approach: Beyond social marketing. In S. White, K. S. Nair, & J. Ascroft (Eds.), *Participatory communication: Working for change and development* (pp. 194–228). New Dehli: Sage.

McLaren, P. & Leonard, P. (1993). *Paulo Freire: A critical encounter.* London: Routledge.

Midgley, J., Hall, A., Hardiman, H., & Narine, D. (1986). *Community participation, social development, and the state.* New York: Methuen.

Morrow, R. A., & Torres, C. A. (2002). *Reading Freire and Habermas: Critical pedagogy and transformative social change.* New York: Teachers College Press.

Pietrykowski, B. (1996). Knowledge and power in adult education: Beyond Freire and Habermas. *Adult Education Quarterly, 46*(2), 82–97.

Population Reference Bureau. (2001). *World population data sheet: Demographic data and estimates for the countries and regions of the world: Book edition.* Washington, DC: Population Reference Bureau.

Pusey, M. (1991). *Economic rationalism in Canberra: A nation-building state changes its mind.* New York: Cambridge University Press.

Rahman, M. A. (1993). *People's self development: Perspectives on participatory action research.* London: Zed.

Ramella, M., & De La Cruz, R. B. (2000). Taking part in adolescent sexual health promotion in Peru: Community participation from a social psychological perspective. *Journal of Community & Applied Social Psychology, 10*(4), 271–284.

Rinehart, W., Rudy, S., & Drennan, M. (1998). GATHER guide to counseling. *Population Reports.* Baltimore, MD: Johns Hopkins University. Series J, Number 48.

Robey, B., Ross, J., & Bhushan, I. (1996). Meeting unmet need: New strategies. *Population Reports.* Baltimore, MD: Johns Hopkins University. Series J, Number 43.

Servaes, J. (1989). *One world, multiple cultures: A new paradigm on communication for development.* Leuven, Belgium: Acco.

Servaes, J., Jacobson, T. L., & White, S.A. (Eds.) (1996). *Participatory communication research for social change.* New Delhi: Sage.

Singhal, A., & Rogers, E. M. (1999). *Entertainment-education: A communication strategy for social change.* Mahway, NJ: Lawrence Erlbaum.

Storey, D. (1999). Popular culture, discourse, and development: Rethinking entertainment-education from a participatory perspective. In T. L. Jacobson & J. Servaes (Eds.), *Theoretical prospects for participatory communication* (pp. 337–358). Cresskill, NJ: Hampton Press.

Storey, D., & Boulay, M. (2001). *Improving family planning use and quality of services in Nepal through the entertainment-education strategy: Summary and update of Field Report*

No. 12. Baltimore, MD: Johns Hopkins University, School of Public Health, Population Communication Services.

Storey, D., Boulay, M., Karki, Y., Heckert, K., & Karmacharya, D. (1999). Impact of the integrated Radio Communication Project in Nepal, 1994-1997. *Journal of Health Communication, 4*, 271-294.

Webler, T., & Tuler, S. (2000). Fairness and competence in citizen participation: Theoretical reflections from a case study. *Administration & Society, 32*(5), 566-595.

White, R. (1999). The need for new strategies of research on the democratization of communication. In T. L. Jacobson & J. Servaes. (Eds.), *Theoretical prospects for participatory communication* (pp. 229-262). Cresskill, NJ: Hampton Press.

White, S., Nair, K. S., & Ascroft, J. (Eds.) (1994). *Participatory communication: Working for change and development*. New Delhi: Sage.

Epilogue

Just as many entertainment-education interventions end with an epilogue, so too does this book, *Entertainment-Education and Social Change*. Here we seek to draw some "big picture" conclusions about the growing worldwide phenomena of E-E, based on the topics explored in this book's chapters. Like many other innovations, the idea of entertainment-education started with a very few people (like Miguel Sabido in Mexico) and initially spread through the efforts of a very few organizations, including Population Communications International (PCI) and Johns Hopkins University's Center for Communication Programs. Then, through the active involvement of a few key individuals like David Poindexter of PCI, Patrick Coleman and Phyllis T. Piotrow at Johns Hopkins University, Miguel Sabido, and others, the idea of entertainment-education gained credence and was incorporated in health interventions around the world. Today, entertainment-education is everywhere, as this volume helps us realize.

This commonly understood history, however, is somewhat of an oversimplification, although it does describe how a dominant form of E-E was created and spread. What is presently called entertainment-education actually had several parents (as good ideas often do). One of these roots of entertainment-education was at the BBC (British Broadcasting Corporation), the main alternative to the commercial broadcasting networks of the United States, and with various institutions and individuals connected to the BBC. For example, as discussed in our Chapter 13, some of the earliest entertainment-education radio broadcasts were (1) *The Lawsons* and *Blue Hills* by the Australian Broadcasting System, and (2) *The Archers*, a long-running BBC agricultural show which began in 1951, created by Godfrey Baseley. The BBC provided training to broadcasting professionals from the Commonwealth nations, including Elaine Perkins of Jamaica, who honed the essence of the E-E soap opera approach at BBC studios in London. Perkins then returned to Jamaica to pioneer this approach in a series of five popular programs broadcast from 1958 through 1989 (Singhal & Rogers, 1999). Perkins' approach to entertainment-education was generally similar to Miguel Sabido's, but the two E-E methodologies were invented independently, one for radio and one for television. They differed in

435

various ways, although both were entertainment-education (as judged by the definitions commonly used).

Another descendent of the BBC approach to E-E radio dramas became important in North India in 1996 with the broadcast of *Tinka Tinka Sukh* (Happiness Lies in Small Things). This E-E intervention was led by Mrs. Usha Bhasin, then the Director of Programs at All India Radio (AIR), and also a former trainee at BBC. Bhasin returned from London to experiment with her own E-E approach in three radio programs broadcast from 1988 to 1995. Her approach came together with Miguel Sabido's E-E methodology in a PCI/AIR workshop in 1995, out of which came plans for *Tinka Tinka Sukh*. This radio drama then led to further E-E interventions in India, both on radio and television, such as the currently broadcast *Taru* (see our Chapter 19) and the BBC World Service Trust's *Jasoos Vijay* (see our Chapter 1). Bhasin and Dr. Arvind Singhal have both been involved, albeit in formal/informal capacities, in both of these E-E interventions.

Yet other variants of E-E are now apparent in the social merchandising telenovelas of Brazil's TV Globo (see our Chapters 14 and 21), in the *Soul City* approach in South Africa (see Chapter 8), in the E-E cartoons of *Meena* in Asia (Chapter 18), and in other illustrations discussed in this book, such as the insertion of health content in U.S. soap operas (see Chapters 10 and 11). Clearly, E-E is a communication tool for social change that can be applied in numerous ways, many of which we have probably not yet thought of. The new media of the Internet and the World Wide Web offer alternative forms to convey entertainment-education to increasingly larger audiences, and for these individuals to provide feedback to E-E professionals (see Chapters 1 and 15).

One could imagine a vast and complicated matrix (1) of the various origins of entertainment-education methodology on one dimension, (2) by the many E-E interventions that are based, more or less directly, on these foundational roots. In most cases, this process is one of continuous evolution and reinvention as the basic idea of entertainment-education is ever changing, in a sequential search for E-E interventions with greater effectiveness, while this basic methodology is being adapted to diverse cultural conditions.

The basic strength of the effects of E-E interventions is illustrated by the two-year ORT (oral rehydration therapy) campaign in Egypt, which led to 90% awareness-knowledge and 70% use of ORT (see Chapter 16). Why does E-E generally have strong effects? A basic reason is the use of formative research in designing E-E interventions. Communication research was an important element in Miguel Sabido's E-E telenovelas since they began in Mexico in 1975 (Chapters 2 and 4). Today, no responsible leader of an E-E project would think of designing an intervention without devoting something like 10% of the total budget to research. Such formative research is particularly important in the case of entertainment-education because of the difficulty in ensuring that the educational meanings interpreted by audience members are those intended by E-E professionals (see Chapter 21). With the important role of communication research in E-E projects, however, comes a special problem, that of achieving collaboration between media professionals and the researchers (as Martine Bouman illustrated in Chapter 12). Every entertainment-education project is a hybrid product of two very different types of expertise. Harnessing these two kinds of professionals to produce an E-E intervention poses important management challenges. But these can be overcome, as Shereen Usdin and others illustrate in Chapter 8.

E-E also has a strong intellectual/scholarly dimension that is generally absent from strictly entertainment. Miguel Sabido drew directly on scholarly theories, such as those of Albert Bandura's social learning theory (see Chapter 5) in gradually forming and reforming his methodology (see Chapter 4). The roots of scholarly study and writing about entertainment-education, however, seem to have really gotten underway only in 1985 at the University of Southern California, when three of the present coeditors (Arvind Singhal, Michael Cody, and Everett Rogers) and William Brown met to analyze why and how episodes of *Hum Log*, the extremely popular E-E television soap opera in India, had effects in changing behavior. We explored the concept of parasocial interaction, positive and negative role models, and other theoretical aspects of E-E (see the Preface of this book). Soon we had a research grant from the Rockefeller Foundation to gather data in India from audience members, so as to test our theoretical insights. This grant may have been the first funded scholarly research on the effects of an E-E intervention.

About this same time, Larry Kincaid, Tom Valente, and other scholars at Johns Hopkins University began conducting scholarly research on the Johns Hopkins entertainment-education interventions underway in various nations. Soon, communication and public health students were conducting research on E-E interventions for their masters and doctoral studies, and courses dealing with E-E were being offered at an increasing number of U.S. and overseas universities. Also important in the scholarly development of entertainment-education thinking has been three international conferences, with the first one hosted in 1989 at the University of Southern California. So progress of the entertainment-education field has been marked by a series of forward steps by E-E media professionals, paralleled by a sequence of scholarly/intellectual/theoretical advances. Promising recent work on the scholarly front includes the importance of media-stimulated interpersonal communication leading to behavior change (see Chapter 22), audience involvement in E-E interventions (see Chapter 7), interpretive study of how audience individuals make sense and give meaning to E-E messages (see Chapter 21), and participatory E-E approaches for empowering the oppressed (see Chapter 20).

What is the future of entertainment-education? Today, it is widely accepted as one useful strategy for social change, with applications beyond family planning and other health topics, and in the United States and Europe, as well as in Latin America, Africa, and Asia. Undoubtedly, these wider applications will be explored in future years, and much will probably be learned to advance our further understanding of entertainment-education, and, more broadly, of the science of human behavior change.

Perhaps one of the unique contributions of the present volume was to rewrite certain of the history of entertainment-education, by showing that the dominant role of Miguel Sabido's E-E methodology was not the only foundation, although it was certainly very important. Like many other useful innovations, variety and diversity in using a basic idea should be recognized, and rewarded.

—Arvind Singhal
—Mike Cody
—Ev Rogers
—Miguel Sabido

REFERENCES

Singhal, A., & Rogers, E. M. (1999). *Entertainment-education: A communication strategy for social change*. Mahwah, NJ: Lawrence Erlbaum Associates.

About the Authors

Rasha A. Abdulla is a doctoral candidate in the School of Communication, University of Miami. Her research interests include development communication and entertainment-education, uses and effects of new media, and music as a medium. She is a citizen of Egypt.

Mira B. Aghi started the tradition of formative research for program development in India in the 1970s. She has been training researchers in South Asia, Eastern and Southern Africa, and South America in qualitative research methodologies for over 30 years. She received her Ph.D. in Psychology from Loyola University, Chicago. She directed the formative research for the *Meena* communication initiative in South Asia, and the *Sara* communication initiative in Eastern and Southern Africa.

Albert Bandura is David Starr Jordan Professor of Social Science in Psychology at Stanford University. The major focus of his work centers on the mechanisms of human agency through which people exercise some measure of influence over personal and social change. His book, *Social Foundations of Thought and Action: A Social Cognitive Theory*, provides the conceptual framework of his theory and analyzes the large body of knowledge bearing on it. His most recent book, *Self-Efficacy: The Exercise of Control*, presents belief in one's personal efficacy to produce effects by one's actions as the foundation of human agency.

Vicki Beck is Director of Hollywood, Health & Society at the University of Southern California's Norman Lear Center, based at the Annenberg School for Communication. Prior to joining USC, Ms. Beck directed the Centers for Disease Control and Prevention's entertainment-education pilot project for research, outreach, and evaluation. A health communication specialist for 20 years, Beck was assistant director of communication at UCLA's Center for Health Sciences, served as Director of Communication for the San Diego-Imperial Chapter of the March of Dimes, and as consultant to the March of Dimes Birth Defects Foundation on national communication planning issues.

Martine Bouman is Managing Director of the Netherlands Entertainment-Education (E-E) Foundation. An independent consultant and researcher, she is involved with several national and international E-E television projects. She previously served as associate researcher in the Department of Communication and Innovation Studies at the University of Wageningen. Bouman investigated the collaboration process in E-E television, which resulted in the publication of her doctoral thesis *The Turtle and the Peacock: The E-E strategy on Television.* She served as the CEO of the Third International E-E Conference in the Netherlands in 2000.

William J. Brown is Professor and Research Fellow in the School of Communication and the Arts at Regent University in Virginia Beach, Virginia. He received a Bachelor of Science degree in Environmental Science from Purdue University, a Master's degree in Communication Management from the Annenberg School for Communication at the University of Southern California, and a Ph.D. degree in Communication, also from the University of Southern California. His academic research interests include media effects, social influence, and the use of entertainment-education (E-E) for social change.

Rachel Carnegie has a B.A. from Cambridge University and an M.A. in Education from Sussex University. From 1991 to 1994 Carnegie was a consultant to UNICEF Bangladesh, responsible for the creative development of the *Meena* communication initiative that promotes the rights of girls. Since 1994 she served as a core adviser to the *Sara* communication initiative for adolescent girls in Africa.

Michael J. Cody received his Ph.D. from Michigan State University and has wide ranging research interests in entertainment media, persuasion, interpersonal communication, health communication, and uses of new technology. He spent the Spring of 2002 in London researching BBC and BBC World Service Trust programs. Cody is Professor, Annenberg School for Communication, University of Southern California.

Galen Cole is Director of Development and Training in the Office of Communication at the Centers for Disease Control and Prevention, Atlanta.

Sangeeta Fernandes (M.A., University of Southern California) is a doctoral student in the School of Communication at the USC Annenberg School for Communication and studies issues in health and entertainment, with an emphasis in international programs and the HIV/AIDS epidemic.

Esta de Fossard has over 30 years' experience in communication for social development and in distance learning. She worked in 70 countries and is an expert in the design, creation, and production of television and radio programs for health education and classroom education. She has written several textbooks about writing and producing radio and television social development projects and more than 50 children's books and textbooks for primary, secondary, and college level. As Senior Technical Advisor for JHU/CCP, she directs design workshops, trains scriptwriters, and reviews scripts for radio, television, and video programs worldwide, including more than 25 serial dramas.

Ben Fraser is an Associate Professor in the School of Communication and the Arts at Regent University, where he is also Director of the Center for the Study of Faith and Culture. He received his Bachelor of Arts in Religion and Psychology at Southern California College, a Master's of Divinity in Theology at Fuller Theological Seminary, a Master's Degree in Psychology at Pepperdine University, a Master's Degree in Communication at California State University, Fullerton, and a Ph.D. degree in Communication at the University of Washington. His academic interests include media effects, celebrities, and international communication.

Sue Goldstein is a public health specialist from South Africa. She is a medical practitioner who qualified at the University of the Witwatersrand, and practiced in primary health care in Soweto and Alexandra, South African townships, for ten years before specializing. She has a special interest in health promotion and health communication, and has written a book on health promotion in South Africa. Since 1995 she has worked with Soul City: Institute for health and development communication in a number of different roles, from managing Soul City series, to research and developing and managing *Soul Buddyz*, the children's series. She has been a health activist since the 1970's, and was a co-founder of the South Africa journal "Critical Health," was an active member of the National Medical and Dental Association, and was a founder member of the National Health Promotion Forum. She is married with three teenage children and enjoys jogging, reading, art, and film.

Bradley S. Greenberg is University Distinguished Professor in the Departments of Communication and Telecommunication at Michigan State University.

Thomas L. Jacobson is Associate Professor in the Department of Communication, University at Buffalo, State University of New York. He earned his Ph.D. at the University of Washington, and has focused much of his research on participatory communication and civic society.

Neill McKee is presently Associate Director for Communication Sciences, Health Communication Partnership, Johns Hopkins University Center for Communication Programs, Baltimore. McKee completed an M.S. in communication theory and research at Florida State University in 1988 and is author of *Social Mobilization and Social Marketing in Developing Communities* (Southbound, 1992) and chief editor and contributing author for *Involving People, Evolving Behaviour* (Southbound, 2000). He initiated and managed

UNICEF's *Meena* and *Sara* communication initiatives while working in Asia and Africa.

Tiffany Menard is a Research Associate at the Michigan Public Health Institute.

Michael J. Papa is a Associate Professor and Chair in the Department of Speech Communication and Dramatic Arts at Central Michigan University.

Antonio C. La Pastina (Ph.D. University of Texas at Austin) is an Assistant Professor in the Department of Communication at Texas A&M University.

Dhaval Patel (Ph.D. Michigan State University) was an Assistant Professor in the School of Rural Public Health in the Health Science Center of the Texas A&M University System before joining UNICEF, New York.

Phyllis Tilson Piotrow established and is the former Director of the Johns Hopkins University's Center for Communication Programs. She played a leading role in family planning and related health communication programs for more than 35 years. A Professor at the Johns Hopkins Bloomberg School of Public Health, Department of Population and Family Health Sciences, she was the Principal Investigator of the Population Communication Services project since its inception in 1982 until 2001. She provided technical assistance in more than 20 developing countries in Africa, Asia, the Near East, and Latin America. Piotrow is the author of numerous publications, including *World Population Crisis: The United States Response* (1972). In 1990 she coauthored *Strategies for Family Planning Information, Education, and Communication*, published by the World Bank, and in 1997 *Health Communication: Lessons from Family Planning and Reproductive Health*. She received the Carl Shultz Award for Distinguished Service from the Population and Family Planning section of the American Public Health Association in 1989, and the Charles A. Dana Foundation Award for Pioneering Achievements in Health and Education in 1991.

David Poindexter is Honorary Chair of Population Media Center. He founded Population Communications International in 1985 and served as its President and Chief Executive until his retirement in 1998. From 1970 until 1984 he Directed the Communication Center of the Population Institute. His B.A. is from Willamette University. He hold two graduate degrees from Boston University. Currently, he undertakes overseas assignments in population mass media work from time to time.

Everett M. Rogers is Distinguished Professor, Department of Communication and Journalism, University of New Mexico. He has been involved in studying the effects of entertainment-education (E-E) for the past 20 years in developing nations, and currently is investigating delivery of E-E health messages by means of the Internet in New Mexico. The author acknowledges the assistance of Professor Michael Slater, Colorado State University, in developing many of the ideas expressed in chapter 15. Rogers and Arvind Singhal are co-authors of *Entertainment-Education: A Communication Strategy for Social Change* (Lawrence Erlbaum Associates, 1999).

William Ryerson is founder and President of Population Media Center (PMC), and previously served as Executive Vice President of Population Communications International. He received a B.A. from Amherst College and an M.Phil. from Yale University. Ryerson is listed in several editions of *Who's Who in the World, Who's Who in America*, and *Who's Who in the East*.

Miguel Sabido is known as the "father of entertainment-education." He is a professional director, playwright, producer and at the same time a communication theoretician. He is the creator and writer of the "theory of the tone in human communications." He was Vice-President of Evaluation and Research for Televisa Network for over 20 years. Presently he is an international consultant for entertainment-education projects around the world. He is the CEO of a Production Company for E-E projects. He is in the process of developing and producing an E-E telenovela for the Hispanic community of the United States. He has published several papers and books. He graduated from the National Autonomous University of Mexico (UNAM).

Charles T. Salmon is Ellis N. Brandt Professor in the Department of Advertising at Michigan State University.

Marcio Schiavo is the Director of Communicarte, a Brazil-based organization promoting social marketing, and Professor in the Master's Program in Sexology at the Gama Filho University in Rio de Janeiro.

Agnes Shabalala is a senior researcher in health communication at Soul City for the past six years. She was a researcher in early childhood education for 12 years at the Institute for Behavioral Science, Unisa (University of South Africa) and the Human Sciences Research Council. She is currently completing a degree in BA Human Behavior at the University of South Africa. She has also written several research papers on early education and health.

Nuzhat Shahzadi works for the UNICEF Regional Office for South Asia, in Kathmandu, Nepal, heading the *Meena* Communication Initiative. Previously, she was in charge of UNICEF's *Sara* communication initiative in East and South Africa. She has an MPH with specialization in health education and has over 17 years experience in the field.

Devendra Sharma is a folk actor-singer and a doctoral student in the School of Communication Studies, Ohio University. He is involved in both the programmatic and the research aspects of the *Taru* Project.

Thuli Shongwe is Senior Researcher for Soul City: Institute for Health and Development Communication. She started working as health researcher in 1978. Before she joined Soul City, she had been a researcher at the Institute for Urban Primary Health Care based at the Alexandra Health Centre. She has been trained in health promotion, epidemiological research and qualitative research methodologies.

Arvind Singhal is Presidential Research Scholar and Professor, School of Communication Studies, Ohio University. He is principal investigator of the *Taru* Project in India. He has analyzed participatory theater in several countries, particularly for HIV/AIDS prevention. Singhal also investigated several interventions in Bangladesh and India that helped clarify organizing for social change as a means of empowerment. Singhal and Everett Rogers are co-authors of *Entertainment-Education: A Communication Strategy for Social Change* (Lawrence Erlbaum Associates, 1999).

Suruchi Sood is Senior Program Evaluation Officer at Johns Hopkins Bloomberg School of Public Health/Center for Communication Programs. She holds a Ph.D. degree in Communications from the University of New Mexico.

J. Douglas Storey is Associate Director of The Health Communication Partnership, Bloomberg School of Public Health, Johns Hopkins University, Baltimore. Since earning his Ph.D. degree at Stanford University, Storey has been researching and designing reproductive health, environmental protection, and other development communication projects.

Negussie Teffera is Population Media Center's Country Representative in Ethiopia. A former Director of the National Office of Population, he wrote the country's population policy and oversaw its adoption and implementation. Negussie holds a Ph.D. in communication from the University of Wales, Cardiff, and has extensive experience in radio production.

Thomas Tufte has an M.A. in cultural sociology and a Ph.D. in media studies, and is Associate Professor at the Department of Film and Media Studies, University of Copenhagen. His recent publications include *Living with the Rubbish Queen: Telenovelas, Culture and Modernity in Brazil (2000)*, *Global Encounters: Media and Cultural Transformation* (coeditor, 2002) and *Media, Minorities, and the Multicultural Society: Scandinavian Perspectives* (editor, 2003). He coordinates a research project, HIV/AIDS Communication and Prevention (www.media.ku.dk/HIV AIDS Comm) and has served as a consultant for DANIDA, SIDA, UNESCO, Rockefeller Foundation, and USAID in health communication and communication for development.

Shereen Usdin is a medical doctor and health communication specialist. She holds a Master degree in Public Health from Harvard University and was a co-founder of the Soul City project, a South African NGO, using media to promote health and devlopment. She is currently Program Manager of the Soul City Series and heads up the organization's Advocacy program. She has worked for many years in the field of communication for social change, HIV/AIDS, gender, health and human rights.

Holley Wilkin (M.A., University of Cincinnati) is a doctoral student in the School of Communication at the USC Annenberg School for Communication, and studies health, entertainment, and media effects.

Kim Witte is Senior Program Evaluation Officer at Johns Hopkins Bloomberg School of Public Health/Center for Communication Programs, on leave from Michigan State University, where she is Professor in the Department of Communication.

Yaşar Yaşer is a graduate of Tarsus American College and Istanbul University, Faculty of Economics. He received a Master?s Degree in Economic Development from Vanderbilt University in Nashville, Tennessee. He currently works as the Executive Director of a nongovernment organization, the Turkish Family Health and Planning Foundation. Previously, Yaser worked in the Turkish Government as President of the State Institute of Statistics, theWorld Fertility Survey in London, and as Director of Administration and Planning.

Author Index

A

Abdulla, R. A., 9, 301, 307
Adler, L., 286
Afuape, T., 251
Aghi, M., 331
Agrawal, J., 100
Aguilar, M., 50
Ahmed, H., 40
Ainslie, R., 44
Airhihenbuwa, C. O., 13, 400
Ajzen, I., 125
Akerelrea, C. A., 286
Alberoni, F., 104
Albert, R. S., 236
Alcalay, R., 259
Alcantara, C., 64
Alemi, F., 286
Alfaro, R. M., 401
Algazy, J. I., 286
Alinsky, S. D., 381
Almeida, H. B., 262
Altman, D., 212, 259
Alva, M. E., 8, 143
Alvarado, M., 259
Ames, F. C., 290
Ang, I., 407
Ansley, D., 290
Apolinario, S., 267
Aquino, J.-S., 285
Aristotle, 56, 68
Arnold, C. L., 286
Ascroft, J., 418
Atkin, C., 99-100
Auwal, M., 368
Azcarraga, E., 28, 64
Aziz, A., 312

B

Badione, L. A., 43
Baer, N., 212, 259

Baezconde-Garbanati, L., 216
Bairnsfather, L. E., 288
Baker, L. H., 288
Baker, M. J., 100
Balcazar, H., 259
Ball, S., 214
Bandura, A., 12-13, 15, 26, 61, 68, 70, 75-76,
    78-81, 83, 85, 119, 125, 132, 144, 196, 216,
    285, 317, 366, 369
Barnas, G. F., 292
Barnhardt, J. M., 287
Barry, E. M., 378
Barth, S., 42
Bartholet, J., 301, 305
Bartlett, K., 286
Basil, M. D., 100, 107, 109
Bautista, A., 401
Beck, V., 9, 191, 207, 210, 212-213, 219, 259
Becker, M. H., 125-126
Bengtsson, B., 288
Benotsch, E., 288
Bentley, E., 26, 61, 68, 119, 128
Berelson, B., 7, 16, 130, 317
Berkanovic, E., 214
Berkel, L., 288
Berko, L., 368
Berland, G. K., 286-288
Bernstam, E. V., 144
Bernstein, L., 288
Berrigan, F., 418
Berutu, H. M., 48
Bharath, U., 8, 394
Bharucha, R., 393
Bhushan, I., 424
Bier, M., 286
Biermann, J. S., 293
Blanco, M., 286
Block, M., 99
Blumler, J. G., 129
Boal, A., 18, 365, 378-379,
    383-390
Bocarnea, M. C., 100
Bogatz, G. A., 214

Bonko, L., 99
Boorstin, D. J., 97-98
Bordenave, J. D., 418
Borelli, S., 263
Borland, R., 286
Boulay, M., 42-43, 55, 130, 143, 428, 430
Bouman, M., 14, 99, 110, 118, 143, 192, 194, 225, 228-230, 232-233, 237, 238, 262
Bourdieu, P., 239-240
Bowman, J., 286
Boyd, D., 302-303
Boyer, J. F., 286
Bradley, C. P., 22
Brake, C., 245, 247
Brand, J. J., 99
Braudy, L., 97-98
Brennan, P. F., 289
Bright, M. A., 211, 216
Brock, T. C., 197, 285
Broder, M. S., 286
Brodie, M., 192-193, 212-213, 259
Brown, J. D., 212, 259, 286, 407
Brown, M. E., 401, 412
Brown, R., 119, 129, 192-193
Brown, W. J., 9, 85, 92, 97, 100, 102-104, 107, 109
Brunsdon, C., 401
Buckingham, D., 246
Buller, D. B., 286
Burciaga, K. D., 286
Burgoon, J. K., 286
Burke, K., 101, 367
Burrell, G., 372
Bushman, B. L., 195
Busler, M., 100
Busselle, R., 193

C

Cacioppo, J. T., 126-127
Caggiano, C. D., 288
Campbell, J., 98
Campbell, N., 288
Cantor, M. G., 231
Carlson, L., 99
Carnegie, R., 331, 342, 345
Carnevale, P. J., 238
Cases, D., 8, 42, 143
Castro, D., 261
Castro, F. G., 288
Catz, S., 288
Chaiken, S., 197
Chalela, P., 289
Chamberlain, M. A., 286
Chambers, R., 380
Chandler, G., 22
Chapel, T., 195
Charnock, A., 302, 307, 313
Chavez, L. R., 286

Chen, H. T., 195-196
Cheney, G., 101
Chi-Lum, B., 286
Chibatamoto, P., 49
Chin, S. Y., 342
Christofides, N., 175
Cody, M. J., 85, 92, 111, 243
Colby, D., 286
Cole, G., 191, 195, 196
Cole, H. P., 285, 286
Cole, J. L., 285
Coleman, P. L., 41, 51, 64, 98, 100, 109, 262
Colle, R. D., 187
Collins, L. M., 288
Convisser, J., 262
Cook, T. D., 193
Cotton, D., 195
Counselman, F. L., 288
Covarrubias, C., 21, 68, 71, 401
Crayford, T., 246
Crouch, M. A., 288
Cummings, M. S., 99

D

Dalrymple, L., 391
Davenport-Sypher, B., 130-131, 133
Davis, J. C., 215-216
Davis, S., 211
Davis, T. C., 288
Dawidziak, M., 208, 219
De Briceno, R. V., 8, 42, 143
De Fossard, E., 7, 12, 39, 54, 192, 262
DeAngelis, C. D., 292
Dearing, J. W., 109, 131, 288
Debowski, S., 292
Deering, M. J., 7, 290
DeJong, W., 109, 214, 259
Dervin, B., 144
Diase, M., 303-304
Dibba, Y., 44, 199
DiClemente, C. C., 123, 131
Diepgen, T. L., 288
Dignan, M., 286
Diop-Sidibe, N., 43
Donohue, G., 317
Drennan, M., 425
Drummond, P., 245
Duane, J. J., 100
Duff, D., 110
Duke, M., 11
Duke, W. E., 215, 218
Duman, M., 251
Dunbar, N. E., 286
Dunlap, J., 110
Dutjuk, F., 48
Dutta, E., 393
Dyer, R., 105

E

Eagly, A. H., 197
Edwards, B., 236-237
El Kamel, F., 50, 302, 307, 310, 313
El Kassaby, S., 304
El Mougi, M., 301, 305, 307
El Sayyad, L. M., 306
El Tohamy, K., 301, 305, 307
Elias, E., 16
Elliot, M. N., 286
Emah, E., 42
Eng, T. R., 288
Erdogan, B. F., 100
Eriksen, A., 403
Evans, S., 246
Everette, J. D., 286
Eysenbach, A. J., 290
Eysenbach, G., 286

F

Fadul, A. M., 265, 402
Faundez, A., 382
Ferguson, D., 99
Fernandes, I., 263, 265
Fernandes, S., 243
Ferrara, M., 49
Festinger, L., 104, 197
Figueroa, M. E., 43, 51, 55, 132, 144, 403
Firme, M., 267
Fishbein, M., 125
Fisher, W., 13
Fiske, J., 407
Flanagin, A. J., 288
Flournoy, R., 212, 259
Foehr, U., 212, 259
Fokkens, P., 200-201
Fong, M., 110
Fotheringham, M. J., 286
Fowler, M., 247
Fraser, B., 9, 97, 100, 102-104, 111
Freimuth, V., 193, 208, 215, 248-249, 259, 284
Freire, P., 365, 378, 382-383, 389-390, 418, 423
Freud, S., 101
Freudenberg, N., 194
Friedman, H. H., 99
Friedman, L., 99
Frith, M., 400
Fuenzalida, V., 402, 410-411

G

Gabr, M., 301, 305
Galavotti, C., 7
Gallion, K. J., 286

Gallo, M., 286
Gamson, J., 97-98
Gandhi, I., 29
Garbanati, J. A., 216
Gaudet, H., 130, 317
George, R. B., 286
Gerbner, G., 78
Germain, A., 175
Giddens, A., 76
Gill, P., 4
Gill, S. S., 29
Gillespie, M., 408
Glass, W., 44, 199
Glik, D., 214
Goldman, K., 100
Goldstein, S., 153, 175, 262
Golladay, G. J., 289
Gonzalez, J., 402
Gramsci, A., 130, 372
Green, M. C., 285
Greenberg, B., 9, 14, 191, 193, 215
Greenfield, M. V. H., 288-290
Greenspon, 10, 11, 13, 15, 193, 197, 208, 249, 259, 284
Grisolli, P., 402
Gross, L., 78
Guadamos, N., 53
Guerini, E., 267
Guillermoprieto, A., 264
Gujral, I. K., 28-29
Gulino, C., 15
Gumed, M., 377
Gumucio D. A., 20
Gunther, A., 13, 431
Gustafson, D. H., 15
Gustafson, G. H., 15

H

Ha, L., 289
Habermas, J., 418, 420-422
Haji, R., 184
Hall, A., 418
Hall, J. R., 286
Halverson, H., 286
Hamburger, E. I., 262, 273
Hanlon, E., 215
Hansen, K., 285
Hardiman, H., 418
Hardyman, R., 248
Harold, C. M., 264
Harris, C., 302, 304
Hartman, M. P., 291
Hasan, K., 54
Hau, B., 286
Heckert, K., 42, 428
Heider, F., 104
Heimberg, F., 100

Heise, L., 175
Herb, R., 110
Hernandez, L. J., 62
Hernandez, O., 264
Hindman, D. B., 286
Hines, J. M., 286
Hirschhorn, N., 310
Hisserich, J. C., 289
Hobson, D., 400–401, 407
Hoeke, S. A., 99
Hoffman, D. L., 286
Holcomb, J. R., 286
Holland, T., 245–246
Hooper, R., 246
Hornik, R., 54
Horton, D., 103, 129
Horton, P. B., 366
Houran, J., 111
Hovland, C. I., 104
Hubell, F. A., 294
Huerta, E., 259
Huesca, R., 403, 418
Huesmann, L. R., 195
Huntington, D. L., 262
Hussey, J., 294

I

Ibarra, L., 214
Ilott, P., 22

J

Jabre, B., 50
Jacks, N., 402
Jackson, R. H., 289
Jacobson, T. L., 9, 13, 379, 417–418, 427
Jacoby, R., 200–201
Janis, I. L., 104
Janz, N., 126
Japhet, G., 104, 175, 262
Jara, J. R., 71, 100
Jato, M. N., 55
Jensen, K. B., 407
Jensen, S., 403, 408
Jensen, T. D., 99
Jibaja, M. J., 286
Jimerson, A., 215
Johnson, A. M., 101
Jones, M. C., 214
Jung, C. G., 27, 61, 69, 128

K

Kahle, L. R., 104
Kalichman, S. C., 288

Kamins, M. A., 99, 104
Kanouse, D. E., 290
Karchi, Y., 42
Karki, Y., 428
Karmacharya, D., 42, 428
Karmakura, W. A., 100
Karya, T., 53
Katz, E., 129, 317, 368
Katz, J., 15, 402
Kazmi, S., 47
Kazungu, T., 33, 35, 184
Kean, T., 290
Keller, S. N., 45, 212, 259
Kelley, H. H., 104
Kelman, H., 100, 102–103,
    105–106
Kemprecos, L. F., 50
Kennedy, M. G., 210, 215, 259
Kennett, R. L., 281
Keoun, B., 291
Kiingi, L. R., 45
Kim, Y. M., 44, 49, 55, 199
Kimmal, P. L., 290
Kincaid, D. L., 13, 42–43, 46, 51, 53–55, 98–100,
    109, 128, 131–132, 144, 262, 284, 321, 368,
    403
Kingery, P., 286
Kiragu, K., 42
Kirby, S. D., 288–291
Kok, G. J., 229
Kolluri, S., 427
Kols, A., 49
Koplan, J., 213
Kotler, P., 315
Kottak, C. P., 276, 400, 402
Kravitz, R. L., 286
Kreuger, U., 301
Krippendorff, K., 402

L

La Pastina, A., 262, 266, 269, 400, 402, 407
Ladin, K., 216
Lalonde, B., 259
Lange, R., 111
Langholz, B., 15
Lansky, A., 7
Lara, M., 286
Lasswell, H. D., 101
Latham, G. P., 81
Lau, D., 110
Law, S., 16, 34, 92, 119, 194, 356
Lazarsfeld, P. F., 130, 317
Leal, O. F., 400, 402, 407–408
Lear, N., 14, 184
LeBlanc, M. M., 286
Lebo, H., 285
Lentz, B., 15

Leonard, P., 22
Leslie, E., 286
Lesser, G. S., 199
Lettenmaier, C. L., 44, 199
Lettermaier, S., 15
Levy, M., 6
Lewis, G., 51
Lewis, P., 22, 50, 55, 403, 418
Leydan, G., 248
Liebes, T., 368, 402
Linnan, H. W., 215
Lippman, W., 131
Locke, E. A., 81
Loots, L., 390
Lopes, M. I. V. de, 406-407
Lopez, A. M., 263
Lougrhan, G., 248
Loza, S., 312
Lozare, B. V., 46-47
Lull, J., 408
Lumsdaine, A. A., 104
Lundberg, G. D., 289
Lunn, B., 285
Lyra, P., 400

M

Maas, L., 229
Maccoby, N., 197
MacLean, P. D., 27, 61, 64-65, 126-127
Maguire, P., 286
Maibach, E., 216
Main, S., 286
Maker, A., 175
Makinwa, B., 400
Malepe, L., 175
Malone, M. E., 215
Mandelblatt, J., 291
Mangan, P., 290
Manoff, R. K., 28
Manoncourt, E., 342
Marangwanda, C., 49, 55
Marceau, L. D., 15
Marks, G., 289
Martin-Barbero, J., 399-400, 402,
    405-406
Mathur, I., 100, 357
Mathur, L. K., 100
Mato, D., 418
Mattelart, A., 263, 273
Mattelart, M., 263, 273
Mattos, S., 264-265
Mayer, J. A., 41
Maxfield, A., 216
Mazziotti, N., 263, 402
McAlister, A., 288
McAnany, E. G., 264-265
McBean, G., 337

McCombs, M., 130
McConnaughey, J., 286
McCutcheon, L. E., 111
McDougall, L., 4-5, 11
McGlynn, E. A., 286
McGuire, W. J., 104, 106, 123, 131
McHugh, M. P., 103
McKee, N., 8, 331, 333, 337, 342, 431
McKinlay, M., 15, 13
McLaren, P., 22
McMichael, A. J., 15
McQuail, D., 129
Meenaghan, T., 100
Mehra, J., 4
Mehra, S. S., 4
Melo, E. G. d. C., 262
Menard, T., 117
Meyer, R. C., 51, 194
Middleham, G., 245, 247
Middlestadt, S. E., 7
Midgley, J., 418
Miles, A., 251-252
Miller, C., 100, 212, 259
Miller, J. D., 286
Miller, P., 313
Minassian, L., 214
Miranda-Ribeiro, O., 269
Mishra, S. I., 289
Mitchell, E. W., 3
Moe, J. C., 99
Monahan, J. L., 144
Montgomery, K. C., 193, 231
Morales, L. S., 286
Morales, O., 265
Morgan, M., 78
Morley, D., 407-408
Morris, N., 405
Morrison, D., 402
Mumby, D. K., 130, 372
Munoz, J. A., 286
Munoz, S., 391
Murdoch, G., 194
Murphy, S. T., 144
Musacchio, R. A., 292
Musen, M. A., 290

N

Nair, K. S., 379, 418
Nariman, H. N., 9, 12, 61, 71, 104,
    193-194, 234, 236
Narine, D., 418
Nasser, S., 308-310, 313
Nebergall, R., 126
Negussie, T., 7, 35, 87, 177, 180, 181, 187
Neurath, P., 357
Newman, E., 259
Ngirwamungu, E., 33

Noer, A., 48, 53
Noff, N. E., 286
Novak, T. P., 286
Nucklos, E., 286
Nyakauru, R., 49
Nzyuko, S., 117

O

O'Conner, J. B., 291
O'Leary, A., 208, 210, 259
O'Mahony, S., 100
O'Malley, A., 288
Obadina, E., 42
Obregon, R., 12, 61, 63, 100, 118, 400
Obwaka, E., 42
Odallo, D., 42
Okigbo, C., 175
Olien, C., 317
Ordonez, M. E., 49, 53
Orozco, G., 406
Ortiz, R., 263
Osman, N., 53
Ostman, R. E., 187
Owen, N., 286
Owies, D., 286

P

Paiva, V., 391, 395-396
Palmer, A., 49
Pant, S., 119, 194, 356
Papa, M. J., 6, 13, 15, 34, 92, 111, 119, 144, 194,
    351, 356, 366, 368, 372
Pappas-Deluca, K. A., 7
Parvanta, C. F., 215
Paskett, E. D., 289
Pastina, A., 9, 261
Patel, D. S., 118, 191, 261
Patton, M. Q., 195
Payne, J. G., 288
Pechmann, C., 198
Pelsinsky, N., 41
Pennick, M., 286
Pepper, J., 289
Pereira, R., 32
Perse, E. M., 6, 7, 19, 103, 366
Petty, R. E., 126-127, 197
Piet, D., 44
Piotrow, P. T., 7, 39, 44, 49, 51, 54, 64, 98, 118,
    123-124, 192, 194, 262, 284, 321
Pitanguy, J., 175
Pleasant, A., 286
Plotnick, C., 193, 197, 208, 249, 259, 284
Poindexter, D., 7, 21, 64, 71, 87, 180,
    184

Pollack, R. E., 289
Pollard, W. E., 210, 212, 219, 259
Poppe, P. R., 8, 42, 143
Portillo, C. J., 216
Potter, P., 215
Powell, R. A., 103
Pranato, J., 53
Press, A., 402, 408
Prochaska, J. O., 123, 132
Prudencio, N., 53
Pruitt, D. G., 238
Puyol, J-A, 289

R

Rabinowitz, P., 259
Radway, J., 401, 407-408
Rafaeli, S., 288
Rahman, M. A., 418
Rahoi, R., 128
Rainie, L., 289
Ramella, M., 22
Ramirez, A., 289, 290, 292
Ramirez, V., 289, 290, 292
Ramos, R., 263
Rangan, N., 100
Rani, M., 51, 55, 403
Rao, N., 1, 2, 5, 7, 8, 10, 15, 81, 119, 179,
    182
Rapoport, A., 251
Rasmussen, F., 403
Ratzan, S. C., 288
Regis, A., 17, 34
Ren, L., 32
Restrepo-Estrada, S., 379
Reviere, P., 395
Reynolds, T., 286
Rice, R. E., 293
Richardes, D., 214
Richardson, J. L., 288
Rideout, V., 212, 259
Rimon, J. G., 16, 42, 49, 51, 53, 98, 108-109, 262,
    284
Rinehart, W. E., 51, 284, 425
Rionda, G., 26
Risopatran, F., 26
Robey, B., 424
Robinson, T. N., 294
Robinson, W., 50, 55
Rodriguez, G., 93
Rogers, E. M., 3-10, 12-18, 26, 29-30, 33-35, 51,
    61, 70-71, 81, 85, 88, 92, 94-95, 98, 103,
    108-110, 118-119, 123-124, 131-133, 143,
    154, 155, 175, 179, 182, 186, 193-194, 199,
    214, 231, 246, 259, 262, 281-293, 309, 312,
    315-316, 353, 356-358, 366, 368, 377,
    394-396, 399, 401-402, 408, 411, 418
Rokeach, M., 14, 107, 125-126

Rose, R. L., 289–290
Rosen, B., 214
Rosenbaum, J., 215
Rosenfield, L. B., 101
Rosenstock, I. M., 125
Ross, J., 424
Ross, M. I., 288–293
Ross, R. K., 288–293
Rossi, P. H., 195
Rost, J. D., 289–291
Rouner, D., 13, 127, 283–285
Rubin, R. B., 103, 366
Rudy, S., 425
Runco, M. A., 236
Rushton, J. P., 373
Ryerson, W. N., 7, 33, 35, 85, 87, 177

S

Saba, W. P., 55
Sabido, M., 9, 21, 26, 28–30, 35, 51, 61–62, 82–85,
     87–88, 89–90, 104, 124, 177, 184
Salazar, M. K., 290
Salmon, C. T., 191, 199–203, 214–215
Sarlo, B., 405
Scheepers, E., 175
Schiavo, M., 261
Schiltz, W., 75
Schriebman, G. L., 214
Schlosser, J., 192
Schmale, J., 291
Schmidt, A., 39
Schmuck, P., 75
Schramm, P., 285
Segura, F., 100
Servaes, J., 379, 418
Seyoum, G. S., 180
Shabalala, A., 153
Shaffer, A., 10
Shahzadi, N., 331
Shai, P. M., 166–167
Shamdasani, P. N., 402
Shanaham, J., 78
Shannon, C. E., 124
Sharan, M., 290
Sharf, B. F., 193, 197, 208, 212, 248–249,
     259
Sharma, D., 351, 358
Shaw, D., 130
Shaw, R., 23
Sheffield, F. D., 104
Shefner-Rogers, C. L., 1, 2, 5, 6, 10, 12, 19, 103–104,
     119, 194, 231, 356
Shefshy, M. L., 259
Sherblom, S., 286
Sherif, K., 126
Sherif, M., 126
Sherry, J. L., 13–14, 261

Shongwe, T., 153
Sienche, C., 42
Signorielli, N., 78
Silayan-Go, A., 3, 6, 14, 109, 262
Silberg, W. M., 288
Silva, F., 261
Simpson, P., 210, 259
Sinclair, J., 264
Singh, J., 29
Singh, R., 285
Singhal, A., 3–10, 12–18, 29–30, 32, 34, 51, 61, 63,
     70–71, 85, 92, 94–95, 97, 98, 103–104, 108,
     110, 118–119, 123, 128, 133, 143–144, 153,
     154, 155, 159, 163, 171, 175, 179, 186,
     192–194, 199, 214, 246, 259, 262, 283–286,
     309, 312, 351, 353, 356–358, 368, 377, 379,
     383, 394–396, 399, 401–403, 408, 411,
     418, 423
Singletary, S. E., 291
Sinha, V., 99
Sisay, W., 179
Slack, J. O., 130
Slater, M., 13, 127, 283–286
Smith, J., 245–246
Smith, Q., 286
Snyder, L. B., 43
Solis, J. M., 288
Solomon, D., 315
Sood, S., 9, 13, 16, 42, 81, 101, 103, 111, 117, 119,
     129–130, 143, 179, 182, 262, 356, 366, 405,
     431
Soule, J. B., 288
Spain, P. L., 26
SRI-Nielson, 44
St. Catherine, E., 17, 34
Stamm, K., 288
Stephenson, W., 13
Stewart, D. W., 198, 402
Stolberg, S. C., 213
Stone, K., 214
Stone, M. P., 301, 305
Storey, J. D., 9, 13, 42–43, 125, 130, 132, 143, 417,
     427–428, 430
Straubhaar, J., 262–263, 264–265, 286
Suarez, T., 288
Suman, M., 285
Sutherland, L., 391–393
Svenkerud, P., 1, 2, 5, 7, 8, 10, 15, 81, 119, 128, 179,
     182
Swalehe, R. M. A., 1, 2, 5, 7, 8, 10, 15, 35, 81, 94,
     119, 179, 182, 184
Sweeney, M. A., 288
Sypher, B. D., 13, 16

T

Tabar, L., 290–292
Tagg, S., 100

Talukdar, R. B., 54
Tata, J. R. D., 32
Tatum, C., 288
Taylor, J., 288
Termini, S., 99
Tesfaye, A., 180
Thabang, 158, 160
Thekiso, M., 169
Tichenor, P. J., 317
Till, B. D., 100
Tipton, M. L., 286
Tomaselli, K., 377
Tompkins, P. K., 101
Tripp, C., 99
Tufte, T., 15, 399-401, 403, 405,
    407-409

U

Uken, J., 289-294
Underwood, C., 42-43, 50, 132
Unger, E., 286
Uphoff, N., 379
Ureda, J. R., 294
Uribe, B. A., 402
Usdin, S., 6, 15, 153, 156, 159-160, 163, 169, 175

V

Valdeavellano, E. E., 130
Valdez, R. B., 288
Valente, T. W., 8, 42, 44, 55, 143, 199, 394
Van Bel, D., 285
Van Empelen, P., 229
Van Italie, J.-C., 22
Van Woerkum, C. M. J., 236
Vaughan, P. W., 17, 33-34, 81, 93-94, 119, 124,
    131-132, 179, 182
Velez, R., 290
Ventsam, S., 130
Vidmar, N., 14,
Vistisen, H., 403
Vorderer, P., 13
Vysokolan, R., 53

W

Wafai, M., 50
Waisbord, S., 405
Wallack, L., 6
Wallerstein, N., 144
Walther, J. B., 291
Wang, M., 32
Wardle, J., 251-252

Washienko, K., 259
Washington, R., 99
Watkins, K. E., 286
Weaver, W., 124
Weick, K., 373
Weinberg, N., 293
Weisbord, S. D., 289
Weisen, R. B., 342
Weiss, C. H., 195-196
Wells, G. L., 197
Wendo, C., 45
Wessel, K., 291
Westoff, C. F., 93
White, J., 289
White, M., 302
White, R., 418
White, S. A., 379
Whitney, E., 54
Wiard, N., 220-221
Wieberdink, E. A. M., 228-229,
    232-233
Wilkin, H., 243
Williams, D. M., 288
Wilson, A., 288
Wilson, K. E., 218
Winkler, M. A., 288
Winnard, K., 3, 7, 14, 15
Winsten, J. A., 109, 193, 214, 259
Witte, Kim, 117
Wober, J. M., 245, 247
Wohl, R. R., 6, 19, 103, 129, 366
Wolfe, K., 39
Wood, R., 288
Woodall, P. B., 286
Woodall, W. G., 286
Wothen, B, R., 195

Y

Yabroff, K. R., 291
Yang, H., 286
Yasser, Y., 9, 321
Young-Jehangeer, M., 377-378
Yun, S. H., 321

Z

Zajonc, R. B., 144
Zalduondo, B. O. de, 404
Zandvliet, A., 229
Zarcadoolas, C., 286
Zhang, J., 32
Zillman, D., 13
Zimmerman, D., 286
Zulu, B. A., 194

Subject Index

A

Aabat, 46
Acompáñame, 27-28, 64, 68, 90
Addresing poverty, 48-50
Advocacy, 169-170
Affectively-oriented parasocial interaction, 367-368
Alexandra Township, 159
All in the Family, 14, 25
All India Radio (AIR), 34, 352
American Federation of Television and Radio
    Executives (AFTRA), 218
And the Nile Flows On, 46
Anglo-Saxon tradition of cultural studies, 407-408
Applying E-E theory, 69-70
Appropriate Web content, 287
Apwe Plezi (After the Pleasure Comes the Pain), 17,
    37
Archers, The, 9, 12, 244
Archie Bunker effect, 14
Audience-centered theories, 129-130
Augusto Boal's theater of the oppressed, 383-385

B

Baixing (Ordinary People), 93
Bandura's social learning theory, 68
    Acompaname, 68
    self-efficacy, 68
Banging pots and pans, 154, 163
BBC (British Broadcasting Corporation), 243-245
BBC World Service Trust, 3, 7, 253-254, 336
    combating leprosy, 254-256
    E-E interventions, 256-258
Beginnings of entertainment-education, 62-64
Behaviorally-oriented parasocial interaction,
    368-369
Bentley's dramatic theory, 68
Beverly Hills 90210, 207

Berdel, 327
Bienvenida Salud! 16
The Bill Cosby Show, 99
Body Spies, 251
The Bold & The Beautiful, 9, 208, 210, 285
Brazilian telenovelas, 263-264
Breast cancer and mammography screening,
    289-290
Bridging paradigms, 404-405
Broadcasting and Film Commission (BFC), 22
Broadcasting time-slot structure, 271-273

C

Cancer Information Service (CIS), 211
Cartoons and comic books for changing social
    norms, 331-348
    birth of *Meena*, 332-334
Casualty, 251, 259
CDC entertainment-education programs, 214-215
    Healthstyles survey, 215-216
Celebrities, 98
Celebrities in entertainment-education, 108-110
Celebrity causes, 100-101
Celebrity endorsements, 99-100
Celebrity identification in entertainment-education,
    97-111
    antecedents and consequences of identification,
        106-108
    dimensions of celebrities, 105
Center for Development and Population Activities
    (CEDPA), 427
Centers for Disease Control and Prevention (CDC),
    7, 191, 208, 304
    2000 Conference on E-E, 201-203
Cognitively-oriented parasocial interaction, 366
Changing social norms, 157
Choice: The Imperative of Tomorrow, 22
Collective efficacy, 15, 80-81, 174

Collective efficacy stimulated by *Taru*, 370-372
Communication research, 71
Communicative action and participation, 419-422, 425-430
Community case study, 363
Contextual theories, 130-131
Convention of the Rights of the Child (CRC), 335-336
Coronation Street, 245-246
Costa, 227
The Cost of Cool, 95
Creative design process, 236-238
Creative development and formative research process, 337-340
Cuando Estemos Juntos, 42
Current state of social merchandizing, 262, 266-269
Cut Your Coat According to Your Cloth, 42

D

Delivering E-E health messages through the Internet, 281-294
Department of International Development, 3
Détente, 42
Dialogic pedagogy, 381-383
Dialogo, 26
Differential modeling, 82
Diffusion of innovations, 315-317
Diffusion of the Internet, 286-287
Digital divide, 286-287
Dividing the Mango, 340
Doctors, 251, 259
Domestic Violence Act (DVA), 160-167
Domestic violence on *Soul City*, 160-167
Domestic violence storyline, 160-167
Drama AIDS Education, 390-393
Drama theories, 128-129
Dual path of influence, 76-77

E

Eastenders, 243, 245, 247-249, 259
Effects of the E-E strategy, 284-286
Egyptian oral rehydration therapy campaign, 305-309
  ORT E-E strategy, 306-307
  ORT target audience, 306
Egyptian Ministry of Health (MOHP), 305
Ek Hi Raasta, 46
El Extensionista, 387-388
Entertainment-education, 3-20, 21-39, 46, 61-74, 191, 227, 233-234, 261, 283, 302, 331, 400-403

and HIV/AIDS, 404
and participation, 417-431
as a public health intervention, 39-60
in Egypt, 302-303
in the Middle East, 301-319
Entertainment-education partnership arrangements, 230-233
Entertainment-education practice and research, 6-8
Entertainment-education programs for public health, 212-214
Entertainment-education radio dramas, 185-188
  capacity-building through training, 186-187
  launching serial dramas, 186
  poems and short stories, 186
  stage dramas, 185-186
  video production, 186
Entertainment-education strategy, 181, 227-229
Entertainment-education television dramas, 225-241
  in Egypt, 303-304
Entertainment-education television spots, 304-305
Entertainment-education theories, 123
Entertainment-education theoretical research, 143-145
Entertainment-education through participatory theater, 377-396
Entertainment-education worldwide, 3-20
Entertainment industry resources, 216-218
  collaborations and their results, 218-219
E.R., 213
Ethiopia and entertainment-education, 179-180
Evaluation of *Meena*, 345-346
Evaluation research on the ORT campaign, 313-314
Evolution of the E-E research agenda, pp. 191-203
Ey Megh, Eyi Roudro, 46
Explanation of behavior change, 14-15

F

Facilitators and impediments of collective efficacy, 82
Fat Free, 251
Fighting Fat, Fighting Fit, 251
Formative research, 156-160
Freirean strategies for empowering the oppressed, 377
Functional adaptation, 91

G

Getting started in Ethiopia, 180-181
Goals and aspirations for collective efficacy, 81
Global AIDS Program, 7

Global application of the sociocognitive model, 87-88
Globo Television Network, 264-266

H

Habermas applied to a population program in Nepal, 424-425
Happy Days, 97
Hard-to-reach audiences in the Southwestern United States, 281-290
Health and social issues, 50, 52-55
  creative ability, 52-53
  cultural sensitivity, 53
  practice in the field, 53
  technical knowledge, 53
  time and patience, 54-55
Health information needs of Internet users, 288-289
Health messages through the internet, 281-294
History of entertainment-education, 21-36
Hollyoaks, 250, 259
Hybrid models of E-E, 131-132
How to write a radio serial drama, 54
How to design and produce radio serial dramas, 54
Hum Log (We People), 7, 9, 16, 21, 30, 91, 97, 108

I

Impacts of *Taru*, 365-366
Implementing the entertainment-education strategy, 8
Importance of social norms, 46-47
Informing and motivating audience individuals about health, 208-212
  breast cancer, 210-211
  Tony's HIV, 209-210
Institute for Communication Research, 61
Integrating E-E, 351-374
Internet-delivered E-E for breast cancer screening, 292-293
Internet health messages, 283-284
International Development Research Centre (IDRC), 304
International Population Communication, 26-28
Interpersonal communication/counseling, 425-427

J

Jasoos Vijay, 3-5, 10
Johns Hopkins University's Center for

Communication Programs, 7, 42-46, 49, 51, 131, 180, 241, 304, 425
Jung's theory of archtypes, 69

L

Lacos de Familia, 270-271
Launching serial drams, 187
Listen Up, 54
Los Hijos de Nadie (Children of No One), 35

M

MacLean's theory of the triune brain, 64-65
Malhacao, 269-270
Mammography screening, 282-283, 289-290
Mass media, 427-428
Maude, 9, 25, 207
Meena, 8, 338, 343
Media campaign for family planning in Turkey, 327-328
Media to mediation, 405-407
Methodological characteristics of E-E, 133-143
  characters, 143
  formative research, 133
  measuring exposure, 133-143
Modification of consumatory lifestyles, 94-95
Monitoring and evaluation of E-E radio dramas, 188-189
Multiple levels of entertainment-education, 6-11
Mumbaki, 44

N

Nasebery Street, 7
National AIDS Control Program (in India), 7
National plan for entertainment-education, 177-189
Nepal's population program, 424-425
Networks for behavior change, 429-430
Nine Ps of E-E, 51
NNVAW (National Network on Violence against Women), 156
Nodes, 65-67
  intellectual nodes, 66
  limibic nodes, 66
    emotional nodes, 66
  reptilian nodes, 65-66
    drive nodes, 65
    intraspecific aggression, 66

Non-linearity of social change, 372–373
NYPD Blues, 191, 207

O

Office of National Drug Control Policy, 214
Oral rehydration therapy (ORT), 9, 301, 315
Orchestrating audiences through folk performances, 358–359
Origins of entertainment-education, 61–74
ORT campaign and communication theory in Egypt, 315–317
ORT campaign E-E strategy in Egypt, 306
ORT communication channels in Egypt, 309–310
ORT communication messages in Egypt, 311–312
Our Neighborhood, 50
Outcome expectations and collective efficacy, 81–82

P

Parameters of E-E, 192–195
Parasocial interaction with *Taru*, 366–369
Participatory and community involvement, 403–404
Participatory communication, 379–380, 422–424
Participatory E-E in Brazil, 396
Participatory photography, 365
Participatory theatrical techniques, 385–387
    forum theater, 386–387
    image theater, 385–386
    invisible theater, 388
    legislative theater, 389
Participatory theater, 390
Pedagogy of prevention in Brazil, 395–396
Pedagogy of the oppressed, 382
Perceived self-efficacy, 78
Pilot testing for the ORT campaign in Egypt, 310–311
Planning workshops for entertainment-education for Ethiopia, 182–183
POFLEP, 33
Population Bomb, 24
Population Communication Center, 23
Population Communications International (PCI), 7, 31–32, 85, 95, 266–267, 352
Population Media Center (PMC), 35, 85, 179, 181, 183
Population Communication Services, 417
Preliminary research for the ORT campaign in Egypt, 307–309
Psychological models, 126–128
Programs of the BBC and BBC World Service Trust, 243–259
Promoting national literacy with E-E, 88–90

R

Radio listening clubs, 356–357
Radionovela da Camisinha, 396
Reaching Hispanic people in the Southwest, 290–292
Reality television and entertainment-education, 10–11
Recognition of exemplary health storylines, 219–221
Research agenda, 198–201
Research on E-E program impacts, 430
Research impacts of E-E telenovelas, 410–413
Resistance to entertainment-education, 13–14
Rubbish Queen, The, 409–410

S

Sabido's methodology, 28–29
Sabido's methodology in India, 29–30
Scriptwriting for *Soul City*, 158–159
Secrets of the Village, 48
Self-efficacy, 15, 68, 174
Serial dramas, 51
Service Brings Rewards, 42, 425
Sesame Street, 49
Shabuj Chhaya, 40
Shabuj Shathi, 54
Simplemente María, 12, 64, 119, 128
Soap opera programs, 246–247
Soap operas and sense-making, 399–413
Social change processes, 101–104
Social cognitive theory, 75
Social cognitive theoretical model, 77–78
Social diffusion model, 76, 85–87
Social learning theory, 317
Social learning through peer conversations, 369–370
Social marketing of ORT in Egypt, 315
Social merchandizing in Brazil, 261–277
Social merchandizing pro-social themes in Brazil, 267–269
Social modeling, 78
Social psychological theories, 124–126
Society strategy for E-E in Ethiopia, 178–179
Soul City, 7–8, 15–17, 153–175
    impacts, 170–173
South Africa, 153–175
South Asian Association for Regional Cooperation (SAARC), 333
Sparrows Don't Migrate, 50
Stemming population growth, 90

Steps/stages model of E-E, 123–124
Symbolic coding aids, 84

T

Talk Back, 21
Taru, 7, 353, 355, 359, 362
Taru Project, 357–358
Taru's listenership, 362
Telenovelas, 12, 408–409
Time for Love, 47
Time to Care: A Question of Children, 45
Tinka Tinka Sukh (Happiness Lies in Small
       Pleasures), 37, 119, 129, 355, 365
Tinka to *Taru*, 355–356
Theater for empowerment in India, 393–395
Theatre of the Oppressed, 18, 383, 385
Theoretical characteristics of
       entertainment-education programs, 119
Theoretical vigor and sophistication, 12–13
Theory behind entertainment-education, 117–145
Tone, 67–68
Threat of commercial television, 245–246
Translational and implementational models, 76, 82
Turkish Family Health and Family Planning
       Foundation, 321–329
   campaign objectives, 322
   campaign effects, 325–327
   campaign strategy, 323–324
   media reach and media mix, 324–325
   social marketing, 328–329
Turkish Radio and Television (TRT), 324,
       328
Tushauriane (Come with Me), 30
Twende na Wakati (Let's Go with the Times), 5–7,
       33, 35

U

UNFPA, 33
U.S. national television, 22
Ushikwapo Shikimana (When Given Advice, Take
       It), 7, 31
Using *Meena* to foster social change,
       340–345
Using multiple media, 251–252
Using Web sites with soap operas, 250–251

V

Ven Conmigo (Come with Me), 64,
       70–71, 90
Vicarious motivators, 84
Video testimony of *Taru* Project, 364
Villa Borghese, 226, 229, 232, 235,
       240–241

W

Wife abuse, 154

Y

Yellow Card, 200

Z

Zhongguo Baixing (Ordinary Chinese People),
       32